QUAKERS, CREATION CARE, AND SUSTAINABILITY

Quakers and the Disciplines:
Volume 6

Edited by:
Cherice Bock
Stephen Potthoff

Series Editor:
Paul Anderson

A Friends Association for Higher Education Book

Quakers
and the
Disciplines

Full Media Services
http://www.fullmediaservices.com

Friends Association for Higher Education
http://www.quakerfahe.org

Volume 1.
Quaker Perspectives in Higher Education
May 2014

Volume 2.
Befriending Truth: Quaker Perspectives
June 2015

Volume 3.
Quakers and Literature
June 2016

Volume 4.
Quakers, Business, and Industry
June 2017

Volume 5.
Quakers, Politics, and Economics
June 2018

Volume 6.
Quakers, Creation Care, and Sustainability
June 2019

Longmeadow, MA | Philadelphia, PA | Windsor, CT

Copyright © 2019
All rights reserved.
ISBN: 1-7336152-1-0
ISBN-13: 978-1-7336152-1-1

Quakers and the Disciplines Editorial Committee:

Paul Anderson
(Series Editor, 2014-Present)

Donn Weinholtz
Abigail E. Adams
Ben Pink Dandelion
Barbara Addison
Don Smith
Jean Mulhern
Stephen W. Angell

As a venture of the Friends Association for Higher Education, the Quakers and the Disciplines series gathers collections of essays featuring the contributions of Quakers to one or more of the academic disciplines. Noting historic values embraced within the Religious Society of Friends regarding particular fields of inquiry, each volume includes essays highlighting contributions by Quakers as means of addressing the needs of contemporary society. Each volume is designed to be serviceable within classroom and other discussion settings, fostering explorations of how pressing issues of the day might be addressed with creativity and passionate concern, informed by a rich heritage of faith, discovery, and action.

ACKNOWLEDGMENTS

It takes a community to create a book, and we feel deep gratitude for those who worked with us and supported us to bring this volume into existence.

Our student editors, **Jack Ferguson** and **Mallory Mishler**, offered insightful feedback regarding the volume's content and helped create the discussion questions. They also aided with many of the mundane tasks of formatting manuscripts and editing citations, for which we are eternally grateful. **Jeanette Mayo** offered her excellent copy-editing skills, working tirelessly to ensure the completion of a polished final manuscript. Likewise, we appreciate the work of Full Media Services publishers **Philip Weinholtz** and **Donn Weinholtz**, who offered timely and smooth service as we moved this volume to print. Thank you all for your time, attention to detail, and care in this process.

The **Clarence & Lilly Pickett Endowment for Quaker Leadership** made it possible for Cherice Bock to attend the Friends Association for Higher Education (FAHE) conference in 2018 to witness presentations that became part of this volume. Thank you, Pickett Endowment, for all the work you do to support emerging Quaker leadership. Cherice Bock also wishes to thank **North Valley Friends Church**, her home meeting, which provided financial support for her to attend the 2018 and 2019 FAHE conferences. She also appreciates North Valley's support of her ministry in the form of a Traveling Minute, recognizing her calling to minister among Friends under a concern for the environment. Cherice's spouse, **Joel Bock**, made this project possible by caring for their children and providing emotional support in countless ways. Thank you!

Our academic institutions, **Wilmington College** (Stephen Potthoff) and **Portland Seminary of George Fox University** (Cherice Bock) supported our research and writing. We appreciate the institutional backing we receive in order to contribute to ongoing scholarship around Friends higher education and building momentum for care of creation.

This volume would not have been possible without the excellent contributions of each of the chapter authors. Thank you to each of this volume's **contributors** for sharing your stories and expertise relating to your academic disciplines, experiences as educators, and activism.

We also thank you, dear **readers**, for your interest in the Quaker role in addressing environmental concerns including anthropogenic climate change, pollution, environmental injustice, and creating a sustainable future for our planet. Thank you for all you already do to care for our earthly home, and we hope this volume offers inspiration, ideas, and motivation as you discern your future actions.

CONTENTS

Appendices

LIST OF CONTRIBUTORS

Rebecca Artinian-Kaiser is currently assistant director at the Center for Theology, Science, and Human Flourishing at the University of Notre Dame. After graduating from George Fox University, she pursued master's degrees in theology at Duke Divinity School (MTS) and at the University of Edinburgh (MTh in ecological ethics). In 2015, she completed a PhD in environmental and theological ethics at the University of Chester (UK). Her dissertation, "The Resurrection and the Restoration of Nature: Towards a Theological Framework for Christian Environmental Action through Ecological Restoration," aims to construct a theological and ethical framework for the practice of restoring degraded ecosystems. Her publications include *Theology and Ecology Across the Disciplines* (edited with Celia Deane-Drummond, 2018) and *Animals as Religious Subjects* (edited with Celia Deane-Drummond and David Clough, 2013). In the fall of 2019, she will take up a new position as associate director of the *Laudato Si'* Research Institute at Campion Hall, Oxford University. Her sojourn with the Quakers during her undergraduate and young adult years continues to influence her thinking on the role of discernment in the moral life, nonviolence, equality, and simplicity.

Cherice Bock (PhD candidate and MS, environmental studies, Antioch University New England; MDiv, Princeton Theological Seminary; BA, psychology, George Fox University) co-edited this volume with Stephen Potthoff. Bock teaches in the creation care program at Portland Seminary of George Fox University, and served as visiting professor of environmental studies at the Oregon Extension in 2018. She is co-clerk of Sierra-Cascades Yearly Meeting. Growing up Quaker in Oregon, USA, Bock connects with God through the natural landscape of the Willamette Valley, the Pacific Ocean, and the mountains. Caring for creation through her personal life, teaching, writing, and advocacy forms the heart of her current call to ministry. Bock has been a GreenFaith Fellow, a Re:Generate Fellow through Wake Forest School of Divinity, and a scholar-in-residence sharing about Quakers and creation care at Reedwood Friends Church (2017) and Berkeley Friends Church (2018).

Douglas J. Burks, PhD, is emeritus professor of biology, Department of Biology, Wilmington College. Burks taught 37 years at Wilmington College including courses in molecular biology and genetics. He was instrumental in developing and teaching the department's bioethics course for over 25 years. In his last seven years of teaching he developed a senior seminar in the general education program for non-majors where he focused on the science and ethics of sustainability.

Kyle Dell (PhD, political science, Boston College; MA, political science, Boston College; BA, political science, Kalamazoo College) is associate academic dean at Guilford College in Greensboro, North Carolina. Dr. Dell holds a joint appointment as associate professor in the departments of political science and environmental and sustainability studies. Dr. Dell's research examines the intersection of democracy and environmental policy, and challenges conventional explanations on the rise of environmental policy. He has lectured as an invited speaker across the United States and internationally as a Program Scholar for the US Department of State. Dr. Dell also serves as board vice president of Project Vote Smart, the nation's leading voter information organization. In 2014–2015, Dr. Dell was awarded a year-long fellowship with the American Council on Education in Washington, DC, where he engaged with higher education leaders from over fifty colleges and universities in the United States and abroad.

Craig Goodworth is an Oregon-based artist working in installation and poetry, and he teaches at George Fox University. His practice encompasses drawing, object-making, research, teaching and farm labor. He received a Fulbright fellowship to the Slovak Republic in 2015, where he worked with themes of blood and honey, his ancestry in the area, and the collapse of pollinators. Goodworth collaborated with ecologists in Slovakia and the American Southwest to explore the topic of forest fires. In the summer of 2017, Goodworth did an art and science residency at the PLAYA in Southern Oregon exploring Earth as body/body as earth. The following summer, he continued this theme at Ucross, a residency on a 25,000-acre cattle ranch in Wyoming. In the fall of 2018 he collaborated with a soil scientist on a multi-site project in the Willamette Valley addressing sustainable burial practices at a historic cemetery. His art often includes objects found on the landscape, or installations incorporating the land as a collaborator. Originally from Arizona, his interests include land, place, mysticism, and folk traditions.

Mike Heller is professor of English emeritus at Roanoke College, Salem, VA, where he taught courses in peace and justice studies as well as spiritual autobiography and American literature. He recently published "John Woolman and Economics: 'A Feeling Knowledge' of 'the Connection of Things,'" an essay in *Quakers, Politics, and Economics* (volume 5 in the Friends Association for Higher

Education Quakers and the Disciplines series). He is a member of the Roanoke Quaker Meeting.

James W. (Jim) Hood teaches courses on nineteenth-century British literature, American nature writing, literature and ethics, first-year writing, and (occasionally) woodworking at Guilford College in Greensboro, North Carolina. His publications include *Divining Desire: Tennyson and the Poetics of Transcendence* (Ashgate, 2000), *Quakers and Literature* (editor, FAHE, 2016), *The Ecology of Quaker Meeting* (Pendle Hill, 2018), and articles on nineteenth-century gift books and early Victorian Quaker reading practices. A longtime member of the Friends Association for Higher Education, Jim worships at Friendship Friends Meeting in Greensboro.

Robert Howell's primary interest is working to understand the links between ecological degradation, economic and financial systems, and ethics, with particular focus on ethical investment, economic and financial reform, and shareholder activism. He works to further public awareness of the threats to human life that current systems bring and, where possible, to mitigate and adapt to a fragile future. He published *Investing in People and the Planet* (2017). He has written about Quaker ethics and spirituality, and how to apply these principles to the social and ecological challenges we face. He spent 12 years working with Quaker Project to provide training in non-violent conflict resolution skills to the Indonesian Police in the 1990s. An active member of Aotearoa New Zealand Religious Society of Friends since the late 1980s, he was an attender for a number of years before then. He holds a master of arts in philosophy, and a postgraduate diploma and PhD in health management. Now retired, Howell's wide-ranging experience includes advisory, teaching, and CEO positions in the health, local authority, international education, and non-profit sectors.

Laurel Kearns, PhD, co-founded the Green Seminary Initiative, and is professor of ecology, society, and religion at Drew Theological School in New Jersey, where she has taught religion, ecology, and social justice for 25 years. Her research is focused on religious involvement in ecological issues and movements, with a particular interest in environmental justice, climate change, and food. She has identified as a Quaker since the late 1980s, serving as the Southern Appalachian Yearly Meeting and Association (SAYMA) delegate to the Friends Committee on National Legislation, and subsequently as a member of the FCNL policy committee in the early 1990s. This was during a time when FCNL started to add environmental issues to their lobbying portfolio, piquing her interest in the foundation for Quaker ecological concern.

Jon R. Kershner earned a PhD in theology from the University of Birmingham (UK) in 2013. His books include *John Woolman and the Government of Christ: A Colonial Quaker's Vision for the British Atlantic World* (Oxford University Press, 2018), *"To Renew the Covenant": Religious Themes in Eighteenth Century Quaker Abolitionism* (Brill, 2018), and a co-authored *Quaker Studies: An Overview* (Brill, 2018). His articles have been featured in several academic journals, including *Quaker Studies*, *Quaker Religious Thought*, and *Quaker History*. He has also written chapters for *Quakers and their Allies in the Abolitionist Cause, 1754–1808*, *Quakers and Literature*, and *The Cambridge Companion to Quakerism*.

Judy Lumb has a PhD in medical microbiology from Stanford University. She retired early from an academic career as a microbiologist studying leukemia at Atlanta University in Atlanta, GA. She began publishing in 1992 in Belize as *Producciones de la Hamaca*, which has over 40 books available in online bookstores. She keeps her feet in two worlds. For Belize, she publishes life stories and the results of environmental and cultural work. For Quakers, she serves on editorial teams for Quaker Earthcare Witness, Quaker Institute for the Future, and *What Canst Thou Say?* (a Quaker mystical journal).

Susanna Mattingly is sustainability and communications manager at the World Office of Friends World Committee for Consultation (FWCC). Brought up a Quaker in the United Kingdom, Susanna worked in the field of sustainability with non-governmental organizations and businesses in London before joining FWCC to run the sustainability program at the world Quaker body.

April Mays is a 2011 alumna of Wilmington College, Ohio, with a double major in accounting and political science, a concentration in international studies, and a minor in economics. She went on to intern with the Friends Committee on National Legislation in the 2011–2012 term as the program assistant for economic policy. After completing the internship, she left Washington, DC to return to her family in the Midwest and began a career as an accountant, eventually getting her CPA license.

Marlene McCauley (PhD, geochemistry, University of California – Los Angeles; BA, chemistry with specialization in earth science, University of California – San Diego) is a professor of geology and environmental and sustainability studies at Guilford College. She has led student and professional field seminars in North Carolina, the Colorado Plateau, Africa, and the Galapagos, and study abroad semesters in Dorf Tirol and Siena, Italy. Her recent research focuses on the design of innovative and engaging interdisciplinary lab science courses in the liberal arts curriculum, including "Terroir: the Science of Wine." She has served as department chair or program director for geology, environmental studies, and sustainable food systems, and as division director for interdisciplinary studies.

Jean Mulhern recently retired from the S. Arthur Watson Library, Wilmington College (Ohio), where she was the director after previously serving for 23 years as the library director at Wilberforce University. At Wilmington she worked with Dr. T. Canby Jones to organize and preserve his papers, and with Dr. D. Neil Snarr to digitally preserve Quaker historical documents held in private collections. She earned her PhD in leadership in higher education from the University of Dayton with previous degrees from Kent State University and Heidelberg University (Ohio). She continues to be active in historical and genealogical research and as a library consultant.

Stanley Chagala Ngesa is a fourth-generation Kenyan Quaker raised in the Maragoli Hills of Western Kenya in the traditions of both Christian Quakerism and the traditional spirituality of his people, the Maragoli. He is currently a postgraduate student of Quaker Studies at Earlham School of Religion in Richmond, Indiana. He has an MDiv degree from San Francisco Theological Seminary, and has worked as an itinerant minister in Kenya and as a chaplain at Marin General Hospital in Greenbrae, California.

Cathy Pitzer recently retired from Wilmington College (Ohio) where she taught sociology. During her 18 years of teaching she designed many innovative projects to encourage students to engage with their local communities in courses such as society and business, and rural sociology. She holds degrees from the University of Pennsylvania and Emory University and is on the executive board of the Friends Association for Higher Education. She is currently an agricultural researcher for the US Department of Agriculture in southern Ohio. She is an avid golfer and reader of mystery novels.

Stephen Potthoff teaches as an associate professor of religion and philosophy at Wilmington College (Ohio, USA). His academic background is in archaeology and the history of religion, and his principle research interests include indigenous religious traditions, ecospirituality, and the psychology of dream and visionary experience. As co-editor, along with Cherice Bock, of the present volume, his publications also include *The Afterlife in Early Christian Carthage: Near-Death Experiences, Ancestor Cult, and the Archaeology of Paradise* (Routledge, 2016). A birthright Friend who grew up in New Garden Friends Meeting in Greensboro, North Carolina, Stephen worships at the Wilmington College Campus Friends Meeting.

Christy Randazzo is a convinced Friend and a member of Haddonfield Friends Meeting in Haddonfield, NJ, USA. Currently an independent scholar, Randazzo is a theologian and activist, whose work has engaged in bridging the divide between the contemplative nature of theological writing with the active, lived theology of congregational life. They have done ministry across multiple religious communities in diverse settings, including youth and young adult ministry in the Episcopal Church, chaplaincy and religious education in Friends schools, social ministries amongst unhoused populations, and peacemaking in situations of ethno-religious conflict. They have earned several degrees in theology, including an MA in general theology from St. Mary's Seminary and University, an MPhil in reconciliation theology from Trinity College Dublin, and most recently a PhD in Quaker theology from the University of Birmingham.

Donald A. Smith is a professor in the physics department at Guilford College. Don graduated from the University of Chicago in 1992, worked as a research assistant at the Max Planck Institut für Extraterrestrische Physik for a year, and then got his PhD from MIT in 1999. He worked as a postdoctoral scientist and lecturer at the University of Michigan for five years, including three years as a National Science Foundation Fellow, before starting work at Guilford College in 2005. A convinced Friend since his teenage years, Don enjoys exploring the boundaries of scientific and religious exploration of the Universe.

Walter Hjelt Sullivan is the director of Quaker affairs at Haverford College. He serves as treasurer on the board of the Earth Quaker Action Team. He has joined Meeting for Worship in bank branches, corporate headquarters, and prison cells. He is a member of Green Street Friends Meeting (PA).

Shelley Tanenbaum is the General Secretary for Quaker Earthcare Witness (QEW). She also serves on the boards of Quaker Institute for the Future and Friends Committee on Legislation in California. Prior to becoming QEW's General Secretary, she researched air quality trends and has a background in environmental science and policy. Her current focus is climate change and environmental justice. She is a member of Strawberry Creek Monthly Meeting in Berkeley, California.

Lonnie Valentine is professor of peace and justice studies at the Earlham School of Religion where he has taught for 30 years. He has sought to bring together his love for process philosophy and theology, focusing on the thought of Alfred North Whitehead, with peace and justice concerns.

Gail Webster (PhD and MS, analytical chemistry, North Carolina State University; BS, secondary chemistry education, Virginia Commonwealth University) is a professor of chemistry and serves as the chair of the Department of Chemistry at Guilford College. Her research focuses on pedagogical reform and development of student-centered curricular materials in chemistry. Professor Webster has authored POGIL (Process Oriented Guided Inquiry Learning) activities to teach general chemistry using climate change concepts and also to teach non-science majors chemistry in the course "Chemistry of Food and Cooking." A proponent of active learning, Professor Webster has facilitated over twenty faculty development workshops through The POGIL Project. Gail is a member of the American Chemical Society, serves on the Women Chemists Committee, and is an active member of the Division of Chemical Education.

Emily Wirzba is the Legislative Representative for Sustainable Energy and Environment at the Friends Committee on National Legislation (FCNL). She leads FCNL's lobbying work to achieve bipartisan recognition of climate change and action in Congress. Emily meets with members of Congress and their staff to promote FCNL's environmental priorities. She also works closely with FCNL's network across the country to organize constituents to lobby, write, and advocate for bipartisan environmental action in Congress. She serves as co-chair of the Washington Interreligious Staff Community's Energy and Ecology Working Group.

Emmett Witkovsky-Eldred was the communications program assistant for the Friends Committee on National Legislation (FCNL) from 2017–2018, and helped Emily Wirzba write the piece "Lobbying for an Earth Restored: Friends Committee on National Legislation" for this volume. While at FCNL, Emmett's primary responsibility was to help write and edit FCNL's various materials, including emails, website content, publications, and social media posts.

Sara Jolena Wolcott, MDiv, is a minister, healer, writer/artist, and entrepreneur. Her work in international sustainable development led her to Union Theological Seminary where her thesis, "ReMembering the Anthropocene Age," re-originated climate change into the legacies of colonization. Upon graduation, she launched the ecotheology company Sequoia Samanvaya, LLC, where she now teaches leaders committed to societal change and is actively training others to do the same. She is an international speaker, loves the Sequoia trees, and is member of Strawberry Creek Monthly Meeting in Berkeley, California. She is active on the board of the Quaker Institute for the Future. She currently lives in the Bronx, New York, in the historical homeland of the Lenape/Siwanoy peoples.

Introduction

By Cherice Bock and Stephen Potthoff

Global climate change. The sixth extinction. The Anthropocene. As we stand ready to enter the third decade of the twenty-first century, humankind faces a global environmental crisis unprecedented in the history of the human species. The Cenozoic Era, which began 65 million years ago with the extinction of the (large) dinosaurs and many other species, and ushered in an age of extraordinary biodiversity, is coming rapidly to a close. In recent decades, humanity has become increasingly aware of the pivotal role we have played as a single species in instigating this latest episode of mass extinction. Though many question whether people themselves will survive the death throes of the terminal Cenozoic, ecotheologian Thomas Berry insists in *The Great Work* that we all stand at the brink of a new Ecozoic Era, in which human beings must learn to live in harmony and right relationship with the Earth and the natural, living world.[1] According to Berry, our task is to align ourselves with and participate in the "dream of the earth" by honoring and drawing upon the foundational creative principle animating all life and the cosmos as a whole, a principle early Friends knew as the Word (*Logos*, Wisdom) of God.[2]

As various contributors to this volume elucidate, the distinctive Quaker conviction that God dwells in all people implies by extension God's indwelling presence in the entire natural and living cosmos. God's immanent presence in the natural world is thus inherently relational, grounding and enveloping all

---

[1] Thomas Berry, *The Great Work: Our Way Into the Future* (New York: Bell Tower, 1999), 7–8.
[2] Thomas Berry, *The Dream of the Earth* (San Francisco: Sierra Club Books, 1988), 196–197.

human beings in reverential, intimate communion with the Divine at the heart of the entire created order. In the words of the biblical psalmist, whenever "deep calls to deep" (Ps 42:7),[3] and human beings recognize God's Self simultaneously in their own hearts and the living cosmos, a relationship is affirmed that is necessarily one of awe, gratitude, and reciprocal care. As Stanley Chagala Ngesa reminds us in this volume, such an intimate experience of God's presence in ourselves and the universe connects us to our most distant ancestors. This wisdom, shared by many indigenous peoples around the globe, also lies at the heart of Thomas Berry's Great Work. Several of this volume's contributors emphasize the crucial concept among Friends of "that of God" in each person, and recognize it is time for us to look within our tradition as well as humbly receive wisdom from other traditions as we seek a way forward regarding human and planetary health and flourishing.

In this volume, we seek to highlight and celebrate the manifold ways in which early and modern Friends, as well as non-Friends affiliated with Quaker organizations and institutions, are participating in this Great Work by drawing on our collective creative energies to usher in a new Ecozoic Era. Given the magnitude of the global ecological crisis and the small number of Friends, the temptation to succumb to resignation and despair is great. It is easy to forget, though, that the early Friends movement, like the early Christian movement centuries earlier, emerged in an era of extreme crisis characterized by a sense that the world itself was about to end. Faithfully attentive to the guidance and prophetic leadings of the Light within, Friends have found the hope, courage, creative inspiration, and inner resources not merely to persevere, but to transform the larger communities, societies, and political systems in which they live.

Part I of this volume, Ecological Themes in Quaker History, begins by seeking a basis for ecological action within the writings and experiences of George Fox, who catalyzed the formation of the community that became known as the Religious Society of Friends (Quakers). Becky Artinian-Kaiser and Cherice Bock examine the theme of wisdom in the writings of Fox, and discuss his understanding of the wisdom motif as a basis for ecological action in the lives of modern Friends. Next, Mike Heller's essay discusses the life and actions of Quaker abolitionist John Woolman, showing his awareness of issues that would later be called environmental justice and concern for animal welfare. In his essay, Douglas J. Burks places the more ecocentric views of Woolman and a few other prominent Friends within a wider historical and socio-economic context of the

---

[3] All biblical quotations in this volume are from the New Revised Standard Version (NRSV) unless otherwise noted.

colonial and early republic era in what became the United States; among these Friends were many farmers who adopted a more anthropocentric view of how human beings relate to the natural world. Part I concludes with an essay by Jean Mulhern and Cathy Pitzer, who profile the life story and contributions of Ruth Stout (1884–1980), a Midwestern Quaker writer widely recognized as the founder of modern organic gardening. Examining the lives and writings of these individual Quakers reveals that Friends throughout their history have embraced creation care, although not always in a fully conscious or developed form.

Part II of the volume, entitled Developing a Quaker Ecotheology, begins the work of constructing an ecotheology from within the Quaker tradition in conversation with theologians and ideas drawn from outside of Friends. Speaking mainly to the Christ-centered branches of Friends, Cherice Bock's essay reflects on the aspects of Quaker theology and practice that lend themselves to but also complicate the construction of a Quaker ecotheology. Next, Christy Randazzo's essay focuses on Liberal Quaker theological metaphors for an interdependent relationship between creation and the Divine, establishing an ecotheological starting point for Liberal Friends. Building on the historical view of John Woolman in Heller's Part I essay, Jon Kershner identifies a Quaker sacramental ecology in the work of John Woolman. Kershner describes common approaches to viewing the value of the natural world, and distinguishes Woolman's phenomenological view of nature from the Romantics and Existentialists, from the anthropocentric view that nature takes on the cultural meaning we place on it, and from those who view wilderness as a place to be tamed. Kenyan Quaker shaman Stanley Chagala Ngesa's essay compares and contrasts Quaker Christianity in Africa with traditional Maragoli shamanism, enjoining Friends worldwide to embrace more fully the panentheistic view of the Divine both traditions share as a crucial element in addressing the global environmental crisis. Next, Lonnie Valentine analyzes the process theology of Alfred North Whitehead from a Quaker perspective, focusing on how process metaphysics might inform a Quaker response to global ecological challenges, utilizing Whitehead's philosophy of organism. To conclude Part II, Laurel Kearns directs our attention to the work of ecotheologian Thomas Berry, whose enthusiastic embrace of the Universe Story and synthesis of ecology and spirituality intersect in multiple ways with traditional Quaker testimonies, attitudes toward science, and understandings of God.

In Part III, Quaker Approaches to the Environment in the Academic Disciplines, contributors working in various disciplines in higher education explore the ways their Quaker values and concern for the environment inform their teaching approaches and research pursuits. In this section's first essay,

Wilmington College religion professor Stephen Potthoff continues the analytical thread of Laurel Kearns's piece by describing his hands-on approach to telling the Universe Story in the classroom, guided and inspired by the closely-aligned nature mysticism of George Fox and French Jesuit paleontologist Teilhard de Chardin. The following essay, by Guilford College English professor James W. Hood, describes an interdisciplinary course he offers which engages students not only through the written word, but also through direct experiential investigation of local natural history. Hood reflects upon the link between this class and earlier Friends in his consideration of natural history as a field of study embraced by such prominent Quaker naturalists as eighteenth-century botanist John Bartram. Next, artist Craig Goodworth explores in an interview with Cherice Bock various ways his own artwork engages with nature and the themes of ecology and sustainability. He discusses the prophetic role of both artist and Friends, and the need for creative voices to speak in this age of climate change. In the following essay, New Zealand economist Robert Howell first outlines the historical roots of our present unsustainable economic system, based on long-outdated scientific theories, and then discusses key ethical and scientific principles that should underlie sustainable economic models with a foundation in the human-Earth relationship. Sara Jolena Wolcott's essay takes the discussion of current unsustainable and unethical economic systems one step further, underscoring the importance of acknowledging and understanding the interconnections between colonization and climate change. Wolcott urges Friends to confront in ourselves and in our pedagogy the role Quakers played as participants in colonial systems of oppression, and particularly in the way we re-member and share our individual and collective stories. Guilford College physics professor Donald A. Smith explains the science of nuclear energy in his essay, emphasizing that though nuclear energy is neither completely safe nor a perfect long-term solution to the energy crisis, the dangers of fossil fuel-based energy generation have been significantly underestimated in comparison to those of nuclear power. Finally, geochemist Marlene McCauley, political science professor Kyle Dell, and chemistry professor Gail Webster describe the recent genesis and framework of Guilford College's popular interdisciplinary Sustainable Food Systems major. The authors reflect on the program's grounding in Guilford's Quaker core values and its success in not only supplying food for the college cafeteria and a campus-based CSA, but also in addressing the acute food insecurity faced by so many residents in the surrounding county.

Part IV of the volume, Stories of Sustainability: Individuals and Organizations Living Quaker Ecotheology in Action, highlights the work and activism of individuals and Quaker organizations in putting Quaker ecotheology into practice. In the first essay, Shelley Tanenbaum, General Secretary of Quaker Earthcare Witness (QEW), describes QEW's origins and mission, issuing an urgent, prophetic call for Quakers working for peace and social justice to address the global ecological crisis on both an individual and collective level. Next, Walter Hjelt Sullivan describes the historical roots and activism of Philadelphia-based Earth Quaker Action Team (EQAT), reflecting on EQAT's campaigns as a vibrant, modern continuation of the Lamb's War declared by seventeenth-century Friends. EQAT has so far targeted PNC Bank and the local utility company with nonviolent direct action toward renewable energy sources and responsible fiscal investment. In the next essay, Judy Lumb presents the work and accomplishments of Quaker Institute for the Future (QIF), emphasizing the ways QIF's grounding in Quaker process and testimonies guides the organization's efforts to address economic sustainability, climate change, and related concerns through intentional study, discernment, and writing 11 *QIF Focus Books* (so far). In his essay, New Zealand Quaker and QIF member Robert Howell summarizes the efforts of Aotearoa New Zealand Friends to live in right relationship with the Earth, grounded through silent worship in the Spirit as experienced in all people and the entire natural world. Next, Susanna Mattingly, sustainability and communications manager for Friends World Committee for Consultation (FWCC), addresses FWCC's recent efforts to support and promote concerted and collaborative action among Friends worldwide to address climate change and the global ecological crisis. She traces FWCC's recognition of Friends' developing sense of call in relation to the environment, and highlights stories of worldwide Friends working on this issue. In the next essay, Wilmington College alumna April Mays recounts her work as a student to build a recycling program on campus, and to introduce food waste reduction initiatives in the school cafeteria. In the closing essay of Part IV, Emily Wirzba and Emmett Witkovsky-Eldred describe the lobbying work of Friends Committee on National Legislation (FCNL) over many decades to address environmental issues and the climate crisis, in recent years through the successful promotion of bipartisan legislation on climate change.

Concluding each part of the volume is a list of discussion questions to promote further reflection and consideration of some of the fundamental points and issues raised by each essay. These questions could be used by college classes, book groups, and adult education gatherings at local meetings. The Appendix offers a collection of statements and minutes from various Quaker organizations related to the global environmental crisis and how Friends and others could respond to it.

The essays in this volume represent decades of impassioned scholarship and activism among Friends as we have begun to recognize Western cultures' impact on the health of our planet. These contributors showcase the excellent work that is already in progress, which we hope encourages other Friends to get involved in this growing movement. We hope these essays also point the way toward future work at this nexus of Quaker studies, activism, and environmental awareness. Subsequent scholarship must recover the threads of our denominational history that help us face the environmental crisis, while also exposing and dismantling aspects of our denominational history and theology that have contributed to the present unsustainable and unjust situation. Perhaps our tradition's activist tactics coupled with contemplative spirituality could prove a useful offering as future Friends and others seek ways to engage in the work of personal and societal transformation without burning out. Furthermore, American, Canadian, and European Friends could learn much from listening to the voices and stories of Friends from the Global South as we seek to disentangle Quaker truths from the destructive story of Western empire. It is our hope that this volume can serve as a source of inspiration, a call to collective global action, an encouragement to listen to each other's stories, and a reminder to seek and honor the Divine Spirit in others and the entire living cosmos.

PART I
Ecological Themes in Quaker History

1| "Do What You Do in the Wisdom of God": Theological Resources for Quaker Ecological Action in the Writings of George Fox[1]

By Rebecca Artinian-Kaiser and Cherice Bock

Abstract: In a time when intentional action to care for our planet is of increasing importance, Friends drafted the Kabarak Call for Peace and Ecojustice (2012) to call Quakers to ecological action as an expression of faithfulness. The following work represents one starting point for drawing Friends' awareness to the theology and practice of early Friends in relation to creation by exploring the writings of George Fox. In this essay, we examine Fox's use of the motif of "wisdom," his view of the connection between wisdom and creation, his understanding and experience of the Word of wisdom (that is, Christ), and the way the experience of the wisdom of God in Quaker worship can inspire ethical action in the world.

I. Introduction: A Plea for Ecological Action Among Friends

At the Sixth World Conference of Friends held in Kenya in April 2012, Friends released the Kabarak Call for Peace and Ecojustice.[2] It declares,

> We have heard of forests cut down, seasons disrupted, wildlife dying, of land hunger in Africa, of new diseases, droughts, floods, fires, famine and desperate migrations—this climatic chaos is now worsening. There are wars and rumors of war, job loss, inequality and violence.

---

[1] An earlier version of this essay—"Wisdom and Love: A Theological Basis for Quaker Ecological Action"—was presented to the Quaker Studies Group at the American Academy of Religion in Chicago, IL on November 19, 2012.

[2] "The Kabarak Call for Peace and Ecojustice" (Kenya: Friends World Committee for Consultation World Conference of Friends, 2012), http://fwcc.world/call.pdf. See Appendix F for full text.

The statement calls Quakers around the world to recognize earthcare as a justice issue and to become "careful stewards of all life," "a light in the darkness of greed and destruction," and "examples in a 21st century campaign for peace and ecojustice." Statements such as these are important for mobilizing Friends to care for the earth and its creatures, as well as for affirming environmental efforts already underway. Moreover, they also reflect a growing recognition of the ecological problems pressing themselves into our line of sight and of the tight connection between human flourishing and the flourishing of the ecosystems humans inhabit.

Within the context of religious responses to the ecological crisis, Quaker approaches tend to focus on practical action discerned through attentive listening to the Holy Spirit, and they have historically worked for wider social change through focused responses to injustice. Such strategies contrast with the more common approach of formulating broad religious-ecological frameworks that then set the agenda for actions in the environment.[3] Quakers, therefore, offer a unique and concrete example for those seeking more action-based responses to the ecological crisis. At the same time, we believe there is insufficient articulation among Quakers of a theological basis that can both inspire and resource such actions; this is particularly important for those within the tradition who need to see the connection between faith and ecological action more explicitly.

While early Friends did not place an unambiguous emphasis on ecological practices (and we do not intend to anachronistically assign such motives to George Fox or other early Quakers), we suggest that the tradition holds potent theological resources for Quaker ecological practice.[4] In this essay, we call attention to the motif of wisdom[5] and its connection to creation in the writings of George Fox, particularly in volume 7 and 8 of his *Works*. We aim to explore some of the features of this wisdom motif and show how it may prove fruitful for developing Quaker thought and action on the environment, and for enriching

---

[3] This preference for constructing or retrieving religious-ecological cosmologies over more contextual approaches can be traced back to the agenda set by Lynn White, Jr. in his landmark essay "The Historical Roots of Our Ecologic Crisis," *Science* 155, no. 3767 (March 10, 1967): 1203–1207. For more on White's impact, see Willis Jenkins, "After Lynn White: Religious Ethics and Environmental Problems," *Journal of Religious Ethics* 37, no. 2 (2009): 283–309.

[4] Douglas Gwyn goes so far as to suggest that there is a "proto-environmental awareness and ethic" present in their writings. Douglas Gwyn, *A Sustainable Life: Quaker Faith and Practice in the Renewal of Creation* (Philadelphia, PA: QuakerPress of Friends General Conference, 2014), xv.

[5] This motif also appears in the Kabarak statement's use of biblical wisdom literature in Job 38:4 ("Where were you when I laid the foundations of the world?") and reinforces the contemporary relevance of wisdom for the development of a Quaker approach to environmental action.

the wider discussions on wisdom in ecotheology and ethics. To achieve this, we will explore how Fox understands wisdom as the basis of creation, as it is revealed in Christ, and as it bears upon human action before briefly noting the "ethical mysticism"[6] in Fox's approach to discerning the wisdom of God in corporate worship as a basis for action in the world.

II. George Fox and the Motif of Wisdom

In a well-known narrative in his *Journal*, George Fox recounts an experience of being caught up "in the spirit…into the paradise of God."[7] In this vision, he witnessed a creation made new, a creation that was open to him so that he could see "how all things had their names given them, according to their nature and virtue."[8] He also saw that those who stood in the "power and light of Christ" could have knowledge of "the admirable works of creation, and the virtues thereof…through the openings of the divine Word of wisdom and power, by which they were made."[9] In another account, Fox tells of a meeting in which the wisdom of God powerfully settled upon those gathered. Through wisdom they "saw" that they were "heirs of the power of God, were to take their possession of the power of God, the gospel and its order."[10] This experience of God's wisdom and power led them to the "practice of true religion"—visiting the sick and aiding the widow and orphan—acts through which they could have "the wisdom of the Lord, and of his creation, and to administer his creatures."[11]

What these narratives reveal is that for Fox right knowledge and right action are closely linked through the wisdom of God. It is in wisdom that one is given to see the true nature of things, and it is in wisdom that one can respond in accordance with this reality, both in the human and nonhuman spheres. In fact, the wisdom that prompts ethical action on behalf of the marginalized is in Fox understood to be the same wisdom by which all things were made. What are often depicted in the modern context as two opposing claims—one ecological, the other social—vying for our moral concern, are shown in Fox's writings to be

---

[6] Howard H. Brinton, *Ethical Mysticism in the Society of Friends*, Pendle Hill Pamphlet 156 (Wallingford, PA: Pendle Hill Publications, 1967), 5.

[7] George Fox, *Journal of George Fox, Vol. I* (Glasgow: W. G. Blackie and Co., 1852), 66.

[8] Fox, *Journal, 1*, 66.

[9] Fox, *Journal, 1*, 66.

[10] George Fox, *The Works of George Fox, Vol. VII* (Philadelphia: Marcus T. C. Gould, 1831), 15.

[11] Fox, *Works, VII*, 15.

connected by wisdom. Indeed, what emerges is a vision of interconnection between the nature of reality, the experience of God in worship, and human activity in society and creation. In connecting wisdom with creation, Fox draws upon an ancient tradition of wisdom found throughout the Scriptures, which he develops in a Quaker key.[12] Echoing this tradition, he points to wisdom as the basis of creation, affirming that it was by wisdom that "all things were made and created" by God.[13]

The nature of wisdom's role in creation must be approached from one angle through the concept of "order," a word that frequently appears in close proximity to "wisdom" in his *Works*. For Fox, the "God of truth is a God of order,"[14] and thus God governs and orders the heavens and the earth in wisdom and power.[15] It appears to be the nature of God's wisdom to order creation[16] according to "that wisdom which made them, and doth not change."[17] The image here is not of some arbitrary ordering or divine decree concerning what something will be; rather, God is shown to be ordering creation according to wisdom—in other words, according to what creation is recognized to be. Thus, for God to create the world in wisdom is to create a world that is ordered, a world in which creatures have names, natures, and virtues.[18]

In addition to ordering creation, he also sees wisdom preserving and directing creation toward its rightful end. Fox asserts, "the wisdom from above is gentle and pure, and preserves you, yea, and the whole creation, to the glory of God."[19] The wisdom that creates and orders creation is the same wisdom that upholds that order and ensures creation's continued existence; moreover, wisdom directs creation towards its *telos* or fulfillment, which for Fox is conceived

---

[12] This is an area of increasing interest within ecotheology from a variety of Christian perspectives. For more on the connection between creation and wisdom, see Celia Deane-Drummond, *Wonder and Wisdom: Conversations in Science, Spirituality and Theology* (London: Darton, Longman & Todd, 2006); Celia Deane-Drummond, "Creation," in *The Cambridge Companion to Feminist Theology*, ed. Susan Frank Parsons (Cambridge: Cambridge University Press, 2002), 190–205; Dianne Bergant, "The Bible's Wisdom Tradition and Creation Theology," in *God, Creation, and Climate Change. A Catholic Response to the Environmental Crisis*, ed. Richard W. Miller (Maryknoll: Orbis Books, 2010), 35–48; Brandon Lee Morgan, "Reimaging Aesthetics: Sergius Bulgakov on Seeing the Wisdom of Creation," *Irish Theological Quarterly* 83, no. 2 (2018): 149–163; Andrea L. Robinson, "The Ecosapiential Theology of Psalms," *Evangelical Review of Theology* 42, no. 1 (2018): 21–34.

[13] Fox, *Works, VII*, 149.

[14] George Fox, *The Works of George Fox, Vol. VIII* (Philadelphia: Marcus T.C. Gould, 1831), 163.

[15] Fox, *Works, VIII*, 186.

[16] Fox, *Works, VIII*, 34.

[17] Fox, *Works, VII*, 149.

[18] Fox, *Journal, I*, 66.

[19] Fox, *Works, VII*, 343.

as the glory of God.[20] He writes, "By the wisdom of God were all things made, and by the wisdom of God must all things be ordered again to God's glory."[21]

Having briefly explored wisdom's ordering and preserving role in creation, we now turn to what is perhaps for Fox the most important aspect of wisdom, namely, as it is known in Christ. For Fox, the possibility of knowing the world as it is only comes through Christ, who himself is understood to be the wisdom of God and the creator of all things.[22] Fox writes that if a person wants to know the things of God, one "must come to the spirit of God and to Christ the wisdom of God."[23] Christ is "the treasure of wisdom and knowledge,"[24] and by living and walking in Christ a person can have the "wisdom and knowledge that is heavenly from this treasure."[25] Again, he writes, "And now, my friends, if you do want wisdom and knowledge to order you in the affairs and service of God, Christ is the treasure of your wisdom and knowledge; and so receive them from his treasury which is above."[26] It is only in Christ, the wisdom of God and creator of all, that the nature of the created order becomes something to which humans have real access. Thus, when Fox exhorts his listeners to "wait for wisdom and in it walk"[27] and "Dwell in the wisdom and power of God,"[28] he is pointing to a new reality that Christ has made possible for the human person to live into.

Once this wisdom, which orders all creation, has been received from God through Christ, it becomes possible for human beings to take up the role that Fox sees has been given to them: that of ordering the creation with the wisdom by which it was made.[29] And so, we turn to the final aspect of Fox's motif of wisdom, that of its bearing upon human action. First, Fox's wisdom framework provides key parameters for this action. With the ordering of creation to "God's glory" an important check has been placed on human activity, namely, creation is ordered to God and, thus, is not a meaningless entity awaiting the human creature's determination of what its good will be. This is particularly important given the tendency in modernity to view creation as the raw material for human progress. Acting in wisdom, therefore, will entail upholding creation and

---

[20] Fox, *Works*, *VII*, 149.

[21] Fox, *Works*, *VII*, 149.

[22] Fox, *Works*, *VIII*, 283.

[23] Fox, *Works*, *VIII*, 283–84.

[24] Fox, *Works*, *VIII*, 63. It is important to note that what Fox terms "wisdom" connects with the Quaker term "Inward Light," but is not congruent with it.

[25] Fox, *Works*, *VIII*, 201, 192.

[26] Fox, *Works*, *VIII*, 192.

[27] Fox, *Works*, *VII*, 150.

[28] Fox, *Works*, *VII*, 116.

[29] Fox, *Works*, *VIII*, 34.

enabling it to be ordered toward its fulfillment in God's glory. Second, as created beings, humans have also been ordered by the same wisdom of God that orders the rest of creation. Therefore, in order for human beings to be what they are, they too must act in accordance with the wisdom that made them. For Fox this means that humanity must take its place in creation by ordering, ruling, and governing "all things which are under [their] hands" in the wisdom of God, that is, in Christ.[30] Again, he writes that by living in Christ the wisdom of God "ye may order, rule, and govern all things which are under your hands (which God hath given you) to his glory. Govern and order with his wisdom all the creatures that ye have under you, and all exchangings, merchandising, husbandry. Do what you do in the wisdom of God."[31]

In order to fulfill this role, human beings must attend to the "counsel of the Lord" from which they receive wisdom from God—the same wisdom that orders creation—so that they may "come to know how to order in the creation with the wisdom by which all was made."[32] Although for Fox this seems to entail refraining from harming other creatures,[33] it can also be drawn out further in terms of the ethical category of love. Fox writes, "And so let all things be done in peace and love, in the name and power of Jesus amongst you…being all ordered with the wisdom of God."[34] And, "Be at peace with one another, and in love and tenderness, and in the wisdom of God order and preserve, and nourish and cherish all things to his glory."[35]

Passages such as these make an explicit connection between being in wisdom and acting in love, including in our actions in the natural world. The wisdom of God that orders, preserves, and directs the creation and is manifest in Christ is a critical component of what it might mean to act in the world in love. Of course, this wisdom, as the Hebrew Scriptures make plain, is not something easily grasped or attained, and so there is a necessary humility and openness to new understandings (and changes in course) that accompany the search for

---

[30] Fox, *Works*, *VII*, 15. While one might be tempted to view such statements as providing a Quaker theology of stewardship, Fox is arguing for a more complex human/creation interaction than is allowed for in stewardship models, which tend to depict the human person acting in creation in the absence of God's action. For an interpretation of George Fox's writings on wisdom through the lens of stewardship, see Virginia Schurman, "A Quaker Theology of the Stewardship of Creation," *Quaker Religious Thought* 24, no. 4 (1990): 27–41.

[31] Fox, *Works*, *VII*, 191.

[32] Fox, *Works*, *VIII*, 34.

[33] Fox writes, "suffer no creature to perish for want of the creatures, and that none be lost through slothfulness, laziness, and filthiness," and also: "With this wisdom…you do good unto all and hurt no one." Fox, *Works*, *VII*, 191.

[34] Fox, *Works*, *VIII*, 192.

[35] Fox, *Works*, *VII*, 85.

wisdom. Acts of love in the natural world that spring from wisdom, therefore, would need to be those that move humbly and patiently, seeking to understand and appreciate it in all its complexities and to "preserv[e] you, yea, and the whole creation, to the glory of God."[36]

II. Wisdom, Worship, and Loving Action

In linking the experience of God in worship and ethical action among Friends, George Fox offers a way to think about the connection between wisdom and responsive and loving action. In one meeting for worship, Fox describes how the wisdom of God settled on those gathered in such a way that they were enabled to practice "the pure religion" through caring for others.[37] For Quakers, a central theological principle[38] is that "Christ has come to teach his people himself."[39] Thus, in traditional Quaker worship, individuals listen together to hear Christ speaking to them directly, and what is discerned in worship has often led to the mitigation of injustices. Friends heard calls to end slavery, to reform prisons and mental health institutions, to reject the use of violence to resolve conflicts, and to work for the rights of women.[40] Howard Brinton describes this movement from worship to action as "ethical mysticism," which "first withdraws from the world revealed by the senses to the inward Divine Source of Light, Truth, and Power, and then returns to the world with strength renewed, insight cleared, and desire quickened to bind all life together in the bonds of love."[41]

The mystical experience of the wisdom of God in worship was for Fox and early Quakers indispensable for the subsequent movement into action in particular contexts. Fox's own experience warrants mention, though it can only be traced briefly here. In the accounts of his experiences, Fox draws inward and away from the world (even spending years wandering the countryside seeking deeper spiritual fulfillment); at particular times, he has a mystical encounter with

---

[36] Fox, *Works*, *VII*, 343.

[37] Fox, *Works*, *VII*, 15.

[38] Pink Dandelion, *The Quakers: A Very Short Introduction* (Oxford and New York: Oxford University Press, 2008), 2, 56.

[39] This was a catchphrase of Fox. He often used this phrase (or a variation) when he preached in new towns. George Fox, *The Journal of George Fox*, ed. John L. Nickalls (Philadelphia: Cambridge University Press, 1997), 304; c.f. 8, 48, 80, 90, 98, 104, 107, 112, 149, 236.

[40] For more on these themes, see *The Oxford Handbook of Quaker Studies*, eds. Stephen W. Angell and Pink Dandelion (Oxford: Oxford University Press, 2013).

[41] Brinton borrows this term from Albert Schweitzer, who thinks of mysticism as an outlook on the world that "brings [people] into a spiritual relation with the Infinite." Brinton, *Ethical Mysticism*, 5. See also Albert Schweitzer, *Out of My Life and Thought* (New York: Henry Holt and Company, Inc., 1949), 235.

the divine, for example, by going up "in spirit through the flaming sword to the paradise of God"[42] or witnessing visionary oceans of darkness and light.[43] These experiences in the spirit, it is important to note, do not yield a disembodied or merely rational comprehension of wisdom; rather, Fox experiences a heightening of his senses in which he becomes more conscious of all creation and its goodness or virtue.[44] As Brinton suggests, Fox became aware of the "inward Divine Source of Light, Truth, and Power"[45] and of himself connected to the rest of creation through "the Word of wisdom, that opens all things, and come to know the hidden unity in the Eternal Being."[46] His encounter with wisdom illuminated his sense-experience of creation and his place within it, and this same wisdom also drew him into loving action in the world. He resisted inequitable laws and famously lived in ways that got him into trouble, speaking the truth he heard from God in prophetic (though not always popular) ways; attending to the wisdom he encountered inwardly, he acted "in the virtue of that life and power that took away the occasion of all wars."[47]

In times of worship, Quakers still wait in expectation for the wisdom of God, the same wisdom that orders all creation and works to preserve it to the glory of God. Seeking to behold and apprehend "the Gospel and its order"[48] in heavenly form, as in Fox's vision of Eden, is not an escape from the material world, but arguably may be a more complete experience of it. In this way, Quakers seek wisdom by cycling through times of withdrawal into an inward awareness of God and God's wisdom in creation before discerning outward possibilities for concrete environmental actions. By attending to wisdom made accessible through waiting worship and mystical encounters with God, Fox offers a way to participate in the wisdom of God at work in creation.

III. Conclusion

As human beings navigate the environmental challenges facing our planet (as a whole and in particular contexts), wisdom is essential for seeing into the pertinent issues and for discerning actions that reflect and respond to the realities of each

---

42 Fox, *Journal*, ed. Nickalls, 27.
43 Fox, *Journal*, ed. Nickalls, 19.
44 Fox, *Journal*, ed. Nickalls, 27.
45 Brinton, *Ethical Mysticism*, 5.
46 Fox, *Journal*, 28. Other historical examples of mystical oneness include Meister Eckhart, Mechthild of Magdeburg, and Julian of Norwich, to name a few. Contemporary ecotheologians discussing mystical oneness in relation to caring for the planet include Thomas Berry, Denis Edwards, Ivone Gebara, Aruna Gnanadason, Sallie McFague, and many others.
47 Fox, *Journal*, ed. Nickalls, 65.
48 Fox, *Works, VII*, 15.

context. Given the complexities of ecological systems and their entanglements with human culture, it will entail approaching environmental actions with humility; at the same time, too great an emphasis on humility can become an evasion of human responsibility and the call to move through the world in wisdom and responsive love. It will entail a commitment to drawing from a wide array of disciplinary and religious perspectives to gain purchase on the issues in play in any given context; from a Quaker perspective, this gathering of knowledge will also include that which is gleaned from the tradition and from corporate discernment. And so, the goal of this essay has been a modest one: to point to (and elevate) the motif of wisdom in the writings of George Fox as a potent resource for scholars seeking to develop a stronger theological basis for Quaker ecological action. Fox's understanding of wisdom and creation, connected as it is to mysticism and action, as well as to corporate discernment, is also a contribution to wider discussions on wisdom in environmental theology and ethics. More work is needed to uncover how this motif functions in Fox's understanding of creation, and how it may be reimagined and deployed to shape the kind of world envisioned by the World Conference of Friends in the Kabarak Call for Peace and Ecojustice.

2 | John Woolman's Environmental Consciousness

By Mike Heller[1]

Abstract: John Woolman (1720–1772) has been greatly admired for his antislavery and economic writings, his self-denying witness, and his Journal, *one of the most widely read Quaker spiritual autobiographies. He has been less often recognized for his environmental insights. He saw pollution, sanitation problems, and abuse of animals as a degradation of the earth, which for him was a gift from God to humanity. His perspective had far-reaching implications. He recognized his own location and that of the Society of Friends within the systemic problems that permeated British culture and the Atlantic community. At the same time, he believed he was experiencing the Kingdom of God both in the present and emerging as a new order. By examining recent scholarship on Woolman, this essay explores how he expressed an environmental consciousness that was part of a prophetic vision of the relationship among humanity, God, and creation.*

In the summer of 1772, when he was nearly fifty-two, John Woolman left London walking on foot toward the north of England. He had several motivations for going to England that included wanting to do what he could to promote peace, to strengthen unity among American and British Friends, and to see the region that he felt was "an ancestral and spiritual home."[2] He knew even before departing, however, that the trip would challenge his beliefs about the economic

---

[1] Great thanks to Katherine A. Hoffman and Charles M. Katz for their ideas and suggestions about this essay.

[2] Geoffrey Plank, *John Woolman's Path to the Peaceable Kingdom: A Quaker in the British Empire* (Philadelphia: University of Pennsylvania Press, 2012), 198.

system, labor, and the environment. The Atlantic voyage would mean traveling on a ship involved in supporting the exploitive and corrupt practices of empire. He knew once he arrived that he would be confronted with practices that he could not approve. One example was he felt he had to avoid riding in the English stagecoaches because they were held to schedules that abused horses and the boys who worked on the coaches. Even though he suffered from poor health and bodily weakness, once in England, he felt he had to walk. As he writes in his *Journal*, "Stagecoaches frequently go upwards of a hundred miles in 24 hours, and I have heard Friends say in several places that it is common for horses to be killed with hard driving, and many others driven till they grow blind. These coaches running chief part of the night do often run over foot people in the dark."[3] Despite trying to avoid towns because of the prevalence of disease, he came down with smallpox and died in early October in York.

While on this journey he wrote what would become the last chapter of his *Journal*, in which he noted the filth and pollution in the streets. Through such observations, he became one of the early observers of industrial pollution, sanitation, and animal abuse. Woolman is known for numerous accomplishments such as his antislavery writings and actions, his essays on the relation of the rich and the poor, his faithfulness to Quaker testimonies, and his *Journal*, which is considered one of the world's great spiritual autobiographies. But he also deserves recognition for environmental insights far ahead of much of Western culture. Woolman remains important to Quaker history because he expressed an environmental consciousness that was part of a prophetic vision of the relationship between humanity and God's creation.

For at least the last two decades of his life, he wrote about how wealth and power, when misused, alienate the wealthy from the Kingdom of God and lead to numerous kinds of harm to people and the environment. Children growing up in luxury are especially vulnerable to the misuse of power. The theme of inheritance was at the center of his first essay against slavery, begun in 1746 and completed in 1754, in which he addressed the dangers to children inheriting slaves.[4] Similarly, he wrote about recognizing God's gifts, which all humanity inherits. In an essay written in 1763, "A Plea for the Poor," he called upon the wealthy who abused their laborers "to consider the connection of things," a recognition that resonates with perspectives today on economics, nonviolence,

---

[3] John Woolman, *The Journal and Major Essays of John Woolman*, ed. Phillips P. Moulton, 1971 (Richmond, IN: Friends United Press, 1989), 183.

[4] Woolman, *The Journal and Major Essays*, 198–209.

and ecology.[5] In a late essay written in 1772, "Conversations on the True Harmony of Mankind & How It May Be Promoted," he wrote about the theme of inheritance and a concern for future generations: "The produce of the earth is a gift from our gracious Creator to the inhabitants, and to impoverish the earth now to Support outward greatness appears to be an injury to the succeeding age."[6] This statement expresses his strongly held belief that we should not use the God-given gifts of the earth more quickly than they can be replenished—to do so is "an injury" to future generations.

In his *Journal*, which he began writing when he was 35, Woolman recorded a sensitivity to animals and his thoughts about the place of human beings in creation. He tells of a boyhood memory of killing a mother robin. At first he felt pleased, but then was "seized with horror, at having in a sportive way killed an innocent creature while she was careful for her young."[7] Knowing that the robin's babies would then perish from starvation, he climbed the tree and killed the baby birds. From this experience he drew a lasting lesson about his own capacity for cruelty. He quotes from Proverbs: "The tender mercies of the wicked are cruel" (Prv 12:10). A few pages later, Woolman makes a more complete statement about how "true religion" is inward and calls a person "to exercise true justice" toward all people and animals:

> I...was early convinced in my mind that true religion consisted in an inward life, wherein the heart doth love and reverence God the Creator and learn to exercise true justice and goodness, not only toward all [people] but also toward the brute creatures; that as the mind was moved on an inward principle to love God as an invisible, incomprehensible being, on the same principle it was moved to love him in all his manifestations in the visible world; that as by his breath the flame of life was kindled in all animals and sensitive creatures, to say we love God as unseen and at the same time exercise cruelty toward the least creature moving by his life, or by life derived from him, was a contradiction in itself.[8]

In these passages from the *Journal's* first chapter, he emphasized the importance of his childhood feelings for the beauty of God's creation and the sacredness of life. Here, writing as an adult, he realized the importance of these feelings. As an

---

5 Woolman, *The Journal and Major Essays*, 247.
6 John Woolman, "Conversations on the True Harmony of Mankind & How It May Be Promoted," in *John Woolman and the Affairs of Truth: The Journalist's Essays, Epistles, and Ephemera*, ed. James Proud (San Francisco: Inner Light Books, 2010), 169.
7 Woolman, *The Journal and Major Essays*, 24.
8 Woolman, *The Journal and Major Essays*, 28.

adult, he was still confronted with the difficulty of reconciling how people can say they love God "while at the same time exercise cruelty toward the least creature moving by his life."

In the *Journal's* next-to-last chapter about the voyage to England, he again describes a feeling of tenderness toward animals. In this case, he feels for the suffering "dunghill fowls" kept in cages on the ship. He writes about how "the pining sickness" of the birds reminds him of "the Fountain of Goodness, who gave being to all creatures, and whose love extends to that of caring for the sparrows."[9] If God's love is extended even to caring for the sparrows, humanity must also seek a caring relationship with the animal world. He writes, "[I] believe where the love of God is verily perfected and the true spirit of government watchfully attended to, a tenderness toward all creatures made subject to us will be experienced, and a care felt in us"; a sense of good stewardship and care for animals should guide decisions "under our government."[10] He concludes the passage by recommending that fewer birds should be carried on these voyages.

Phillips P. Moulton did some of the best scholarship on Woolman's writings in the mid-twentieth century. More than twenty years before completing the most authoritative version of Woolman's *Journal,* Moulton was drawn to studying Woolman's ethics. Mary Moulton writes about how her husband first encountered Woolman in the 1940s: "A student in a course [Phil] taught for the Cleveland YMCA…loaned him a copy of Woolman's *Journal,* saying 'I think you'll find ideas similar to yours.' Phil said it was like a homecoming, a validation and a great expansion of what he had been trying to work out by himself."[11] Moulton decided to study Woolman for a sabbatical in 1964. One of his advisors, learning of his plan for the sabbatical, asked, "Whoever heard of Woolman?"[12] But Moulton knew the value of Woolman. In an essay, which grew out of that sabbatical and was published in *Quaker History,* he writes, "Woolman's perception of the long-range, and often obscure, effects of an act is especially evident in the passages where he advocated simple living. He dealt frequently with the harmful effects of seeking to maintain a standard of living higher than was really essential for the doing of God's will. He traced a multitude of evils to the pursuit of wealth, luxury, status, honor, or easy living."[13]

---

[9] Woolman, *The Journal and Major Essays,* 178.

[10] Woolman, *The Journal and Major Essays,* 178–79.

[11] Mary Moulton, "In Honor of Phillips P. Moulton," in *The Tendering Presence: Essays on John Woolman,* ed. Mike Heller (Wallingford, PA: Pendle Hill Publications 2003), 311.

[12] Mary Moulton, "In Honor of Phillips P. Moulton," 312.

[13] Phillips P. Moulton, "John Woolman: Exemplar of Ethics," *Quaker History* 54 (1965): 86.

For Woolman, wealth, luxury, status, and easy living were all connected directly or indirectly to environmental issues. His aspiration to live simply was about not living beyond one's needs and understanding the layers of harm excessive living caused, but more importantly it was about fulfilling God's will. "Living on a material level," Moulton writes, created "its own chain of evils."[14] Woolman illustrated this "chain of evils" this way: "One person continuing to live contrary to true wisdom commonly draws others into connection with him, and when these embrace the way the first hath chosen, their proceedings are like a wild vine which springing from a single seed and growing strong, its branches extended, and their little tendrils twist around all herbs and boughs…within their reach, and are so…locked in that without much labor…they are not disentangled."[15] Living "contrary to true wisdom" is a phrase Woolman often used. In this regard, he wrote about connections that led from the wealthy's desire for luxuries to the oppression of the poor, and about the connections that led from the desire for luxuries to the causes of war. He saw that the chain of evils gradually entangles humanity and has long-range implications about the environment, even if these were not stated directly.

He thought a great deal about "the connection of things."[16] As a result, he decided to give up his dry-goods business because its success was out of proportion to how he felt he was being called to live. He made numerous decisions about leading a simpler life. He decided to wear undyed clothing, partly because it would be cleaner and partly because the dyes were made by slave labor. He gave up using sugar because slave labor was used in its production. On his journeys in the ministry to meet with slave owners, he often chose to walk rather than ride horses in order to communicate what slaves endured. He chose to give up the use of silverware and silver goblets because of oppressive mining conditions. In addition to avoiding the stagecoaches in England because of the abuse of horses, he objected to the child-labor conditions, writing: "Postboys pursue their business, each one to his stage, all night through the winter. Some boys who ride long stages suffer greatly in winter nights, and at several places I have heard of their being froze to death. So great is the hurry in the spirit of this world that in aiming to do business quick and to gain wealth the creation at this day doth loudly groan!"[17] Like a biblical prophet, he boldly addresses harmful business practices that put profits above the safety of the poorest workers. Reading the

---

[14] Moulton, "John Woolman: Exemplar of Ethics," 87.

[15] Woolman, "A Plea for the Poor," in *John Woolman's Journal and Major Essays*, 258–259; quoted in Moulton, "John Woolman: Exemplar of Ethics," 87.

[16] Woolman, *The Journal and Major Essays*, 247.

[17] Woolman, *The Journal and Major Essays*, 183. He is referencing a passage from Romans 8:18–23, which has become an important passage for ecotheologians.

Journal, we realize he did not work out all of these ethical decisions early in life; they evolved for him over the course of three decades.

Sometimes he must have appeared difficult to his contemporaries not only because of how he stood out in his undyed clothing, but also in his firm positions. When Woolman was preparing to leave for England, several Friends wrote letters to ease his way on his journey. The Philadelphia Quaker leader, John Pemberton, wrote the following in a letter to Joseph Row in London:

> This goes per Capt. Sparks with whom our dear Friends John Woolman and Samuel Emlen embarks, [sic] Thou knows the latter who is grown a sound good minister and I hope will have acceptable service. The first is a truly upright man but walks in a straiter path than some good folk are led, or do travel in. He is a good minister, a sensible man, and though he may appear singular, yet from a close knowledge of him he will be found to be a man of a sweet clean spirit and preserved from harsh censure of those who do not see and conform as he does.[18]

Pemberton made a point of reassuring Joseph Row that although Woolman seemed strange, he walked "in a straiter path" than most. He must have seemed extreme to many of his contemporaries. Pemberton's letter goes on to say the following:

> It will be safest for Friends with you to leave him much to his own feelings, and to walk and steer in that path which proves most easy to him, without using much arguments or persuasion. He will do nothing knowingly against the Truth, and has had long experience in the Truth. He is much beloved and respected among us, and I doubt not will on close acquaintance be so to the truly religious with you.[19]

Perhaps leaving "him much to his own feelings" meant that Woolman came across as overly self-assured, that he was difficult to talk with, or that he really liked being left alone. At any rate, he was not one who could be persuaded to act counter to the Truth as he saw it revealed to him.

---

[18] Sterling Olmsted and Mike Heller, eds., *John Woolman: A Nonviolence and Social Change Source Book,* second edition (Wilmington, OH, and Richmond, IN: Wilmington College Peace Resource Center and Friends United Press, 2013), 139.

[19] Olmsted and Heller, *John Woolman: A Nonviolence and Social Change Source Book,* 139.

In *If John Woolman Were Among Us: Reflections on the Ecology of Flush Toilets and Motor Vehicles*, Keith Helmuth contends that Woolman's stances would probably raise eyebrows if he were alive today. As examples, he says Woolman would likely refuse to use the flush toilet and he would likely refuse to use motor vehicles, much the same way he refused to ride stagecoaches in England. Woolman would look at large issues such as the fact that "Flush toilets are an extravagant use of water resources": our mind-set about "waste" is wrong headed, and "The flush toilet is biologically destructive technology because it systematically removes nutrients from the soil-plant-animal-soil cycle."[20] Woolman would object to polluting our water supply with toxins, for "We all live downstream."[21] About Woolman, Helmuth writes: "no other figure in Quaker history has retained such continuing relevance across such a broad front of spiritual and socio-economic issues."[22] He goes on to argue:

> There is a key factor behind the enduring character of John Woolman's thought. He had the gift of relational perspective, an ecological consciousness. He saw clearly, felt strongly and articulated convincingly an ecology of spiritual life which included economic and social activity.... He understood that an economic and social system supported by unjustly rewarded labour imperiled the true Spirit of Christ, even in those only marginally connected with its operation....[23]

This "relational perspective" and "ecological consciousness" brought Woolman to many of the same conclusions others are coming to today regarding the inevitable result of unjust actions toward other people and creatures.

Helmuth lists the devastating effects of motor vehicles, which he thinks would have horrified Woolman, including that the internal combustion engine "has turned farming from an activity of ecosystem preservation into an activity of industrial extraction," and has shaped our communities and market systems. "[M]otor vehicles have ruptured the orderly development and self-renewing patterns of human settlements," depopulating rural areas; they have promoted "a grossly wasteful economic style" and "habits of consumerism...[which have] become a complete political-economic ideology"; further, motor vehicles are a major cause of air pollution and the greenhouse effect. "The loss of life, injury and

---

[20] Keith Helmuth, *If John Woolman were Among Us: Reflections on the Ecology of Flush Toilets and Motor Vehicles* (Argenta, BC: Argenta Friends Press, 1987), 20–23.

[21] Helmuth, *If John Woolman were Among Us*, 25.

[22] Helmuth, *If John Woolman were Among Us*, 1.

[23] Helmuth, *If John Woolman were Among Us*, 1.

property damage…of the motor vehicle system is annually equivalent to a major war."[24] What Woolman would think of motor vehicles, Helmuth claims, would go even further:

> If it seems to Woolman that 'creation…doth loudly groan' under the stress of the stage-coach transportation system, imagine what metaphors he would have to reach for to represent the effect on Creation of our present motor vehicle transportation system. The groan must surely become a shriek issuing from the tens of thousands of humans and millions of animals which are killed and maimed annually on our highways.[25]

The systemic problems in the eighteenth century, which Woolman witnessed and felt so deeply, must have seemed to him just as devastating.

There is much in Woolman's writing that will speak to readers' ecological consciousness today, but he does not address sustainability as a separate issue. Reginald Reynolds writes, in *The Wisdom of John Woolman*, "Woolman's mind was in no sense 'departmentalized.' … [V]ery often a single paragraph, or even a single sentence, covers such a range that it is only by trying to feel where the main emphasis lies that I have been able to assign it a place in one of my categories."[26] His perspective was thoroughly grounded in a Christian universalism in which the heart's sympathy grows from a "principle" from God, "placed in the human mind," and available to everyone:

> There is a principle which is pure, placed in the human mind, which in different places and ages hath had different names. It is, however, pure and proceeds from God. It is deep and inward, confined to no forms of religion nor excluded from any, where the heart stands in perfect sincerity. In whomsoever this takes root and grows, of what nation soever, they become brethren in the best sense of the expression.[27]

He felt that this sympathy, growing from a spiritual "principle" in the mind of all humanity, was the great source of reform.

---

[24] Helmuth, *If John Woolman were Among Us*, 33–35.

[25] Helmuth, *If John Woolman were Among Us*, 31.

[26] Reginald Reynolds, *The Wisdom of John Woolman* (London: Friends Home Service Committee, 1948), 41.

[27] Woolman, *The Journal and Major Essays*, 236.

Woolman's environmental consciousness was shaped by his concern for future generations and a "universal love" that opens one's heart to being content to live simply:

> The greater part of the necessaries of life are so far perishable that each generation hath occasion to labour for them; and when we look toward a succeeding age with a mind influenced by universal love, we endeavour not to exempt some from those cares which necessarily relate to this life, and give them power to oppress others, but desire they may all be the Lord's children and live in that humility and order becoming his family. Our hearts being thus opened and enlarged, we feel content in a use of things as foreign to luxury and grandeur as that which our Redeemer laid down as a pattern.[28]

He had faith in the power of "universal love," as the leadings of the divine Spirit, which could guide one's life, including the choices to limit luxury and grandeur. In a Philadelphia Yearly Meeting epistle of 1759, Woolman asks whether Friends feel "an affectionate regard for posterity."[29] It's an attractive phrase for expressing not just near-term concerns but rather the long-range implications of actions for generations to come.

In a recent biography, *John Woolman's Path to the Peaceable Kingdom: A Quaker in the British Empire*, Geoffrey Plank offers an historical context for understanding Woolman's life and reformist efforts. He argues that: "the broad range of controversies [Woolman] joined…stemmed from his insistence that humanity should reform itself comprehensively."[30] He writes that the religious vision "to establish that kingdom foreseen by the prophet Isaiah…inspired Woolman's detailed and sweeping critique of the material culture and economy of the British Empire."[31] Woolman's ability to see "the connection of things" gave him an understanding of what we would term the systemic problems which permeated the British culture and the Atlantic economy: "that purchasing products of slave labor promoted slave-raiding and warfare in Africa and that concentrating wealth in the hands of the landed elite on the American East Coast had the effect of pushing landless whites onto Indian lands in the west."[32] Woolman's attention was not focused so much on ecological concerns as it was on slavery, relations

---

28 Woolman, *The Journal and Major Essays*, 250.
29 Woolman, *The Journal and Major Essays*, 101.
30 Plank, *John Woolman's Path to the Peaceable Kingdom*, 3.
31 Plank, *John Woolman's Path to the Peaceable Kingdom*, 3.
32 Plank, *John Woolman's Path to the Peaceable Kingdom*, 3.

between "the landed elite" and the "landless whites," relations with the American Indians, and Quaker expansion of material wealth. Nevertheless, Woolman's interests reveal concerns that touched significantly on environmental issues.

In the mid-1750s, as Woolman's dry goods business was growing, he sold products like sugar, rum, and pork to his customers. Plank observes, "Sugar, molasses, and rum were so prominent in the diet and customs of the Delaware Valley Quakers that even the most adamant opponents of slavery had trouble avoiding them."[33] He raised and sold pork until 1758, when his account books show that his trade in pork abruptly stopped. Plank suspects this might have come about because he realized the pork was being shipped to the Caribbean islands.[34] It wasn't until the 1760s that he made the decision to give up wearing dyed clothing and stopped eating sugar because of the oppressive conditions in which they were produced. Woolman was not a vegetarian, but he was sensitive to animals' lives. Plank observes that: "Domestic animals played an essential role in Woolman's conception of moral order. They demanded love and care while implicitly calling on their keepers to behave responsibly. They also modestly accepted their place in God's creation."[35] Woolman's experience growing up on his parents' farm must have given him a life-long affection for animals and being on the land, and must have intensified his later revulsion from the pollution in cities.

He writes in the *Journal* about walking northward in England and becoming disgusted by the filth he saw in cities, a feeling that led him to express how he wished people would give up urban life for the country. He observed sewage in the streets, the slaughtering of animals, and industrial waste from textile dyes:

> Having of late travelled often in wet weather through narrow streets in towns and villages, where dirtiness under foot and the scent arising from that filth which more or less infects the air of all thick settled towns, and I, being but weakly, have felt distress both in body and mind with that which is impure. In these journeys I have been where much cloth hath been dyed and sundry times walked over ground where much of their dye-stuffs have drained away.[36]

---

[33] Plank, *John Woolman's Path to the Peaceable Kingdom*, 152.
[34] Plank, *John Woolman's Path to the Peaceable Kingdom*, 87.
[35] Plank, *John Woolman's Path to the Peaceable Kingdom*, 27–28.
[36] Woolman, *The Journal and Major Essays*, 190.

Living continually in these filthy conditions, Woolman felt, equated with urban living. He takes a position that is counter to our largely urban lifestyles today. Living in these conditions, he believes, could obstruct one's ability to be sensitive to "the pure operation of the Holy Spirit":

> Near large towns there are many beasts slain to supply the market, and from their blood, etc., ariseth that which mixeth in the air. This, with the cleaning of many stables and other scents, the air in cities in a calm, wettish time is so opposite to the clear pure country air that I believe even the minds of people are in some degree hindered from the pure operation of the Holy Spirit, where they breathe a great deal in it.[37]

Yet, despite being discouraged, he follows this with the observation: "With God all things are possible, and the sincere in heart find help under the greatest difficulties, but I believe if Truth be singly attended to, way may open for some to live a country life who now are in cities."[38] This faith, that God's ongoing work in the world makes "all things possible," supported his motivation to persevere, regardless of how helpless he may have felt. Despite the systemic problems he saw, he believed that the power of the spirit might lead to solutions that he could not imagine.

He believed that port cities were particularly terrible places because they were centers of the slave economy. "He called the economic system that existed in those urban ports a 'deviation…from that simplicity that is in Christ…. [He] interwove his condemnation of urban apostasy with Isaiah's eschatological vision of an impending age of agrarian harmony."[39] Woolman specifically condemned not only Britain's entanglement with the slave trade, "the trade from this island to Africa," but also the oppressive conditions of "inhabitants being employed in factories" for the sake of those "growing outwardly great by gain."[40] He compares this degeneracy to "the right use of things where…we might inhabit [a] holy mountain" and thus be "disentangled from connections" to the oppression:

> the weight of this degeneracy hath lain so heavy upon me, the depth of this revolt been so evident, and desires in my heart been so ardent for a reformation, so ardent that we might come to that right use of things

---

[37] Woolman, *The Journal and Major Essays*, 190.
[38] Woolman, *The Journal and Major Essays*, 190.
[39] Jon R. Kershner, *John Woolman and the Government of Christ: A Colonial Quaker's Vision for the British Atlantic World* (New York: Oxford University Press, 2018), 101.
[40] Woolman, *The Journal and Major Essays*, 185.

where, living on a little, we might inhabit that holy mountain on which they neither *hurt nor destroy*! and may not only stand clear from oppressing our fellow creatures, but may be so disentangled from connections in interest with known oppressors, that in us may be fulfilled that prophecy: "Thou shalt be far from oppression" [Is. 54:14]. Under the weight of this exercise the sight of innocent birds in the branches and sheep in the pastures, who act according to the will of their Creator, hath at times tended to mitigate my trouble.[41]

The memory with which he ends this passage refers to his personal experience of finding comfort from animals.

In an article titled "John Woolman and the Land," Plank interestingly observes that readers often look for lessons in what Woolman refused to do, but to understand him "we need to think not only about the activities he opposed, but also those he pursued."[42] Plank uses issues regarding the land to argue that Woolman was a complex person. For one thing, he was a relatively wealthy landowner himself, compared with his neighbors. Therefore, he was not poor—an observation that shifts how one sees Woolman's "scathing" criticism of social hierarchy. Plank writes that "Land, wealth, and social hierarchy preoccupied Woolman for most of his adult life, and his writings on these subjects expose the complexity of his historical circumstances."[43] In some respects, despite his radicalism, his views were much like his fellow Quakers. For example, Woolman shared the Quaker perspective that "granted unusual respect and authority to women," but "[his] vision was patriarchal" in the disposition of his own real estate."[44] Plank points out that, unlike the confrontational style of Benjamin Lay who was censured by Friends, "Woolman was careful in every part of his ministry to proceed with support from his Quaker meetings."[45] Yet, Woolman championed the belief that the wealthy must be benevolent toward enslaved people and American Indians, and set an example for the poor. Plank concludes the article by saying that Woolman hoped for a future where people "with great landed

---

[41] Woolman, *The Journal and Major Essays*, 185.
[42] Geoffrey Plank, "John Woolman and Land," in *Quakers, Politics, and Economics*, eds. David R. Ross and Michael T. Snarr (Philadelphia: Friends Association for Higher Education, 2018), 304.
[43] Plank, "John Woolman and Land," 314.
[44] Plank, "John Woolman and Land," 316.
[45] Plank, "John Woolman and Land," 318.

estates would live and work face-to-face with their poorer and younger neighbors…. They would work hard, trade only locally, and live off the produce of the land."[46]

A recent book that directly addresses climate change is Kevin J. O'Brien's *The Violence of Climate Change: Lessons of Resistance from Nonviolent Activists*. With a chapter on each nonviolent activist, O'Brien writes about Woolman, Jane Addams, Dorothy Day, Martin Luther King, Jr., and Cesar Chavez. He calls them "a cloud of witnesses" regarding climate justice. O'Brien includes Woolman, because:

> he offers a lesson about the importance of transforming oneself. He sought not only to make the moral case against slavery but also to cleanse his life of all the privileges that slavery afforded to white men, leading him to give up his business and refuse to dye his clothes. His attempt to purify himself is an example to concerned people in the twenty-first century, who must decide how to deal with our own complicity in climate change.[47]

Woolman had to transform himself, not for his own sake, but because he felt called to address members of the Society of Friends and the broader society who saw slavery as just "a part of how the world worked" and who believed slavery was "not worth questioning." To do this, he needed to find "creative ways to raise awareness about the evils of slavery to everyone he encountered."[48] O'Brien adds that "nonviolence must be creative because it is countercultural—it always works against conventional wisdom and societal norms…. [and to] 'envision alternatives.'"[49] Woolman used his self-denying actions, as well as his ability to have conversations with people, to raise awareness of their own selfishness. In O'Brien's words,

> This selfishness lures many of us to continue enjoying the comforts of a middle-class lifestyle in the industrialized world, eating whatever we want, flying regularly on planes, running an air conditioner when it gets hot, and politely keeping our opinions to ourselves so as not to be rude. But the better and purer voice within us calls for a different way of life,

---

[46] Plank, "John Woolman and Land," 320.

[47] Kevin J. O'Brien, *The Violence of Climate Change: Lessons of Resistance from Nonviolent Activists* (Washington, DC: Georgetown University Press, 2017), 9.

[48] O'Brien, *The Violence of Climate Change*, 51.

[49] O'Brien, *The Violence of Climate Change*, 52.

a resistance to cultural patterns that cause violence. If we listen to the best voices within ourselves this will help us to cultivate empathy for those who suffer as the climate changes, and will help us to set an example of resistance against the systems that are responsible.[50]

Woolman seems to have had an extraordinary ability to talk with people and share his concerns about their behavior without them completely turning away. To listen to one's own "purer voice within" is at the heart of Woolman's own actions but also what he expected from others.[51] One would think that Woolman might have come across to his contemporaries as being self-righteous and off-putting. At times, he must have been difficult to accept for some people, because he pushed them in ways that were uncomfortable. He does not seem, however, to have been self-righteous, but rather expressed an unusual degree of humility and sincerity; at the same time, he was able to express his ideas to others. He appealed to others not by preaching how they should act, but by speaking in ways that left space for others to decide for themselves what actions were needed. He trusted that others, particularly his fellow Quakers, could turn to their own inward teacher to find the guidance they needed.

O'Brien concludes his book by emphasizing that Woolman, Addams, Day, King, and Chavez were all flawed individuals and all left unfinished work for their followers. He writes, "None of these witnesses defeated structural violence.... Day cautioned her readers against a sense of responsibility for solving the world's problems or seeking affirmation from any form of success. She asked, 'And why must we see results? Our work is to sow. Another generation will be reaping the harvest.'"[52] Woolman also wrote about the importance of not looking too much for one's own successes: "Travelling up and down of late, I have had renewed evidences that to be faithful to the Lord and content with his will concerning me is a most necessary and useful lesson for me to be learning, looking less at the effects of my labour than at the pure motion and reality of the concern as it arises from heavenly love."[53] Rather than being overly concerned with his

---

[50] O'Brien, The Violence of Climate Change, 85.

[51] The word "purity" is problematic for many people because of its association with oppressive cultural practices, but the word is useful in the ecological context for discussing the "purification" that Woolman sought in an impure world, but a more complete discussion relating to Woolman's understanding of purity and its connection to today's environmental concerns will have to wait for a future essay.

[52] O'Brien, The Violence of Climate Change, 202.

[53] Woolman, The Journal and Major Essays, 72.

own success, Woolman found it necessary to return again and again to the inward "motion of love" that was his source of guidance.[54]

Woolman's ideas and actions—those he refused to do and those he advocated—were guided by his mystical, prophetic vision. His environmental consciousness is rooted in his understanding and experience of the Kingdom of God. The best book on this is Jon Kershner's *John Woolman and the Government of Christ*. Kershner argues that Woolman's religious faith thoroughly shaped his alternative vision for society. He explains that Woolman's understanding of the Kingdom of God was based on divine revelation, which was not based upon "destruction of the present order" but on "the hopeful creation of a new order."[55] From this perspective, Woolman as an apocalyptist "stands as God's agent commissioned to make known the divine revelation and, so, is a harbinger of the new world unfolding in the present."[56] The purpose of Christ's incarnation was ongoing, "as Christ continually comes to humanity so that God's 'will be done on earth as it *is* in heaven.'"[57] Kershner emphasizes the degree to which Woolman believed he was already experiencing Isaiah's peaceable kingdom in the present.[58] In an article on Woolman's prophetic voice, Kershner writes: "Woolman believed that the physical world and the spiritual world were intertwined and that God was bringing about a new world that repudiated the values, politics, economics, and structures of a world alienated from God and God's purposes."[59] The desire to be responsive to God's ongoing revelation is evident throughout the *Journal* and essays.

In the *Journal*'s first paragraph, after stating his purpose for writing, which Woolman says is to "leave some hints of my experience of the goodness of God,"[60] he includes an early vision of creation, which appealed to him as a child. While the other children played, he tells the reader that he went off alone to read the Bible, and remembers reading the last chapter of Revelation: "He showed me a river of water, clear as crystal, proceeding out of the throne of God and the Lamb, etc." (Rev 22:1). William Barclay's *The Revelation of John* states, "the river of life may well stand for the abundant life God provides for his people

[54] Woolman, *The Journal and Major Essays*, 23, 127.
[55] Kershner, *John Woolman and the Government of Christ*, 9.
[56] Kershner, *John Woolman and the Government of Christ*, 10.
[57] Kershner, *John Woolman and the Government of Christ*, 85–86.
[58] Kershner, *John Woolman and the Government of Christ*, 102.
[59] Jon R. Kershner, "'Diminish Not a Word': The Prophetic Voice of John Woolman," in *Quakers and Literature*, ed. James W. Hood (Philadelphia: Friends Association for Higher Education, 2016), 21.
[60] Woolman, *The Journal and Major Essays*, 23.

which is there for the taking."[61] In *Breaking the Code: Understanding the Book of Revelation*, Bruce Metzger claims that the last chapters of Revelation elaborate "on the promise God had long before given to Isaiah that he would 'create new heavens and a new earth' (Is 65:17).... The new creation will have some continuity with creation as we now know it, yet it will be radically different.... God is continually making things new here and now.... The angel shows John a sparkling river that flows crystal clear from the heavenly throne, which indicates its boundless supply."[62] If one is reading with the environment and sustainability in mind, it's remarkable that Woolman emphasizes at the beginning of his *Journal* the importance of what he called "that pure habitation which I then believed God had prepared for his servants," a place of crystal clean water emanating from God for humanity.[63]

In *Journal* chapter 10, Woolman writes about prayer, saying, "The place of prayer is a precious habitation."[64] To equate "the place of prayer" with a "precious" place to live is a remarkable statement of one's home, or for that matter the earth, becoming a sacred space. The word "habitation" is particularly significant as it relates to a place of safety and "the throne of God and the Lamb."[65] He puts special emphasis on children by saying that "a trumpet was given me that I might sound forth this language, that the children might hear it and be invited to gather to this precious habitation, where the prayers of saints, as precious incense, ariseth up before the throne of God and the Lamb. I saw this habitation to be safe, to be inwardly quiet, when there was great stirrings and commotions in the world."[66] The passage seems to come full circle to the *Journal*'s first page where he told of his boyhood memory of reading Revelation. It is all the more significant because there is evidence that he thought to end the *Journal* here. Before sailing for England, not knowing if he would return, he left his manuscripts with Friends for possible editing and publication, and at that time the manuscript ended with this passage.[67] Here, possibly at what he thought might be the *Journal*'s final page, he brings together inward prayer, safety, and a place before the throne of God. Kershner writes of the significance of this passage, saying:

---

[61] William Barclay, *The Revelation of John*, Vol. 2 (Philadelphia: Westminster Press, 1976), 221.

[62] Bruce M. Metzger, *Breaking the Code: Understanding the Book of Revelation* (Nashville: Abingdon Press, 1993), 98, 99, 102.

[63] Woolman, *The Journal and Major Essays*, 23.

[64] Woolman, *The Journal and Major Essays*, 160.

[65] Woolman, *The Journal and Major Essays*, 160.

[66] Woolman, *The Journal and Major Essays*, 160.

[67] Woolman, *The Journal and Major Essays*, 160 n7.

Woolman did not attempt to identify the precise way God's "habitation" with humanity would be consummated…the location of this state of "habitation" was both in heaven and in the hearts of the faithful, the timing of the "habitation" was both in the future and at every moment. Woolman believed the reign of God had already begun within time, even as the reign of "the world" appeared to be in control…. [Through] faithfulness to that revelation, the individual served as a harbinger of the age to come.[68]

Woolman thus felt it was his duty to be an advocate for "the age to come." His authority, as Kershner explains, was grounded in his belief in his place in the eschaton.[69] Woolman "was simultaneously a citizen of God's kingdom and a sojourner on earth. He had the tenuous position of maintaining one foot in the eschaton and one foot in the world of eighteenth-century society, and so he felt commissioned to challenge the social practices of his fellow colonists with his alternative vision of the kingdom."[70] This belief, then, was a "realizing eschatology because it was at once a present reality and still unfolding."[71]

Kershner uses a 1755 epistle, drafted by Woolman, which he and thirteen other Friends signed, to illustrate this realizing eschatology. The epistle's purpose was to urge fellow Quakers not to support or participate in the French and Indian War by advising Friends:

to hold fast the profession of our faith without wavering—that our trust may not be in [humanity], but in the Lord alone…. We (being convinced that the gracious design of the Almighty in sending his son into the world was to repair the breach made by disobedience, to finish sin and transgression that his kingdom might come and his will be done on earth as it is in heaven) have found it to be our duty to cease from those national contests productive of misery and bloodshed, and submit our cause to him…. And we trust [that] as there is a faithful continuance to depend wholly upon the Almighty arm from one generation to another, the peaceable kingdom will gradually be extended "from sea to sea and from the river to the ends of the earth," to the completion of those

---

[68] Kershner, *John Woolman and the Government of Christ*, 91.
[69] "The 'eschaton' is that eon in which God's revealed purposes would be fulfilled." Kershner, *John Woolman and the Government of Christ*, 82.
[70] Kershner, *John Woolman and the Government of Christ*, 88.
[71] Kershner, *John Woolman and the Government of Christ*, 88.

> prophecies already begun, that "nation shall not lift up sword against
> nation nor learn war any more." (Is 2:4; Zec 9:10)[72]

This is a statement of the peace testimony as well as a statement of humanity's relationship to the Kingdom of God. Key phrases point to a shared belief in ongoing revelation. The epistle refers to "the gracious design of the Almighty" and the belief that by being faithful to God's will, which Woolman emphasizes by invoking the Lord's prayer ("his will be done on earth as it is in heaven"), the peaceable kingdom may be restored "from sea to sea." The work of God and humanity is ongoing, and Friends must follow through "to the completion of those prophecies already begun."

Kershner also argues that Woolman "had a greater focus on the emergence of a spiritualized eschaton within history" that distinguishes him from his peers and helps explain the extent and breadth of his radicalism.[73] For Woolman, revelation took precedence over all earthly possessions and power.

> The "Government of the Prince of peace," Woolman believed, was the reigning power established through the "Dominion" of God's love. The government of Christ was already present, he claimed, but individuals and society could interrupt its dominion if they acted outside of the divine revelation, or, as he put it, when "Power is put forth separate from pure Love." Oppressive labor practices, wealth accumulation, and opulence were against the "Nature of his Government," because they signified a rejection of God's perfect ordering of the "visible Creation."[74]

Woolman expressed this conflict of loyalties as the opposition of "customs" and "Truth," where Truth takes on meanings that encompass the spirit of Christ and the Kingdom of God. One place where he emphasizes this opposition is at the beginning of his first essay against keeping slaves. There he states that harmful practices are often "Customs generally approved and received by youth from their superiors," but he goes on to say that "the highest wisdom [is] to forego customs and popular opinions, and try the treasures of the soul by the infallible standard: Truth."[75] By contrasting "customs" with "Truth" Woolman has summarized a great deal of the conflicts felt by many today.

---

[72] Woolman, *The Journal and Major Essays*, 48–49.
[73] Kershner, *John Woolman and the Government of Christ*, 12.
[74] Kershner, *John Woolman and the Government of Christ*, 90.
[75] Woolman, *The Journal and Major Essays*, 198.

As a college professor, I have often felt that I failed to teach John Woolman's *Journal* adequately. His *Journal* and essays are a difficult read for many people. But there are always a handful of students who take Woolman's writings to heart. One of them, Emily Densmore, who is a recent Roanoke College graduate, wrote me the following:

> While I know little to nothing about economics, the way Woolman lived life so intentionally—practicing what he preached for lack of a better phrase—really gave me a lot to reflect on. I've been thinking a lot about living intentionally and the small practices I can implement to spread peace....
>
> I was very struck by the quote "As servants of God, what land or estate we hold, we hold under him as his gift.... Nor is this gift absolute, but conditional, for us to occupy as dutiful children"—humbling and powerful. I'm not sure I have the words to properly describe how this quote struck me, but it renewed in me a sense of greater purpose, of gratitude, and responsibility.[76]

Emily's heartfelt response to Woolman is uplifting. It speaks to me of our ongoing work, as activists, advocates, and educators. We are wise when we follow Woolman's example of "looking less at the effects of my labour than at the pure motion and reality of the concern as it arises from heavenly love."[77]

---

[76] Emily Densmore, email to the author, May 8, 2018, used by permission; Woolman, *The Journal and Major Essays*, 256.

[77] Woolman, *The Journal and Major Essays*, 72.

3| Quakers and Quaker Farmers in the Colonial and Early Republic Era and the Development of Two Views of Nature

By Douglas J. Burks

> *What people do about their ecology depends on what they think about themselves in relation to things around them. Human ecology is deeply conditioned by beliefs about our nature and destiny—that is, by religion.*

> —Lynn White, Jr. [1]

Abstract: *In colonial and pre-republic America we see the nascent development of two types of Quaker environmentalism stemming from differing attitudes towards the natural world: an ecocentric and anthropocentric environmentalism and view of nature. These two views can be understood in the context of early Quaker farmers and artisans and their experiences on the land.*

Many Quaker farmers came from poorer areas of Great Britain in a time when the commons were being enclosed; they came not only to escape religious persecution but also for economic opportunity and a chance to provide for their families. Their industriousness and hard work built farms not only for subsistence but to produce cash crops, leveraging earnings to buy more land to provide for their children and future generations. These farmers saw the land as a means to an end and as a gift from the Creator to be used for their sustenance, believing that natural resources were not to be wasted and misused but utilized efficiently to maximize return. This anthropocentric view of nature as a gift to be used for human benefit, prioritizing land use for the needs of current and future generations, was consistent among other farmers across the mid-colonies. A loss of soil fertility resulted within a generation, driving many Quaker farmers

---

[1] Lynn White, Jr., "The Historical Roots of Our Ecologic Crisis," *Science* 155, no. 3767 (1967): 1203–1207, at 1205.

to develop more arable land or to move to other areas where land was available for a cheap price. Decisions about land use were driven by economic considerations.

Meanwhile, a second view emerged from artisans and spiritual leaders such as William Penn, Anthony Benezet, and John Woolman. This view developed into ecocentric environmentalism. These Friends perceived the natural world as a personification of God: nature reflected God's beauty and essence—therefore, to harm nature was to harm God's kingdom. Nature had moral standing as God's creation; animals and the natural world needed consideration when making choices. Benezet did not eat animal flesh because he believed animals held the light of the Creator. Woolman refused to ride in stagecoaches in England because horses were treated immorally. This is a nascent ecocentric view of the environment, a view that at times meant nature would take precedence over human convenience.

I. The Context

To understand the views of nature that developed during the colonial era among American Quakers, one must first look at the setting and context: the availability of cheap and fertile land along with strong family values shaped how early Quaker farmers responded to the pioneer colonial world. They built communities to sustain their families both physically and religiously. During the colonial and early republic years of what became the United States of America, two ways of relating to the natural world can be viewed among Friends, and these can now be identified as precursors to today's anthropocentric and ecocentric views of nature.

II. Colonial and Early Republic Period

1. Mid-Atlantic States

A wealth of knowledge about early Quaker farmers in the Mid-Atlantic States in America's colonial and early republic period exists. In many ways they resembled other New England and Mid-Atlantic farmers: they came to the American Colonies seeking both religious freedom and economic opportunity, searching for a place that could nourish their families and protect them from outside corruption. In this, they shared the view of Puritans who, like Quakers, were also escaping a changing family structure in Great Britain. In the sixteenth and seventeenth centuries, England "experienced an alarming increase in population, a rapid rise in prices, the enclosure of traditional common lands, and the sudden appearances of a large class of propertyless men and women who flocked to the growing cities," disrupting family and religious life.[2]

Welsh Quakers were especially focused on family, children, and remaining faithful to their religion. Levy observed that these Welsh Friends "now accepted a religious obligation to protect their children's gift of grace from 'carnal talkers,' not simply by protecting and cherishing them when young children but also by settling them in morally protected situations. This task required more wealth than most northwestern Welsh middling households had. Most of their children left Quakerism."[3] This led these early Quaker settlers to seek places where they could prosper and provide for children.

Quaker farms, like farms more generally during this period, were enterprises involving all nuclear and extended family members, serving the purposes of producing a commodity and sustaining the family. However, Quaker farmers in New Jersey, the Delaware Valley, and Appalachia differed from other early farmers in this era because of the higher status of women and the greater focus on providing for and sustaining children. At the same time, the Quaker practice of buying up farmland for their children to inherit contributed to an erosion of the commons in both the Mid-Atlantic and Appalachian regions. As Barry Levy states:

> The middle colonies were where the virtuous and prosperous family farm of legend and lore actually existed. Although this phenomenon was primarily due to the superior farmland of the middle Atlantic region, Quaker domesticity did play a role. Delaware Valley Pennsylvania Quakers and their New Jersey neighbors were the leaders and pace-setters in the construction of a family-based wheat and flour trade.[4]

Quaker fathers in New Jersey and Pennsylvania were driven to "buy enormous quantities of land, which were devoted to their sons, and which they distributed generously."[5]

The first farmers recruited by William Penn for his colony were Quakers from upland provincial British areas. Quakers from this region were of limited means, lacking the resources to raise their families with "the high costs inherent in radical Quaker domesticity, particularly the costs of controlling the placement

---

[2] Steven Mintz and Susan Kellogg, *Domestic Revolutions: A Social History of American Family Life* (New York: The Free Press, 1988), 8.

[3] Barry Levy, *Quakers and the American Family: British Settlement in the Delaware Valley* (New York: Oxford University Press, 1988), Kindle loc. 176–178.

[4] Levy, *Quakers and the American Family*, Kindle loc. 205–207.

[5] Levy, *Quakers and the American Family*, Kindle loc. 187–188.

and marriages of Quaker children, and the stringent economic limitations of [their] original, upland homelands."[6] Pennsylvania and the Delaware Valley offered an opportunity to succeed and live out their deep family values. An estimated 200 or more upland British families settled in the Delaware Valley between 1682 and 1700. These farmers were industrious and innovative compared to other farmers in the Delaware Valley; they were driven to accumulate wealth and land to provide for their offspring. Quakers possessed double the area (500 acres compared to 200 acres) owned by other settlers.[7] In his history of Quakers in America, Jones states that early settlers recruited by

> Penn were Englishmen, mostly yeomen. They had bought their lands from Penn from rough maps before leaving England, at the very moderate price which he asked of £100 for 5000 acres or smaller tracts in proportion, with a quit-rent annually of one shilling for each hundred acres. This enabled many a poor English renter to become a landowner in Pennsylvania, and, as a matter of fact, these farmers greatly prospered, though Penn had difficulty in collecting his quit-rents.[8]

These early Quaker immigrants came to an undeveloped frontier and elected to alter the land and build shelter. Woods needed clearing, fields plowing and planting for the first time. First crops were seeded by hand and "cut with a sickle, threshed with a flail. Spelt wheat, barley and rye were first cultivated."[9] Each year these settlers plowed more land and improved their housing. Within four years of establishing their first farms, early Quaker settlers produced enough wheat surplus to begin trading with the West Indies, and commerce eventually extended into southern Europe.[10]

Quaker women played an important role in readying farm crops for market, particularly in the linen and the butter trades. It is estimated that 47,860 pounds of butter were shipped to the West Indies in 1710. In his diary, Benjamin Hawley describes purchasing 170 pounds of butter for market from neighboring Quaker women in 1763.

---

[6] Levy, *Quakers and the American Family*, Kindle loc. 181.

[7] Levy, *Quakers and the American Family*, Kindle loc. 181.

[8] Rufus M. Jones, Isaac Sharpless, and Amelia M. Gummere, *The Quakers in the American Colonies*, reprint edition (London: Macmillan and Co., Ltd., 1901, 1923; Charleston, SC: BiblioBazaar, 2010), Kindle loc. 8673.

[9] George R. Prowell, *History of York County Pennsylvania, Volume I* (Chicago: J. H. Beers and Co., 1907), 120.

[10] Jones, Sharpless, and Gummere, *The Quakers in the American Colonies.*

Delaware Valley Quaker farmers treated their land as a resource for commodity production. They were business oriented, always focused on the bottom line of generating yield for profit:

> The soil was carefully cultivated and gave rich returns, the principal crop being wheat, although there was much variety of products. There were some small manufactories, and a good export trade in grain, flour, and furs was carried on with England and the West Indies. So prosperous was Pennsylvania that it became one of the richest and most populous of the American settlements; and before the Revolution, Philadelphia, the great market of the province, became the largest town in the thirteen colonies.[11]

Farms above all provided for the family. In describing the farming of Jacob and Hannah Peirce with their sons Johnathon and David in the 1790s, Walter Peirce offers from Jacob's diary a rich description of farm life. Meat raised, cured, and consumed on the farm included mutton, beef, and pork, as well as leather for the production of shoes and clothing. The family garden produced potatoes, turnips, cabbage, peas, sweet potatoes, cucumbers, strawberries, pumpkins, and watermelons. From their orchards they harvested apples, pears, plums, peaches, grapes and chestnuts. They milled lumber for their homes and buildings, produced lime from quarried limestone, and used a kiln to turn clay into bricks. The Peirce farm was typical of agrarian Quakers of the colonial and republic period: they developed a self-sustaining operation to provide for their needs as well as excess yield to accumulate wealth.[12] Quaker farmers were pragmatic, holding a scientific view of farming; technical education in agriculture was highly valued in the early republic period. Woody cites a 1796 letter from Philadelphia Yearly Meeting, which "stated that Friends are engaged in an undertaking to furnish Quaker farmers with some of the comforts of civilized life. A fund is raising to supply the expense of instructing them in Agriculture, in mechanic arts, and in some useful branches of learning."[13]

---

[11] William S. Stob, *The Life and Times of William Pettit Raley and His Family in America: A Glimpse at Life in the 18th and 19th Centuries* (N.p.: Trustees of the Stob Living Trust, 1993, 2017), Kindle edition, 40.

[12] Walter Peirce, "A Farmer of the Early Republic," *Bulletin of Friends' Historical Association* 19, no. 1 (1930): 7–15, Project MUSE.

[13] Thomas Woody, *Early Quaker Education in Pennsylvania*, Kindle edition (New York: Teachers College, Columbia University, 1920), 263.

2. The Southern Colonies

Life on the Pennsylvania frontier was pleasant and profitable for many Quaker settlers, yet farmers from New Jersey and Pennsylvania began moving south to Virginia and the Carolinas and north into western New York as early as the 1770s in search of more land; for example, "The Raleys were in York County for about 10 years, yet always looking for a better opportunity elsewhere."[14] They along with many others from Pennsylvania moved into northern Virginia a few years before the American Revolution. In the spring of 1772 the family "journeyed some 100 miles south to Loudoun County, VA, settling near Waterford, about 10 miles south of Harpers Ferry and the Potomac River."[15]

Early settlers came to Virginia because land was cheap. Alexander Ross, member of the Nottingham Meeting in southern Chester County, PA, and Morgan Bryan obtained about 100,000 acres of land in about 1730 near the Opeckan River.[16] In 1733, Amos Janney and his wife Mary Janney purchased 400 acres on the Catoctin Creek. They had come from Bucks County, PA looking for greater opportunity. Amos built a gristmill and a sawmill, which were successful enterprises that provided farmers the opportunity to send their grains to market.[17] Francis Hague, the husband of Mary's sister Jane, bought a farm in the area soon after.[18] The county began to build and improve local roads, facilitating the movement of goods to and from Janney's Mill. The village of Waterford had begun to grow rapidly by 1780, becoming a town with a large Quaker community.[19] Werner Janney and Asa Moore Janney note that like the relatives they left behind in Bucks and Chester counties, "Goose Creekers, moreover, were not so overwhelmingly meek and pious as the writing of their ministers may have presented them. They were industrious, innovative farmers, aggressive business people, and stern but fair in their financial dealings."[20]

Inevitably, grain crops quickly depleted soils of minerals and needed nutrients. Phillip Price in Chester County began using lime in the form of gypsum

---

[14] Stob, *The Life and Times of William Pettit Raley*, 58.

[15] Stob, *The Life and Times of William Pettit Raley*, 58.

[16] James Pinkney Pleasant Bell, *Our Quaker Friends of ye olden time; being in part a transcript of the minute books of Cedar Creek meeting, Hanover County, and the South River meeting, Campbell County, VA*, Google Books (Lynchburg, VA: J. P. Bell Company, 1905), 193.

[17] "History," Waterford Foundation, Inc., accessed July 2018, http://waterford-foundation.org/history/.

[18] "Quaker research in Virginia — Hopewell Meeting," Hay Genealogy, accessed July 2018, http://haygenealogy.com/hay/quaker/quaker-VA.html.

[19] Waterford Foundation, Inc., "History."

[20] Werner Janney and Asay Moore Janney, *Ye Meetg Hous Smal: A Short Account of Friends in Loudoun County, Virginia, 1732–1980* (Elkton, VA: X-high Graphic Arts, 1980), 1.

and manure to replenish his fields. His wife Rachel brought these practices to Loudoun County in Virginia along with Israel Janney, who brought some limestone back after attending Yearly Meeting in Philadelphia to use on an oat field.[21]

Land degradation and family growth would lead Virginia Friends to migrate south and west in search of better and cheaper land. Quakers in migration followed kin who struck out as pioneers to new areas. These pioneers would encourage Quakers to follow, guiding relatives and friends to good, cheap parcels of land; this is reflected in the Quaker settlement of Virginia, where family names from Loudoun County parallel those in Bucks County, PA:

> In the first Quaker settlement of Loudoun, surnames such as Mead, Hague, Janney, Palmer, Clowes, Yardley, Bond, and Hough figure large. Why did a relatively few names count for so much? The answer is relatively simple. They were neighbors in Loudoun because they were neighbors in Bucks. They were neighbors—a term synonymous with family. The neighbors might not be your brothers and sisters or in-laws, but they were kin. And where your kin went and spied out good land, you were likely to go too.[22]

The deep religious commitment of Friends encouraged marriage within the faith during the colonial period; this led to concentrated Quaker settlements as families moved in search of farmland and opportunity.

Most Quakers came from Pennsylvania and Virginia to the Piedmont section of North Carolina for cheap farmland. Following patterns in settlement and migration, economic factors attracted Quakers to the area. Besides cheap land, the climate was more favorable in North Carolina, where the growing season was longer, although the soil was not as fertile as in the Delaware Valley. They sought land on which they could make a living and build tight-knit Quaker communities to practice their faith.

III. Spiritual Leaders of the Colonial and Early Republic Period: Savory and Weighty Friends in Public Ministry

Early Quaker leaders and more urban Friends expressed a different view of the natural world: a perception of nature as a part of God and as a reflection of divine essence to be savored and protected; from that foundation, an ecocentric environmentalism took root.

---

[21] Janney and Janney, *Ye Meetg Hous Smal*, 1.
[22] Janney and Janney, *Ye Meetg Hous Smal*, 6.

1. William Penn

William Penn (1644–1718) was the son of Admiral Sir William Penn, a favorite in the court of King Charles. Penn was a serious young man: "while at a high church Oxford College he was surreptitiously attending the meetings and listening to the preaching of the despised and outlawed Quakers."[23] He professed membership in the Religious Society of Friends or Quakers at the age of 22. In 1668 he was imprisoned for writing a tract, *The Sandy Foundation Shaken*, which attacked the doctrine of the Trinity, and he was imprisoned on several occasions for his beliefs.

King Charles II of England had a large loan with Penn's father. After the death of Sir William Penn, King Charles II settled the loan by granting the younger Penn a large area west and south of New Jersey on March 4, 1681. A few months later, the Duke of York granted him the three "lower counties" (later Delaware). Penn named the territory Sylvania (woods) and the King added Penn to the name: Penn's Sylvania became Pennsylvania, to honor the elder Sir William Penn.

Penn wrote *The Frame of Government of Pennsylvania* in 1682, which guaranteed religious freedom and developed a provincial representative council and general assembly.[24] Penn had hoped that Pennsylvania would be a profitable venture for himself and his family; he marketed the colony throughout Europe in various languages and, as a result, settlers flocked to Pennsylvania. Despite its rapid growth and diversity, however, the colony never turned a profit for Penn or his family; in fact, Penn would later be imprisoned in England for debt, and at the time of his death in 1718, he was penniless.

William Penn's actions and directives displayed a view of nature broader than mere utilitarian use for sustenance. When he designed Greene Countrie Towne (Philadelphia), Penn insisted settlers preserve one acre of trees for every five acres they cleared. He also required oak and mulberry trees to be preserved for shipbuilding and for the silk industry. He imported many trees from England, including fruit trees, hawthorn, walnuts, and hazelnuts to grow alongside the native trees.[25]

[23] Sydney George Fisher, *The Quaker Colonies, a chronicle of the proprietors of the Delaware*, Kindle edition (New Haven, CT: Yale University Press, 1919), 5.

[24] William Penn, "Excerpts from *Frame of Government of Pennsylvania*," Constitution Society, 1682, accessed July 2018, http://constitution.org/bcp/frampenn.htm.

[25] Shan Holt, "Open Space Adventures in William Penn's 'Greene Countrie Town,'" from the Supplement to the 120th Annual Meeting (American Historical Association, 2005), http://historians.org/annual-meeting/past-meetings/supplement-to-the-120th-annual-meeting/open-space-adventures-in-william-penns-greene-countrie-town.

In *Fruits of Solitude* he wrote, "It were Happy if we studied Nature more in natural Things; and acted according to Nature; whose rules are few, plain and most reasonable."[26] He also wrote, "The Country is both the Philosopher's Garden and his Library, in which he Reads and Contemplates the Power, Wisdom and Goodness of God. ... A Sweet and Natural Retreat from Noise and Talk, and allows opportunity for Reflection, and gives the best Subjects for it."[27]

A nascent spiritual value of the natural world can be seen: "Despite the obvious need for the production of food for [people] and livestock in this new land, Penn encouraged the growing of ornamentals as well as the planting of fruits and grains. As early as 1698, Edward Shippen, a Quaker merchant, was said to have had an 'extraordinary fine and large garden' in Philadelphia."[28] One can see the influence of his aristocratic status on Penn's appreciation of the beauty of nature, and his belief in the importance of maintaining gardens for the enjoyment of these aesthetics. While Penn's suggestions remain anthropocentric in the sense that the trees and gardens were to be planted for people to enjoy, this practice leans more toward an ecocentric view in that the plants were seen as valuable in themselves, rather than for a strictly utilitarian purpose.

2. Anthony Benezet

Anthony Benezet (1713–1784), a child of French Huguenots, immigrated with his family to Philadelphia in 1731. He joined the Religious Society of Friends as an 18-year-old and became an early abolitionist, along with John Woolman, with a ministry to relieve the suffering of slaves. Benezet was never very successful as a merchant and turned to teaching at Germantown School in 1739. In 1754, he left the Friends English School to set up the first public girls' school in the Americas.

In teaching, Benezet told students: "[The One] who made us, made the bird and the fish; [the One] who made them loves to do them good. Bird and fish can feel pain, even as we do: So be sure that thou hurt them not in thy play."[29]

He also founded the Negro School at Philadelphia for black children in 1770. He wrote several treatises on slavery, including: "A short account of that part of Africa inhabited by the negroes. And A Caution and Warning to Great

---

[26] William Penn, *Some Fruits of Solitude In Reflections And Maxims*, reprint edition (London: Headley Brothers, 1905), 23.

[27] Penn, *Some Fruits of Solitude*, 61.

[28] Penn, *Some Fruits of Solitude*, 7.

[29] Anthony Benezet, *The Pennsylvania Spelling-Book*, third edition (Providence, Rhode Island, 1782), 16.

Britain and her Colonies, in a short representation of the calamitous state of the enslaved negroes in the British Dominions." [30]

Perceiving the value of all human beings as children of God containing the Light within, he began to enlarge that view to include all animals. He saw equality among not only all people but also in God's creatures. Central to Benezet's view of the world was the conviction that creation and all of its inhabitants were the special conception of God, worthy of respect and consideration. Benezet saw beauty in nature and appreciated animals as a gift from God.[31]

Benezet condemned wasting the gift of God's creation and castigated those who mistreated animals. His regard for nature is reflected in his inability to sacrifice animals for food, or even kill vermin and insects. As he expressed, he had early on formed "a kind of a League of Amity and Peace with the animal Creation, looking upon them as the most grateful, as well as the most reasonable Part of God's Creatures."[32] Benezet could not bring himself to harm or injure animals that God had created. "If the Geese must be slain," preparatory to their presentation as gifts, Benezet informed his friend John Smith of Burlington, NJ, "I shall chuse to be excused from being the Executioner.... I shall scarce ever imbrue my Hands in the Blood of any Creature, having in a measure left off eating Meat, as it conduces to my Health."[33]

Benezet was not a conservationist in the modern sense, however, and saw no need to protect the "wilderness." He believed land should be used effectively to produce the most bounty possible; though he felt ill at ease with commerce he did not condemn the use of the creation for profit. He accepted the need to sell agricultural commodities for fair gain.[34] Benezet's attention to the experiences of animals, and his willingness to do without meat rather than harm them, is a further step toward an ecocentric view from that of Penn.

---

[30] Robert Vaux, *Memoirs of the life of Anthony Benezet*, Kindle edition (Philadelphia: J.P. Parke, 1817), Kindle loc. 233–237.

[31] Vaux, *Memoirs of the life of Anthony Benezet*.

[32] George S. Brookes, *Friend Anthony Benezet* (Philadelphia: University of Pennsylvania Press, 1937), 39.

[33] Donald Brooks Kelley, "'A Tender Regard to the Whole Creation': Anthony Benezet and the Emergence of an Eighteenth-Century Quaker Ecology," *The Pennsylvania Magazine of History and Biography*, 106, no. 1 (1982): 69–88, at 76. jstor.org/stable/20091642.

[34] Vaux, *Memoirs of the Life of Anthony Benezet*.

3. John Woolman

John Woolman (1720–1772) was born in New Jersey, and worked on his father Samuel Woolman's farm until he was 21. In his *Journal* he later described a youthful experience, sharing a story about thoughtlessly killing a mother robin, and then out of pity the babies he noticed in her nest.[35] This experience weighed on his heart, inspiring him to love and protect all living things from then on.

He left the farm to enter a trade and felt a calling to traveling ministry, speaking most famously against slavery. He traveled the colonies to Maryland's east shore and the Rhode Island coast, among other places, where he carried his message of abolition, bringing his antislavery doctrine to the attention of ship-owners.

Woolman also strongly believed animals should not be mistreated. While in England, he refused to take stagecoaches because of the abuse of the horses. He wrote in his *Journal*: "Stage-coaches frequently go upwards of one hundred miles in twenty-four hours; and I have heard Friends say in several places that it is common for horses to be killed with hard driving, and that many others are driven till they grow blind.... So great is the hurry in the spirit of this world, that in aiming to do business quickly and to gain wealth the creation at this day doth loudly groan."[36] Woolman's view draws close to a modern ecocentric view of nature. He stood strongly for causes of justice through love, speaking firmly and before his time for the rights of all people, and perceiving that the right to live justly extends to non-human life as well.

IV. Two Views of Nature

We see among colonial and early republic Quakers two views of nature and the environment in nascent forms. These two views are predominant in our environmental thinking today in the United States of America; the first is an anthropocentric view of nature, and the second an ecocentric view of nature and the environment.

---

[35] John Woolman, *The Journal of the Life, Gospel Labours and Christian Experiences, of that Faithful Minister of Jesus Christ, John Woolman, to which are Added, His Last Epistle, and Other Writings*, Google Books (Philadelphia: Friends' Bookstore, 1883), 20–21.

[36] Woolman, *Journal*, 199.

1. Anthropocentric View of Nature

An anthropocentric view perceives nature as serving humanity, lacking any intrinsic value, and worthy of conscientious consideration only in terms of its value to human activity and needs. Nature exists as a means to an end, with no moral standing in and of itself; environmental concern and action exists solely in relation to the impact on humanity. The anthropocentric view of nature widely held by Quaker farmers in the colonial and early republic period continues with many Quaker farmers in the Midwest today. In this we see that Friends have varying views of nature even in our modern era.

Genesis 1:26–28 says, "And God blessed them, and God said unto them, 'Be fruitful, and multiply, and replenish the earth, and subdue it: and have dominion over the fish of the sea, and over the fowl of the air, and over every living thing that moveth upon the earth.'"[37] Based on this Genesis command, many early Quakers assumed God had given them dominion over creation. Both George Fox and Robert Barclay believed God intended humanity to use nature for human benefit. Barclay, in his *An Apology for the True Christian Divinity*, contends: "For it is beyond question, that whatever thing the creation affords is for the use of [humanity], and the moderate use of them is lawful." He went on to state that people had the right to feed and clothe themselves well if their income and education could afford it, and if they did so without "superfluity, nor immoderately."[38]

Quaker farmers viewed their farms as a resource to produce commodities for profit, allowing the purchase of more acreage for maintaining and expanding their religious communities and families. They saw their land and animals through the utilitarian lens of providing sustenance and profit; land was a gift from the Creator to be used for human benefit. They believed they were called to use their land efficiently and to its full potential for the betterment of their kin and community. Because of this, they also felt obliged to treat animals humanely, but as no more than food sources and beasts of burden.

By exploiting their land to maximize production, they ran it into the ground. As these early settlers farmed, their soil decreased in fertility:

> Like pioneer farmers of all ages and all lands, the first settlers took little thought of soil conservation.... Within a generation after the first farms

---

[37] King James Version (KJV).

[38] Robert Barclay, *An Apology for the True Christian Divinity: Being an Explanation and Vindication of the Principles and Doctrines of the People Called Quakers*, ed. Edward Marsh, eleventh edition, Google Books (London: Arthur Wallis, Printer and Bookseller, 1849), 489.

were established along the Delaware there were signs that the soil fertility account in the land was getting low, if not already over-drawn. By 1730 many Bucks County farmers were complaining about poor yields.... [W]heat yields had declined from an average of 20 to 30 bushels an acre to ten bushels or less.[39]

Like most of the European American settlers who first cultivated the land, early Quaker colonists did so for agricultural purposes, not practicing crop rotation, and without the use of natural fertilizer such as manure.[40] As productivity decreased, fields were abandoned, while new areas were cleared and cultivated, reflecting their belief that land was a capital resource to be used for human benefit. Thomas Jefferson summed up this view of land as a means to an end by stating, "We can buy an acre of new land cheaper than we can manure an old one."[41] The decrease in fertility drove many Quaker farmers to migrate to better farmland.

2. Ecocentric View of Nature

An ecocentric environmentalism ascribes intrinsic value to the natural world. Further, it perceives nature as having equal value to human beings and their interests. As understood by many present-day Friends, ecocentric environmentalism attributes a spiritual value to nature as the creation of God, which means that at times we are called to make sacrifices for its good. This is reflected in the mission statement of Quaker Earthcare Witness:

> WE ARE CALLED to live in right relationship with all Creation, recognizing that the entire world is interconnected and is a manifestation of God.

> WE WORK to integrate into the beliefs and practices of the Religious Society of Friends the Truth that God's Creation is to be respected, protected, and held in reverence in its own right, and the Truth that human aspirations for peace and justice depend upon restoring the earth's ecological integrity.

---

[39] Stevenson Whitcomb Fletcher, *Pennsylvania Agriculture and Country Life: 1640–1840* (Harrisburg, PA: Pennsylvania Historical and Museum Commission, 1950), 123–124.

[40] Robert V. Smith, "Soil Survey of Adams County, Pennsylvania," US Department of Agriculture, 2005, 12, accessed January 2019, http://nrcs.usda.gov/Internet/FSE_MAN-USCRIPTS/pennsylvania/PA001/0/PA_Adams.pdf.

[41] Smith, "Soil Survey of Adams County, Pennsylvania," 125.

WE PROMOTE these Truths by being patterns and examples, by communicating our message, and by providing spiritual and material support to those engaged in the compelling task of transforming our relationship to the earth.[42]

Early Quaker spiritual leaders demonstrated beliefs and practices moving toward this view of nature. Friends in the eighteenth century interpreted the use of land and the environment through the lens of the Bible, though different people came to different conclusions about what that meant. Anthony Benezet and John Woolman saw creation as the special creation of God, a divine gift to be revered and respected. They began to articulate a Quaker view that creation care extends to animals, and in fact to all life.

In our modern world, the early conceptions of environmental concern mentioned above can feel somewhat lacking, but Woolman's and Benezet's views were the leading edge in their era, forming the seeds of an environmental concern and ethos. As Kelley notes:

We need to study Benezet and others in his circle to begin a reassessment of the powerful role of religious values in the formation of America's environmental concern. We need especially to reassess the influence of religion on ecology and on attitudes regarding the relationship of living things one to another. We may discover that the Quaker love for "God and his Creatures" in the eighteenth century ran deeper and contained more durability of purpose and more breadth of implication than did the better known Puritan or Transcendentalist visions of an earlier or later era.[43]

Several Friends including John Woolman, John Churchman, Joshua Evans, John Hunt, and Anthony Benezet experienced what it meant to be a Christian by direct encounter with the Inner Light and a growing mysticism.[44] Their God was not as similar to the Old Testament God as to the God of the Sermon

---

[42] Learn more at Quaker Earthcare Witness at http://quakerearthcare.org, or in chapter 18 of this volume: Shelley Tanenbaum, "Earthcare as a Quaker Value: The Formation and Continued Work of Quaker Earthcare Witness." See also Appendix D, Quaker Earthcare Vision and Witness.

[43] Kelley, "A Tender Regard to the Whole Creation," 87.

[44] Donald Brooks Kelley, "Friends and Nature in America," *Pennsylvania History: A Journal of Mid-Atlantic Studies* 53 (1986): 257–272.

on the Mount, a God of love and beneficence: "There, amid the insights of collective mysticism, they sensed the presence of their Creator and saw in his radiance, if he vouchsafed it, the world transformed to a new order and harmony."[45] This led them to see God, nature, and humanity living "in balance with God's environment, in sheltering regard to his 'plants,' 'seeds,' and 'vines,' and in ecological equilibrium with all God's 'beasts' and 'creeping things.' Religion, in powerful fashion, had spawned a new eighteenth-century ecology, or at least a distinctive ecological perspective on the world." [46]

V. Conclusion

Early Quakers in the United States of America expressed two differing views of nature: anthropocentric and a nascent ecocentrism. Many Quaker farmers displayed a different view of nature derived from pragmatically working the land and raising animals for human gain, perceiving the natural world as a gift from God who commanded dominion over the earth. These Friends took seriously their moral duty to be good stewards of nature, determining decisions about land use and animal husbandry by prioritizing human needs. This attitude is "often agrarian (farming-oriented) and can be productivist/productionist (seeks to maximize and privilege the economic productivity of ecosystems or altered forms thereof for human financial gain). The latter aspect relates to a theology that holds that Creation is God's exclusive gift to 'Man' and that to not maximize the utility of it is disrespectful of God and His creation as long as such use is not excessive (e.g. driven by sins such as greed)."[47] Quaker farmers were pragmatic and saw the land and nature as gift from God for their use. They were to be fruitful and build a kingdom of God on earth in which their future generations would be sustained. Nature was to be used for human good but in a wise manner.

In contrast, weighty leaders and urban Friends attributed aesthetic and spiritual value to the natural world. Aristocrat William Penn encouraged settlers in his colony to save woodlands and grow gardens. Woolman and Benezet also perceived creation as reflecting the nature of God, and encouraged a moral duty to protect and not harm animals, believing them God's creatures. They had a

---

[45] Donald Brooks Kelley, "The Evolution of Quaker Theology and the Unfolding of a Distinctive Quaker Ecological Perspective in Eighteenth-Century America," *Pennsylvania History: A Journal of Mid-Atlantic Studies* 52 (1985): 242–253, at 248.

[46] Kelley, "The Evolution of Quaker Theology," 248.

[47] Steve Douglas, "Religious Environmentalism in the West. I: A focus on Christianity," *Religion Compass* 3, no. 4 (2009): 717–737, at 722, doi-org/10.1111/j.1749-8171.2009.00161.x.

strong and consistent vision that humanity must live in harmony with nature; this included making sacrifices for its protection. Benezet's perception of nature was a spiritual one in which "his solutions to ecological abuse centered on reformation of the individual—individual self-restraint."[48] This early, non-Darwinian, ecocentric view of nature upholds the intrinsic value of creation, and is centered in a spiritual unity with nature.

We still see these two major views of environmentalism in the Society of Friends; they expose both a philosophical and religious difference that creates a tension within the Quaker community and reflects the surrounding culture.

---

[48] Kelley, "A Tender Regard to the Whole Creation," 70.

4 | Ruth Stout, the Queen of Mulch

By Jean Mulhern and Cathy Pitzer

Abstract: Ruth Stout (1884–1980) was an American Quaker considered to be the mother of organic gardening. Ruth's popular books focused on her "no-work" gardening system, all published after she was 60 years old. Her columns were featured in Mother Earth News and Rodale's Organic Gardening. At a time when chemical fertilizers and pesticides were becoming popular (the 1950s), Ruth promoted the use of mulch to raise vegetables organically and control weeds without back-breaking labor. Her no-till philosophy was decades before its time; however, with several of her mulch and plain living books still in print, she continues to inspire new generations of organic and permaculture gardeners.

Ruth grew up in Kansas with deep Quaker family roots in Ohio and Indiana. Her grandmother was on the governing board of Wilmington College (OH). Sister of noted mystery writer Rex Stout, Ruth was quite independent, smashing bars with Carry Nation, working with Quaker relief in Russia, hosting a Depression-era retreat on her Connecticut farm, and even admitting to gardening au naturale.

"Mulch Queen" Ruth Stout (1884–1980) might be amazed to learn that she has become a central figure, decades after her death, in the emerging movement of those who value living in "right relationship" or more generally, "sustainable living."[1] Indeed she provides an inspiring example for those seeking to align their

---

[1] Thomas Berry, "Living in Right Relationship," Quaker Earthcare Witness, accessed February 2019, http://quakerearthcare.org/article/living-right-relationship. "Mulch Queen" is a nickname Stout used of herself and others continue to use to describe her, e.g.: "Ruth Stout's System for Gardening," *Mother Earth News*, February/March 2004, accessed

lifestyles with the natural environment. Her books are still relevant today to those who advocate for organic gardening,[2] permaculture, and sustainable agriculture.[3] This article outlines how birthright Quaker Ruth Stout's life and gardening practices intersect with the Quaker testimonies of simplicity, peace, integrity, community, equality, and stewardship (judicious care for and use of resources).

I. Early Life

Ruth Stout was born in 1884 in Kansas, the middle child among nine, to Quaker parents John Wallace Stout, a teacher, school superintendent, and later salesman, and his wife, Lucetta Todhunter Stout. Both parents were graduates of Earlham College, founded by the Society of Friends. Lucetta, in particular, continued to attend Quaker meeting when one could be found nearby. Though her children were less attentive to meeting and Sabbath school, they did receive strong guidance in Quaker values from their two sets of devout Quaker grandparents, Nathan and Sophia Stout and Amos and Emily Todhunter. For example, when one of the family dogs died, Ruth watched tearfully from the window as her brothers dug its grave in the yard. Her grandfather Stout saw her distress and gently guided her to another window overlooking her mother's flower garden as he commented, "Thee was looking out the wrong window."[4]

Lucetta herself was an exemplar of wise and gentle discipline, allowing her children opportunities to make mistakes as long as no one was harmed. She protected her own private time to read or sew by keeping a bowl with a wet washcloth nearby. Should a child come near her, perhaps to tattle or voice a minor complaint, she would invite them closer and while consoling, also wipe their faces and hands with the cloth. Ruth said such *kind* attention discouraged them from bothering their mother so much. "When we were growing up," Ruth wrote, "Mother gave us very few rules to live by; she was a Quaker and followed her own Inner Light, encouraging us, as far as possible, to do the same."[5]

The Stout children were a rambunctious group, engaged in performing assigned chores and farming tasks, planning surprise parties, and writing and

February 2019, http://motherearthnews.com/organic-gardening/ruth-stouts-system-zmaz04fmzsel.

[2] Sue Robishaw, "A Few Good Gardening Books," Many Tracks Organic Gardening, accessed February 2019, http://manytracks.com/Garden/Books.htm.

[3] Robert Scott, "A Critical Review of Permaculture in the United States" (PhD diss., University of Illinois at Urbana/Champaign, 2010), http://robscott.net/2010/wp-content/uploads/2010/01/Scott2010.pdf.

[4] John McAleer, *Rex Stout: A Biography* (Boston: Little, Brown, 1977), 160.

[5] Ruth Stout, *As We Remember Mother: A Lifetime of Love and Laughter With a Mother Light Years Ahead of Her Nineteenth Century Peers* (New York: Exposition Press, 1975), 80.

performing plays for their family and neighbors. None of the Stout children attended college. They did, however, grow up in a house full of 5,000 books and with parents who were prolific readers.[6] All were self-motivated and pursued worthwhile careers in business, banking, medicine, editing, and writing. Ruth's brother Rex Stout became a well-known mystery writer and for many years had his own small farm about 20 miles from Ruth's farm in Connecticut. He also was an avid gardener, specializing in growing irises.[7]

While still in high school, Ruth, her sister Juanita, and their mother became interested in the prohibition activist Carry Nation. They attended Carry's meetings, and she even visited their home on several occasions. Lucetta, who was against violence, did not attend the saloon raids, but the sisters did. Ruth reported that at one Kansas raid, she cut her hand smashing a window with a hatchet in full view of a police officer, but was not arrested, much to her disappointment.[8] Lucetta also had no problem with card-playing or dancing, activities often frowned upon in conservative Kansas and among Quakers at the time. Ruth wrote of her mother Lucetta: "One had to know Mother rather well to realize that she followed nobody's rules, not even God's, without giving them some thought—to find out if they made sense to her."[9] Ruth was certainly influenced by her mother's example and wrote an appreciative biography in tribute to her mother in 1975, titled *As We Remember Mother.*[10]

After high school, Ruth joined her brother Robert and his wife Esther who were working their way from Topeka to New York City. Rob and his wife read palms (Ruth knew that it was a fraud), and Ruth worked as a nursemaid and later a telephone operator in Indianapolis. Ruth was in Indiana so long she convinced her mother and a couple of her siblings to move there to be nearer to relatives and Lucetta's elderly mother, Emily Todhunter, who lived in Wilmington, Ohio. The family also needed to pool their resources because Ruth's father was living on the road as a traveling salesman. During the five years in Indiana, Ruth's sister May, a doctor, died in Colorado, perhaps by suicide. She had been having business trouble with a partner/mentor but Ruth believed she herself had contributed to May's depression. May had asked to move to Indiana to be with Ruth and their mother but Ruth had refused her request, suggesting

---

[6] Sandra Knauf, "The Whole Ruth," *Greenwoman,* vol. 5 (Colorado Springs, CO: Greenwoman Magazine, 2013), 34.

[7] Ruth Stout, "Verdict: Iris Are Wonderful, Interview with Rex Stout," *Popular Gardening,* June 1956, 48–52.

[8] Ruth Stout, *Company Coming: Six Decades of Hospitality, Do-It-Yourself and Otherwise,* reprint edition (New York: Exposition Press, 1958; Norton Creek Press, 2012), 32.

[9] Knauf, "The Whole Ruth," 34.

[10] See footnote 5.

May should try harder to make a success of her medical practice. Later Lucetta counseled Ruth that she could keep May alive in her heart by keeping hold of the good memories, advice Lucetta herself would follow a few years later when her young son Donald died of tuberculosis.[11]

Ruth began the next 20-year-long chapter in her life with the family's move to New York City in 1909 to join brothers Robert and Rex. They lived in a four-story brownstone, sparsely furnished but perfectly roomy for parties and house guests. Ruth made the most of her expert writing and editing skills with a series of office jobs. On the side, she sold a few short stories and at one point opened a tea room with a friend and then a tea room on her own called the Klicket in Greenwich Village. Her clientele included artists and political activists of the World War I era, and it was at the Klicket that she met Scott Nearing, a well known Socialist and pacifist who spearheaded a back-to-the-land "simple living" movement.[12] She volunteered to be Nearing's administrative assistant and learned to convert his dynamic speeches into text for publication. She also met her eventual husband, Fred Rossiter, at her tea room. Fred was married at the time, and they agreed to stop seeing each other after Fred's wife would not give him a divorce.[13]

Although Ruth had plenty of friends and a full work schedule and social life, she did not feel fulfilled. Looking back at her life, she commented that youth was overrated: the "flowers have to mature before they give you blossoms."[14] It was during this period that Ruth advanced in her clerical career to positions such as bookkeeper and business manager, showing increasing self-confidence with a feminist edge. She bluffed her way into the bookkeeping job with Rex's encouragement and technical advice. She said she learned that "it was a mistake to submit to things you do not agree with (unless you had no choice) and more importantly, the job taught her the importance of thinking for oneself."[15] She successfully stood her ground by advocating for flexible hours for the women in her department, arguing that they were highly productive but could cost the firm overtime pay unless allowed to balance out long hours with shorter hours on less busy days. Her least favorite job was filling glue pots in a factory for a year, a monotonous job that she took on principle as an act of worker solidarity: she believed that she should experience factory work if she used factory-made products.

---

[11] Knauf, "The Whole Ruth," 35.

[12] Helen Nearing and Scott Nearing, *Living the Good Life* (New York: Schocken Books, 1954).

[13] Stout, *Company Coming*.

[14] Knauf, "The Whole Ruth," 36.

[15] Knauf, "The Whole Ruth," 37.

II. Ruth Stout and Her Year in Russia (October, 1923–September, 1924)

As time went on Lucetta Stout grew concerned with Ruth's aimlessness and her stalled relationship with the married Fred Rossiter. Alert to Ruth's passion for the works of Dostoyevsky, she urged Ruth to consider volunteering with the American Friends Service Committee famine relief work in Russia, a cause for which Quakers in England and the United States were actively raising funds.[16] Quakers were providing resources for famine relief in the Orenburg oblast (administrative district) in southwest Russia. Quakers were also coordinating donations and relief from other organizations.

Ruth immediately seized the opportunity. Her passport, issued to her at age 39, outlined her plans to work with American Friends Service Committee relief efforts in Russia and to travel as a tourist in Germany and England. She left New York for Europe on September 15, 1923, aboard a White Star Line ship and made her way to her assignment at an orphanage for 200 children in the village of Grachovka.[17] The service area was about the size of Indiana. The AFSC mission in the region was: "To combine faith and works, to render practice and spiritual service, to save life, and to help make a better world in which to live."[18] For Ruth, the mission validated her Quaker upbringing and her mother's emphasis on experiential education and living an active, purposeful life. Through her experience in Russia, Ruth would transform from a sociable New York working girl to a principled woman with first-hand experience dealing with humanitarian crises.

The famine in Russia had been ongoing for several years as a result of high temperatures, drought, and unproductive farming practices. Thousands died, parents starving to give what little food they had to their children. Horses and camels, essential for farm work and transportation, died of starvation or were sacrificed as food, causing a downward cycle with less large-scale grain production. The Quakers had just opened their third orphanage in the Orenburg area, where Ruth helped provide relief services. She personally raised funds to assist individual children with unique needs by sending out appeals through her network of family and friends in New York.[19]

---

[16] Stout, *As We Remember Mother.*

[17] "Ruth Stout, September 8, 1923," US Passport Applications, 1795–1925, database, Ancestry.com.

[18] American Friends Service Committee, "Bulletin No. 62, Eighth Annual Report, June lst, 1924–May 31st, 1925," *American Friends Service Committee Bulletin,* Issues 51–100, cover, accessed in Google Books.

[19] Stout, *Company Coming.*

As one of 29 workers, Ruth immersed herself in the Quaker-led initiatives to assist the peasants of Grachovka. Urgent health issues included the rampant spread of malaria and tuberculosis. Relief work included food and clothing distributions, orphan education, crop seed, medicine, and the purchase of horses and tractors to pull plows.[20] In 1923, the Quaker mission imported 15 tractors and 1,000 horses from Turkistan and Siberia.[21] To encourage self-sufficiency, the peasants received material assistance from the Quakers in exchange for their labor in village construction and sanitation projects.

At first the Quakers focused on feeding children, only to discover that starving adults who could not care for their children were more likely to abandon them to the orphanages. Even as the drought abated, the 1924 AFSC Report showed that the Quaker Mission in the Orenburg oblast had fed 10,000 children and additional starving widowed mothers. Ruth saw the survivors, without horses or camels, struggling to grow grain crops with hand tools, only to have their meager crops fail.

Like her fellow relief workers, Ruth became discouraged as the critical needs only worsened with continuing famine and then widespread disease. At one point during her service, Wilbur Thomas, the executive secretary of the AFSC, arrived to inspect relief and reconstruction operations.[22] He bolstered their spirits and assured them their difficult work was necessary and productive. His message was similar to the following excerpts from AFSC annual reports at that time:

> The greatest objective has been to create good-will in the world; the saving of life and the giving of relief have been a means to that end.[23]

> We all feel that our relief work should be done by people who have a real message to give and a committee such as this can gather up all this kind of spiritual relief and unify it. During the past year a number of workers have gone over with the object of doing all in their power to

---

[20] American Friends Service Committee, "Bulletin No. 59, Seventh Annual Report, June 1st, 1923–May 31st, 1924," *American Friends Service Committee Bulletin*, Issues 51–100, accessed in Google Books.

[21] American Friends Service Committee, "Bulletin No. 58, Sixth Annual Report, June 1st, 1922–May 31st, 1923, *American Friends Service Committee Bulletin*, Issues 51–100, accessed in Google Books.

[22] David W. McFadden, Clare Gorfinkel, and Sergei Nikitin, *Constructive Spirit: Quakers in Revolutionary Russia* (Altadena, CA: Intentional Productions, 2004), 56–58.

[23] American Friends Service Committee, 1923, 2.

strengthen the faith and trust of suffering individuals, and to try to conciliate conflicting classes and peoples.[24]

Ruth felt her work in Russia was fulfilling and she corresponded with her family and friends to share her experiences. She exchanged letters with Scott Nearing, whose "Save the World" lectures (her words) had inspired her to extend herself and to reach out to others less fortunate.[25] Nearing was interested in the political changes occurring in Russia, or, "what was cooking in the Kremlin."[26] Ruth provided him with the details of her work but said she "just wasn't politically-minded and never would be."[27] Ruth made her point to Nearing by sharing human interest details: "How happy Ivan was with the cow I had managed to scrape up money for," she wrote Nearing, "and I told him that Masha's operation had been successful, and that I had collected enough money from friends at home to send Seryozha to a Conservatory of Music."[28] Ruth's own admitted typically-youthful desire to save the world had evolved into a recognition that, as an individual, she could not save the whole world but she could help improve the lives of those in one Russian village and one orphanage in important, practical ways.

By the summer of 1924 the drought around Grachovka began to diminish and farming became more productive. Most Quaker relief workers, other than medical workers, began returning to their homes or other assignments.[29] Ruth returned to New York aboard the *Aquitania* out of Southampton September 27, 1924, arriving after a seven day transatlantic crossing October 3, 1924.[30]

Ruth's Russian experience was transformative. She counted it among her three most exciting adventures: opening her own tearoom, her first sight of the Russian steppes, and the purchase of her Poverty Hollow Farm in Connecticut.[31] Forty years later, Ruth noted her increasing appreciation for the values of simplicity and stewardship:

My natural lack of interest in material things was accentuated when I spent a year in Russia with the Quakers doing famine relief work.

---

[24] American Friends Service Committee, 1924, 10.

[25] Stout, *Company Coming*, 58.

[26] Stout, *Company Coming*, 58.

[27] Stout, *Company Coming*, 59.

[28] Stout, *Company Coming*, 59.

[29] American Friends Service Committee, 1925, 7.

[30] New York Passenger Lists, 1820–1957, Ancestry.com database.

[31] Stout, *Company Coming*.

Somehow, when you are in close touch with a large orphanage (the parents had died of starvation), where the children decorate their rooms with the bright-colored labels from tomato cans, sent from America, the lavishness of things revolts you somewhat when you get back home. One way of spending money that insults my intelligence is to pay a disproportionately high price for something. I recall that a small dish of peas in a restaurant I was taken to once cost more than a bushel of fresh picked ones.[32]

In Grachovka, Ruth's work had clarified for her the brevity of life and the importance of living a principled life in community. She had first-hand knowledge that a basic human need was being able to feed oneself and others. She saw for herself the cyclical human tragedies of famine, poverty, disease, and death, complicated by years of revolutionary war, local violence, and drought. She shared in the relief workers' hopefulness in providing seeds, tools, and horses, only to share also the Russians' frustration with crop failure. She enjoyed brief moments of laughter with the orphans and shed tears for untimely deaths. For the next fifty years, Ruth defended the Russian people against expressions of Cold War animosity, saying that one should visit Russia and become acquainted with the Russian people. She believed criticism should be placed on the Soviet government but not on its long-suffering residents.[33]

III. Ruth in New York City

After her return to the United States from Russia in 1924, Ruth sought ways to act upon her expanded worldview. She joined Rex at various Socialist organizing meetings and rallies. Ruth spent two weeks at a summer camp for Socialist and trade union activists, but her experience there soured her on the purity of the Socialist cause. She observed camp leaders treating employees with apparent class bias, and later observed members of The Liberal Club treating those with less means unfavorably. Ruth decided not to associate with those without the integrity to abide by their own stated philosophy and rules about equality.[34]

She obtained a part-time job to pay the bills and donated her volunteer time to Scott Nearing who had begun publishing a leftist magazine entitled, *The New Masses*. She performed administrative and editing work for Nearing. After seven years apart from Alfred "Fred" Rossiter, she boldly contacted him again

---

[32] Stout, *Company Coming*, 102.
[33] Stout, *Company Coming*.
[34] McAleer, *Rex Stout: A Biography*.

and found that he still maintained interest in her. Three years later he finally obtained a divorce, and in 1929 married Ruth, who was by then age 45.

Shortly after their marriage, but before the 1929 stock market crash diminished their finances, Fred, a Columbia-educated psychologist, suggested moving from New York City to the country. In early 1930, the couple purchased 55 acres of farmland with a house and barn in Redding, Connecticut, in an area called Poverty Hollow, a small region that once sheltered an enclave of unemployed workers stranded by the failure of several water-powered industries in the late nineteenth century.[35] Ruth recalled that she agreed to the move "without a second's hesitation."[36] Fond remembrances of her childhood on a Kansas farm played an important role in Ruth's decision.[37] Fred devoted his time to creating artistic, museum-quality turned wood bowls and she focused her early-morning work time on learning to grow vegetables by the most efficient, nature-friendly means possible.[38] Together they formed a community with countless old and new city friends whom they welcomed to stay for weeks or months at a time in their converted barn, enjoying healthful country living and the garden harvest.[39] One eccentric guest stayed so long he built his own retreat shack in a distant field. Ruth was not equally fond of all of her many guests. Some guests she had to will herself to tolerate, yet she strived to find ways to treat them all equitably.[40] Fred and Ruth lived at Poverty Hollow until their deaths; Fred died in 1950 and Ruth in 1980.

Oddly enough, considering the importance of gardening to her in later life, Ruth does not fully explain her attraction to and preoccupation with gardening in any of her books. As a child, her primary duty on the Kansas farm had been gathering corn cobs for use in the cook stove, not working in the garden.[41] Most of her life after Kansas was spent in urban areas. Contributing factors may have been her mother's love of growing flowers, brother Rex's interest in gardening, and Scott Nearing's "simple life" philosophy.[42] Ruth, a vegetarian at the time she moved to the farm, likely valued highly the potential harvest from her own land. When the Depression struck, there were obvious

---

[35] Brent M. Colley, "Redding Ridge, Connecticut (CT) History, Past and Present," History of Redding, last modified June 4, 2007, accessed February 2019, http://historyofredding.net/HRreddingridge.htm.

[36] Ruth Stout, *How to Have a Green Thumb Without an Aching Back: A New Method of Mulch Gardening* (New York: Exposition Press, 1955), 12.

[37] Stout, *How to Have a Green Thumb*, 13.

[38] Knauf, "The Whole Ruth."

[39] Stout, *Company Coming*.

[40] Stout, *Company Coming*.

[41] McAleer, *Rex Stout: A Biography*, 49.

[42] Nearing and Nearing, *Living the Good Life*.

cost savings in "growing your own." Finally, Ruth's year in Russia working with famine relief showed her how people suffer when the cycle of self-sufficient food security breaks. Throughout her Connecticut years, brother Rex and Scott Nearing were her gardening mentors. Nearing, who had left political activism to promote subsistence farming in rocky Vermont, never convinced Ruth that gardening was all about the nobility of sweaty hard work. Instead, she valued making time for reading and socializing with her farm guests and sought to eliminate needless garden labor and still produce good-quality vegetables. Ruth's husband, Fred, encouraged her gardening efforts but was not an active participant in them.

Ruth's first attempt at a garden was a 240x100 foot plot—more than half an acre. Even after plowing during the wrong season, hauling away "thousands" of stones, planting seeds at the wrong time of year, failing to add enough lime to balance the soil's pH, and losing much of her corn crop to crows, Ruth's enthusiasm remained undimmed.[43] The second year her efforts netted "two or three meals of peas" and "about five little beets."[44] A few dozen tomato plants, planted too early, froze.[45] The third season, Ruth reduced the size of her garden by half and was able to eat vegetables in season as well as can over 300 quarts. While the results of her efforts were improving, Ruth worked so hard she feared "it was inevitable that some day I would drop in my tracks."[46] Indeed, by May the following year she was flat on her back with sciatica.

It was not until 14 years later, in 1944, that what would become the Ruth Stout system of no-till, no-work mulch gardening began to take shape. Restless after the farmer who plowed her field every year was a no-show because of a broken down tractor, Ruth had a revelation: Why plow? She impatiently planted her seeds in rough shallow furrows in the midst of untilled soil, and they grew. Soon, she began using kitchen garbage for fertilizer and spoiled hay for mulch.[47] Ruth simply parted the hay and threw her seeds into small furrows made quickly by the stroke of a hoe. She reduced the size of her garden again, to 50x60 feet.[48] Eventually, Ruth's minimalist garden would provide more than enough vegetables to feed two people each year, and Ruth would boast that she had not

---

[43] Stout, *How to Have a Green Thumb*, 18.
[44] Stout, *How to Have a Green Thumb*, 26.
[45] Stout, *How to Have a Green Thumb*, 27.
[46] Stout, *How to Have a Green Thumb*, 55.
[47] Stout, *Company Coming*, 69.
[48] Stout, *Company Coming*, 72.

set foot in a grocery store for 17 years.[49] It was in that post-World War II period that Ruth abandoned the traditional labor-intensive tasks of gardening (digging, weeding, watering, plowing, hoeing), by simply adding an 18-inch layer of hay on the ground. Her garden was not formal with neat rows; it was unruly, apparently crowded, and very productive. Ruth began sharing her "growing" success first with her family and visitors, then through articles in a few magazines, and finally through a series of books.

IV. The Ruth Stout Method

The Stout method can be described as no tilling, no watering, no weeding, and no composting—all the result of a thick layer of permanent mulch. Ruth recommended a bottom layer of household food waste covered by at least eight inches of rotted hay, although straw, leaves, or grass cuttings would also do (the bags of woodchip "mulch" sold in stores today are unsuitable). A separate compost pile was not necessary, she declared, because the mulch and garbage would decompose over time, providing nutrients to the soil, keeping the ground moist, and preventing the propagation of weeds. In order to plant, one simply pulled back the mulch and placed the seeds on the ground. Brother Rex was cynical at first, calling her yard, hopefully humorously, a "garbage dump."[50] Rex grew 186 varieties of iris and extolled their easy care, with no mulching needed (although he had a full-time gardener). Ruth shared that she, too, had a clump of irises that she never divided and always mulched, and they continued to bloom.[51] Years later, after many spirited discussions, Rex finally took her advice and tried mulching his prized irises. He also designed and built a raccoon-proof enclosure for her garden.[52]

Does the Ruth Stout method work? Recent reviews of her books by readers suggest it does.[53] Hundreds of readers who have tried her method have testified to its effectiveness in all but clay soils, although critics such as the late Gene Logsdon, popular twenty-first century Ohio organic gardening author,

---

[49] Gloria Stashower, "Poverty Hollow," *The New York Times,* May 29, 1977, 377, accessed February 2019, http://nytimes.com/1977/05/29/archives/long-island-opinion-poverty-hollow-priestess.html.

[50] Barbara Bamberger-Scott, "Ruth Stout: The No-Dig Duchess," accessed February 2019, http://homestead.org/gardening/ruth-stout/.

[51] Stout, "Verdict," 1956.

[52] Ruth Harley, "Pest-Proofing Your Garden," *Storey's Country Wisdom Bulletin*, A–15, January 11, 1997, 18.

[53] Readers can perform searches for Ruth Stout on Amazon or Goodreads to find similar reviews.

have critiqued Stout's method as too simplistic, while providing his own techniques to make it more effective.[54]

V. The Historical Context

The foundation for Quaker interest in simplicity and environmental sustainability can be traced to the works and life examples of earlier Quakers such as the American shopkeeper and preacher, John Woolman (1728–1772). Woolman sparked the historic debate and informs the contemporary conversation about preserving our natural environment and its gifts versus defending an economic system built on using (or exploiting) the natural environment and its inhabitants: "The produce of the earth is a gift from our gracious Creator to the inhabitants, and to impoverish the earth now to support outward greatness appears to be an injury to the succeeding age."[55]

It also is important to understand the historical context of gardening in the 1950s. During World War II more than 20 million Americans grew "victory gardens," but interest in gardening waned post-war. In the 1950s a number of products were introduced that seemed to simplify home gardening: insecticides such as Sevin, fungicides such as Daconil, soil conditioners, fertilizers that eliminated the need for manure, improved hybrid seeds, and the introduction of gasoline powered garden tractors, rototillers, and other equipment.[56]

At the same time, a nascent organic farming movement was taking shape. In 1942, Jerome Rodale began publishing *Organic Farming and Gardening* magazine. Later during that decade, Louis Bromfield operated Malabar Farm in Mansfield, Ohio, the best known of several experiments in sustainable, pesticide free agriculture. Ruth actually did not set out to be an organic farmer. In fact, she decried organic farmers as "faddists," who were "never able to talk about much else."[57] She considered her method to be superior to organic gardening, as it required no composting or watering. Yet she wrote, "I was an organic gardener,

---

54 Gene Logsdon, "Ruth Stout: Mulch Can Cover a Multitude of Sins as Well as Weeds," The Contrary Farmer Memorial Blogsite, December 16, 2008, http://thecontrary-farmer.wordpress.com/2008/12/16/mulch-can-cover-a-multitude-of-sins-as-well-as-weeds/.

55 John Woolman, *A Journal of the Life, Gospel Labours, and Christian Experiences, of that Faithful Minister of Jesus Christ, John Woolman* (Philadelphia: T. E. Chapman, 1837), 364.

56 Jolene Hansen, "An American Timeline: Home Gardening in the US," accessed February 2019, http://gardentech.com/blog/gardening-and-healthy-living/ an-american-timeline-home-gardening-in-the-us.

57 Ruth Stout, *Gardening Without Work for the Aging, the Busy and the Indolent*, reprint edition (New York: Devin-Adair, 1963; Norton Creek Press, 2011), 173–4.

if a somewhat unorthodox one, for years before I ever heard the expression."[58] Clearly Ruth's gardening methods were compatible with the organic gardening philosophy: both require no pesticides, no herbicides, no chemical fertilizers, no burning leaves, and no wasted water.

VI. Ruth Stout, Author

Ruth's early attempts to publicize her method on the radio and in magazines ran into a major problem: she was not allowed to say that she did not use chemical fertilizer. "It was unfortunate," she wrote, that the use of chemical fertilizer was a problematic choice not only for practical and scientific considerations but also for commercial profit issues. "I wouldn't expect any magazine that advertises chemical fertilizer and poison sprays to take kindly to my way of gardening."[59] Even Consumers Union, which did not accept commercial advertising, rejected her articles. Only Jerome Rodale, an ardent opponent of chemical pesticides and proponent of healthy soil, was willing to publish her. She became a regular contributor to the Rodale magazine *Organic Farming and Gardening* from 1953 to 1971, and won thousands of fans over to her gardening techniques with her intimate and humorous writing style.[60]

As the Stout method gained popularity, Ruth began to receive hundreds of letters and visitors to her farm. As a consequence, she decided to compile her ideas into a book. Her first book, *How to Have a Green Thumb Without an Aching Back,* was self-published in 1954, when Ruth was 70. She did not recall where she found the money to publish but was sure that her husband Fred was not the source.[61] The next year Exposition Press published *Green Thumb* commercially, eventually selling hundreds of thousands of copies.

In 1961 Ruth published *Gardening Without Work for the Aging, the Busy, and the Indolent.* The title suggests as much about Ruth's philosophy of life and sense of humor as it does about her method of gardening. This second book was met with much skepticism by Ruth's sister Mary, who said, "You told the whole story in one 1500-word article; how do you expect to fill a book?"[62] Ruth replied that over the years she had refined her method, taking into account not just her own experience, but comments of people who visited the farm or heard her speak at garden clubs, libraries, or on the radio. One visitor to the farm, for

---

[58] Stout, *Gardening Without Work,* 157.

[59] Stout, *How to Have a Green Thumb,* 75.

[60] "Ruth Stout System of Permanent Hay Mulching," last modified June 18, 2013, Veganic Agricultural Network, accessed February 2019, http://goveganic.net/article182.html.

[61] Knauf, "The Whole Ruth."

[62] Stout, *Gardening Without Work,* 4.

example, said that instead of planting potatoes she simply threw them on the ground and covered them with mulch. Ruth tried this and it worked.[63]

A third book on gardening, *The Ruth Stout No Work Garden Book*, a compilation of articles she had written for *Organic Gardening and Farming* magazine, was published in 1973 with her helper Richard Clemence as co-author. Ruth's books and methods became even more popular after the publication of Rachel Carson's *Silent Spring* in 1962.[64]

Ruth also wrote five books expounding on her family history and her philosophy of life. Her gardening books have been translated into German, Danish, Croatian, Swedish, and Dutch. A complete list of her books is located at the conclusion of this essay.

Her approach to gardening, as well as life, reflected a Quaker upbringing that emphasized practicality and common sense. She bragged that she had personally tried everything she recommended in her book, decrying "armchair gardeners" who had not done the same. Ruth wrote in the first person, in a style that was informal, personal, and chatty. She often anthropomorphized her vegetables, having imaginary conversations with them. Readers describe her books in terms such as "witty," "laugh-out-loud-delightful," "practical, to the point, and funny," and "like sitting down with the author on a rainy day."[65]
After Fred's death in 1960 when Ruth was 76, she kept busy by gardening, writing, giving lectures, and welcoming some 7,000 visitors to Poverty Hollow, feeling they gave her something to do as well as something to contribute to the world.[66] She starred in a documentary about her no-mulch gardening in 1976.[67] Ruth used her books on gardening and her film to expound upon her philosophy of life. Her books reflected a positive mental attitude that she credited for her long and healthy life: "I just am, by nature, an optimist," she stated. Always a self-described "people person," Ruth gave parties, operated a guest hostel in her barn, and surrounded herself with many people even as she maintained a zone of privacy for balance.[68]

No account of Ruth's gardening would be complete without mentioning her propensity for gardening in the nude, a practice that often

---

[63] Ruth Stout and Richard Clemence, *The Ruth Stout No-Work Garden Book: Secrets of the Year-round Mulch Method* (Emmaus, PA: Rodale Press, 1973), 47.

[64] Rachel Carson, *Silent Spring*, fortieth anniversary edition (Boston and New York: Houghton Mifflin Company, 2002).

[65] Quotes from reviews of Stout's work found at Goodreads.com.

[66] Knauf, "The Whole Ruth."

[67] Arthur Mokin, dir., *Ruth Stout's Garden*, filmed with audio in English in 1976, 23:00, http://youtube.com/watch?v=GNU8IJzRHZk.

[68] Stout, *Company Coming.*

stopped traffic on the road adjoining Poverty Hollow. She took delight in retelling the story and mentioned it in her film, interviews, and in her books: "I would go down there to garden and the minute I got down there I would take off all my clothes and garden naked. I've always loved the air on my body. And I never said a word about it to Fred."[69] Fred figured out what she was doing, however, because, from his barn woodshop, he heard cars slowing and stopping along the road adjoining their farm whenever she was gardening.

In 1933 Ruth's father, John Wallace Stout, died. Her mother, Lucetta, and sister, Mary, then came to live at Poverty Hollow during the warmer months, while continuing to winter in New York City. At Poverty Hollow, Lucetta built a small house for herself and Mary. When she wanted to build on an addition, Fred disagreed with her plan. Ever independent, Lucetta waited until the Rossiters were away and contracted for the addition to be built to her own design. It was too far along to change when Ruth and Fred returned.[70] Ruth grew flowers to please her mother, including a number donated by Rex from his gardens. Lucetta, a committed pacifist, died in 1940, heartsick about the impending war in Europe. Ruth's sister Mary continued to live on at Poverty Hollow in the small cottage. Mary became Ruth's full-time companion in later years and died in 1977. Rex Stout died in 1975 at his property called High Meadow in Brewster, New York, at age 88. Ruth Stout died nearby in Connecticut in August 1980 at the age of 96. Many members of the family are buried in Villeau Cemetery in Ridgewood, New Jersey but Ruth Stout Rossiter is buried in Evergreen Cemetery, Redding, Connecticut.[71]

VII. The Legacy of Ruth Stout

Ruth Stout's works have become celebrated classics of organic gardening through Rodale Publishing and recent republishing through Norton Creek Press. Now a new generation of author/gardeners are building on Ruth's experiments in no-till gardening that she popularized in her articles and books.

Happily for gardeners, like Ruth's no-till methods, organic gardening at home is an accessible choice, requiring fewer steps than traditional gardening. They can skip tilling the soil twice a year, hoeing and weeding, watering, and controlling pests artificially. Here is how an agent with the North Carolina Extension Service defines organic gardening: "In an organically managed yard or

---

[69] Knauf, "The Whole Ruth," 45.

[70] Stout, *As We Remember Mother.*

[71] "Ruth Imogen Stout Rossiter," Find a Grave, accessed February 2019, http://findagrave.com/memorial/147399267/ruth-imogen-rossiter.

vegetable garden the emphasis is on cultivating an ecosystem that sustains and nourishes plants, soil microbes and beneficial insects rather than simply making plants grow."[72] Various practitioners of organic gardening today use methods similar to Ruth's. Patricia Lanza, for example, popularized a method she called "Lasagna Gardening" that involves a six- to eight-inch layer of peat moss and grass clippings that require no digging or weeding. "Perhaps," she wrote, "I am Ruth Stout reincarnated, only neater and…I never take my clothes off in the garden, no matter how much I would like to."[73]

Robert Kirchner, a Canadian Quaker, acknowledged the influence of Ruth upon the permaculture movement:

> The fundamental ethical principles of Permaculture are: (a) Care for the earth, (b) Care for people, and (c) Share the surplus [Fair Share]. Permaculturists seek to design and implement systems that allow humans to meet their basic needs (food, shelter, clothing, etc.) in an ecologically sustainable manner. Because food is one of the most basic human needs, Permaculture ideas have been principally applied to the problem of food production, and it is perhaps best known as a method of organic gardening. Typically, Permaculture gardeners emphasize edible perennial plants, including fruit trees and bushes, to create a self-sustaining "food forest." I might add that it was a Quaker, Ruth Stout, who pioneered the no-till, mulch-intensive organic gardening techniques which became central to Permaculture.[74]

In 1978, Australian Rosemary Howe Morrow became a convinced Quaker about the same time she discovered Permaculture. She said: "I was also intrigued by a [Permaculture] course which began with ethics…. [N]one of my other studies had ever mentioned the word. There was a correspondence between Quakerism and permaculture. They had in common things like care for people, simplicity, community, ethical use of money and right livelihood. I was

---

[72] Charlotte Glen, *What is Organic Gardening?* North Carolina Cooperative Extension, March 22, 2012, accessed February 2019, http://pender.ces.ncsu.edu/2012/03/what-is-organic-gardening/.

[73] Patricia Lanza, "Lasagna Gardening," *Mother Earth News*, April/May 1999, accessed February 2019, http://motherearthnews.com/organic-gardening/lasagna-gardening-zmaz99amztak.

[74] Robert Kirchner, "On Quakers and Permaculture: Making a Living, Not a Killing," Neighbour Grow: An Edmonton Quaker transitions to a livelihood in urban permaculture, April 9, 2014, http://neighbourgrow.wordpress.com/2014/04/09/ on-quakers-and-permaculture-making-a-living-not-a-killing/.

at home."[75] She began exploring how Permaculture might be useful in addressing redevelopment issues in countries affected by war and global warming. Morrow's implementation of Permaculture in Afghanistan was documented in the film *Garden at the End of the World: Permaculture and the Forgotten, Teaching Permaculture in Places that Absolutely Need It, a Message of Hope with Rosemary Morrow*. This documentary won the 2010 Human Rights Award from joint sponsors, the World Association for Christian Communication (WACC), and SIGNIS (the World Catholic Association of Communication).[76]

Rosemary Morrow was honored to present the 2011 James Backhouse Lecture on a contemporary issue, a series begun in 1964 by the Australia Yearly Meeting of the Religious Society of Friends (Quakers).[77] Backhouse, an English Quaker and botanist, was a Quaker missionary in Australia and South Africa between 1831 and 1841.[78] Morrow described how Permaculture has made significant improvements in people's lives and noted in a preface to her published lecture:

> In projects first offered in Vietnam and Cambodia I did not know, and nor did Quaker Service Australia (QSA), that permaculture would be more than re-establishing food supplies for starving people. Permaculture, as more than gardening, proved to be a physical and social healer restoring peace, food culture and self-respect to damaged people and landscapes. It provided a remembering of how to live again.[79]

Ruth's no-till methods align well with the currently-popular sustainable agriculture movement, the production of food in a manner that protects air, water, and land, encompassing the Quaker testimony of stewardship. In fact, her

---

[75] Russ Grayson, "A Short and Incomplete History of Permaculture," Pacific Edge, last modified 2007, http://pacific-edge.info/2007/07/a-short-and-incomplete-history-of-permaculture/.

[76] Gary Caganoff, *Garden at the End of the World: Permaculture and the Forgotten, Teaching Permaculture in Places that Absolutely Need It, a Message of Hope with Rosemary Morrow* (Sydney, Australia: Lysis Films, 2009), accessed February 2019, http://thegardenattheendoftheworld.info/.

[77] Rosemary Howe Morrow, *A Demanding and Uncertain Adventure*, ebook (Religious Society of Friends [Quakers] in Australia, Interactive Publications, 2011).

[78] William N. Oats, *Backhouse and Walker: A Quaker View of the Australian Colonies, 1832–1838* (Sandy Bay, Tasmania: Blubber Head Press in association with the Australian Yearly Meeting of the Religious Society of Friends, 1981).

[79] Morrow, *A Demanding and Uncertain Adventure*, 3.

No-Work Garden Book (1973) is cited as a seminal work in textbooks for sustainable agriculture[80] and permaculture.[81]

VIII. Conclusion

John Woolman and other early Friends, though they did not set out to do so, fashioned the foundational Quaker worldview grounded in stewardship and a strategy for personal responsibility and individual action to preserve the natural environment. That Ruth Stout's life philosophy evolved from her immersion in a Quaker family, her AFSC service in Russia, and her decades of hands-on Poverty Hollow garden experiments is well-documented in her many books. To borrow from Rosemary Morrow's comment on the impact on Permaculture, Ruth herself continues to inspire many in the art of "remembering how to live again" through her online video, her reprinted books, and social-media sharing by new generations of her fans. Ruth lived life full-on, always active, always impatient with the general social current. When Ruth asked herself what had happened to her old resolve to do something for humanity, brother Rex prompted her, "Can you do anything more fundamental than to raise food? Even Einstein has to eat."[82]

Ruth was more than a gardener; she was a philosopher, always willing to share her successes, failures, and philosophy of life.[83] Ruth's books document how she lived a gardener's life aligned with the Quaker testimonies of simplicity, peace, integrity, community, equality, and stewardship. Stout biographer Sandra Knauf summed up Ruth Stout's philosophy: "If you live yourself to suit yourself, how can you fail to make the most of it?"[84]

---

[80] Marion Henkel, *21st Century Homestead: Sustainable Agriculture I* (Morrisville, NC: Lulu.com, 2015), 188.

[81] Peter Bane, *The Permaculture Handbook: Garden Farming for Town and Country* (Gabriola Island, BC: New Society Publishers, 2012), 7, 445.

[82] McAleer, 257–258.

[83] Barbara Damrosch, "More Vegetables, Less Work: Lessons from the Mother of Mulch," *Washington Post*, March 9, 2017.

[84] Knauf, "The Whole Ruth," 45.

Books by Ruth Stout

Stout, Ruth. *How to Have a Green Thumb Without an Aching Back: A New Method of Mulch Gardening.* New York: Exposition Press, 1955, reprinted by Fireside, 1990.

Stout, Ruth. *Company Coming: Six Decades of Hospitality, Do-It-Yourself and Otherwise.* New York: Exposition Press, 1958, reprinted by Norton Creek Press, 2016.

Stout, Ruth. *It's a Woman's World: A Buoyant Guide to Easier, More Enjoyable Living.* Garden City, NJ: Doubleday, 1960.

Stout, Ruth. *If You Would Be Happy: Cultivate Your Life Like a Garden.* Garden City, NJ: Doubleday, 1962, reprinted by Norton Creek Press, 2016.

Stout, Ruth. *Gardening Without Work: For the Aging, the Busy and the Indolent.* New York: Devin-Adair, 1963, reprinted by Norton Creek Press, 2011.

Stout, Ruth and Richard Clemence. *The Ruth Stout No-Work Garden Book: Secrets of the Year-round Mulch Method.* Emmaus, PA: Rodale Press, 1973.

Stout, Ruth. *As We Remember Mother: A Lifetime of Love and Laughter With a Mother Light Years Ahead of her Nineteenth Century Peers.* New York: Exposition Press, 1975.

Stout, Ruth. *I've Always Done It My Way.* New York: Exposition Press, 1975.

Stout, Ruth. *Don't Forget to Smile: How to Stay Sane and Fit Over Ninety.* Bookstore Press reprint, 1984, 2002.

Part I: Ecological Themes in Quaker History – Discussion Questions

1. **Chapter 1. "Do What You Do in the Wisdom of God": Theological Resources for Quaker Ecological Action in the Writings of George Fox, by Rebecca Artinian-Kaiser and Cherice Bock**

   1. Based on what you learned through reading the essay on George Fox's wisdom motif, how do you think Fox might comment on contemporary environmental issues using these ideas if he were alive today?

   2. In what ways does Fox's motif of wisdom connect to creation?

   3. What is the relationship between wisdom and social action among Friends, according to this essay, and how does this relate to current environmental concerns? In what ways, if any, does this movement between wisdom and action align with your own experience?

2. **Chapter 2. John Woolman's Environmental Consciousness, by Mike Heller**

   1. John Woolman argued for the importance of challenging "customs" with "Truth." Relating to environmental concerns, what deep-rooted "customs" does humanity hold that are in conflict with the "Truth" that Woolman refers to? What does this commitment to "Truth" look like today compared to what it looked like for Woolman?

   2. How did John Woolman's mystical experiences and approach to Quakerism and Christianity shape his actions and social commentary? What can you imagine Woolman doing or saying today regarding the climate crisis?

3. **Chapter 3. Quakers and Quaker Farmers in the Colonial and Early Republic Era and the Development of Two Views of Nature, by Douglas J. Burks**

    1. Given the differing perspectives of the anthropocentric and ecocentric views of nature within the Quaker community, is it possible, or beneficial, to find a middle ground between the two? What commonalities could Friends of both perspectives agree on pertaining to nature and the environment?

    2. How might the anthropocentric Quakers and the more mystical, ecocentric Quakers from history tackle the environmental problems we face in the present day?

    3. According to this article, how did Quaker farmers differ from non-Quaker farmers regarding their business, farming, or environmental practices? In what ways, if any, do you think this difference related to their Quaker beliefs?

4. **Chapter 4. Ruth Stout, the Queen of Mulch, by Jean Mulhern and Cathy Pitzer**

    1. How do Ruth Stout's gardening methods contribute to making a sustainable lifestyle feasible for a wider audience? Why do you think her techniques are still appealing to gardeners today?

    2. Stout was not as vocal about the influences of Quakerism on her actions as were some of the other Friends in this section. What do you notice about her methods and lifestyle that seem consistent with the stories of Friends in chapters 1–3, and what strikes you as significantly different from them? Is it important to do what we do as an expression of Quaker values? Why or why not?

5. **Part I General Questions**

1. Burks uses the terms ecocentric and anthropocentric to describe different views of nature. Which of these terms do you think describe the other Friends detailed in Part I?

2. Since earlier Friends did not specifically discuss environmental concerns or climate change, do you find it helpful or unimportant (or somewhere in between) to look for themes relating to creation and ecology in historical Friends' writings? Why?

PART II
Developing a Quaker Ecotheology

5 | Quakers and Creation Care: Potentials and Pitfalls for an Ecotheology of Friends[1]

By Cherice Bock

Abstract: While Friends have a strong tradition of activism around the social justice issues of each era, we also tend to spiritualize our faith, disconnecting it from the material world. Environmental concerns are arguably one of the most important social justice issues of our time, and in many ways, activism, advocacy, and lifestyle witness seem like natural ways for Friends to engage in social justice in this time in history. This essay will explore some of the historical and theological strengths Friends can draw from our tradition that can help build a particularly Quaker ecotheology, as well as some of the portions of the Friends tradition that get in the way of practicing our faith in a more sustainable way.

I. Quaker Context for Building an Ecotheology

"What is the social justice issue of our time?" I pondered this question for many years. Growing up a birthright Quaker in Oregon, I became a convinced Friend during my high school years as I learned the stories of historic Friends who stood up against injustice and actively worked toward peace in loving and courageous ways. And yet, I wondered which social justice issue to focus on now; there are many from which to choose.

I continued laboring with this question until one night in 2008, standing on a rooftop in the West Bank of the Palestinian Territories, I sensed the beginnings of an answer. I was a member of a Christian Peacemaker Teams

---

[1] With gratitude to Reedwood Friends Church (Portland, OR) and Berkeley Friends Church (Berkeley, CA) for invitations to serve as scholar-in-residence at their Center for Christian Studies (2017) and Quaker Heritage Day (2018), respectively, at which I presented these ideas and received feedback from the gathered communities.

(CPT) delegation, learning about their important work of peacemaking through accompaniment and nonviolent direct action.[2] Our group listened to stories about the conflict in Israel/Palestine and its history, visited and learned about the Israeli settlements in the West Bank, and heard about the unequal laws regarding water access, planting and harvesting olives and other crops, and permits to build and renovate Palestinian homes. We journeyed through West Bank checkpoints and roadblocks, our CPT hats and American or European passports allowing us relatively easy access to places Palestinians could not travel. It was easy to point righteous fingers at the Israeli government and its people for enforcing unjust policies, to see the settlers taking land that was not legally theirs, to condemn the soldiers who shoot holes in Palestinians' illegal water catch systems for fun.

But that summer night, standing on a roof in Dheisheh refugee "camp" near Bethlehem,[3] overlooking the illegal Israeli settlement Har Homa, I realized there is very little difference between Israeli settlers and me, except a couple hundred years of settlement expansion and creation of laws. I, too, live on land systematically taken from its original owners through war and broken treaties; I, too, live in the midst of a culture that strategically hordes natural resources, enjoying flush toilets and water enough for lawns while others do not have enough potable water to drink. I felt overwhelmed and complicit in the injustice experienced by Palestinians. I also felt a leading that night to work on the many injustices in my own culture.

Continuing to discern about my particular calling, I became increasingly aware of environmental concerns and their impact on human and interspecies conflict in the present day, and in the future we are creating. As the context within which all other social justice issues take place, it became clear to me that caring for the planet is the social justice issue of our time. Resource competition, pollution, and climate change exacerbate all other interpersonal and international conflicts, and my understanding of social justice expanded as I recognized the Quaker call to peacemaking may also include reducing human conflict with other species and with future generations. Add to that habitat fragmentation and human population expansion, which make it difficult for other species to thrive, and I can imagine a peace testimony that attends to not only interpersonal

---

[2] "Palestine," Christian Peacemaker Teams, accessed January 2019, www.cpt.org/programs/palestine.

[3] Refugee "camps" have existed since the 1948 Arab–Israeli War (Nakba), and families displaced from properties in what is now Israel have since built multi-story structures, each generation adding rebar and cement dwellings above existing levels.

conflict, but also to equitable treatment of other species throughout God's creation.

I share this story as part of the process of doing Quaker theology: as Friends, our theology flows out of our individual and communal lived experience of the Present Teacher, in line with understandings of what it means to be a follower of the Way across time, and responding to the particular context of the time and place in which we reside. Acknowledging my context is part of my theological reflection on what it means to be a faithful Friend here and now.[4] My own sense of leading is that we as the Religious Society of Friends need to become more actively involved in the work of environmental care, for the sake of present and future human beings, as well as for the sake of other creatures. In many ways, our denomination is well situated to do this work, based on our heritage, but there are other aspects of our tradition that may hold us back from living faithfully and sustainably.

Therefore, in this paper, I will 1) share a bit more about my own Quaker background and my assumptions about the unifying factors of Friends theology (recognizing the difficulty or impossibility of doing so), 2) offer a brief explanation of the field of ecotheology and why it is important, 3) describe some areas of Quaker thought and practice that make it difficult for Friends to move in the direction of a more ecologically informed theology, and 4) focus on areas of potential Quaker strength when it comes to living out our tradition in ways that lead to addressing the environmental situation.

II. Central Tenets of Quakerism

My Quaker background falls firmly in the Christ-centered branches of Quakerism, and it is from this perspective that I will mainly speak in this piece.[5] However, I hope that many portions of this essay will be applicable to any Friend. In that vein, I will name a few ideas that are central to much of Friends theology, while recognizing individual Friends' beliefs vary. The areas with strong agreement across Friends traditions include personal experience of the Divine, corporate discernment, testimonies centering around the idea of "that of God in

---

[4] C. Wess Daniels, *A Convergent Model of Renewal: Remixing the Quaker Tradition in a Participatory Culture* (Eugene, OR: Wipf & Stock, 2015).

[5] For a perspective on an ecotheology stemming from Liberal Quakerism, see chapter 6 in this volume: Christy Randazzo, "'The Divine Light of Creation': Liberal Quaker Metaphors of Divine/Creation Interdependence."

every one," and the calling to direct action in this time and place to participate in the reconciling work of the Spirit in our time.[6]

The Religious Society of Friends began to coalesce as a movement after 1652, when George Fox experienced "one, even Christ Jesus, that can speak to thy condition."[7] That direct experience gave him confidence and passion to encourage others to seek a similar experience themselves. He recognized there is no need for a priest or ritual sacrament in order to encounter the Present Teacher: each one has access to experiencing God. In several places, Fox emphasized: "Christ was come to speak to his people himself," and many Friends recognize this as central to what it means to be Quaker.[8] At the same time, early Friends on through the present day recognize the importance of collective discernment, listening together for the leading of the Spirit, and helping one another discern whether or not a word or idea is from God. Each one can encounter the Inward Light of Christ as mediated through our own conscience, and the interplay between individual and corporate discernment helps keep ourselves and our communities accountable.[9]

As the Friends tradition continued, consistent themes connecting belief and practice emerged and came to be called testimonies or distinctives. Though the particular practices change over the years, the main thrust of the actions to which Friends have consistently felt called have been grouped into testimonies, often referred to using the acronym SPICE(S): simplicity, peace, integrity, community, and equality or equity; some update the acronym to include a second S for stewardship (which includes stewardship of the planet) or sustainability.[10]

---

[6] While it is true that not all Friends use the same language to describe the entity with whom we come in contact through direct experience, and indeed some Friends are non-theist, most historical and current Friends use language such as God, Christ, Jesus, Divine, and Spirit to describe the One they encounter. In this essay I will use these terms and write from a Christian Quaker perspective.

[7] George Fox, *The Journal of George Fox,* ed. John L. Nickalls, revised edition (Philadelphia: Philadelphia Yearly Meeting, [1694] 1997), 11.

[8] Fox, *Journal,* 304; c.f. 8, 48, 80, 90, 98, 104, 107, 112, 149, 236. Examples of Friends emphasizing the centrality of this idea to Quakerism: Elton Trueblood, *The People Called Quakers* (Richmond, IN: Friends United Press, 1989), 64. Pink Dandelion, *The Quakers: A Very Short Introduction* (Oxford and New York: Oxford University Press, 2008), 2, 56. Margery Post Abbott, *To Be Broken and Tender: A Quaker Theology for Today* (Western Friend, Friends Bulletin Corporation, 2010), 29.

[9] Robert Barclay, *An Apology,* ed. Dean Freiday (Manasquan, NJ: Hemlock Press, 1967). Rachel Hadley King, *George Fox and the Light Within 1650–1660* (Philadelphia: Friends Book Store, 1940).

[10] The inspiration for these SPICE testimonies comes from Howard Brinton, *Friends for 300 Years* (Philadelphia: Pendle Hill Publications, 1964), 120ff. Not all Friends find it useful to codify our testimonies in this way, feeling it limits our understanding of what we might be

Central to the testimonies is the focus on equality and equity, and that is based on the idea of "that of God in every one," as Fox described.[11] Further, this testimony is based on biblical passages such as Gal 3:28: "There is no longer Jew or Greek, there is no longer slave or free, there is no longer male or female; for all of you are one in Christ Jesus."

Finally, Friends emphasize the importance of living out the good news of Jesus in the present day. Jesus described his mission as proclaiming good news to the poor, release to the captives, recovery of sight to the blind, letting the oppressed free, and proclaiming the year of Jubilee (Lk 4:18–19). He talked about the Kingdom of God being "among you" (Lk 17:21).[12] It is not only something we experience after we die, but it is something we participate in as a community in this life. Early Friends talked about the Lamb's War (Rv 14:1–5), which was the nonviolent struggle to enact the Kingdom of God in their collective lives in ways that impact the social and political world of their day.[13]

Having explored the grounding of the (nonviolent) Lamb's War in the central Quaker ideas of individual access to the Divine, corporate discernment, and living out the good news proclaimed by Jesus through the testimonies, I will now briefly describe the field of ecotheology and why we need it. I will then discuss areas of weakness in Quaker theology and practice in relation to building an ecotheology from a Friends perspective, and the areas where Friends theology and practice can naturally develop in the direction of environmental care.

---

called to, but I find it useful to use these categories as long as we see them as descriptive of previous callings rather than prescribing or proscribing what we may be called to in the future.

[11] Fox, *Journal*, 263.

[12] NRSV. Various versions translate this passage differently: the New King James Version says, "the Kingdom of God is within you," and the New International Version (NIV) and New American Standard Version (NASV) says "in your midst." What is important to note is that the Greek word for "you" here is plural: the Kingdom of God is present in and among us collectively, and presently.

[13] For more about the Lamb's War, see especially: James Nayler, "The Lamb's War" in *The Works of James Nayler* (Farmington, ME: Quaker Heritage Press, 1657), accessed January 2019, www.qhpress.org/texts/nayler. According to Barbour, many leading Quakers wrote about the Lamb's War, and he has a useful chapter on this topic: Hugh Barbour, *The Quakers in Puritan England* (New Haven and London: Yale University Press, 1964), 33–71. George Fox often referenced the chapters about the Lamb's War in Revelation in many of his writings (Rv 15:2, 17:14, 18:20), and referred to himself as the "Lamb's Officer" (David Loewenstein, "The War of the Lamb: George Fox and the Apocalyptic Discourse of Revolutionary Quakerism," in *The Emergence of Quaker Writing: Dissenting Literature in Seventeenth-Century England*, ed. Thomas M. Corns [Frank Cass and Company Limited, 1995], 25–41, at 26, 30). Gwyn discusses the connection between the Lamb's War and sustainability at length: Douglas Gwyn, *A Sustainable Life: Quaker Faith and Practice in the Renewal of Creation* (Philadelphia, PA: QuakerPress of Friends General Conference, 2014), 113–127. See also chapter 23 in this volume, Walter H. Sullivan, "Earth Quaker Action Team: Reclaiming the Lamb's War for Justice and Sustainability in the Twenty-first Century."

II. What Is Ecotheology, and Why Do We Need It?

Ecotheology has emerged in the last several decades as a response to the environmental situation in which we find ourselves, looking for indications within sacred texts and church history regarding right relationship between humanity and the rest of creation. The term "ecotheology" appears first in publication in a 1973 review article detailing emerging directions in the religious academy relating to the environmental crisis: ecological theology, Christian environmental ethics, the Bible and nature or the environmental crisis, and practical or pastoral works geared toward ministers or Christian lay people in regards to their actions toward the Earth.[14] Therefore, although the term directly names theology, it has been used as a catchall term to refer to the entire scope of environment-related fields within the Christian disciplines.[15] Already in 1973, Gowan references "Lynn White's famous article": a 1967 paper entitled, "The Historical Roots of Our Ecological Crisis" that critiques Christianity's role in legitimizing the culture that created the environmental problems we now face.[16] While theologians recognize the truth in much of White's critique of church history, they also have been working to point out that this is not the only way to read the Christian tradition. Therefore, the work of ecotheology and biblical hermeneutics related to the environment has largely been to recover an ecological paradigm within Christian scripture and tradition.[17] Within an ecological reading of Christianity, human beings are *part of* creation rather than *apart from* creation. People are charged with taking care of the environment, and participating in co-creation

---

[14] Donald E. Gowan, "'Ecotheology': a review article," *Perspective (Pittsburgh)*, 14, no. 2 (1973): 107–113.

[15] The term has also since been used by people of faiths other than Christianity to do similar work in their own faith traditions. For example: Kaveh L. Afrasiabi, *Mahdism, Shiism, and Communicative Eco-Theology: Selected Articles in Comparative Theology* (Scotts Valley, CA: CreateSpace Independent Publishing Platform, 2015). Soumaya Pernilla Ouis, "Islamic Ecotheology Based on the Qur'ān," *Islamic Studies* 37, no. 2 (1998): 151–181. Lawrence Troster, "Tikkun Olam and Environmental Restoration: A Jewish Eco-Theology of Redemption," *Jewish Education News* (Fall 2008): 1–6.

[16] Gowan, "'Ecotheology': a review article," 108. Lynn White, Jr., "The Historical Roots of Our Ecological Crisis," *Science* 155 (1967): 1203–1207.

[17] A few good resources on ecotheology and biblical hermeneutics relating to the environment include: Stephen Bouma-Prediger, *For the Beauty of the Earth: A Christian Vision for Creation Care,* second edition (Grand Rapids: Baker Academic, 2010). Daniel L. Brunner, Jennifer L. Butler, and A. J. Swoboda, *Introducing Evangelical Ecotheology: Foundations in Scripture, Theology, History, and Praxis* (Grand Rapids: Baker Academic, 2014). Ernst M. Conradie, Sigurd Bergmann, Celia Deane-Drummond, and Denis Edwards, eds., *Christian Faith and the Earth: Current Paths and Emerging Horizons in Ecotheology* (London: Bloomsbury T&T Clark, 2015). Ellen Davis, *Scripture, Culture, and Agriculture: An Agrarian Reading of the Bible* (New York: Cambridge University Press, 2008).

with God through that caretaking. Considered a form of contextual theology, ecotheology relates to the particular context of our world at this point in history, and it requires an awareness of one's particular time, place, and political and economic situation in historical reality.[18]

As it becomes increasingly impossible to ignore the reality of anthropogenic climate change, consideration of the environmental impact of our actions is of vital importance. Ecotheology is an attempt to identify parts of the Christian tradition that help us live in an environmentally friendly manner, and to critique ways the Christian tradition has promoted unhealthy actions. Much good work has been done in this area, showing that an ecological paradigm does exist within the biblical text and within some streams of church history. However, the Western church has much work to do in order to separate true and essential parts of Christianity from Western culture, and particularly from the aspects of Western culture that have tended toward empire building, colonization, and overconsumption of natural resources. While much of the work we need to do is very practical and relates to our actions and interactions in the world, much of the work is spiritual. For those of us in "developed" nations, it will require us to be transformed toward recognizing our place in the community of creation; it will require a hard examination of our actual needs; and it will require us to do the hard work of caring for those unjustly impacted by our lifestyle of overconsumption, including living human beings, future generations, and other species whose very existence is threatened by our current trajectory.[19]

Based on our heritage of standing up for social justice causes from a basis in contemplative spiritual grounding in the Inward Christ, Friends are in many ways well situated to do the work of cultivating a Quaker ecotheology that is not only written, but is also lived—that is not only made up of changes in outward behavior, but is primarily a conversion of the heart. However, given our tradition's roots in Western Christianity and our heritage in American and other colonies, those of us from the "first world" still have much work to do in order to live into this potential.

---

[18] Celia Deane-Drummond, *Eco-Theology* (London: Darton, Longman and Todd, 2008).

[19] Joanna Macy and Chris Johnstone, *Active Hope: How to face the mess we're in without going crazy* (Novato, CA: New World Library, 2012).

III. Pitfalls within Friends Theology and Practice for Developing a Quaker Ecotheology

Quakerism contains many helpful aspects that can lead us toward a more faithful relationship to the rest of creation, and I will get to those in the next section. However, I believe it is important to point out our areas of weakness as well. Most of these critiques are based on what I consider an incomplete expression of the fullness of what Quakerism is meant to be.

Friends came into existence in England scant decades following René Descartes's publication in France of texts which became foundational to the Enlightenment and the modernist worldview. While the Enlightenment did not come into full force until the middle of the eighteenth century, the premodern worldview was noticeably eroding, with its focus on divine right of monarchs and a strict hierarchy based on one's social position at birth. Quakerism emerged in the midst of political unrest: the English Civil Wars, the Commonwealth under Oliver Cromwell, and the Restoration of the monarchy with the return of Charles II to the throne. Whereas authority in a premodern worldview resided in tradition and established hierarchies, with ultimate authority to name divine revelation limited to those with the church-ordained right to speak for God, a modernist worldview shifted authority to the individual. This is evidenced in Descartes's famous dictum, "I think, therefore I am," and the move toward democracies rather than inherited systems of power.

Quakerism, emerging in the midst of this shift, retained some of a premodern worldview with its strong belief in divine revelation, but shifted the location of revelation from church hierarchy to the individual, or the community listening together. While this democratization of religion also occurred in many other denominations emerging during the movements making up the Reformation, Quakers took the idea of "priesthood of all believers" to an extreme not seen in other emerging denominations, eradicating church hierarchy and claiming God could speak to and through any individual.

While this is positive in many ways, it also opened Quakerism up to some of the more problematic aspects of Enlightenment and modernist thought: namely, too great a focus on objectivity and rationality, and with them, a propensity toward dualistic understandings of reality. As researchers began understanding themselves as a subject viewing a series of objects, way was paved for many advances in science. When done well, objectivity can be a useful tool. However, it also creates a false dichotomy between humanity and nature, with human beings as subjects in a world of objects—objects there for our use. Much of the resulting implications were based on a neoplatonic understanding of the dualistic separation between matter and logic or reason, with the latter considered more godly. Thereby, a patriarchal hierarchy was also established: males were thought to be more rational and females more emotional (irrational), and women were more connected to the material world. Dualisms including nature vs. culture, indigenous vs. civilized, object vs. subject, and animal vs. human being were seen as forming a chain of being that represented one's place in relation to godliness. Following this line of thinking, pure reason and objectivity were extolled as closest to God, and connection to the material world was seen as ungodly.[20] Anything connected to the less important side of these dualities is still unconsciously considered more associated with the material world by those with cultural roots in the Western traditions, and this has major impacts on the way we treat the planet and creatures we consider less important. It also creates a situation in which we must always be trying to prove ourselves worthy of the more important sides of these dualities in order to be more godly, and to be worthy of being treated as a subject rather than an object.[21]

This neoplatonic dualism occurred throughout the Western church, and in some ways Quakers resisted this simple dualistic categorization, actively working to undermine portions of the hierarchy. However, this dualism creeps into Quaker practice in myriad ways.

The main way I see Quaker practice giving in to hierarchical dualism is in our treatment of the spiritual and the material. Since traditional Quaker worship takes place in silence and without the use of physical sacraments, this can come across as placing more importance on spiritual matters to the exclusion of the physical world. Worshiping in silence can feel like an attempt to transcend our physical bodies and their distractions in order to focus on what is higher, the spiritual plane. The original intention of getting rid of physical sacraments and worship aids such as stained glass and incense was to emphasize that all of life is a chance to encounter the holy: an authority figure in the church hierarchy is not necessary in order for us to encounter God, and being in a church building surrounded by particular smells or sights is not necessary in order to sense God

---

[20] Whitney Bauman, *Theology, Creation, and Environmental Ethics: From Creatio Ex Nihilo to Terra Nullius* (New York & London: Routledge, 2014). Heather Eaton and Lois Ann Lorentzen, eds., *Ecofeminism and Globalization: Exploring Culture, Context, and Religion* (Lanham, MD: Rowman & Littlefield Publishers, Inc., 2003). The connection between the treatment of women, people of color, the natural world, and other oppressed and marginalized populations has given rise to the term "intersectionality," which describes the way all justice issues are connected because they are caused by the understanding of a dualistic hierarchy I have just described, based on the neoplatonic idea of a great chain of being, which supports an exploitative and extractive society and relationship to the rest of creation.

[21] Sallie McFague, *Super, Natural Christians: How We Should Love Nature* (Minneapolis, MN: Fortress Press, 2000).

at work. However, getting rid of these physical reminders also has the effect of removing any material objects or sensory experiences from our worship times. In this way, we unconsciously imply that our focus is on the interaction with God that happens on the spiritual level, and that the material world is only a distraction.

When not at our best, Friends tend to also infer rationality is a sign of closer proximity to godliness, distancing ourselves from emotional expressions of our experience of God. Rationality, intellectualism, and traits considered "masculine" are often conflated with spirituality. In Liberal Quaker circles, this can result in elitism, where Friends intellectualize Quakerism and valorize education, making it difficult to be a Quaker if one is not interested in or educated enough to participate in abstract conversations. Among pastoral Friends, the emphasis on rationality can be expressed in ways that lead to discrimination against gender, race, and sexual orientation: the more Western ideal of "masculine" forms of leadership are recognized and valued in "released" pastoral ministry, while nontraditional leadership gifts are not. In relation to the environmental situation, if Friends emphasize only rationality (to the exclusion of other types of leadership and spiritual gifts that are then termed irrational or emotional), this means that a) Friends have a vested interest in continuing the status quo because they are defining what they value based on the aforementioned dualistic hierarchy, and b) Friends miss out on creative and prophetic solutions to environmental concerns that require a broader range of skills, intelligences, and awareness of the relationships that make up the community of creation. In other words, when we spiritualize and intellectualize Friends theology and practice, we only reiterate the systems of power we say we stand against.

One other major way Friends theology and practice is often clouded by Enlightenment and modernist thinking and the unexamined participation in Western culture's dualistic hierarchies is in our propensity to individualize our faith. While it is important and necessary, as Fox suggested, for us each to experience that "Christ is come to speak to his people himself," it is equally important that we test our leadings with others and work together toward communal understanding of what we hear from God. It is one of our strengths that we work toward group discernment, and I will discuss that more in the next section, but we also strongly value the individual. Finding a balance here is of utmost importance. Individualism is a hallmark of Enlightenment thought; Cartesian thought is based on the premise that the only thing we can truly know is the existence of "I," and everything else is formed around the self. The subject views objects, considered separate from the self, and it is very easy to slide into understanding the objects in the world as present for the sake of the subject, the self. When placed in combination with the dualistic hierarchy, the individual who wishes to be understood as a subject, as an "I," must be as high on the hierarchy as possible in order to not be understood within the system as an object, something to be used by and for the sake of the subjects. This creates a system of competition, where one must always be competing for the power to name who is a subject and who an object. Within Quakerism, when we use our individual understanding of our personal Light Within to compete with others for the power to name who is subject and object, we play into this same dualistic hierarchy. When we must compete for power rather than collectively humbling ourselves to listen for Divine direction, we miss the point of Quakerism, and yet this is a pattern I have seen occurring in many Quaker circles today (Liberal and pastoral) and across history. With our radical and core belief of that of God in every one, we must humbly listen to that of God in one another in our worshiping communities, and also recognize God may be speaking through those outside the group.

In relation to the environment, interestingly, the emphasis on individualism among (particularly pastoral) Friends can lead to anti-intellectualism, which seems contrary to the propensity toward elitism and intellectualism mentioned in relation to our emphasis on rationality, above. However, Friends in the pastoral tradition sometimes give extra weight to their own understanding rather than trusting experts in the field. This can occur in the case of interpreting the Bible and theology: Friends trust their own reading of scripture, hopefully inspired by the Spirit, and are at times skeptical of those trained in the history and culture of biblical times and languages. This can also happen in relation to people's trust of those who talk about climate change. If Friends do not experience (or recognize) its impacts themselves and do not read the Bible in such a way that caring for this world is important to them theologically, they may trust their own individual understanding of what God is saying to them in relation to the environment rather than listening to the perspectives of those trained in climate science.

Additionally, Friends' focus on individualism can lead to us treating one another and the planet as disposable, only here as objects for us to use and discard. If Friends treat one another as individuals with whom to compete rather than as a group with whom to work together, we reproduce the unhealthy patterns of our Western culture rather than the radically prophetic and communal message of early Friends, and of Jesus. This has implications for the way we imagine ourselves in relation to the economy: when we think of our economic status and choices as a mark of our individual achievements, when we think of our money and possessions in an individualized way, we uphold a system that opposes Jesus's "good news for the poor." When we advocate for policies in which pollution happens "Not In My Back Yard" (NIMBYism), but support environmental degradation in other people's backyards by purchasing products that pollute and destroy land, water, air, and ecosystems elsewhere, we contribute to environmental injustice. This can only occur because we buy into an economic and social system offering more rights to some than to others. Collectively, first-world Friends are, quite frankly, not doing much better about resisting or offering an alternative to this system than many other groups.

IV. Potentials within Quaker Theology and Practice for Developing a Quaker Ecotheology

Although these problem areas exist within the Religious Society of Friends, largely due to our legacy in connection with Western culture, I am hopeful about the areas of positive potential within the Friends tradition that can help us move toward a more complete expression of caring for creation. The pitfalls mentioned in the last section stem from distortions of Quaker theology. While not limited to Quakerism, these pitfalls occur uniquely among Friends because of our particular emphases. When practiced well, these emphases can be positive. Indeed, when I presented on this topic to a group of Friends and said the pitfalls among Friends were our emphasis on spirituality, individual connection to God, and a focus on rationality rather than emotional religiosity, one Friend said these were the very things that drew him to Friends from the nondenominational Christian congregation in which he was raised. And I agree—the convictions that we do not have to be doused in hierarchically-blessed water and that God communicates with each one are of central importance to what it means to be Friends, and these are good and important ways to understand our relationship to God and one another. When this emphasis on individual spirituality is coupled with radical submission to our communal discernment, when the rejection of limited sacraments is enlivened by our experience of sacramental encounter with the Divine in and through all our embodied moments, these Friends convictions retain their power and call us all to a heart-opening expression of Christ's message.

The pitfalls described above stem from the strong tendency of human beings to desire power and control. This grows out of fear: fear that we are not worthwhile and lovable, and fear our basic needs will not be met—fear of not having and being enough.[22] We all experience fear, so it's a matter of how we deal with it. As Friends, when we are at our best, we face our fear with courage and vulnerability: we prophetically speak the truth we have found, and we listen with others, trusting that together we can hear the voice of the Spirit. Rather than making decisions that are easy or safe, we engage in the sometimes painful work of discernment. We open ourselves to the Inward Light, which shines on our individual and corporate places of darkness. We hold the tension of mystery and paradox, not creating creeds that can serve as a shortcut to nominal faithfulness, but practicing holy obedience one faltering step at a time. We do all this work from the location of belovedness, knowing there is that of God in every one: we do not need to prove ourselves to God or one another; we are already loved. Christ is already present to us, speaking to us—his people—himself. When we act out of a space of love, we no longer have to be ruled by fear and the desire for control. Instead, we can make choices that benefit the group, and we can let go of our own opinions and humbly listen together.

In relation to caring for the Earth, letting go of our fear and acting through love and trust helps us to attend to long-term implications of our actions, and to recognize the impact of our actions on other people, creatures, and natural systems. When reacting to the world around us out of fear, we tend to make decisions with short-term benefits for ourselves and our families, seizing the largest piece of the pie we can—but these self-focused actions can have detrimental long-term effects as well as unjust outcomes for many contemporary people and other creatures. The Quaker tradition of radical discipleship can help us acknowledge our fears, offer them to God and the group, and seek a way forward that is ethical and loving.

In that vein, I will describe eight ways in which the Quaker tradition holds much potential for developing and enacting an ecotheology with foundations in our denominational story and values: 1) our propensity toward mysticism and emphasis on the Spirit, 2) our focus on community, 3) the ability to strip away forms and get back to the heart of faithfulness, 4) the emphasis on taking the Bible seriously in many of our Quaker families, 5) our focus on reconciliation, equality, and peacemaking, 6) our testimony of simplicity, 7) our historical willingness to recognize the Spirit at work in other traditions, and 8) our vision of all of life as sacramental.

---

[22] For a more complete treatment of this topic, see Cherice Bock, "Scarcity vs. Abundance: Moving Beyond Dualism to 'Enough,'" *Christian Feminism Today*, June 2015, http://eewc.com/scarcity-vs-abundance-moving-beyond-dualism-enough/.

1. Mysticism and Emphasis on the Spirit

The Religious Society of Friends sees as its starting point the mystical encounter George Fox had with "one, even Christ Jesus," who spoke to his condition and filled him with joy. This unmediated access to the Divine became the heart of the Quaker message, and underpins the other testimonies; if all have access to the Divine, all are equal. If we can speak to that of God in one another, perhaps we can "take away the occasion of war."[23]

In relation to care for the planet, what happens when we imagine that of God not only in every one, but also in every thing? While in many ways we are just beginning to recognize this in the last century as we have become more aware of ecological concerns, we can see this idea already present in earlier Friends' writings. Regarding Fox's famous vision where he returned to the Garden of Eden "through the flaming sword," Fox described himself feeling "opened" to the natural world even in his senses, and connected to the rest of creation. He describes a mystical union he believes other wise people have also experienced, and it is enacted through "the Word of wisdom, that opens all things, and [Fox and other wise people have] come to know the hidden unity in the Eternal Being."[24] This "hidden unity in the Eternal Being" sounds very similar to the concepts developed in ecotheology relating to interconnectedness between God and creation, particularly through the work of the Spirit.

Likewise, according to John Woolman: "true religion consist[s] in an inward life, wherein the heart doth love and reverence God the Creator and learn to exercise true justice and goodness, not only toward all [people] but also toward the brute creatures."[25] Woolman here emphasizes that the inward spiritual life led him to outward action based in love for all creation. Woolman, discouraged on one of his journeys, found comfort and certainty that "Love was the first motion,"[26] propelling him on that journey. He sought to test whether his leadings derived from an experience of God's love and called him to loving action.[27] He was not only concerned about being in right relationship with God and other people, but also "the brute creatures," showing that his inward life, his mystical connection to the Divine, drew connections across all creation.

---

23 Fox, *Journal*, 379.

24 Fox, *Journal*, 28. Gwyn interprets this *Journal* passage similarly: Gwyn, *A Sustainable Life*, xxiii.

25 John Woolman, "Journal," in *The Journal and Major Essays of John Woolman*, Philips P. Moulton, ed. (Richmond, IN: Friends United Press, 1989), 28.

26 Woolman, *Journal*, 127.

27 Michael Birkel, *A Near Sympathy: The Timeless Quaker Wisdom of John Woolman* (Richmond, IN: Friends United Press, 2003), 91.

The focus of these earlier Friends and Friends today on the movement of the Spirit among us connects easily to a major theme in ecotheology regarding the importance of the Spirit as a connector. In Hebrew, רוּחַ (*ruach*) means spirit, Spirit, wind, breath, or that which animates or gives life. The Greek word for spirit, πνεῦμα (*pneuma*), means wind, breath, or the creative force of a person. In both languages, the word used to denote the Spirit has to do with creativity and the force that enlivens. Since we share this breath with other creatures, understanding the Spirit as the breath of life, the One who creates and sustains, offers a vision for our interconnectedness with the rest of creation, and also the participation of God in every breath of creation history.[28]

2. Communalism

This participation in the life of God helps move to the next point regarding a potential within Quaker theology: that is, the importance of community. "In the beginning was relationship, so says the Trinity," according to Sallie McFague, referring to God speaking about God's self as "us" and "our" in Genesis 1:26.[29] While the theological concept of the social Trinity is more associated with Eastern Orthodoxy than with Western theological traditions, it is an understanding of God that Friends seem to have also discovered. Rather than a linear (verging on hierarchical) understanding of the Persons of the Trinity as in Western theology, where the Father sends the Son who sends the Holy Spirit, or other variations on this theme, the social Trinity is all about interdependence and mutuality: there is movement between the Persons as they interact and work together, and they invite creation into their economy. When we think of the community of all life as participants in this mutual, creative, and interdependent relationship, the life-breath of the Spirit enlivens us all and we become co-creators with God of an emerging community.

This makes good sense alongside Quaker theology and practice. Historical Friends did not create clear distinctions in their writing regarding the work of each Person, but the different names for the Godhead were used interchangeably and various metaphors were created or discovered from the Bible and used, such as Seed, Light, Present Teacher, and so forth. The work of the Divine Being was seen as dynamic and present, with little emphasis on which

---

[28] Laurel Kearns, "Con-spiring Together: Breathing for Justice," in *The Bloomsbury Handbook on Religion and Nature: The Elements*, eds. Laura Hobgood and Whitney Bauman, Bloomsbury Handbooks in Religion series (New York: Bloomsbury Academic, 2018), 117–132. Sallie McFague, *A New Climate for Theology: God, the World, and Global Warming* (Minneapolis, MN: Augsburg Fortress Press, 2008), 159–174. McFague calls this pan*en*theism.

[29] McFague, *A New Climate for Theology*, 165.

part of God was in charge of which action.[30] Friends saw themselves as participants in bringing about the work of God in the world, not through creating a separatist city on a hill, but through active participation in government and in matters of social concern through speaking truth to power. William Penn attempted to create a place in which all were welcome to participate in forming a fair government in Pennsylvania, a community not limited to Quakers. Friends from the early decades of the movement attempted to advocate for more just laws regarding social status, ability to worship freely, participation in war, and the conditions of prisons. In this way, emphasis on communalism is two-fold in Friends tradition: the community of Friends who gather to worship and discern the voice and direction of the Divine, and the community of all humanity in which Friends are called to actively collaborate with God and others to usher in the Kingdom of God.

In imagining the potential for this aspect of Friends practice to be an asset regarding environmental concerns, I see that Friends already understand the Godhead to be participatory and dynamic, and see ourselves as co-creators with God of God's work in the world. I see that Friends are already concerned with collaboratively working toward a human community that is just and equitable, and so as Friends recognize the disproportionate impact of environmental injustice on marginalized populations, Friends are already well situated to care about this problem and to mobilize to do something about it.[31] And finally, since Friends already have an understanding of who their community is that extends beyond the in-group of Quakers to include all humanity, it is possible that we can take the next step toward understanding ourselves as participants in the community of all life, seeing the work of God in the world as not only right relationships between people, God, and one another, but also the entirety of creation.

3. Ability to Deconstruct or "Remix"

While we have this potential to extend our understanding of who is included in our community to include all life, it will take a great deal of internal work individually and communally for Friends, particularly in first-world countries, to recognize our participation in a harmful system that perpetuates environmental

---

[30] For a more complete discussion of Friends' understanding of the Trinity, see Cherice Bock, "Quaker Pneumatology," in *T & T Companion to Pneumatology*, eds. Daniel M. Castelo and Kenneth M. Loyer (London: Bloomsbury T & T Clark, forthcoming).

[31] Gwyn also discusses the importance of community and corporate discernment in the Quaker tradition and their potential for aiding us in moving toward a more sustainable future; see especially: Gwyn, *A Sustainable Life*, 61–63, 69–72, 75–93.

injustice against people and other creatures, and to dismantle the pitfalls mentioned in section III. We have the resources within our tradition to do this work, but it remains to be seen whether we are willing to do so.

C. Wess Daniels explains the work of deconstructing tradition that Friends did in the emergence of the movement, showing how this process relates to the ideas found in twentieth century philosophies of deconstruction. Daniels shows historical Friends deconstructing their received tradition down to its essentials and "remixing" it with elements of their current culture.[32] In the early years of the Friends movement, Friends stripped away all the non-essential elements of Christianity, rejecting the need for church buildings, hierarchically ordained leadership, rituals that had become dead, and the cozy mutual legitimization of church and state to prop up an unjust social and economic system. They did this by focusing on listening to the present Spirit and reading the Bible to discover the essential elements of "primitive Christianity." Daniels suggests (and I agree) that while this work was important for that original generation, their work is not enough: the work of deconstructing received tradition and remixing it with current context must occur in each generation, and even in each individual Quaker. This does not mean the essentials of what it means to be a Quaker change from generation to generation or individual to individual, but that each of us does the work of knowing the Inward Christ experimentally, as did Fox, in order to discern our individual and collective calling based on the needs of our current time and place.

Early Friends removed the forms and trappings of organized religion that had built up around the essential parts of what it means to be a follower of Christ. In our own time, however, the rejection of phyical sacraments, the importance of silent worship, use of Quaker terminology and "Quaker process" in business sessions, and a range of other practices depending on one's branch of the Quaker family have often become our very own religious forms, often lacking in the essential ingredient of personal and corporate encounter with the Divine, and the impetus to following the direction we hear. Since we have this tradition of deconstruction and remixing with current culture in our denominational heritage, perhaps it is embedded enough in our Quaker DNA that we can again deconstruct the problematic areas of our theology and practice in order to course correct, focusing again on the essential elements of what it means to be Friends of Jesus in the Quaker way. This is a strong potential due to our particular history, and I hope we can use our collective story to build

---

[32] Daniels, *A Convergent Model of Renewal.*

momentum for focusing on environmental justice and caring for creation as an expression of what it means to be Quaker now.

As Friends have developed an understanding of our testimonies in the last century, we have worked to name that which is essential about our denomination. While the SPICES acronym may not sufficiently cover the entirety of what it means to be a Friend, it labels guideposts so each generation of Friends can learn from the wisdom of previous generations. The testimonies of simplicity, peace, integrity, community, equality, and stewardship are open enough that they can be adapted for the particular concerns of each time and place, but can help focus on what is and is not the work of the Quaker community. For those of us from Christ centered Quaker traditions, the Bible offers a foundational guidepost as well, with the testimonies emerging as threads of the biblical tradition that we as Friends have continued to carry forward. In this way, we can hopefully see care for creation as a concern that connects us to our Judeo-Christian and Quaker past, while remixing these important themes (testimonies) in a way that is novel in our own time and place as we face unprecedented environmental injustice, degradation of natural systems, and anthropogenic climate change.

4. Taking the Bible Seriously

Refocusing on the essentials of our tradition must take the Bible seriously, as Friends from Christ-centered traditions. Doing so can help us deconstruct our theology and practice responsibly, connecting us to the story of people of faith while allowing us to step faithfully into a new situation. Early Friends knew the Bible well, and used it as a measuring rod for any leadings they felt. Robert Barclay explained that all leadings should be tested based on what we learn from the Bible, but he also cautioned about reading the Bible without the inspiration of the Holy Spirit: he likened reading the Bible without the Spirit to examining a corpse compared to a living person.[33]

As early Friends read the Bible in the Spirit, they recognized the main thrust of the biblical witness: love and reconciliation, living as a society tending toward equity and shalom. They named themselves the Religious Society of Friends because they understood their main role as Friends of Jesus, not servants (Jn 15), as disciples walking alongside a Present Teacher. They took the Bible at its word regarding the intention of Jesus to remove the legalism that had emerged within the Jewish practices of his day and to reclaim the heart of the law and the

---

[33] Barclay, *Apology*, 32, 40.

prophets, summed up in loving God and loving neighbors as oneself (Lk 10). They took Jesus at his word regarding peacemaking (Mt 5:9, 21–22, 38–48) and the integrity to always tell the truth (Mt 5:37). In short, they recognized his command to live out the Spirit of the law rather than the letter of the law. Because of this, they were able to discern through the reading of scripture in the Spirit that the letter of the Bible was not always literally true: for example, they understood that the passages interpreted to support slavery or the subjugation of women were not intended that way, as they read other passages supporting the equality of all people in matters both social and spiritual.

Taking the Bible seriously as we discern our role as Friends in relation to environmental concerns requires us to again approach the text seeking guidance from the Spirit. With our eyes opened to this new area of awareness, what do we see when we read about our spiritual forebears and their relationship to the rest of creation?[34] What portions of scripture might we be interpreting in unhelpful ways, and what parts might we find that help us see the intention of caring for creation that we might not have noticed when we weren't looking for them? Ecotheologians and biblical interpreters are helping us understand and uncover an ecological paradigm present in the biblical witness, reminding us that the cultures who produced these texts were agrarian.[35] Rereading the covenants between God and the people, we become aware that many of the covenants included right treatment of the land, and the health of the land was used as an indicator of how well the people were living up to their side of the covenant. When reading the Bible with this in mind, the land and other creatures become almost another character in the story. Romans 8:19–23 states in part: "We know that the whole creation has been groaning in labor pains until now," reminding us that it is not only humanity involved in the story of salvation history, but the entire creation is participating with us in the birthing of the new creation. If we take the Bible seriously as Friends, we can attune ourselves to the Spirit speaking through these ancient texts to our current condition, inviting us to participate in that same story, and to recognize that reconciliation extends to God, ourselves, other people, and all of creation. We can listen to the Spirit regarding scriptural interpretations that have been unhelpful regarding our treatment of other parts of the natural world, and humbly invite the Spirit to redirect us into a more faithful path.

---

[34] *The Green Bible* highlights passages relating to creation in green, similarly to many Bibles' use of red lettering for the words of Jesus. It is instructive to flip through a copy of *The Green Bible* to get a sense for what is present in the biblical text that relates to the rest of the natural world, treatment of the land and other creatures, and so forth. *The Green Bible*, reprint edition (New York: HarperOne, 2010).

[35] Davis, *Scripture, Culture, and Agriculture.*

5. Emphasis on Reconciliation, Equity, and Justice

The testimonies of equality and peacemaking form, perhaps, the clearest connection between Friends tradition and environmental concerns. A collective focus on reinterpreting these testimonies in light of the environmental situation could offer a unifying Quaker witness regarding creation care.[36] Four potential areas of crossover between the Friends traditions of peace and justice with environmental issues are worth mentioning specifically: 1) the ability to take away the occasion of wars and increasing conflicts over natural resources, 2) the conviction about the equality of all people and the problem of environmental injustice, 3) that of God in every one extending to that of God in every thing, and 4) the potential for nonviolent direct action and peacemaking tactics and networks already familiar to Friends to be utilized in the work of addressing environmental concerns.

In this historical moment, those of us who heed Christ's call to peacemaking must recognize the underlying issues in present global conflicts. Wars over control of natural resources and access to key geographical features such as ports or mountain passes are not new. What is perhaps new is our awareness of this underlying cause, and the fact that in previous centuries there were other areas into which to expand or escape when one's land was under threat or when one experienced climatic threats such as drought. Currently, refugees are attempting to escape from places that are unsafe due to war as well as a changing climate, leaving places such as Africa and the Middle East for Europe, and Latin America for the United States and Canada. The compounded problems relating to land loss due to multinational corporations' land grabs, environmentally harmful mining and fossil fuel extraction, destruction of rain forests for profit, and many other economic factors have created a situation in which people's homelands are destroyed and communities are fragmented. Peacemaking in this time, as I mentioned in the introduction to this piece relating to Israel and Palestine, requires us to work on the root causes of conflict: overuse and hoarding of natural resources by a few while many do not have what they need. This strategy is at the heart of the colonization process, which has been active in Western cultures for at least the past 500 years, but at this point, there is nowhere new to colonize.[37]

---

[36] In fact, Gwyn suggests "that sustainability is not just one more concern among many, but the framework in which Friends today must contemplate, even rethink, every aspect of Quaker faith and practice," so that rather than seeing sustainability or stewardship as one more distinct testimony, it helps tie the testimonies together. Gwyn, *A Sustainable Life*, xii.

[37] "There is no Planet B" has become a catchphrase in environmental circles, and is the title of a helpful book about the problems facing us and what we can do to ameliorate

Current economic models, as I allude to in the section on pitfalls above, are based on objectifying human beings as interchangeable and disposable parts of a labor pool, and seeing natural resources as interchangeable inputs in a linear system of consumption that does not have a plan for what to do with the outputs (waste and byproducts). The Quaker testimony of equality, however, invites us to resist the dehumanization necessary in this economic system: people are not interchangeable cogs in a machine of production, but are beloved individuals with gifts, talents, and that of God in them. No one is more deserving of the basic necessities of life than anyone else, including breathable air, potable water, healthy soil, a loving community, and the opportunity to engage in meaningful work. The wealthy and powerful are no more worthy of a tip of the hat or honorific language than anyone else; each person is deserving of respect and care. As already mentioned in subsection 1 on mysticism and the Spirit, a deeper interpretation of our testimonies on equality and peacemaking needs to occur in order for this potential strength of Quakerism to help us in relation to the environmental situation. Friends already do well at emphasizing the importance of social and economic justice as an expression of our faith (although we do not always do well at living out our ideals). We see peacemaking as a process of reconciliation between God, ourselves, and other people. Adding the dimension of reconciliation with the land to our call to peacemaking helps bring in the material world and nonhuman creatures to our thinking—and hopefully our action—toward right relationship. In Quaker language, we are extending our understanding of that of God in every *one* to include that of God in every *thing*.[38]

As Friends with a call to peacemaking, reconciliation, and equitable treatment of all, we hold great potential for moving into a new understanding of

---

them: Mike Berners-Lee, *There Is No Planet B: A Handbook for the Make or Break Years* (Cambridge, UK: Cambridge University Press, 2019).

[38] I was already aware of this idea of "that of God in every *thing*" popping up in various Quaker settings, and as editor of this volume, I noticed this seems to be an emerging theme in this volume. See particularly the essays by Laurel Kearns, S. Chagala Ngesa, and Shelley Tanenbaum. The concept of watershed discipleship may also be helpful to Friends as we re-envision our understanding of where we encounter "that of God." Mennonites Ched Myers and Todd Wynward describe one aspect of watershed discipleship as seeing the elements and creatures in the world around us as potential rabbis, intentionally learning from creation as from a respected teacher who knows more about God than we do, and through whom God chooses to be embodied. Early Christians such as Augustine referred to the "book of created nature," stating that while the written Word is important, we also learn about God through the world God created and placed us within. Augustine, "Sermon 68," in *Sermons III (51-94)*, ed. John E. Rotelle, transl. Edmund Hill (Brooklyn, NY: New City, 1991). Ched Myers, ed., *Watershed Discipleship: Reinhabiting Bioregional Faith and Practice* (Eugene, OR: Cascade Books, 2016). Todd Wynward, *Rewilding the Way: Break Free to Follow an Untamed God* (Harrisonburg, VA: Herald Press, 2015).

our own testimonies, seeing the natural world not simply as the stage on which salvation history happens to occur, but as an integral set of subjects with whom we are called into reconciling relationship, as partners and even teachers along the Jesus Way. The final area of potential relating to these testimonies is the years of community organizing, nonviolent direct action, civil disobedience, and advocacy for more just laws in which Friends have engaged in the past. If we can offer what we know in those areas, holding to our commitment to nonviolent resolution of conflicts and our commitment to working toward a more equitable civil society by protesting unjust laws, we may have something to offer to the broader environmental community. When we do this work well, it is steeped in the strength of individual and corporate contemplative practices, offering an undergirding of spiritual depth that can, perhaps, help ease the tendency of activists to burn out. By offering with humility the truth we have found as Friends, that we believe all people have access to that of God in themselves and can recognize the Spirit at work in others, Friends have the potential to be vibrant members of an Earth community tending toward shalom.

6. Emphasis on Simplicity

A final Quaker testimony I will mention is that of simplicity. The Friends emphasis on plain language and plain dress has a long history with the purpose of focusing Friends on following God rather than being distracted by the latest fashions or giving different amounts of honor to people based on class and wealth.[39] Although plain dress has at times been used legalistically and hypocritically (my favorite is Elizabeth Gurney Fry adhering to the letter of the law regarding Quaker grey by wearing fahsionably cut grey dresses made from the finest fabrics),[40] when done as a personally chosen testimony rather than a collectively enforced marker of inclusion in the community, it can be a powerful witness. Friends famously began wearing clothing that had not been dyed by slaves, and some Quaker businesses sold only products that had not been procured by slave labor.[41] Quaker chocolatiers were some of the first to find

---

[39] Fox, *Journal*, e.g. ch. X where Fox describes the problem with hat honor and his refusal to swear oaths.

[40] Elizabeth Gurney Fry, *Memoir of the Life of Elizabeth Fry: With Extracts from Her Letters and Journal*, eds. Katharine Fry and Rachel Elizabeth Cresswell (Philadelphia: H. Long-streth, 1847).

[41] John Woolman's testimony against using products requiring slave labor was inspirational in changing Friends' beliefs and actions regarding their consumption patterns, and his witness is dealt with masterfully in the chapters in this volume by Mike Heller, "John Woolman's Environmental Consciousness," and Jon R. Kershner, "Woolman and Wilderness: A Quaker Sacramental Ecology."

alternatives to slave-produced cacao.[42] When simplicity is practiced collectively based on each person's conscientious choice, Friends can embody a collective witness that is visible and that encourages more just practices in social and economic spheres. In these and many other ways, the Friends testimony of simplicity has been a way to signal and enact the testimonies of equality, peace, and integrity.

The testimony of simplicity has at least as much to do with our spiritual state as it does with our outward actions, and it is this work of simplicity that many of us as Friends in "developed" nations need most. The inward work of allowing God to remind us what we truly need and to receive satisfaction from the joyful state of having enough sounds so easy and yet it is incredibly challenging and often painful to our egos. In a culture in which bigger (or smaller, in the case of technology), better, more, and newer is advertised continually around us, it is difficult to know where to draw the line between that which is necessary, that which is a luxury offering joy and meaning to life, and that which is taking us too far into materialism or greed. While it is not easy, the work before us is spiritual in nature, with practical implications: working to not feel guilty for all we have, to not judge others who have more than us and see ourselves as pious in comparison, and to not rationalize our need for more stuff. Instead, this work of simplicity invites us to open ourselves to trust God, recognizing we are interdependent with one another as creatures embedded in the natural world, and to learn to celebrate joyfully that our needs are met collectively.

Relating to the environmental situation, the testimony on simplicity takes on even more important dimensions. In our time, plain dress might mean only wearing clothing acquired secondhand so as not to support companies with unjust practices and to keep useable items out of landfills. Or it might mean purchasing only a few items of high quality from companies with good labor and environmental practices and wearing one's small wardrobe for years. Ambitious Friends with the knowledge and means to do so might make their own clothing or purchase it from local clothiers. Likewise, the testimony of simplicity could be utilized as we make choices regarding the food we eat. Perhaps we select mostly foods grown in our local region, with only a few favorite items imported from other parts of the globe. Maybe we grow our own food, or support local farmers. We can become involved in gleaning groups that pick fruit from abandoned fruit trees or pick produce left behind in fields already harvested and take it to food banks so that not only the wealthy benefit from local food. We can focus on eating foods that are in season, not requiring extended storage in refrigerated

---

[42] Deborah Cadbury, *Chocolate Wars: The 150-Year Rivalry Between the World's Greatest Chocolate Makers* (New York: PublicAffairs, 2010).

facilities or shipping from another part of the world using fossil fuels. Our testimony of simplicity may extend to advocacy for organic agriculture or small-scale farming, emphasizing simple methods for pest control and honoring the work of small, local growers who invest in the land using methods that can continue for generations.[43]

Many of us in the global north are accustomed to the false "simplicity" of not knowing where our food and other items come from. Rethinking our testimony of simplicity, therefore, means recognizing the complexity of the global systems in which we are participating. It means opening our hearts to the painful work of letting the Spirit simplify our lives so that we focus solely on God for validation, and not on others who judge us based on what we wear or where we live. It means humbling ourselves to remember that each person is equal to us, and we do not have a right to products requiring practices that are unjust, inequitable, or unhealthy to current and future generations.

7. Willingness to Recognize the Spirit at Work in Other Traditions

At times in our collective history, Friends have been cognizant of the presence of the Spirit already at work in people of other traditions. John Woolman felt called to visit the Delawares, and encountered the same Spirit in their gathered meetings as he knew.[44] Friends have often partnered with those from other denominations or religions to do the social justice work to which they feel led. Barclay assumed that God is at work and speaking to all people, whether or not they know the name of Jesus or have access to the Bible.[45] We can answer that of God in every one, meaning that we can trust that God is already at work in others' lives.

This practice holds potential for Friends to learn from others regarding how we are to live in light of environmental problems and climate change. If God is at work in other cultures and and religious communities, perhaps we can learn from those who have traditional practices that lead them to care for the planet and its creatures more directly than does our understanding of the Judeo-Christian tradition. Perhaps we can find areas of common ground such as the concept of shalom and find groups whose care for the land on which we reside was more skillfully honed, and we can learn from them how best to care for the

---

[43] Further thoughts on the connection between the testimony of simplicity and the practice of sustainability can be found in Gwyn, *A Sustainable Life*, 129–146.

[44] John Woolman, *The Journal of John Woolman*, ed. John G. Whittier (Boston & New York: Houghton Mifflin Co., 1909), 201.

[45] Barclay, *Apology*, Propositions 5 and 6.

places we now inhabit as an act of faithfulness.[46] Further, we may be able to listen to and learn from those Friends in the two-thirds world who are drawn to the same Spirit and now share much of our religious tradition, and who may be able to teach those of us from European backgrounds how to live in greater harmony with the rest of creation.[47]

8. No Strict Delineation Between Sacred and Profane: Sacramentalism

The final area of potential I will point out in regards to Quakers and the environment is the flip side of our de-emphasis on physical sacraments. While it can be a problem that we do not practice the physical sacraments because we may tend to spiritualize everything, the Friends teaching regarding sacraments is not that there are none: instead, it is that everything is a potential sacrament. Every moment and each relationship is a chance to encounter the Divine at work in and through the world around us. To the extent that we aproach life with this sacramental mentality, our de-emphasis on particular physical sacraments can be an asset rather than a drawback.

How do we keep ourselves focused on the sacramentality of all life and each moment when we do not set aside particular days or rituals to remind ourselves? This is an important question Friends need to ask ourselves if we hope to build on this potential as a denomination. For programmed Friends, we can build in reminders of the importance of partnering with creation and hearing God through other created entities through our programmed elements. While most Friends do not adhere to a liturgical calendar, we can pay attention to the seasons, listening to God through the rhythm of the world around us. As programmed Friends, we can look intentionally for ways the other-than-human world shows up in biblical passages we feel called to give messages about, and we can sing songs and offer prayers that remind us of our connection to the rest of creation as an important aspect of what it means to be a Friend of Jesus. While most of us do not practice communion with physical elements, Friends of all types do often share food with one another, and we can express gratitude for the food, drawing our awareness to the ways in which the food was produced and brought to us, and recognizing who derives economic benefit from our food purchases, deciding to support sustainable and local food systems. All Friends

---

[46] Randy S. Woodley, *Shalom and the Community of Creation: An Indigenous Vision*, Prophetic Christianity series (Grand Rapids, MI: Eerdmans Publishing Co., 2012).

[47] The essay by S. Chagala Ngesa in this volume is an excellent example of the rich wisdom we may learn from if we ask these kinds of questions of worldwide Friends and are willing to listen.

can be stewards of our buildings and grounds in ways that recognize the sacramental spaces in which we gather to worship: yes, our buildings and grounds are not *more* holy than other places, but they are *as* holy, and perhaps we can spark a sacramental reverence for the places in which we connect with God through intentional care of our spaces, and through talking about the reasons why we are doing so.

The list of ways in which we can draw our attention to the holy in each moment and place could continue through many more examples. The overall point is that this piece of the Quaker tradition can potentially serve to connect us with the work of God in the world, as long as we invite in the mystery, the wonder, the curiosity, the extravagance of being alive in this miraculous world, and the joy of participating with the Spirit who gives us breath in the process of co-creating a reconciling, shalomic community of all life. If we can simultaneously hold the Quaker truth that no one day or place is more sacred than another, with the constant state of holy expectancy that God shows up in each moment, our small but feisty denomination has immense potential to step into an environmentally aware moment in our shared history with grace and Spirit-deepened power.

V. Building a Quaker Ecotheology

Imagining the work before us as Friends feels daunting, and at the same time I am hopeful that it is possible. If we wish to make this transition to a Friends theology and practice that meets the environmental challenges of our time, we must find our anchor in the true Light which gives light to everyone (Jn 1:9), the One who became flesh and dwelled among us (Jn 1:14), the same One who spoke to George Fox's condition and can speak to ours.

In building a Quaker ecotheology, we can gain much from grounding ourselves in our denominational tradition, particularly the testimonies we have found useful and meaningful across time.[48] We have much in our history upon which we can build in a positive direction. Many of the pitfalls in our theology are shared across the myriad denominations formed out of the Reformations and Awakenings: they arise out of a shared value system loosely defined as Western culture. We have our own particular pitfalls as well, our particular brand of emphasis on the spiritual over the material and rationality over other ways of knowing such as spiritual wisdom.

---

[48] Gwyn, *A Sustainable Life.*

The strengths we have developed as a spiritual community, however, far outweigh the weaknesses, if we can avoid falling to one side or the other on the areas of our tradition that can cause us problems. We are from a spiritual tradition that values each one's access to the Divine. We believe God can and does speak to us today, and speak to us about our particular situation. We believe we are called to live in a way that takes away the occasion for all wars—a way that actively works toward reconciliation and shalom. Our tradition requires each person and generation to deconstruct the trappings of religion and focus on the essentials of deep connection to the everlasting wisdom and creative power who sustains us through a current of love, lavished on all. When we become convinced Friends, we are participating with God and with people from all times and places whose lives center around co-creating this loving and just community with our relational God. We recognize we do not have all the answers or understand the fullness of God, but we each have our own valuable piece to offer, and we can learn and grow from attending to the wisdom of others.

To the extent that we as Friends have allowed our cultures to cloud our understanding of God and what loving community looks like, we have much work to do. Many the world over are calling this work "decolonizing," and Friends from the global north must engage the practice of decolonizing Quaker theology and practice with humility and tenacity. I fervently hope we can learn from the wisdom of our Quaker siblings in the global south as we delve into these topics, as well as Friends of color and from other marginalized populations in our own countries. The way we treat "others" is integrally connected to the way we treat the planet and non-human creatures.

To the extent that Friends have continually worked to break free from religiosity and unjust cultural norms, to the extent that we have listened for and followed the still, small voice speaking to us individually and communally, to this extent there is hope for our denomination yet. When we remember to live with the expectation of the holy breaking through at any moment, when we attend to the ways God works through us as physical bodies embedded in ecosystems and interdependent with other creatures for our shared survival, we live out a Quaker ecotheology.

Uncertainty exists regarding how Friends received our pejorative name "Quaker," but it is clear that early Friends were experiencing a response to the intense work of the Spirit in their bodies as they worshiped and testified. I hope and pray we can likewise pay attention to the Spirit at work in us as embodied beings. May we extend our awareness of our communal work beyond economic and social equity to include the environment in which we reside, participating in the breath of the Spirit enlivening all creation.

6 | "The Divine Light of Creation": Liberal Quaker Metaphors of Divine/Creation Interdependence

By Christy Randazzo

Abstract: *Quaker theology has throughout its history heavily depended upon metaphors for the relationship, and inter-relationship, between the Divine and the created order, whether that involves the particular (such as the "seed" of Christ placed in the specific person) or the comprehensively cosmological (such as the "Light," emanating from God into all people). This reflects a long-standing Quaker concern to see the action and presence of the Divine in the current reality, concerned with the health and thriving of creation while it is still alive. Through its project of expanding the vision of what the Divine is and does, Liberal Quaker theology has placed an even greater emphasis on developing metaphorical language for the Divine, which speaks to the human experience of interdependence with a Divine entirely present within its creation, including expanding the metaphorical palette to include other traditions.*

In this essay, I first develop an understanding of the Liberal Quaker theological imaginary, examining how Liberal Quakers place experience as a pillar upon which constructive theology can be developed. I then explore the wide scope of Liberal Quaker metaphorical theology regarding the interdependence of Divine and creation, both from a historical perspective as well as a thematic one, examining the multiplicity and variety of Liberal Quaker metaphorical language of Christ and of Light. I develop three main frames for developing theologies of interdependent Light: as Incarnate Incarnation, as the Divine within the Human, and as the Divine Healer of Sin—particularly structures of sin and injustice.

I. Introduction

The strong emphasis on interdependence between the Divine and the creation in the metaphorical theology of the Light lends itself well to adaptation as an alternative model of divine interdependence for ecotheologies and theologies of creation care. Interdependence between human beings, and between humanity and God, provides the impetus for pursuing the practical work of healing the creation on the human level. Since these processes are imprecise and dynamic, these theologies depend upon the creative use of metaphor and a flexible theological imagination. Therefore, they require metaphorical theologies that can adapt to the fluctuations inherent in constantly changing relationships and the failure of language to precisely describe the "unspeakable" nature of inter-relationality with the Divine.

In this essay, I argue the openness and flexibility of the Quaker metaphor of Light would prove an invaluable asset to theologies of eco-stewardship and creation care, due to their insistence on integrated inter-relationship between the Divine and the Creation, with a particular focus on human response to Divine inter-relationality. I first develop an understanding of the Liberal Quaker theological imaginary, examining how Liberal Quakers place experience as a pillar upon which constructive theology can be developed. I then demonstrate the importance of metaphor in Liberal Quaker theology by demonstrating how Liberal Quakers have developed the Light as the central metaphor for the interdependence of the Divine and the creation, as well as an experienced reality of the inter-relationality of the Divine and humanity. I explore this metaphor through two perspectives: 1) the thought of one Liberal Quaker theologian, Rufus Jones, with a particular focus on ways the Divine-human interdependence of the Light necessitates a strong social justice witness and practice, and 2) the collective thought of the authors of the Swarthmore Lecturers, with particular focus on Light as healer of individuals and social structures.

II. Liberal Quaker Experiential Theology

Liberal Quakerism, as a distinct and definable branch of worldwide Quakerism, applied liberal theology to Quaker thought in the late nineteenth century. Quakerism at that point was still mainly located within the United Kingdom and countries at one time connected to the British Empire, most particularly the United States. Due to the history of Quaker settlement patterns in the United States and the subsequent impact of time, geographical distance, and a variety of other theological and cultural influences, Quakerism in the United States became quite diversified, leading to distinct and divergent branches with marked differences in theology and practice. These include several broad categories: liberal, conservative, pastoral, evangelical, and Pentecostal. While Quakerism in the UK developed a significant evangelical focus in the nineteenth century, the relatively small size of the British Quaker community, and subsequent lack of theological diversity, shielded British Quakers from the separations experienced in the United States. However, due to the strong cultural and theological ties between British and American Quakerism, the "liberal theology" movement of the late nineteenth century washed over Quakerism in both countries, leading to the development of a distinct form of Quakerism now known as Liberal Quakerism.

Two correlative traits dominate the Liberal Quaker approach to the development and subsequent expression of theological beliefs and statements: 1) the negative dictum that Liberal Quakers reject any theological statement or structure which resembles a creed, and 2) the positive dictum that theological truth is to be known through the interaction between the experience of individuals and the community in worship and the testing of these experiences in the lives of both individual Quakers and the Quaker community.

The first trait, rejection of creeds, is stated plainly in Britain Yearly Meeting's *Faith and Practice* with the words, "truth cannot be defined within a creed."[1] The second, regarding experimental understanding of truth, is developed through the emphasis on the interaction between the experiences and beliefs of the individual and the community. Included with this framework is the informal nature of discipline within the community, where formal structures of managing belief and doctrine are replaced with "advice and counsel, the encouragement of self-questioning, of hearing each other in humility and self-love."[2] These two traits are based upon the core theological conviction of Liberal Quakers: as *Faith and Practice* claims, no one person (or ecclesial entity, one can assume) can ever completely comprehend or speak the whole truth about God.

Liberal Quakers insist God can only be known in any meaningful sense through the personal experience of the Divine.[3] This forms what could be termed an "empirical epistemology," where theological statements about God

---

[1] Yearly Meeting of the Religious Society of Friends (Quakers) in Britain, *Quaker Faith and Practice* (London: Britain Yearly Meeting, 1994), 12. (Hereafter, BYM Faith and Practice.)

[2] BYM Faith and Practice.

[3] This is a core tenet of Liberal Quakerism, stated as such in the first passage in *Quaker Faith and Practice*. "Friends maintain that expressions of their faith must be related to personal experience" (BYM Faith and Practice, 1.01).

must reflect the Liberal Quaker experience of God, both individually and communally.[4] This stance of experiential epistemology is reflected in the hazy outlines of much of Liberal Quaker theology, where metaphor is a more effective theological tool than the precision of doctrine and where all truth about God is open to continuous reinterpretation.[5] This aversion to establishing rigid doctrinal statements means neither that Liberal Quakers deny the possibility of universal truth about God, nor that such truth cannot be expressed on a human level.[6] Rather, Liberal Quakerism shifts the proof of the truth of their theology to the experience of God: if a theological construct can aid individual Liberal Quakers to experience God in a more complete manner and demonstrate that experience in a reformed life, and through their experience influence their community, the theological construct has been demonstrated to be proven.[7]

Richenda Scott describes "experience" as composed of two elements: the relationship human beings have with the outer, physical environment, which is mediated through the use of the physical senses and can be termed the material experience; and the relationship human beings have with the inner environment of emotions, thoughts, and "those frontiers of consciousness beyond words."[8] The inner experience is mediated through the mind and spirit and can be said to be the emotional and spiritual experience. She argues that these two elements combine in a unified human experience of the body in space and the soul in God. The human person is not simply receiving experience as a response to sensory and spiritual input, but the person is also actively interacting with the environment in a dialogic exchange. This applies to the personal nature of the experience of God. Scott asserts the experience of God is an immediate and personal one, and does not require any outside mediator to establish the connection. She argues that, due to the inherently subjective nature of human experience, no singular experience of God could be said to be either universally applicable to all people

---

[4] George H. Gorman, *The Amazing Fact of Quaker Worship* (London: Friends Home Service Committee, 1973), 2.

[5] Alex Wildwood represents an expression of this perspective which is non-Christian: "I felt I was finally beginning to square the circle, to bring what I had experienced in diverse other places and forms: experiences of the Spirit in spontaneous rituals, in seasonal circles, in being real with one another and in simple acts of human kindness—with the faith and practice of the Quaker-Christian community which I had felt led amongst. For Hicks was pointing to an experience central to Quaker faith: not a *belief* in something external but an inner knowing; Truth not as a concept, an idea or a doctrine, but as a reality we experience." Alex Wildwood, *A Faith to Call Our Own: Quaker Tradition in the Light of Contemporary Movements of the Spirit* (London: Quaker Home Service, 1999), 5.

[6] Gerald Priestland, *Reasonable Uncertainty* (London: Quaker Books, 2007), 21.

[7] Silvanus P. Thompson, *The Quest for Truth* (London: Headley Brothers, 1915), 14.

[8] Richenda C. Scott, *Tradition and Experience*, Swarthmore Lecture (London: Allen and Unwin, 1964), 2.

or authoritative over all other experiences.[9] Kenneth Barnes makes a similar argument, emphasizing that much of the critique experiential religion faces comes from a glorification of the intellectual, reasoned interpretation of what is inherently an a-rational experience. According to Barnes, the emotional and spiritual experience of God cannot be accurately expressed using verbal and intellectual means.[10]

This insistence on individual experience does not mean, however, that a person could not gain insight through another's interpretation of their individual experience.[11] The Liberal Quaker emphasis on bringing all leadings from God to the gathered community demonstrates the importance of not celebrating the individual experience as the exclusive basis from which to make authoritative claims about God. While emphasizing the importance of the dialogue between individual and community, both for Liberal Quakers and throughout Christian history, Scott acknowledges it can present challenges if an individual feels they experience God in a vastly different fashion from the rest of the gathered community.[12] This can lead to the individual experience of the communal God separating people, thus introducing loneliness into what should be a shared and communal event.[13]

This is not to claim Liberal Quaker theology is developed in a structural vacuum; rather, Liberal Quakers place religious experience as the primary locus for theological reflection and development. This is not a common theological approach, as the inherently fragmentary and dynamic nature of experience can make it an unreliable foundation upon which to say anything certain and universal about God.[14] By viewing other theological sources through the lens of religious experience, however, Liberal Quakerism makes the claim that theology must be contextual, dynamic, non-universal, and developed through the dialogic interplay between the interpretation of the religious experience of individuals and the community.

---

[9] Scott, *Tradition*, 12. This is not a perspective unique to Scott; this is also common language amongst Liberal Quakers. Charles Carter stated, "religious knowledge has existence or validity if it is not welling up in individual experience. No structure or church authority will maintain it then. In fact, the spiritual can be defined by the nature of our apprehension of it." Charles Carter, *On Having a Sense of All Conditions*, 3.

[10] Kenneth Barnes, *The Creative Imagination* (London: George Allen and Unwin, Ltd., 1960), 9.

[11] Scott, *Tradition*, 12.

[12] Scott, *Tradition*, 13.

[13] Scott, *Tradition*, 24.

[14] Lonnie D. Kliever, "Experience-Religious," in *New & Enlarged Handbook of Christian Theology*, eds. Donald W. Musser and Joseph L. Price (Nashville, TN: Abingdon Press, 2003), 190–93, at 190.

As Rachel Muers notes, it is thus "highly unlikely" present-day Liberal Quakers will ever accept a definitive work of Quaker systematic theology, which seeks to develop the one British Quaker vision on the common theological questions of soteriology, Christology, hamartiology, and the like.[15] Individual Quakers might find satisfactory theological answers that fit within Liberal Quaker theological frameworks, and even claim some answers are more helpful than others; yet, these answers will always be open to reinterpretation and re-examination in light of new experiences. This reflects the Liberal Quaker rejection of creeds which, as Pink Dandelion argues, is actually more an acknowledgement by Liberal Quakers of the dynamic nature of human experience, precluding the establishment of any theological statement as authoritative.[16] Thus, if a belief can be changed in light of new evidence, at conceivably any time, any claim to authority would be meaningless. As any ecclesial theology is arguably dependent on some texts or beliefs common to the community, the Liberal Quaker aversion to granting authoritative status to any text or belief precludes the development of anything resembling a "Liberal Quaker theology." Instead, there would be as many Liberal Quaker theologies as there are Liberal Quakers. As Dandelion notes, this is the stance of most Liberal Quakers towards the development of a Liberal Quaker ecclesial theology.[17]

The Liberal Quaker aversion to ecclesial theology is contradicted by the existence of what, in British Liberal Quakerism, is arguably the common ecclesial document which not only provides the "orthodox" British Liberal Quaker approach to issues of administration and structure, but also provides an "orthodox" set of perspectives on issues of theological belief and ethics: *Quaker Faith and Practice*.[18] Reflecting the historical, cultural, and theological connections across the Liberal Quaker world, this emphasis on the importance of *Faith and Practice*-type documents in other Liberal Quaker yearly meetings is a fundamental similarity across the Liberal Quaker world. This is not a controversial statement, for these books claim such an authority for themselves, in particular the British one.[19]

If the *Faith and Practice* documents of Liberal Quaker yearly meetings are thus the authoritative document for Liberal Quakers in terms of theology, practice, and polity, it can be seen as the structural rubric upon which any Liberal

---

[15] Rachel Muers, *Testimony: Quakerism and Theological Ethics* (London: SCM Press, 2015), 20.
[16] Pink Dandelion, *A Sociological Analysis of the Theology of the Quakers: The Silent Revolution* (Lewiston, NY: The Edwin Mellen Press, Ltd., 1996), 151.
[17] Pink Dandelion, *A Sociological Analysis of the Theology of the Quakers*, 147.
[18] Pink Dandelion, *A Sociological Analysis of the Theology of the Quakers*, 151.
[19] BYM Faith and Practice, 12.

Quaker ecclesial theology can be built. The structure of the book, the manner through which ideas are developed, and even the themes emphasized in the book all provide a framework for how Liberal Quakers develop theology.

The Liberal Quaker theological method is therefore informal in its approach to the development of common theological ideas, valorizes experience as the primary source for theological information and reflection, and is suspicious of attempts to either systematize the theological thought of Liberal Quakers or to establish permanent and universally binding structures of belief upon Liberal Quakerism. Anyone seeking to develop a Liberal Quaker theology must take into account this creative interplay between the experiences, context, and beliefs of both individuals and of the community. This interplay must be examined in light of the rejection of claims to authority that other theological approaches allow, such as the inherent authority of time (as in, beliefs which have stood the test of time), scripture, or the authoritative nature of ecclesial sponsorship (in the form of official doctrine or ecclesially-sanctioned theologians).[20] A prime example of this method involves Liberal Quaker use of metaphorical theology to construct models of God reflecting their experience.

III. Liberal Quaker Metaphors of Interdependence

Liberal Quakers often use metaphor in a creative attempt to explain their experience of God. The Light is one such central metaphor, yet Inner Seed, Inner Guide, Light of Christ, and Inner Light are also attempts to explain the Liberal Quaker experience of an immanent God who is concomitantly connected to all of creation. This use of images reflects the difficulty Liberal Quakers often have in expressing the fullness of their experience of the Divine, resulting in metaphors that might not work beyond specific circumstances or for all people. This

---

[20] Carole Dale Spencer argues that while Liberal Quakers have a "wide diversity of belief, they are not without a 'source of authority'." Spencer claims that that final authority rests with Britain Yearly Meeting, and the *Quaker Faith and Practice* (Spencer, 156). This claim rests within the context of the Liberal Quaker business process, where any text written, or action taken, by BYM is made with the awareness that it is not definitive, permanent, or free from critique. This applies to *Quaker Faith and Practice,* which claims that Liberal Quakers are both individually and collectively "holders of a precious heritage of discoveries," which, it can be assumed, were discovered through experience. Yet, even these discoveries must be held onto somewhat lightly, as the Quaker "vision of the truth will, again and again, be amended" (BYM Faith and Practice, 16). Thus, "authority" for BYM is far less certain and definitive than it might be in other ecclesial structures that claim theological authority. I argue that, since this authority is built upon the collective experience of Liberal Quakerism, they still place their main understanding of authority with experience. Carole Dale Spencer, "Quakers in Theological Context," in *The Oxford Handbook of Quaker Studies,* eds. Stephen W. Angell and Pink Dandelion (New York: Oxford University Press, 2013), 141–157.

is not to argue against the use of such metaphorical language, however: metaphorical language and models of God are necessary tools for framing the complexity of the experience of God, as long as they are vessels for moving human understanding toward the deeper reality of the God who was experienced and are not held as definitive statements of the fullness of the reality of God.[21]

Liberal Quakers often hold very tightly to well-loved models of God that reflect deeply held perceptions of Quaker values and beliefs, but which may not be entirely accurate or fully express a complex God.[22] One of the most consistent models in Quaker theology is the language of Light. The theological meaning of this language has not remained static across Quaker history, however. In the following section, I explore how this language has developed over time, with a particular focus on the role of Light in the development of Liberal Quaker theologies of interdependence. In the history of Quaker theology, the term Inward Light has a very specific meaning, relating to the Light of Christ that shines from God inward toward the person.[23]

The early Quaker vision of Light emphasized the potential for actual union with God or Christ which lay dormant within a person until it was awakened by faith and, if attended to, could help people attain a state of perfection in which they could resist temptation and thus avoid sin.[24] A notable trend within Liberal Quakerism is to reinterpret the metaphor of Light by emphasizing the theological aspect of human union with God through the Light of Christ, which is accessible to all, and the ethical aspect of a responsibility to care for each individual due to the presence of the Light Within. Reflecting the general Liberal Quaker trend toward a flexible and open approach to theological language, where even Quaker theological terms with a specific meaning began to shift and morph as Liberal Quakers struggled to explain their experience of God and used whatever tools were at their disposal, the early Quaker concept of Inward Light morphed into Inner Light, which carries a variety of theological meanings. The Light

[21] Beth Allen, *Ground and Spring: Foundations of Quaker Discipleship* (London: Quaker Books, 2007), 25.

[22] Brenda Clifft Heales and Chris Cook, *Images and Silence: The Future of Quaker Ministry* (London: Quaker Home Service, 1992), 80. Reflecting this, Clifft Heales and Cook argue that this has the potential to frame an understanding of the Divine which only serves as a mirror to reflect Liberal Quakers and their values. As a corrective, they argue for Quakers to adopt a willingness to consistently subject their long-standing models to a process of review, measuring them against the experience of both individual Quakers and the community to determine if they continue to help the community make meaning of experiences of the Divine.

[23] Edgar G. Dunstan, *Quakers and the Religious Quest* (London: Allen & Unwin, 1956), 25.

[24] Rosemary Moore, *The Light in their Consciences: Early Quakers in Britain, 1646–1666* (University Park, PA: The Pennsylvania University Press, 2000), 21.

is thus an expansive term for the interdependence of God and humanity, and for the human experience of being in relationship with the Divine.

In what follows, I will describe the ways Liberal Quaker scholars have approached and developed the concept of the Inward Light, and how, seen collectively, their descriptions show a Light that connects humanity, God, and creation in interdependent ways. I examine this from the perspective of both an individual scholar, Rufus Jones, as well as a collection of voices from across the spectrum of Liberal Quaker history, the authors of the Swarthmore Lectures, in order to gain both a nuanced and comprehensive understanding of Liberal Quaker interdependence theologies of Light. I first explore the role of Christology in shaping Jones's social interdependence theology of Light. I then examine two main strands of the interdependence theology of Swarthmore Lecturers: the Light as Divine within the Human, and the Light as Divine Healer of Sin.

1. Interdependence in Rufus Jones' Theology

The interdependence theology of Rufus Jones is important to examine due to the influence of his theology on Liberal Quaker theological developments in his own time and the intervening years, specifically the Swarthmore Lecturers. I first chart some foundational elements of Jones's understanding of the role of the Incarnation on establishing a relationship of interdependence between humanity and the Divine, transitioning towards a development of Jones's understanding of interdependence within the Divine. I then analyze the implications of these ideas on Jones's social theology, and the role of interdependence in shaping Quaker testimony. A key element in that theological reflection has been Jones's insistence that human beings are already in an interdependent relationship with the Divine, without the need to engage in any practices of self-abnegation to "clear out the human" in order to connect directly with the Divine.[25]

Dialogically, this both shaped, and was shaped by, Jones's strongly incarnational Christology. As a Quaker, Jones's theology had been shaped by the consistent theological conviction that "every human life partakes of God."[26] Jones's liberal reading of Quaker tradition led him to understand George Fox's experience of the Divine as, what he termed, a "continuous sense of the Divine life enfolding his own."[27] This is an experience which, as Jones admits, is never

---

[25] Rufus Jones, *The Testimony of the Soul* (New York: The Macmillan Company, 1936), 152–153.

[26] Rufus Jones, *Social Law in the Spiritual World: Studies in Human and Divine Inter-Relationship* (Philadelphia: The John C. Winston Co., 1904), 165.

[27] Jones, *Social Law in the Spiritual World*, 165.

stated as such anywhere within Fox's journal, but which is certainly strongly implied—or so Jones argues.[28] A continuous sense of God's enfolding presence within human life is not entirely without warrant within Christian theology, however, especially when one takes seriously the Christian claim to Christ as the Divine incarnate within humanity.

Jones did, indeed, take this claim seriously, and took this incarnation to its logical conclusion, or at least logical to a Quaker formed by a vision of the Light of Christ actively present within every single person, continuously inviting the human being into deeper relationship.[29] Jones placed strong emphasis on a close reading of the Apostle Paul, particularly Paul's imagery of the interconnected relationship between Christ and humanity within the letters to the Corinthians and Ephesians. This reading gave Jones scriptural warrant for his understanding of the interdependence between the incarnate Christ and humanity. Again, Jones is not engaging in a complex game of eisegesis with this effort. To be completely fair: Christian tradition emphasizes that through Christ's human nature all of creation is capable of being in relationship with the Divine. This establishes the path along which Jones can create a doctrine of God as interdependent with humanity. In many ways, Jones can be said to be a confessional theologian, and an apologist: not only was his reading of scripture and Quaker theological history deeply bound by his identity as a Quaker in a specific context, he felt a very insistent calling to develop theology to serve that context and community.

Through the image of Christ, the being who straddled the Divine and the human, Jones establishes the process through which God develops interdependence with humanity. First, Jones demonstrates that by straddling the seemingly insurmountable divide between Divine and human, Jesus establishes himself as the channel through which God reaches out to humanity, and pulls human beings back through the channel into an intimate relationship with the Divine. As incarnation transforms human existence into something capable of being completely inhabited by the Divine, human beings are incomplete until they can live in relationship with the Divine.[30] Next, through Christ, the Divine experiences everything which human beings experience, including the suffering of human existence in its entirety.[31] This establishes the foundational aspect of interdependent relationship: what one experiences, the other experiences, and thus are both bound in mutual experience. This roots Jones firmly in Quaker tradition,

---

[28] Jones, *Social Law in the Spiritual World*, 163.

[29] Rufus Jones, *The World Within* (New York: The Macmillan Company, 1918), 33.

[30] Jones, *Social Law in the Spiritual World*, 253.

[31] Jones, *Social Law in the Spiritual World*, 101.

which has always emphasized the personal experience of the Divine as the primary element of Quakerism.[32] Finally, through the working of the Divine within the human person, the person is perfected through the process of the Divine changing the human being into the image of God, the inward self which is from henceforth "always at home with the Lord."[33]

The theological implications of this progression are profound. For one, Jones claims God suffers as human beings suffer, meaning that eliminating human suffering is both a human *and* a Divine imperative. Second, Jones argues people are created to be incomplete without the presence of God. Yet, this does not presume human beings are capable of ever *actually* existing without the presence of God within. Instead, they are in relationship proleptically with the Divine, their relationship being existent foundationally, in that to be human ontologically is to be in relationship with the Divine. This is explained in Jones's formulation, "it is impossible to make immanence intelligible without *transcendence,* even in the case of our personal spirits."[34]

Third, Jones envisions a panentheistic Divine, a Spirit who is both immanent within and transcendent beyond the world, who is, as Jones states, the "Ground and Source of all we can call Mind or Reason in the universe."[35] A God who experiences everything human beings experience is a God who experiences what *every* person experiences. If all human beings are bound to a God whose incarnation in the world makes the world closer to God, this binding also makes Godself closer to the entire world, enfolding the entire world within the Divine. Thus, the panentheistic God brings all of humanity into relationship with the entire creation, opening the horizon for new possibilities for humanity. This brings with it a rippling of consequence for individuals, however: human interconnection.

The ethical implications of this interconnection are clear: when you make any person suffer, you also make God suffer—an untenable situation crying out for remedy. Yet, as God is present throughout the entire creation, and within human beings as the Inner Light,[36] then harm to any one human being is untenable as it carries with it a tripartite harm: to the individual as themselves (human), to the individual as a part of the Light (Divine), and to the individual

---

[32] Rufus Jones, *The New Quest* (New York: The Macmillan Company, 1928), 125.

[33] Jones, *The World Within*, 35.

[34] Jones, *The Testimony of the Soul*, 110. By "personal spirits," Jones appears to mean the individual human soul, that which makes the human being recognizably human—as opposed to the Spirit of God.

[35] Jones, *The New Quest*, 186.

[36] "Inner Light" is the term Jones preferred, and through his continuous use, aided in its spread amongst Liberal Friends.

as a member of humanity (human and Divine). Jones understands the human person to be an individual only as they are a member of the created order, and thus only as they are a member of the interdependent community of God and the creation. Their personhood existed through connection to others, or as he stated, "personality at every stage involves interrelation."[37]

This is the final step of the process that begins with God's creation of a human being who requires relationship with God, and a God who in turn desires relationship with every person. Through God, human beings are interconnected to each other. As human beings cannot be truly human without relationship with God, through God human beings cannot be truly human unless they are in interconnected relationship with other human beings.[38] In other words, following Jones down the rabbit hole here leads to the inevitable conclusion that people do not seek to free others from oppressive structures of war, famine, and homelessness—the work Rufus Jones, through the aegis of American Friends Service Committee, initially did for millions of refugees of the First World War—simply out of obligation to God, or even only to aid other people in need. In fact, I argue the most radical implication of Jones's theology is that people do relief work *because they are human*, because failing to serve the other is to fail as a human person, and it is only through service to the other that the self truly becomes the self.

2. Light as Divine Within the Human

There appears to be general consensus within Liberal Quakerism on the acceptance of the Liberal Quaker doctrine of the Light as God's presence within the human person, an incarnate presence with the capacity to bring a person into greater levels of relationship with God. Beliefs about the capacity of that Light to influence humanity differ, however, depending upon one's opinion about the potential of human nature to be improved, or even perfected. A minority perspective exists which argues for a chastened view of human nature where human sinfulness creates a barrier with God that only the incarnate Christ could overcome. The majority view maintains a positive view of human nature that can be perfected by the presence of God: the Light opens space for humanity to develop a fully interdependent relationship.

---

[37] Jones, *Social Law in the Spiritual World*, 58.
[38] Rufus M. Jones, *New Studies in Mystical Religion* (New York: The Macmillan Company, 1927), 170.

This is significant because it claims the incarnate presence of the Light within the human person works in partnership with the inherent human potentiality to improve and to reject sin in a continuous effort to heal division among human beings, and between people and God. Thus, this vision of the Light makes the claim that the partnership with the incarnate Light confers upon human beings the capacity to heal the damage caused to humanity and to the entire creation through division and human destructiveness. Human beings are thus active agents in their own reconciliation with each other and in their atonement with God.

William Charles Braithwaite argues that the universal witness of Quakers has proclaimed that the "Spirit of God" is best expressed—in terms of its incarnation within the creation—in the "spirit of man," Braithwaite's term for the human soul.[39] In Braithwaite's designation, all of humanity is thus created to be in relationship with the Light, and is made whole through the union of Light and human being.[40] This inevitable union between God and humanity was the result of the continuous improvement of the human condition, reflecting the Liberal Quaker concept of human perfectibility and continuous evolution.[41] Braithwaite assumes humanity has the responsibility to respond to this invitation. The initiative for acceptance must come from humanity, as the Light has already done all of the work that it is capable of doing to invite the individual into relationship without creating the relationship unilaterally.[42]

This inherent capacity for unity with the Light is actually a potentiality, an active response of the human person to the initiative of God towards humanity. Henry Hodgkin argues the early Quakers developed this doctrine as a reflection of their own experience of such a response from their souls to God. Hodgkin argues the insistence on such a potentiality resulted from the early Quakers' strong reaction against the doctrine of total human depravity, a doctrine whose falsehood the Quakers realized due to their experience of their own goodness.[43] This same experience amongst Liberal Quakers informs their hopefulness that each person can be inspired to reach out to, and thus to experience, the same Spirit of God as the early Quakers experienced.

---

[39] William C. Braithwaite, *Spiritual Guidance in the Experience of the Society of Friends* (London: Headley Brothers, 1909), 81.

[40] Braithwaite, *Spiritual Guidance*, 88.

[41] Braithwaite, *Spiritual Guidance*, 87.

[42] Braithwaite, *Spiritual Guidance*, 81.

[43] Henry T. Hodgkin, *The Missionary Spirit and the Present Opportunity* (London: The Swarthmore Press, Ltd., 1916), 90.

By 1968, this analogy of human perfectibility had begun to be generally accepted amongst Liberal Quakers.[44] It should also be noted humanism also began to grow in acceptance amongst Liberal Quakers during this time period. This positive attitude towards the human potential for perfectibility is not universal in Liberal Quaker theology, however. In light of this context, in his 1968 Swarthmore Lecture, William Thorpe addressed his concerns about this trend by reassessing H.G. Wood's earlier critique of the Liberal Quaker doctrine of the universal Light. Thorpe echoed Wood's rejection of the inevitability of human perfectibility, especially in relation to the presence of the Inner Light within the human being. Thorpe considered this to be an unfortunate optimism regarding the human condition, especially the belief in the expansive capability of human reason that resulted from the Liberal Quaker belief in the human capacity to reason itself into union with the Light.[45] Thorpe argued Wood only acknowledges a chastened vision of the Inward Light, which requires the graceful action of God in order to come to its full development within the human person. For Wood, this aversion to human perfectibility results from both his intense awareness of the extent of human sinfulness and his insistence that faith in Christ be the necessary avenue through which the individual gained any sense of union with God.[46] As a result, Thorpe argued Wood rejects the equating of the Inner Light and Christ. Wood instead insists the Inner Light is the spirit of humanity seeking union with Christ.[47] In this, Wood agrees with Braithwaite's vision of a humanity created to be in relationship with God. Both Wood and Thorpe chasten that vision, however, insisting on a greater level of human sinfulness and separation from God than Braithwaite accepts.

Despite Thorpe's argument for the value of Wood's chastened view of human nature, Beth Allen argues this concept (that humanity has been designed for relationship with the Divine) has become the dominant strand within contemporary Liberal Quakerism. Allen stresses this concept is both hopeful about the possibility of human perfectibility and rooted in a positive view of human goodness.[48] Allen argues this inherent "God-shaped hole" within gives humanity the ability to respond to God's invitation for relationship.[49] This design has epistemic significance for humanity, Allen asserts, in that it provides the means for

---

[44] Thorpe's commentary refers to: Herbert G. Wood, *Quakerism and The Future of the Church* (London: The Swarthmore Press, Ltd., 1920).

[45] William H. Thorpe, *Quakers and Humanists* (London: Friends Home Service Committee, 1968), 16.

[46] Thorpe, *Quakers and Humanists*, 17.

[47] Thorpe, *Quakers and Humanists*, 18.

[48] Allen, *Ground and Spring*, 24.

[49] Allen, *Ground and Spring*, 24.

having a complete knowledge of the ontological reality of human existence: an existence foundationally marked by relationship with God.

While the Liberal Quaker theological tradition may not be in union about the nature of the element within humanity that desires relationship with God, it does appear to be in unity about the universality of the Light that reaches out to the creation. Playing with this concept, some Liberal Quakers argue that due to the unique subjectivity of the individual, it would be most appropriate to state that the universal Light interacts with individuals by means of a light unique to that specific individual. In this construction, "light" would mean the truth of that individual person's experience of God. This view takes the subjectivity of human experience seriously.

In that vein, T. R. Glover argues a light comes to each individual from God, analogous to the individual lights of a string of lamps at a railway station. All of the lamps give forth light, which, when combined with the other lamps, creates a unified light for the station. However, each lamp is still radiating its own individual light, which could be said to be unique to that one specific lamp. Glover insists one can confirm one's light is the "real light" from God by comparing one's own light to that of others. Yet, Glover argues God has many lights, all of which may serve to illumine the truth of God in ways that might seem confusing and contradictory when compared to each other.[50]

Glover's analogy reflects the Liberal Quaker sense that truth is not the reserve of one tradition, and that there are in fact many equally valid perspectives on truth. This is still an extant perspective, as Christine Davis uses very similar language when claiming each individual must follow the Light in each person. She asserts that God gives each person what could be termed an individual task and God grants each person their own light with which to illuminate their path toward achieving that task.[51]

The ambiguity of this poetic language means Glover and Davis could be interpreted to say the Light is not universal and does not unite humanity in an interdependent whole. However, that would be an incomplete reading of Glover and Davis's metaphorical use of light. It appears they are instead explicitly recognizing each individual will have an inevitably subjective experience of the Light.

Other Liberal Quakers engage with the universality of the Light by focusing on the unity this universality creates between subjective human beings. In this construction, the universal nature of the Light is experienced subjectively by

---

[50] T. R. Glover, *The Nature and Purpose of a Christian Society* (London: Headley Brothers Publishers Ltd., 1912), 8.

[51] Christine A. M. Davis, *Minding the Future* (London: Quaker Books, 2008), 48.

each individual, yet the commonality of the experience transcends human individuality, thus creating unity.

Hugh Doncaster emphasizes the element of unity between God and humanity, arguing Liberal Quaker experience has demonstrated unity with the Light is available to all who seek such unity.[52] This experiential theology of human unity is developed through the experience of unity in worship, yet may not be initially obvious to plain observation. Doncaster acknowledges the individual experience of Liberal Quakers can sometimes lead a person to proclaim an understanding of a truth that the rest of the gathered community of Quakers may not have experienced, demonstrating spiritual unity does not immediately lead to a unity on the plane of lived human reality. Doncaster stresses, however, that the spiritual unity of all human beings in the Light will eventually bring humanity into unity on the lived plane, and those who are consistently in disunion with the rest of the group may not actually be in true pursuit of unity within the group.

G. K. Hibbert hints at the belief that the presence of the Light within the human person can lead to human perfection, both through the influence of the perfect God within the human person and through the mechanism of the Light's guidance of human behavior towards the divine ideal. Hibbert asserts God's incarnation within the human person is actually a necessity. Hibbert argues that since God's love for humanity demands relationship, God must therefore become incarnate in order to grant humanity the inward experience necessary to provide complete awareness of the joy that can come through relationship with God. This inward experience, Hibbert argues, is far more effective in converting the human desire for God than any outward doctrine could ever be. This direct experience of God occurs whenever people experience anything lifting them out of their mundane existence and compelling them to engage in compassionate behavior toward others. Hibbert suggests these experiences occur at the point where God and humanity are in relationship, the point where human beings are "most truly human," and are thus made perfect by their relationship with God.[53] Hibbert asserts these experiences, and the perfection that results, can only occur due to the action of the Light within the human person.[54]

Hibbert makes the rather paradoxical claim that the presence of the Light within the human person grants one the ability to either deny relationship with God, and thus to sin, or to seek relationship with God, and thus to be made perfect in God. This occurs due to Divine efforts toward converting the human

---

[52] BYM Faith and Practice, 26.65.

[53] G. K. Hibbert, *The Inner Light and Modern Thought* (London: George Allen and Unwin, Ltd., 1924), 55.

[54] Hibbert, *The Inner Light and Modern Thought*, 12.

heart to seek relationship with God, as described above. Hibbert asserts God desires true relationship with humanity, a relationship chosen by humanity and pursued as a result of the human desire for such a relationship and not simply due to some Divine command that would compel humanity into relationship.[55] This introduces the element of choice into the Divine/human relationship. The logical claim follows, contends Hibbert, that a choice can only be truly said to be a choice if it is made freely and without compulsion. Thus, the Light has the task of guiding the human person toward relationship with the Light. As this relationship involves human decision, resulting ethical choices impact not only humanity, but the rest of creation as well.[56]

E. B. Castle agrees with the view of the Light as an active force, terming the Light a "catalyst." The "catalytic action" of the Light inspires human action through the power of the love God has for humanity and which flows from God to humanity through the action of the Light reaching out to humanity.[57] Castle asserts the Light is thus a guiding force, both inspiring humanity toward change and actively pushing humanity toward relationship with each other through the active redirection of human conduct toward others.

While the Light guides human behavior and sentiment, caution should be taken to remember the necessarily communal element of the action of the Light. The guidance given by the Spirit is actually a communal guidance, due to the presence of each individual in the wider spiritual community of the Light. This communal nature of the spiritual community ensures individual judgement does not become the supreme arbiter of right and wrong. Viewing the Light as communal event and presence thus ensures the Light is shared amongst all people in the community both as a communal experience and a gift from God to the individual.[58]

3. Light as Divine Healer of Sin

The salvific significance of the Light for Liberal Quakers falls along two tracks: the Light as liberator from the oppressiveness of human sinfulness, both as self-imposed guilt about human weakness and from literal imprisonment and torture, and the Light as divine warrior against the forces of evil on both the spiritual and physical planes. Salvation is thus, for Liberal Quakers, a question of liberation

---

[55] Hibbert, *The Inner Light and Modern Thought*, 15.

[56] Hibbert, *The Inner Light and Modern Thought*, 27.

[57] E. B. Castle, *The Undivided Mind* (London: George Allen & Unwin, Ltd., 1941), 42.

[58] Shipley N. Brayshaw, *Unemployment and Plenty* (London: George Allen and Unwin, Ltd., 1933), 120.

from evil and violence as opposed to the traditionally Christian soteriological views of salvation from a tormented afterlife. Liberal Quakers may be concerned with spiritual forces, but only as they deleteriously impact the present condition of life, and transfer their spiritual evil to a physical evil of oppression, violence, abuse, and the systemic evils of racism, misogyny, and economic inequality.

Adam Curle argues the Light provides a counterbalance to the oppressive messages of worthlessness and guilt that pervade so many aspects of culture, especially regarding human sinfulness. The effect of these messages, Curle argues, is to destroy the human spirit and to eventually become the evil monsters these voices, both interior and exterior to the human mind, claim humanity is at its core. These messages lead people to forget that the Light resides at the core of humanity and the immeasurable love of God for all of creation resides at the core of the Light. Feeling ourselves bereft of the love of God, or the inherent worth stemming from such powerful love, Curle argues human beings choose to fill the hole with lies about the inherent superiority of some individuals above others. This is truly a lie: human superiority makes no sense in the context of the equal, immanent presence of God within each individual person. Curle suggests, therefore, the Light liberates humanity from the necessity to prove their worth by some ultimately flawed human definition and, as a corollary, casts away the dark emptiness of worthlessness by filling each person with the love of God, regardless of any metric of worth.[59]

Following on his emphasis on social sin relating to Truth, Gerhart von Shulze-Gaevernitz developed a model of the Light as liberator of human beings from the evils of oppressive social sin, and as liberator of the imprisoned. Social sin, for von Shulze-Gaevernitz, is a nexus of oppression, rooted in the pursuit of power and money. Von Shulze-Gaevernitz envisioned a long flow of money through banks, the hands of laborers, and oppressive taxation, all feeding the wars of nationalist governments, finally resting in the hands of war profiteers. This social vision of sin has a strong echo in liberation theology, with an obvious socialist critique of capital.[60] Von Shulze-Gaevernitz acknowledges this powerful nexus of oppression can be overwhelming and may lead people to apathetic resignation in the face of its implacable power.[61] The Light, von Shulze-Gaevernitz argues, provides a means of liberation from imprisonment in this system of social sin through action to redeem the social order and a strong and consistent effort

---

[59] Adam Curle, *True Justice: Quaker Peace Makers and Peace Making* (London: Quaker Home Service, 1981), 24.

[60] Jon Sobrino, *Christology at the Crossroads: A Latin American Approach* (Maryknoll, NY: Orbis Books, 1976), xix.

[61] Gerhart von Shulze-Gaevernitz, *Democracy and Religion: A Study in Quakerism* (London: George Allen and Unwin, Ltd., 1930), 88.

to redeem the souls of the people enmeshed in this order. The Light's immanence is thus transcendent, as it seeks to reform the entire system even as it is
held captive by the system.[62]

Von Shulze-Gaevernitz does not claim the Light is physically involved
in the breaking of physical chains. Instead, von Shulze-Gaevernitz argues the
Light strengthens those who are imprisoned and oppressed through the immanent presence of the Light within each human soul.[63] When a person rests on
the Light for support in desperation, the Light gives that person a "liberty of
Spirit" through the love of God flowing through the Light into the person.[64] He
suggests this flow of love breaks the oppressive power of the chains, and defeats
the purpose of the imprisonment, which is to destroy the spirit of the imprisoned
person. This form of salvation finds its echo in the Gospel messages of freedom
to captives and the prophetic messages of freedom from oppression (Lk 4:18–
19).

IV. Conclusion

Liberal Quakerism assumes the greatest possible Divine immanence within the
creation: an Incarnation that infuses every particle of creation. Liberal Quakers
are not in unity about the implications of this, however. Some Liberal Quakers
claim this leads to an inherent goodness and sacredness of the entire creation,
with the corollary that humanity must therefore be inherently good. Others insist
on chastening that view, acknowledging the human potential for both evil and
good. The Light is active in the process of human transformation, striving to
guide humanity toward both a greater awareness of the presence of the Light,
and of the ethical consequences of that presence. Liberal Quakers view this intimate guidance as the truest expression of human freedom, because it allows human beings to develop faith in the presence of the Light on their own terms.

---

[62] Von Shulze-Gaevernitz, *Democracy and Religion*, 91.
[63] Von Shulze-Gaevernitz, *Democracy and Religion*, 88.
[64] Von Shulze-Gaevernitz, *Democracy and Religion*, 89.

7 | Woolman and Wilderness: A Quaker Sacramental Ecology[1]

By Jon R. Kershner

Abstract: The Quaker minister, tailor, and abolitionist, John Woolman (1720–1772), was influenced by a tradition of apophatic spirituality of openness that led him to view all places as places where God was already present and could instruct the person sensitive to divine leading. He did not romanticize nature, but responded to the specific features of each landscape. Believing that God's will could be reflected in wilderness, pastoral, and urban locations, Woolman suggests an intersubjectivity between place, humanity, and the divine that supports a Quaker sacramental ecology.

In 1763 the New Jersey Quaker minister, tailor, and abolitionist, John Woolman, and two others, a companion and a guide, began a two week trek into the Pennsylvania wilderness to visit the Native American town of Wyalusing.[2] Woolman's encounter with wilderness along the way speaks broadly to his reception of the various natural and constructed spaces of the eighteenth-century world, whether they be urban, pastoral, or wild. Instructed by an apophatic spirituality of openness that believed all physical spaces promised to be places of divine instruction, Woolman did not overlook, ignore, or romanticize the physical features of the landscape in an attempt to get beyond or behind the specificity of each location. Rather, in Woolman's spiritual ecology one encounters the way the individual, God, and the specific realities of each physical place exist with intersubjectivity,

---

[1] A version of this essay was given at Quaker Heritage Day at Berkeley Friends Church, Berkeley, CA, February 23, 2019.

[2] John Woolman, "Journal," in *The Journal and Major Essays of John Woolman*, ed. Phillips P. Moulton (Richmond, IN: Friends United Press, 1971), 117–137.

such that all places and all landscapes provide affordances that can draw the sensitive wanderer into spiritual places of insight, conviction, awareness, and awe.[3] Woolman's interactions with the natural world build on the spiritual sacramentalism of the Quaker tradition that understood the presence of Christ to be in a fundamental unity[4] with all humanity and all creation, and, therefore, always in the process of revealing God's self through the whole of the spiritual and natural world.

Woolman's 1763 journey into the wilderness took place during what in America became known as the French and Indian War (1754–1763): a conflict between the two great European imperial powers, France and England, each power, among other things, vying for control of the Ohio River Valley, which encompassed western Pennsylvania. Some Native American groups sided with the French, some sided with the English, some wished to be neutral. The constant pushing westward of the frontier by British settlers led to conflict with the Native American groups who witnessed their land invaded and their treaties transgressed.[5] To make things more complicated, European settlers believed that the promise of fertile and plentiful land that had convinced them to leave their homelands and move their families to America was not as promised. Indeed, many of these European settlers were frustrated to learn upon arrival in America that the ownership of the land they had purchased was under dispute. These European immigrants had purchased the land from colonial land brokers, so they thought their claim was legitimate. Native Americans held a very different understanding of land ownership than did the Europeans and resented the cheating that European brokers and proprietors used to expand their claims on traditionally Lenape and Conestoga lands. The dispute was ugly. There were massacres on all sides.[6]

Many of the European settlers on the frontier eventually fashioned a conquest theory of ownership, wherein those who could take the land by force had a sovereign claim to it.[7] Alongside that conquest theory of ownership was a

---

[3] Jay David Miller, "'Nature Hath a Voice': John Woolman's Wilderness Habitus," *Religion and Literature* 45, no. 2 (2013): 36–37.

[4] Hilary Hinds, "Unity and Universality in the Theology of George Fox," in *Early Quakers and Their Theological Thought, 1647–1723*, eds. Stephen Angell and Pink Dandelion (New York: Cambridge University Press, 2015), 56–57.

[5] Andrew Newman, *On Records: Delaware Indians, Colonists, and the Media of History and Memory* (Lincoln, NE: University of Nebraska Press, 2012), 175–76.

[6] Judith Ridner, *A Town In-Between: Carlisle, Pennsylvania, and the Early Mid-Atlantic Interior* (Philadelphia: University of Pennsylvania Press, 2010), 8–9, 92–93, 104.

[7] Kevin Kenny, *Peaceable Kingdom Lost: The Paxton Boys and the Destruction of William Penn's Holy Experiment* (New York: Oxford University Press, 2009), 4–5; Newman, *On Records*, 27–30.

racialized view of Native Americans where the crimes of some were attributed to all. For many settlers, there was no distinction between "friendly" and "enemy" Native Americans.[8]

The political background of Woolman's 1763 journey into the wilderness is helpful for understanding the situation Woolman was entering when he journeyed to Wyalusing. It helps to shatter those preconceptions and romantic notions that sometimes obscure contemporary understandings of the way people in centuries past experienced nature and wilderness. Going into the wilderness in the eighteenth century was not to be taken lightly. It was not like a week spent camping in Yellowstone, Yosemite, or some other National Park today. It was dangerous and difficult, and despite it all, Woolman found it to be a journey through a physical landscape that offered sometimes troubling spiritual lessons with implications for the landscape of the soul.

The idea that nature and place could say something about God, could in some way reflect God's nature, could provide lessons that are not confined to the material world, but that integrate the spiritual and physical—that idea is not new, nor is it particular to any group. It stretches the length of Christian history. For most of the first thousand years of the history of Christianity, few Christians could read books about God. Without being able to read the Bible or other spiritual texts, many Christians looked to the physical and natural world around them to inspire the soul, to reflect back to them in ways obvious for all to see the ways of God.[9]

Ancient theologians said there was the book of Scripture, and there was the equally important and by far and away more accessible "Book of Nature."[10] The faithful Christian could and must learn from both. But it was the book of nature that was readily available for all to see. For them, the visible world mediated God's invisible presence and attributes. The view that physical objects and practices can reflect God is called sacramentalism, the capacity to see the holy and sacred in what is otherwise considered mundane. For these early Christians, the natural world was a vehicle to knowledge of God and God's will.[11]

---

[8] Kenny, *Peaceable Kingdom Lost*, 230–31.

[9] Jame Schaefer, *Theological Foundations for Environmental Ethics: Reconstructing Patristic and Medieval Concepts* (Washington, DC: Georgetown University, 2009), 65.

[10] Saint Augustine, "The Writings Against the Manichaeans and Against the Donatists," in *Nicene and Post-Nicene Fathers*, ed. Philip Schaff, vol. 4 (Hendrickson Publishers, Inc., 1995), 339, http://ccel.org/ccel/schaff/npnf104.iv.ix.xxxiv.html.

[11] Schaefer, *Theological Foundations for Environmental Ethics*, 65.

The fourth century theologian, Ephrem the Syrian, was one of many early church leaders who saw the natural world as a revelation of divine attributes, and, even more than that, many believed nature was a sacred symbol for God:

> In every place, if you look, His symbol is there,
> and when you read, you will find His types.
> For by Him were created all creatures,
> And He engraved His symbols upon His possessions.
> When He created the world,
> He gazed at it and adorned it with His image.[12]

Ephrem taught his congregation that everywhere they looked, everywhere they went, they encountered the symbols and types of God. Not only was the created world good, the created world would lead the careful and faith-filled observer to God. The ubiquity of God's symbols across natural places meant that it was not only in cultivated and pristine environments that God would be recognized, but even the harsh, rough, and uncomfortable spaces could be reverenced because they exist, and because they exist they were a doorway to the knowledge of God. Reading the book of nature was a sacred calling, made possible through the eyes of faith, but fully open for all to see.

Woolman was aware of frontier hostilities between Native Americans and British settlers before he left the safety of his home, but felt a sense of divine "leading" to visit "the natives of this land who dwell far back in the wilderness."[13] On one particularly soggy day *en route*, Woolman recorded in his journal the severity of the mountain slope, downed logs that obstructed his path, and the swamps he and his companions crossed. As he sat in his tent, unable to travel due to heavy rain, Woolman noted that the wetness of the season and the threat of hostilities made his journey more difficult than it would have been at another time.[14] However, he credited the political and environmental difficulties of traversing the wilderness with heightening his reliance on God and concern for others:

> And as it pleased the Lord to make way for my going at a time when
> the troubles of war were increasing, and when by reason of much wet
> weather travelling was more difficult than usual at that season, I looked

---

[12] Quoted in Schaefer, *Theological Foundations for Environmental Ethics*, 68.
[13] Woolman, "Journal," 122–24.
[14] Woolman, "Journal," 127.

upon it as a more favourable opportunity to season my mind and bring me into a nearer sympathy with [the Native Americans]. And as mine eye was to the great Father of Mercies, humbly desiring to learn what his will was concerning me, I was made quiet and content.[15]

That night his guide's horse wandered off in the rain. Woolman's companion went in search of the horse and found it on its way back to Philadelphia. Seven hours later, he returned to camp with the horse, where the party spent another night because it was too late in the day to travel.[16]

Woolman paid attention to the physical realities of the wilderness around him, and the hardships they occasioned. This is an important point. Woolman did not romanticize nature or wilderness; he did not and he could not lose sight of wild spaces as life threatening and potentially dangerous, as was so much of life in the eighteenth century. And here is the point: Woolman's conviction that God could speak in and through nature was distinct from a view of nature as convenient, benevolent, or pleasant.

Woolman did not idealize the wilderness like Henry David Thoreau would a century later.[17] Even though some of the nineteenth century Romantics, like Thoreau, looked back to Woolman as the type of simple, agrarian spirituality they venerated,[18] Woolman was not one of them. Woolman and many colonists of his generation had in their recent memories the dangerous and uncertain struggle with wilderness that their parents and grandparents had known as settlers in a new-to-them land. Moreover, colonists continued to hear accounts from the frontier where existence remained tenuous and settlers struggled to survive, and where the expediency of survival was sometimes pitted against the teachings of one's religion, occasioning compromise and anxiety.[19] For some Quaker meetings along the Pennsylvania frontier, day-to-day life meant negotiating the external dangers of attack and the more mundane uncertainties of securing a livelihood in a rough environment. For these scattered frontier Quakers, far from the security of Philadelphia, living on the margins of colonial civilization sometimes meant living on the margins of Quaker discipline. Those Quaker meetings had

---

[15] Woolman, "Journal," 127–28.

[16] Woolman, "Journal," 128.

[17] Roderick Frazier Nash, *Wilderness and the American Mind*, 4th edition (New Haven, CT: Yale University Press, 2001), 84–85.

[18] Phillips P. Moulton, "The Influence of the Writings of John Woolman," *Quaker History* 60, no. 1 (1971): 12–13.

[19] Karen Guenther, *"Rememb'ring Our Time and Work Is the Lords": The Experience of Quakers on the Eighteenth-Century Pennsylvania Frontier*, The Pennsylvania History and Culture Series (Selinsgrove, PA: Susquehanna University Press, 2005), 18.

to make their own way, even if it sometimes transgressed the sensibilities of Philadelphia Quakers who did not know what it was like to live as a religious minority, nor did they have to reconcile their resistance to violence with the danger of Native American attacks experienced by those Quakers on the frontiers.[20] The difficulties of life on the frontier and the economic concerns of colonialism meant for many eighteenth-century colonists, both Quaker and non-Quaker, the wilderness was an obstruction to be subdued, rather than Thoreau's mid-nineteenth century Romantic understanding of wildness as a "source of vigor, inspiration, and strength."[21]

Woolman's response to wilderness was distinct from many of his fellow colonists, because he did not view wilderness as an obstruction, but neither did he idealize it as an objective purveyor of wisdom like Thoreau would. Woolman's interactions with wilderness coincide with what Belden Lane has called a phenomenological perception of nature.[22] That is, Woolman did not view nature as inherently one thing or another, neither an obstruction like other colonists nor an innate "source of vigor" like Thoreau. Rather, nature and wilderness simply were, and because of the empirical fact of their existence, they were agents of providence and solicited a response that reflected God's provision for all beings. Two other views of nature contrast with Woolman's phenomenological view. One is the "cultural perception" of nature and physical place that views geography as a blank slate—something with no meaning outside of what human beings attribute to it. In the "cultural perception" of nature, the individual's or group's personal affinities and dispositions are projected onto nature in a way that turns nature into nothing other than the observer's projected desire.[23]

A modern example of this cultural perception would be those who see economic utility as the reason for nature's existence, and hence practices like mountaintop removal are believed to be justified. Cultural perceptions of nature and place need not be destructive, as is the case in the example of mountaintop removal. Cultural perceptions could lead to neutral or protective interactions with place; the key feature of cultural perceptions is that place is understood as only carrying meaning and value that is attributed to it by human beings without regard to the specific features of the place itself. It is a view that starts with the human person's or community's needs and projects those needs onto physical places. More positively, the cultural perception of place contends that all physical

---

[20] Guenther, "Rememb'ring Our Time and Work Is the Lords," 17–18.

[21] Nash, Wilderness and the American Mind, 88.

[22] Belden C. Lane, "Giving Voice to Place: Three Models for Understanding American Sacred Space," Religion and American Culture: A Journal of Interpretation 11, no. 1 (2001): 66–67.

[23] Lane, "Giving Voice to Place," 57–58.

spaces can be sacred in so far as they reflect the social construction of sacredness. Cultural perceptions of place recognize that nature does not carry a specific predetermined and inherent meaning isolated from the cultural construction of meaning that is projected onto it.[24]

The second view of geography and nature that Woolman rejected was what Belden Lane has called "environmental determinism,"[25] which contrasts with the cultural perception of nature in that it assigns a predetermined and fixed, inherent meaning to nature and place. It is deterministic. This view claims that human views of nature and place have no bearing on the meaning and interpretation of places. Rather, nature and place will evoke, unbidden, a predetermined response. However, changing interpretations of nature across cultures and history would suggest that simply coming into contact with a geography does not carry the same meaning across contexts, and so the possibility of objective meanings is questionable. For example, a grove of oak trees may have been important to New England Puritans, but the meanings they found there would have been different from the meaning of an oak grove to Celtic Christians in pre-modern Britain, who carried the memory and legacy of Druid spirituality with its veneration of oak groves as spiritual places.[26]

In the view of environmental determinism, simply going to a natural place would occasion a predetermined spiritual transformation. So, entering the wilderness would occasion growth and vitality simply by being there, without any conscious effort or changes within the individual. It supports the "illusion that changing places is the simplest way of changing ourselves,"[27] and that the natural world promises automatic transformations. However, while there may not be a set of predetermined and preordained meanings that correspond with natural settings, the example of Woolman teaches us that nature's power of suggestion is great.

Unlike cultural perceptions that view wilderness as a blank slate onto which the subject projects their own meanings, and unlike the "environmental determinism" that assigns predefined and inherent meanings to natural objects, supposedly independent of human perception,[28] a phenomenological perception of wilderness is "never a purely cognitive process."[29] This type of perception is

---

[24] Lane, "Giving Voice to Place," 57–58.

[25] Belden C. Lane, The Solace of Fierce Landscapes: Exploring Desert and Mountain Spirituality (New York: Oxford University Press, 1998), 14–16.

[26] Celia Deane-Drummond, A Handbook in Theology and Ecology (London: SCM Press, 1996), 36–37.

[27] Lane, Solace of Fierce Landscapes, 37.

[28] Lane, Solace of Fierce Landscapes, 14.

[29] Lane, "Giving Voice to Place," 66.

not simply a projection and neither is it purely a human-assigned meaning. Woolman's experiences in the wild demonstrate the "intersubjectivity" that exists between people and the natural world in which there is reciprocity between subjects.[30] From this phenomenological perspective, the wild is present to and with the human subject "only to the extent that [the human being] participate[s] in the various affordances it offers, responding to the striking geographical features it projects."[31] Woolman brought to the wilderness, as he did to all physical spaces, an apophatic spirituality in which the divine will could fill his own.[32]

This apophatic spirituality can be seen in one of Woolman's favorite terms, "resignation." For Woolman, "resignation" did not mean giving up. It did not mean ceasing human effort. What Woolman called "resignation" was the spiritual practice of becoming one with God's will. It meant to recognize that human beings are complicated and conflicted and that their truest selves are realized when they trust God and seek to pursue in their daily lives all those things that comprise the righteous and just life. It was not an apophatism that required the "annihilation of the self" or a denial of the integrity of personality and human effort. "Resignation" was a precondition for true discernment. Woolman's practice of "resignation" operated on the assumption that there were supernatural powers at work within the natural world and that the most authentic response of the human being to God was to see the physical world and the spiritual world as a piece.[33]

In "resignation," or yieldedness to God, Woolman believed the individual could be transformed from the false-self lost in a spiritual wilderness of alienation to God, into a true-self that could identify in the physical wilderness the continuous revelations of God, which gave form and structure to the human experience.[34] This apophatic spirituality is best understood as an openness to the sacramental experience of nature; an experience that allows natural places the freedom of their existence, as they are, without human projections of meaning. Thus, Woolman did not idealize the wilderness as inherently positive, or having any inherent meaning at all beyond its existence as a part of God's creation, of which he was also a member. He did not gloss over the physical difficulties and dangers wilderness occasioned. However, in his apophatic spirituality he discerned in the wilderness particular "affordances" of place that led him to reflect

---

[30] Lane, "Giving Voice to Place," 59.

[31] Lane, "Giving Voice to Place," 67.

[32] See: Lane, *Solace of Fierce Landscapes*, 62–65; Miller, "'Nature Hath a Voice': John Woolman's Wilderness Habitus," 36–37.

[33] Jon R. Kershner, *John Woolman and the Government of Christ: A Colonial Quaker's Vision for the British Atlantic World* (Oxford, New York: Oxford University Press, 2018), 34.

[34] Kershner, *John Woolman and the Government of Christ*, 43.

inwardly on the presence of external stimuli, and therein to learn new spiritual insights.[35]

The day after their guide's horse went on its escapade in the rain, the party set off again for Wyalusing.[36] Woolman recorded in his journal: "The sun appearing, we set forward, and as I rode over the barren hills my meditations were on the alterations of the circumstances of the natives of this land since the coming in of the English."[37] Woolman observed that Native Americans had lost to the English the best lands and their own livelihoods, so that they were forced to "pass over mountains, swamps, and barren deserts, where travelling is very troublesome" in order to trade with the English.[38] Wilderness phenomena were present to Woolman as the phenomena themselves.

Swamps, mountains and barren landscapes maintained their physical integrity. He did not try to imagine his way through the physical objects in search of metaphors for independence and vitality, like the Transcendentalists would a century later.[39] To do so would have diminished the injustice of Native American displacement and the difficulties of life on the frontier. To project a meaning onto nature that does not reflect the physical reality of nature would have been to reduce nature itself to a purely human construction, because no honest person who had any other options could idealize the rain-soaked, mosquito-infested, dangerous, and difficult realities of traversing, living in, and finding a livelihood in fierce landscapes. It was the poor and the oppressed who were forced to live with those realities in the eighteenth century.

Rather, the wilderness was present to Woolman as it really was, even though interpreted through the individuality of his own apophatic spirituality. The affordances of the wilderness landscape illumined economic injustice and, as Jay Miller argues, "destabiliz[ed] and reorder[ed]" his sense of self, human relations, and his understanding of divine will for human organization.[40] The wilderness was both threatening and instructive,[41] and so Woolman did not avoid it. He did not view it as only an obstruction. Rather, wilderness was a present subject with him in his desire to be transformed by God, and therefore, would be used by God to extend his compassion and spiritual insight.

---

[35] Jon R. Kershner, "'A More Lively Feeling': The Correspondence and Integration of Mystical and Spatial Dynamics in John Woolman's Travels," *Quaker Studies* 20, no. 1 (December 1, 2015): 109, doi.org/10.3828/quaker.20.1.103. For Lane's use of "affordances," see also: Lane, "Giving Voice to Place," 67.

[36] Woolman, "Journal," 128.

[37] Woolman, "Journal," 128.

[38] Woolman, "Journal," 128.

[39] Lane, *Solace of Fierce Landscapes*, 17.

[40] Miller, "'Nature Hath a Voice': John Woolman's Wilderness Habitus," 7.

[41] Miller, "'Nature Hath a Voice': John Woolman's Wilderness Habitus," 7.

After noting the barrenness of the wilderness landscape and the consequences of British colonial policy on Native Americans, Woolman examined his own complicity in injustice:

> My own will and desires being now very much broken and my heart with much earnestness turned to the Lord, to whom alone I looked for help in the dangers before me…. And a weighty and heavenly care came over my mind, and love filled my heart toward all [hu]mankind, in which I felt a strong engagement that we might be obedient to the Lord while in tender mercies he is yet calling to us…. And here I was led into a close, laborious inquiry whether I, as an individual, kept clear from all things which tended to stir up or were connected with wars…and my heart was deeply concerned that in future I might in all things keep steadily to the pure Truth and live and walk in the plainness and simplicity of a sincere follower of Christ.[42]

On this journey into the wilderness, Woolman's understanding of faithfulness to God's will was expanded into new arenas of personal piety and economic justice. Wilderness affordances were not incidental to the spiritual insights he discerned and the extension of compassion he experienced. The specificity of the wilderness landscape, and his own spirituality, were both prerequisite for the experience.

The approach to wilderness places I have identified in Woolman is distinct from the perception of wilderness by other colonists, which was often unambiguously negative. The whole colonial endeavor was predicated on the notion that distant wilderness places could be cultivated for lucrative resources to enrich the homeland. When William Penn received the royal charter for what would become Pennsylvania in 1681—about the time John Woolman's grandfather immigrated to the colonies[43]—Penn simultaneously became the single largest landlord in the British Empire.[44] In order to pay for his settlement and some of his vast debts, he needed to sell his land and expand the colonial infrastructure inland.[45] The entrepreneurial land speculators who purchased land from Penn set up towns between the port city of Philadelphia and the frontier.[46] These land speculators then recruited settlers to purchase smaller tracts from them, and to

---

[42] Woolman, "Journal," 128–29.
[43] James Proud, "A Note on John Woolman's Paternal Ancestors: The Gloucestershire Roots; The West New Jersey Plantation," *Quaker History* 96, no. 2 (2007): 28.
[44] Kenny, *Peaceable Kingdom Lost*, 2.
[45] Kenny, *Peaceable Kingdom Lost*, 2.
[46] Ridner, *A Town In-Between*, 4.

set about the work of harvesting Pennsylvania's natural bounty to trade back to the port cities and on to the major European capitals.[47] Penn's descendants succeeded him as executors of the colony and continued to view the wilderness as something to be tamed.[48] The Quaker colony was not alone in this; the Puritan vision for New England was "an errand unto the wilderness" that entailed turning the wilderness into a "city on a hill," a vision that was spiritual and metaphorical, but also evocative of the designs that would be exerted on the landscape itself.[49]

Colonialist ventures were founded on the assumption that the wilderness was either an obstruction to economic expansion, or a resource to be tamed and commodified. Over the course of the eighteenth century colonial markets became seen as places of commercial expansion by homeland mercantilists and industrialists. Extensive transatlantic shipping networks grew to accommodate the movement of natural resources from colonial ports to Europe, and, in return, European luxuries and fashions were shipped back to colonial ports for consumption and distribution inland.[50]

If the monied colonialist interests wanted to commodify the wilderness and its resources, individual colonists knew their survival depended on subduing it. Quakers generally agreed that wilderness places needed cultivation. Carla Gerona's work on Quaker dream culture has found that colonial Quaker dreams often featured visions in which wilderness places were groomed into pastures with fences, and tamed.[51] In Quaker spiritual writings, the "wilderness" was synonymous with depravity and willful spiritual regression.[52] And here Woolman's

---

[47] Ridner, *A Town In-Between*, 4.

[48] Carla Gerona, *Night Journeys: The Power of Dreams in Transatlantic Quaker Culture* (Charlottesville, VA: University of Virginia Press, 2004), 146–47.

[49] Sacvan Bercovitch, *The American Jeremiad* (Madison: University of Wisconsin Press, 1978), 25–26.

[50] T. H. Breen, *The Marketplace of Revolution: How Consumer Politics Shaped American Independence* (New York: Oxford University Press, 2004), 41, 53.

[51] Gerona, *Night Journeys*, 14, 120.

[52] Samuel Fothergill, "Memoirs of the Life and Gospel Labours of Samuel Fothergill, with Selections from His Correspondence. Also an Account of the Life and Travels of His Father, John Fothergill; and Notices of Some of His Descendants.," in *The Friends' Library; Comprising Journals, Doctrinal Treatises, and Other Writings of Members of the Religious Society of Friends*, eds. William Evans and Thomas Evans, vol. 9 (Philadelphia, PA: Joseph Rakestraw, 1845), 170; Michael L. Birkel, *A Near Sympathy: The Timeless Quaker Wisdom of John Woolman* (Friends United Press, 2003), 90; John Churchman, *An Account of the Gospel Labours, and Christian Experiences of a Faithful Minister of Christ, John Churchman: To Which Is Added a Short Memorial of the Life and Death of a Fellow Labourer in The Church...* (Philadelphia: Printed by Joseph Crukshank, 1779), 179; Woolman, "Journal," 171; John Woolman, "An Epistle to the Quarterly and Monthly Meetings of Friends," in *The Journal and Essays of John Woolman*, ed. Amelia M. Gummere (New York: Macmillan Company, 1922), 482.

complexities challenge generalizations and sweeping characterizations, for Woolman, too, used the term "wilderness" as a metaphor to describe Quaker spiritual laxity and divine displeasure.

> A trust is committed to us, a great & weighty trust, to which our diligent attention is necessary. Wherever the active members of this visible gathered church use themselves to that which is against the purity of our principles, it appears to be a breach of this trust, and one step backwards toward the wilderness; one step towards undoing what God, in Infinite Love, hath done through his faithful servants, in a work of several ages, and appears like laying the foundation for future sufferings.[53]

For Woolman, a spiritual wilderness is a place to avoid. Like the Hebrew people wandering in the desert because they failed to fulfill what God required of them, so Quakers could experience a spiritual wandering in a wilderness of their own making if they did not live up to their end of their covenant with God. If they participated in oppression, if they were more focused on their pocket books than on God's voice, if the divinely appointed designs of their liberation from persecution and ecclesial oppression in England were not realized in the life of their community, then they had already entered a wilderness place.[54] But even in this spiritual metaphor, wilderness is not described as evil; it is an accurate reflection of the spiritual reality. It does not call for a response of destroying the wilderness, it calls for a conversion of the heart so that the lessons of the wilderness can be learned. Woolman's warning about spiritual wilderness is mild compared to his peers, like John Churchman, who understood spiritual wilderness to be a type of punishment that purified the wayward through their suffering.[55]

These views reflect the cultural assumptions about wilderness most Quakers maintained.[56] Woolman believed that if people were faithful to God's intent for social organization, fewer people would live in colonial or European cities, fewer would be involved in the transatlantic economy, and more people would undertake what Woolman called "the sweet Employment of Husbandry."[57] For Woolman, this agrarian vision was an eschatological one in which

---

[53] Woolman, "An Epistle to the Quarterly and Monthly Meetings of Friends," 482.

[54] Jon R. Kershner, *"To Renew the Covenant": Religious Themes in Eighteenth-Century Quaker Abolitionism* (Leiden: Brill, 2018).

[55] Churchman, "Memoirs," 179.

[56] Geoffrey Plank, "'The Flame of Life Was Kindled in All Animal and Sensitive Creatures': One Quaker Colonist's View of Animal Life," *Church History* 76, no. 3 (2007): 587.

[57] John Woolman, "On a Sailor's Life," in *The Journal and Essays of John Woolman*, ed. Amelia M. Gummere (New York: Macmillan Company, 1922), 505–506.

Isaiah's peaceable kingdom would be enacted on earth, and the social harmony that characterized the Garden of Eden would be restored on earth.[58]

For eighteenth century Patriots like Thomas Jefferson and Thomas Paine, the image of "sturdy yeomen" working the pastoral landscape was grounded in a secular vision of historical progress, not a religious one of fulfilling God's will.[59] Yet, in either Woolman's religious vision or the Jeffersonian one, the ideal society to be established in America would be one of subsistence farmers engaged in animal husbandry. For many colonists, a pastoral, agrarian vision was the "equilibrium" between the two extreme poles of wilderness and European-style cities.[60] The agrarian ideal tamed the wilderness but did not fall into the dislocation of industrializing, urban centers.[61] In the context of the colonial endeavor, then, wilderness places were usually seen as hindrances in need of cultivation. For colonists, it was cultivation, not wilderness, that was the ideal. Where colonists differed was on the type of cultivation desired, and the degree to which European-style development should be emulated in the colonies.

This context helps to highlight two important aspects of Woolman's perspective on wilderness that he did not share with many of his fellow colonists. First, while Woolman did view farming as a noble employment, he did not reject wilderness places as merely hindrances and obstructions. In his apophatic spirituality the affordances of every landscape could be divinely filled with meaning, and so could become active subjects evoking insights unavailable in another setting. The wilderness, then, was not kept at arm's length as that which needed to be tamed, but was taken into himself as a fellow participant in God's creative paradigm and, thus, as a fellow shaper of meaning and a co-interpreter of the divine will. Jay Miller says, Woolman "does not separate who he is from where he is."[62] Later on his journey to Wyalusing, Woolman wrote about a rainstorm he and his fellow travelers encountered, "which was so heavy that it beat through

---

[58] Another Quaker wrote enthusiastically in 1761 that the day had arrived when "the wilderness and the solitary place will be made to rejoice and become as the Garden of the Lord." Geoffrey Plank, *John Woolman's Path to the Peaceable Kingdom: A Quaker in the British Empire* (Philadelphia: University of Pennsylvania Press, 2012), 246; John Woolman, "A Plea for the Poor, or A Word of Remembrance and Caution to the Rich," in *The Journal and Major Essays of John Woolman*, ed. Phillips P. Moulton (Richmond, IN: Friends United Press, 1971), 258; Woolman, "Journal," 48–49; John Woolman, "Considerations on the True Harmony of Mankind and How It Is to Be Maintained," in *The Journal and Essays of John Woolman*, ed. Amelia M. Gummere (New York: Macmillan Company, 1922), 443.

[59] Otto Kraushaar, "America: Symbol of a Fresh Start," in *Utopias: The American Experience*, eds. Otto Kraushaar and Gairdner Moment (Metuchen, NJ: Scarecrow Press, 1980), 17.

[60] Nash, *Wilderness and the American Mind*, 94–95.

[61] Nash, *Wilderness and the American Mind*, 90.

[62] Miller, "'Nature Hath a Voice': John Woolman's Wilderness Habitus," 17.

our tent and wet us and our baggage."[63] As a result of the storm, the large number of trees that fell across the path further mired their journey.[64] The wetness of the path, the downed trees, and more swamps, led Woolman to write, "we got through with extreme difficulty."[65] And directly after this description of the environmental conditions, Woolman wrote: "I had this day often to consider myself as a sojourner in this world, and a belief in the all-sufficiency of God to support his people in their pilgrimage felt comfortable to me, and I was industriously employed to get to a state of perfect resignation."[66]

Severe wilderness conditions led Woolman to consider the transitory nature of human pursuits, and fostered a spiritual conviction that abandoning oneself to the will of God and to the establishment of God's will on earth was the goal of human existence. The trees, rain, and swamps destabilized the logistics of the trip to Wyalusing and corresponded with a spiritual destabilization of Woolman's sense of self that deepened his dependence on God.[67] For Woolman, destabilization was not to be avoided, and thus the wilderness was not to be avoided, because it was in such experiences that one's vision was expanded. While the wilderness was a place of physical obstruction, the physical wilderness was not necessarily a spiritual obstruction, and further, a spiritual wilderness could be a place of instruction and transformation.

What was required for all of these transformations was not something external to the human subject, but an internal disposition of openness to the affordances of every place, a "sacra-mentality" that responds to the affordances of every place as a place of humility and wonder, struggle and the sacred, weeping and confession, because these are all honest responses to the presence of God. This "sacra-mentality" is a pervasive sacramentalism founded in the apophatic conviction that the life of faith is a life of responsiveness to the God who wishes to be known. It trains the sensitive soul to see that every journey is a journey into God because every physical place, as wild and brutal as it may be, is also a place that already bears God's presence. This is not to deny the danger and trouble of fierce landscapes, neither is it to romanticize nature in ways only possible among the philosophical elite who extract refreshment from nature and then retreat to comfortable, urban lives. Rather, it is to honestly respond to the geographic features that exist in nature and to honestly reflect on the less than ideal, less than romantic contours of the landscape of the human soul.

---

[63] Woolman, "Journal," 131.
[64] Woolman, "Journal," 131.
[65] Woolman, "Journal," 131.
[66] Woolman, "Journal," 131.
[67] See also, Miller, "'Nature Hath a Voice': John Woolman's Wilderness Habitus," 17–18.

A second difference between Woolman and many other colonists was that he did not wish to subdue or eradicate the wilderness.[68] He thought the British expansion into the wilderness of his day was already an economic injustice to the Native American population, and that if colonists rejected materialism, they would be able to subsist comfortably on modest farms with no need for expansion into wild places.[69]

Thus, in Woolman's vision for colonial America, the wilderness would always be near at hand.[70] When Woolman returned home from his journey to Wyalusing, he again recounted in his journal the difficulties occasioned by the wilderness: the bushes, trees across the path, and even rattlesnakes. He then reflected, "people who have never been in such places have but an imperfect idea of them. But I was not only taught patience but also made thankful to God, who thus led me about and instructed me that I might have a quick and lively feeling of the afflictions of my fellow creatures whose situation in life is difficult."[71]

Woolman did not overlook the wilderness landscape, neither did he assign it a purely metaphorical value of his own determination. Rather, the specificity of the wilderness landscape was spiritually instructive and stayed with him as a permanent part of his understanding of the life of faith. In this way, Woolman's spirituality was always a spirituality of place, a habit of being, such that any physical landscape could become a heavenly gateway. Woolman's perspective contrasts sharply with the view of those colonists whose commercial exploits sought to carve up the wilderness, whose agrarian vision wanted to subdue it, or who thought of the wilderness as a problem to be solved.

Woolman's view of the wilderness also differs significantly from Thoreau's.[72] At times, Thoreau ventured into nationalistic interpretations of wilderness. For example, Thoreau saw in the American wilderness a source of human vitality that could nurture the American spirit in ways unavailable in what he considered to be the tame and effete European existence. Thoreau said the American wilderness was to the American spirit what the she-wolf who suckled Romulus and Remus was in Roman legend: it nurtured a cultural and moral vigor absent in countries that lacked the abundance of wilderness America enjoyed.[73]

---

[68] See Woolman's rejection of the transatlantic economy. Woolman, "Considerations on the True Harmony of Mankind," 444–445.

[69] Woolman, "Journal," 128–129; Woolman, "Plea for the Poor," 260.

[70] Woolman, "Journal," 128–129; Woolman, "Plea for the Poor," 260.

[71] Woolman, "Journal," 137.

[72] There is evidence that Thoreau was familiar with Woolman's *Journal*. William Jolliff, "The Economy of the Inward Life: John Woolman and Henry Thoreau," *The Concord Saunterer*, New Series, 15 (2007): 91–111.

[73] Nash, *Wilderness and the American Mind*, 90.

The abundance of wilderness in early nineteenth century America, and the potential for moral formation Thoreau attached to it, would lead him to say, "all good things are wild, and free."[74]

Woolman would not attach such nationalistic or moral weight to wilderness itself. The religious compromises faced by Quakers on the frontier were evidence that the wilderness could lead to moral imperilment as much as it could to moral vigor. There was nothing inherently good in the wilderness. The wilderness was difficult and dangerous. However, Woolman found in the real difficulties of wild places affordances that extended his compassion for humankind universally and heightened his sensitivity to divine leading. The only good that could come from the wilderness was that of being resigned to God's will.

In addition to taking dangerous journeys into the wilderness periodically, Woolman was also a farmer, he had an orchard, and he observed the landscape wherever he went. This spiritual sensitivity and awareness of landscape combined to reveal insights while tending the orchard or walking the city street. There was no need to attribute to wilderness an inherent spiritual meaning, such that one must leave one's domestic surroundings to enter the wild in search of spiritual wisdom, because the spiritual habit of being that was resigned to God's will found God's presence everywhere. The suggestive power of nature was great, but the affordances of each place, each location, each vista, from the most mundane to the magnificent, were places for the receptive soul to live in communion with the God who is already active and present in every place.

However, one suspects that Woolman felt it inevitable that God would call everyone into wilderness places. The particularity of the wilderness landscape can afford an intersubjectivity of being that is largely unavailable in other landscapes. The wilderness wayfarer can thus find new spiritual insights in barren landscapes, insights as threatening and destabilizing to the spiritual self as the wilderness is to the body. For Woolman, though, the goal was to be resigned to whatever journey God called one to, and then to accept the affordances of those landscapes, people, and situations, as gifts from God.

Woolman's encounter with the wild is useful for a Quaker sacramental ecology because it provides an alternative perspective to those encounters that 1) view wilderness as an instrument toward spiritual self-fulfillment, 2) view wilderness as primarily a means to inner strength and peace, or 3) look to wilderness for its utility and material value. In contrast, Woolman's experience of destabilization in the wilderness directed his attention outside of himself: to a heightened sense of dependency on God, and to the extension of social compassion. To

---

[74] Nash, *Wilderness and the American Mind*, 88.

walk through every place, natural or constructed, wilderness or domestic, busy or barren, comforting or challenging, serene or obscene—to walk through all of these spaces open to the affordances of every landscape, and every place, is to foster the sacra-mentality that takes the realities of place seriously. This awareness of the sacred sees other entities as they are, and yet in full intersubjectivity, honors and respects each place. And, it challenges and destabilizes one's spiritual state in a way that admits growth, conversion, and conviction. An ecology like Woolman's resists the temptation to imagine ecological concern as something that only happens "out there," in far off places, the concern of other people. Instead, "out there" is right here, and right here (wherever that may be) is a holy place because God already fills every landscape.

8 | Maragoli Shamanism Marries Quaker Christianity

By S. Chagala Ngesa[1]

Abstract: The author was raised an "orthodox" Christian Quaker in a family that included his maternal great-grandmother, one of the first Kenyan converts to Quakerism. He was also initiated by her, during his teens, as a traditional Maragoli shaman. What she taught, and he learned, was that the Christian and indigenous traditions taught the same ethics, and the same supremacy of the One God, whom the Maragoli call Nyasaye, whom they understand to be gender-free. However, while Christianity additionally taught a gospel of the ever-present Savior Jesus Christ and the ever-availability of the Holy Spirit, the indigenous Maragoli tradition emphasized the immanence of God in everything that is, both living and nonliving. True, an understanding of the immanence of God can be found in Christian tradition, too, from the earliest times, but historically, it has not been universally respected among Christians, or among Quakers.

The author pleads for a panentheist view of God and creation, particularly at this time when the very earth is imperiled by environmental catastrophe. He attributes this growing threat to negligent stewardship and a dominant culture that devalues the creation, excuses war and waste, and glorifies and protects selfish behavior. Quakers and other people of the dominant world religions, he argues, have important lessons to learn from tribal faith traditions if they would fulfill their destiny: to show the world both the bankruptcy of this ethic of selfishness and the all-inclusiveness of the divine love that humanity is called to express—not just to our human neighbors but also to every created being and thing, and creation itself.

---

1 I would like to thank John Jeremiah Edminster for working as my editor and advisor on this project.

I. Introduction

Quaker Christianity and Maragoli shamanism, spiritual traditions from widely divergent origins, have surprisingly "married" harmoniously among my people, the Maragoli of the hill country of western Kenya. For over a century, the Maragoli have walked in simple, peaceable, compassionate ways, teaching their children to treat all creation as sacred and worthy of respect, in a spirit that it would be hard to identify as either "Quaker" or "indigenous Maragoli," for indeed it is both. Quakerism today upholds many values—integrity, community harmony, nonviolence, truthfulness, sustainability, individual and group discernment—with a view to finding unity with God and one another, and encouraging spiritual equality across divides of gender, age, ethnicity, and class. These were also the values of the Maragoli before the missionaries came among them. More importantly, both traditions hold that God talks—that the Supreme Deity *Nyasaye*, who is gender free, wants to communicate directly with humans, and in fact does so, if we will but open our hearts, listen, and obey. One of the most important beliefs of modern Friends is that "there is that of God in every one."[2] While Maragoli shamanism agrees with this Quaker claim in principle, it also points out something else: that there is "that of God" in all things, living and nonliving.

This information was given to me when I was still a teenager by my great-grandmother, Dorika Bweyenda (1883?–1983), who was both an initiated Maragoli shaman (*umusalisi*) and one of the first convinced Friends in Kenya.[3] In answer to my question as to the distinction between Maragoli shamanism and Quaker Christianity, she explained to me that our native tradition recognizes the presence of God in everything that is. Because for the most part ours is an orally

---

2 Wilmer Cooper, *A Living Faith* (Richmond, IN: Friends United Press, 1990), 12. Lewis Benson writes: "The phrase 'that of God in every man' has been widely used in the twentieth century as an expression which signifies the central truth of the Quaker message. Many present-day Quakers, when asked what the Quakers believe, are likely to reply: 'They believe that there is that of God in every man,'" although Benson then cautions that "[George] Fox does not use the declarative sentence, 'There is that of God in every man,' and he never makes it the central theme of any of his sermons or writings" (Benson, 2). Benson notes, "Between 1700 and 1900 'that of God in every man' virtually disappeared from the Quaker vocabulary, but early in the present [twentieth] century it came back into use" (Benson, 17). Benson attributes its revival to Rufus Jones who, in an "Introduction" to his 1903 abridged version of Fox's *Journal*, explains Fox's that-of-God concept in a way that, Benson claims, seriously distorted Fox's meaning (Benson, 17). The modern-day usage tends to downplay Fox's understanding that "that of God" in people is often engaged in reproving selfish and wicked behaviors so as to correct them. Lewis Benson, "'That of God in Every Man'—What Did George Fox Mean by it?," *Quaker Religious Thought* 24 (1970): 2–25.

3 Like most Maragoli of her generation, Dorika did not know her date of birth. I am dating it by circumstantial evidence.

transmitted culture, Dorika's wisdom has never been put into writing before. But having spent the formative years of my life living with her, and being initiated and taught by her as my spiritual teacher, I now feel a great sense of duty and urgency to share her teachings with the world, for no one but me—out of over a hundred of her then-living descendants—carries these memories. She and I would often stay awake all night, talking in the dark, doing without sleep. I felt no need of sleep then, for I experienced her, in Brother Lawrence's memorable phrase, as if I were at the breasts of God.[4]

More than 40 years ago, Dorika prophesied that I would one day be among the first from the village to travel overseas (*engeleka*) to the "land of the ghosts," *avasungu*, from which the first Quaker missionaries had come to Kenya, there not only to learn about Quakerism, but also to share our precious Maragoli shamanic wisdom.

Dorika was in the habit of inviting many of her descendants to dine with her, in keeping with our tradition that one should never eat alone. There is always room for one more around any eating circle, and we must always sit down to eat, as standing or walking is considered disrespectful not just to other persons present, but also to the food itself. This is because we believe that all of us humans are walking cemeteries, the graveyards of once-living animals, fish, vegetables, grains, fruits, water, and air. The least we can do is show some respect!

But this night she invited only me. We were speaking in Lulogooli, our local dialect of the Luhya language. That conversation is still vivid in my memory as I write:

It is just past sunset, and already dark, in the Maragoli Hills, which lie right on the equator. Dorika, the mother of my late maternal grandfather Ngeresa and grandmother of my late mother Dinah Happiness Mmbone, is seated facing me in the red glow of her smoldering cooking fire. To my right is the three-stone fireplace near the wall of her hut, her soot-covered clay cooking pot held above the embers by the stones' points. We have washed our hands in preparation for the food on the earthenware plate set on the green mat between us. The plate, like the cooking pot, is the handiwork of her daughter-in-law, Joyce Kisia Asiaba Kivizi, Ngeresa's late wife.

---

4 Lawrence's exact words are *mamelles de Dieu*: "Ma maniere la plus ordinaire, est cette simple attention, & amoureux en Dieu; où je me sense souvent attaché avec des douceurs & des satisfactions plus grandes que celles que goûte un enfant attaché aux mamelles de sa nourrice, aussi si j'osois me servir de cet terme, j'appellerois volontiers cet état mamelles de Dieu, pour les douceurs inexprimables que j'y goûte & dont j'y fais l'experience." Laurent de la Résurrection, *Maximes spirituelles fort utiles aux âmes pieuses, pour acqerir la presence de Dieu* (Paris, 1692), 136–137, http://gallica.bnf.fr/ark:/12148/bpt6k64657654.

We lock gazes as Dorika begins to chant a long prayer that blesses all the elements that made the food: the rain, the sun, the soil, the plants, the worms, the bees, and the water; the fire that cooked it; the people who planted, tended, and harvested the food; the hands that prepared it; and all our human ancestors, both dead and living. Then she blesses me before we begin to eat. It is our everyday meal, but it is ample: gluten free, brown, cornbread-like uvuchima vwa ovolo, made from a mixed flour of locally grown finger millet, millet, and cassava. Uvuchima is bland until covered by our aromatic, tasty sauce of smoked dried tilapia, ikivambala, boiled with locally made salt, umunyu mukereka. On a separate plate is umutó, a local dandelion, cooked with umutere, okra[5]. It is bitter, but Dorika taught me to love it: "Every bitter herb that is not poisonous, and every thorny plant and fruit that is not poisonous, is medicinal." We sit on a circular green mat plaited by Joyce from papyrus reeds, laid over the dried green cow dung-smeared mud floor in her round mud hut with a conical thatched roof, which has only one small wooden window and one door, both of which stand ajar, but not enough to fully vent the smoke that stings our eyes.

As we both eat contentedly, Dorika suddenly stops chewing, as if struck, perhaps even jolted, by something important that she must urgently convey. "Listen, my beloved 'husband,'" she says. "I have something very important to tell you."

"What is it, my dear Friend?" I answer. These were the pet names we called each other.

Still holding my gaze, she points her right forefinger directly at my left eye. "One day you will go to the country where the ghost Friends came from, to learn about their religion and tell them about ours." A rush of excitement seizes my body and I break out in goose bumps.

I am awestruck as I imagine hobnobbing with Bruce Lee in Hollywood.

II. "That of God in Everyone"

Friends from different strands of Quakerism understand the concept of "that of God in every one" in different ways. Wilmer Cooper says: "Some have held that the Light, Spirit, Seed, Measure, 'that of God in Everyone,' and Christ Within had a common meaning for early Friends and therefore can be used interchangeably."[6] But some Friends today have distanced themselves from the early

---

5 I have all these ingredients in my house here in Richmond, IN, and I am always happy to invite and welcome locals and travelers from afar to come and share a meal with me. I enjoy cooking.

6 Cooper, *A Living Faith*, 18.

Friends' identification of the Light with Christ, preferring not to theorize about what "the Light" is. Cooper writes, "There is the Quaker Universalist movement, for example, which regards historic Christ-centered Quakerism as too narrow in a world where we need to join hands with persons of other religious faiths. They see Quakerism as a bridge to these people, as expressed in the commitment to 'that of God in every one.'"[7] Quaker Universalists of this tendency would shy away from saying "Christ, the Light." But it must be remembered that there are Christian Quakers who are also "universalists" in the sense of believing that God (and Christ!) saves good souls of all religious traditions! Such, in fact, were the first Quakers.

Those who hold a more Christ-centered view are often affiliated with Friends United Meeting (FUM) or Evangelical Friends Church International (EFCI), of which the majority today are found in East Africa and Latin America.[8] An explicitly Christian faith is also found among Conservative Friends, who are concentrated in the USA, and among the many Christ-centered Friends world-wide who are scattered among Liberal and unaffiliated Friends meetings. A majority of Friends believe in the peace testimony, Cooper says, "because Friends place such emphasis on the dignity and worth of the individual, perhaps best expressed in George Fox's phrase, 'that of God in every one.'"[9] Violence against any person negates this very principle because everyone, being created in the image of God, has a certain sacredness.

Margery Post Abbott sees the shadow-side of this phrase: "Much of my struggle with 'that of God in everyone' lies in the intensity of its optimism about

---

7 Cooper, *A Living Faith*, 152. In 1656, Fox writes, "I was moved to give forth the following exhortation to Friends in the ministry: … 'In the power of life and wisdom, and dread of the Lord God of life…dwell, that in the wisdom of God over all ye may be preserved, and be a terror to all the adversaries of God, and a dread, answering that of God in them all…. [B]e patterns, be examples…wherever you come; that your carriage and life may preach among all sorts of people, and to them. Then you will come to walk cheerfully over the world, answering that of God in every one." George Fox, *The Journal of George Fox,* edited by John L. Nickalls, revised edition (Philadelphia: Religious Society of Friends, 1997), 263. This "exhortation" contains what are perhaps Fox's best-known uses of the phrase "that of God." See its use in Margery Post Abbott, *To Be Broken and Tender* (Friends Bulletin Corporation, 2010), 47.

8 Kelly Kellum, the current General Secretary of FUM, remarks that for the first time since Quakers arrived in Kenya, an FUM Triennial gathering is to be held there in July 2020. Part of the reasoning behind this is that FUM-affiliated Quakers' numbers are dwindling in the US, but growing in Kenya, and US Quakers report being both encouraged by this numerical growth and inspired by the celebratory enthusiasm of Kenyan Quakers' worship (personal conversation with Kelly Kellum, February 22, 2019). In general, US Quakers can more easily travel to Kenya than Kenyan Quakers to the US, being both richer (on the average) and more certain to get the necessary visas.

9 Cooper, *A Living Faith*, 107.

humanity and temptation to over-expectation."[10] In other words, the assertion of "that of God in every one" implies that the default condition of humanity is to will and do only good, as God does. As we all know, this assumption is far removed from the reality of the human condition: human beings often will, and do, what they know to be wrong; this is what most Christians mean by saying that we are all sinners. It often takes great effort of the will on the part of individuals, *and* divine aid, to do the life-giving thing. Fox was well aware of human fallibility; he had often been painfully victimized by the very people who claimed to represent Jesus Christ. Where was "that of God" in them as they were abusing him? He knew it was there, but it did not guarantee moral goodness when people resisted it. It might merely make them uncomfortable, and they could refuse to heed the discomfort.

III. The Maragoli Context

The Maragoli are a Bantu-speaking people who have long been practicing settled agriculture in the Maragoli Hills of western Kenya, situated on the equator a few miles north of the Kavirondo Gulf of Lake Victoria (*Inyanza*), the second largest freshwater lake in the world (after Lake Superior) and the source of the River Nile. The Maragoli people believe they have lived in their present location for centuries, after having originally come from *Misri,* Egypt, by following the Nile upstream.

The Maragoli are also known as the Mulembe people, after the Lolugooli word *mulembe,* "peace." By synecdoche, "the Mulembe nation" has now come to refer to the entire Luhya tribe. The Maragoli's pacific inclinations were well known not only throughout Kenya, but widely throughout East Africa, even before the coming of Quaker missionaries in 1902. As both a fourth-generation Kenyan Quaker and an initiated Maragoli shaman, I have been fascinated by the history of the meeting of these two cultures—my own Maragoli culture and that of the peace-loving American Friends—that amazingly, as if providentially, blended without one erasing the other. Much of the responsibility for this blending may lie with the extraordinary character of the early Quaker convert Dorika Bweyenda, my great-grandmother and my initiator into the Maragoli shamanic tradition.

Dorika Bweyenda was about 19 years old when the missionaries came. Her husband of perhaps four years, Mmboga, was himself the village shaman

---

10 Abbott, *To Be Broken and Tender,* 46. It might be said that for Fox, "that of God" functioned primarily as an inward rebuke of sinners, but for modern Friends it was primarily an inward sanctifier of "fundamentally good" human beings.

then, having been trained and initiated by his father, the renowned shaman Votega, after whom "Votega's stone" in the heights of the Maragoli Hills is named. Dorika became one of the Quakers' first Kenyan converts. Votega declined to become a Quaker himself, explaining that he carried more power to heal the people, the land, and creation in general than the white newcomers did. Mmboga, at first resistant, was persuaded by Dorika to become a Friend. Long unable to conceive a child, Dorika at last became pregnant, with the help of Votega's medicine, on the eve of the First World War. Three months into her pregnancy, Mmboga was conscripted by the occupying British into the King's African Rifles. Notwithstanding his Maragoli and Quaker pacifist principles, Mmboga, with many other young Maragoli men, was drafted to fight in a war about which he knew nothing. He and the other Maragoli never returned home, and to this day nothing is known about their fate. Had they been British lads killed in action, the Crown would never have allowed their records to be lost; but such was the colonizers' attitude toward subjugated peoples: they were not seen as fully human.

When Dorika gave birth to her little bouncing bundle of human destiny, my grandfather, in 1914, she named her destiny's child Ngeresa, "English," after the British occupiers who had kidnapped her husband. Everyone agreed that her naming her son after the people who had robbed her of her husband and her child of his father was an act of unbelievable forgiveness. That is one of the reasons village elders proposed that she be made the village's next shaman. She was initiated by Votega.

Dorika lived to be about 100 years old; I was born when she was about 82. One day I asked her why she had named my grandfather "Ngeresa." She looked me straight in the eye and answered, "As a shaman, I know that no one can crush a person. I gave your grandfather that name to remind myself of that. They took away Mmboga's body, but his spirit still lives right here, where we are. His spirit lives in me, and"—she pointed directly at me—"his spirit lives in *you*."

IV. Maragoli Reverence for Creation

The Maragoli people's current literacy is superimposed on a traditional oral culture that has for centuries been passing along our history, culture, spirituality, and values by word of mouth, through deliberate and cherished strategies. This is done through rites of passage such as rituals surrounding childbirth, marriage, death, immigrating to a different land and settling, planting season, harvesting season, and building and occupying a new home. One of the more intense is our rites of passage from childhood to adulthood, different for each gender, which introduce young Maragoli boys and girls into the responsibilities of adulthood. These take several days, with long-term follow-up, in which elders teach the new initiates (roughly between ages five and ten) what had been passed down to them during their own initiation.

Traditionally, we circumcise boys just before they leave the sacred initiation space, which may be a forest or the side of a river or lake.[11] The girls' initiation is also rigorous, but involves no genital surgery. There are multiple reasons for the removal of the boy's foreskin, for example hygiene, and as a mark of membership in a distinct age group, but the most important reason for circumcision is to give boys a sense of the pain that the ancestors suffer when we neglect, disrespect, and mistreat them. It teaches us empathy and compassion, enables us to celebrate and remember our traditions, and helps us clarify and affirm our cultural roots. It makes us feel important as little guys, giving us authority to be adults. It is meant to feed our healthy passions without holding back, and to tame our unhealthy ones. All circumcision age groups are given a name relating to current major events.

The pain we go through enables us to appreciate the pains and joys of life and in our world. We are prepared for this intense pain several days in advance, and advised not to cry, even though in the old days there was no anesthesia and the knife used was deliberately left blunt to make the experience painful.[12] Should any of the boys cry because of the extreme pain, all the boys in the circle, who may number up to one hundred, converge around him to assure him that it is understandable for him to cry, but he is not going through the pain alone, but rather with all of us together. Outsiders might consider this cruelty, and unnecessary traumatizing of the innocent, but for us it is a procedure that bestows honor, and we see the pain as a small price to pay for gaining the authority of a community elder at that young age. I was circumcised at age five.[13] In fact, immediately upon the removal of the foreskin, we look the circumcising elder straight in the eye and thank him for gifting us with this honor. Becoming an elder is not a matter of age or gender, but rather, of having passed through some

---

11 The urbanized tend to have the procedure done in hospital, which means the boys miss out on learning the cultural, historical and spiritual significance of the rite of passage. The same fate has befallen the Luloogoli language, as most of the educated speak and pass on to their offspring only Kiswahili and English in their households because they are convinced the latter has high status compared to Luloogoli.

12 Due to HIV/AIDS concerns, nowadays the family of a child brings the knife to be used.

13 All circumcision age-groups are given a name relating to current major events. For example, my age-group was named "Ambrosia," after the variety of hybrid bicolor white-and-yellow maize that was introduced into Maragoli agriculture that year.

kind of initiation ritual that teaches us how to care for our fellow human beings and all creation.

When the circumcision is done near a river, our blood flows into the river. When it is done in a forest, the blood shed onto the dry land eventually percolates into the groundwater and thence into the plants, animals, and human beings who drink the water. At this point, our elders tell us that our blood is carried by the water downstream to Lake Victoria, where some of the water will evaporate into the sky and be dispersed throughout the cosmos, while the remainder, released into the River Nile, will begin its long journey into *Misri* and the Mediterranean Sea, and thence to all the oceans of the world. (Girls are taught to bury their menstrual blood, and their placentas after giving birth. Therefore, women's blood makes a similar journey through the soil and into all living things.) Our life-blood has thus been shared with the whole universe through our circumcision. It is as if we boys have now had our first sexual intercourse, a very painful one, with all creation as our partner.

During initiation, each child must name his or her totemic animal, plant, number, and spiritual teacher. The animal or plant is one that the initiate is committed to protect. If a boy's special number happens to be seven, then every time the boy sees seven of a certain thing, he knows to be on the alert: he is being given a message. A child may choose anyone who has been initiated as their spiritual teacher. I chose Dorika.

Another menas of for continuing and communicating our cultural traditions is the sharing of dreams during the bonfire circle, which occurs nightly except when it is raining. Dreams are recognized as an important part of life, and the sharing of them is an important part of the life of the community, which up to this day has lacked the distractions of radio and television, except that a few have acquired these in recent years. In this circle, we share our hopes for the future and the dreams experienced during the previous night. Everyone around the circle is welcome to give an interpretation of another's dream, though only the person holding the talking stick is permitted to speak. The discipline of the talking stick trains every Maragoli to be a good listener. The talking stick, which is considered a member of the circle in its own right and a respected citizen, represents the non-human creation as a whole. As soon as one is given the talking stick, one stands and greets the others in the circle before saying anything else; greetings, in the form of courteous inquiries to which one expects answers, are known to take up to an hour. A speaker may ask each other person how the members of their household are doing, how their domestic animals are, their plants, their soil, the water, what they ate and drank today, inquire whether they slept well and what they dreamed about last night, and so on and so forth, and the next speaker will be asked the same questions all around the circle. The same protocol applies whenever two neighbors meet on the road or elsewhere.

We believe that our dreams are important because *Nyasaye*, and our ancestors, speak to us through dreams, and we believe that no dream is without significance: there *are* no trivial dreams. People we know, our animals, plants, birds, insects, water, fire, air, wind, rainbow, rain, and lightning can all be communicating with us through our dreams.

When we say that our ancestors speak with us through dreams, we do not confine the meaning of "ancestors" merely to past blood relatives. Rather, we are taught that our ancestors include *Nyasaye*, our own bodies, our blood, the plants, the soil, the rivers, the lakes, the mountains, the valleys, trees, animals, creeping things, the Sun, the Moon, air, fire, wind, rain, our brothers and sisters, our parents and grandparents, and so on. It is made clear to us that all these are our ancestors because without them, we could not exist. *We are,* because these ancestors are; and because these ancestors are, therefore *we are.* We are taught to be thankful, and to honor, respect, and protect and care for all of these ancestors, because they look to us, and also because by being thankful for their lives, we are valuing, honoring, and being thankful for our own lives.

We are taught to honor and respect the animals that give us food by slaughtering them quickly, with a minimum of suffering. When we have to slaughter a chicken, a goat, or a cow for food, we face them in humility and tell the animal that we honor and respect them for giving up their lives for our sustenance, because killing should only be life giving. The same reverence is called for when we harvest vegetables and fruits: the kale and tomato that we harvest from the garden give up their lives so that we can have life ourselves. While I fully understand why some people are vegetarians for reasons of health, I am always surprised when I hear people say that they are vegetarians because vegetables have no blood. To our mind, vegetables have as much life as animals, and their own kind of life-blood, which is their sap. They are therefore respected and honored in the same way animals are thanked, not only for relieving our hunger, but also for giving us life. For this reason, whenever I am at a place where food is served and people start eating before giving thanks for the meal, as I have often witnessed in the United States, I stop them and insist on saying a prayer of thanksgiving to honor the food, the soil, the sunlight, the water, the God who gave it, and the people that planted, harvested, transported, cooked, and served the food. The wastage of food that I see here in the USA breaks my heart, especially as I know there are millions of people all over the world who go to sleep on empty bellies. I can never wrap my head around seeing many people fill up their plates with food, only to dump it all in the garbage bin after eating a small portion of it. I wonder why they had to fill up their plate when they knew they did not need that much food.

V. What is Maragoli Shamanism?

When the Maragoli speak about shamanism, they refer to particular people set aside by the whole community to perform certain functions that involve healing not only the body, but also the mind and the spirit. Maragoli shamanism also involves healing of the natural world. Maragoli shamanism is life giving. It has no evil intentions and does not involve casting spells against anyone. For example, when there is no rain in the village for an extended period of time, the village shaman is called upon to intervene by offering prayers and animal sacrifices, such as a cow or a goat, to *Nyasaye*. To the happy surprise of every villager, the rains come down in torrents after the shaman has performed the sacrificial rituals at a designated sacred place, which the village has a hand in choosing. Here we honor our happy and supportive ancestors, and appease whatever ancestors may have been troubled, through various specific rituals. A similar procedure is followed when we have unexplained epidemics or other calamities in the village.

The shaman is always someone from the village that he or she serves. Since time immemorial that person had to be male, but during Dorika's lifetime, this requirement was waived to allow her to become the first known female shaman.[14] After the shaman's consecration comes the consecration of a specific hut in a forest, in an elevated place, or by a body of water, for the chosen one to occupy—both as a recognition of the powers conferred on them, and also as a place for seekers of healing to access their services, or pay homage, during specified times of the day or the night. The shaman can also decide where exactly the hut can be built.

For one to be chosen as shaman, a number of criteria must be met. One has to show integrity and interest in becoming a shaman by understudying a shaman. This means clinging to them, seeking to be trained in the arts of local medicine and divination, and studying the elements of how to conduct the rituals.

---

14 Dorika had both the shamanic gifts and the shamanic knowledge, passed on to her by her father-in-law, Votega, who cured her infertility and taught her all she knew about herbal medicine. He perhaps foresaw that Mmboga would not come back from the war and that she would have to be the successor to his knowledge. She was not recognized as the village shaman until it was clear that Mmboga must have died and would not return. While the presence of other Quaker converts in the village must have made it easier for the village as a whole to accept a female shaman, Quakers would still have been a small minority in the village then. The real deciding influence for accepting Dorika as a shaman would have been Votega, who had initiated her as a shaman before she became a Quaker, and who told the villagers they must accept her as their shaman.

Another criterion of shamanship is natural giftedness with extraordinary powers, such as foreknowledge of such events as the birth of a child born with extraordinary powers, the outbreak of war, a plague of locusts, or the death of a person or animal. One type of shamanic giftedness is the ability to use bodily fluids for healing, such as by spitting saliva into an ailing individual's mouth in the wee hours of the morning, before the shaman has eaten, drunk, or cleansed their mouth. My great-great-grandfather Votega, Dorika's father-in-law, carried all the above gifts, which were in high demand and which he put to good use, earning him a reputation for greatness that endures to this day. Finally, one must be chosen for initiation as a shaman by the previous shaman, and be willing to undergo the initiation. Once made a shaman, one may not cease to be a shaman except by death.

A key gift is moral wisdom, and the ability to forgive what most people would find unforgivable. This gift was carried by Dorika, along with her remarkable gifts of intuitive herbal medicine, community organizing, philanthropy, clarity of mind, compassion, and revolutionary and prophetic foresight. Her community recognized her moral wisdom after she named her son "English," *Ngeresa*. Everyone agreed that to name her son after her husband's kidnappers was an act of unbelievable forgiveness. That is why she was proposed by some elders (in addition to Votega) to succeed her husband as the village shaman in 1915.

Between 1902 and the 1930s, a number Quaker missionaries came to Kaimosi and Maragoli. Among the first who arrived in Maragoli territory were Orthodox Quaker Midwesterners Arthur Chilson, Edgar Hole, Willis Hotchkiss, and Emory Rees. They translated the Bible into Lulogooli with the help of Joel Litu, an early Maragoli Friend, and understood their mission as the establishment of a "self-supporting, self-propagating native church."[15] After traveling by ship from New York to Mombasa in 1895, they waited until the new railroad was laid from the coast to Kisumu on Lake Victoria. When they arrived among the Maragoli, they quickly learned the local language and were able to explain to the local people the most important tenets of their religion. They said that they followed a Teacher called Jesus Christ who walks in the Light, lives the Light, shares the Light, and in fact *is* the Light. They believed in pacifism, simplicity, justice, human perfectibility, and their commission by Christ to spread the word of God and to serve, feed, and heal people. They also taught that there is that of *Nyasaye* in everyone.

---

15 Stephen W. Angell, "Quaker Women in Kenya and Human Rights Issues," in *Freedom's Distant Shores: American Protestants and Post-Colonial Alliances with Africa*, ed. R. Drew Smith (Waco, TX: Baylor University Press, 2006), 111–130, at 114. Here, "Orthodox" refers to the branch of Friends that emerged from the Hicksite-Orthodox split in the 1820s.

After listening to this, Dorika said to herself, "This sounds like our own shamanism. I see Jesus Christ as our Ancestor." She successfully persuaded her husband to join her in adopting Quakerism; but his father Votega declined to join, recognizing that his own powers to heal people and nature exceeded that of the missionaries. Dorika, however, respected the Quakers' moral wisdom, particularly in regard to truth telling. She remembered once having greeted Bwana Lisi (Luloogoli rendering of Rees) and after shaking his soft hand with her hardened rough palm, for days she did not wish to wash off that feeling.[16]

But she knew something important that the missionaries were *not* saying. She agreed that there is that of God in everyone, but she also knew, from shamanic tradition, that there is also that of God in everything living *and* nonliving, and that God feels the feelings of every creature capable and incapable of feeling. With her adoption of Quakerism and Christianity, Dorika Bweyenda let Jesus Christ bless the Maragoli with the way of peace and universal forgiveness, and at the same time, she led her people into a Christian Quakerism enriched by the reverent panentheism of her inherited shamanic tradition.

Among Dorika's remarkable gifts was her memory for what she had heard. She had no formal education, and never learned to read; however, after the Bible had been translated into Lulogooli, in the 1930s, she memorized it in its entirety, and, if someone cited a chapter and verse from it, she could recite it without hesitation. She also knew the entire hymnal by heart. Her record of church attendance was exemplary: rain or shine, she never missed a Sunday service, and on Thursdays, when the women's group that she led met, she attended from 8am to 1pm.

Having become a convinced Friend, she donated her own land as a site for the first Friends church building in her village, Lyavugulu, and mobilized the other villagers and their resources to build it on a hilltop where it could be seen from all directions.[17] The church building stood until 2012, when Brian Young,

---

16 "Bwana" is a Kiswahili word meaning master, and is used as an honorific before the name of a respected individual. It is used alone as a form of polite address, similar to the use of the word "sir" or "mister" in English. At the time the Friends missionaries arrived in East Africa, this term was used for all white men.

17 Before Dorika gave land and mobilized villagers to build the first Lyavugulu Friends Church, all the new convinced Friends used to walk for 20 kilometers (almost 12.5 miles) to and from Friends Church Kaimosi to attend Sunday worship. The Friends from Lyavugulu village would wake to their "alarm clock," the first crow of the rooster, between 3 and 4am. They would arrive at 8am in time for the worship service and then walk back in the afternoon. The villagers from Lyavugulu would often share tea with Bwana Lisi when in Kaimosi. While they used large silver mugs (*lisuvila*), Rees drank out of a small white china teacup. Dorika noticed that although they filled theirs to the brim as a mark of fullness or fullbodiedness, he only filled his small cup three quarters full. This disturbed the locals, as this was a sign that he was not fully grown up. But Dorika wondered whether the reason he didn't fill up his

then pastor of Berkeley (CA) Friends Church (and now pastor of West Richmond Friends Church in Richmond, Indiana), attending the Sixth World Conference of Friends held at Kabarak University near Nakuru, Kenya, visited Lyavugulu and, finding the old building in disrepair, reported its need for replacement back to his home church. The church's treasurer, Giuseppe Rensi, promptly raised the funds that built the new Lyavugulu Friends Church of brick and corrugated iron sheets that stands today.

In addition to Dorika's gift of land to the church, she also bequeathed to me, her successor as the village shaman, three acres of land to be held in trust for community use.[18] This bequest was unusual in several ways: culturally, it was unheard of to grant property to a granddaughter's son. Secondly, it was outrageous to sign over the title in the presence of her bullheaded son, who nonetheless, though bluntly bypassed, obeyed her direct command not to interfere. Third, it was unprecedented to give land to the whole community. Fourth, it was remarkable indeed to make only one person the trustee, and that, a youth. Local land use in this densely populated area is such that three-acre plots are as rare as thousand-acre plots would be in suburban New Jersey. I asked her, "Why are you doing this?"

She answered, "Because you remind me of Votega. You look exactly like him. And like him, you are left-handed. I do not know any other of his descendants who are left-handed." In Maragoli we believe that left-handedness comes from the mother's side; In Lulogooli, the left hand is called "the woman's hand," and the right, "the man's hand." Indeed, I would have inherited Votega's left-handedness through my mother, but then through a succession of three of her male ancestors.

One day, I hope to build a solar powered library and a community center for my village on this acreage to honor Dorika's wishes for the community.[19] Solar panels there might provide electricity for the village, which suffered a catastrophic loss of firewood, the traditional energy source, when the forest was razed after Dorika's death. I hope, at the same time, to replant the Maragoli Hills with native trees and underbrush, hoping to invite back the rain, the birds, and the other wildlife. When the forest returns, our traditional religious life—our rites

---

cup to the brim was that he feared that his long nose would drink the tea before it reached his mouth.

18 Upon her visit to the village about five years ago, I initiated my daughter, Ema Makungu, as my shamanic successor. My other two daughters are Sarah Adiero and Victoria Mmbone. Ema is the mother of my three grandchildren, Faith, Naomi, and Isaiah.

19 To decide what to do with the land that would meet the needs of the community, I held a clearness committee in the village. This project of a community center and library was unanimously affirmed.

of passage and our healing ceremonies—may resume. This is exactly what Dorika would have wished her successor shaman to do. It is to be remembered that the shaman is not a chief or a political leader, but a servant: of God, of the people, and of the creation, which means if the creation and the people are injured, it is the shaman's duty to see to their repair.[20] This is my role in my community, in all creation, and in the world at large.

One of Dorika's major legacies is that she mobilized the villagers, just after World War II, to plant additional trees in Maragoli Forest. But then this magnificent, mature forest, whose rich underbrush provided fuel and medicine for the villagers and habitat for birds and other wildlife, whose canopy drew the precious rain for our drinking and irrigation, and whose deep roots held fertile soil, was clear-cut in the late 1980s and early 1990s. A profiteering Vihiga District Commissioner, an appointed representative of the President of Kenya, brought in lumber companies to enrich himself and his cronies, leaving the villagers without cooking fuel or adequate rainwater, and the Maragoli Hills denuded of topsoil. This devastation of our land went on in spite of extensive, prolonged, and ultimately fruitless protests, which were suppressed by Administration Police, who answered to the District Commissioner. When it was over, villagers grieved individually and together in their evening circles. The Maragoli Forest, once our sacred space for initiations and other holy rituals even as recently as my own childhood, is now gone, its place taken by what are now disparagingly called the Maragoli Stone Hills. I am afraid that the same fate now threatens the only remaining equatorial forest in Kenya, Kakamega Forest, and its neighbor across the Uganda border, Mabira Forest. I am afraid, but I remain hopeful and prayerful that all humanity will come together and do all it takes to save these lungs of the world.

VI. Panentheism Within Christian Tradition

With that history and hope in mind, I feel it important to find places of connection within Christianity and Quakerism with the Maragoli understanding of that

---

20 My late grandfather, Buyusi, father of my late father Jafether, as well as my maternal grandfather Ngeresa, were both volunteer community leaders (*amagutu*) for different periods and villages. In my early twenties, opinion leaders in the village asked my permission to forward my name to the District Commissioner to be hired as a paid chief (*umwami*). I politely declined, preferring my work as an itinerant minister. Asked why I was rejecting such an honorable and lucrative civil service position, I labored and used all the humility I could muster to say that I considered myself a global citizen of the cosmos who, although passionately believing in acting locally to have impact globally, would only accept a call to *global* civil service to help bring about peace in the world.

of God in all creation. A belief in the omnipresence of God is to be found in Christian tradition since its very beginnings—although, significantly, there is suggestive evidence that many other Christians have regarded nature as though it were neither inhabited by God nor much cared about by God. This ambivalence among Christians about the status of nature led Dorika to conclude that Christians did not recognize "that of God" in non-human things.

The word "panentheism" was not coined until 1809, but the idea that the Divine is present everywhere in creation, though self-existent and not identical with the creation, has been present in Christian thought since biblical times.[21] Psalm 139:7–10 marvels at God's ubiquity. In Matthew 5:34–35, Jesus calls heaven God's throne, and the earth, God's footstool; Paul preaches to the Athenians that God cannot be confined in "shrines made with human hands.... For 'In him we live and move and have our being'" (Acts 17:24, 28).[22] Orthodox Christianity, unlike the more ambivalent Catholic and Protestant traditions, has tended to preserve this panentheistic understanding.

But there has also been an ancient tendency among Christians, in part brought in from Greek philosophy and the mystery-schools of the Hellenistic era, which scorned the "material" and exalted the "spiritual," to regard the earth as too impure or "unclean" to house its Creator. In Genesis 3:17 this Creator pronounces the ground "cursed" because of Adam's transgression, and in Genesis 6:7 is "sorry" for making the creatures. The Christians' "Old Testament" ends with God's threat to "strike the land with a curse" (Mal 4:6). Indeed, in the Book of Revelation, God bombs the earth with a star called Wormwood, pelts it with 100-pound hailstones, and replaces it with a new and better earth (Rv 8:11, 16:21, 21:1). Can the transcendent God love earth, or nature, enough to clothe Godself in it and be its immanent God also? Does God live within and through the creatures, or are they too "dirty"? This is not merely an abstract theological question. Does God feel the feelings of creatures? When Jesus suffered pain, did God feel it, or did God merely infer it? Every believer must wonder: does God feel *my* pain? If not, how can God know me?[23]

---

21 Philip Clayton points out: "Historians generally claim that the word 'panentheism' was first coined by Karl Christian Friedrich Krause in 1829. This is actually incorrect; the term '*Pan+en+theismus*' occurs already in 1809 in the famous *Essay on Freedom* by Friedrich Schelling. The word literally means 'all in God.' The etymology is a bit misleading, however, since in most cases the 'in' actually has at least *two* meanings: all things are in God, and God is in all things." Philip Clayton, "Panentheisms East and West," *Sophia* 49, no. 2 (2010): 183–191, at 183.

22 All biblical quotes are from the New Revised Standard Version (NRSV), unless otherwise noted.

23 The Council of Nicaea condemned the idea that God the Father could have suffered the pain that the Son suffered on the cross, declaring "patripassianism" a heresy. But

Christian tradition, especially in the West, preserves a persistent dissensus between these two views of nature, each of which can find support in scripture. The first regards nature solely as a kind of disposable stage for the drama of God's salvation of certain "elect" individuals, while the rest of the individuals—"anyone whose name was not found written in the book of life" (Rv 20:15)—along with animals, plants, and the earth itself, are destroyed by fire (2 Pt 3:10) or made to vanish with the rest of the "old" creation (Rv 21:1). Paul snorts: "Is it for oxen that God is concerned?" (1 Cor 9:9). In this view, subhuman nature has no intrinsic worth in God's eyes, and the feelings of oxen and sinners are of no concern to God.

The second Christian view of nature remembers that the Creator pronounced the entire creation "very good" on completing it (Gn 1:31). Psalms celebrate God's kindness to wild creatures (Pss 104:10–30; 145:15–16); God sports with the monster Behemoth (Jb 40:15) and calls each of the stars by name (Ps 147:4). A Christian holding this view may see in the Fourth Gospel that nothing was made that was outside the confines of Christ, the Word of God (as both John Scotus Eriugena in the ninth century, and George MacDonald in the nineteenth, read John 1:3).[24] Gregory Palamas in the East, and Meister Eckhart and Jakob Boehme in the West, express panentheistic views.[25] The intended end of all created things is not to be trashed in an apocalyptic lake of fire (Rv 20:10–15) but to be reconciled to God through Jesus Christ (Col 1:20).

---

this would limit God's omniscience, allowing the Creator to see, hear, smell, and experience all other actual and possible senses except the feeling of pain. If the Father could not feel the Son's pain, of course, then neither could the Father feel the pain of any other creatures: human, ox, tree. If this is true, the only way to preserve God's omniscience would be to declare pain illusory and without any real existence, as the currently popular *A Course in Miracles* seems to do.

24 The Greek original of John 1:3 reads καὶ χωρὶς αὐτοῦ ἐγένετο οὐδὲ ἕν, "and outside of him not one thing came into being," which the Vulgate (though permissibly) renders *et sine ipso factum est nihil,* "and without him nothing was made," i.e., without his agency. Eriugena puts a period to end the sentence here—the original manuscripts, of course, having no punctuation—and reads the following words ὃ γέγονεν as properly belonging with John 1:4, making it read *"What came to be* in him was life." The twenty-fifth of George MacDonald's *Unspoken Sermons,* "The Creation of Christ," also argues for this division of sentences. George MacDonald, *Unspoken Sermons, Series I, II, and III, Complete and Unabridged,* Classics Reprint Series (CreateSpace Independent Publishing Platform, 2016).

25 While these figures were "accused of pantheism by their contemporaries, their systems can be identified as panentheistic because they understood God in various ways as including the world rather than being the world...." John Culp, "Panentheism," in *Stanford Encyclopedia of Philosophy,* December 4, 2008, last updated June 3, 2017, accessed February 2019, http://plato.stanford.edu/entries/panentheism/.

Christian poets, on the whole, have done a better job than the theologians of celebrating the omnipresence of God in the non-human creation. Francis of Assisi's *Cantico di Frate Sole* praises the Lord for His manifestations in "Brother Sun," "Sister Moon," "Mother Earth," Fire, Water, and even "Our sister Bodily Death."[26] Peter Abelard sings,

> Now to the King Eternal
> Be praise eternally,
> From whom are all things, by whom
> And in whom all things be.[27]

The English metaphysical poet George Herbert sees created things as windows into Heaven, hailing this way of seeing as "The Elixir," another name for the legendary Philosopher's Stone:

> A man that looks on glasse,
> On it stay his eye;
> Or if he pleaseth, through it passe,
> And then the heav'n espie.
>
> This is that famous stone
> That turneth all to gold,
> For that which God doth touch and own
> Cannot for lesse be told.[28]

"Everything that lives is holy,"[29] cries William Blake, who also quips in "Auguries of Innocence":

> If the sun and moon should doubt,
> They'd immediately go out.[30]

---

26 Francis of Assisi, *Francis of Assisi in His Own Words: The Essential Writings*, ed. Jon M. Sweeney (Brewster, MA: Paraclete Press, 2013), 88.

27 Helen Waddell, translator, included in Betty Radice, translator, *The Letters of Abelard and Heloise* (New York: Viking Penguin, 1974), 293.

28 George Herbert, "The Elixir," in *The Poems of George Herbert*, edited by Helen Gardner (London: Oxford University Press, 1961), 175–176.

29 From the last line of William Blake, *The Marriage of Heaven and Hell* (Boston: John W. Luce & Co., 1906), 47, accessed February 2019, http://gutenberg.org/files/45315/45315-h/45315-h.htm.

30 William Blake, *The Complete Poetry and Prose of William Blake*, ed. David V. Erdman, revised edition (Berkeley, CA: University of California Press, 1982), 490.

And Gerard Manley Hopkins's sonnet "God's Grandeur" begins:

> The world is charged with the grandeur of God.
> It will flame out, like shining from shook foil.[31]

In addition to the poets, panentheist philosophers such as Hegel and Whitehead, and translators of panentheist Hindu classics such as the Bhagavad Gita have influenced Christian thought in more modern times. A watershed moment may have occurred on Easter Sunday 1955, when the Jesuit priest and eminent pale-ontologist Pierre Teilhard de Chardin died of a sudden heart attack. He had been forbidden by the Roman Catholic Church since 1941 to publish his crowning work, *Le phénomène humain,* but his death allowed its posthumous publication in the same year, followed four years later by its appearance in English translation as *The Phenomenon of Man.* In Teilhard's foreword, he writes, "[Humanity], the centre of perspective, is at the same time the *centre of construction* of the universe."[32] In its concluding pages he writes, "Christ invests himself organically with the very majesty of his creation."[33]

A survey of panentheistic thought within Christian tradition would not be complete without mention of what has recently been called Celtic spirituality. J. Philip Newell, one of its foremost contemporary exponents, credits it with "a passion for finding God at the heart of all life."[34] Among its exemplars he lists the ninth-century Irish expatriate John Scotus Eriugena, mentioned above, who taught at the court of the Holy Roman Emperor Charles the Bald. Eriugena's sermon on the Prologue to the Fourth Gospel (Jn 1:1–17), *Vox Aquilae* ("the Voice of the Eagle"), argues that in the creation, everything that came to be, came to be within the boundaries of the Creative Word of God—a teaching pre-served in the Greek text of the gospel, but lost in the Latin-speaking West, which

---

31 Gerard Manley Hopkins, *The Major Works, including all the poems and selected prose,* Oxford World's Classics series, ed. Catherine Phillips (London: Oxford University Press, 2002), 128.

32 Pierre Teilhard de Chardin, *The Phenomenon of Man* (New York: Harper & Row, 1959), 33.

33 Pierre Teilhard de Chardin, *The Phenomenon of Man,* 297.

34 J. Philip Newell, *Listening for the Heartbeat of God: A Celtic Spirituality* (New York: Paulist, 1997), 2. But Power critiques many of the claims made for the "Celtic Spirituality" tradition: "one of the weaknesses of the movement [is] that people may find what they seek, and possibly what they want, rather than what actually existed." Rosemary Power, *The Celtic Quest: A Contemporary Spirituality* (Blackrock, Ireland: The Columba Press, 2010), 18.

had only Jerome's translation, the Vulgate, for scripture.[35] To paraphrase Eriugena, all creation abides forever within a Creator who has given us both a book of scripture and a book of nature by which to teach us divine truths.[36] This suggests that God might not only experience through such "inanimate" creatures as rocks and water, but also communicate with people through them.

Unfortunately, the eye that can see all things as in God and God as in all things cannot ordinarily be given to one whose will is opposed to receiving it. One with an emotional investment in seeing nature as "dead" will not welcome a revelation that all nature is alive with God's life: the earth, for such a person, is not Mother Earth but real estate, ready to be claimed as property and done with as the owner pleases. This seems to have been the attitude of the Vihiga District Commissioner who ordered the razing of the Maragoli Forest. The danger is that Christians and other people of faith who lack a sense of the creation's livingness, or holiness to God, may unwittingly ally themselves with such persons.

VII. Panentheism within Quakerism?

In 1648, George Fox had his celebrated epiphany: "Now was I come up in spirit through the flaming sword into the paradise of God. All things were new, and all the creation gave another smell unto me than before, beyond what words can utter." Fox made no further attempt to explain this new "smell," but his mystical ascent "into the paradise of God" clearly altered his perception of the creation, "opening" to him "the nature and virtues of the creatures."[37] There is no evidence that his ascent made him a panentheist, however. Rather, he came to see that Christ would teach his followers "the right use of the creatures," both ani-

---

35 Eriugena's *Vox Aquilae* is translated in Christopher Bamford, *The Voice of the Eagle: The Heart of Celtic Christianity*, new edition (Great Barrington, MA: Lindisfarne Books, 2000), 69–114; Eriugena's exegesis of John 1:3 is on 82–83. Eriugena continues: "All things, therefore, that were made by the Word, live in him unchangeably and are life.... [A]ll are one in him, above all times and places, and subsist in him eternally" (86).

36 Bamford (2000), 198–200. Newell (1997), 34, writes, "Eriugena taught that Christ moves among us in two shoes, as it were, one shoe being that of creation, the other that of the Scriptures." Deirdre Carabine, in *John Scottus Eriugena* (New York: Oxford University Press, 2000), 25, identifies "the central idea" of Eriugena's *Periphyseon* as "that creation is the manifestation of God and, therefore, is sanctified." In that work Eriugena writes of the "ineffable descent of the Supreme Goodness, which is Unity and Trinity, into the things that are so as to make them to be, indeed so as itself to be." Carabine (2000), 49, citing *Periphyseon*, Book III, 678D. The pagination is that used in the *Patrologia Latina*, vol. 122 (Paris, 1853), as Carabine notes, 114, footnote 12.

37 Fox, *Journal*, 27.

mate and inanimate, and bestow a wisdom "with which… [humanity] must order, and use the creatures, and order the Creation to the glory of God."[38] To retain that wisdom, Fox insisted, one must abide in the Light of Christ: "[W]ait in the light, from him to receive power, which brings out of the world's lusts and defilements, …but you will come to know the right use of the creatures, waiting in the light."[39]

The twelfth and thirteenth maxims from William Penn's *Some Fruits of Solitude* express a clearly panentheistic view of creation, though this author has found no evidence that panentheism was ever articulated as a conscious doctrine in the writings of early Friends:

> 12. And it would go a great Way to caution and direct People in their Use of the World, that they were better studied and knowing in the Creation of it.

> 13. For how could [People] find the Confidence to abuse it, while they should see the Great Creator look them in the Face, in all and every Part thereof?[40]

I suggest that Fox's reverent attitude toward "the creatures" for the sake of God to whom they belong is the functional equivalent of panentheism, which is reverent toward the creatures for the sake of God who dwells in them. In either case there is respect for creation because of its relation to God, and a wholesome fear of offending God by abusing creatures, whether God is seen as the creatures' Owner or as their Inhabitor. This natural sympathy between the two views is important to consider when we acknowledge that panentheism never gained a firm foothold in Quaker thought—until Quakerism came to Kenya. It is my observation that Kenyan Quakers today, of whatever ethnic origin, will respect the word of a shaman if he tells them, "Respect this forest," or, "Don't defile this lake." All traditional Kenyans are attuned to the indwelling life of created things.

---

38 Fox, "To the Parliament and Protector of England," 10, Digital Quaker Collection, http://esr.earlham.edu/dqc/. In Fox's Epistle No. 128 (*Works*, vol. 7, 121) he uses virtually identical language, adding a caution about "covetousness" and what we would today call utilitarian thinking about the creatures. George Fox, *The Works of George Fox*, 8 volumes, reprint of the 1831 American edition (State College, PA: George Fox Fund, 1990), Digital Quaker Collection, http://esr.earlham.edu/dqc/.

39 Fox, "Christ's Light," *Works*, vol. 4, 305.

40 William Penn, *Some Fruits of Solitude, in Reflections and Maxims, Relating to the Conduct of Humane Life*, in *Collection of the Works of William Penn*, vol. 1 (London: J. Sowle, 1726), 821.

The Maragoli have a saying: "Talk to a stone. Even though a stone will not reply to you, when you talk to it, it hears you."

Almost a century after Fox, the Quaker John Woolman famously avoided using dyed clothing because of the damage done to both the human workers and the environment by the dyeing process, just as he avoided using postal and other services that abused horses. He did not theorize that there was "that of God" in the horses, but he was as compassionate to them as if he felt "that of God" in them. Similar compassion led Quaker abolitionists from Woolman onward to avoid trafficking in goods produced by enslaved labor. Numerous other Quaker witnesses have arisen from Quakers' tender-hearted refusal to misuse creatures, from the creation of humane mental hospitals and the Underground Railroad to the witness against the internment camps of World War II.

In North American Quaker thought there are now more direct panentheistic glimmerings. Douglas Gwyn writes:

> When God says in Genesis 1:26, "Let us make humankind in our image, according to our likeness," who does God address? In the story thus far, only God and the cosmos have appeared. Can it be that God speaks to the entire creation, inviting that stupendous panoply to collaborate in creating humans? We indeed bear the image of the universe in our bodies. We are literally "stardust," formed from the elemental wreckage of a star that died billions of years ago. Adam, literally "dust," is the child of the universe. We bear witness in our bodies to the laws of thermodynamics. The genetic inheritance of life on earth is encoded in us. Yet we also bear the image of a divine origin and destiny. The image of God is manifest in our sense of a reality beyond ourselves, beyond everything we know, and in our longing for it. We yearn toward God as a plant leans to the light. The image of God is "that of God," the light that is life itself in all men and women (John 1:4, 9). Thus, to live with integrity and universal love is to honor both our mother and our father (see Exod. 20:12), the divine and the cosmos. It is to live gently upon the earth, peacefully with our fellow humans, and faithfully to the knowledge of God in us. [41]

Within the past 40 years, Quaker Earthcare Witness (QEW) emerged in the United States. Though Fox's language about "right use of the creatures" is no longer in use, the idea of it remains alive in QEW. However, Fox's sense of

---

41 Douglas Gwyn, *A Sustainable Life: Quaker Faith and Practice in the Renewal of Creation* (Philadelphia: FGC Quaker Press, 2014), xviii.

connection between the "right use of the creatures" and the "mind of Christ" or "light of Christ" is not evident on QEW's website; this is an age when activists tend to keep their theology to themselves. Many may have panentheistic views, but the spiritual source of Quaker activists' activity may be more often felt in the heart than named by the mind.

I hope, in any case, that the wisdom of Christianized Maragoli shamanism, along with the wisdom of other earth-revering tribal peoples' traditions, will strengthen the spiritual anchoring of Quaker and other religiously-based earth-care witnesses in the trying times to come, as the day grows ever closer "that shall burn as an oven" (Mal 4:1). If we come to see that God actually inhabits the creation, we may become more wary of abusing or destroying it. And if we know that Christ is leading us in our struggle, we may move forward with both humility and confidence. Weighty Friend, minister, teacher, and writer, Douglas Gwyn, has hailed the Maragoli synthesis of native panentheism with Quaker Christianity as "one that can contribute to Friends and other Christians finding the earth as part of God's redemptive purposes."[42]

VIII. Conclusion

"Where there's smoke, there's fire," goes a Maragoli saying. "Where there's fire, something is cooking. Where something is cooking, there is food for thought." We humans are now cooking the life out of the earth.

In spite of the peril to all life presented by the environmental crisis and climate injustice of our time, and in spite of the human ignorance, greed and selfishness that have brought this about, it is possible that God is using the crisis for God's own life-giving goals. This would not exonerate those responsible for the war, waste, and destruction that have wrought such toxic conditions on earth—the destabilization of ecosystems with runaway species extinctions, the desertification of arable land, mass murders of the innocent, the acidification and the defiling with plastic of the oceans—but God may be meaning to bring a great good out of this great evil. How? Perhaps by letting conditions get to such a crisis-point that no one can survive unless the world's political and economic institutions agree to put the common good ahead of the selfish interests of nations, corporations, and individuals. But perhaps this agreement, which would include the abolition of war and a widespread consensus to sacrifice self-will to the goodwill of the Beloved Community, cannot be reached and put into practice

---

42 Douglas Gwyn, personal communication, February 9, 2019.

without a general metamorphosis of human consciousness—which can only come as a gift from God.

Tribal peoples' traditions must come to be explored with respect by the peoples of the world's dominant cultures. The Abrahamic religions agree that only the Creator is worthy of worship, and that any reverence shown to normally invisible creatures (such as the "gods," "angels," or "spirits" of elements and localities) would constitute idolatry, a forbidden sin. In their zeal to suppress the supposed idolatries of "paganism," they have taught that these normally invisible creatures are either nonexistent or diabolical, and today the ruling consensus in the industrialized world is that they simply don't exist at all. And yet, Christians, Jews, and Muslims would agree that one should never dump trash on a *human* neighbor's property!

What tribal peoples like the Maragoli have to teach the industrialized world is that the tutelary spirits of water and wind—call them "gods," "angels," or "spirits"—are real neighbors, ancestors, bearing a kind of consciousness that is as capable of being offended by trash-dumping as human neighbors would be. Perhaps the Water God cries to the Supreme Creator for justice, and the Creator hears its prayer! If the Creator were to call us human beings to repentance for our offenses against the other creatures in nature, could we hear the Creator's rebuke? Not if we're trained to categorically disbelieve in invisible entities bearing messages! Then we can hear neither the Water God nor the God and Father of our Lord Jesus Christ, neither the Angel of El Niño nor the voice of Allah. But God is not mocked, as the Scriptures say (Gal 6:7). Nature becomes ever more disorderly as human beings grow ever more persistent in our disrespect, and as it does, drought-afflicted Iowa farmers may grow ever more ready to call on Lakota shamans to conduct a rain dance.[43]

But I am looking forward filled with hope to a time when the majority of humanity might affirm the all-inclusiveness of the Divine love humanity is called to express—not just to our human neighbors, but also to every created being and thing. There is life in all things that we can be trained to be aware of, and it is one with the life of our Creator. How would the world change if the Abrahamic religions—Christians, Jews, and Muslims—could embrace that of God in nature and all creation, animate and inanimate?

---

43 The success of such a rain dance is recorded in the thought-provoking Eliot Cowan, *Plant Spirit Medicine* (Newberg, OR: Swan•Raven & Co., 1995), 98–99.

Afterword

I am very grateful to the still-living spirit of Dorika Bweyenda for her gift of Christ's light, which I have been privileged to bring to the wider world, along with the Maragoli culture and spirituality of which she taught me to be a spokesperson. I am grateful for her deeply grounding me in those wisdoms, and for teaching me such skill in my mother tongue, and in my history, tradition, and aspirations. I embody her prophecy, her spirituality, and her soul, which teach me compassion, openness, accountability, hope, and love. In my own humble way, by the grace of God, I have attempted to do what she sent me out into the world to do. I now hope to return to my village, in keeping with her request, with the gift of a solar-powered library and a community center, which will bring together all peoples of the world. I intend to name this space in her honor, and to renew the forest from which the Maragoli have always drawn life. In her spirit, I invite Friends of all branches of Quakerism, and indeed all people of good will from around the world, to join me in making this dream a reality.

Acknowledgements

I am grateful to Earlham School of Religion (ESR) for the scholarship that is allowing me two years of postgraduate study in Quaker Studies. According to Matthew Hisrich, the Dean of ESR, far fewer Kenyan women have applied than men, and those that have, have often been denied visas to come.[44] I strongly urge the many capable East African Quaker women leaders and pastors, like the gifted Judith Ngoya, minister at Friends International Center in Nairobi, to consider applying for admission to any of ESR's excellent postgraduate programs to share your gifts with the world.

---

44 Matthew Hisrich, personal conversation, February 25, 2019.

9 | Process Metaphysics for Ecological Survival: Alfred North Whitehead in Conversation With Friends

By Lonnie Valentine

Abstract: Process philosophy and theology reject the substance metaphysics of the dominant Western tradition for a relational metaphysics, developed most fully by Alfred North Whitehead. Quakers have embodied such a relational vision in their practice, but have done little to reflect upon the metaphysics suggested by an incarnational experience of God, one another, and our planet. Such theological reflection can deepen our sense of how the earth is incarnated in us and we in the earth. Such thinking can, literally, contribute to our world's survival.

After losing his son, Eric, in World War I and witnessing the destruction wrought in the next world war with that new weapon, the atomic bomb, Whitehead saw two stark possibilities for us and our world: a new age of liberation, or humanity's self-destruction.

This paper will explicate Whitehead's vision of the "philosophy of organism" (Whitehead's term from his book, Process and Reality*) in relation to Quaker thought and practice for the sake of creation care. With the aid of process thought, Quakers can better help cultivate a deep ecological sensibility.*

I. Introduction

Alfred North Whitehead (1861–1947) sought a systematic account of how reality works, a quest few dare anymore. This rejection of systematic thought adds to the dangers of our present moment: "Without vision the people perish" (Prv 29:18). In his long effort to think systematically, Whitehead consistently sought to overcome the dualism running through most understandings of our world and ourselves since the advent of Greek rationalism. Falling into dualism is the foundational sin of thought. Dualisms such as God and the world, nature and humanity, matter and mind, body and soul, senses and thinking continue to impact Western thought.

Before the modern and postmodern periods, early Quakers sought a holistic understanding of how reality works. They did not divide the spiritual from the material, God from the world, or the inward Christ from outward actions. A rough ecological sensibility appears in the form of the emerging testimony of simplicity. They sought to overcome the dualities promulgated by those around them, focusing on communion with the Spirit as the connection between the many divisions in their world. Therefore, Quakers today have a heritage of thinking ecologically that precedes Whitehead, but Whitehead can help Quakers think more systematically about our environmental sensibilities. This paper will first present Whitehead's vision of the "philosophy of organism" and then relate that to Quaker faith and practice.[1]

II. Whitehead's Vision

Whitehead lost his youngest son, Eric, in World War I and lived to see the devastation of another world war and the dropping of the atomic bombs before he died at age 87 at the end of 1947. In one of his final dialogues with his students, he remained positive in hopes for us and our world, but warned of our possible self-created annihilation:

> The conditions of our lives have been basically more altered in the past fifty years than they were in the previous two thousand—I might say three thousand. I think that we are on the threshold of an age of liberation, a better life for the masses, a new burst of liberated creative energy, a new form of society; or [humankind] may all but exterminate itself and desolate this planet.[2]

Some seventy years past Whitehead's death, humanity has now created even more ways to exterminate itself and desolate the planet. Can we still say with Whitehead that our planet and we are "on the threshold of an age of liberation"? I seek to maintain such hope, but it is difficult. Perhaps you find hope difficult, too. Whitehead did not believe there was some force, be it the power of God or the wisdom of humanity, that would inevitably stop us if we continue

---

[1] Whitehead, *Process and Reality*, 18.
[2] Alfred North Whitehead, *Dialogues of Alfred North Whitehead: As Recorded by Lucien Price* (Boston: Little, Brown & Co., 1954), 276.

down the road to destruction. He would probably point to the myriad stars with millions of planets and say that God's effort to create life—and life abundant (Jn 10:10)—would not be defeated everywhere, though it could certainly be defeated here on this planet. Whitehead's metaphysics moved beyond dualism, and I will now explore how his ideas opened up further possibilities that can aid us in thinking about our ecological situation.

1. Overcoming Dualism: The Actual Occasions of All Experience

Whitehead's first and foundational ecological point is his argument that we in the West have mistakenly understood the world of nature as composed mostly of inanimate matter, and we have reduced the mind to nothing but a complex manifestation of matter. Quakerism began just prior to the Enlightenment as scientific consciousness emerged. As Quakerism began, many thinkers in the seventeenth century insisted that the materialistic form of empiricism was the only way we know truth. Others with religious concerns disagreed and, following Descartes, maintained the existence of mind or soul as the basis of human subjectivity that was not reducible to mere matter.

Whitehead notes that this trend continued into the twentieth century, pointing out how the dogmatism of the church was giving way to the dogmatic "creed" of science that "matter in motion is the one concrete reality in nature" that rules out any claim for mind or soul or God.[3] Each camp insisted they could claim the final real foundation of the world. Dualism persisted. However, Whitehead offered a systematic bridge between these two worlds with his philosophy of organism.

Rather than arguing on one side of this matter/mind or any other dualism, Whitehead sought an underlying way to relate the two poles. He argued there is no merely dead matter, inert and lacking subjectivity, nor any subjectivity free from the material of the world. In studying the development of modern physics his vision was that at the base of everything were "actual occasions" which are dynamic, processional events rather than fixed, unchanging substances. These events then contain elements of both mentality and materiality. Such "occasions" actually have subjectivity as they take the events of the past into themselves as objects of their experience and also seek goals beyond what has been given from the past. Thus, no division exists between what we call matter and what we call mind or soul. Rather, life embraces both the material and

---

[3] Alfred North Whitehead, *Science and the Modern World* (New York: Macmillan, 1925), 204.

the spiritual. Reality is fundamentally relational, and so is not composed of separate substances and essences, either as fixed material particles or free transcendent mind or soul. In this way, there is no essential separation between earth and us.

Therefore, in Whitehead we do not have the billiard ball notion of material particles interacting randomly with each other. Neither do we have a mental or spiritual realm untouched by the material world. His metaphysics denies the Cartesian separation between pure mentality and the rest of a mechanistic world. The dynamically alive and experiential events in Whitehead's schema manifest elements of both materiality and subjectivity. If reality does not fit the usual models of Western philosophy, how then *does* reality work?

In Whitehead's understanding, each new event that arises must take into account the past and decide how to shape past events. New interpretations of past events are incarnated in the emerging new event. That is, reality is not finally static, but always in process. Emerging events incorporate the reality of the previous events and shape them toward a future: "The organic starting point is from the analysis of process as the realization of events in an interlocking community. The event is the unit of things real."[4] This means that, though life is organized in very complex ways, there is no dualism between dead and living, or higher and lower forms of life. We ourselves are a complex interaction of a multitude of events that connect our body and mind together, ourselves to other selves, and our many communities of selves to the entire world. We are built from events that are, in turn, at work in all things. Thus, to destroy our larger world of "nature" is at the same time to destroy human "nature." We can simplify the earth and ourselves, but each small event will continue to generate more events. Our world may become inhospitable to life, as hot as Venus or as cold as Mars. However, the universe contains vast potential to again create complex life.

2. The Experiential-Reflective Ways of Knowing

Whitehead's second ecologically specific contribution is his encouragement to fully experience the ways of knowing reflected in this metaphysics. Whitehead did not think abstract concepts are sufficient, but that such abstract reflection is a necessary part of our experience: "Philosophy begins in wonder. And, at the end, when philosophic thought has done its best, the wonder remains. There have been added, however, some grasp of the immensity of things, some purification of emotion by understanding."[5] His very rejection of a world built of static

---

[4] Whitehead, *Science and the Modern World*, 138.

[5] Alfred North Whitehead, *Modes of Thought* (New York: Macmillan, 1938), 232.

material blocks forms an implicit emphasis on the experiential: "There is no going behind actual entities to find anything more real."[6] These occasions of experience are what lie at the base of all things. Our intellectual recognition of this leads us to focus on the experiential nature of all reality, including ourselves. The active and dynamic events, past and present, are the final real things of our world. There is no unchanging material substance nor unchanging spiritual soul or mind underlying emerging events. However, each emerging event takes account of its past in its own way. The objects of the past became subject in the emerging actual occasion and, in turn, become an object for future emerging occasions:

> Each actual entity is conceived as an act of experience arising out of data. It is a process of "feeling" the many data, so as to absorb them into the unity of one individual "satisfaction." Here "feeling" is the term used for the basic generic operation of passing from the objectivity of the data to the subjectivity of the actual occasion in question.[7]

That is, the true foundation of the world is neither object nor subject in isolation from one another or collapsed one into the other, but the "throb of experience" that unites past events into the felt unity of a present event.[8]

Whitehead thought Western Christianity has been too influenced by the modern scientific worldview, suggesting everything is simply bits of matter, but we also have been too influenced by those elements of Greek thought coming from Plato, who understood that the realm of the Forms, the abstract realities we can touch by our thought, were more real than our embodied experiences. Again, we have inherited a struggle to fix reality as either material or spiritual. However, as Whitehead's epigraphs for this paper insist, the function of high abstract thought is to help life here below. Both the material pole and the mental pole are needed in the ongoing creation of the world. It is the incarnated expression of thought in what is manifested that is truly real. The realm of abstract thought is important in directing our work, but our work is not solely directed to thought.

When Whitehead was asked what was more important—facts or ideas—he responded that ideas *about* facts were most important.[9] Such thinking in abstractions, then, is vital to directing our attention to elements in our world, but we cannot fly off to some Kingdom of Heaven where we escape the actual,

---

[6] Whitehead, *Process and Reality*, 18.
[7] Whitehead, *Process and Reality*, 40.
[8] Whitehead, *Process and Reality*, 190.
[9] Whitehead, *Dialogues of Alfred North Whitehead*, 271.

living world. Some current Christians claim that when this earth is destroyed, we will be taken (or at least some of us will be taken) to a better world. Such thinking contributes to the danger that we will indeed exterminate ourselves. However, if we truly understand that embodied life, here on this world, is as real as it gets, we may work to keep life going on this planet.

Another influence that leads us to fail to realize the processional nature of our world—events which are alive and interactively changing with the events around them—is that our Western languages deceive us. How so? We structure thought in terms of subjects and objects: "I saw the whale." In this linguistic structure we can miss the fundamental interrelation between subject and object:

> The doctrine of the individual independence of real facts is derived from the notion that the subject-predicate form of statement conveys a truth which is metaphysically ultimate. According to this view, an individual substance with its predicates constitutes the ultimate type of actuality.... With this metaphysical presupposition, the relations between individual substances constitute metaphysical nuisances: there is no place for them.[10]

Therefore, we seek a way out of this dilemma not by denying there are fundamental essences or substances to the things in the world, but by insisting that our troublesome relations with other events are but "accidental" to our true and unchanging essential nature. In this way there arises a barrier between us and all else. We then see ourselves separated from nature, to say nothing of being separated from other human beings. And thus the false doctrine of essentialist individualism prevents us from truly seeing that we are incarnating the world into ourselves, and that the world is likewise incarnating us into it. Therefore, our very thought processes tend to drive us away from realizing the metaphysically unavoidable truth that we do not live without being formed to our core by the world, and of course we form that world. If we mistreat our world, it will return the favor. Therefore, the world we shape will in its turn form us, for good or ill.

Whitehead's philosophy of organism suggests the whole world—including humanity—is capable of changing course toward a goal that is not fully determined by our past. That is, though there are "efficient causes" in the sense that we truly must deal with what the world has become through its long history before our species arrived and since we have misshapen the world for our selfish desires, the future is not irrevocably determined by that past. We can envision

---

[10] Whitehead, *Process and Reality*, 137.

and act upon final causes or purpose—a *telos* that can truly shape our direction now. Much of science deals exclusively with past causes, seeing how present circumstances derive from the past. However, at times this approach turns into the rejection of any purpose. That is, what we call "purpose" is nothing but that which is already completely determined by the past. Whitehead rejects this thinking: "Scientists animated by the purpose of proving that they are purposeless constitute an interesting subject for study."[11]

3. Whitehead's God as Radically Immanent and Transcendent

The third ecological point in Whitehead's philosophy of organism is that in our very ability to sense the potentialities for our world is the way to save ourselves. For Whitehead, as stated in the epigraph for this paper, it is the elucidation of this actual world that is the purpose of all thinking. For him, we desperately need creative thought if we are to save our planet and ourselves. There are in the realm of potentiality those ideas that can address our dilemma. To get lost in the pain of this hurting world would leave us unable to see what might be possible. To stick with what we have always done or assume we can think our way out of our problems by ourselves serves only to cut ourselves off from the flights of imagination that open us to more than we currently do or think. This imaginative openness can yield concrete solutions to our ecological problems.

In the early part of the twentieth century, philosophy was rejecting the strand of imagination that Whitehead was drawing upon for scientific materialism. So, in his magnum opus, *Process and Reality*, Whitehead had to issue a "Defense of Speculative Philosophy," where he gives this analogy:

> The true method of discovery is like the flight of an airplane. It starts from the ground of particular observation; it makes a flight in the thin air of imaginative generalization; and again lands for renewed observation rendered acute by rational interpretation. The reason for success of this method of imaginative generalization is that...factors which arc constantly present may yet be observed under the influence of imaginative thought.[12]

In his speculative philosophy, God was necessary to make sense of the assessment of the facts of the order that has emerged from the interactions of the

---

11 Alfred North Whitehead, *The Function of Reason* (Boston: Beacon Press, 1929), 16.
12 Whitehead, *Process and Reality*, 5.

events found at the base of things.[13] As with our fundamentally relational and processional interactions with the world, God shares these same characteristics: "God is not to be treated as an exception to all metaphysical principles, invoked to save their collapse. [God] is their chief exemplification."[14] God is both radically immanent in the world, as we are, and God is also transcendent to the world, as are we. Of course, the difference is that ours is a limited portion of the world that is incarnated into us and we offer but a limited transcendence to that world. God is related to *all* the universe. That means that God is immanent in all events everywhere, and that means that God also transcends all those events. God then operates in the same way that all "actual occasions" do, those final real things that make up everything.[15] However, where our experience is limited to our particular past and our particular purposes, God is aware of all the past and all possibilities.

From God's vision of potentialities, God offers into each emerging event an "initial aim" that would provide the most harmony for that event in relation to everything else. For Whitehead, such a God (very different from the usual vision of God) is posited just because we do see that there is emerging order in the world:

> The things which are temporal (actual occasions) arise by their participation in the things which are eternal (pure potentials). The two sets are mediated by a thing which combines the actuality of what is temporal with the timelessness of what is potential. This final entity [God] is the divine element in the world, by which the barren inefficient disjunction of abstract potentialities obtains primordially the efficient conjunction of ideal realization.[16]

If there were no such element of ordering of possibilities, creation would be mere chaos. Now, after creation makes its "choice" about how to move forward given what it makes of the past and God's "aim" for creation, God then takes in all of what has happened and is changed because of creation's choice. To complete the circle, after creation acts, then God must adjust the new possibilities for the world based upon what creation has chosen. For Whitehead, we can say that the potentialities offered to the world are God's desire for justice in the sense of a harmony given to the world. We then can say that God's taking in

---

[13] Whitehead, *Process and Reality*, 343.
[14] Whitehead, *Process and Reality*, 343.
[15] Whitehead, *Process and Reality*, 18.
[16] Whitehead, *Process and Reality*, 16.

of the world's choices is God's love for the world. God, as we do, "feels" the world. When humanity turns away from God by choices that create harm, then God suffers just as we do: "God is the great companion—the fellow-sufferer who understands."[17]

God interacts with the world by offering possibilities for realization of the "initial aim." These possibilities provide the direction for actions that will be most harmonious for creation. God then responds to the choices of creation by offering a new aim that takes account of the past choices made. In this non-coercive way, God provides a "lure for feeling" toward a more harmonious creation.[18] That is, God does not wield coercive power over creation, and human beings—like all creation—have real freedom. We can deny God's offering for a more beautiful and livable world and God will continue to offer choices toward a better world, given our choices. God is not omnipotent and does not intervene in coercive ways in creation, either in time or at some end time.

In Whitehead's view, the three mistakes in philosophical or theological thought that haunt the Western world flow from this mistake about how God interacts with the world. God is not the "unmoved mover" of Aristotle who causes creation through complete power over the creative act and who is un-changed by what creation does. God is also not the "ruthless moralist" who is-sues rigid divine commands that humanity must not refuse, or risk peril. Finally, the worst of all is that the West saw God "in the image of the Egyptian, Persian, and Roman imperial rulers…. The church gave unto God the attributes which belonged exclusively to Caesar."[19] For Whitehead, Christianity then missed the alternative vision of God presented by Jesus: God fits none of those three ver-sions of deity but Jesus' vision "dwells upon the tender elements in the world, which slowly and in quietness operate by love; and finds purpose in the present immediacy of a kingdom not of this world."[20]

III. The Quaker Vision

This section on the Quaker theological vision in relation to process thought will move through the three ecological points from the foregoing section on White-head's process vision. This section will also offer some reflections on how en-gaging in theological reflection might help enrich Quaker practice.

---

[17] Whitehead, *Process and Reality*, 351.
[18] Whitehead, *Process and Reality*, 189, 344.
[19] Whitehead, *Process and Reality*, 342.
[20] Whitehead, *Process and Reality*, 343.

Working back from the third point above, Quakers have been reluctant to engage in theological reflection: "the fact is that Quakers are not given to speculation about God."[21] This is true both at the beginning of Quakerism and into our era. Cooper quotes Rufus Jones: "There is, it must be said in all frankness, no distinctly Quaker conception of God."[22] In Wilmer Cooper's view, Quakers have understood that "God must be experienced spiritually within," and so "Friends have never begun their search for God in the realm of logic, nor in the external world of nature, nor in the far reaches of space and time. For them God is infused Spirit rather than abstract external being."[23] Howard Brinton also notes that Quakers were wary of theological speculation as well as any demand to submit to creeds.[24] However, both Cooper and Brinton do insist that Quakers did engage in theological reflection upon their experience. Cooper indicates that Quakers were rooted enough in the Puritan movement to insist upon God's transcendence that is beyond their own immediate experience of the Light: our personal experience did not capture God's transcendence.[25] Brinton notes that the earlier theologians of the Quaker movement, Robert Barclay and William Penn, "were fully aware of the importance of a consistent system of ideas."[26]

Reflecting upon the process approach engages these trends in Quaker theological reflection about God because process theology affirms the Quaker claim that the reality of God is to be experienced and not just thought about.

1. God Present in Experienced Reality in Both Process Thought and Quakerism

However, process thought insists that thought itself can be spiritual. Our thinking can shape and correct our experience just as our experience will shape our thought. That is, spirit and thought are not set in a dualist separation or necessary conflict. Early Quakers rightly, then, did not want their experience of the Light to be either reduced to doctrine or (as they experienced) rejected because of the doctrines of their opponents. However, as both Cooper and Brinton indicate, Quakers did engage in theological reflection—though affirming that our thinking

---

[21] Wilmer A. Cooper, *A Living Faith: An Historical and Comparative Study of Quaker Beliefs,* second edition (Richmond, IN: Friends United Press, 1990), 33.

[22] Rufus M. Jones, "The Quaker Conception of God," *Beyond Dilemmas: Quakers Look at Life,* ed. S. B. Laughlin (Philadelphia: J. B. Lippincott Company, 1937), 29.

[23] Cooper, *A Living Faith,* 34.

[24] Howard Brinton and Margaret Hope Bacon, *Friends for 350 Years: The History and Beliefs of the Society of Friends Since George Fox Started the Quaker Movement,* updated edition (Wallingford, PA: Pendle Hill Publications, 2002), 40.

[25] Cooper, *A Living Faith,* 34.

[26] Brinton and Bacon, *Friends for 350 Years,* 40.

does not capture the fullness of God. Therefore, as Friends we need to engage in theological reflection as a check upon our experience. After all, the early Friends did this by studying and reflecting on the Bible, arguing that Quaker experience was both affirmed and checked by what was given in the Bible.

One element of Quaker practice that most clearly coincides with process thought is the idea of getting a leading from the Spirit. This relates us to the great vision of harmony of God but in a way particular to us. That is, we do know something directly from God, but that does not mean we know everything that God is doing. Our task, then, is to work to develop our capacity to attend to these leadings. Like anything else, this takes practice. All the spiritual disciplines, within Quakerism and beyond, can be means to opening ourselves to those leadings, to being guided by the vision of God in our context.

2. Listening to and with Past and Present Friends as Process Theology

In relation to the second point in the process vision above, Quaker practice has stressed that we need, individually and corporately, to seek guidance from the Spirit. This corresponds to the process claim that God is incarnated in every emerging event. In the words of Cooper, "Friends have insisted that to know and claim God…, God must be experienced spiritually within…. For them God is infused Spirit rather than abstract external being."[27] In addition to the stress upon individual spiritual practices to equip one to so experience the "infused Spirit" of God, the practice of corporate waiting worship recognizes the inherent relationality of all experience. That is, Quaker practice has sought to avoid the problems that may come when we individually decide just what those leadings are by urging one another to engage the wisdom of the Meeting about our leadings.

As Howard Brinton puts it, Quaker "group mysticism" is not focused upon just the individuals but this "mysticism of the Quakers is directed both toward God and toward the group. The vertical relation to God and the horizontal relation to [others] are like two coordinates used to plot a course; without both the position of the curve could not be determined."[28] This image suggests, in line with the process vision, that not only do we seek to be aware of God's presence in our experience, but we also need to be aware of the influences of those around us and our corporate past. That is, we must attend to others in order to have some sense of what is influencing the present time in our corporate life together as well as our individual experience. Quaker ways of discernment

---

[27] Cooper, *A Living Faith*, 34.
[28] Brinton and Bacon, *Friends for 350 Years*, 4.

have often been used when we feel unsure about our leadings, but they need to be used also when we believe we are pretty clear about our leading. Since we have held, like process thought, that we are always in relationship with each other as we are in relation to God, we need to actively draw upon our various ways of discernment. The corporate insight can guide individual discernment just as an insightful individual can guide corporate discernment.

In addition to the insights of our Quaker contemporaries we need also to draw on the witnesses of faith in the past. This agrees with the process view. That is, though tradition can be felt as a dead weight, in part because we can easily see its mistakes, we can relate to past tradition as if we are in dialogue with it. Rather than seeing the past as demanding us to think and act in certain ways or demanding of the past what it cannot give, we can engage the past conversationally. We sometimes believe we can cut ourselves off from the past of our tradition since we see its problems. That is, whether liberal or conservative or other version of Friend, we may want to separate ourselves from aspects of our past tradition by rejecting the entire tradition. However, in process thought as in Quakerism, we need to have some understanding of the past to be able to understand the influences it has on our present. It is not that we seek to mechanically repeat the good that has been done in the past. Rather, engaging with that past gives us some way to learn from past mistakes while also gaining courage from past successes. Further, even with all the mistakes and horror of the past, there are also insights that transcend those very mistakes and horrors. As with our contemporaries, witnesses from the past can talk to us to help us get more clarity on what we are to do.

3. Process Theology Moves Quakerism Toward Ecological Care

This final reflection relates some Quaker views of the natural world to the first point of the process vision presented above. That is, Quakers recognized, as does process theology, that the natural world is not made up of dead matter formed by mechanistic processes driven by past events. Nature is alive and so God is being incarnated in all events of nature, just as God is incarnated in us. Our intellectual understanding of this will help us live out an ecological commitment to care for the natural world. Further, intentionally putting ourselves within the natural world, seeking to be open to what both God and that world are guiding us to do, may deepen both our enjoyment and work to preserve nature. As early Quakers said, God is not confined to any church structure and is in no need of having others mediate God to us. Fox provides an account of his own mystical experience that changed his view of the natural world:

Now I was come up in spirit through the flaming sword, into the paradise of God. All things were new; and all the creation gave unto me another smell than before, beyond what words can utter. I knew nothing but pureness, and innocency, and righteousness; being renewed into the image of God by Christ Jesus, to the state of Adam, which he was in before he fell. The creation was opened to me; and it was showed me how all things had their names given them according to their nature and virtue.[29]

Fox notes that this experience moved him to consider practicing medicine for the good of humanity, "seeing the nature and virtues of things were so opened to me by the Lord."[30] Such an experience may be ours by working not only to protect the natural world, but to immerse ourselves within it so that we may learn to feel its presence within us. Establishing such a relation may help us learn what we must do to protect this natural world from which we, after all, have been formed.

John Woolman has been often noted for his concern for the creatures of the earth and the treatment of the land. For example, in *A Plea for the Poor*, Woolman connected the poverty of many (due to those who misuse wealth) to the mistreatment of animals. When the poor are so dependent on animals for their own survival, they may be pushed to mistreat them in a desperate effort to survive. Woolman demonstrates both his empathy for the suffering of poor people and the suffering of poor animals:

Oxen and horses are often seen at work when, through heat and too much labor, their eyes and the emotion of their bodies manifest that they are oppressed. Their loads in wagons are frequently so heavy that when weary with hauling it far, their drivers find occasion in going up hills or through mire to raise their spirits by whipping to get forward.[31]

Therefore, if we desire to deepen our understanding of and commitment to the world of nature in which we have our being, then working to connect nature to our worship, both individually and corporately, is necessary. Just as we will not

---

[29] George Fox, *The Works of George Fox, in Two Volumes*, vol. 1 (Philadelphia: Marcus T. C. Gould, 1831), 45, Hathi Trust Digital Library, http://babel.hathitrust.org/cgi/pt?id=hvd.32044020662334;view=1up;seq=5.

[30] Fox, *Works*, 48.

[31] John Woolman, *The Journal and Major Essays of John Woolman*, ed. Phillips P. Moulton (Richmond, IN: Friends United Press, 1971), 238.

understand how our past human history shapes us without immersing ourselves in that history, we cannot understand how the natural world has shaped us without directly experiencing that natural world. Moreover, as with both the process and Quaker view of the immediacy of God in and through all things, the more we are in direct contact with nature, the more we are able to hear what it speaks to us. That is, process theologians and Quakers have said that our intellect does help us understand how God, human beings, and our world work, but our deepest understanding is gained by direct experience.

In conclusion, there are strong correlations between the metaphysics of process theology and the Quaker vision. Engaging with process thought can highlight emphases within Quaker faith and practice that might be deepened by engaging in theological reflection from a process view. When I found Quakers, I thought they were seeking to enact the process metaphysics I had read about in college. I also thought that in my Meeting, where theological exploration was not much of a focus, we could enhance our practice by engaging with process thought. There are strands within Quakerism that see nature as alive and emphasize our deep relation with it. There are strands that see the divine, by whatever name, as radically immanent in all things. There are Quaker practices that work to relate us to both the divine nature and our natural world. This dialogue with process thought can be of benefit and joy to us, and help us live into aspects of our tradition that lead toward a future in which humanity can participate.

10 | Quaker Ecological Foundations and the Universe Story[1]

By Laurel Kearns

Abstract: In contrast to the contemporary tension in some conservative Protestant theological circles over science that leads some to be skeptical about climate change, that tension is primarily absent for Quakers. The long tradition of Quakers in the study of science, shown in this essay, provides epistemological and spiritual grounding for grappling with environmental concerns. Resonance between Quaker worldviews and science can be found in the spiritual understanding of the evolution of the universe found in the work of the Catholic "geologian" Thomas Berry. With Berry, scientists and theologians concerned about the human relationship with the natural world have teamed up in recent decades to tell the Journey of the Universe, weaving together scientific and spiritual epistemologies to celebrate the beauty and mystery of the unfolding story of creation in which we find ourselves. This story can help shape the foundation for our response to the ecological crisis. This essays seeks to extend the conversation on Quaker foundations for ecological concern and their resonance with the work of Thomas Berry and Brian Swimme.

I. The Universe Story and Its Links to Quakerism

As renowned Quaker scholar of religion and science Philip Clayton comments in the introduction to the book *Quakers and the New Story*, "a variety of interpreters of science" are "suggesting that the 'new story' that science is telling actually

---

[1] Parts of this essay come from my contribution, "Quakerism and the Journey of the Universe," to *Living Cosmology: Christian Responses to Journey of the Universe*, eds. Mary Evelyn Tucker and John Grim (Maryknoll, NY: Orbis, 2016), 300–310, used here with the permission of the editors of that volume.

supports something very much like traditional Quaker ways of conceiving reality."[2] Clayton is referring in particular to the work of "geologian" Thomas Berry, who advocates that through understanding the evolution—"the journey"—of the universe, people can gain new insights from the "mystical dimension of the universe…. [W]e can see that every being in the universe is cousin to every other being in the universe."[3] Berry is perhaps best known for his work with the physicist Brian Swimme on the book *The Universe Story*, which lays out the implications of the evolution of the universe as a "new story" of common origin, a new understanding of the Genesis story.[4] This new story helps us realize our human place in the magnificence of the cosmos, that we are not separate from the creation. As Berry eloquently pronounced: "the human story is inseparable from the universe story. Then we can see that this story of the universe is in a special manner our sacred story, a story that reveals the divine…the singular story that illumines every aspect of our lives—our religious and spiritual lives as well as our economic and imaginative lives."[5] With this recognition comes responsibility for how human activities now disrupt planetary systems, imperiling all.

The "new story" or "universe story" resonates with many Quakers. The movement for Earth Literacy, or the knowledge of the complexity of the earth's systems and the interconnectedness of everything, is closely associated with the work of Thomas Berry and Brian Swimme, and has been very influential among Friends.[6] One popular Quaker presenter, Brad Stocker, describes his work in ways that are directly related to Berry's telling of the universe story: "My simplest definition for Earth Literacy, the elevator one I use is this: Earth Literacy begins with knowing and understanding the implications of the science story of the cre-

---

[2] Philip Clayton, "The New Story and Quaker Belief & Practice," in *Quakers and the New Story: Essays on Science and Spirituality*, eds. Philip Clayton and Mary Coelho (Burlington: Quaker Earthcare Witness, 2007), 6–7, at 6, http://newuniversestory.com/images/QuakersNewStory.pdf.

[3] Thomas Berry, "The Universe Story: Its Religious Significance," in *The Greening of Faith: God, Environment and the Good Life*, eds. John E. Carroll, Paul Brockelman, and Mary Westfall, twentieth anniversary edition (Durham, NH: University of New Hampshire Press, 2016), 208–218, at 214.

[4] Brian Swimme and Thomas Berry, *The Universe Story* (San Francisco: HarperOne, 1994). Brian Swimme and Mary Evelyn Tucker, *Journey of the Universe* (New Haven, CT: Yale University Press, 2014). Swimme and Tucker also produced a film of the same name after Thomas Berry's death. Learn more at http://journeyoftheuniverse.org/film.

[5] Thomas Berry, *The Sacred Universe: Earth, Spirituality, and Religion in the Twenty-first Century* (New York: Columbia University Press, 2009), 94.

[6] To learn more about Earth literacy, see: "What is Earth Literacy?" Earth Ethics Institute, accessed February 2019, http://earthethicsinstitute.org.

ation and the evolution of our Universe and Earth told with an infusion of spirituality."[7] It is a way of seeing the presence of God in all things, or as William Penn put it: "to see the Great Creator…in all and every part thereof."[8]

A special edition of the *Quaker Eco-Bulletin* in 2006 highlights how the current worldview that devalues people and creation "is now being challenged by new scientific stories about the emergence of the Universe, the planet Earth, and its life forms, and the processes that have evolved to sustain life. In many ways these scientific stories reflect and support ancient Earth-centered wisdom about the human-Earth relationship now being reclaimed and incorporated into some contemporary spiritual practice."[9] The need for such a reclamation indicates that part of the problem is that we have forgotten we are part of the earth, seeing ourselves as separate with "dominion" over it,[10] and seeing the universe as a "collection of objects," as Berry comments.[11] This divorce of our connectedness, many argue, has left us spiritually bankrupt. Quakers often have a different sensibility, grounded in both our recognition of that of God in every one (for some, "in every living thing," as discussed below) and our embrace of what can be learned from science, as Daniel Seeger, a past director of Pendle Hill, beautifully illuminates in this 2011 *Friends Journal* article:

> Both science and religion rest ultimately on our contemplation of the natural world…. To survey any beautiful scene without distraction is to become aware of an incredible creative process that has raised all things up from the formless dust that infuses everything with vitality and energy, that maintains balance and lawfulness, and that illuminates each order of living things with a degree of wisdom suitable to its estate. We

---

[7] Brad Stocker, "Earth Literacy?" *Befriending Creation* 27 no. 3 (2014): 4–5, http://quakerearthcare.org/bfc/volume-27-number-3.

[8] William Penn, "Some Fruits of Solitude in Reflections and Maxims," in *Franklin's Way to Wealth and Penn's Maxims* (Mineola, NY: Dover Publications, 2006, reprint of 1837 edition), 21.

[9] Keith Helmuth, Judy Lumb, Sandra Lewis, and Barbara Day, "Changing World View and Friends Testimonies," *Quaker Eco-Bulletin* 6, no 4 (July-August 2006), 1, http://quakerearthcare.org/node/133.

[10] The term "dominion" comes from the King James Version translation of Genesis 1:26, and is a much-contested term in ecotheological scholarship. It is interpreted by many Christians to mean that all of creation is put here for human use, and that humans are to rule over creation, and is contrasted with the notion of stewardship. For more on the tensions between the concepts of dominion and stewardship, see: Laurel Kearns, "Cooking The Truth: Faith, The Market, And The Science of Global Warming," in *Eco-Spirit: Religion, Philosophy and the Earth*, eds. Laurel Kearns and Catherine Keller (New York: Fordham University Press, 2007), 97–124.

[11] Swimme and Berry, *The Universe Story*, 243.

become aware that human existence is a part of this great web, we are humbled, and we ask what response is called for from us so that we might play our role properly in this great unfolding drama. Some religionists disparage what they call nature mysticism as a counterfeit spirituality. In truth, it is not a counterfeit spirituality but the foundation, the essence, and the core of the religious sensibility.[12]

Key here is how Seeger grounds this core religious sensibility in an awareness of our participation in the universe, and our understanding that we are one part of a "great web" gained through contemplation of the natural world, and as explored below, this practice goes deep to our Quaker roots. His assertion that religion and science "rest ultimately" in an understanding of the natural world resonates with the contemporary connection between science and religion seen in Berry and Swimme's universe story. But before exploring that further, it is worth briefly tracing the Quaker grounding for such contemplation through the study of science.

Clayton, in his introduction to *Quakers and the New Story*, comments, "Quakers are not known as a particularly scientific folk. During much of our history, Friends have worried that the attitudes and results of the sciences might stand in tension with the inner experiences and ethical testimonies that lie at the center of our tradition."[13] Seeger speaks to counter this worry in his *Friends Journal* article, and in that vein, I offer an examination of key figures in the first 150 years of the Society of Friends in order to demonstrate that there should not be a tension. In fact, the significant engagement of early Friends in the sciences demonstrates the Quaker embrace of science and evolutionary theory. This can aid us in making environmental concern central to our faith and action unhindered by any of the tension Clayton mentions between our inward ethical convictions and the sciences. Further, expanding recognition of the insights of science to include an understanding of the universe story can lead to a more complete religious sensibility in line with what Seeger names: one that expands our Quaker ethic beyond human beings.

---

[12] Daniel A. Seeger, "Why Do the Unbelievers Rage? The New Atheists and the Universality of the Light," *Friends Journal* (January 2011): 6–11. Pendle Hill is a Quaker study center outside of Philadelphia, PA.

[13] Clayton, *Quakers and the New Story*, 6.

II. Historical Roots of Quakers and Science

George Fox, one of the founders of the Society of Friends, sought "unity with the creation,"[14] and Fox's contemporary, Jacob Bauthumley, pronounced that "I see God is in all Creatures...and every green thing."[15] William Penn, the noted seventeenth century Quaker behind the founding of Pennsylvania, expressed a similar interpretation in his admonition to study nature: "It would go a long way to caution and direct people in their use of the world that they were better studied and known in the creation of it. For how could [humanity] find the confidence to abuse it, while they should see the Great Creator stare them in the face, in all and every part thereof?"[16] All of these early Quakers admonished their followers to contemplate the natural world, and to see God there.

These words of Fox and Penn should sound familiar to contemporary Quakers who profess to "see God in all things" or "God in all Creation," and also to Fox's and Penn's contemporaries: this was not an uncommon sentiment among other English dissenters.[17] One of the founders of Methodism, John Wesley, writing roughly a century later (1748), declared "that God is in all things, and that we are to see the Creator in the face of every creature; that we should use and look upon nothing as separate from God, which indeed is a kind of practical atheism."[18] These words might sound heretical to some conservative Protestants (even Methodists) today, who have paid little heed to Wesley's writings on animals and science, but it did not seem heretical to his Methodist and Quaker contemporaries. Indeed, Penn's and Wesley's statements echo the theology of Martin Luther, the well-known Protestant Reformer, who stated: "God is substantially present everywhere, in and through all creatures, in all their parts and places, so that the world is full of God and [God] fills all, but without...being

---

[14] Os Cresson, "QEW: A Nature Walk for All Friends," Quaker Earthcare Witness, accessed February 2019, http://quakerearthcare.org/article/qew-nature-walk-all-friends. This article contains many other instances of such beliefs among Quakers.

[15] Bauthumley later became a Quaker, having visited George Fox during one of his many imprisonments. As quoted in the QEW Nature Walk article (fn 14), where it is referenced from Nigel Smith, *A Collection of Ranter Writings from the 17th Century* (London: Junction Books, 1983), 232.

[16] Penn, "Some Fruits of Solitude in Reflections and Maxims," 21.

[17] For examples of the use of these phrases in more contemporary settings, see: Bill Howenstein, "Loving the Universe," 1992 Jonathan Plummer Lecture, McNab, IL: Illinois Yearly Meeting of the Religious Society of Friends, July 26, 1992, http://quaker.org/legacy/iym/plummer/1992.html.

[18] John Wesley, "Sermon 23: Upon Our Lord's Sermon on the Mount, Discourse III," I.11, http://ccel.org/ccel/wesley/sermons.v.xxiii.html#v.xxiii-p0.3.

encompassed and surrounded by it."[19] All of these Protestant reformers were familiar with the tradition of reading the creation as the first revelation of God to be found in the "Book of Nature."[20] Such an attitude stands in stark contrast to the Utilitarian view of nature as having worth only through its utility to human beings, and indeed, their insights should cause all to contemplate the tension between recognizing God in all things, and environmental destruction and degradation.

This tradition of careful observation of the Book of Nature can be seen in the preponderance of Quaker naturalists and botanists in our history. Both George Fox and William Penn emphasize that Quakers should be "competent botanists" with Fox suggesting that children be taught the "nature of herbs, roots, plants and trees."[21] William Penn admonished, "It were Happy if we studied Nature more in natural Things; and acted according to Nature; whose rules are few, plain and Reasonable."[22] Later, the famed American botanist, William Bartram (1739–1823), known for his detailed observations on his travels through the American South, (Bartram's Trail is named for him) was Quaker.[23] Historian Larry R. Clarke notes that the book *Bartram's Travels* is a "combination of scientific objectivity with a deep appreciation of nature as the bountiful creation of God," noting that this "double approach to nature" was not as present in scientists of the eighteenth century.[24] Rather, it revealed Bartram's underlying Quaker awareness of the immanent presence of God in everything.

---

[19] Martin Luther, "The Sacrament of the Body and Blood of Christ—Against the Fanatics," in *Martin Luther's Basic Theological Writings*, ed. Timothy F. Lull (Minneapolis, MN: Fortress Press, 1989), 224–239.

[20] For the history and frequency of this concept see: Arjo Vanderjagt and Klaus van Berkel, eds., *The Book of Nature in Antiquity and the Middle Ages* (Leuven, Belgium: Peeters Publishers, 2005); and Arjo Vanderjagt and Klaus van Berkel, eds. *The Book of Nature in Early Modern and Modern History* (Leuven, Belgium: Peeters Publishers, 2006).

[21] As quoted in John Brooke and Geoffrey Cantor, *Reconstructing Nature: The Engagement of Science and Religion* (Edinburgh: T & T Clark, 1998), 302.

[22] Penn, "Some Fruits of Solitude in Reflections and Maxims," 20.

[23] Bartram's Garden in Philadelphia was the Bartram estate where William grew up. It is the oldest surviving botanical garden in the US Bartram's Trail, which flows through many of the southern states, is named for him. His father John was also a recognized botanist and Quaker, although he was disfellowshipped by the Darby Meeting for denying Jesus' divinity. For more on Bartram and other American Quakers, see: Ellen M. Ross, "The Solace of History: Reflections on Quakers and the Environment," *Friends Journal*, February 17, 2012, accessed February 2019, http://friendsjournal.org/the-solace-of-history-reflections-on-quakers-and-the-environment/.

[24] Larry R. Clarke, "Quaker Background of William Bartram's View of Nature," *Journal of the History of Ideas* 46, no. 3 (1985): 435–448, at 435. See also Donald Brooks Kelley, "Friends and Nature in America: Toward an Eighteenth-Century Quaker Ecology," *Pennsylvania History: A Journal of Mid-Atlantic Studies* 53, no. 4 (October 1986): 257–272.

Taking heed of such admonitions as Penn's may be one reason that, from the early decades of the Society of Friends, as John Brooke and Geoffrey Cantor point out, Quakers were disproportionately present in the Royal Society of London (whose full name indicated its purpose: Improving Natural Knowledge), a preeminent association of scientists and mathematicians with a royal charter and an exclusive membership.[25] The Royal Society and the Society of Friends were founded about ten years apart in the mid-1600s. The number of Quakers in the Royal Society rose steadily so that by 1900, they made up 35% of the Society's membership. Quakers saw no conflict between their faith and studying science, as they saw science as one avenue to the truth they sought.[26] This was apparent in their embrace of Darwin's writings, a pivotal moment in the dialogue between science and religion in the Christian West, as exemplified in the writing and illustrious career of the Quaker physicist Silvanus Thompson, known for his textbook on calculus (still in print), and his work on electric current.[27] Brooke and Cantor describe an essay Thompson wrote in 1871, roughly a decade after the publication of Darwin's *On the Origin of Species*: "he found nothing upsetting in Darwin's theory since it did not conflict with religion.... He welcomed evolution because, like other scientific theories, it displayed God's design and purpose in the physical world."[28]

For some Protestant groups, and not just historically, Darwin's understanding of evolution is construed as contradicting the biblical passages in Genesis, and thus becomes a basis for their rejection of climate science.[29] However, Quakers have recognized that the Bible is not a science textbook. Rather, Brooke and Cantor point out, the Quaker embrace of science was furthered, like that of many Protestant groups, by their approach to the Bible not as a rigid account and rule book, for which scientific knowledge might prove to be a challenge, but as a source of inspiration for understanding God's presence throughout the cre-

---

[25] Brooke and Cantor, *Reconstructing Nature*, 218-313.

[26] Interestingly, Brooke and Cantor point out that there were very few Quaker physicists and mathematicians in the first hundred-plus years of the Society, although many did research on meteorology and astronomy. This lack of physicists and mathematicians may be due to the fact that for most of the eighteenth century, Cambridge, the primary educational institution for physicists and mathematicians, refused to grant degrees to dissenters. Brooke and Cantor, *Reconstructing Nature*, 302.

[27] Silvanus Thompson, *Calculus Made Easy*, second edition (London: Macmillan and Co., Ltd., 1910, 1914).

[28] Brooke and Cantor, *Reconstructing Nature*, 297.

[29] For more on the tensions between science, economics and the climate denial of some evangelicals, who nevertheless present themselves as "green" evangelicals, see: Kearns, "Cooking The Truth."

ation and across time. Because of their commitment to the individual's responsibility to listen to their own Inner Light and, from that, form their own views and seek to live a life of moral responsibility, any doctrinal emphasis on biblical literalism and creationism had no appeal to earlier Quakers. Thus, most branches of Quakerism have not been haunted by a rejection of evolutionary theory and a select suspicion of science that underpins many Christians' failure to respond to the current ecological crisis of global climate change.[30] Revisiting our earliest beginnings leads to the conclusion that Quakers have seen science as compatible with and complementary to our faith.

III. There is That of God in Every Thing

It is out of the same tradition of studying the Book of Nature that Thomas Berry, in a frequently misunderstood quote, advocated putting the scripture on the shelf for 10–20 years, and studying the universe, so as to understand the Bible in a whole new way.[31] The goal of Berry, Swimme, and so many others in telling the journey of the universe story is to shift us out of a human-centered view of the world, where everything else is of lesser value. Brian Swimme, in the film *Journey of the Universe*, comments that understanding the evolution of the universe means that "we aren't living on the Earth, we are participating in it" because, as Berry frequently notes, the "universe is a communion of subjects" and not "a collection of objects."[32]

This resonates with the statement on the "Quaker Finder" webpage of the Friends General Conference (the organization that represents "unprogrammed" or silent Quakers): "We hold ourselves open to the Light and reach for the divine center of our being. We know the center to be a place of peace, love, and balance, where we are at one with the universe and with each other."[33] It is worth noting that this understanding of Quaker faith and practice is on the

---

[30] Thankfully, it appears there is diminishing adherence to climate denial in the US, but not yet any real diminishment of the powerful economic interests that still hinder any substantive shift in socio-cultural, political, and economic systems to address the anthropogenic sources of climate change. See Anthony Leiserowitz, et al., *Climate Change in the American Mind: December 2018*, Yale University and George Mason University (New Haven, CT: Yale Program on Climate Change Communication, 2018), accessed February 2019, http://climate-communication.yale.edu/publications/climate-change-in-the-american-mind-december-2018/.

[31] Berry was not dismissing the Bible, so much as saying that when one understood the magnificence of the universe and its intricacy and complexity, then all the passages about the Creation jump out at you, passages that many skip over or think little about.

[32] Swimme and Berry, *The Universe Story*, 243.

[33] "Quaker Finder," Friends General Conference, accessed March 6, 2019, http://fgcquaker.org/connect/quaker-finder.

webpage for seekers or those inquiring about the Society of Friends—it is that central. This awareness of the life force of all things that connects us has allowed many Friends to reinterpret the central Quaker tenet (as much as there are tenets in the Society of Friends) that there is "that of God in every one."[34] Recognizing this phrase might be seen as anthropocentric in light of the ways Western worldviews and economic systems have led to environmental degradation, some Friends are beginning to expand (or perhaps, as suggested above, even reclaim an early understanding) this central tenet to "there is that of God in every thing" or "there is that of God in all creation," as illustrated in this quote from the *Quaker Eco-Bulletin*:

> Since Earth itself, and everything on it, is an expression of this essentially unnamable, yet pervasive, fecundity of the Universe, we can understand "that of God" as moving in all forms and creatures. The motion of Creation is in every animal, every plant, every rock, every form and process of Earth. In worship, we seek to find the inner light of the divine, to be open to that of God. [35]

Although the latter insight, as expressed in the statement that there is that of God in every thing, is contested in some circles that insist the traditional understanding is that there is "that of God in every one," it is clear in revisiting the works of early Quakers that this more encompassing expression has deep roots in our history. Thus, the theological affirmation of the divine presence in others, which has always formed the basis of Quaker ethical practice, can also serve as the foundation for a Quaker ecological ethic when we expand the circle of others. Becoming aware of that of God is essentially a recognition of relatedness: we acknowledge a kinship with others and their sacred worth. Therefore, moving toward recognizing "that of God in every thing" is an invitation to enter into right relationship with all the planet's inhabitants, as addressed by the following query: How would we act in the world differently if we took seriously the words of Fox and Penn, and worked to recognize, and respond to, that of God in all things?

Perhaps this larger Quaker vision of ethical responsibility extending beyond humanity is best summed up in a Quaker Earthcare Witness (QEW) statement: "we are called to live in right relationship with all Creation, recognizing

---

[34] George Fox, *The Journal of George Fox,* ed. John L. Nickalls, revised edition (Philadelphia: Religious Society of Friends, 1997), 263.

[35] Helmuth, et al., "Changing World View and Friends Testimonies," 1.

that the entire world is interconnected and is a manifestation of God…that Creation is to be respected, protected, and held in reverence in its own right, and the Truth that human aspirations for peace and justice depend upon restoring the Earth's ecological integrity."[36] This notion of right relationship can be seen in QEW's motto: "Seeking emerging insights into right relationship and unity with nature."[37] It cannot and should not be dismissed as nature mysticism, just as some dismiss Thomas Berry's work as only about ideas. Instead, the insights of both Berry and Quakers insist that such a change in perspective toward a radically relational ethic demands action toward a just, sustainable, and inclusive world.

IV. Quaker Testimonies and the Universe Story

It is not only the long tradition of learning from science as part of our process of discerning "that of God" that motivates Quakers to respond to the ecological crisis. Other aspects of Quaker ecological concern are similarly grounded. Quakers trace their commitment to sustainability to the testimonies of simplicity, right relations (equality), and integrity that have been central themes of Quakerism. These Quaker testimonies are expanded by seeing God in all things.[38] For instance, who/what are we to be in right relationship with? Or, how does the testimony to integrity change if we expand where we recognize the presence of God? Such an awareness can lead us to question the integrity of our business and economic practices that lead to environmental degradation and environmental injustice. These expanded testimonies thus provide a religious cosmology similar to that advocated by Berry as a result of understanding the story of the universe: one that locates "the human in the larger contexts of the universe and Earth processes that provide a deep framework for valuing nature."[39]

Historically, the testimony to simplicity meant plainness in dress, speech, buildings, and lifestyle. Plainness, as one aspect of simplicity, was seen as a tool of personal discipline and spiritual practice to cultivate an inner connection to the Light of Christ, of God, of the sacred in one's heart, and as a path of personal virtue to avoid the distractions of worldly things and the accumulation of wealth. Thus, there has been an anti-consumption, anti-consumerism orientation built in from the beginning. George Fox argued that the accumulation of wealth contributed to war and was a form of violence. Instead, he advocated the

---

[36] See Appendix D, Quaker Earthcare Witness Vision and Mission.

[37] See Quaker Earthcare Witness, http://quakerearthcare.org.

[38] For examples of this phrase see Howenstein, "Loving the Universe."

[39] John Grim and Mary Evelyn Tucker, *Ecology and Religion* (Washington, DC: Island Press, 2014), 154.

right sharing of economic resources in the interest of social justice. The commitment to simplicity not only allows the individual to be less distracted and therefore closer to God, but also to sense the presence of God in nature. For more contemporary Friends, simplicity is valued as an approach to a sustainable lifestyle that is more connected to nature and economic justice and less focused on consumption. This environmental side of the simplicity testimony reaches across the Quaker world, connecting theologically liberal and evangelical organizations of Friends.

A key organization of Friends' work on sustainability, Quaker Earthcare Witness (QEW), points out that the current concepts of balance and sustainability are already present in the Quaker understanding of equality. The concept of right relationship requires seeing others as valuable and worthy, and this can be traced back to John Woolman (1720–1772). If humanity is not in right relationship with the more-than-human natural world, then the Quaker dedication to a world without war and with just social relations cannot be achieved.[40]

In a special 2006 edition of the *Quaker Eco-Bulletin* devoted to "changing worldview and Quaker testimonies," the authors, after laying out the story of the evolution of the universe, go on to discuss the "cultural evolution" and the "economics and the new consciousness" before explicitly connecting it with the guiding "testimonies" of Quaker life: simplicity, peace, integrity, equality, community.[41] Since this special edition explicitly makes the connection between Quaker values and the insights of the story of the universe, I will quote in its entirety the section concerning Quaker testimonies and the suggested ecological interpretation (in italics) of each testimony as a result of the needed "changed worldview."

Simplicity—Functional approach to the arrangements of life and work; non-acquisitive; frugal; unadorned; spiritually centered; attentive to direct experiences and relationships.

Subsidiarity—*Direct decision making at the most immediate level of participation on matters of local and regional concern; anchoring life and livelihood in local and regional communities; production, use, and recycling of goods and services within local and regional economies.*

---

[40] See chapter 18 of this volume, Shelley Tanenbaum, "Earthcare as a Quaker Value: The Formation and Continued Work of Quaker Earthcare Witness." For more on the Quaker notion of right relationship as an expansion of an understanding of sustainability, see: "Living in Right Relationship," Quaker Earthcare Witness, accessed February 2019, http://quakerearthcare.org/article/living-right-relationship.

[41] Helmuth, et al., "Changing World View and Friends Testimonies," 4.

Peace—Nonviolent living; conflict prevention; conflict resolution; relationship building; reduction and elimination of the causes of conflict, violence and war.

Human-Earth Relationship—*Ways of life and means of livelihood that do not violate ecosystem resilience and integrity, or depend on violent and exploitative control of resources; mutually enhancing human-Earth relationship within a context of right sharing of resources.*

Equality—Recognition and practice of dignity and respect; human solidarity; equitable access to the means of life and life development resources.

Ecological Footprint—*Shared life space and life development resources; habitat preservation; biodiversity preservation; cultural preservation.*

Integrity—Truthfulness; ethical consistency; devotion to right relationship; valuing direct experience and accurate information.

Ecological Adaptation—*Ways of life and means of livelihood that are congruent with the resilience and functional integrity of the biotic environment; active enhancement of ecosystem resilience and integrity.*

Community—Mutual support relationships; cooperative reciprocity; sharing of spiritual and physical commons; ceremonial representation of social life.

Social Ecology—*Mutually enhancing human-Earth relationship; fully responsive to environmental processes; mindful participation in the dynamics of interdependence and ecosystem reciprocity.*

Service—Life and work orientation around contribution to human betterment; e.g., human service work, education, provision of useful goods and services, public policy and civic engagement, social justice, economic security.

Stewardship—*Life and work orientation around contribution to mutually enhancing human-Earth relationship; e.g., ecosystem restoration; energy use conserva-*

tion; transition from nonrenewable to renewable energy and materials; local production for local use; green building; environmental education; ecological footprint reduction; overall ecologically sound economic adaptation.[42]

For those who know Berry's work,[43] this Quaker vision of the fleshing out of what it means to be human in relation to the universe mirrors Thomas Berry's *The Great Work* to "give shape and meaning to life by relating the human venture to the larger destinies of the universe."[44] This involves rethinking our systems of economics, politics, religion, education, agriculture, and so forth that were all predicated on the human being as separate from the larger dynamic biosystems. The individualism and utilitarianism in our Western culture's relations and systems belie the need to recognize our interdependence and mutual thriving.

As rooted in Quaker history, the conviction that there is that of God in everything opens us, like Berry and Swimme's universe story, to understanding the cosmos as a source of divine revelation. In recognizing God throughout the creation, we find a greater vitality and sense of connection. Berry suggests, "we are most ourselves when we are the most intimate with the rivers and mountains and woodlands…with the air we breathe, the Earth that supports us, the soil that grows our food."[45] As Quakers recognize, there is much in global economic and socio-cultural unjust relations that keep us from that sense of connection; indeed, these unjust relations lead to the current ecological crisis as we watch the "un-creation" of healthy planetary systems.

In Berry and Swimme's presentation of the universe story, Quakers can find their mystical insights, their testimonies and principles of living, and their centuries long commitment to understanding the world through science united in a vision for the twenty-first century. It is a new understanding of being in right relation that resonates with Berry's view of the universe as "a communion of subjects."[46] *Journey of the Universe*, in its rich portrayal in text and film, is a new vision, a new understanding of what it means to be human, to be a creature of the universe, although as has been detailed here, it is not a completely new story for us as Friends. As *Journey of the Universe* aptly states: "every time we are drawn

---

[12] Helmuth, et al., "Changing World View and Friends Testimonies," 4.

[43] Indeed, *The Great Work* and Berry and Swimme's *The Universe Story* are all sources recommended in this *Quaker Eco-Bulletin* special edition.

[44] Thomas Berry, *The Great Work: Our Way into the Future* (New York: Random House, 1999), 1.

[45] Berry, *The Sacred Universe*, 95.

[46] Swimme and Berry, *The Universe Story*, 243.

to look up into the night sky and reflect on the awesome beauty of the universe, we are actually the universe reflecting on itself. And this changes everything."[47]

Quakers—throughout the centuries—have worked to change socio-cultural and economic systems that degrade others. As we now work to change how those systems interconnect with the disruption of the very planetary systems upon which we depend for life, we can draw upon the same source of inspiration as throughout our history: recognizing that of God in all things.

---

[47] Swimme and Tucker, *Journey of the Universe*, 2.

Part II: Developing a Quaker Ecotheology – Discussion Questions

1. **Chapter 5. Quakers & Creation Care: Potentials and Pitfalls for an Ecotheology of Friends, by Cherice Bock**

    1. What "pitfalls" to developing a Quaker ecotheology does Bock outline? In what ways do these ideas and practices pose a problem for the development of an ecotheology? Do you agree or disagree with this assessment, and why?

    2. Reflecting on the "potentials" to building an ecotheology of Friends, which of these areas do you find most energizing or fruitful as you think about your own understanding of addressing environmental concerns?

2. **Chapter 6. "The Divine Light of Creation": Liberal Quaker Metaphors of Divine/Creation Interdependence, by Christy Randazzo**

    1. In what ways does Randazzo describe the connection between the Quaker concept of the Light, divine/creation interdependence, and environmental concerns? How might these ideas help Quakers develop an ecotheology?

    2. What are some examples from your own experience of the Light that show how this concept may affect human action relating to the environmental crisis?

3. **Chapter 7. Woolman and Wilderness: A Quaker Sacramental Ecology, by Jon R. Kershner**

    1. How does Woolman's phenomenological view on the environment relate to your own experiences with nature? Why is this perception that emphasizes intersubjective experience important to distinguish from the many other environmental worldviews when approaching Quaker ecotheology?

    2. How did Woolman's negative experiences with the harsh realities of nature influence his understanding of the connection between God and

the environment? Based on Kershner's descriptions of other interpretations of the natural world, how might other colonists at the time have responded to the same experiences Woolman endured on his trek through the wilderness?

4. **Chapter 8. Maragoli Shamanism Marries Quaker Christianity, by S. Chagala Ngesa**

   1. What can the culture of the Maragoli people teach the rest of the world about the environment, God, and indigenous traditions? How could this wisdom shape or affect Quaker ecotheology?

   2. How does the theme of ancestry influence Maragoli attitudes towards nature? What can the Friends and others learn from this, and how does it relate to how we treat other parts of the natural world?

   3. On its surface, Christianity does not incorporate this understanding of ancestors, though some groups include important roles for saints, relics, and holy sites. Can you imagine reverence for human and nonhuman ancestors fitting into a Christian and/or Quaker framework? Why or why not?

   4. Do you think climate change and other environmental crises can be God-given opportunities for humanity to pull together as a global community? Why or why not?

5. **Chapter 9. Process Metaphysics for Ecological Survival: Alfred North Whitehead in Conversation with Friends, by Lonnie Valentine**

   1. What are some events or trends that could be interpreted as divine leadings to steer away from ecological destruction and toward a more sustainable potentiality or *telos*? In what ways have you (or we) accepted or denied these leadings as individuals, as the Society of Friends, and as a global human culture?

   2. In a time when many human beings are highly dependent on modern technology that indirectly reinforces a dualistic worldview, in what ways does Valentine suggest process thought can help Friends and others incorporate the human-Earth relationship in our worship and other practices? Do you agree? Why or why not?

6. **Chapter 10. Quaker Ecological Foundations and the Universe Story, by Laurel Kearns**

    1. How, according to your own experience and Kearns's insight, can science aid in moving humanity closer to a state of right relationship with the rest of the natural world? Is science an inherently positive force?

    2. What does Thomas Berry's universe story have in common with other universe narratives and creation stories? How is it different? What can these stories teach about science, culture, and theology, and how does this relate to the construction of an ecotheology in the Quaker community?

7. **Part II General Questions**

    1. What are some of the themes for building a Quaker ecotheology that you see emerging across these essays?

    2. After reading these essays, what does Quaker theology and practice have to offer the broader conversation about ecotheology? What can Quakers learn from other branches of theology and other environmental fields that may help Friends build a more complete ecotheology?

PART III

Quaker Approaches to the Environment in the Academic Disciplines

11 | A Quaker Educator in Dialogue with Teilhard on the Universe Story

By Stephen Potthoff

Abstract: As is evident from George Fox's life-changing visionary return to the Garden of Eden, the biblical accounts of creation were of primary importance to early Friends. As a mystic, George Fox accessed the original reality of Eden, experiencing the universe as a new creation while simultaneously retelling the Eden story. Similarly, the French Jesuit paleontologist Teilhard de Chardin experienced a deeply mystical connection to the natural world, a connection that informed in profound ways his synthesis of Christian theology and eschatology with the evolutionary story of life on planet Earth.

In this essay, I engage in dialogue with George Fox and Teilhard in reflecting on what a new Quaker universe story might encompass, drawing on my own experience not merely with nature mysticism, but also as an educator who regularly tells and retells the universe story in the classroom and workshop settings in a hands-on fashion using a collection of fossils to narrate the story of life on this beautiful planet we inhabit. As revolutionary as Teilhard's synthesis was at the time, what new insights from paleontology, biology, astronomy, cosmology and quantum physics might now need to be included in this generation's telling of the universe story? How do/ might contemporary Friends connect with the universe and living world through mystical awareness as well as in more direct, physical relationship with the natural world?

As a Quaker educator, nature mystic, and student of earth science and evolution, I have long been drawn to the writings and insights of French Jesuit paleontologist Pierre Teilhard de Chardin (1881–1955). Had I spent my boyhood, like Teilhard, in the beautiful volcanic landscape of Clermont Ferrand, we might very well have become fast friends, both drawn to rocks as an expression of what is "permanent, enduring, eternal" in the universe.[1] Like Teilhard, I was also fascinated from a very young age with the evolution of life and human beings on this extraordinary planet, Earth. Reading some of Teilhard's account of his experience working as a paleontologist in England, I recognize a fellow nature mystic who senses the Divine Presence in the natural world all around him. Teilhard could be describing my own experience discovering Ordovician marine fossils in the Ohio shales and limestones when he reflects on:

> the extraordinary solidity and intensity I found then in the English countryside, particularly at sunset, when the Sussex woods were charged with all that "fossil" Life which I was then hunting for, from cliff to quarry.... There were moments, indeed, when it seemed to me that a sort of universal being was about to take shape suddenly in Nature before my very eyes.[2]

As I explore next, such a mystical sense of the Divine Presence in nature also found expression in the visionary experiences of George Fox.

I. George Fox's Mystical Encounter with the Incarnate Word

Early in my childhood, I was introduced to George Fox (1624–1691), founder of the Quaker tradition, and his visionary openings, which revealed to him God's presence and work in the natural world. At the beginning of his *Journal*, Fox recounts that God instructed him as an eleven-year-old boy how to live faithfully, avoiding excess and wantonness in word and deed. For Fox, to live faithfully is to live in harmony and unity with creation in the context of covenantal relationships in which all creatures fulfill their divine purpose and role. At the foundation of all existence, the Word (Jn 1) upholds, sanctifies, and unifies all of creation:

> For the Lord showed me that though the people of the world have mouths full of deceit and changeable words, yet I was to keep to 'yea' and 'nay' in all things, and that my words should be few and savoury, seasoned with grace; and that I might not eat and drink to make myself wanton but for health, using the creatures in their service, as servants in their places, to the glory of him that hath created them; they being in

---

[1] Kathleen Duffy, *Teilhard's Mysticism: Seeing the Inner Face of Evolution* (New York: Orbis Books, 2014), 10.

[2] Pierre Teilhard de Chardin, *Human Phenomenon* (Portland: Sussex Academy Press, 1999), 25–26.

their covenant, and I being brought up into the covenant, as sanctified by the Word which was in the beginning, by which all things are upheld; wherein is unity with the creation.[3]

As a young man of 24 in 1648, Fox undergoes a transformative visionary experience in which he journeys back through the gates of Eden, guarded by cherubim and a flaming sword (Gen 3:24), into the original garden of paradise before the Fall of Adam and Eve. In this state, he beholds the unity, purity, harmony, and beauty of the original creation underlying this world, held together by the Word, illuminated by the Light of Christ, and open to all Christ's faithful followers:

> Now was I come up in spirit through the flaming sword into the paradise of God. All things were new, and all the creation gave another smell unto me than before, beyond what words can utter. I knew nothing but pureness, and innocency, and righteousness, being renewed up into the image of God by Christ Jesus, so that I say I was come up to the state of Adam which he was in before he fell. The creation was opened to me, and it was showed me how all things had their names given them according to their nature and virtue…. But I was immediately taken up in spirit, to see into another or more steadfast state than Adam's innocency, even into a state in Christ Jesus, that should never fall. And the Lord showed me that such as were faithful to him in the power and light of Christ, should come up into that state in which Adam was before he fell, in which the admirable works of the creation, and the virtues thereof, may be known, through the openings of that divine Word of wisdom and power by which they were made. Great things did the Lord lead me into, and wonderful depths were opened unto me, beyond what by words can be declared; but as people come into subjection to the spirit of God, and grow up in the image and power of the Almighty, they may receive the Word of wisdom, that opens all things, and come to know the hidden unity in the Eternal Being.[4]

As Mel Keiser observes, Fox's visionary return to paradise is catalyzed by his experience the year before of Christ—God's Divine Word and Wisdom, the Inner Light—dwelling within him, which reveals and illuminates the present world

---

[3] George Fox, *The Journal of George Fox,* ed. John L. Nickalls (London: Religious Society of Friends, 1986), 2.

[4] Fox, *Journal,* 27–28.

simultaneously as the original Eden and the New Creation.[5] As Rebecca Artinian-Kaiser and Cherice Bock note, in emphasizing the Logos, the Divine Word of wisdom that all may receive, "Fox draws upon an ancient tradition of wisdom found throughout the Scriptures, which he develops in a Quaker key."[6] The Gospel of John's description of Jesus as the Logos incarnate draws in part on the Hellenistic Greek philosophical concept of the Logos derived from Plato's concept of the World Soul, which Plato defined as the "intelligent and harmonious principle of proportion or relatedness that exists at the heart of the cosmic pattern and allows all things to unfold in the best possible way."[7] Drawing equally on the biblical wisdom tradition exemplified in Proverbs 23, John's Logos Hymn celebrates the Divine Word, by which God not only creates the universe, but also orders, sustains, and holds it together in all its beauty and complexity. As described in key biblical passages embraced by both Fox and Teilhard, through the Word/Christ, "All things came into being," and "in him all things hold together" (Jn 1:3; Col 1:16-17).[8] Fox thus understood himself to live in a "covenant of light" encompassing all human beings and the entire creation. As Douglas Gwyn summarizes:

> The light is a covenant in that it is God's unconditional, loving presence with us, always ready to lead, always ready to forgive and begin again. The covenant of light is the presence of Christ, the Word who created and upholds all things.... As one turns to the light, attends to it and learns to live according to its leading, one lives into the covenant.... The Word that created all things is a light in each person that guides into unity with the creation.[9]

II. Teilhard and Logos-Sophia as Source of Love and Union

Like George Fox, Teilhard perceived and delighted in the radiance and "hidden unity in the Eternal Being" he experienced and sensed in the natural world all

---

[5] Melvin R. Keiser, *Inward Light and the New Creation* (Philadelphia: Pendle Hill Publications, 1991), 7-8.

[6] See chapter 1 of this volume, Rebecca Artinian-Kaiser and Cherice Bock, "'Do What You Do in the Wisdom of God': Theological Resources for Quaker Ecological Action in the Writings of George Fox," 5.

[7] David Fideler, *Restoring the Soul of the World: Our Living Bond with Nature's Intelligence* (Rochester: Inner Traditions, 2014), 47, 57.

[8] Douglas Gwyn, *A Sustainable Life: Quaker Faith and Practice in the Renewal of Creation* (Philadelphia: FGC Quaker Press, 2014), xvi; Duffy, *Teilhard's Mysticism*, 12.

[9] Gwyn, *A Sustainable Life*, xvi-xvii.

around him. In the sunlit meadow, the cloud-shrouded mountains, the fossil bra-chiopod, Teilhard perceived a Divine Light "gleaming at the heart of matter," such that all of nature was "bathed in an inward light."[10] With deep intensity and intimacy, both men entered into union with the Original/New Creation through all their senses. Fox remarks of his Eden vision that "all creation gave another smell unto me than before," while Teilhard saw, tasted, heard and smelled the Divine Light, music, and fragrance in nature. Like all mystics, though, Teilhard struggled to articulate his experiences, often turning to music instead as a more complete expression of the union, harmony and beauty he perceived with the eyes of the spirit.[11]

Like George Fox, Teilhard thus came to identify this Divine Presence at the heart of matter and of ongoing creation as Christ, the Divine Word (Logos) celebrated at the beginning of the Gospel of John as incarnate in the person of Jesus. John's Logos is equivalent to *hokmah*, or divine wisdom, personified in Proverbs 23 as a woman (Sophia in Greek). Like the Logos in John 1, Sophia is present with God before creation, and it is with and through her that God creates the entire cosmos. Teilhard comes to see Sophia as central to the original and ongoing creation of the universe, for it is through the infinite and radiant power of her love that the entire universe is woven together in a single unified whole. As Kathleen Duffy eloquently summarizes: "She is the raiment who is forming as she is being formed, continually creating the mystical milieu in which the forces of love encourage all things to become one."[12] Teilhard experienced So-phia's presence also in human gentleness and compassion, like the Word in George Fox's experience that dwells within and guides people into union with the entire cosmos. Teilhard's mysticism reaches its ultimate synthesis in his real-ization that Sophia is also the Universal, Cosmic Christ dwelling at the heart of matter, guiding and inspiring humanity ever forward into ultimate union with God and the entire created order.[13] For George Fox and for Teilhard, then, the cosmos was alive, filled with the spirit of God, and held together in Divine Wis-dom and Love.

---

[10] Pierre Teilhard de Chardin, *Journal*, (Paris: Fayard, 1975), 13, and Pierre Teilhard de Chardin, *Divine Milieu* (Paris: Editions du Seuil, 1957), 130.

[11] Duffy, *Teilhard's Mysticism*, 28–31, 34.

[12] Duffy, *Teilhard's Mysticism*, 111.

[13] Duffy, *Teilhard's Mysticism*, 113–114.

III. Creating Space for Mystical Encounter in the Quaker Classroom

As a Quaker educator, I strive to facilitate in my students some small semblance of the transformed, expanded vision Teilhard and Fox describe, which allowed them to perceive this Divine Light at the center of the cosmos and of every human being. In my global course on indigenous religions, we watch the movie *Avatar,* and read African Dagara shaman Malidoma Somé's experience of being initiated back into his native village culture, a process of education whose first component is "enlargement of one's ability to see" so that one learns "to be a part of nature and to participate in a wider understanding of reality."[14] In a pivotal episode of his initiation, Malidoma, after much effort and resistance, encounters a radiant spirit of pure, divine love in the yila tree before him.[15] In my comparative religion class, we read of a similar expansion of vision in the Great Vision of Lakota shaman Black Elk, who journeys skyward and receives the power of life and healing from the Six Grandfathers of his people. In my first year seminar, I accompany students to Lytle Creek on the edge of campus, encouraging them to explore this local ecosystem through all their senses, while also telling them the story of the death and resurrection of this stream after chemical runoff from the nearby airpark killed all life in the creek in the late 1990s. In my dreams and world mythology class, as well as in my work with student dreams on tropical ecology field expeditions, I join students in exploring through personal dream and visionary experience our connection with the deeper spiritual dimension of the natural world.

My commitment to fostering in my students a sense of familiarity and intimacy with the natural world and living cosmos has emerged as a response to the life and work of ecotheologian Thomas Berry, a native of Greensboro, North Carolina, my home town, and disciple of Teilhard. In his book, *The Great Work,* which has been a required text in my values and ethics class, Berry critiques the modern university because it "prepares students for their role in extending human dominion over the natural world, not for intimate presence to the natural world."[16] Cultivating such intimate presence to the natural world involves recognizing that the entire universe has "a psychic-spiritual as well as a physical-material aspect from the beginning."[17] This psychic-spiritual aspect—the workings of

---

[14] Malidoma P. Somé, *Of Water and the Spirit: Ritual, Magic, and Initiation in the Life of an African Shaman* (New York: Tarcher/Putnam, 1994), 226.

[15] Somé, *Water and the Spirit,* 221.

[16] Thomas Berry, *The Great Work: Our Way Into the Future,* (New York: Bell Tower, 1999), 73.

[17] Berry, *The Great Work,* 81.

the Logos or World Soul, in other words—is exemplified in the miraculous ability of an acorn to grow into an oak tree:

> While no sense faculty can experience it directly and no equation can be written to express it, our immediate perception tells us that there is a unifying principle in the acorn that enables the complex components of the genetic coding of the oak tree to function as a unity—send down roots, raise the trunk, extend the branches and put forth leaves and fashion its seeds, then to nourish all this by drawing up tons of water and minerals from the Earth and distributing them throughout the life system. That such a vast complexity of functioning should have some unifying principle, known traditionally as the "soul" of the organism, is immediately evident to human intelligence.[18]

To foster awareness of and participation in this spiritual dimension of unity and interconnection of the Earth and living cosmos, Berry concludes that students must study and learn the universe story—the narrative of the origin of the universe in the primal flaring forth of the Big Bang on through the present moment as we witness the terminal phase of the Cenozoic era and the beginning of the Ecozoic era.[19] It is only through such intimate presence to the universe that students can come to understand that the universe is not merely "a collection of objects," but rather a "communion of subjects."[20]

It is in the environmental ethics unit of my values and ethics class that I strive to foster some sense of awe, wonder, curiosity, and most importantly union with the natural world through a hands-on telling of the universe story, focusing on some of the highlights in the evolution of life on planet Earth. The more students can actually participate in the interconnected unity and the cosmogenesis—ongoing creative process—that characterizes the universe, the more they are able to experience their own role in this extraordinary story. I begin with awe-inspiring photos from the Hubble space telescope to give some sense of the vastness of the known universe after its birth in the Big Bang from a point of infinite potential 13.7 billion years ago. Panning in on our Milky Way galaxy and solar system, I recount the birth of our present sun and orbiting planets out of the supernova death of a previous, parent star. Out of this massive explosion come elements such as calcium, carbon, iron, and oxygen, essential for the emergence of all life on planet Earth—we are literally made of stardust, the dust of

---

18 Berry, *The Great Work,* 79.
19 Berry, *The Great Work,* 85.
20 Berry, *The Great Work,* 16.

the earth out of which God, according to the Genesis 2 creation story, fashions Adam, the first human being.[21]

The first stone I hand around to students is a nickel-iron meteorite 4.5 billion years old, which dates to the birth of our solar system. Iron not only forms (along with nickel) the molten core of our planet, generating the magnetic field which protects us from the Sun's radiation, but also courses through our veins, turning bright red when our blood encounters the oxygen in the air we breathe. This same red, iron-oxide color characterizes the first, and oldest, fossil I pass around to the class, a two billion year old silicified stromatolite from Minnesota. The photosynthetic bacteria that created these ancient mat-like stromatolite structures in Earth's primordial seas still exist today, and were responsible for filling our planet's early atmosphere with the oxygen necessary for so much of life on the planet in coming eons.

Passing around examples of 450 million-year-old Ordovician marine fossils—brachiopods, horn corals, trilobites, crinoids—from the nearby Caesar Creek spillway brings the focus down on the local area here in southwest Ohio, though this area existed as a shallow tropical sea just south of the equator in Ordovician times. As students hold these ancient sea creatures in their hands, I invite them to reflect on how their own bodies are supported by bones consisting of calcium carbonate, the same mineral these early marine creatures learned to synthesize from seawater in constructing their exoskeletons. Together, we remember, every time a baby is born, or a tear shed, our birth in the oceans, whose salt water we still carry in our bodies to this day.

Carboniferous plant fossils from the nearby Appalachian coal deposits, and more recent fossil leaves from the Paleocene-Eocene Thermal Maximum 55 million years ago, allow me to discuss the carbon cycle, fossil fuels, the green-house effect, and how human beings fit into this picture. Drawing a tree on the board with the Sun shining in the background, I invite biology and agriculture students to describe what happens in the miraculous process of photosynthesis, whereby plants capture carbon from atmospheric carbon dioxide and use it to construct their bodies, emitting the oxygen we need to breathe. We then discuss how the burning of wood, coal, oil, and other fossil fuels releases CO_2 back into the atmosphere, which causes global warming. Passing around the 55 million-year-old leaf fossil provides an example of significant global warming in the past due to a natural build-up of carbon dioxide in the atmosphere. Paleobotanical

---

[21] *Adamah*, the Hebrew word for the humus out of which God creates the first person, sounds strikingly similar to the original person's name, Adam.

studies of insect predation patterns on leaves from the Paleocene-Eocene Thermal Maximum strongly suggest population increases and northward movement of leaf-eating insects from more tropical latitudes during this period.

This very brief, hands-on telling of the universe story serves as an entrée into reading David Suzuki's wonderful book, *The Sacred Balance: Rediscovering Our Place in Nature*, which draws extensively on indigenous wisdom and religious traditions from around the world.[22] Suzuki's book, though more scientific in its focus than Berry, expands upon, solidifies, and deepens the overarching, experiential lessons of union and interconnectedness with all life I introduce in my telling of the universe story. *The Sacred Balance* serves as a perfect companion volume to Louise Diamond's *The Courage for Peace*, which we read as part of our preceding unit on peacebuilding in the values and ethics class. Diamond builds her book around certain basic lessons, which in various ways also lie at the heart of Suzuki's book. Briefly, Diamond teaches that we are all part of one larger, interconnected whole held together through love, and out of that divinity and wholeness we can act as peacebuilders in every moment.[23] As a culminating service learning project for the class, students participate in our Grow Food, Grow Hope community garden, which not only fosters participation in the miraculous cycles of life that sustain us, but also supports work for social justice in our local community by teaching and providing space for low-income families to grow their own food.

IV. Conclusion

Connecting the wider universe story to more familiar stories of creation in the biblical Book of Genesis encourages students to consider that the biblical and scientific accounts of origin intersect with one another in some remarkable ways and need not be in conflict with one another.[24] Holding and beholding a silicified stromatolite or fossil brachiopod helps students experience in a concrete, physical fashion their interconnection with and ultimate dependence on these ancient ancestral (and contemporary) life forms. As Laurel Kearns points out in this volume, the universe story and the nature mysticism underlying it not only are in alignment with the fundamental Quaker witness to that of God in every person

---

[22] David Suzuki, *The Sacred Balance: Rediscovering Our Place in Nature* (Toronto: Greystone Books, 2007).

[23] Louise Diamond, *The Courage for Peace: Daring to Create Harmony in Ourselves and the World* (Berkeley: Conari Press, 2002), 21, 67, 126, 189.

[24] Berry, *The Great Work*, 83.

and even all of creation, but also necessarily evoke "an ethical response" by enabling us "to focus on the local, the particular, as worthy of care and action."[25]

In my values and ethics course, as well as in many of my other classes, then, I invite students to reflect upon, and perhaps also to experience, the Divine Light George Fox and Teilhard de Chardin saw gleaming at the heart of the natural world. It is my hope that they might learn to revel in and celebrate our union and interconnectedness with one another and the natural world, thus entering into the covenant of light which George Fox and many other mystics embrace, in the service of building a more harmonious relationship with the living universe that births and sustains us all.

---

[25] See chapter 10 of this volume, Laurel Kearns, "Quaker Ecological Foundations and the Universe Story."

12 | Reclaiming Natural History: Quakers, Nature, and Education

By James W. Hood

Abstract: This article describes and explores the meanings of a course I have been teaching at Guilford College for five years. The course, entitled "Animal Stories of the Cape Fear River Basin," focuses on natural history accounts of central North Carolina from the late seventeenth century to the present. While the course fulfills a general education writing requirement, and is therefore necessarily concerned with helping students develop their research-based argumentative writing skills, the course content provides an opportunity to rethink how we might teach our students about the natural world from a non-specialist perspective.

The article also traces some of the history of Quaker engagement with natural history, discussing the work of eighteenth- and nineteenth-century naturalists like John and William Bartram and describing how Friends publications in the nineteenth century promoted the value of natural history education. Inspired by this long-standing Quaker interest in teaching about the natural world, I discuss how my own course seeks to recover some key pedagogical territory for general study of natural history.

In a world where students increasingly interact with things coming at them through screens—removed from direct sensory engagement with the tangible world—it is critical to introduce students to other creatures that inhabit, however invisibly to most of us, the ecosystems our incredible human success as a species has systematically destroyed.

I. Morning in the Woods

The air temperature is 30 degrees Fahrenheit as I walk down the hill from my office toward the Guilford College lake and the entrance to the two hundred acres of woods that are part of the campus. I'm meeting a group of students there, my 8:30 a.m. section of a research-based argumentative writing course I've been teaching for the last five years at this Quaker liberal arts college in North Carolina. I worry that it might be colder than I bargained for, though I told them to dress appropriately and I'm snug in my wool upper layers and insulating long johns. The sun is rising, the air is clear, and my weather app tells me we're headed for 45 degrees soon.

We gather at the yellow metal swinging gate that marks the start of the main trail down a short hill into the woods, a mix of mature oaks, beech, hickory, and tulip poplar in large stands, then Virginia and shortleaf pine mixed with smaller hardwoods (like the hillside up to our right as we walk down the gravel path). Sweet gum, sycamore, ash, and walnut populate the lower areas along the small stream that empties the lake we've left behind, beginning as a pipe disgorging water below the lake's twenty-foot earthen dam. The lake was created in 1952 to provide recreation for students, but for many years now swimming and boating have been forbidden there. Enough stories survive about detritus lining the lake's mucky bottom, strange chemicals that might flow in from the small watershed that feeds the lake (which includes run-off from nearby streets, homes, and parking lots), and prehistoric-size snapping turtles that the students don't bother to break that particular prohibition. Who needs an old swimming hole anyway when Netflix beckons?

Our destination is a swath of stream a few hundred yards on, part of the lake outflow's confluence with another small rivulet that collects rain and uprising ground water over another portion of the forest. We pass the point where these two courses join and snug their way together through a culvert under our trail. The students are mostly quiet, complaining a bit about the cold. I seek whatever sunlight is passing through this early April's as-yet-leafless trees.

We veer off to the left, away from a boggy part of the woods, cross over a small mound, and gather streamside. I unload my backpack on the bank stones: four white dishpans; a pH test kit; a Ziploc bag of small, plastic Petri dishes, droppers, and two small hand lenses; two laminated sheets with pictures and descriptions for identifying macroinvertebrates; a waterproof thermometer; a dip net. An inch-and-a-half diameter, clear plastic tube, marked with one-inch increments and closed at one end with a glued-on plastic cap, rounds out the cache of supplies. We will fill the tube with stream water, tipping out bits until we can see the black-and-white triangle pattern through the water at the closed-off end, an easy—if somewhat less-than-perfect—way of gauging turbidity, the amount of sediment suspended in the water.

I make some assignments, directing one student to measure the turbidity, another to check air and water temperature. Another pair measure the water's pH by adding ten drops of reagent to each of two small vials of water filled to the marked level, shaking the vials, then figuring the pH by holding the now-greenish water in the vials up to the sunlight next to a color chart. Another student takes out her phone, touches the screen a few times, and calls out the GPS coordinates to the student scribe, the one who will record all the collected data on a form provided to us by the Haw River Assembly, the grassroots organization that's been working to protect the Haw River (into which this unnamed stream eventually flows) since 1982, by which time textile mill pollution had made it one of the nation's dirtiest rivers.

Most of the students fan out up- and downstream. Their assignment: find a riffle where the water is flowing well, turn over rocks, and collect any and all macroinvertebrates they find on the undersides, placing these insects gently in one of the white dishpans (filled now with a little stream water) for us to count after our collecting period concludes. Other students take the flat-ended dip net and work the stream's bottom, jigging the net upstream for two or three yards in a riffle, emptying it carefully of leaves and stones, picking out whatever larvae, snails, or crustaceans have found their way in, and placing these in the white dishpans as well. The fingerling fish that get netted go back into the stream immediately. We're glad to see them, but we're not counting vertebrates today.

A student squeals; all heads turn in the direction of the sound. "It's a huge one," the student shouts, and I amble over to find a three-inch crayfish in the net. We gingerly extract this small "lobster" and place it in one of the dishpans, picking it up carefully at the point where the tail joins the main part of its body to avoid being pinched by the wildly articulating claws. We will count crayfish, small and large, in our tally.

Another student has found a dusky salamander, a common inhabitant of Piedmont North Carolina seeps and streams. It's another vertebrate, but we hold it temporarily in another dishpan so that everyone will have a chance to see it. The mayfly and caddisfly larvae are washed by students off the undersides of the stream rocks into the white containers. A cranefly larva undulates horrifically in one dishpan, looking like a creature only Hollywood could conjure.

I call everyone back to the central starting point where we can line up the white tubs and count out the critters in different categories: pollution sensitive, semi-pollution sensitive, pollution tolerant. We're pleased to find a number of caddisfly, mayfly, and water pennies (tiny beetle larvae that look like miniscule limpets and eat algae on a rock's surface). They are all pollution sensitive. The crayfish tolerate lower water quality, but they are still indicators that the water isn't wretched. We input the data on the tally sheet, conclude the water quality rating is "good," and walk back up the hill, happy that the day has warmed already, even if the water (at 42 degrees) felt like glacial melt.

II. Whiteboards and PowerPoints

This stream monitoring activity constitutes the community-engaged learning portion of the writing course I teach entitled "Animal Stories of the Cape Fear River Basin." Community-engaged learning is a pedagogy that has developed out of service learning, a movement that has grown rapidly at colleges and universities in recent decades.[1] It recognizes the importance of engaging with community partners—in the case of my course, the Haw River Assembly—to enhance the applicability of higher education. The Quaker college where I teach emphasizes this pedagogical engagement with the world outside our campus boundaries, though this occurs mainly with agencies that support the well-being and endeavors of human animals, not non-human ones.

The "animal stories" we read and tell in my interdisciplinary writing skills/historical analysis/natural history course focus on the interactions between non-human and human animals over time in central North Carolina. We read about the arrival of human animals in North Carolina thousands of years ago and their relatively small, but perceivable, impact on the natural environment. We analyze early written accounts by Europeans exploring North Carolina (William Hilton, John Lawson, John and William Bartram) to understand the attitudes they expressed towards non-human animals and the plant life they found here. For the most part, understandably, they considered the non-human animals they discovered here in such abundance a God-granted meat locker, just as they viewed the impressively tall and remarkably straight longleaf pines—as well as oaks, hickories, and other trees—a divinely-deeded lumber yard.

We also read more recent accounts of North Carolina's non-human animals, like John Terres' extensively-detailed observations of turkey vultures, rabbits, quail, raccoons, barred owls, flying squirrels, and others in *From Laurel Hill to Siler's Bog: The Walking Adventures of a Naturalist*, published in 1969, as well as two books that tell the stories of major North Carolina rivers: Anne Cassebaum's *Down Along the Haw* (2011) and Philip Gerard's *Down the Wild Cape Fear* (2013). The students write brief historical analyses of one early European account of encountering wildlife and the landscape of coastal North Carolina; a researched

---

[1] The Corporation for National and Community Service reported in 2005 that 33 percent of students in the US had had at least one service learning experience. The National Survey of Student Engagement in 2014 indicated that 52 percent of all first-year students and 62 percent of those graduating from colleges and universities had participated in at least one course that was based in service learning. Caryn McTighe Musil, "Department Designs for Civic Impact," *Peer Review*, Association of American Colleges & Universities 19, no. 4 (2017): 2.

essay on the natural history and population change over time in North Carolina of a native non-human animal; and a longer, carefully-documented paper about some aspect of human animals' impact on the environment of the Cape Fear River Basin. They share their research in class presentations and, by the end of the course, they know a lot about North Carolina's history, non-human animals, and major environmental problems in the Basin (like the pollution caused by textile mills from the nineteenth century to the 1990s and the major problems with industrial hog farming in eastern North Carolina). And they have learned a little natural history of the place where they are currently living, mostly from their research and other students' presentations, but also through our stream monitoring sessions and some other walk-and-talks we take around campus.

Although the natural history portion of the course is relatively small— as a general education course it has to focus on writing instruction and historical perspective development—I've realized more and more that it's the natural history I really want them to learn. It feels critical for my students to discover that red foxes were brought to North Carolina (before it was North Carolina) from Europe for sport hunting, that the native gray fox can climb trees, that longleaf pine savannas depend upon fire to maintain open space between individual trees and that the orchids and carnivorous plants growing underneath them have adapted for surviving such fires, that beaver disappeared completely from North Carolina in the late nineteenth century but were reintroduced (imported from Pennsylvania) in the 1930s. I want them to wonder at the endangered Cape Fear shiner, which only lives in spotty, separated populations in the Rocky, Deep, and Haw Rivers (feeder rivers of the Cape Fear), and be astonished that 1,500-year-old bald cypress still grow in the Three Sisters Swamp area of the Black River (another river that flows into the Cape Fear). They should know that Jordan Lake, a human-made, nutrient-overloaded recreation area and water source for the towns of Apex and Cary, houses an impressive population of bald eagles, having proved a key habitat area for the national bird during its post-DDT recovery here in the lower 48 states. These are some among the many "animal stories" we learn from our readings and discussions. Students perform research about loggerhead sea turtles, mockingbirds, wood ducks, coyotes, the red wolf (the only wild—and very endangered—population of which lives in Alligator River National Wildlife Refuge in eastern North Carolina), and other non-human animals, and they have the opportunity for brief but significant encounters in the field with dusky salamanders, crayfish, caddisfly larvae, Canada geese, and ring-necked ducks in late winter on the college lake. Finally—and this is the best part—students become more aware of "animal stories" and begin relating spontaneous accounts of sighting deer, fox, Muscovy ducks, wild turkey, and other creatures as the semester progresses.

In the age of the Internet, when more and more of our interactions with the world outside the doors of our homes or residence halls are curated for us through Amazon Prime algorithms and Facebook preferences, so many of my students have lost the need or the desire to explore that world on their own. At my college, we see fewer and fewer students simply spending time out-of-doors; this has changed drastically in the nineteen years I have been teaching on my stunningly beautiful mature oak-, hickory-, maple-, and beech-canopied North Carolina campus. So much comes mediated to us through our screens, and the vast majority of the information we absorb concerns human animals alone. Think about how many academic disciplines and how much of the academy's resources are devoted to human animal concerns. My own discipline—literature—is one of the most self-absorbed, fixating upon human artistic productions made only for other human beings (and often for an elite subset of humanity). I want my "animal stories" students, in some small but hopefully significant ways, to open their minds to the world of non-human narratives, to the lives and miraculous beings of blue crabs, Atlantic sturgeon, pileated woodpeckers, black bears, muskrats, and shad. Their stories are potent, life giving, sometimes funny, sometimes poignant, always valuable, and definitively real.

III. Quaker Naturalists, Quakerism, and Natural History Education

The idea of reclaiming natural history for our students in the context of a writing course may first appear odd, a disconcerting amalgamation of disciplines so disparate—English and biology, for lack of better terms—as nearly to be meaningless. Admittedly, in teaching the course I sometimes think I am only managing to give short shrift to two things (the teaching of writing and teaching students about some of the fauna and flora of a particular place) instead of providing a rich experience in one or the other of those academic arenas. But the course is designed to be interdisciplinary for some very particular reasons, the most prominent of which is my conviction that solving environmental problems requires a broader, less-specialized point of view than is typical when we limit ourselves to a single discipline (or a single sub-specialty of a discipline). The problems caused by industrial hog farming in eastern North Carolina, for example, cannot be overcome solely by studying the bacteria associated with fecal lagoons, although such study is clearly critical. Key economic, political, social, historical, and environmental racism concerns also pertain to that issue, concerns always in need of careful articulation in writing if positive changes are to come about. So even as I lament my course's apparent lack of disciplinary focus, I recognize that one of its great strengths lies in its more general, cross-disciplinary approach. And since the course is for first-year or sophomore students, it makes sense to be broader in the approach rather than deep.

The history of Quaker involvement in natural history study, particularly in the mid-to-late eighteenth century when such study blossomed in the United States, suggests that I am working in a small way to reclaim an educational emphasis consistent with long-standing Quaker values and practices. Quakers played important roles at the forefront of modern American natural history study, which is not surprising given their prominence in colonial and early postcolonial America as well as—perhaps more importantly—their strong beliefs in egalitarianism, continuing revelation, honoring with reverence the wonders of creation, proper and moral education, and the development of practical skills. Eighteenth-century Friends are likely to have been drawn to natural history study for a number of different reasons—including the fact that some had the leisure time to pursue collecting and cataloging—but there were (and are, I would argue) some particular Quaker sensibilities that suited members of the Religious Society of Friends especially both to become naturalists and to promote natural history education. Historical investigation regarding Quaker involvement with natural history has tended to focus either on particular naturalists—the most prominent of whom are of course John Bartram (1699–1777) and his son, William (1739–1823), renowned Quaker botanists/naturalists from Philadelphia whose writings (John's journals and diaries, William's *Travels*) and involvement in scientific work and societies make them key figures in eighteenth- and early nineteenth-century American natural history—or more generally on Quaker attitudes towards the natural world, particularly as expressed in the writings of eighteenth-century Quaker reformers like John Woolman and Anthony Benezet.[2] I will review here

---

[2] Multiple studies of the Bartrams exist, and William's *Travels* has received significant discussion from environmental and literary historians in the past thirty years. For extensive information on John Bartram, see Hoffmann and Van Horne's *America's Curious Botanist*. For a thoroughgoing comparison of John's and William's different understandings of the natural world, see Thomas P. Slaughter's *The Natures of John and William Bartram*. Larry R. Clarke's article outlines carefully the notably Quaker aspects of William's views on nature, often contrasting those with his father's thoughts. More recently, Robert Sayre has argued that William Bartram's "environmental vision" was far-reaching and consistent enough that he deserves the title of "the first ecologist" (67). For additional insight into eighteenth-century Quaker environmental sensibilities, see the articles by Kerry S. Walters and Donald Brooks Kelley. Nancy E. Hoffmann and John C. Van Horne, eds., *America's Curious Botanist: A Tercentennial Reappraisal of John Bartram, 1699–1777* (Philadelphia: American Philosophical Society, 2004). Thomas P. Slaughter, *The Natures of John and William Bartram* (Philadelphia: Alfred A. Knopf, 1996). Larry

some of the main reasons why Quaker beliefs and sensibilities could have attracted Friends to natural history study in the 1700s and then discuss how Quakers promoted natural history as a key part of education in the nineteenth century.

Central to George Fox's explanations of his encounter with divine truth is the idea that he came to know God "experimentally," by which he meant through direct, personal experience. For Fox, God was neither an idea apprehended by the cogitating mind nor something interpreted and delivered to believers through an intermediary priest. God was knowable through somatic experience, a truth manifested by Friends' quaking bodies in meeting for worship. As Larry R. Clarke has argued, this fundamental Quaker emphasis on direct experience of the divine had a profound effect on Friends' attitudes toward the natural world, primarily in their belief that experiential encounters with nature could lead to knowledge of God. For Clarke, Quaker theology was "apophatic" in its refusal to make intellectual, positive statements about God, choosing instead to derive knowledge of God inductively through intuition and experience.[3] Coming to understand God more fully through natural world encounters, therefore, aligned neatly with extant Quaker theological dispositions.[4] Clarke also notes that on a more practical level Quakers in eighteenth-century Pennsylvania would have valued the study of nature as an excellent alternative to the frivolous distractions that led into vice, things such as music, novel-reading, play-going, and dancing, activities Quakers inveighed against publicly from their beginnings well into the latter part of the nineteenth century.[5] Such practicality also meant that Quakers thought of nature study as closely related to agricultural pursuits. Indeed, John Bartram has been described by one biographer as a "simple Quaker

---

R. Clarke, "The Quaker Background of William Bartram's View of Nature," *Journal of the History of Ideas* 46, no. 3 (1985): 435–448. Robert Sayre, "William Bartram and Environmentalism," *American Studies* 54, no. 1 (Mar. 2015): 67–87. Kerry S. Walters, "The 'Peaceable Disposition' of Animals: William Bartram on the Moral Sensibility of Brute Creation," *Pennsylvania History: A Journal of Mid-Atlantic Studies* 56 (1989): 157–176. Donald Brooks Kelley, "The Evolution of Quaker Theology and the Unfolding of a Distinctive Quaker Ecological Perspective in Eighteenth-century America," *Pennsylvania History: A Journal of Mid-Atlantic Studies* 52, no. 4 (1985): 242–253.

[3] Clarke, "Quaker Background," 439–440.

[4] Bruce Silver disagrees somewhat with Clarke's attribution of distinctively Quaker dispositions to William Bartram's conception of nature. Bruce Silver, "Clarke on the Quaker Background of William Bartram's Approach to Nature," *Journal of the History of Ideas* 47, no. 3 (1986): 507–510.

[5] Clarke, "Quaker Background," 442.

farmer,"[6] in addition to being a naturalist and explorer of the American continent, and he was very much engaged in the sale of American plant seeds he collected or produced at his garden. A bent toward practicality also informed the ways in which other Quakers engaged in natural history pursuits.

The origins of the distinctions we now hold between the professional practice of science (think university-employed biologists, geologists, etc.) and lay interests in such areas (think bird watching and mineral collecting) may go back to an eighteenth-century distinction between natural history—a more practical, less systematic, non-theoretical pursuit involving plants, animals, landforms and their change over time—and natural philosophy, the systematic and more theoretical study of fundamental natural principles, especially in the arenas of physics, chemistry, and astronomy. As Edward Baltzell suggests, since natural philosophy required mathematical training, it became the province of more highly educated specialists as Enlightenment science developed, whereas the naming and collecting of nature's plants, rocks, and animals was left to the natural historians.[7]

Baltzell, in his study of the religiously based differences between Boston and Philadelphia in the colonial period, notes that Quakers "were indeed leaders in eighteenth-century science," but they tended to be more interested in natural history as opposed to the more theoretical scientific pursuits.[8] It was a group comprised mainly of Quakers who helped reorganize the American Society for the Promotion and Propagating of Useful Knowledge (which came to be referred to as the American Society) in Philadelphia in 1766, which later joined with the American Philosophical Society as one group under that name in 1769. The American Society focused on the science of things useful and uplifting—agriculture, technology, natural history—pursuits that aligned well with a Quaker religious emphasis on the utilitarian and being self-taught, not (at that time) university-educated. As Baltzell puts it, "To most Quakers theory was as useless as theology. Fact collecting better fitted the Quaker preference for things over words and was infinitely amateur, democratic, and egalitarian."[9]

It makes sense, then, that Quakers played an important part in the founding and development of the Academy of Natural Sciences in Philadelphia in 1812, the first natural history museum in the United States. One of the important founders of that institution was Thomas Say (1787–1834), a Quaker who

---

[6] Whitfield J. Bell, Jr., "John Bartram: A Biographical Sketch," in *America's Curious Botanist: A Tercentennial Reappraisal of John Bartram, 1699–1777*, eds. Nancy E. Hoffman and John C. Van Horne (Philadelphia: American Philosophical Society, 2004), 5.

[7] Edward Digby Baltzell, *Puritan Boston and Quaker Philadelphia: Two Protestant Ethics and the Spirit of Class Authority and Leadership* (New York: The Free Press, 1979), 173.

[8] Baltzell, *Puritan Boston and Quaker Philadelphia*, 174.

[9] Baltzell, *Puritan Boston and Quaker Philadelphia*, 174.

was John Bartram's great-grandson. Say's Quaker wife, Lucy Way Sistaire Say (1801–1886), an accomplished artist who completed the seventh number of her husband's serial *American Conchology* following his death, was a naturalist in her own right and became the first woman elected to membership in the Academy of Natural Sciences in 1841.[10] A number of other prominent natural historians in the nineteenth century were Quakers as well, including Solomon White Conrad (1779–1831) and his son, Timothy A. Conrad (1803–1877).

Thomas Say's contributions to American natural history study went beyond the founding of the Academy of Natural Sciences and the publication of *American Conchology*, the first publication about American shells. He also published *American Entomology, or Descriptions of the Insects of North America* between 1824 and 1828 following his participation in Stephen Harriman Long's expeditions to the Rocky Mountains in 1819–1820 and to Minnesota and Lake Superior in 1823.[11] *American Entomology* was the first book about insects indigenous to the United States published in America. Say's Quaker background seems to have informed his natural history perspective quite powerfully. During the 1819–1820 government-sponsored expedition to the American West, he observed and described differences between Native American and white approaches to hunting bison, noting how Indians utilized each part of a bison they had killed while white hunters slaughtered large numbers of bison almost indiscriminately, "from mere wantonness and love of this barbarous sport," keeping only the bison's tongues to actually use. He even suggested that "some law for the preservation of game might be extended to, and rigidly enforced in the country where the bison is still met with; that the wanton destruction of these valuable animals, by the white hunters, might be checked or prevented,"[12] an indication of a proto-environmentalist ethic.

Some of Say's writing about the creatures he encountered during the 1819–1820 expedition clearly demonstrates a Quaker appreciation for the divine order operating within the natural world. Here, for example, is his description of sandhill cranes observed near Council Bluffs:

---

[10] Patricia Tyson Stroud, "'At What Do You Think the Ladies Will Stop?' Women at the Academy," *Proceedings of the Academy of Natural Sciences of Philadelphia* 162 (2013): 198.

[11] Patricia Tyson Stroud, "Forerunner of American Conservation: Naturalist Thomas Say," *Forest & Conservation History* 39, no. 4 (1995): 187–89.

[12] Edwin James, ed., *Account of an Expedition from Pittsburgh to the Rocky Mountains, performed in the years 1819, 1820, by order of the Hon. J.C. Calhoun, Secretary of War, under the command of Maj. S.H. Long, of the U.S. Top. Engineers. Compiled from the notes of Major Long, Mr. T. Say, and Other Gentlemen of the Party* (London: Longman, Hurst, Rees, Orme, and Brown, Paternoster-Row, 1823) 2:168.

They were now in great numbers, soaring aloft in the air, flying with an irregular kind of gyratory motion, each individual describing a large circle in the air independently of his associates, and uttering loud, dissonant, and repeated cries. They sometimes continued thus to wing their flight upwards, gradually receding from the earth, until they become mere specks upon the sight, and finally altogether disappear, leaving only the discordant music of their concert to fall faintly upon the ear.[13]

The writing here delicately combines factual description, painting a clear, realistic portrait of crane flight, with a hint of religious metaphor, which reverberates slightly in the idea of these majestic birds "gradually receding from the earth" as they wing their way toward the heavens.

Say's Quakerism seems to have informed his sympathetic attitudes toward Native Americans as well as his proto-environmentalist ethic regarding non-human animals. His interest in things small and apparently insignificant (insects and mollusks) may also suggest a Quakerly attention to that which often goes unnoticed. But it is important to note that his attitudes toward the natural world may also be seen as a product of the more general religious and cultural sympathies of his time. Richard Judd argues that a number of American naturalists engaged in cataloging the vast floral and faunal riches of colonial and early-Republic America emphasized in their writings the key concepts of balance and the interrelatedness in the natural world as well as the practical and spiritual importance of nature to human beings. In the hundred-year period (1730–1830) from the work of Mark Catesby to that of John James Audubon, many other naturalists—among them John and William Bartram, François and François-André Michaux, Alexander Wilson, Benjamin Silliman, Thomas Nuttall, and Benjamin Smith Barton (only the Bartrams being Quakers among them)—conveyed ideas about the natural world in much the same vein as those promoted by Thomas Say. Judd argues that the proto-environmentalist ethic communicated by these early American naturalists, informed by Enlightenment versions of religious piety, laid the groundwork for the more explicit arguments for conservation—especially forest conservation—that would come from George Perkins Marsh in his monumental *Man and Nature* (1864) and then John Muir and others in the late nineteenth and early twentieth centuries.

Although Judd does not discuss Thomas Say's work, he does attend to William Bartram, who was Say's uncle. Judd suggests that Edward Hicks' vision of the peaceable kingdom helped shape his fellow Philadelphian Bartram's "well-

---

[13] James, *Account of an Expedition,* 2:68.

known sympathy for animals,"[14] a sentiment perhaps most poignantly expressed in Bartram's account in his *Travels* of the trauma experienced by a bear cub on approaching the body of its recently killed mother. Traveling with his party along the east coast of Florida, Bartram encountered quite a few deer and bears. He writes that they saw eleven bears in the course of one day, none of which looked "surprized or affrighted at the sight of us."[15] Bartram's hunter determined to shoot a bear, "for the sake of the skin and oil, for we had plenty and variety of provisions," and did so, laying the largest of a pair "dead on the spot."[16] What happened next is remarkable, both in the fact of it and for the manner in which Bartram describes it:

> presently the other, not seeming the least moved, at the report of our piece, approached the dead body, smelled, and pawed it, and appearing in agony, fell to weeping and looking upwards, then towards us, and cried out like a child. [W]hilst our boat approached very near, the hunter was loading his rifle in order to shoot the survivor, which was a young cub, and the slain supposed to be the dam; the continual cries of this afflicted child, bereft of its parent, affected me very sensibly, I was moved with compassion, and charging myself as if accessary to what now appeared to be a cruel murder, and endeavoured to prevail on the hunter to save its life.[17]

Of course there may be more behind Bartram's sensitivity to non-human animals here than simply a Quaker sensibility (as Judd's article would suggest). But Kerry S. Walters has argued convincingly that Bartram's attitudes—developed less from theological conceptualizing and more through empirical observation and inductive reasoning—derived powerfully from his Quaker background even as it differed from arguments about how to treat non-human animals promulgated by Bartram's proto-ecological, Quaker, and slightly older contemporaries John Woolman, Anthony Benezet, and John Churchman. These

---

[14] Richard W. Judd, "A 'Wonderfull Order and Ballance': Natural History and the Beginnings of Forest Conservation in America, 1730–1830," *Environmental History* 11, no. 1 (2006): 24.

[15] William Bartram, *Travels Through North & South Carolina, Georgia, East & West Florida, The Cherokee Country, The Extensive Territories of the Muscogulges, or Creek Confederacy, and the Country of the Chactaws: Containing an Account of the Soil and Natural Productions of Those Regions, Together With Observations on the Manners of the Indians. Embellished with Copper-Plates*, Documenting the American South (Philadelphia: James & Johnson 1791), xxv.

[16] Bartram, *Travels Through North & South Carolina*, xxvi.

[17] Bartram, *Travels Through North & South Carolina*, xxvi–xxvii.

writers, Walters contends, grounded their arguments concerning non-human animals in the Quietist and reforming eighteenth-century Quaker idea that it was "the human duty to cultivate humility in the service of God"[18] and that "benevolence to brute creation was a manifestation of one's proper attitude and duty towards the deity."[19] Bartram, however, felt that human beings owed right treatment to their fellow creatures not because of some theocentric notion that being kind to non-human animals helped align rightly one's relationship with the creator, but because non-human animals, by themselves demonstrating "their apparently intelligent ability to invent, act purposively, communicate, teach, learn and adapt" as well as to engage in "moral reason,"[20] have "intrinsic rights…to moral consideration."[21] Bartram's empirical and practical observations of animal behavior led him to conclude (in a short treatise he wrote about his understanding of nature) this: "if we examine minutely the morality or manners of animals and compare them with those nations of the human race…[,] we shall find but little difference between their manners and the animal creation in general."[22]

Bartram's compassion for the bear cub in his *Travels*, as well as his remarkably understanding and kind comments there about rattlesnakes as "generous" and "magnanimous"[23] and wolves as creatures nowhere as rapacious as others might think,[24] are remarkable for his time period (perhaps even for our own in some ways), and his reminder that the realm of non-human animals follows a consummate form of "economy"[25] toward a purposeful end surely attests to an early type of ecological awareness that is consonant with the particularly Quaker understanding of the interrelatedness of all things, grounded in the belief that that of the divine dwells in all human beings and therefore, by extension, in the entirety of the universe.

This all-too-brief survey of some of the history of natural history and early natural historians makes it clear that Quakers were key developers of the field in America and that there appear to be multiple ways in which Quaker sensibilities intersected with an interest in collecting, describing, and cataloging items from the non-human world. Nineteenth-century Quakers also vigorously promoted natural history education, particularly in some articles that appeared in *The*

---

[18] Walters, "Peaceable Disposition," 159.
[19] Walters, "Peaceable Disposition," 163.
[20] Walters, "Peaceable Disposition," 171.
[21] Walters, "Peaceable Disposition," 165.
[22] Bartram in Walters, "Peaceable Disposition," 171.
[23] Bartram, *Travels Through North & South Carolina,* 264.
[24] Bartram, *Travels Through North & South Carolina,* 159.
[25] Bartram, *Travels Through North & South Carolina,* xxvii.

Friend (Philadelphia) and *The Friends' Intelligencer*. One unsigned piece, written specifically for *The Friend* and entitled "On the Study of Natural History," laments that many remain uninstructed in the ways of the natural world because of the less-than-effective usual mode of lecturing, a pedagogical method (this writer claims) that "uniformly fails of fixing principles and definitions in the mind of the student," pummeling that learner instead with an all-too-quick "succession of objects" that pass by so quickly that the student becomes confused by nature's variety instead of first gaining a clear framework within which to comprehend.[26] This writer recommends not just "a course of lectures" in order to learn botany, but rather a course of study that can "fix distinctions and principles in the mind, and put the student in possession of a key to decypher [sic] the great book of nature,"[27] thereby attracting students to botanical (or other natural history) study where they now find it "repulsive."[28] The writer also suggests that class size should be more limited than is generally the case and that the instructor, since a course on such a model would demand more time, "should receive a greater compensation than has been usual."[29]

The article closes with its author noting that "the very competent and respected naturalist whose lectures are now announced in the daily papers" would be willing to offer just such a special course that the article describes as the very best kind. It is perhaps no accident that, on the very same page on which this article appears, a notice is thereupon printed for a series of "Lectures on Botany" to be given by "S.W. Conrad," no doubt the Quaker naturalist Solomon White Conrad (1779–1831) who ran a less-than-successful printing and bookselling business in Philadelphia, preferring to spend his time in the field searching for plants and minerals to display and discuss at a natural history salon he organized regularly. He was a lecturer in mineralogy at the University of Pennsylvania and later, for a brief period, professor of botany there.[30]

The concern for a proper education in natural history expressed in this article finds a strong echo in a book review published in *The Friend* a few years later. This unsigned review, of *Letters to a Young Naturalist on the Study of Nature, and Natural Theology*, written by James L. Drummond and published in London in 1831, opens with an argument for the inclusion of natural history in a general course of education: "Amongst the many improvements which a more diffused and liberal system of education is every where producing around us, there are

---

[26] "On the Study of Natural History," *The Friend: A Religious & Literary Journal* 26 (April 1828): 203.

[27] "On the Study of Natural History," 203.

[28] "On the Study of Natural History," 203.

[29] "On the Study of Natural History," 203.

[30] "Conrad, Solomon White," *Global Plants*.

none to be contemplated with greater satisfaction, than those which serve to render mankind familiarly conversant with the works of nature."[31] This very positive review sounds familiar notes regarding the salutary effects of studying the phenomena of nature, remarking that such study ought to be "generally made a necessary branch of education"[32] and noting that "[i]t would not be possible for men to treat the lower beings of creation with cruelty, or even to look upon them without interest and admiration, if natural history were more generally cultivated, and especially if it were taught and attended to, as Dr. Drummond insists it ought to be, 'as a part of natural religion.'"[33] The review supports what Judd has argued: that natural history writing in the 1730–1830 period emphasized natural theology, basing proto-environmentalist arguments in religious sensibilities.

This review of Drummond's *Letters* also echoes British Romantic writers' ideas about the soothing powers awash in the natural world, the way nature can occupy and console the human mind when burdened by the vicissitudes of life. For this reviewer, "[i]f we once acquire the habit of examining with attention the works of nature, we need never be without employment."[34] Where most people might "be overcome with ennui, the naturalist would feel his bosom full, to overflowing, with cheerfulness and benevolence."[35] Indeed, as Drummond says in one of the many passages from his book quoted in this review, "the habit of contemplating nature, is an inestimable and endless source of happiness."[36] It would seem that early nineteenth-century Quakers, facing the changes wrought on their lives and the natural world by the beginnings of the Industrial Revolution, avidly promoted simple encounters with nature as a calming antidote to the increasing complexities of human existence. Such sentiments sound all too familiar.

Twenty years later, in a review of Susan Fenimore Cooper's *Rural Hours: by a Lady* (New York, 1851), *The Friend* once again proclaimed the positive, educational value of natural history study, noting "[w]e cannot too highly recommend to our youth the importance of early cultivating a taste for natural history, either as a useful training of their observing powers, or as a cheap and ready

---

[31] "Review of *Letters to a Young Naturalist*," *The Friend: A Religious & Literary Journal* 5, no. 11 (December 1831): 81.

[32] "Review of *Letters*," *The Friend*, 5 no. 11, 81.

[33] "Review of *Letters*," *The Friend*, 5 no. 11, 82.

[34] "Review of *Letters to a Young Naturalist on the Study of Nature and Nature Theology*," *The Friend: A Religious & Literary Journal* 5, no. 12 (December 7, 1831): 89.

[35] "Review of *Letters*," *The Friend*, 5 no. 12, 90.

[36] "Review of *Letters*," *The Friend*, 5 no. 12, 90.

source of pleasure and instruction."[37] *The Friends' Intelligencer* also published extensive extracts from Cooper's *Rural Hours* two years later (1853) in volume ten of that publication ("Rural Hours" *Friends' Intelligencer*, "Further Extracts"; "Continued Extracts"). The *Intelligencer* also ran an extensive reprint from the *Massachusetts Teacher* entitled "Importance of the Study of Natural History as a Branch of Elementary Education" across four numbers of volume nineteen in June and July of 1862, and this article repeats reasons for studying natural history we have already seen:

> there is one point of view which should make the study of Natural History an object of no small importance in the education of every human being. It is its moral influence upon us; it is the fact, that unless we study nature extensively, we remain strangers to the wonders of the universe; we remain unconscious of the beautiful harmony there is in creation; we fail to perceive distinctly that there is in nature a revelation of the Supreme Intelligence, which teaches us every thing has been done with order, with a view to a plan, and with reference to the creation of that privileged being to whom God has revealed himself in another manner; it is the fact that the revelation of God in Nature, the manifold manifestations of His power, His wisdom, His intelligence, which are displayed throughout nature, remain a sealed book to those who are not early taught to read it, or they remain as a sort of undeciphered hieroglyphics, which man may easily misinterpret from want of sufficient knowledge of the characters in which they are written.
>
> The study of nature is worthy of our attention in this respect; and its importance in this point of view is as great as that of any other branch of study.[38]

The ideas about the value of nature here represent a somewhat less vatic and difficult to comprehend expression of thoughts presented earlier by Ralph Waldo Emerson in his 1836 essay, *Nature*, or Henry David Thoreau in *Walden* (1854) and other pieces, but the fact that this Quaker publication strongly promoted early education in natural history remains striking and important.

---

[37] "Review of *Rural Hours* by Susan Fenimore Cooper," *The Friend: A Religious & Literary Journal* 24, no. 25 (March 1851): 194.

[38] "Importance of the Study of Natural History as a Branch of Elementary Education," *Friends' Intelligencer* 19, no. 16 (June 1862): 249–250.

To conclude this far from comprehensive account of late eighteenth- to mid-nineteenth-century Quaker promotions of the study of natural history, it is good to return to the idea that Quakers found such an education consistent with their egalitarian ideals. As one brief quotation in *The Friend* from Mary Matilda Howard's 1846 book, *Ocean Flowers and their Teachings*, put it in 1856, "The study of *Natural History* is within the reach of every one."[39] Nature study, the inclusion of this quotation in *The Friend* implies, can benefit everyone, teaching them "the art of thinking clearly and accurately…with a much less degree of weariness, than that which usually accompanies the study of simple quantities and mere abstract forms."[40] This quotation specifically names natural history study as more beneficial in disciplining human judgment than "Mathematics," a point that recalls the natural history/natural philosophy distinction with which we began this historical survey, reminding us that Quakers valued less esoteric study of the practical facts of this world more than the sorts of scientific investigation that led, ultimately, to the development of technologies like the atomic bomb. It would seem there is a lesson here for us about being mindful regarding where our human inquisitiveness might lead.

IV. Attentiveness

When *The Friend's* 1831 review of *Letters to a Young Naturalist* extols "the habit of examining *with attention* the works of nature" (emphasis added),[41] it clearly anticipates the connection being drawn in our own day between mindfulness and engagement with the natural world. Many writers have articulated this link powerfully, though perhaps most directly in recent years by Thomas Lowe Fleischner in his essay, "The Mindfulness of Natural History," the introductory piece in *The Way of Natural History*, a collection Fleischner edited. In this book that argues for reclaiming a powerful role for natural history at this critical time in our planet's history, Fleischner asks, and answers, the fundamental question: "Why does attentiveness to nature matter? In a very fundamental sense, we *are* what we pay attention to. Paying heed to beauty, grace, and everyday miracles promotes a sense of possibility and coherence that runs deeper and truer than the often illu-

---

[39] ["The study of Natural History,"] *The Friend: A Religious & Literary Journal* 29, no. 28 (March 1856): 231.

[40] ["The study of Natural History,"] 231.

[41] "Review of *Letters*," *The Friend*, 5 no. 12, 89.

sory commercial, social 'realities' advanced by mainstream contemporary cul-ture."[42] I teach Fleischner's essay at the start of the "Animal Stories of the Cape Fear River Basin" course, hoping that my students will catch the lesson that pay-ing attention to those small, apparently insignificant things like caddisfly larvae tubes, riffle beetles, and pond snails, affords their lives something beyond post-ing bathroom selfies on Instagram.

In using the terms "human animals" and "non-human animals" throughout the course, I want continually to remind my students that we are also animals, thereby further bringing (hopefully) non-human animals into the circle of "us," the group of beings deserving of our consideration and care. I want to engage my students in gestures of empathy, and paying attention to something beyond our own selves is the beginning of such empathetic gestures. To be amazed at the number of nuts a flying squirrel can gather in the course of a night—something John Terres reveals—can be the genesis of seeing beyond the confines of my individual needs and desires, into the lives of others.

When some students recall Fleischner's essay in their final reflective writing on what they have learned during our stream monitoring sessions, and say that they saw and came to appreciate things they would not otherwise have seen and come to know more about, I sense something may have just gone right in the course. As we humans, simply by exercising the skills and abilities we have perfected over years of evolution, continue to have such a profoundly negative impact on the quality of our earth's water, its air, its soil, and the well-being of its other inhabitants, I hope my course provides one small hedge against the hu-bris that has led us into the Anthropocene and its environmental obscenities. Because we now know better, because we *know* that the enemy of our own envi-ronment is *us*, we need to engage in multiple means of unseating such recalcitrant human animal pride. In trying to do some of this upending, I find solace in know-ing that fellow Friends have long called themselves and others to attend to nature and its wonders in an attempt both to improve human thinking and to cherish the lives of other beautiful and marvelous things that have flourished upon this planet for so much longer than we human animals have held their fate in our all-too-dexterous hands.

---

[42] Thomas Lowe Fleischner, "The Mindfulness of Natural History," in *The Way of Natural History,* ed. Thomas Lowe Fleischner (San Antonio, TX: Trinity University Press, 2011): 9.

13 | Ecotone: Quakerism, Sustainability, Art, and the Boundaries Between

By Craig Goodworth with Cherice Bock

Abstract: Land-based artist and poet, Craig Goodworth, shares about his art, his work (physical labor), and his spirituality, describing the place where they meet as an ecotone. After spending time at an Eastern Orthodox monastery, Goodworth discovered Friends and attended Earlham School of Religion. He describes the similarities and differences between art and work, using an art installation he created, Playa Study #8 (Trench), and a ditch he dug for a Quaker camp as examples. Cherice Bock interviews Goodworth and asks him to describe how his understanding of art relates to Quakerism and sustainability. Goodworth invites Friends to ever-deepening communion with all life as embodied and creative beings-in-relation.

I. Editorial Introduction

Craig Goodworth, an Oregon-based artist working in installation and poetry, often situates his art making at physical, disciplinary, and spiritual ecotones—the liminal spaces between two ecosystems. According to ecologists, ecotones often hold the most biodiversity. They teem with life, as creatures thrive amongst the abundant resources of both water and land, for example, or prairie and forest. Ecotones are also fraught with danger, however: land creatures can only spend so much time in the water, and unseen dangers can lurk below the surface. Creating art in such liminal spaces enables a richness and fecundity of materials and inspirations, but also requires hard work from the artist—some in his interior landscape, some in the exterior, physical landscape, and some in the relational world of society and academia.

217

His practice encompasses drawing, object-making, research, teaching, and farm labor. He has received fellowships in art and writing, including a Fulbright Fellowship to the Slovak Republic (2015). Along with exhibiting his artwork nationally and internationally, he's engaged in various collaborations and residencies relating art to science and religion. Goodworth holds master's degrees in fine art and sustainable communities. His art includes themes of land, place, mysticism, and folk traditions. Influenced by time spent at an Eastern Orthodox monastery and finding a home in Quakerism, Goodworth teaches at George Fox University while also practicing visual art and poetry through exhibitions, lectures/readings, and various artist residencies.

A native of Arizona, Goodworth has spent much of his life in the West. Influenced by the desert landscape of the American Southwest and the fertile Willamette Valley of Oregon, he also delves into his connection with the landscape and culture of his ancestors in Eastern Europe. In recent years, his art has explored environmental topics both social and ecological: the experience of human immigration and its ecological and justice connotations, the aesthetic qualities of bees and honey as well as the ecological concern of hive collapse, and the power and horror of wildfires. He returns again and again in his art to the theme of the body: the individual body and interior landscape of the self, and the connection between and responsibility to the broader body of the Earth and its community of life.

We invited Goodworth to share about his journey toward Quakerism, sustainability, and art, and the ecotone where they meet. He will also share photographs illustrating the ecotone between art and work, and the individual and earthly body. He shares his experiences as an artist-practitioner, Quaker, and professor.

II. Art, Sustainability, and Quakerism: Exploring the Ecotone

Cherice Bock: Can you please share with us a bit about your journey toward art, sustainability, and Quakerism?

Craig Goodworth: It's been a pilgrimage. After some college football and being unwilling to give a decade of my life to West Point and the Army, I went to art school in Baltimore. Following undergraduate studies in sculpture, I was chomping at the bit to see the world another way besides art. I returned West to begin interdisciplinary graduate studies in sustainability. My thesis explored self-emptying as prerequisite to envisioning good and sustainable communities, and I worked on it while living at an Eastern Orthodox monastery in the desert Southwest. I stayed on with the monks in rural northern New Mexico and did some work with a logger in a nearby canyon until moving to Richmond, Indiana. There, this combination of art, sustainable communities, working with my hands, and self-emptying expanded and extended in my poetry and prose while I attended Earlham School of Religion under the Thomas Mullen Writing Fellowship.

Bock: *When you discovered Quakers, what in particular made you feel this might be a spiritual home?*

Goodworth: I don't know if pilgrims ever fully find a home. But I can say that while I've become disenchanted with American Christianity, and enchanted with monasticism, Quakers at their best offer a way of being spiritually alive and fully in the world—the one that, for me, includes my wife and kiddies.

Initially—and still—I felt drawn to unprogrammed worship, or what some Friends call "primitive Quakerism." The active non-violence of the Quaker peace testimony challenges and encourages me. "Acquire the spirit of peace," the monks were fond of saying, "and thousands will be saved through you."

I still draw from the desert tradition, and my journey with Friends in Indiana and Oregon has added layers of depth to my experience of both spirituality and community.

Bock: *In what ways does your art incorporate your concern for sustainability and your practice of Quakerism?*

Goodworth: Robert Barclay described the Catholic and Anglican Churches' sacraments as having degenerated into a kind of religious magic. He said, "Your communion is too small."[1] In essence, the Quaker witness that all of life is a sacrament opens the way for art to be sacramental, an act of participation in communion with all life.

As to how my art specifically relates to my concern for sustainability, I've been playing with the phrase, "preconditions for caring beyond one's skin." While my art has included collecting, recycling, and repurposing of materials, perhaps my art explores sustainability in so far as it explores the preconditions for a kind of caring that extends beyond one's skin. While I've done my share of living carelessly, since having children I've been particularly concerned with taking care of who and what belongs to me. I think a lot of us today are learning to

---

[1] Quoted in Jack L. Willcuts, *Why Friends are Friends* (Newberg, OR: Barclay Press, 1984), 35.

expand our definitions of community to include the young, the old, the land, and the non-human other.

Working in narrative poetry demands I empathetically imagine the voice of the other on the page. Poetry, I think, can be a form of bearing witness, which is an act I see Quakers valuing across time. Bearing witness can be both a willingness to feel one's own pain, and also a willingness to bear others up. It is the opposite of apathy, according to Kathleen Greider, and the embodiment of passion. Greider says the avoidance of power—what could also be called unethical passivity—is the unwillingness to suffer with the human situation. That form of passivity, Greider suggests, lacks the aspect of bearing witness. In my own work, bearing witness requires me "to suffer an active sense of power in relation," letting the other reach human credibility on the page.[2]

In my ongoing studies at the Earlham School of Religion I've been wondering about grafting the work of the chaplain onto my primary work as an artist. When I ran this idea by an artist/educator friend, he responded by saying, more than anything else he sees my work as prophetic and concerned with a kind of truth telling and repairing or returning to connections we have lost to land and the body. He went on to say that he sees my work as using art as a method of making relationship, of integrating and holding disparate elements such as cultural narratives, science, and faith. I agree with this. Because I am so close to the praxis, this kind of broader conceptual framing is often more intuitive or unconscious for me.

My art making makes use of the Quaker processes of individual and group discernment and meetings for clearness. My spiritual community tethers me to place: for example, I bookended the year spent on a Fulbright Fellowship in the Slovak Republic with clearness meetings, and having a holding community in Oregon to leave and return to was both precious and practical.

---

[2] Kathleen Greider, *Reckoning with Aggression: Theology, Violence, and Vitality* (Louisville, KY: Westminster John Knox Press, 1997), 64.

Image 1: Craig Goodworth creating "Playa Study #8 (Trench)," Summer Lake, OR, 2017

III. Art/Work as Embodied Communion with All Life

Bock: *Describe how your work (art and labor) relates to caring for the planet and working toward sustainability.*

Goodworth: An interview with the painter Jackson Pollock I read years ago in an art history course remains with me and has influenced the way I view my own art. Asked how nature figures into his paintings, Pollock responded: "I am nature."[3] That spoke to my condition. So often in our talk we separate humanity from nature.

    While my primary work is my art practice, I do some teaching and farm labor. In a grounds-care capacity on the 90-acre property of Tilikum Center for Retreats and Outdoor Ministries outside Newberg, OR, I do a lot with firewood, pruning, and various kinds of semi-skilled tasks. This labor, combined with work (teaching) and action (art) is a kind of three-legged stool that provides stability and sustains my practice. Or better yet, I think of orchard ladders, designed with a third leg allowing one to work on uneven ground. I've settled into this triad of labor, work, and action since moving to Oregon and caring for orchards.

    If I understand Hannah Arendt's distinction correctly, we've got our repeated chores, necessary larger works, and symbolic endeavors such as kinds of art and activism.[4] These acts can overlap and mutually support one another.

    The lay of the land in the Willamette Valley serves as an apt metaphor: Oregon's Cascades sharply divide the wet and the dry. Living in a valley between the cultural terrains of urban and rural, folk and elite, farm and vineyard, the borders are porous, bleeding into one another. These liminal spaces are at times fecund, yet they are not always familiar or safe. It seems art happens best when on the edges: both cultural/geographic and when straddling labor, work, and action.

IV. Trenches as Art and Labor, Connecting Bodies of Artist and Land

Bock: *Describe the two bodies of work we'll be discussing in this interview: Playa Study #8 (Trench) and a grounds work ditch you dug at Tilikum (see Images 2–6).*

---

[3] Lee Krasner in "Oral history interview with Lee Krasner," interviewed by Dorothy Seckler, December 14, 1964, in the Lee Krasny Papers, Archives of American Art, Smithsonian Institution, Washington, DC.

[4] Hannah Arendt, *The Human Condition* (Chicago, IL: The University of Chicago Press, 1958, 1998).

Goodworth: In the summer of 2017, I received a four-week residency to work on integrating art and science themes at PLAYA in Oregon's Great Basin Desert.[5] I worked on poems and did a series of land-based artworks. One of these involved digging a trench on the playa about four feet deep, three feet wide, and 14 feet long. It culminated in placing my body directly in the earth's body and documenting it from an aerial perspective with a drone a couple hundred feet above ground. It came to symbolize unity for me. Visually from that distance, the body in the trench appears like a seed.

The following winter, with the ground still wet and soft, I dug ditches on Tilikum's property. We were putting in some water pipes and an electric line. It's on a hill with some pockets of heavy brush. Getting a machine in there isn't really practical, so I had to dig the ditches by hand with a pick, routing the ditch around larger fir and oak roots. When the direction of the ditch changed, I wasn't thinking about art, but saving my back. Nevertheless, when I was about finished digging, I looked back at the ditch and couldn't help but think about land art.

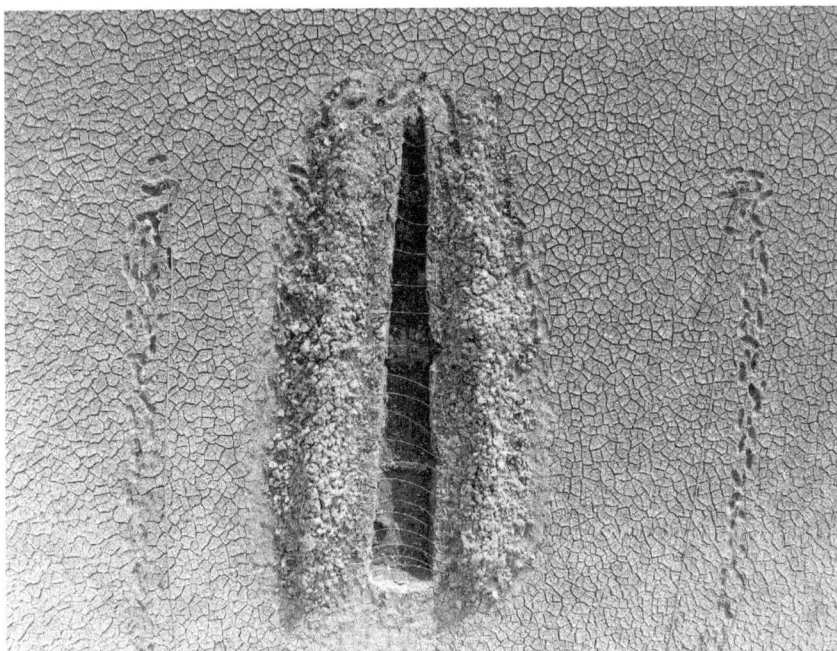

Image 2: Playa Study #8 (Trench), Summer Lake, OR, ©Craig Goodworth, 2017

---

[5] "PLAYA offers residencies of soul-expanding space, solitude, and community to artists and scientists whose creative inquiry and innovative dialogue help bring positive change to our environment and world." "Home," PLAYA website, accessed January 2019, http://playasummerlake.org/.

Image 3: Playa Study #8 (Trench), Aerial View, Summer Lake, OR, ©Craig Goodworth, 2017

Image 4: Playa Study #12 (Corpus), Aerial View, Summer Lake, OR, ©Craig Goodworth, 2017

Image 5: Craig Goodworth, grounds work (ditch), Tilikum Center for Retreats and Outdoor Ministries, 2017

Image 6: Craig Goodworth, grounds work (ditch) 2, Tilikum Center for Retreats and Outdoor Ministries, 2017

Bock: In what ways were the experiences of digging the trench and ditch as art and as work similar and different?

Goodworth: The experiences felt similar in so far as the body: the tooling and the labor overlaps. If I was a contractor pouring cement foundations, and one week I lay one for a church, the next week for a brothel, what changes in my work? It's the same materials, the same process of problem solving—essentially there is no difference.

And yet, they are different because the contexts and purposes of the trench and ditch vary so largely: the one symbolic, the other utilitarian. For the trench, the digital artifact (the photograph) is for an art audience. The ditch has no audience except that I decided to photograph it and bring it up in this piece of writing.

Digging the trench on the playa and the ditch in the woods—I am listening in both cases. I am listening to my body and the tools, as well as the earth as body, the soil, depth, and the direction and scale of my work. If not undertaken carelessly, both can be prayerful.

I am thinking of the British Sculptor David Nash who observed: "The spiritual is absolutely dovetailed into the physical and the two are essentially linked with each other. To work the ground in a practical, basic common sense way is a spiritual activity."[6]

And I am thinking of Thomas Kelley's understanding of living on two levels. I actually first read that book about a decade ago. Our neighbors, Lon and Raelene Fendall, had a very large oak tree come down. I had Kelley's *A Testament of Devotion* in my tool bag. I remember it was hot. After bucking the trunk with a saw, I was splitting the rounds by hand on a hill. It made practical sense to pace that job with small chunks of reading. I could listen in different ways and on both levels to the tree and the book. Digging the ditch in the forest, I recall having my dog with me most of the time, and a notebook and pen in my shirt pocket. Digging the trench on the playa is about tools and form but it is also about grief—the land, my own (we had a baby started that didn't make). In each case, there's the level of physical labor and embodied movement, and that opens up internal space to do work at another level, a level of meaning making through interior work that can't be disconnected from the labor. Psychologists tell me embodied action allows access to a different part of our being, of our brain.

---

[6] In John K. Grande, *Art Nature Dialogues: Interviews with Environmental Artists* (Albany: State University of New York Press, 2004), 6.

The way art and life happens for me is that it generates meaning over time. I didn't know in July I'd be digging ditches the following February. However, the utilitarian ditch in Oregon's Willamette Valley, in a way, completes or is a companion piece to the land-art trench in Oregon's Great Basin Desert.

Bock: *It sounds like the type of care you put into something is what gives it meaning as either work or art, and also, work becomes art.*

Goodworth: Yes. Theologian Martin Buber stated it is not the nature of the task but its consecration that is the vital thing.[7] Perhaps the mundane—and even the profane—through consecration (the act of respecting, honoring, and noticing) becomes the sacred. I am thinking of:

- A Slovak artist who resisted Communist toil and stacked hay bales in sculptural ways, insisting on the symbolic dimensions of labor.
- Cool Hand Luke and the chain gang, spreading the street tar above and beyond the expectation of the guards.[8]
- Viktor Frankl cleaning the latrine with a toothbrush once for the concentration camp guard and a second time for God.[9]

Art seems to come down to intention: in this way, the contractor pouring a cement foundation for a brothel could do that work as unto the Lord.

V. Quakers and Art

Bock: *As Friends, we haven't always valued aesthetics or artwork very highly, and therefore Friends might applaud your practical ditch and wonder why a piece of ephemeral art is necessary. In what ways do you feel making art is necessary, and how does this relate to Quakerism? (This can be a critique of Quakerism, too.)*

Goodworth: I've wondered about Ernst Becker's assertion that the essence of the human being is his or her paradoxical nature, the fact that he or she is half animal and half symbolic. Some thinkers and poets claim our health as human beings is determined by how well we hold together the symbolic with the animal.

---

[7] Martin Buber, *Tales of the Hasidim* (New York, NY: Schocken Books, 1947, 1991).

[8] *Cool Hand Luke*, directed by Stuart Rosenberg (Burbank, CA: Warner Brothers, 1967).

[9] Viktor E. Frankl, *Man's Search for Meaning* (Boston, MA: Beacon Press, 1959, 2006).

Edward Hicks's "Peaceable Kingdom" paintings can be experienced on three levels: theological, historical, and personal. They are loaded with animals functioning symbolically. In the last century, art has often separated beauty from use—fine art from craft. Quakers, perhaps, have separated use from beauty. From what I've read, many in Hicks's meeting were more comfortable with him painting carriages than painting rich folks' farms and prophetic biblical passages.[10] Even though Quakers may not be as comfortable with high art as with craft, Hicks's paintings, as early American folk art, have secured a foothold in museums and art history. They sell for an un-Quakerly amount of money.

The distinction between art and work/craft may not always be necessary or useful. In some instances it's clean and clear, in others it's more porous. This makes me think of the Balinese saying: "We have no art. We do everything as well as we can."[11] Here, the distinction is no distinction.

While art and life may not be the same thing, for me they get pretty close. I tire of talk of the artist as some extra-creative and sensitive, special kind of being, and that tricky, three-letter word A-R-T being wrapped up in elitism and highbrow snobbery.

VI. Art as Embodied Ecotone

Bock: *Ecotone is a word you use often to describe your work (art, labor, and teaching work), and it is an important concept in ecology. What do you find symbolically meaningful about imagining the confluence of these actions as an ecotone?*

Goodworth: In ecology, an ecotone refers to the transition between two landscapes. The boundary can be clear and defined, or complicated and ambiguous. My art mirrors an ecotone by crossing boundaries between farm labor and land art, audiences and cultures. What's interesting about an ecotone is that while it is a space that allows for mutual clarification, it also makes a third thing: in pairing actions that seem to occupy different terrains, I am interested in how each may be better understood, and what third thing might be found.[12] For example, I understand Orthodox monks better from being with Quakers, and Quakers better from having been with monks.

---

[10] Carolyn J. Weekley, *The Kingdoms of Edward Hicks* (New York, NY: The Colonial Williamsburg Foundation, 1999).

[11] Marshall McLuhan, *Understanding Media: The Extensions of Man* (Cambridge, MA: MIT Press, 1994): 73.

[12] With appreciation to my friend and Friend, Roy Gathercoal, for this wording.

While I see myself as an artist who is journeying with Quakers, I want to avoid assuming the role of a "Quaker artist": I see myself on an ecotone, living on the fringe of Quaker culture, perhaps able to speak in and also to bridge beyond. And I want to be careful to avoid the "I am the self declared artist-prophet" thing.

Bock: *What ways do artists—or you as an artist—embody ecotones?*

Goodworth: In August of 2018, making a series of temporary land-based artworks in Ucross, Wyoming, I interacted with various kinds of folks, like placing myself at an intentional ecotone where all sorts of people overlap.[13] At the residency, I had regular dinners with a Navajo poet, novelists from New York and Bolivia, a sculptor from Santa Fe, and a Muslim painter. I sought permission from a rancher to engage cattle in the project; I borrowed tools from the maintenance guys and moved cows with the Peruvian shepherds. I talked poetry at the table and football by the chutes.

I wonder how the artist can be of use socially as an ecotone in our divided times, holding in tension diverse geographies and communities. I do this to the degree that I hold different places in meaningful relationship—various parts of the map including the desert Southwest, the lush Northwest, the Old Country of my Slovak heritage, even the landscape of my grandfather's Pennsylvania farm remembered from childhood. And I seek to find coherence, honoring boundaries and differences between places. Interior and exterior ecotones I regularly work with include:

Quaker / monk
Quaker Midwest / Northwest
The American West / Central Europe
Farm labor / art work

And conceptually, within various projects I've been concerned with straddling the worlds of:

earth as body / body as earth
temporary / permanent
secular / religious

---

[13] Ucross Foundation is a working ranch that hosts residencies for artists of all kinds. Learn more at http://www.ucrossfoundation.org/.

VII. Conclusion

Bock: *As you think of yourself as an artist in this time and place, in the Quaker community, developing a sacramentality that makes an art of intentional practices, what do you think the work of an artist is in the face of the current environmental situation? Are there ways in which this flows from your Quaker values?*

Goodworth: Kathleen Norris, in her essay, "Jeremiah as Writer: The Necessary Other," draws similarities between the prophet and the artist whose task is "to reveal the *fault lines* hidden beneath the comfortable surface of the world we invent for ourselves, the national myths as well as the little lies and delusions of control and security that get us through the day."[14] Much of my work as a poet is about the fault lines, and my land-based art is made on and from physical fault lines. I think the task of the prophet and the artist is to witness to fault lines and ecotones.

Our divisions today go deep, nationally as well as within the Quaker family. We don't have a common culture. Our religious language is problematic. It is fair to wonder if there is a center, something that holds between Quakers. It seems to me, more than anything else, the common ground we seek may be the ground—our shared earth, or "common *casa*," or fouled nest.

In Slovakia, I was moved by how folks in the villages seemed to care about everything inside their gates—garden, meat-hog, firewood cribs, outdoor kitchens—all represented evidences of a kind of caring for one's plot, however large or small. As one whose primary self-understanding is that of a pilgrim, I've been thinking about what it means to practice home: how house is an extension of the body and caring for something beyond one's immediate skin. Caring for my own home, I confront questions of hospitality, neighbor, watershed. This means finding and potentially crossing boundaries, accepting obligations, and answering the other in both practical and creative ways.

Practicing home includes, at times, leaving home to make art in social spaces and places outside the neighborhood. I wonder if my role as an artist amongst Quakers is to be more at ease with being "other": that is, simply letting my life and work speak for what it is and from where it is on the boundary, and listening for ways to engage in life-giving ecological give-and-take. This might include envisioning new kinds of practices—perhaps even for quiet and still Quakers—that would be grounded in the body and aesthetics and usefulness, and that can open us to participating in place. To participate means to reckon

---

[14] Kathleen Norris, *The Cloister Walk* (New York, NY: Riverhead Books, 1997), 34.

with our place in the community of creation, and assume the responsibility of making a home. And making sure, as Barclay warned about sacraments, our communion is not too small.

14 | How Are We to Live? An Overview of Ethics, Economics and Science

By Robert Howell

Abstract: Continued human life on Earth is threatened by such risks as climate warming, human population growth, toxins, and strains on supplies of quality water and food. Each of these imperils our current way of life, and the survival of the human race. They challenge the assumptions of our economic and social practices in a fundamental way, and especially the ethical principles of human-human and human-Earth relations. This essay provides an overview of significant historical developments of our ethical, economic, and scientific principles and the relationships between each. It shows that in the main streams of ethical traditions that primarily dealt with human-human relationships (such as Aristotelian, Utilitarian, and social contract), a number of modern philosophers have extended these to include human-Earth considerations. It describes how the dominant economic model was developed prior to the scientific understanding of thermodynamic laws, and hence has left the current economic framework in conflict with modern science. A number of economists have written about the limitations of the dominant neoclassical model, but unfortunately the dominant model is still mainstream. As a result our way of life is based on principles that exploit the world's resources so that we are not living within the capacity of the Earth.

An example of the need for consistency between ethics, modern science, and an ecologically sustainable economic model is illustrated in this essay, including some of the ethical debate involved in the scientific discussions of the Intergovernmental Panel on Climate Change and the United Nations Framework Convention on Climate Change.

Until the human-Earth ethic is reflected in our economic and social behavior, our future is very bleak. Any relevant discussion of Quaker principles and ethics and the policy options that follow from these need to recognize these matters.

I. Introduction

In thinking about what ethical principles could be considered by the Quaker reader, it is important to appreciate significant historical trends in ethics, economics, and science and their relationships, for three reasons. First, a Quaker ethic should be able to stand a critical appreciation. Understanding the strengths and weaknesses of the main non-Quaker ethical positions can allow the reader to work toward a more considered, principled position and support policies that follow from that. Second, in engaging with non-Quakers about how we are to live, an understanding of the issues in ethics, economics, and science, and how they have affected each other, puts the Quaker reader in a better position for that dialogue and engagement to argue for principles and their application for policies based on those principles. Discussion of what policies should be adopted (example: how we should invest our money) is more considered when the different ethical, economic, and scientific underpinnings are appreciated.[1] Third, the current science indicates that the risks from climate warming alone are serious enough that mitigation alone is not sufficient, and that we need to urgently plan and prepare how to adapt to an ever increasingly hostile world.

So, how are we to live to get what we want from life, to enjoy the love of family and friends, the comforts of the Earth, and the pleasures of the good life? A normal pattern for many of us is to seek an education, to get a good job, to enable us to buy a house and various goods and services to feed ourselves, travel, and keep in good health. We expect the collective arrangements by the people who live with us—locally, nationally, internationally—to provide security for our safety, and protection of the rewards of our work and effort.

Yet there are numerous signs that these expectations cannot be met in the immediate future. These indicators include climate warming, water pollution, energy pricing, food shortages, banking failures, government incompetence and paralysis, and the destructive behavior of many business operations.[2] In each of these indicators, let alone their combined impact, significant evidence shows we cannot continue business-as-usual. A pragmatic and innovative problem solving approach within the current framework will not deal with these issues. Instead, we need to think in a different way. We need to rethink the basic assumptions that underlie what we have understood by the good life: the beliefs that we have about how to relate to our fellow human beings and the Earth we live on.

---

[1] I offer a place-based Quaker approach to these topics in chapter 21 of this volume: Robert Howell, "How Aotearoa New Zealand Quakers Care for the Planet."

[2] Wayne Cartwright, ed. "Strong Sustainability for New Zealand: Principles and Scenarios," Earth Limits, 2009, accessed January 2019, http://earthslimits.org/.

Many of the intellectual frameworks of ethics and economics are based on innovative approaches for their time, over one or two or more centuries ago. These shaped the way we built our institutions: the governmental, commercial, and civil society sectors commonplace today, and that we take for granted. The purpose here is to discuss the various strands, traditions, or schools of thought in ethics, science, and economics and how they fit together. Until we release ourselves from these historical straitjackets of how to think about how we are to live, the future will be captured by the limitations of outmoded principles that underpin current thought and practice.

Ethics traditionally has dealt with human-human relations and ignored human-Earth matters. The dominant international economic model is based on outdated scientific principles. Yet there are many writers and thinkers who have recognized these weaknesses and have extended the traditional ethical and religious traditions to include a human-Earth perspective, and an economics that is based on modern scientific principles. These are described here. Figure 1 summarizes the major thinkers and concepts in Western ethical, economic, and relevant scientific traditions in a diagram.

II. Ethics

This section describes the differences between moral language, codes, and ethics. It then briefly describes the key concepts used by the major Western ethical traditions of Aristotle (1 in Diagram [hereafter in D]), Kant (2A in D), Social Contract (3A in D), and Utilitarianism (4C in D). It notes that traditionally they have dealt with human-human concerns: it was often environmentalists who introduced the human-Earth relationship (7B in D). This section looks at how some modern philosophers have extended the traditional ethical frameworks to include a human-Earth focus (1, 2A, 3A, 4c in D), and how modern theologians and religious thinkers have done this also (5 in D). The section concludes with a personal suggestion using the Aristotelian notion of *phronesis* or practical wisdom.

Everyday discourse includes words such as "right," "ought," "duty," "obligations," and "responsibilities." We talk about obligations parents have toward their children for their care and nurture. Organizations have responsibilities toward their employees. Entitlements can be rights, or what people are owed. This is moral language.

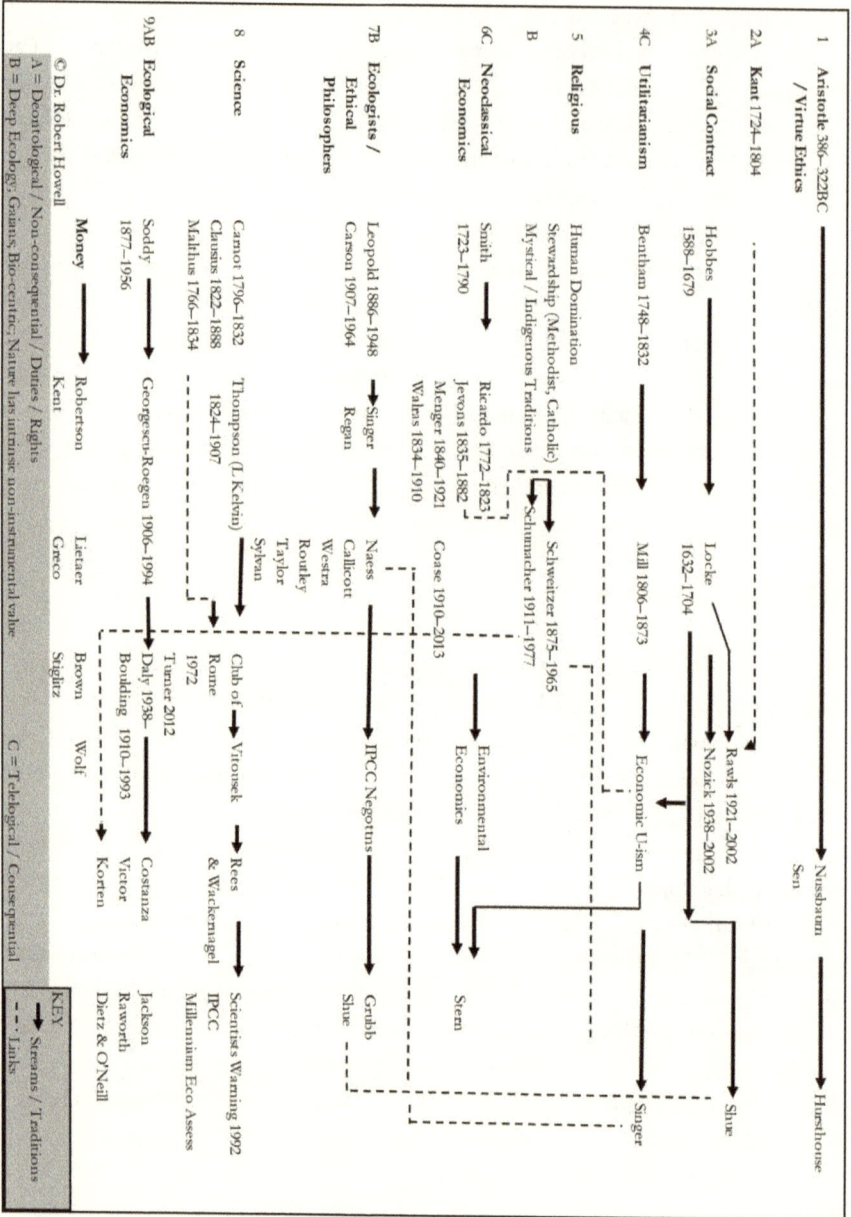

Figure 1

1   Aristotle 386–322BC / Virtue Ethics → Nussbaum → Hursthouse

2A   Kant 1724–1804 → ... → Sen

3A   Social Contract   Hobbes 1588–1679 → Locke 1632–1704 → Rawls 1921–2002; Nozick 1938–2002 → Shue

4C   Utilitarianism   Bentham 1748–1832 → Mill 1806–1873 → Economic U-ism → Singer

5   Religious   Human Domination / Stewardship (Methodist, Catholic)

B   Mystical / Indigenous Traditions → Schweitzer 1875–1965

6C   Neoclassical Economics   Smith 1723–1790 → Ricardo 1772–1823; Jevons 1835–1882; Menger 1840–1921; Walras 1834–1910 → Coase 1910–2013 → Environmental Economics → Stern

   Schumacher 1911–1977

7B   Ecologists / Ethical Philosophers   Leopold 1886–1948; Carson 1907–1964 → Singer; Regan → Naess; Callicott; Westra; Rowtley; Taylor; Sylvan → IPCC Negotns → Grubb; Shue

8   Science   Carnot 1796–1832; Clausius 1822–1888; Malthus 1766–1834 → Thompson (L. Kelvin) 1824–1907 → Club of Rome 1972; Turner 2012 → Scientists Warning 1992; Rees & Wackernagel; IPCC; Millennium Eco Assess

9AB   Ecological Economics   Soddy 1877–1956 → Georgescu-Roegen 1906–1994 → Daly 1938–; Boulding 1910–1993; Korten → Costanza; Victor; Dietz & O'Neill; Jackson; Raworth

   Money   Robertson; Kent; Lietaer; Greco; Brown; Stiglitz; Wolf

© Dr. Robert Howell

A = Deontological / Non-consequential / Duties / Rights
B = Deep Ecology; Gaians, Bio-centric; Nature has intrinsic non-instrumental value
C = Teleological / Consequential

KEY
→ Streams / Traditions
-- Links

Everyday discourse includes words such as "right," "ought," "duty," "obligations," and "responsibilities." We talk about obligations parents have toward their children for their care and nurture. Organizations have responsibilities toward their employees. Entitlements can be rights, or what people are owed. This is moral language.

When these descriptions of intention or behavior are gathered together in a set they can take the form of professional rules, organizational charters, national constitutions, policies, codes of conduct, creeds, doctrines, and cultural customs through myths, stories, and traditions. For example: organizational employment rules describe the expected behavior between an employee and their employer about matters such as racial or sexual discrimination, a safe workplace, drinking alcohol, or taking certain drugs while at work. Schemas describe standards, sets of rules, customs, or policies, and are attempts to give system, clarity, and intellectual power to everyday moral activity and discourse. Other examples of codes are the Earth Charter, the Universal Declaration of Human Rights, and the World Charter for Nature.[3]

In these codes are certain primary moral concepts or principles. When we talk about these principles, we are using a meta-language: we are talking about the moral language or schema. Philosophers have developed theories about these primary moral principles, and argued that a certain notion or notions could be used to derive explanations about what is ethical. Theories can also aim to advocate for different understandings about how to behave where there are contradictions between different discourse and behavior, and between different schemas. Within the classical Western ethical traditions, Immanuel Kant relied on the notion of duty,[4] the Utilitarians on the concept of happiness or utility (where the right action is the one that will produce the greatest good and least amount of pain for the greatest number of people),[5] and John Rawls on the idea of equity

---

[3] "The Earth Charter," Earth Charter, accessed January 2019, http://earthcharter.org/. "The Universal Declaration of Human Rights," United Nations, accessed January 2019, http://un.org/en/universal-declaration-human-rights/. "World Charter for Nature," United Nations, 1982, accessed January 2019, http://un.org/documents/ga/res/37/a37r007.htm.

[4] Robert Johnson, "Kant's Moral Philosophy," *The Stanford Encyclopedia of Philosophy*, 2008, accessed January 2019, http://plato.stanford.edu/archives/sum2014/entries/kant-moral/.

[5] Jeremy Bentham, *Introduction to the Principles of Morals and Legislation* (Oxford: Basil Blackwell, 1948). John Stuart Mill, *Utilitarianism* (Oxford: Oxford University Press, 1998). William K. Frankena, "Utilitarianism," in *Dictionary of Philosophy*, ed. Dagobert D. Runes (Whitefish, MT: Kessinger Publishing, 1942), accessed January 2019, http://ditext.com/runes/u.html. David O. Brink, "Mill's Moral and Political Philosophy," in *Stanford Encyclopedia of Philosophy* (Redwood City, CA: Metaphysics Research Lab, Stanford University, 2007), accessed January 2019, http://plato.stanford.edu/entries/mill-moral-political.

or fairness.[6] Aristotelians use a set of virtues coordinated by *eudemonia* (understood as "a flourishing life").[7] Thomas Hobbes and John Locke were early advocates for the idea of a social contract that described the responsibilities between a ruler and their subjects.[8] That approach has been very influential in French, American, and international thought (such as the Universal Declaration of Human Rights). The latter included individual property rights that excluded notions of collective ownership developed by many indigenous peoples. These traditional Western ethical theorists or theories primarily focus on human-human relations, although Utilitarians were reformers in regard to such attitudes and behavior toward animals.

The social contract theories deal with the authority that rulers could and should have, deciding the responsibilities of leaders and the range of social institutions to be included in a government's obligations to its citizens. Earlier, social contract theory dealt with the divine right of kings, and then over time was widened to include ideas about parliamentary participation and extension of voting rights away from only male and usually white landowners. In the 1970s Rawls (3A in D) gave a new impetus to the social contract tradition by describing persuasive arguments for the importance of the notion of fairness. Rawls's theory recommends equal basic rights, equality of opportunity, and promoting the interests of the least advantaged members of society by social institutions (such as education and welfare), addressing the disadvantages over which individuals have no control and yet limit one's life choices.

Differing from Rawls is Robert Nozick (3A in D), who argued for a libertarian ethic (maximizing individualism and freedom of choice) and a minimalist state with very wide disparities in access to the resources necessary for living.[9] But a minimalist state will have very few of the functions that are critical for a safe and sustainable world. Nozick tries to explain how a police force can be theoretically established by voluntary association while granting the individual

---

[6] John Rawls, *A Theory of Justice* (Cambridge, MA: Harvard University Press, 1971). Martha Nussbaum, "The Enduring Significance of John Rawls," *The Chronicle of Higher Education*, accessed January 2019, http://evatt.org.au/papers/enduring-significance-john-rawls.html.

[7] Aristotle, *Ethics*, translated by J. A. K. Thomson (London: Penguin, 1948).

[8] Ian Shapiro, ed., *Two Treatises of Government and A Letter Concerning Toleration: John Locke*, Rethinking the Western Tradition series (New Haven, CT: Yale University Press, 2003). Alex Tuckness, "John Locke," in *Stanford Encyclopedia of Philosophy*, 2005, accessed January 2019, http://plato.stanford.edu/entries/locke/.

[9] Robert Nozick, *Anarchy, State, and Utopia* (New Jersey: Blackwell, 1974). Edward Feser, "Robert Nozick," in *Internet Encyclopedia of Philosophy*, accessed January 2019, http://iep.utm.edu/nozick/.

rights without social coercion, but admits it cannot be done.[10] His theory fails. The major differences between the two lie in the extent that governments should act to address the disadvantages that arise through factors beyond the individual's control, such as where one was born, the family one was born into, their sex and color (human-human obligations). Both Rawls and Nozick ignore human-Earth relationships.

While traditional Western ethics has primarily dealt with human-human relationships, people throughout history have included human-Earth relations in their ethic (7B in D). These include people from many indigenous cultures, Francis of Assisi, William Blake, William Wordsworth, John Muir (founder of the Sierra Club), Mahatma Gandhi, Jean-Jacques Rousseau, and Albert Schweitzer. German foresters, influenced in part by Rousseau, and the movement promoting wilderness, included a human-Earth perspective into their thinking.[11] But it was twentieth century scientists such as Rachel Carson[12] and Aldo Leopold[13] who led the modern development in environmental ethics. Their focus on a human-Earth relationship was picked up by some of the animal rights writers (e.g. Peter Singer, Tom Regan),[14] and then environmental philosophers such as Arne Naess (deep ecology),[15] J. Baird Callicott (the leading contemporary exponent of Leopold's land ethic),[16] Laura Westra (ecological integrity),[17] Richard Sylvan (the intrinsic

---

[10] Jonathan Wolff, *Robert Nozick* (Cambridge, UK: Polity Press, 1991).

[11] Richard H. Grove, *Green Imperialism: Colonial Expansion, Tropical Island Edens, and the Origins of Environmentalism, 1600–1860* (Cambridge, UK: Cambridge University Press, 1995). Ramachandra Guha, *Environmentalism: A Global History* (New York: Longman, 2000).

[12] Rachel Carson, *Silent Spring* (London: Hamish Hamilton, 1963). See also http://rachelcarson.org/.

[13] Aldo Leopold, "The Land Ethic," in *Environmental Ethics: An Anthology*, eds. Andrew Light and Holmes Rolston, III (Oxford: Blackwell Publishing, 2003), 38–46. Aldo Leopold, *A Sand County Almanac* (Oxford: Oxford University Press, 1949). See also http://aldoleopold.org/.

[14] Peter Singer, *Animal Liberation: A New Ethics for Our Treatment of Animals* (New York: HarperCollins, 1975). Tom Regan, *The Case for Animal Rights* (Berkeley, CA: University of California Press, 1983).

[15] Arne Naess, "The Deep Ecological Movement: Some Philosophical Aspects," in *Environmental Ethics: An Anthology*, eds. Andrew Light and Holmes Rolston, III (Oxford: Blackwell Publishing, 2003), 10–31.

[16] J. Baird Callicott, *In Defense of the Land Ethic: Essays in Environmental Philosophy* (Albany: State University of New York, 1989).

[17] Laura Westra, *Living in Integrity: Toward a Global Ethic to Restore a Fragmented Earth* (Lanham, MD: Rowman Littlefield, 1998).

value of the non-human, natural world),[18] Paul W. Taylor (respect for nature),[19] and Holmes Rolston, III (value in nature),[20] amongst many others.

We have seen that scientists and environmentalists have acknowledged the ethical issues involved in their discussions. A number of modern philosophers have also recognized the traditional approach needs to be extended to include the human-Earth relationship. Rosalind Hursthouse (1 in D) is an example of someone who has used the Aristotelian approach, which bases the good life on the cultivation of virtues. She argues for "respect for nature" as a new virtue.[21]

Peter Singer is a modern Utilitarian or consequentialist (4C in D). He devotes two chapters of the third edition of *Practical Ethics* to climate change and the environment, respectively.[22] He describes an environmental ethic arguing from a human-centered ethic. He argues that we have a responsibility to avoid harming people. Individually and collectively through our emissions we are causing harm. We have an obligation to act individually and to change the policy of governments to slow climate change.

The philosopher, Henry Shue (3A in D) uses the social contract tradition to advocate for a rights approach based on fairness.[23] He states that the purpose of a right is to provide protection for human beings against a threat to which they are vulnerable and against which they may be powerless without such protective action. To be effective, such protective action must be international and intergenerational. Rapid climate change places current and future generations in the kind of circumstances that call for the construction of rights-protecting institutions. Climate change threatens the right to life, the right to health, and the right to subsistence. He argues that rights-protecting institutions are required on the principle of fairness for the right of all current and future generations to life, and for immediate action to reduce this environmental destruction.

Within Christian thought, the Genesis story has been used to support human dominion over nature for human benefit, as pointed out by White in a

---

[18] Richard Sylvan, *Transcendental Metaphysics* (Cambridgeshire, UK: White Horse Press, 1997).

[19] Paul W. Taylor, *Respect for Nature: A Theory of Environmental Ethics* (New Jersey: Princeton University Press, 1986).

[20] Holmes Rolston, III, *Environmental Ethics: Duties to and Values in the Natural World* (Philadelphia: Temple University Press, 1988).

[21] Rosalind Hursthouse, "Environmental Virtue Ethics," in *Working Virtue*, eds. Rebecca L. Walker and Philip J. Ivanhoe (Oxford: Oxford University Press, 2007).

[22] Peter Singer, *Practical Ethics* (Cambridge, UK: Cambridge University Press, 2011).

[23] Henry Shue, "Ethics, the Environment and the Changing International Order," *International Affairs* 71, no. 3 (1995): 453–461. Henry Shue, "Global Environment and International Inequity," *International Affairs* 75, no. 3 (1999): 531–545. Henry Shue, "Human rights, climate change, and the trillionth ton," in *The Ethics of Climate Change*, ed. Denis G. Arnold (Cambridge, UK: Cambridge University Press, 2011), 292–314.

1967 article, "Historical Roots of Our Ecologic Crisis."[24] But many Christian churches and theologians have argued that there are other ways to view the biblical story. For example, for Methodists, the theology of creation proclaims the consistent message of Christian stewardship, of humanity's obligation to care for the whole of the earth and its creatures. While historically some groups may have emphasized human dominion over creation, much modern church teaching explicitly denies this interpretation.[25]

Many Quaker Yearly Meetings have adopted statements and minutes such as those found in the Appendix of this volume. Other religions have affirmed a human-Earth ethic that recognizes interdependence between humanity and nature.[26] Eric Schumacher's *Small is Beautiful: A Study of Economics As If People Mattered* was a very popular book in the 1970s.[27] It brought a Buddhist approach to economics and ethics. Pope Francis' historic encyclical "Laudato si': On Care for our Common Home" described an integral ecology, with implications for human-human and human-Earth relationships in all areas of the Christian life.[28] The Forum on Religion and Ecology at Yale is the largest international multireligious project of its kind.[29] Its conferences, publications, and website explore religious worldviews, texts, ethics, and practices in order to broaden understanding of the complex nature of current environmental concerns. The Forum is a valuable source to identify many religious views that take a human-Earth relationship other than one of exploitation of the Earth.

These are just a few examples of philosophers, ethicists, and theologians from many traditions who have included a human-Earth relationship in their ethical framework. Respect for nature, care, integrity, oneness, intrinsic value, resilience, stewardship, wholeness, and reverence for life: these are some of the

---

[24] Lynn White, Jr., "The Historical Roots of Our Ecologic Crisis," *Science* 155, no. 3767 (March 1967): 1203–1207.

[25] E.g., this report created for the Methodist Church in the UK: *The Theology of Creation: A Position Paper for the Church's Investment Policy Relating to Environmental Ethics*, London: Central Finance Board of the Methodist Church, 2009, accessed January 2019, http://cfb-methodistchurch.org.uk/downloads/position_papers/cfb_climate_change_position_paper.pdf.

[26] Gary Gardner, "Invoking the Spirit: Religion and Spirituality in the Quest for a Sustainable World," *Worldwatch Paper* 164, Worldwatch Institute (2002).

[27] Eric Schumacher, *Small is Beautiful: A Study of Economics As If People Mattered* (Vancouver, BC: Hartley and Marks Publishers, 1973).

[28] Francis, "Laudato Si': On Care for Our Common Home," Washington, DC: United States Conference of Catholic Bishops, 2015. The Encyclical's implications for how we invest are described in *Catholic Investment: Principles and Practice*. The authors are Thea Ormerod (Australian Religious Response to Climate Change), Jacqui Remond (Catholic Earthcare Australia) and Robert Howell (Quaker, Aotearoa New Zealand), http://catholicearthcare.org.au/wp-content/uploads/2016/08/Catholic-Investment-Principles-and-Practice.pdf.

[29] See: Religion and Ecology at Yale, http://fore.research.yale.edu/.

concepts to choose for a core ethical principle or principles from which to build a more ecological ethical framework.[30] If we choose one principle, it needs to be rich enough to generate the secondary concepts, schema, and sets of obligations to be able to define a relationship that guides behavior. If more than one concept is chosen, then they need to be integrated together to avoid conflicts and contradictions.

Do we give priority or equal weight to righting the injustices that led to developing countries being much poorer, against a need to drastically reduce carbon emissions by all countries including poor countries that might have large deposits of fossil fuels? Does the United Nations Declaration of Human Rights (including property rights) take precedence over the World Charter for Nature ("Nature shall be respected and its essential processes shall not be impaired")?[31] There is a need to select and use a core ethical concept, or set of concepts, that do not see the world as solely or mainly for human utility. In addition to the arguments above, I would put forward a more pragmatic argument. If we start with the notion that nature is mainly to be seen for instrumental utility for humankind, but subject to certain limits, it is much harder to develop a relationship with nature that enables a fit that works for human beings, and where nature is able to provide a sustainable place for human life. It is the same as having a competitive ethic for business, but within some limits. If the basic value of business is maximization of self-interest, it is very difficult for a business executive to leave the office for home and change into a loving, caring spouse or parent. And to develop a society as a whole that is a loving and caring place to live in, while a significant portion of it works to contrary standards, is very difficult. People do not find it easy to live simultaneously in a contradictory or disjointed way.

Aristotle talked about *phronesis* or practical wisdom: that is a complex, learned, and nuanced ability to be virtuous. It is like an apprenticeship. It is not something that can be switched on and off. If humans value and respect nature, but recognize that it is also of utility for food, shelter, and warmth, it will be much easier to design an economy and society that has the right relationship with nature, than if we start with the belief that the world is primarily for our use, but within certain limits. Rather than start at one end (the world is for us to exploit) but then impose some limits, start at the other end (we should ensure nature's

---

[30] The Earth Charter uses a number of concepts including respect, ecological integrity, care, equity, and justice; see http://earthcharter.org/.

[31] "World Charter for Nature," United Nations, 1982, accessed January 2019, http://un.org/documents/ga/res/37/a37r007.htm.

health and resilience are paramount) and then see what resources are needed for humanity and how they can be used wisely.

III. Mainstream Economics

This section describes how the neoclassical economic model came about (6C in D), and a fatal weakness of the theory in explaining how money is created below (AB in D). The current dominant economic model, classical or neoclassical, is based on Adam Smith's work, and has been developed by economists such as David Ricardo, William Stanley Jevons, Carl Menger, and Léon Walras, amongst others.[32] Classical economics posits that, if individuals pursue their self-interest in a competitive free-market system, the market will eventually reach an optimal and stable equilibrium that will benefit everyone. Competition will bring about the most efficient price for goods and services through a balance of supply and demand. The price mechanism will also deal with scarcity, encouraging substitution of diminishing resources. The model assumes a Utilitarian ethic.

The neoclassical tradition recognizes that the market is not always perfect. There are externalities (costs that are not included in prices). Pollution created in the production of certain goods is an example and the cost usually falls on the government or non-polluters to pay.[33] Ronald Coase is a more recent economist who suggests market pricing be used to deal with the environmental hazard[34] of chlorofluorocarbons (CFCs).[35] But Nicholas Stern argues that the greatest market failure was the lack of factoring in of the cost of climate warming.[36] Environmental economics is a subset of the neoclassical position where attempts are made to identify externalities and internalize them in prices.

---

[32] David Ricardo, *On the Principles of Political Economy and Taxation*, first edition (London: John Murray, 1817). William Stanley Jevons, "The Mathematical Theory of Political Economy," *Journal of the Statistical Society of London* 37, no. 4 (December 1874): 478–488. doi: 10.2307/2338697. Carl Menger, *Principles of Economics* (Auburn, AL: Ludwig von Mises Institute, 1871, 2007). Léon Walras, *Elements of Pure Economics*, reprint edition (London: American Economic Association and the Royal Economic Society, Allen and Unwin, 1874, 1954).

[33] Hence the "polluter pays principle," which is a concept in environmental law that places responsibility on the entity causing the pollution to pay for its remediation. See: http://lse.ac.uk/GranthamInstitute/faqs/what-is-the-polluter-pays-principle/.

[34] Ronald H. Coase, "Ronald H. Coase – Biographical," in *Les Prix Nobel*, Nobel Lectures Series, The Nobel Prize website, accessed January 2019, http://nobelprize.org/prizes/economic-sciences/1991/coase/biographical/.

[35] CFCs are the particle responsible for creating the hole in the ozone layer, and regulated by global agreements in the 1990s.

[36] Alison Benjamin, "Stern: Climate change a market failure," *The Guardian*, November 29, 2007, accessed January 2019, http://theguardian.com/environment/2007/nov/29/climatechange.carbonemissions.

When economists developed classical economic principles, they believed in the existence of natural laws of economics that were analogous to the laws of physics. They substituted economic variables for physical ones; however, the physics they used was soon to be outmoded. By copying the equations of mid-nineteenth century physics, economists fell victim to the assumptions of the time. As a result, the ability of their theories to accurately describe and predict economic activity is seriously flawed.[37]

John Reed, CEO at Citicorp, became disillusioned with the predictions of economists. He funded a 10-day cross-disciplinary workshop in 1987 where he brought major scientists and economists together. The scientists were amazed at economic assumptions that were out of step with modern science: they said that it was like visiting Cuba—completely shut off from the Western world with vintage cars of the '50s.[38]

A more recent example is the inability of mainstream economists to predict the 2008 financial collapse. Mainstream economists did not predict the 2008 crash because the behavior of the financial sector was not included in their models. This exclusion is due to neoclassical economists' inadequate understanding of how money is created by privately owned banks. The theory supposes that only the private market has a role in the creation of money, and that money has a neutral role in economic behavior. Ingham calls this orthodox concept of money for monetary policy "incoherent."[39] The expectation that the state has no role to play, and that money can be created only by market means, Wray calls "Peter Pan Never-Never Land," a theory based in fantasy.[40] The obsessive reliance on the market in money creation is ideological: the theory refuses to acknowledge the roles of the government monetary authority, the banking system, and the agencies of production. It refuses to recognize that the financial sector is a cost to the general economy. The cost of money creation is excessive and the system is unstable.[41]

---

[37] Cartwright, ed., *Strong Sustainability for New Zealand: Principles and Scenarios*, New Zealand: New Zealand National Commission for UNESCO, Sustainable Aotearoa New Zealand, Inc., Nakedize Ltd., 2009.

[38] Eric Beinhocker, *The Origin of Wealth* (Cambridge, MA: Harvard Business School Press, 2006).

[39] Geoffrey Ingham, *The Nature of Money* (Malden, MA: Polity Press, 2004).

[40] Randall Wray, *Modern Money Theory* (New York: Palgrave Macmillan, 2012).

[41] Other authors who have described this problem include: Joseph Stiglitz, "Macroeconomics, Monetary Policy and the Crisis," in *In the Wake of the Crisis*, eds. Olivier Blanchard, et al. (Cambridge, MA: MIT Press, 2012), 31–44. James Robertson, *Future Money: Breakdown or Breakthrough?* (Devon, UK: Green Books, 2012). Deirdre Kent, *Healthy Money, Healthy Planet: Developing Sustainability Through New Money Systems* (Nelson, NZ: Craig Potton, 2005). Ellen Brown, *Web of Debt: The Shocking Truth about Our Money System and How We Can Break Free* (Baton Rouge: Third Millennium Press, 2007). Ellen Brown, *Public Bank Solution* (Baton Rouge: Third

Many authors have written about this problem, including Martin Wolf, associate editor and chief economics commentator at the *Financial Times*. He is widely considered one of the world's most influential writers on economics, and "staggeringly well connected" within elite financial circles.[42] As a young man Wolf supported Keynesian economics, which saw the need for governments to intervene in the economy, but gradually became disillusioned and moved to become an influential advocate of globalization and the free market.[43] This changed after reflecting on the 2008 meltdown. He writes that he is guilty of working with a mental model of the economy that did not allow for the possibility of another Great Depression. He states that the economic, financial, intellectual and political elites have misunderstood the consequences of headlong financial liberalization. The policymaking elites failed to appreciate the risks of systemic breakdown; the intellectual elites failed to anticipate the crisis and agree on what to do; and the political elites were discredited by their willingness to finance the rescue. He argues that the current international economic model is too unstable and needs to be changed. In particular he recommends changing the privatization of money-creation carried out by banks, and making that function the responsibility of government.

The current mainstream neoclassical economic system is based on a Utilitarian ethic that sees the Earth as a resource for human utility. It is based on a version of the libertarian social contract that sees a minimal role for government, yet its most sophisticated advocate, Nozick, is unable to justify the establishment within society of a police function within his scheme. It ignores the instability of the financial sector through the privatization of money creation: it is linked to a monetary policy that is incoherent.

IV. Science (8 in D)

Sadi Carnot published only one book, the *Reflections on the Motive Power of Fire* in 1824, in which he expressed the first successful theory of the maximum efficiency of heat engines.[44] In this work he laid the foundations of an entirely new

---

Millennium Press, 2013). Thomas H. Greco, Jr., *The End of Money and the Future of Civilization* (White River Junction, VT: Chelsea Green Publishing, 2006). Bernard Lietaer, et al., *Money and Sustainability: The Missing Link* (Devon, UK: Triarchy Press, 2012).

[42] Martin Wolf, *The Shifts and Shocks — What We Have Learned and Have Still to Learn from the Financial Crisis* (London: Penguin, 2014).

[43] John M. Keynes, *The General Theory of Employment, Interest and Money* (Eugene, OR: Harvest / San Diego, CA: Harcourt 1936, 1964).

[44] Sadi Carnot, *Reflections on the Motive Power of Heat*, ed. and transl. Robert Henry Thurston (New York: J. Wiley & Sons, 1890).

discipline, thermodynamics. Carnot's work attracted little attention during his lifetime, but it was later used by Rudolf Clausius and Lord Kelvin to formalize the second law of thermodynamics and define the concept of entropy.[45]

The First Law of Thermodynamics states that all matter and energy in the universe is constant, that it cannot be created or destroyed. The Second Law (sometimes called the entropy law) states that matter and energy can only be changed in one direction, from usable to unusable, from ordered to disordered. The earth is a closed system except for the entry of energy in the form of sunlight. In earth's system what goes into part of the system must come out, and it does so with its productive potential irrevocably diminished.[46]

The thermodynamic laws are in direct contradiction with the equilibrium law that is one of the foundational principles of the current dominant neo-classical economic model. The belief that there is no limit to growth, and that there is always a substitute for scarce resources, are in conflict with the thermodynamic laws of modern science.

The Club of Rome produced a book, *Limits to Growth*, in 1972, which was based on computer simulations of exponential economic and population growth with finite resource supplies.[47] Scenarios based on business-as-usual, with its belief in unlimited inputs to the economic system, could not be sustained. Recently, Graham M. Turner has shown that their predictions about limits to growth were justified.[48]

Peter M. Vitousek and others in 1986 calculated that 40 percent of the solar energy converted by photosynthesis available to counter the entropic effect of the Second Law is already captured by humans.[49] The ecological footprint was conceived by William E. Rees and developed in conjunction with Mathis

---

[45] Rudolf Clausius, *The Mechanical Theory of Heat – With Its Application to the Steam Engine and to Physical Properties of Bodies* (London: John van Voorst, 1867).

[46] W. F. Magie, ed. and transl., *The Second Law of Thermodynamics: Memoirs by Carnot, Clausius and Thomson* (New York: Harper, 1899).

[47] Donella Meadows, et al., *The Limits to Growth: a Report for the Club of Rome's Project on the predicament of Mankind* (New York: Universe Books, 1972). The book developed issues like population that had been earlier identified by Malthus. Thomas R. Malthus, *An Essay on the Principle of Population* (London: J. Johnson, 1798).

[48] Graham M. Turner, "On the Cusp of Global Collapse? Updated Comparison of the Limits to Growth with Historical Data," *GAIA — Ecological Perspectives for Science and Society* 21 no. 2 (2012): 116–124.

[49] Peter M. Vitousek, et al., "Human appropriation of the products of photosynthesis," *Bioscience* 36, no. 6 (1986): 368–373.

Wackernagel and others.[50] Current use of the footprint shows that 1.7 Earths would be required to meet the demands humanity makes on nature each year.[51] If there is any uncertainty about how scientists think about the perilous state of the Earth, the "1992 World Scientists' Warning to Humanity," signed by 1,700 of the world's leading scientists, including the majority of Nobel laureates in the sciences, leaves no doubt.[52] Their statement contains the following:

> The earth is finite. Its ability to absorb wastes and destructive effluent is finite. Its ability to provide food and energy is finite. Its ability to provide for growing numbers of people is finite. And we are fast approaching many of the earth's limits. Current economic practices which damage the environment, in both developed and underdeveloped nations, cannot be continued without the risk that vital global systems will be damaged beyond repair.[53]

V. Ecological Economics (9AB in D)

Ecological economics is an economic system that accepts the thermodynamic laws as given. Frederick Soddy was one of the early founders of ecological economics. He received the Nobel Prize for Chemistry in 1921. From 1921–1934 he carried on a quixotic campaign for a radical restructuring of global monetary relationships. This economy would be rooted in physics (particularly the laws of thermodynamics) and he was roundly dismissed as a crank. Most of his proposals (abandoning the gold standard, letting international exchange rates float, using government surpluses and deficits as macroeconomic policy tools, and establishing economic statistics) are now conventional practice. One remaining recommendation, eliminating fractional-reserve banking, is still outside conventional wisdom.[54]

---

[50] William E. Rees, "Ecological Footprints and Appropriated Carrying Capacity: What Urban Economics Leaves Out," *Environment and Urbanization* 4, no. 2 (1992): 120–130.

[51] Global Footprint Network, accessed January 2019, http://footprintnetwork.org/our-work/ecological-footprint/.

[52] For a second warning issued in 2018, see: William J. Ripple, Christopher Wolf, Thomas M. Newsome, Mauro Galetti, Mohammed Alamgir, Eileen Crist, Mahmoud I. Mahmoud, William F. Laurance, and 15,364 scientist signatories from 184 countries, "World Scientists' Warning to Humanity: A Second Notice," *BioScience* 67, no. 12 (December 2017): 1026–1028, doi.org/10.1093/biosci/bix125.

[53] "1992 World Scientists' Warning to Humanity," Union of Concerned Scientists, accessed January 2019, http://ucsusa.org/about/1992-world-scientists.html#.VHuZd6SUc5k.

[54] Eric Zencey, "Mr. Soddy's Ecological Economy," *The New York Times*, April 11, 2009.

The Quaker Kenneth Boulding, in an influential article, "The Economics of the Coming Spaceship Earth," contrasted an open-ended economy with a closed economy. The open economy he called the "cowboy economy," the cowboy being symbolic of the illimitable plains and also associated with reckless, exploitative, romantic, and violent behavior, which is characteristic of open societies. The closed economy of the future might similarly be called the "spaceman economy." Here the earth is seen as a single spaceship, without unlimited reservoirs of anything, either for extraction or for pollution.[55]

Building on this concept, Herman Daly proposes three rules for an economics based on modern science.[56] The Output Rule states that wastes should be kept within the assimilative capacity of the local environment. The Input Rule states that the harvesting rates of renewable inputs shall not exceed the regenerative capacity of the natural system that generates them. The third rule says that the non-renewable depletion rate shall equal the rate at which renewable substitutes are developed by human invention and investment.

There are many other economists who have made valuable contributions to ecological economics.[57] For instance, Robert Costanza's contribution was to value the world's ecosystems and natural capital estimated to be in the range of US$16-54 trillion per year, with an average of US$33 trillion per year. Because of the nature of the uncertainties, this must be considered a minimum estimate. Global gross national product total is around US$18 trillion per year.[58] Another example is Kate Raworth, who developed an image of "The Doughnut" of social and planetary boundaries, showing how social and ecological limits are related.[59]

---

[55] Kenneth Boulding, "The Economics of the Coming Spaceship Earth," in *Environmental Quality in a Growing Economy,* ed. Henry Jarrett (Baltimore, MD: Resources for the Future/John Hopkins University Press, 1966), http://arachnid.biosci.utexas.edu/courses/THOC/Readings/Boulding_SpaceshipEarth.pdf.

[56] Herman Daly, *Steady-State Economics,* second edition (Washington, DC: Island Press, 1991). Herman Daly, *Beyond Growth* (Boston MA: Beacon Press, 1996). Herman Daly, *Ecological Economics and Sustainable Development* (Cheltenham, UK: Edward Elgar, 2007).

[57] Other economists amongst many who have contributed to economic analysis based on the foundations of ecological economics include: David Korten, *The Great Turning: From Empire to Earth Community,* second edition (Oakland, CA: Berrett-Koehler, 1997, 2007). Peter Victor, *Managing Without Growth* (Cheltenham, UK: Edward Elgar, 2008). Tim Jackson, *Prosperity Without Growth? The Transition to a Sustainable Economy* (London: Earthscan, 2009). Rob Dietz and Dan O'Neill, *Enough is Enough* (Oakland, CA: Berrett-Koehler, 2013).

[58] Robert Costanza et al., "The Value of the World's Ecosystem Services and Natural Capital," *Nature* 387 (1997): 253–260.

[59] Kate Raworth, *Doughnut Economics: Seven Ways to Think Like a 21st-Century Economist* (White River Junction, VT: Chelsea Green Publishing, 2017).

VI. IPCC and UNFCCC (7B in D)

This essay has described significant historical developments of our ethical, economic and scientific principles and the relationships between each. The relevance for this and the need for consistency is clearly illustrated with some of the ethical debate involved in the scientific discussions (7B in D) of the Intergovernmental Panel on Climate Change (IPCC). It was set up to advise the United Nations Framework Convention on Climate Change (UNFCCC) on the issues of climate change.[60] The UNFCCC states in Article 2:

> The ultimate objective of this Convention…is to achieve…stabilization of greenhouse gas concentrations in the atmosphere at a level that would prevent dangerous anthropogenic interference with the climate system. Such a level should be achieved within a time-frame sufficient to allow ecosystems to adapt naturally to climate change, to ensure that food production is not threatened and to enable economic development to proceed in a sustainable manner.[61]

The UNFCCC states there are five guiding principles to use for working toward this objective. The first is that protection should be on the basis of equity in accordance with common but differentiated responsibilities. The second states that full consideration should be given to those parties, especially developing countries, that are particularly vulnerable and would have to bear a disproportionate burden. The third says that parties should take precautionary measures in the absence of full scientific certainty, but that policies should be cost effective. The fourth states that parties should promote sustainable development. The fifth says that parties should promote an open international economic system, and climate change measures should not unduly restrict international trade.

One of the writers on the IPCC Working Party Group III in the early 1990s, Michael Grubb (7B in D), recognized a number of the ethical issues in the discussions.[62] Grubb noted the economic calculations by economists such as William Nordhaus relied on a Utilitarian philosophy. He noted that countries will

---

[60] United Nations Framework Convention on Climate Change, accessed January 2019, http://unfccc.int/.

[61] UNFCCC, 2008, http://unfccc.int/essential_background/convention/background/items/1353.php.

[62] Michael Grubb, "Seeking Fair Weather: Ethics and the International Debate on Climate Change," *International Affairs* 71 no. 3 (1995): 463–496. Michael Grubb, "The economics of climate damages and stabilization after the Stern Review," *Climate Policy* 6 (2006): 505–508.

have different impacts, with the developing countries experiencing the effects of climate change more acutely than developed countries. They would be less able to avoid damage caused by climate warming. Nordhaus and others argued that it would be cheaper for developing countries to adapt to climate change rather than abate it. Kamal Nath, the Indian Environment Minister, publicly rejected these policies because of the discrimination between rich and poor people.

The UNFCCC's Articles and Principles are not based on sustainable, economic, ethical, and governance models that will enable the UNFCCC to achieve the purpose of avoiding dangerous climate change because some of their premises rest on a neoclassical economic model using Utilitarian principles.[63] The first three principles are in conflict with the last two. It should be noted that the agreements reached in Paris in 2015 at the United Nations Climate Change Conference abandoned these ethical principles and agreed to accept voluntary targets set by each individual country.[64] The Climate Action Tracker estimate of the total warming of the aggregate effect of Paris Agreement commitments and of real-world policy shows that if all governments achieved their Paris Agreement commitments the world will likely warm 3.0°C, twice the 1.5°C limit agreed to in Paris.[65] The world's leading climate scientists have warned only 11 years remain for global warming to be kept to a maximum of 1.5°C,[66] and a more recent report by the Met Office has reduced this to 5 years.[67]

VII. Conclusion

The traditional ethical philosophers and schools, such as Aristotle, Kant, the Social Contract, and Utilitarianism, dealt with human-human relations. Ecologists

---

[63] Robert Howell, "Talking Past Each Other: Economics, Ethics, the IPCC and the UNFCCC," *International Journal of Transdisciplinary Research* 4 no. 1 (2009): 1–15.

[64] "The Paris Agreement," United Nations, accessed January 2019, http://unfccc.int/process-and-meetings/the-paris-agreement/the-paris-agreement.

[65] Climate Action Tracker, http://climateactiontracker.org/publications/warming-projections-global-update-dec-2018/.

[66] V. Masson-Delmotte, P. Zhai, H.-O. Pörtner, D. Roberts, J. Skea, P.R. Shukla, A. Pirani, Moufouma-Okia, C. Péan, R. Pidcock, S. Connors, J.B.R. Matthews, Y. Chen, X. Zhou, M.I. Gomis, E. Lonnoy, Maycock, M. Tignor, and T. Waterfield, eds., *Global Warming of 1.5°C. An IPCC Special Report on the impacts of global warming of 1.5°C above pre-industrial levels and related global greenhouse gas emission pathways, in the context of strengthening the global response to the threat of climate change, sustainable development, and efforts to eradicate poverty*, Intergovernmental Panel on Climate Change, 2018, World Meteorological Organization, Geneva, Switzerland, accessed January 2019, http://ipcc.ch/sr15/.

[67] "Forecast suggests Earth's warmest period on record," Met Office, February 6, 2019, accessed February 2019, http://metoffice.gov.uk/news/releases/2019/forecast-suggests-earths-warmest-period.

such as Carson and Leopold, followed by later environmental ethicists, included in their writings human-Earth relations. More recently philosophers such as Hursthouse, Singer, and Shue, extended the traditional ethical streams to include human-Earth relations.

Science, through the work of people such as Carnot, Clausius, and Kelvin, developed the laws of thermodynamics. Unfortunately, the dominant international economic model developed by Jevons, Menger, and Walras is based on scientific understandings predating the introduction of thermodynamic concepts. The neoclassical economic model uses a form of Utilitarianism premised only on human-human relations, and sees the Earth simply as there for human utility and exploitation. Based on outdated science and ethics, neoclassical economics also identifies with a version of the social contract that minimizes the role of government and maximizes the place of the market, leading to an incoherent monetary policy causing major instability. Ecological economic systems that do recognize the laws of thermodynamics are not mainstream enough to have significant influence.

A number of ethical concepts and principles can be used to develop an ethic that takes into account both human-human and human-Earth relationships. Until we adopt and use such concepts as equity and respect for nature, enabling us to live within the capacity of the Earth to support human life, we will be denying any desirable kind of life to future generations.

The 2018 report by the IPCC states very clearly the serious dangers the world faces through a warming world.[68] Why does the world not take heed? I believe it is because of the mental and organizational straitjackets that we are in because of an unscientific and unethical economic system. Until we change those, we will not significantly tackle climate warming. Wolf, in his criticism of the unregulated, market-based economic system, cannot see it continuing because it is too unstable. Very broadly, he sees two partial solutions: less globalized finance or more globalized regulation. He does not see reform coming very soon and is therefore anticipating further major financial and banking crises. Unfortunately, the dangers of ecological deterioration would only at best be slowed and not halted unless the global economic system reorients itself around a human-Earth ethic that respects our natural world. Even then, the impact on the planet through pollution, greenhouse gas emissions, deforestation, and a host of other ecological problems we currently face will not be easily reversed.

---

[68] IPCC, *Global Warming of 1.5°C.*

The option of a gradual and smooth transition to a world where we live within the capacity of Earth to support us is rapidly fading. The fossil fuel industry, which knew in the 1970s about the threat of climate warming, must bear some of the responsibility, but so must mainstream economists.[69] Today the changes will be forced on us by a rapidly deteriorating Earth, and will be drastic and harsh—and many people will die. The chances of enjoying the love of family and friends, the comforts of the Earth, and the pleasures of the good life will become very limited. Until we release ourselves from these historical straitjackets of how to think about how we are to live, the future will continue to be captured by the limitations of outmoded principles that underpin current thought and practice. It is now time for Quakers to join with others and move beyond these historical restraints to prepare for a difficult future.

---

[69] Shannon Hall, "Exxon Knew about Climate Change almost 40 years ago," *Scientific American*, October 26, 2015.

15 | Seeking Truth in History and Pedagogy: ReMembering and Decolonizing are Crucial for Sustainability

By Sara Jolena Wolcott

Abstract: Creating sustainable cultures necessitates attending to our histories, which gave rise to our current socio-ecological context. This essay first gives a brief historical overview of some of the ways that the Anthropocene Age stems from the Western history of colonization. It then continues to why this history matters for Quakers, before highlighting the pedagogical styles that the author has found useful in her own teaching of this challenging material. Particular focus is on ReMembering our stories, which includes stories of ourselves as Friends and the cultures we belong to. ReMembering requires telling these stories as accurately as possible, particularly from the perspective of marginalized communities. This work of ReMembering also creates spiritual bonds connecting us to the land, other people, and the Divine, and includes working toward personal healing from historical trauma inflicted and experienced.

I. Introduction

Potentially sustainable futures require unsettling current prevailing notions of "truth" which derive from inaccurate histories. Quakers, historically known as the Friends of Truth, have much potential to further speak and live out truth and to support the education of our students as rooted truth seekers. To do so, Quakers must first embrace the process of unlearning inaccurate histories. Our truth-seeking must turn toward our shared history in order to create earth honoring pedagogies that can enhance the needed societal shifts.

To learn history is to come closer to knowing ourselves: where we come from and how we got here. Better understanding the past enables the possibility of creating sustainable futures. Seeking more accurate histories is of relevance for all educators, regardless of their discipline. Pedagogical styles—the *how* of teaching and learning more holistic histories—are as important as the substance of the history itself.

The epistemologies and belief systems that created the Anthropocene Age find an origin point with European colonization, sometimes referred to as the Age of Discovery, which began in the mid-fifteenth century. Early European colonization was inescapably intertwined with Christianity. By the time George Fox founded Quakerism in the seventeenth century in England, the theological and cultural supremacy that infused European colonization was such a part of English culture that it became ingrained in the "revolutionary" Protestant movement. Subsequently, Quakers, including Quaker educators, played a role in the overarching colonial process. Many present-day Friends still struggle to acknowledge the denomination's historical role, and therefore their own benefit and culpability from the denomination's collective role in colonizing the Americas and Africa.

For Quaker educational endeavors to have a chance at success in enabling the creation of sustainable cultures, Quakers need to engage with decolonizing their research and pedagogy, and collaborate to create new ways of approaching knowledge.[1] A key part of this process is unlearning and relearning more accurate history. Quaker historical narratives, as well as social and ecological narratives, need to change. Fortunately, existing initiatives suggest that Quakers can adjust (and many are adjusting) their self-narrations to align with more accurate histories, a key part of both emergent and decolonizing pedagogies.

As a Quaker educator working in a non-traditional adult educational setting, in this essay I encourage other Quaker educators to increase their capacity to engage with historical truth-seeking. Toward that end, I first show some of the key connections between colonization and climate change that are rarely appreciated. This section identifies some of the content Friends need to learn and to teach, and why these historical connections are necessary foundations for enabling a paradigm shift toward a more sustainable future. I subsequently discuss my pedagogical context and style, focusing on what it means to (further) decolonize our pedagogies based primarily on my own experience of teaching this material. Throughout, I refer to the importance of iterative cycles of (un)learning, teaching, reflecting with our students, and listening to the ongoing promptings of the Holy Spirit.

---

[1] For more information on decolonizing research, a hallmark text is: L. T. Smith, *Decolonizing Methodologies: Research and Indigenous Peoples* (Dunedin, NZ: Zed Press, 1999).

II. ReMembering Some Historical Connections Often Left DisMembered

The common story about climate change in particular, but also ecological destruction more generally and the rise of the Anthropocene Age, locates the origins of climate change in the extraction of fossil fuels starting during the Industrial Revolution in England.[2] Almost any textbook on climate change will reference graphs showing the increase in carbon dioxide in the atmosphere starting in the late 1700s and exponentially increasing into the modern era. The narrative accompanying the graph, especially in the humanities and social sciences, increasingly attends not only to the scientific explanation, but also to the underlying worldviews and mentalities that were amplified due to the spike in fossil fuel use. While a variety of values and worldviews can be attributed to this behavior, the primary one is the Industrial Revolution, which separated the mind from the body (rationality) and the earth from the human being (labor and resources), as highlighted in the epistemologies of the scientific revolution and the Enlightenment.

Given this origin story, we tend to focus on fossil fuels as the culprit to the Anthropocene Age. However, the mentalities mentioned above did not originate in the Industrial Revolution, they were simply able to become more powerful due to the aid of fossil fuels. We can more accurately trace the underlying mentalities to the beginning of colonization. I am not suggesting that educators detract attention from fossil fuels and the need to draw down humanity's use of them. I am suggesting that in order to do this, it helps to more accurately locate where the mentalities of the separation of people from place arise. Recently, geologists Simon Lewis and Mark Maslin argue that the discovery of the Americas and the genocide that followed was so profound that it impacted the biochemistry of the earth's atmosphere and geology.[3] They therefore originate the Anthropocene Age, as I do, from the beginnings of colonization.

In stating that non-sustainability emerges in its current form from colonization, one can also say the Industrial Revolution emerged from colonization. During and through colonization, Europeans developed the current unsustainable material and economic models (including capital, models of labor, and natural resources at a global scale) and mindsets, worldviews, and orientations—includ-

---

[2] There are also those who trace the beginnings of the Anthropocene Age to the beginning of the agricultural revolution, or the mid-twentieth century with the proliferation of the atomic bomb.

[3] Simon L. Lewis and Mark A. Maslin. *The Human Planet: How we Created the Anthropocene* (New York: Penguin Books, 2018).

ing the theological arguments that support actions leading to climate change. Below, I give a brief overview of three of these dynamics: economics, worldviews, and religion.

1. Material Context and Economics

Colonization played a critical role in enabling the context and the material flow of resources from which the economics of the Industrial Revolution was possible. The case of the global rise of the sugar industry provides a pertinent example. As Sydney Mentz details in his book, *Sweetness and Power*, the first industrial economies were actually in the colonies: sugar plantations. First, the colonizers destroyed the people who were first there—in the Caribbean, where Columbus first landed, this included the near destruction of the Taino people. Subsequently, the land itself was transformed from the tremendous biodiversity of the lush tropical islands to the mono-cropping of sugar plantations. Africans were stolen from their own land and forced to labor on the Caribbean land.[4]

At least a century before the Industrial Revolution, the basic factory style of work was first developed on the sugar plantations, which were essentially agricultural factories more than a century before this form of industry took hold in Britain. The sugar plantations included around the clock factory-like scheduling and job specialization. During harvest time, there was assembly-line-like production. Not only the production system, but the first fully modern global economy was practiced on slave plantations. Slaves were amongst the first people whose lives utterly depended upon the outside world: their cooking pans, clothes, and much of their food and housing was made somewhere else by someone else. The economy was wholly import-export based; it was utterly dependent upon the world market.

Slave-produced sugar also provided the cheap fuel for human labor. The colonies provided the empire (in this case, Great Britain) with the capital they needed to invest in the Industrial Revolution. Cheap sugar, in many ways, paved the way for oil: financiers, sugar lobbyists, markets, traders, workers, and laborers became connected in a particular structure of a global economic system, so that fossil fuel corporations were able to travel down largely pre-existing market pathways.

Elizabeth Abbott describes the significant impact the sugar industry had on both the people and the local ecology. She writes, "as sugar production took

---

[4] Sydney Mentz, *Sweetness and Power: The Place of Sugar in Modern History* (New York: Penguin Books, 1986). See also: Kirkpatrick Sale, *The Conquest of Paradise: Christopher Columbus and the Columbian Legacy* (New York: Plume, 1991).

root, it uprooted almost everything that had been there before: the peoples and their civilizations, and the agriculture and the very soil and topography of the New World."[5] Columbus' encounters with the Natives were "instrumental" in contributing to the genocide of Native peoples in North and South America, the loss of bio-cultural diversity and the growth of monoculture around the world, the slavery of Africans and Native peoples, the creation of modern trade routes, the redefinition of diets, taste preferences, and diet-related diseases, and the legal frameworks and economic patterns of development that have come to destroy our planet's capacity for good health.[6]

2. Worldviews and Mindsets

As I alluded to above, it is increasingly common, especially in the humanities and social sciences, to attend to the worldviews and mindsets underlying the Anthropocene Age. Most point to: 1) the extractive worldview or mindset of destroying nature for the profit of a few, 2) anthropocentric worldview expressed in a culture of human, especially male, superiority over nature and European white Christian superiority over other cultures, and 3) the growth mindset that privileges economic growth over other forms of growth (e.g., spiritual growth).[7] Technological superiority followed and intersected with these larger trends.

These mindsets do not stem from the Industrial Revolution. The European imperial moment can itself be traced back to Roman imperialism. Indeed, the monarchs of Europe consciously modeled their imperial forces on what they saw to be the golden age of the Roman Empire.[8] The basic human patterns of greed of exploitation can be traced back much further; to some extent, extractive mentalities and the underlying greed beneath them are dimensions of the human experience that can be identified in some of our earliest memories of human society. So why focus on the early European colonial moment of the fifteenth century?

My answer to this question is: because certain patterns of bio-cultural relationships came to dominate global human and ecological interaction during early colonial times that continue to this day. Of particular importance is the role

---

[5] Elizabeth Abbott, *Sugar: A Bittersweet History* (New York: Harry N. Abrams Publishing, 2011), 26.

[6] Abbott, *Sugar*, 27.

[7] For example, Larry Rasmussen, *Earth Honoring Faith: Religious Ethics in a New Key* (Oxford, UK: Oxford University Press, 2016).

[8] Anthony Pagden, *Lords of All the World* (New Haven, CT: Yale University Press, 1998).

of race and its relationship to the dis-association of people from place. The primacy of the human being—anthropocentrism—has within it a distinct racial (and to a certain extent, a gendered) component. It was, especially in the beginning, primarily Christian men of European heritage who assumed they had "dominion" over people and planet. It was a certain group of people, not all human beings, who dis-joined nature from human beings in such a way that people and places became objectified, commodified, and exploited. The legal, theological, moral, and political documents that enabled colonization to occur in this particular way were a series of papal bulls (documents issued by the pope with a high level of significance) in the late fifteenth century. Over time, these bulls became known as the Doctrine of Discovery.[9] I argue that we can trace the beginning of the Anthropocene Age to the Doctrine of Discovery.

To understand the rupture between place and people and the subsequent creation of the concept of race that emerged in the colonial moment, a rupture which continues to tear apart our society today, one of the best guides to turn to is the theologian Willie James Jennings. In *The Christian Imagination: Theology and the Origins of Race,* Jennings points to the beginnings of colonization, including the transatlantic slave trade, as a violent disjoining of people from place.[10] Africans' identity became associated with their skin color instead of their local ecology. This is core to both the mental orientation that separates people from place as well as the creation of race. Alas, too often racial disparities and ecological destruction are seen as separate concerns. A deeper historical perspective helps make the connection between racism and ecological destruction as part of the same historical gesture, done at the same time by more or less the same people.

Similar trends of cultural superiority can be seen in the destruction of both the people and the ecosystems of the land that came to be known as the Americas, first by the Spanish in the 1500s and then the French and the British in the 1600s. The key religious documents that gave the theological, legal, and political power for this colonizing action were a series of papal bulls that came to be known as the Doctrine of Discovery. These are some of the reasons I argue that we can trace the origins of the mindsets of the Anthropocene Age to the beginnings of the Doctrine of Discovery.

---

[9] There are many resources on Doctrine of Discovery. A classic, simple statement by one of the experts in the field is: Steve Newcomb, "Five Hundred Years of Injustice: The Legacy of Fifteenth Century Religious Prejudice," Indigenous Law Institute, 1992, accessed February 2019, http://ili.nativeweb.org/sdrm_art.html.

[10] Willie James Jennings, *The Christian Imagination: Theology and the Origins of Race* (New Haven, CT: Yale University Press, 2011).

The mentalities of domination over nature and the permissibility to exploit nature for human purposes have distinctly gendered dimensions whose historical roots arise from the same time period. Nature, in the worldview of the industrialists and the worldview they spawned, was feminine. Carolyn Merchant, in her groundbreaking book, *The Death of Nature*, points to the connection between the Great European Witch Hunt (which was given Church authority via another papal bull in 1484), the scientific revolution, and the destruction of Indigenous peoples in the Americas.[11]

Thus, the current disconnection of people from place in Western cultures, the pattern of anthropocentric (or, more specifically, androcentric) thinking, and the overarching worldviews and mentalities of control and domination relate to the beginnings of European colonization in the mid-fifteenth century.

3. Religion

The worldviews described above cannot be understood apart from the time period's religious lens. As is commonly known, the long history of colonization was closely tied with the Catholic Church and the Bible. The Doctrine of Discovery is itself a set of Christian documents subsequently inserted into international and US law. These Church documents continue to define the relationship between the US government and Native peoples and groups today.[12] For the first three to four centuries of colonization, from 1450 into the 1800s, the vast majority of settlers and colonists were working within a Christian framework. Their relationship to the land, including their understanding of private property, was framed within the theological interpretations of the Christianities of their times.

To approach the history of the last half millennium is thus to engage in challenging but ultimately rewarding religious and spiritual questions, especially for those of us who have inherited Christian origins. Jennings delves into the theology behind colonization, sourcing it in the Church's self-association with Israel. Thus, Christians have thought of themselves as the chosen people of God, instead of as newcomers to an ancient lineage. (The latter may have encouraged more of a posture of humility.) Jennings traces core Christian values such as hos-

---

[11] Carolyn Merchant, *The Death of Nature: Women, Ecology, and the Scientific Revolution* (New York: Harper Collins, 1990).

[12] E.g., this court case argued this century: *City of Sherrill v. Oneida Indian Nation of N. Y.* (Syllabus), 544 US 197 (US Supreme Court 2005), accessed March 2019, http://supreme.justia.com/cases/federal/us/544/197/. See also: Adam D. J. Brett, "*Sherrill v. Oneida* Opinion of the Court," Doctrine of Discovery, August 1, 2018, accessed March 2019, http://doctrineofdiscovery.org/sherrill-v-oneida-opinion-of-the-court/.

pitality through what he refers to as the "diseased" Christian imagination. In regard to the role Christianity (not simply Catholicism) played in creating the Doctrine of Discovery, Indigenous scholar Steve Newcomb is one of the experts: his book *Pagans in the Promised Land* is one of the authorities on the subject.[13] He traces the cultural superiority to the notion of "dominion" in Genesis that is subsequently carried throughout the Old Testament and was picked up in the New Testament and its interpreters. Newcomb writes, the "Lord of the Bible gave Abram and his people the right to take possession of the land of Canaan, despite the fact that indigenous people [Canaanites] were already living there" (Gen 1:28).[14] From a Christian perspective, this was the premise that justified the divine right of possession or dominion of the "chosen people" to land currently occupied by people who were consistently referred to as "uncivilized," "savages," "heathens," and "pagans."

In exploring the values and worldviews underlying the actions that led to the Anthropocene Age, it is necessary to engage with Christianity, since Christianity was central to the colonial period and to how the Anthropocene Age was formed. Teaching about Christian history, be that to Christians, Quakers, or others, is in itself a complex topic. While those who already teach religion are familiar with the challenges, I share here some of what I have learned, especially for those who may want to bring these ideas into educational contexts that are not explicitly "about religion." Indeed, one of the overarching trends of colonization is the separation of the spiritual and religious from the rest of life, especially the life of the mind. Integrating not only religious history but also a deep spiritual listening into unexpected contexts is part of decolonizing pedagogies.[15]

I find it essential to help people distinguish between the person of Jesus and the institutional church. Students may or may not have a relationship to Jesus independent of the church. Some students need to hear that looking at the historical sins of the church and their contemporary manifestations does not mean we are discrediting the life of Jesus or the long lineage from which he came. While that might sound obvious to a Quaker educator, I often have intelligent, well-educated, adult students who do not know how to talk about Christianity in a nuanced way. Instead, students often either defend or demonize Christianity. Such a dichotomized approach does not aid students navigating a religiously pluralistic society, especially given the tremendous resources that Christianity does

---

[13] Steven T. Newcomb, *Pagans in the Promised Land: Decoding the Doctrine of Christian Discovery* (Golden, CO: Fulcrum Publishing, 2008).

[14] Newcomb, *Pagans in the Promised Land*, 56.

[15] Judy M. Iseke-Barnes, "Pedagogies for Decolonizing," *Canadian Journal of Native Education* 31, no. 1 (2008): 123–148.

offer for responding to and living well in the Anthropocene Age. A more nuanced perspective includes contextualizing the historical Jesus, reminding students how little we know about the actual man, and teasing out the diversity of interpretations of his life and teachings. I emphasize Jesus's struggle against the Roman Empire, the colonizer of his time. I remind students that the early church slowly moved from following a man who refused to bow to unjust power structures to a church associated with the very same Empire: a man of peace became the symbolic head of an international war machine, particularly through the actions of Emperor Constantine. I also emphasize the diversity of Christian traditions that can be found in every historical era. There is not now nor has there ever been a single Christianity. It is not my responsibility to ensure students either keep or break away from their faith, whatever it may be: that is between them and the Holy Spirit. However, as part of the process of decolonizing and of enabling new knowledge formations to emerge, it is critical to support students' spiritual search both inside and outside the classroom as part and parcel of engaging with our shared eco-histories.

The two authors mentioned above, Jennings and Newcomb, have very different approaches to Christianity. Jennings works from within the tradition and aims to help it realize itself. Newcomb shows how Christianity is embedded in the US legal system, which is against the Constitution's own clear separation of church and state. He is not trying to redeem Christianity. My pedagogical approach is to support students in identifying how different authors approach similar histories differently.

Religion played a strong role in colonization, and in the mentalities that undergirded the Industrial Revolution. Drawing students' awareness to this role is important for Quaker educators if we hope to encourage a shift toward a more sustainable cultural pattern—for one thing, it shows the power of faith traditions to impact history, which can be used for collective good or ill. Teaching in this way includes equipping students to challenge received historical narratives of the church in a way that strengthens their understanding of the complexity of Christianity and which strengthens their spiritual toolkit.

III. Why This Matters for Quakers

This history impacts Quakers in particular in at least two major ways: the first is our allegiance to our peace testimony, and the second is our capacity to narrate our own histories more accurately, and subsequently shift our identity to be more in line with truth. Our peace testimony can help us develop a more sustainable worldview. However, we must first be willing to understand our own denominational story more accurately with regard for colonialism and our relationship to the earth, other creatures, and other people.

Quakers are historically, and today, concerned with peace. While organizations such as Quaker Earthcare Witness, Quaker Institute for the Future, Quaker committees for ecological well-being at the Yearly and Monthly Meeting levels across the country, and Friends General Conference have lifted up ecological concerns, the links between ecological well-being and peacemaking are not yet fully entrenched within the body of the Religious Society of Friends.[16] Quakers' historic peace testimony may be far more easily activated when we recognize the deep violence to *both* people and the earth caused by unsustainable action. Many understand that to do violence to the earth is to do violence to God's creation and is, therefore, an act of spiritual violence. Indeed, this forms the basis of Pope Francis' seminal work, *Laudato Si': On Care for our Common Home*.[17] An integrated history of the Anthropocene Age enables the links between peace and environmental concerns to be made more clearly: it quickly becomes impossible to think of ecological well-being and peaceful societies as separate endeavors. Empire, and with it colonization, as mentioned above, has been one of the most violent forms of organization known to humanity. The Roman Empire killed Jesus; Jesus's life bore witness to an alternative to Empire.

Much of Quakers' historic social justice work, from abolition to women's suffrage, has had some anti-colonial flair, which is to say, it understood the dignity of human beings was impossible in the conditions of disparity made possible by the deeply misogynistic and violent tendencies of empires. Some of our most beloved Quaker figures, from George Fox to John Woolman, are people who removed themselves from the "world"—which is to say, from the world created by human imperial power structures. That this imperial structure can, at times, look and sound like a vibrant democracy makes it all the more complex and, for many, hides the violence of the police state that is more clearly revealed in a government that spends significantly more on military expenditures than on public education.[18] I am not discounting the many freedoms and benefits the

---

[16] As of the time of this writing, the American Friends Service Committee has not linked climate change and sustainability to its overarching work for peace and justice. As a whole, the organization itself does not see the direct links between the two, though there is some evidence that this is beginning to shift.

[17] Francis, "Laudato Si': On Care for Our Common Home," Washington, DC: United States Conference of Catholic Bishops, 2015, http://w2.vatican.va/content/francesco/en/encyclicals/documents/papa-francesco_20150524_enciclica-laudato-si.html.

[18] According to the Pew Research Center, in 2017, the US federal government spent 3% on education and 15% on national defense. That said, they also spent a total of 73% on human services, including education, social security, and healthcare. Drew Desilver, "What

United States offers. I am highlighting that these occur on stolen land and have historically been paid for by stolen labor and the destruction of vast, precious, and often precarious ecosystems. Even some of the greatest still-sustainable ecosystems in the country today, many of which exist in our natural parks, were themselves created through expelling the Native Nations, whose land was forcibly taken from them.

Many histories, however, inaccurately overemphasize how "good" Quakers were in relation to social justice issues. Of particular concern are the inaccurate histories about how Quakers treated the land and the Indians. We often hold up Quakers in early Pennsylvania as exceptions to the rule of settlers mistreating Indians. While Quakers often spoke far better of the Indians than did other Christian settler/colonizer communities, Jean Soderlund points out that in Pennsylvania, Quakers significantly benefited from the models of religious and multi-cultural tolerance already established by the Lenape peoples.[19] Similarly, Quakers helped abolish slavery, but did not fully include African Americans in Quakerism.[20]

Quakers perpetuated the general models of land ownership and land cultivation that re-created the European agrarian style of fields, fences, and their accompanying social systems of inequity while adding a particularly American model of property ownership that fed the capitalist models of economic growth. Quakers rarely significantly or systematically questioned the moral superiority of European-American economic assumptions and land management, although several Quakers were aware, in their relationships to Indians, that other models of land management were possible. While some shared values of simplicity and integrity with their Indian hosts and neighbors, they also fully participated in and financially benefited from the growth-based classical economic model that we now recognize as unsustainable.

And let us be clear: Meetings, school administrators, and teachers thought they were doing the morally correct thing at the time. As with any historical period, we must always situate how people saw themselves in their own context. Deconstruction, including how we wish it might have been, can only

---

Does the Federal Government Spend Your Tax Dollars On? Social Insurance Programs, Mostly," Pew Research Center, April 4, 2017, accessed February 2019, http://pewresearch.org/fact-tank/2017/04/04/what-does-the-federal-government-spend-your-tax-dollars-on-social-insurance-programs-mostly/.

[19] Jean R. Soderlund, *Lenape Country: Delaware Valley Society Before William Penn* (Philadelphia: University of Pennsylvania Press, 2014).

[20] Donna McDonnel and Vanessa Julye, *Fit For Freedom, Not for Friendship: Quakers, African Americans and the Myth of Racial Justice* (Philadelphia: Quaker Press of Friends General Conference, 2018).

happen after a proper understanding of the historical situation, viewed as accurately as possible. Looking back, we can see that although Friends had good intentions, they often contributed to violent destruction of Native American cultures and the land, and benefited from the economic structures giving preference to whiteness, as that concept was constructed.

The depth of violence between people and place that has already occurred in the Americas necessitates spiritual engagement and healing of both the land and the people. At our best, Quaker discernment processes and our dedication to listening to the Light can contribute to this healing. Fortunately we are now living in a time when Quakers are taking our own participation in the violence of colonization more seriously.

The work of Paula Palmer and the Toward Right Relationship Project coming out of Boulder Friends Meeting is a powerful and pertinent example of how a Quaker who herself is untrained as a formal historian responded to a call by the Native Nations in the United States to engage in historical research into the role that Quakers played in the Indian boarding schools. She undertook a substantial research project and has since been traveling the country, teaching Quakers about our own history: a history as active participants in the process of "civilizing" Indian children. Often, this involved forcibly removing Native children from their families, their culture, their language, and their land.[21] For Quakers to *not* engage with this history perpetuates the process of dis-membering: living on the land as if we are part of an a-historical reality.

It might not be immediately apparent to many people engaged with growing sustainable cultures that Indian boarding schools have much to do with ecological destruction. The topics are disconnected due to the different bio-cultural ways of living that the Indians practiced compared to the European-American lifestyle, and the Native peoples' relationship to the land itself. Fundamentally, Indian ideas of collective land ownership (made possible through the continuation of Indian culture) was a threat to US sovereignty. Indigenous peoples' relationship with the land was, while not always as romantic as some might lead us to believe, one that did not lead to unsustainable cultures destroying the very land itself. Their way of living, including their fierce love of freedom, as well as their relationship to the land that was historically theirs, fully threatened the "progress" of America as articulated in "manifest destiny" and, after the frontier moved across the entire continent, redefined as the neoclassical economic model of continual economic growth. The economy of the United States was made

---

[21] For more information, see: "Toward Right Relationship with Native Peoples," Boulder Friends Meeting, accessed January 2019, https://boulderfriendsmeeting.org/ipc-right-relationship-2/.

possible in part through the near-complete cultural obliteration of the first peoples. The boarding schools were an explicit part of that process.

To engage in the depth of what it means to come into right relationship with the land and waters that sustain life entails developing right relationship with the previous caretakers of the land. This includes everything from land acknowledgement to actively building relationships with local native peoples and engaging in anti-racism training.

We need to fall in love with our world in order to sustainably inhabit it. To come to fall ever more deeply in love with our land entails learning about the first peoples who lived in our particular space and how they lived, because this can give us clues about how we might live in right relationship with the land today. Further, it means building whatever relationships with land, people, and other species are most appropriate today. When we do so, the meaning of sustainability can shift and new economic and political possibilities can emerge.

IV. Considering Pedagogy

Quakers understand that the means are as important as the ends, exemplified in our peace testimony, which seeks to take away the occasion for all wars, not just to reduce conflict. An appropriate pedagogical approach is necessary to elicit the individual identity and cultural change we seek. In my own teaching, I am developing a process that I refer to as ReMembering and ReEnchanting. I initially was inspired to play with the word "remembering" by African feminist Cynthia Dillard, who reminds us that (re)membering is a process of both re-calling what has been forgotten and putting something once fragmented back together again.[22] I subsequently found that this term has been played with by people across a wide range of disciplines, including feminist theology, human dimensions of climate change, psychology, somatic healing arts of various forms, and narrative therapeutic practices. I have come to adopt the grammar of "ReMembering," and have been developing this into a pedagogical process far more elaborate than simply a play on words. In this section, I share some of what I have learned. However, before I do so, let me first situate myself in my primary teaching context, which is not a traditional one.

Upon graduating seminary, and after having led a series of workshops across the country on material relating to eco-spirituality and decolonization, I founded and continue today to direct Sequoia Samanvaya LLC, an ecotheology

---

[22] Cynthia B. Dillard, *Learning to (Re)Member the Things We've Learned to Forget* (New York: Peter Lang Publishing, 2012).

company wherein education is our primary endeavor.[23] We primarily serve adult learners through teaching ReMembering (historical truth seeking) and ReEnchanting (creative) courses. Our courses primarily occur online. Students meet regularly via videoconference, where they are able to see one another's faces and hear each other talk. I no longer permit students to audit the course by doing readings only, because the face-to-face interaction is a necessary component in the learning process. Students meet regularly in cohorts with a teacher specifically trained in the ReMembering process. Each cohort is limited to nine students or fewer, to ensure each student receives focused attention. Weekly assignments include written, oral, and video material, readings and activities from a work-book, and somatic, meditative, and spiritual exercises. The online classroom itself is primarily a space for discussion with conversation. Another teacher or myself facilitate. Lectures are developed as needed; emerging based on the knowledge students come to the course with and their particular questions. Each cohort develops its own themes, and each cohort's journey through the historical material is unique.

Most of our students are active leaders in their spiritual and religious communities, including seminary professors and pastors. Their ages have ranged from 22 to 90 years old, and their geographical location is usually inside the territories now known as the United States, but students from other countries have also joined since the material is globally relevant. I explicitly approach sustainability as an ecofeminist theologian, which is to say, with the understanding that unsustainable systems derive from an intense spiritual crisis in our relationship to Earth and to one another that has a gendered dimension. In addition to my online courses, I also give in-person talks and run workshops and retreats.

Every online class I offer, even those that do not explicitly address history, starts with students giving self-introductions that include them stating the Indigenous group whose land they are currently on. Often students don't know who was on the land before they were. I consistently introduce myself in this way, modeling this behavior. This simple land acknowledgement does several things: it helps students to link the historical material with their current lives; it forces immediate engagement with the material; it helps create a new culture of how their identity relates to place, as well as to other people. It is also part of the long process of decolonization. Whereas decolonizing was once conceptualized

---

[23] To learn more, visit our website: www.sequoiasamanvaya.com.

as colonial governments handing over the instruments of governance to sovereign powers, "it is now recognized as a long-term process involving the bureaucratic, cultural, linguistic and psychological divesting of colonial power."[24]

As non-sustainability arose from colonization, decolonizing is a necessary component of enabling students to co-create sustainable futures. This is obviously a significant task, requiring ongoing learning on the part of educators and students alike. As educator Paulette Regan writes, "Decolonization is not 'integration' or the token inclusion of Indigenous ceremony. Rather, it involves a paradigm shift from a culture of denial to the making of space for Indigenous political philosophies and knowledge systems as they resurge, thereby shifting cultural perceptions and power relations in real ways."[25] At its best, it incorporates a wide range of practices that acknowledge and deconstruct power structures that continue the invisibility of Indigenous perspectives, philosophies, ontologies, and other manifestations of the continuing legacies of colonization. A range of resources is available for educators engaging with students of all ages.[26] Many of the references cited here lean heavily toward a focus on engaging with Indigenous perspectives. I urge educators to take a wide view of decolonization that integrates anti-racism, alternative governance systems, concerns related to gender and sexuality, destruction of Mother Earth, global inequalities and other ramifications of mentalities of scarcity and models of ownership that lead to strangling levels of competition and overwhelming inequities. I suggest that it is of critical importance to help white folks recognize and have continual inquiry into the damage that colonization has done to white folks as well as to their Indigenous brothers and sisters.

In writing about decolonizing pedagogy in higher education, Judy M. Iseke-Barnes suggests several different components that can be covered. These include: "(a) colonizing and decolonizing agendas, (b) disrupting government ideology, (c) decolonizing government and reclaiming Indigenous governance, (e) decolonizing spirituality and ceremony, (f) disrupting colonizing ideologies and decolonizing minds, (g) reconnecting to land, (h) decolonizing history, and (i) community-based education and decolonizing education."[27] These should not be teacher-centered, but give students a voice and space to hear themselves and one another in community.

---

[24] L. T. Smith, *Decolonizing Methodologies: Research and Indigenous Peoples* (Dunedin, NZ: Zed Press, 1999).
[25] Paulette Regan, *Unsettling the Settler Within: Indian Residential Schools, Truth Telling, and Reconciliation in Canada* (Vancouver, BC: University of British Columbia Press, 2000), 189.
[26] Iseke-Barnes, "Pedagogies for Decolonizing," 123–148.
[27] Iseke-Barnes, "Pedagogies for Decolonizing," 124.

In this section, I offer some examples of what I have learned and what seems to be working, and show how these practices make some small efforts towards decolonization. These are not meant to be prescriptive. Compassionate and thoughtful experimentation is encouraged. Simply teaching history that re-integrates Indigenous and non-white perspectives that have for too long been erased from dominant narratives of "how we came to be here" is an important step in the process of decolonization. It is also important to do so in ways that honor Indigenous epistemologies, cultures, ontologies, languages, and histories as valid not only in the past but also in the present context, without over-romanticizing Indigenous histories. Much more research is needed into decolonizing pedagogies as part of educating for sustainability.

When I first started teaching this material, I quickly noticed that my students found it overwhelming. Despair, grief, and guilt are common emotions in engaging with historical trauma. Informed by my previous work with Joanna Macy, Buddhist scholar and ecofeminist who is known for her despair work, I knew that it was unwise—would even miss the point entirely—if I did not support students in addressing their own despair.[28] It was necessary to go beyond intellectual understanding. After all, one of the main problems in the dominant mindset that has led us on this unsustainable path is the split between the mind and the body, commonly referred to as the Cartesian split. One way this mindset plays out is that certain people are seen as primarily having minds and other people (laborers, slaves, Indigenous peoples, and women) are seen as primarily useful due to their bodies. The re-integration of mind and body for all people is part of the process of re-membering who we are, where we come from, and the value of each one. We need to engage these traumatic histories and their continued legacies with our heart, minds and souls. Iseke-Barnes notes that integrating somatic and spiritual experiences is a key part of decolonizing pedagogies. The intellect alone is necessary but insufficient to the task at hand. I subsequently began experimenting with pedagogical styles within the constraints of online contexts that create space for sharing grief and despair, and experimented with ways to move out of guilt. I now bring prayer, silence, ritual, music, and out-of-the-"classroom" techniques to my teaching.[29] To bring students into a broader awareness of our contentious history (which not all students are even aware of as being contentious in the first place) is itself spiritual work.

---

[28] Joanna Macy and Molly Young Brown, *Coming Back to Life: The Guide to the Work That Reconnects* (Gabriola Island, BC: New Society Publishers, 2014).

[29] By out-of-the-"classroom," I mean not only that my courses do not take place in a traditional classroom (since we meet using online platforms), but also that experiences they have outside of the classroom time are an integral and acknowledged part of the learning process.

1. Moving with Overwhelm: The Importance of the Somatic

Confronted with fear and overwhelm, it is easy to jump too fast into the question, "What do we do?" While this is a crucial question, we first need to let ourselves experience both the pain of the past and the wonder that dwells and quickens within us. We must first touch base with love. We need to strengthen our compassion muscles, as much if not more so than our intellectual muscles—that includes compassion for ourselves. Akin to this is the process of building relationships and being in community, but we must not forget the importance of turning inwards for wisdom and cultivating our inner lives.

Part of this process involves inviting students to engage their bodies and their breath in the learning process. Where in their bodies do they experience the overwhelm or the pain? Do they dissociate? Where is their breathing? When I teach adults in retreat settings, I take time for people to express themselves somatically (through movement) and vocally (through making sounds, moans, or singing). Moving *with* grief enables the emotions to move through the body and not be stagnant. This actually can keep the mind from jumping too quickly into "what do we do" because some kind of "doing" (a physical motion) is already happening.

There is increasing literature on the importance of creating whole selves through integrating the mind, the spirit, the breath, and the body. Thus, Adefarakan writes that "decolonization means becoming conscious of the spiritual dimensions of our physical existence, and this requires particular attention in a Euro-dominant worldview that equates education and progress with the intellect, with written knowledge, and with the visual." She continues to point to the importance of engaging with an educational practice that treats students as whole beings. "Decolonization in the classroom," she writes, "means decolonization in all areas of life."[30]

Course materials, as well as pedagogical styles, are valuable opportunities for integration of the mind, body and spirit. Integrating Indigenous people's voices in sharing their own histories, including mythologies, are part of the process of de-centering Euro-dominant mindsets. Audio recordings, including lectures, interviews, and dialogues, are increasingly easy thanks to the wide array of material available on, for example, YouTube. I consistently give my students music videos made by young Indigenous artists; these are not only appreciated by

---

[30] Temitope Adefarakan, "Integrating Mind, Body and Spirit through the Yoruba Concept of Ori," in *Sharing Breath: Embodied Learning and Decolonization*, eds. Sheila Batacharya and Yuk-Lin Renita Wong (Edmonton, AB: AU Press, 2018), 229–252.

the students, but they give students learning options that are related to oral traditions, not written ones, which is much closer to Indigenous pedagogical styles. They are also valuable insights into Indigenous cultures, as music videos are gaining popularity as powerful forms of self-expression for Indigenous youth. Thus, for example, in 2017 the Indigenous Music Awards in Canada had over 200 submissions from throughout North America.[31]

Another important somatic component is that of historical trauma. People experience fear, despair, overwhelm—and for some, reminders of their own family histories—in their bodies. Historical trauma passes between generations and becomes physically lodged within people's bodies. This *must* be acknowledged, especially when working with ethnically diverse students. There is no way to anticipate what trauma will be re-ignited, or by whom. People's somatic and emotional responses to this material are varied. Part of the pedagogical goal needs to include equipping students to attend to the somatic dimensions of their experiences when engaging in the past-in-the-present as part of their life-long practices of creating sustainable societies.

2. Enabling Complexity

This history is complex material. Pedagogical styles where simplistic responses are the final responses do not sufficiently get to the heart of the matter. It is easy when people hear some variation of, "What we have now is wrong and what was there before was better" (in reference to Native American treatment of the land, for example), to either say, "We must fully reclaim what was lost," or, "But we can't go back to what was!" Both are extreme positions. Surely there are pathways between the extremes.

We can only work with what we have. People from all over the world, whose ancestors were only remotely or not at all involved with much of the histories mentioned above, now live, eat, drink, and defecate in what was once more commonly known as Turtle Island. With climate change, more mass migrations are predicted. The land has already been built upon; the rivers have been re-routed.

Simultaneously, new imaginaries are utterly possible based on what is already happening. Because of the rise in variations of urban gardening, we know it is entirely possible for concrete streets to be torn up and for gardens to be planted. Because rivers once dried have been revitalized, we know waterways can

---

[31] Toyacoyah Brown, "Here Are the Nominees for the 2017 Indigenous Music Awards!" PowWows.com, April 6, 2017, accessed February 2019, http://pow-wows.com/nominees-2017-indigenous-music-awards/.

be brought back to life. Because individuals and churches have given land back to the first peoples in the US and Canada, we know that land can be returned. For example, the United Methodist Church returned 1.5 acres of land to the Nez Perce Tribe that was taken from them in a clear treaty violation in the summer of 2018 in a ceremony in which both groups participated.[32] Reparations for justice can and do happen; more are possible.

However, growing justice requires growing the connectivity of communities bound together by more accurate histories and the blossoming of our spiritual selves. The process has not been, is not now, and I doubt it will ever be, neat or tidy. Thus, the pedagogical style used when discussing these topics and dreaming about future directions needs to enable students to befriend the messiness and complexity of it all, marks of the common humanity we share.

3. Time, Our Relationship to Place, and Emergent Pedagogies

Historical truth seeking is a process of deepening our relationship to place, as part of shifting our relationship to time. History is in the present. Everything in the present comes from somewhere in the past. The candle that is partly burned was made and lit by someone in the past. The tree's life is a result of generations of trees before it; its shape is the result of a lifetime of wind, water, and other creatures or buildings around it. Everything and every being in the present, from the food we eat to the water we drink to the buildings we work in, has a history and its own story, if we but pay attention. Place is shaped by time.

Similarly, time is inherently related to place. Summer in New Haven, Connecticut is different than summer in Boulder, Colorado. How time intersects with space and place are complex topics. They are theological, by which I mean our relationship to them is held within our theological imagination of the nature of time. A key part of decolonizing pedagogies is re-contextualizing students into their particular place-time. Grounding students in their local history is critical for them to understand the contemporary condition of their watersheds. Dams, pollution, sanitation, flood patterns, and urban planning decisions all have histories that can be traced to the colonial experience. These are complex systems.

Complex systems—including learning about the past that is also in the present—are emergent systems. Everyone in the learning process, including the educator, is part of a complex, emerging system: the unfolding of history that has

32 Greg Nelson, "Wallowa Lake Ceremony Honors Return of Land to Nez Perce," Oregon-Idaho Conference of the United Methodist Church, August 2, 2018, accessed February 2019, http://umoi.org/newsdetail/wallowa-lake-ceremony-honors-rightful-return-of-land-to-nez-perce-11627405.

a possibility of influencing new futures. It is inherently unpredictable and insistently social. The individual and the collective are both critical components impacting the learning process. Emergent systems arise in complex systems: such systems require emergent pedagogical styles.[33]

Teaching with awareness to this emergent and unfolding future is not about having a pre-set plan. It is about letting learning and new insights emerge. Blank et al. encourage us to learn to "enjoy the uncontrollable."[34] This is an inherently relational approach to learning. I have learned to enjoy the uncomfortable. It is almost inevitable that there are uncomfortable moments in any classroom that works with uncomfortable histories. More than that, there are unpredictable moments. Students bring in stories, questions, and ideas that I could not possibly predict or be fully prepared for. I never shy from admitting my ignorance—my job is not to know everything! More than that, however, the students' questions dictate where we go: in that sense, it is an emergent process that arises out of their relationships to the material, to their own ancestry, and to one another, as well as to me. The unpredictable is the locus of my focus: the relationships between the students and myself are my primary concern.

For my ReMembering courses, in which there is concrete material I want to teach in a particular order using certain methods, the emergent process is largely within the discussion itself, rather than the entire syllabus. There is always room in the syllabus for certain themes to be explored more deeply than others based on the interest of the class. The relationships between the students—the community that forms—is crucial.

Of course, part of why I can do this is that I am an independent educator: ultimately, I only need to meet the expectations and needs of my students, not an outside administrator or a set of criteria handed to me from larger institutional forces. This gives me amazing freedom in what I can ask of my students and is one of the reasons I love this approach, although it has its own challenges. Most educators in institutional settings must abide by institutional norms and procedures. As a result, it may be difficult, if not impossible, to utilize fully emergent pedagogical systems. In my fully emergent courses, such as my course for women writers, the syllabus simply says, "work on your writing" for each lesson; however, the experience of the class is that an arc naturally evolves, with a particular set of themes and questions. Students continuously sign up for further

---

[33] Doug Blank, Kim Cassidy, Anne Dalke, and Paul Grobstein, "Emergent Pedagogy: Learning to Enjoy the Uncontrollable—and Make It Productive," *Journal of Educational Change* 8, no. 2 (2007): 111–130.

[34] Blank et al., "Emergent Pedagogy," 111.

classes or seek some other way of working with me. Over 75 percent of my students seek to work with me in some capacity after they complete a course.

V. Toward Conclusions: Encouragement

I like to believe Quakers are particularly well equipped for historical truth seeking of the kind I have outlined here, which embraces the past with a big heart as well as a keen mind, listening to where Spirit is moving within our bodies and souls. We are, at heart, truth-seekers. History is a critical part of what enables our truth to emerge. We have a deep respect for the emergent: our entire worship style is based on the emerging movement of the Holy Spirit. We regularly train ourselves to listen to and follow that movement, which is only sometimes verbal, and often moves us in the somatic, the emotional, and the communal. Our tradition of everyday mystics should make this kind of sensitive, open-to-spirit pedagogical approach a natural fit for Quaker educators and Quaker institutions of higher education. It would not surprise me if many Quaker educators are already practicing variations of emergent pedagogical styles within their own classrooms, especially in the humanities and social sciences.

The process of decolonizing education is immense and ongoing. Education, including Quaker education, has too often cooperated with the colonial enterprise (or at least not resistant to it). Quaker educators must recognize the part that our forebears, for all of their good intentions, played in this process. This requires humility and a deep recognition of our own historical faults. We have been part of the problem as well as part of the solution. We need to take time to grieve, to apologize, to unlearn, re-learn, and build stronger relationships with others impacted by these histories. We need to deepen our capacity to listen to nature: such capacities were shunned during the process of colonization, and even though they are key for our collective survival, few of us are well versed in them. I suggest we let ourselves engage in multiple forms of expression as part of our healing process: art, dance, and ritual, as well as silent worship. And we need to encourage our students to enter the uncertain, messy process of unraveling what they have been taught about America and about their particular place in the world.

Beyond the fear, shame, uncertainty, and grief, there are amazing potentials for Spirit to move. We do not go into these waters alone. We are held in this work by a Spirit who flows in and through truth, and seeks conciliation. And so, let this be a word of encouragement, as well as a provocation, to more fully integrate decolonial and spiritual processes into the pedagogical approach of Quaker educators as part of empowering sustainability.

16 | Nuclear Power from a Quaker Physicist's Perspective

By Donald A. Smith

Abstract: We have lived in the shadow of the threat of nuclear weapons for over 70 years. That threat has colored the debate about the benefits of using nuclear energy to power electrical turbines instead of coal or natural gas. In this chapter, I lay out my understanding of energy, based on my experience as a Quaker physicist. I discuss what energy is and why it is important. I explain where nuclear energy comes from, describe how a chain reaction works, and present a simple model of radioactivity. I summarize and contextualize the dangers of taking advantage of the properties of atomic nuclei, both in terms of dosage and the challenges of nuclear waste storage. I close with some thoughts about how my perspective as a Quaker has shaped my reactions to what I have learned as a physicist. Nuclear energy is certainly not safe, nor will it solve all our problems, but in my experience, its dangers are overestimated, while the dangers of our current fossil fuel based power grid are underestimated. As we work toward a sustainable future, in the face of the imminent catastrophe of climate change, I don't think we can afford to completely dismiss nuclear energy as a potential intermediate solution. The debate must be grounded in facts, not fear.

I. Introduction

On July 16, 1945, at 05:29:21am local time, the first nuclear explosion was detonated in the desert outside Socorro, New Mexico.[1] The roughly 100-pound "Gadget" exploded with the equivalent yield of twenty-four thousand tons of dynamite. The mushroom cloud extended over seven miles into the air. The

---

[1] Richard Rhodes, *The Making of the Atomic Bomb* (New York: Simon & Schuster, 1986).

shadow of that cloud has stretched across the intervening seven decades, and shaded all discussion of whether nuclear energy might have other uses. Meanwhile, the average surface temperature of the planet has increased by almost two degrees (Fahrenheit)[2] and the ocean levels have risen by 20 centimeters.[3]

In this chapter, I will attempt to convey the perspective on energy I have gained through working as a professional physicist. In my experience, a lot of well-intentioned misinformation has become part of our common knowledge, and I hope this chapter will help readers understand the science more clearly. I will start with an overview of what energy is, and why it is important. In particular, I will explain where nuclear energy comes from, how people use it, and why a reactor is fundamentally different from a bomb. I will introduce the ethical issues surrounding the use of nuclear energy, from a Quaker perspective, and attempt to argue that, while using nuclear energy certainly has dangers, those dangers are often inflated by fear, while the dangers of the current energy system are underestimated, because we are familiar with them. The imminent, existential threat of climate change must also be taken into consideration when attempting to balance the dangers of different energy sources as we seek ethical means of creating sustainable energy solutions while keeping our planetary environment comfortably livable for the species thriving in current climate conditions.

II. Energy

Energy is a notoriously difficult concept to define. Richard Feynman, as celebrated a physicist as there is, has affirmed we don't really know what energy is.[4] Richard Rhodes recently published an entire book on the history of energy in human society without ever trying to define it.[5] The US government tries to define energy as "the ability to do work,"[6] but this definition is not adequate. First, it gives no definition for "work," which turns out to be defined in terms of changing the value of energy, rendering this energy definition circular. Second, it turns out that there is such a thing as "waste energy," energy that cannot do

---

[2] "Global Warming of 1.5 ºC," Intergovernmental Panel on Climate Change, October 2018, http://ipcc.ch/sr15/.

[3] R. K. Pachauri and L. A. Meyer, eds., Intergovernmental Panel on Climate Change, *Climate Change 2014: Synthesis Report. Contribution of Working Groups I, II and III to the Fifth Assessment Report of the Intergovernmental Panel on Climate Change*, IPCC, Geneva, Switzerland, 2014.

[4] Richard Feynman, *The Feynman Lectures on Physics, Vol. 1* (Reading, MA: Addison-Wesley, 1963).

[5] Richard Rhodes, *Energy: A Human History* (New York: Simon & Schuster, 2018).

[6] See, e.g. "Glossary," US Energy Information Administration, accessed January 2019, http://eia.gov/tools/glossary. This definition pops up in lots of places, despite its inadequacies.

work, which renders the definition of energy self-contradictory. In addition, there is a bewildering variety of different kinds of energy, indicated by modifying adjectives such as kinetic, potential, rest, light, chemical, thermal, and so on. Are these energies all the same, or just related to each other? How?

The best definition of energy is that it is (1) a *number*, (2) associated with a *system*, and (3) calculated according to certain *rules*. This very abstract definition demands further specification to understand those italicized words. We will explore each of these points individually.

(1) *Energy as a number*. The most important aspect of energy to understand is that it is, indeed, a number. It is not a "thing," a "substance," or a "field." It does not exist in space; it cannot be measured, observed, or interacted with. It can only be calculated, based on measurements you can make of your system. For the rest of this chapter, I will often refer to energy as an "energy number" to reinforce this concept.

(2) *Energy associated with a system*. A system is a collection of objects and interactions that one thinks are relevant to the problem one is studying. It is actually amazing that nature even allows us to limit ourselves to a system—if the universe were such that you needed to consider all of it to be able to understand any of it, we would never get anywhere. But if one studies, say, a baseball that has been thrown through the air, one could limit the system under consideration to the baseball, with the Earth and the air as external forces in its environment. Or one could choose the baseball and the Earth as the system, and keep the air in the environment. One would not, however, have to consider the sun, the oceans, the billions of human beings on the planet, and so forth. One doesn't even have to consider that the ball is made of trillions and trillions of atoms, just to understand where the ball is going to fly.

(3) *Energy defined by rules*. To calculate the energy number accurately, one needs to define one's system carefully (and never change it), and one needs to follow the appropriate rules. The rules can be simple (for example: if an object is moving, take half its mass and multiply by its speed, squared, to get the kinetic energy associated with it) or they can be quite complicated. However, each kind of energy has a certain rule or procedure for how to calculate it, depending on the system being considered. Because energy is just a number, the way to allocate that number completely depends on how the system is defined. To use the example of the baseball, the label of the same energy number would be given different names, depending on whether or not the system was just the ball, or the ball and Earth.

Each object or interaction related to a system can have an energy number associated with it (including, under some circumstances, space itself), and therefore it can sometimes be convenient to talk in shorthand as if the energy exists in space, when really it is just associated with something in space. The best illustration I have seen of this concept is the "augmented reality" you can get with internet-connected digital cameras like smartphones. The camera shows the street view you see with your eyes, but the computer overlies extra information associated with the objects in the field of view of the camera. That information isn't there in space, but it is associated with the reality that is there. In a similar way, there is no energy "in" the flying baseball, but you can calculate a kinetic energy number associated with the flying baseball.

For example, consider that flying baseball. For a 100-gram baseball moving at 50 meters per second, the kinetic energy would be 125 joules.[7] However, if you were a gnat sitting on the ball, you would say that from your perspective, the ball is not moving, so its speed and therefore its kinetic energy would be zero joules. So how much energy does the ball *really* have? Both! Neither! The energy isn't really there, and the correct value for the energy number depends on how you define the system.

To a physicist, there are really only four kinds of energy: kinetic (associated with the motion of objects), potential (associated with certain kinds of interactions between objects, like gravity or electricity), light (associated with the color of the light), and rest (associated with the mass of an object). Because energy is not a thing that exists, we can get away with naming it in different ways in different contexts. Thermal energy (associated with temperature) is often considered a fifth form of energy, but it is really just another kind of kinetic energy. Thermal energy is associated with the *random* motion of the atoms that make up an object rather than the *bulk* motion of the whole object. The temperature is just a measure of how fast the atoms in a material are jiggling around.

If energy isn't really real, and can only be defined this abstractly, why is it so important? Why do we have a US Department of Energy? Why are we told it is so important to conserve energy? Why do we fight wars over energy? The answer is that energy has two characteristics that make it so important to us: the first is that the rules by which the energy number is calculated associate that number with aspects of life we do care about, very much: speed, temperature, and light. We don't really care about the energy number for its own sake, whether it's 652 joules or 25 BTUs or what have you. We want to move our goods and ourselves from one place to another. We want to lift material off the ground to build buildings. We want to have our houses at a certain temperature and our

---

[7] See Section III for a description of the various units used to express the energy number.

refrigerators at another. We want to be able to see at night, for comfort and safety. All of these activities have energy numbers associated with them.

The second critical aspect of energy is that for a given definition of a system, the total energy number always stays the same. The type of energy can change, but the total number has to stay the same. If you want to increase the kinetic energy of a car (increasing its speed, for example), then some other kind of energy must go down (by burning gasoline, for example). If the energy of the system does change, then the energy associated with something in the environment must change by the opposite amount (if the energy of a glass of cold water on the kitchen counter goes up as it comes to room temperature, the energy of the air in the room must go down by the same amount).

These two aspects, together, are why energy is so important: it's associated with activities we care about, and the total value of the number does not change. Much as money, in and of itself, is meaningless; the fact that in our society it determines what we can buy and do is what renders it so desirable to people. Energy alone means nothing, but it provides a useful bookkeeping device for aspects of life we think are very important.

With this probably counter-intuitive but accurate definition of energy in mind, we can turn to the question of nuclear energy. In Section IV, we will explore the rules for nuclear energy: where it comes from and how it tends to be used, but first we need a short explanation of the units in which the energy number is expressed.

III. Units of Energy

If we are going to examine real-world implications of nuclear energy, we are going to need to grapple with the problem of energy units. Most physical quantities must be expressed in units: *How* big? *How* far? *How* fast? A unit is a standard that lets two people understand what they're talking about by agreeing on what they will compare it to. It's a ratio. If we say a table is three feet long, we mean that the ratio of the length of the table to the agreed upon standard "foot" is three to one.

For energy, there is a bewildering variety of standards in common use. This is partly due to the fact that the US has stubbornly resisted converting to the international standards, but also due to the history of the context in which energy numbers are used. In part because energy is not a thing, but an abstract number, people developed different standards for different purposes, to keep the ratios to reasonably convenient numbers. The international unit for energy is the joule (J). You can think of a joule as roughly the amount of kinetic energy you would associate with a baseball near the surface of the Earth that has dropped about one meter of height. From the study of thermodynamics, we inherit the energy unit of a calorie, which is the increase in thermal energy of one gram of water when it increases its temperature by one degree Celsius at one atmosphere of pressure. One calorie is about four joules.

To make things even more confusing, in the US food industry, the common unit to describe the chemical energy associated with food is called the Calorie, which is 1000 times larger than the thermodynamical calorie. In Europe, food labels give the units in kilojoules. The electrical companies that provide electrical energy to homes use the units of kilowatt-hours (kWh); one kWh is 1000 joules per second for one hour, so 3.6 million joules. Companies that provide home heating, however, might use "British Thermal Units" or BTUs. My heating bill tells me how much my house has needed each month in "therms," which is 100,000 BTU, or 100 million joules.

Nuclear and particle physicists, on the other hand, like to use the unit of the electron-volt, or eV. Much like if you drop a baseball in gravity, a charged particle released near other charged particles will accelerate, increasing in kinetic energy. A single electron that flows from one side of a 9-volt battery to the other will increase its energy by 9 eV, which is about a millionth of a trillionth of a joule. Such a small unit is useful, because the rest energies of subatomic particles can be expressed in reasonable-sized numbers in these units. An electron has a rest energy of about 500 keV (thousand eV), and a proton has a rest energy of about 1 GeV (billion eV).

All of these, plus others I didn't mention, are expressions of how much energy can be associated with different processes. In principle, any unit could be used in any circumstance; they are all just ratios of each other. However, in practice, traditions have built up in different contexts such that people are used to using certain units for certain purposes, but that is merely human habit and convenience, not because of anything about nature that demands it. There is nothing inherently wrong with measuring speed in furlongs per fortnight, but Americans find miles per hour more familiar. When we talk about nuclear energy in reactors, we will be switching back and forth between the world of atoms and particles, where people use MeV, and the world of electrical power, where people use J or even kWh, so it is useful to be able to switch back and forth between these units.

IV. Nuclear Energy

The electrons are held to the nucleus of the atom by the electrical force, and there is an energy associated with that interaction. To pull an electron off an atom, or to pull two atoms apart that have bonded into a molecule, increases the potential energy associated with that interaction. Some other energy must therefore go down if that is to happen. For example, light can be absorbed by the atom, decreasing the light energy, and raising the potential energy of the electron's interaction with the nucleus. Sometimes, molecules can shift their component atoms around into a new configuration, lowering the potential energy of the interactions of their atoms, which allows some other kind of energy to go up.

Simply speaking, this is how the body gains the energy associated with our motion, temperature, and neural electricity. This is also how oxidation (burning) converts the potential energy of the carbon molecules (in, say, coal or gasoline) into kinetic energy. Since, for practical purposes, we don't burn one molecule of coal at a time, it's more useful to talk about the thermal energy increasing: coal gets hot when you burn it, because the atoms are moving faster. This thermal energy can be used to boil water, increasing the kinetic energy of the water molecules that are turned from liquid into steam. These fast-moving water molecules bounce against a turbine, increasing its kinetic energy by making it spin, which in turn rotates a magnet that pushes electrons around in a wire, leading ultimately to the current in your house that enables you to have light and television and the internet.

There are other ways to increase the kinetic energy of a turbine besides boiling water: a river flowing downhill is decreasing the potential energy number associated with the gravitational interaction of the water and the planet Earth. That decrease can result in the increase of the kinetic energy of a turbine, yielding hydroelectric power. The atmosphere flows from one place to another, yielding a kinetic energy number associated with its motion, and if that flow pushes a turbine, wind power results. Solar power works a little differently, but the light energy associated with sunlight goes down when the light is absorbed, and that can increase the potential energy of electric charges by pushing them apart, creating a voltage.[8] When the charges flow back together (decreasing the potential energy again), that's called a current, which has a kinetic energy number, and so forth.

Another kind of energy that can drop to allow the energy of the boiling water to increase is the rest energy of the nucleus. The protons and neutrons in

---

[8] Sunlight yields about 1400 joules per second per square meter of energy on average at the Earth's surface. Not all of that light's energy is turned into electrical energy. Some of the light is reflected and some goes to increasing the temperature of the solar cells. The cells are therefore not 100% efficient (electrical energy out is less than light energy in—although energy is 100% conserved, we can't use the thermal energy for electrical power). Also, if the light does not fall perpendicularly onto the surface, the energy per square meter goes down, like butter spread over too much bread.

the nucleus are held together by a different force than the electricity that holds the electrons to the nucleus. Physicists call this force the "strong" force, because it can overcome the electrical repulsion of the protons.[9] Although the properties of the strong force are different from those of electricity, the strong force also has a kind of energy associated with it, and the energy number associated with the nucleus tells you its mass. Because the rule for calculating mass energy (called "rest energy" by physicists because an object has this energy associated with it even if it is not moving, or "at rest") is the famous $E=mc^2$, a nuclear particle that can change its mass will also change this energy.

The most fundamental process for understanding nuclear energy is that a neutron (rest energy of 938.565 MeV) can turn into a proton (rest energy of 937.272 MeV) and an electron (0.511 MeV), as well as a neutrino, which has such a small rest energy people thought for a long time it was zero. When this process will happen is essentially unpredictable in the specifics, although on average it won't take much longer than 12 minutes for a given neutron by itself. Note that 0.511 and 937.272 do not add up to 938.565!!! Does this mean energy is not conserved? No! Although the rest energy of the system goes down, the kinetic energy goes up! The pieces left over after the decay will be moving. This process is called beta decay, because the electron was originally called a "beta particle." Beta decay is one of the most common forms of radioactivity, and this is also why you don't tend to see lone neutrons lying around by themselves.

The strong force can hold a neutron together and keep it from decaying if there are other particles around for the neutron to interact with. Those particles could be neutrons or protons, but they have to be very, very close to each other to help. The strong force can only reach about a thousandth of a trillionth of a meter—any particles have to be closer together than this for the strong force to be able to hold them together. Not coincidentally, this is about the size of an atomic nucleus. Any bigger than this, and a nucleus gets more likely to fall apart. For a given number of protons, a group of friendly neutrons can hold them together against their natural repulsion of each other, and the protons and neutrons together can keep the neutrons from decaying. This is why the periodic table of the elements does not go on forever to higher and higher atomic numbers. Eventually, the nuclei get so big that the strong force can't reach across the nucleus to hold them together, and they tend to break apart. This breakup is called fission,

---

[9] Protons repel each other from their electrical force—if it weren't for the strong force, nuclei would fly apart and there would be no atoms at all.

and the pieces tend to have less rest energy than the original nucleus did, so the process allows some other energy to go up.[10]

The number of protons in a nucleus determines how many electrons can swarm around that nucleus in a neutral atom, and the number of electrons determines the chemical properties of that atom, so we call each atom that has a particular number of protons an element. A given atom of a given element can have a range of neutrons, which will change the mass of the atom but not its electrical/chemical properties. Atoms with the same number of protons but different numbers of neutrons are called different isotopes of the same element. Too many neutrons, and the instability of the neutron wins out over the stabilizing efforts of the strong force, and the nucleus will beta decay, spitting out an electron. Too few neutrons, and the strong force can't hold the nucleus together at all. If you can find some way to push two nuclei within the range of the strong force, against the electric repulsion, the strong force can latch them together in a process called fusion, creating a heavier element. Since the potential energy of the interaction of protons goes up as they get closer, some other kind of energy must go down to get them that close. This energy is usually provided by getting the nuclei moving very, very fast, as they do in the enormous temperatures at the core of the sun.

Generally speaking, large elements tend to drop in energy when they break apart, and small elements tend to lower in energy when you smash them together (if you can get them close enough in the first place). Our sun is smashing hydrogen into helium right now, releasing energy that eventually makes its way to Earth associated with sunlight. Under the right circumstances, if you can arrange it so that a lot of heavy nuclei split apart, the energy drop from the splitting will allow a very large increase in the kinetic energy of the pieces. One method of getting a lot of splitting is through a chain reaction.

V. Chain Reactions

Certain large nuclei (uranium and plutonium, in particular) split apart in particularly useful ways. Let's use uranium as an example. Uranium nuclei can stay unchanged for hundreds of millions of years; they are almost stable, from a human lifespan point of view. However, uranium 235, which has 92 protons and 143

---

[10] Usually the type of energy that increases is the kinetic energy of the decay products. If there are lots and lots of decays going on, this can be perceived macroscopically as an increase in temperature. The individual decay particles, however, if they collide with living tissue, can damage the organism. These decays are called radioactivity, the diverse set of decay products that come out at high energy are called radiation, and when that energy is deposited in a living organism, the energy change is called a dose (see Section V).

neutrons, decays ten times faster than uranium 238 (92 protons and 146 neutrons). So if you find a hunk of uranium on Earth, very little of it will be U-235.[11] If you add a neutron to U-235, however, about 82% of the time it becomes highly unstable and splits apart immediately.[12] This particular isotope has the very useful property that when it splits apart, it usually does so in such a way that in addition to two lighter nuclei, it also frees two solo neutrons. If these neutrons hit more U-235 nuclei, they can split again. Those splits release more neutrons, which can cause more splits, leading to what's called a chain reaction. Each split lowers the energy of the nuclei, enabling them to move quickly (increase in thermal energy). The exact direction of the emerging neutrons is completely unpredictable, so the only way to be sure the process will continue is to have many, many other U-235 atoms around.

Let's start with a single split that results from a U-235 nucleus absorbing a neutron. This split releases roughly 200 MeV of energy. That's only about 30 trillionths of a joule; not much energy. However, neutrons have a very small mass compared to a baseball (less than a trillionth of a trillionth), so they move much, much faster than a dropped baseball, up to 10% of the speed of light. But these neutrons can't go very far in a lump of uranium before hitting something else. The time between fission events in a runaway chain reaction is about 10 billionths of a second (10 nanoseconds).

If each of those neutrons hits another U-235 nucleus, and those split apart, that's 400 MeV more, plus four more neutrons. A second time, and you get 800 MeV and eight more neutrons. This still doesn't seem like much, but after a third time, you're up to a total of 2000 MeV. By the time 560 nanoseconds have passed, enough energy has been released to destroy a city. Each splitting only releases 30 trillionths of a joule, but when trillions of trillions of nuclei are involved, trillions of joules can be released.[13]

This runaway chain reaction only occurs if the neutrons are certain to hit other U-235 nuclei. If they hit something else, then the energy release can be slowed down and controlled. If, for example, only one neutron hits another U-235 nucleus, then the process would release a steady power of 3 trillionths of a

---

[11] Less than one percent, now. However, because of the difference in rates, millions of years ago, the percentage of U-235 must have been higher. The uranium in the Earth would have been made during the explosion of a massive star, billions of years ago. Back then, there would have been close to equal amounts of U-235 and U-238, but relatively little of the U-235 is left now.

[12] The other 18% of the time it becomes U-236, which also breaks apart, but more slowly (tens of millions of years—still much faster than U-235).

[13] The yield of Little Boy was about 63 trillion joules. Fusion in the sun releases about 100 trillion trillion joules every second.

joule every billionth of a second. The average fraction of neutrons that hit U-235 nuclei can be controlled by introducing other types of atoms to deliberately get in the way. For example, some reactor designs include carbon rods that can be inserted into the uranium to slow down the chain reaction or removed to speed it up. More than 99% of the uranium found in the ground is U-238, which completely prevents a U-235 chain reaction from even starting. To get the chain reaction fast enough to produce power to boil water and spin a turbine, you need 3% or 4% of the total uranium to be U-235. In other words, you need to more than quintuple the amount of U-235 present, relative to the U-238.

To have the chain reaction run away completely and become a bomb, the uranium must have more than 90% U-235, and there must be enough uranium in close proximity that the neutrons don't just fly out of the sample (and the uranium must hold together long enough for the chain reaction to get through the dozens of cycles necessary). The Little Boy bomb dropped on Hiroshima in 1945 contained almost 150 pounds of uranium, only 2 pounds of which was actually involved in the chain reaction. The role of impurity in the sample in slowing down the chain reaction is why a reactor can never turn into a nuclear bomb. There's just far, far too much U-238 present that gets in the way. A thorough description of the uranium enrichment process (increasing the fraction of U-235 in a sample) is beyond the scope of this chapter, but suffice it to say that it is very difficult. It is a long road from reactor-grade uranium to weapons-grade uranium. In the context of a nuclear reactor, though, how electrical power is produced is not much different from what happens in a coal plant: something rearranges its structure (for coal it's the molecules, for nuclear it's the nuclei), allowing the potential energy of the interaction (electric force for coal, strong force for nuclear) to go down, which allows the kinetic/thermal energy of the pieces to go up, which we perceive as an increased temperature, which boils water, generates steam, and turns a turbine. There is nothing more or less natural or artificial about either process.

In fact, there is evidence that billions of years ago, the conditions were right for uranium deposits in what is now western Africa to have developed sustaining nuclear chain reactions completely on their own.[14] They seem to have run stably without any runaway meltdown for up to a million years before running out of enough U-235 to keep the chain going.[15] Even more significantly, the radioactive products of the chain reaction remained contained in the deposit for

---

[14] F. Gauthier-Lafaye et al., "The last natural nuclear fission reactor," *Nature* 387, no. 337 (1997): 337.

[15] A. Meshik, "The Workings of an Ancient Nuclear Reactor," *Scientific American* 293, no. 5 (2005): 82–91.

billions of years, boding well for the prospect of long term underground storage of human reactor waste.[16] There is nothing unnatural about the nuclear processes. Of course, "natural" does not mean "safe."

VI. Dosage

Radioactivity is a random process. Exactly when a uranium nucleus will decay is unpredictable, how a specific nucleus will decay is unpredictable, where the products will go is unpredictable, and what they will do when they encounter another atom is unpredictable. However, when you consider trillions and trillions of decays, the average properties can be very precisely determined. This is why we can say that that after 703.8 million years, half of a sample of U-235 will have decayed to something else, and we can even know what percentages of that half that decayed will decay into what products, but we cannot predict which half will decay, and we cannot predict what products a specific nucleus will become.

The closest we can get to quantifying how much radiation someone is subjected to is to calculate the amount of energy the radiation has deposited in their tissue. It turns out to matter how much tissue is involved: the damage occurs when radiation particles hit atoms in the tissue, so if the particles are concentrated in a small region, more damage to that region can be expected to result. So, the official definition of "dose" is energy per kilogram of tissue mass, times a fudge factor that attempts to account for the kind of radiation and the kind of tissue. The international unit for this dosage is the sievert (Sv).

Determining what will happen when someone is exposed to a relatively small amount of radiation is almost impossible. For a very large dose (1-10 Sv or more), the effect is clear, fatal, and horrific, but for a small exposure, it's less obvious. Usually it involves developing cancer, but because there are many ways to develop cancer, and because we are always exposed to all sorts of radiation, it is usually impossible to say with confidence that this specific person would not have developed cancer if she had not been exposed to that particular source of radiation.[17] Usually, the best we can do is look at a large population and estimate how many additional cancers developed due to the radiation exposure that would not have happened otherwise. This is a very imprecise calculation, and it is not at all clear how it should be extrapolated to small dose cases.

---

[16] Mossman et al., "Carbonaceous substances in Oklo reactors—Analogue for permanent deep geologic disposal of anthropogenic nuclear waste," *Reviews in Engineering Geology* 19 (2008): 1–13.

[17] One exception is a particular kind of thyroid cancer that results if your body takes up radioactive iodine. However, this exposure can be avoided, and the cancer is treatable.

There is just too much radioactivity around us all the time to isolate out small effects. Eating a banana exposes you to one tenth of a millionth of a sievert, due to the radioactive potassium (which your body needs). Some wags have suggested we use this dosage as a new standard and call it the banana equivalent dose.[18] Then all other dosages could be described in bananas. Since we have radioactive elements in our bodies, sleeping next to a human being for eight hours will give you about half of a banana equivalent dose. Radiation comes from space, and it comes up from the ground. The area around Denver, for example, is high in radon, which exposes Denverites to an additional 3 thousandths of a sievert (mSv) above the average US dosage of 6.2 mSv.[19] Interestingly, the increase in radiation level at which the International Commission on Radiological Protection recommends evacuation is 1 mSv.[20] Should we evacuate Denver? Even more interestingly, the cancer rate in Denver is below the national average, despite the inhabitants receiving a higher radiation dosage.[21] Again, the specifics of low-dose radiation are very difficult to predict.

VII. Dangers of Power: Comparing Real and Perceived Threats of Nuclear vs. Coal

On March 9, 1945, a Japanese city was almost destroyed by American bombs. Over the course of a single night, 1,667 tons of napalm incendiary bombs were dropped on Tokyo, killing more than 100,000 people.[22] Almost five months later, the first nuclear bomb was dropped on Hiroshima. 80,000 people died immediately. Although more people died in Tokyo, it is the Hiroshima bomb that has been seared into our memory and is memorialized every August. There are many reasons for this asymmetry: one bomb vs. many bombs, the nuclear bomb killed a much higher percentage of the population, and last but not least the existential dread that pervaded the Cold War arms race in the era of Mutually Assured Destruction, but I think the "invisible killer"—the slow, disfiguring death of radiation poisoning—adds a extra layer to the horror that a visible threat like a firebomb evokes.

---

[18] "Banana Equivalent Dose," Wikipedia, last modified November 26, 2018, http://en.wikipedia.org/wiki/Banana_equivalent_dose.

[19] "Radiation Sources and Doses," United States Environmental Protection Agency, accessed January 2019, http://epa.gov/radiation/radiation-sources-and-doses.

[20] Richard Muller, *Energy for Future Presidents* (New York: Norton Publishing, 2012).

[21] "Incident Rates Table," National Cancer Institute, accessed January 2019, http://statecancerprofiles.cancer.gov/incidencerates/.

[22] Tony Reichhardt, "The Deadliest Air Raid In History," *Smithsonian Air and Space Magazine*, (March 9, 2015).

On March 28, 1979, at the Three Mile Island nuclear power station, a cooling valve stuck open, allowing too much water to escape from the reactor core.[23] The reactor core began to melt. This accident led to a media storm, exacerbated by miscommunications and misunderstandings between government agencies, inflaming the public's terror of all things nuclear.[24] I was just a kid, but I remember the fear evoked by those three words, "Three Mile Island," and I always thought it must have resulted in terrible, terrible loss of life. I was shocked when I looked into the history as an adult and found that the number of people who were killed because of the reactor meltdown was...zero. One follow-up study concluded that the major cause of loss of life due to the incident was an increase in lung cancer because many people smoked more cigarettes because they were stressed about Three Mile Island.[25]

Obviously, the disasters at Chernobyl and Fukushima were less benign, but the overall point remains that in the six decades of commercial nuclear power production, the average global fatality rate directly due to problems at nuclear reactors is less than one per year. The total number of people whose deaths can be attributed to radiation from the Fukushima disaster is less than 400 and may be as low as zero.[26] Contrast this with the 15,000 people who died from the tsunami, and yet the nuclear plant seemed to get more attention from the media, despite the relative lack of harm. This emphasis made the reactor seem more dangerous than the tsunami.

The annual number of deaths attributable to coal power plants is over 7,500 in the US alone, largely due to pollution. If you are worried about radiation, people who live near a coal plant typically receive three times the radiation dosage compared to people who live near a nuclear plant. Coal plants are radioactive, too.[27] Naturally occurring coal contains trace amounts of uranium and thorium,

---

[23] "Background on the Three Mile Island Accident," US Nuclear Regulatory Commission, last updated June 21, 2018, http://nrc.gov/reading-rm/doc-collections/fact-sheets/3mile-isle.html.

[24] P. L. Cantelon and R. C. Williams, *Crisis Contained, The Department of Energy at Three Mile Island* (Carbondale, IL: Southern Illinois University Press, 1982).

[25] John Kemeny, "The President's Commission on The Accident At Three Mile Island, The Need for Change: The Legacy of TMI," US Government Printing Office (October 1979): 157–163.

[26] Muller, *Energy*.

[27] J. McBride, R. Moore, J. Witherspoon, and R. Blanco, "Radiological impact of airborne effluents of coal and nuclear plants," *Science* 202, no. 4372 (December 1978): 1045–1050.

but when reduced to ash, the leftovers contain up to ten times their natural levels.[28] Coal ash is not subject to as strict regulations as nuclear waste, and it is often dumped into pools where it leaks into streams and rivers.[29]

The point here is not that nuclear power is risk-free or causes no harm, but that we have a tendency to underestimate the risks of the familiar and overestimate the risks of the unfamiliar. If we had no automobile infrastructure, and someone proposed building a transportation grid that would kill 40,000 people a year, I can't imagine that proposal would be enthusiastically accepted, and yet that is how many people die each year in traffic accidents in the US.[30] We accept those losses as part of the cost of our lifestyle. In recent years, public pressure has resulted in many states raising their speed limits to 70 mph or even 75 mph, even though we know beyond a doubt that this will increase the fatality of crashes. There are deaths that we are willing to accept to live the way we want to live. Because this is what we do every day, those deaths seem acceptable, if not inevitable. Similarly, we accept the deaths that happen due to coal power, and recoil at the possibility of deaths due to nuclear power, even though the overall number of deaths would most likely go down if we switched over to nuclear power.[31]

Is nuclear power perfect, clean energy? Of course not. There's no such thing. Even wind turbines and solar cells damage the environment, not least through the construction process. The question is not, is nuclear power 100% safe? The question is, how does its safety compare with our other options? For example, electric cars are a huge improvement over gasoline vehicles, in terms of reducing the emission of greenhouse gases. If the electricity to charge the car's batteries is produced by a coal power plant, per mile driven, an electric car results

---

[28] Mara Hvistendahl, "Coal Ash Is More Radioactive Than Nuclear Waste," *Scientific American* (December 13, 2007).

[29] "Frequently Asked Questions about the Duke Energy Coal Ash Spill in Eden, NC," United States Environmental Protection Agency, accessed January 2019, http://epa.gov/dukeenergy-coalash/frequently-asked-questions-faqs-about-duke-energy-coal-ash-spill-eden-nc.

[30] "General Statistics," Insurance Institute for Highway Safety, accessed January 2019, http://iihs.org/iihs/topics/t/general-statistics/fatalityfacts/state-by-state-overview.

[31] To be fair, there are complexities in this argument that I have skimmed over. Currently, fossil fuel plants are responsible for about 60% of the power produced in the United States (see the materials from the US Energy Information Agency), while nuclear power plants produce about 20%. If we were to make such a massive switch in production scale, it seems reasonable to assume that there would be an uptick in the number of deaths attributable to nuclear power plants (if only due to construction accidents in building them). However, the fact remains that producing power with fossil fuels is much more dangerous than people think, even ignoring the implications for global warming.

in about ten times less mass of greenhouse gases being dumped into the atmosphere. If the electricity comes from a nuclear power station, that discrepancy is even larger. However, the process of making any kind of car causes pollution, and the batteries are full of rare earth minerals and toxic chemicals that aren't exactly environmentally friendly, either. Changing the energy values of a system in ways that are useful to us always results in some kind of waste. We can minimize that waste, we can try to reduce the harm that waste causes, but we cannot eliminate it completely.

VIII. Nuclear Waste

Imagine you have a large bucket full of pennies. You dump the pennies out on the floor, and roughly half of them will come up heads. Set those pennies aside, put the tails back in the bucket, and dump the remaining pennies out on the floor again. Repeat the process until you have no pennies left. I perform this exercise with my students, and I ask them to predict how many times we'll have to dump the pennies until there are none left. They usually wildly overpredict the number, which turns out to be about ten to fifteen.

This process of flipping pennies is an accurate physical model of radioactive decay. The pennies represent unstable nuclei. The flipping process represents time passing, and a result of heads represents the occurrence of a decay. Since roughly half of the pennies will come up heads, one flip is the amount of time that half the pennies "live" in the sample, and so this amount of time is called one half-life.[32] The number of pennies that come up heads, per time, is called the activity of the source, and the more active it is, the more dangerous it is. However, the more active it is, the shorter the half-life, so the material will be dangerous for less time. The longer the half-life, the lower the activity, and the less dangerous it is. In the limit of an infinite half-life, the material is stable, and there is no danger from radioactivity at all. However, in all cases, once you're past ten or 15 half-lives, there's basically none of the radioactive material left.

---

[32] There are two truly staggering implications of this model. First is that the process of radioactive decay seems to be truly random. Ironically, penny flipping is not a truly random process; it's just complicated. If you knew all the forces and conditions under which a penny is flipped, you could absolutely predict the outcome. Subatomic particles are not like that. You could know everything there is to know about a particle, and you could still not predict exactly when it will decay. Second, the pennies are effectively identical; the subatomic particles are truly identical, and yet they decay at different times. This is functionally equivalent to throwing two identical baseballs in exactly the same fashion, and having them fly in completely different directions. And yet, on average, they behave exactly the same.

The reason nuclear bombs are more dangerous than conventional weapons is that the results of the nuclear processes are themselves unstable. In addition to the damage of the actual explosion, the byproducts of the fission hang around, like pennies that have yet to come up heads. They can do damage after the explosion is over. Uranium, once the extra neutron is added, can split in a number of different ways, but one common path is to become xenon-140 and strontium-94 (plus the two neutrons that go on to hit other uranium nuclei and keep the chain reaction going). However, xenon-140 has a half-life of 14 seconds, and Sr-94 has a half-life of 75 seconds, before each undergoes beta decay to a heavier element. Xenon-140 becomes cesium-140, which becomes barium-140 after a half-life of 64 seconds. The barium has a half-life of 13 days to become lanthanium, which has a half-life of 1.7 days to become stable cerium-140. For the other branch, strontium-94 becomes yttrium-94, which in turn becomes zirconium-94 after a half-life of 19 minutes, so what was uranium has turned into stable cerium and zirconium.[33]

These products are what we name "nuclear waste," although the primary component of nuclear waste is leftover uranium from the original supply that didn't get the chance to get involved in the chain reaction before the refinement level dropped below the percentage able to sustain the process. The transport and storage of this waste is what causes many people's anxiety about embracing nuclear power. As with the dangers of production, I argue that the dangers of nuclear waste are overestimated, while the dangers of fossil fuel waste are underestimated.

While there are major oil spills every few years, and phrases like "Exxon Valdez" and "Deepwater Horizon" have become part of the vernacular, there has never been a significant transport accident with nuclear waste.[34] Coal ash, which you will recall from earlier in this chapter is itself radioactive, is dumped in ponds and surface pits and leaks into the surface water system. A major leak dumped 39,000 tons into the Dan River in North Carolina in 2014.[35]

Since fission produces much more energy per mass than chemical burning, there is proportionately less waste produced, per joule. In the whole history

---

[33] A chart of all nuclide properties can be found at "Table of Nuclides," Nuclear Data Center at KAERI, http://atom.kaeri.re.kr:8080/ton/.

[34] "A Historical of the Safe Transport of Spent Nuclear Fuel," Department of Energy, accessed January 2019, http://energy.gov/ne/downloads/historical-review-safe-transport-spent-nuclear-fuel.

[35] "Case Summary: Duke Energy Agrees to $3 Million Cleanup for Coal Ash Release in the Dan River," United States Environmental Protection Agency, accessed January 2019, http://epa.gov/enforcement/case-summary-duke-energy-agrees-3-million-cleanup-coal-ash-release-dan-river.

of the US nuclear power program, we have produced about 72,000 tons of nuclear waste.[36] That seems like a large number, until you consider that it is about a tenth of a percent of the coal we use every year in power plants.[37] In 2017, nuclear power plants accounted for roughly one quarter of our electrical power production, but coal provided roughly a third.[38] This means nuclear provided roughly two-thirds as much energy for a tiny, tiny fraction of the amount of waste, and no carbon dumped into the atmosphere.

Most nuclear waste is stored deep underground (below the water table) in geologically stable places (I described in Section V how the natural reactors in Africa remained isolated for millions of years). Richard Rhodes reports that the facility being developed in New Mexico, one kilometer down through solid rock, part of a 2-km wide salt stratum that stretches under Kansas, could "easily accommodate the world's nuclear waste for the next thousand years."[39]

The particular decay chain described above will be pretty much complete in a year or so (the 13 days for the barium decay is the longest half-life), but there are other decay paths that yield unstable products with much longer half-lives. Nevertheless, according to the World Nuclear Association, after 40 years, the activity of the waste product will have already sunk to less than one-thousandth its original value.[40] Because of the exponential decay of the activity (the penny-flipping), the danger drops faster than most people realize, and again, the longest-lasting isotopes are also the least active. Berkeley physicist Richard Muller points out that after 100 years, the activity of uranium waste is only 100 times the level of the original uranium, so if you design a storage system that has only a 10% chance of leaking 10% of its contents (current standards are much more stringent than that!), you're back to where nature was when you started.[41] Remember that we are surrounded by radioactivity, all the time. Should we let the chance that a small number of people in thousands of years will get an extra dose of a few bananas dictate our policy now?

[36] Government Accountability Office report, "Spent Nuclear Fuel: Legislative, Technical, and Societal Challenges to Its Transportation" GAO-16-121T: Oct 1, 2015.

[37] US Energy Information Agency report, "Today in Energy," December 28, 2018, http://eia.gov/todayinenergy/detail.php?id=37817.

[38] Lawrence Livermore National Laboratory visualization, based on EIA data, April 2018, LLNL-MI-410527, http://flowcharts.llnl.gov/content/assets/docs/2017_United-States_Energy.pdf.

[39] Rhodes, Energy.

[40] "Radioactive Waste—Myths and Realities," World Nuclear Association, last updated May 2017, http://world-nuclear.org/information-library/nuclear-fuel-cycle/nuclear-wastes/radioactive-wastes-myths-and-realities.aspx.

[41] 10% of 10% is 1%, so if the waste is 100 times as active as "natural" uranium, 1% of 100 is 1, so that puts the danger level right back to where the uranium was before you mined it. Muller, Energy.

The problem of transporting and storing materials for nuclear power has been solved on a technical level. The problem that is still facing us is one of politics and cultural psychology.[42] The common perception of nuclear material is usually vastly out of date, overshadowed by fear, and shaped more by popular fiction (e.g. the three-eyed fish on *The Simpsons*) than scientific fact. Of course, if we were to step up nuclear production to seriously offset the amount of coal and natural gas we currently use, there would be problems of scale, but we also know that if we continue dumping greenhouse gases into the atmosphere at our current rate, we will be faced with a whole host of much less solvable problems.

IX. Nuclear Quakers

Quakers have opposed bombs, nuclear and otherwise, as part of our conviction that war is not the right way to settle disputes between nations. During the height of the nuclear arms race, Britain Yearly Meeting's Faith and Practice included the following strong statement: "We believe that no one has the right to use [nuclear] weapons in [one's] defence or to ask another person to use them on [one's] behalf. To rely on the possession of nuclear weapons as a deterrent is faithless; to use them is a sin."[43] The Friends Committee on National Legislation lists nuclear disarmament as one of its lobbying priorities.[44] These are just two easily found examples; there are many, many more.

However, as with many in the non-Quaker population, the differences between bombs and reactors are not reassuring to Friends. The group Quaker Earthcare Witness acknowledges this explicitly: "As Friends, our peace testimony has long led us to witness against nuclear power because of its connection to

---

[42] Public perception of the dangers of nuclear power seem to be largely influencing the architects of the Green New Deal rather than information garnered from the scientific community. Sources below include a letter signed by over 600 environmental groups, faith communities, and other organizations asking for a Green New Deal, and an article describing pushback from scientists regarding the Green New Deal's rejection of nuclear power. "Letter to Address the Urgent Threat of Climate Change," January 10, 2019, in Center for Biological Diversity, accessed January 26, 2019, http://biologicaldiversity.org/news/press_releases/2019/climate-legislation-01-10-2019.php. James Temple, "Let's keep the Green New Deal grounded in science," *MIT Technology Review*, January 18, 2019, accessed January 26, 2019, http://technologyreview.com/s/612780/lets-keep-the-green-new-deal-grounded-in-science/.

[43] Meeting for Sufferings, Quaker Faith & Practice, Britain Yearly Meeting, 1955, 24.41.

[44] "Nuclear Weapons; Advocacy for Disarmament and Nonproliferation," Friends Committee on National Legislation, accessed January 2019, http://fcnl.org/about/policy/issues/nuclear-weapons.

nuclear war."[45] Some people worry that radioactive waste from a reactor could be mixed into a regular bomb to add fallout to its destructive effects.[46] Such a bomb would not be a nuclear bomb, but would use radioactive materials like packing a pressure cooker full of nails and ball bearings. Should we therefore ban pressure cookers? Or ball bearings? A major theme of this chapter is that any form of energy production always carries risks, and we need to consider carefully which risks are worth taking.

California Friend Karen Street published an article in *Friends Journal* in 2008, encouraging Friends to reconsider the science around nuclear power.[47] This article generated such a response (one letter began, "We were aghast, and surely we weren't the only ones, to see such a frighteningly pro-nuclear article"[48]), that she wrote a follow-up article the next year to summarize and address the issues that were raised.[49]

Her two articles cover this material in much more depth than I have room to explore here, but the main question she raises is essentially: can we afford to *not* take the risks associated with nuclear power, in the face of the known impending existential crisis of climate change?[50] In the ten years since Ms. Street published her article, the climate problem has only gotten worse. Especially with the rising standard of living of the developing world, we first worlders must grapple with the integrity question: is it right for us to enjoy an energy-rich lifestyle that was built on the back of fossil fuels, and then react with horror when poor countries want to follow in our footsteps? Bill McKibben, among others, has sounded the warning bell that there is an actual limit to how many tons of greenhouse gasses we can pump into the atmosphere,[51] and if we wait for market forces to inhibit fossil fuel extraction, we will cross that limit.[52] If we want to

---

[45] "Minute on Nuclear Power," Quaker Earthcare Witness, last updated October 14, 2007, http://quakerearthcare.org/article/qew-minute-nuclear-power. See Appendix E in this volume for full text.

[46] Although Muller argues the panic after such a bomb would be a bigger problem than the bomb itself. Richard Muller, "The Dirty Bomb Distraction," *MIT Technology Review* (June 2004).

[47] Karen Street, "A Friend's Path to Nuclear Power," *Friends Journal* (October 2008).

[48] Ace Hoffman, "Another View on Nuclear Power," *Friends Journal* (January 2009).

[49] Karen Street, "The Nuclear Energy Debate among Friends: Another Round," *Friends Journal* (July 2009).

[50] An impressive bibliography of Street's sources can be found at http://quaker.org/legacy/fep/FJ-Nuclear-Energy-Debate.html.

[51] Bill McKibben, "Global Warming's Terrifying New Math," *Rolling Stone*, July 19, 2012, http://rollingstone.com/politics/news/global-warmings-terrifying-new-math-201207 19.

[52] Indeed, according to NASA, we crossed that limit in the spring of 2018. "NASA Scientists React to 400 ppm Carbon Milestone," Global Climate Change, last updated May 21, 2013, http://climate.nasa.gov/400ppmquotes/.

avoid catastrophe, that carbon has to stay underground. We cannot be blind to the real dangers of fossil fuels while acting on the fears of possible dangers of nuclear power.

X. Conclusions

Personally, I am not convinced that nuclear power is *the* answer to our energy challenges. In the long term, the only energy source that makes sense to me is the sun. If we can increase the efficiency of photovoltaic technology, the sun can deliver up to 1400 watts of power per square meter of surface. The US Federal Energy Information Administration estimates the electrical power usage of the US at about 40 quads (or about 4×10^{19} joules), of which 70% comes from fossil fuels. At 50% efficiency, it would take a square field 100 km on a side to power the entire US electrical power grid. That's a lot, and there are also challenges with storage and transport, but solar panels can be distributed in ways that power plants can't. Also, people are working on clever ways to extract solar power from otherwise useless surfaces, such as transparent solar panels that can capture electricity from infrared sunlight.[53] Windows made of such cells could provide power for a building while still being transparent for people to be able to look through.

However, in the short term, we need something to quickly replace fossil fuels, and I am convinced that our decisions on this question have been guided by fear rather than knowledge. Fear from the shadow of the mushroom cloud. Fear from the specter of radiation poisoning. Fear from a lot of ignorance and misinformation about the real dangers of nuclear power, combined with blindness to the damage being done right now by the familiar fossil fuel industry. We need to look at the problem and possible solutions with clear eyes.

While certainly dangerous, there is nothing unnatural about gaining energy from changes in the nucleus. It's no less natural than gaining energy from changes in molecules, also known as burning, and arguably less dangerous. There have been far fewer deaths attributable to nuclear power plants than other forms of power production. Coal plants emit more radiation than nuclear plants, and far, far more pollution. Even hydroelectric power, which emits no greenhouse gases, has led to human disaster, such as when 30 dams in China failed in 1975,

---

[53] Peter Dockrill, "Transparent Solar Cells Like This Could Deliver 40% of America's Power," *Science Alert*, October 24, 2017, http://sciencealert.com/transparent-solar-cells-satisfy-40-of-american-power-needs-see-through-light.

leading to the deaths of 230,000 people.[54] The 2012 tsunami killed far more people than the Fukushima reactor disaster, and even the evacuation caused more death than the radiation. The Three Mile Island disaster that so scared me as a child: zero deaths. Demanding complete and total safety from nuclear is unrealistic, and it represents an inconsistent standard when compared with other forms of energy generation.

At a Friends General Conference gathering, probably in July 1997, an attender spent the whole week wearing a sandwich board sign that protested the impending launch of the international Cassini mission to Saturn. I believe her sign said something like, "No nukes in space." At the time, it made me sad and somewhat bewildered. Did she think there is no radioactivity outside the planet Earth in the universe? Where did she think the uranium in the Earth came from? Did she not understand how vast space is; was she worried about contamination? I never approached her at the time, being conflict-averse (as many Quakers are), but I wonder now at what that conversation might have been like. Could we have found common ground? Could we find ways to work together to solve problems we did agree on? Or would fear and our lack of a common language (physics, not English) lead to misunderstanding and conflict? Now, in 2018, I believe the threat facing us from global climate change is so severe, we need to consider carefully *all* the possible solutions at our disposal, and I don't believe we can afford to dismiss nuclear power so quickly. It's no panacea, but unless we come up with something better, we shouldn't dismiss it purely out of fear.

---

[54] Phil McKenna, "Fossil Fuels are Far Deadlier than Nuclear Power," *New Scientist,* March 23, 2011, http://newscientist.com/article/mg20928053.600-fossil-fuels-are-far-deadlier-than-nuclear-power/.

17 | The Sustainable Food Systems Major at Guilford College: Food, Environment, and Community

By Kyle Dell, Marlene McCauley, and Gail Webster

Abstract: Guilford College's Sustainable Food Systems (SFS) major was developed in 2015 by an interdisciplinary team of faculty and students. We were moved to develop an SFS major with clear connections to Guilford's mission and values in response to strong interest in the field on the part of students, faculty, and staff. Such a major is also important to the greater Greensboro community, as our area experiences high levels of food hardship.

We developed the SFS major rather quickly, taking advantage of partnerships between members of the college community and the surrounding community. We were able to devote considerable time and resources for a team to research and benchmark similar programs. As a second-wave food studies program, Guilford's SFS curriculum now reflects not only qualities important to the mission of the institution, but also best practices of the discipline. The Guilford College Farm is an integral part of the major. Located on campus, the farm is a living laboratory for our students.

The Sustainable Food Systems major brings Quaker ethos into the college curriculum. The success of this program is evidenced by the rapid growth of the number of majors, by funding from foundations, alumni, and individuals in support of program development, and by the connections made by SFS with the community. Our experience in developing the Guilford College Sustainable Food Systems major should be useful for other institutions interested in establishing similar programs.

I. Introduction

Guilford College was founded by the Society of Friends in 1837 and has a mission to provide a "transformative, practical and excellent liberal arts education…necessary to promote positive change in the world."[1] Guilford College's new Sustainable Food Systems (SFS) major is deeply rooted in this mission. The Sustainable Food Systems major was approved at Guilford College in December 2015 and became available to students in Spring 2017. By Spring 2018, over 30 students were declared majors in the program, placing it midway in the ranking of small to large programs at Guilford. SFS is a unique major that reflects Guilford's core values, already producing graduates poised to make a difference in the world.

Developed in Summer 2015 by an interdisciplinary faculty, staff, and student team, the curriculum reflects Guilford's heritage as a Quaker college, incorporating practical engagement by students in many aspects of food systems. Among the key components for success in developing the program were attention to consensus-building activities, inclusion of staff and students in the team, effective benchmarking with a prominent consultant and relevant alumni, and deepening of relationships to existing campus facilities. As a second-wave food studies program, Guilford's curriculum reflects classroom learning, practical skill-building, and community engagement informed by the college's mission, specifically environmental sustainability, social justice, and peace.

The Guilford College Farm represents an integral part of the major. Our 120-year farming tradition began as a practical necessity in 1837. In 2011, the farm was revived and by 2016 it was recognized as one of the Top 30 Sustainable College Run Farms in the United States.[2] In celebrating the launch of the program that year, food scholar Michael Pollan celebrated the new program as a "path-breaking move" for a college. No four-year college in the country has a sustainable farm like ours: located on campus and practicing sustainable management principles while inside the boundaries of a metropolitan area experiencing serious food hardship. This working farm provides an authentic experience for students, a living laboratory for research, and it is a physical representation of our mission of transformational education, allowing us to offer farm-based skills courses and practicums right on campus. The farm supplies food to the college cafeteria, a CSA (community supported agriculture program), the Mobile Oasis Farmers Market (providing fresh produce to food desert areas in Guilford County where fresh produce is otherwise scarce), an on-campus farmer's market, an at-risk refugee community, and several off-campus grocery stores and restaurants. The farm has 2.5 acres currently under production for

[1] "Guilford College Catalog (2018–19)," 7, Guilford College website, retrieved from http://guilford.edu/media/18231.
[2] "Top 30 Sustainable College Run Farms," College Values Online, 2016, http://collegevaluesonline.com/features/sustainable-college-run-farms/.

fruits and vegetables, a greenhouse, two high tunnels to extend the growing season, a barn, and a farmhouse. This working farm not only provides real-world experience for students, but is also a new venue for community collaborations.

II. Why Sustainable Food Systems?: An Important New Major for Guilford and Beyond

A core team of faculty was moved to develop the SFS major for a number of reasons. First, the program and its unique approach to food systems reflects the interests and needs of our community. Only 25 other colleges in the country have programs similar to our SFS major. Only four of these colleges are in the Southeast, two being located at community colleges. Local and national job growth in sustainability and sustainable food is very rapid and a new generation of leaders in food systems is desperately needed by our communities.[3] Guilford has already graduated a number of students in recent years that are working in fields connected to Sustainable Food Systems, and our new majors are already engaging in serious study and practical work related to food systems.

The program allows faculty and students to live the mission and core values of Guilford College. Graduates in Sustainable Food Systems will be prepared to promote positive environmental and social change in the world. SFS provides a values-rich practical education that challenges students to see a larger, systems view of food, society, and the environment, and embodies Guilford's mission, values and Quaker heritage. Existing community partnerships in our local community and in sustainable food studies abroad programs also support community-based and global learning. The partnerships are constructed to remove artificial barriers between faculty, staff, and students, emphasizing a college core value of equality. Thousands of hours of student labor already supported the farm and its operation when we developed the program. Now, the SFS major integrates the farm into the academic program as an essential component of our curriculum, with practicum and skills courses providing the experiential learning that is important to student success. The farm is integral to the new major, and serves as a model of cooperation and synergy between Guilford faculty and staff of the Office of Sustainability.

Motivation for creating the program did not simply emerge from an internal commitment to inward-facing mission statements. The Greensboro-

---

[3] James Hamilton, "Is a Sustainability Career on your Horizon?" Bureau of Labor Statistics, 2012. "Employment Opportunities for College Graduates in Food, Agriculture, Renewable Natural Resources, and the Environment, United States, 2015–2020," United States Department of Agriculture, accessed January 2019, http://purdue.edu/usda/employment/.

High Point community continues to experience serious food system failure reflecting social, economic, and racial inequality. In 2015, the Food Research Action Center named Greensboro-High Point as the worst area in the United States for food hardship, and we continue to rank poorly in more recent years.[4] The report measured the percentage of families reporting that they did not have enough money to buy food in the past 12 months. The rate for Greensboro-High Point in 2014 was 27.9%, higher than many other communities experiencing economic hardship (see Fig. 1).

Metropolitan Statistical Areas (MSA) with Highest Food Hardship Rates (2014)

MSA	Food Hardship Rate
Greensboro-High Point, NC	27.9
Baton Rouge, LA	24.9
Fresno, CA	24.9
Bakersfield, CA	24.3
Jackson, MS	22.9
Augusta-Richmond County, GA-SC	22.8
Columbia, SC	22.8
Memphis, TN-MS-AR	22.7
Dayton, OH	22.6
Riverside-San Bernardino-Ontario, CA	22.4

Figure 1. Metropolitan Statistical Areas with highest food hardship rates in 2014. Statistics from Food Research and Action Center, 2015.

---

[4] Randy Rosso, "How Hungry is America? FRAC's National, State, and Local Index of Food Hardship," Washington, DC: Food Research and Action Center, June 2016, accessed January 2019, http://frac.org/wp-content/uploads/food-hardship-2016-1.pdf. Randy Rosso, "How Hungry is America? Food Hardship in America: A Look at National, Regional, State, and Metropolitan Statistical Area Data on Household Struggles With Hunger," Washington, DC: Food Research Action Center, August 2018, accessed January 2019, http://frac.org/wp-content/uploads/food-hardship-july-2018.pdf.

The SFS program will support better solutions for meeting the food hardship of our community and beyond. The program empowers our students to engage with community partners already addressing food hardship needs and gives students experiential community-based learning that is identified as a high-impact practice in higher education today.[5]

Because of the centrality of the community for the Sustainable Food Systems program, the team proposing the new SFS program devoted one-third of our time during the summer the major was created to researching and making contact with existing community partners who could provide effective support for engaging our faculty, students, and staff in addressing food hardship in our area. The following organizations became strategic community partners for our new program and empowered Guilford to enter into efforts to address local food hardship:

- Guilford County Health Department Mobile Oasis Market
- Renaissance Food Co-op
- Guilford County Food Council
- Food Not Bombs
- Greensboro Farmers Curb Market
- North Carolina Agricultural and Technical State University Farm

Community partners like these were already engaged in food hardship initiatives in the region, and the SFS program sought to learn from these partners ways to engage with this issue and provide the best learning opportunities for our students as our wider community confronts these challenges.

Closer to home, the SFS program proposal also benefited from the partnership and advice of the college's Bonner Center for Community Service and Learning, which has worked for many years engaging Guilford students with a wide variety of community partners addressing this issue. Guilford College is one of 27 in the country to have the Bonner Scholars program. At Guilford, 60 Bonner Scholars are selected annually based in part on their commitment to service-learning. Every year, the Bonner Scholars complete more than 24,000 hours of community service. Bonner Scholars operate a Farm Stand selling produce on campus to raise money to support their other initiatives such as donating fresh produce weekly to at-risk refugee and immigrant communities.

---

[5] George D. Kuh, "High-Impact Educational Practices: What They Are, Who Has Access to Them and Why They Matter," Washington, DC: Association of American Colleges and Universities, 2008, accessed January 2019, http://aacu.org/leap/hips.

They also partner with Guilford County to run the Mobile Oasis Market, which brings fresh produce to local food deserts and underserved communities.[6]

III. Development of the SFS major: A Unique Learning Community

1. Background

The SFS curriculum was developed after extensive research by a team of faculty and students in summer 2015, who were supported by the college's Summer Research Scholars Program. The curriculum incorporates high-impact experiential learning courses, such as internships, study abroad, research, service learning, and skills courses. Our program also includes a core of required courses, as well as a focused group of electives. Examples of focus areas include food production, food enterprises, food justice, food advocacy, food policy, food economics, food education, and food and health.

While the new curriculum reflects best practices of successful programs across the country, our new program is also distinctive. Students and faculty engage with food systems in a way that emphasizes the environment, sustainability, food justice, and food advocacy, guided by Guilford's core values, and reflecting Guilford's Quaker heritage.

Many land grant universities across the country have long histories of traditional agriculture programs that promote factory and mass farming practices, many of which reject or ignore basic principles of sustainability. The mission of Guilford College seeks to provide a "transformative, practical and excellent liberal arts education...guided by Quaker testimonies...necessary to promote positive change in the world."[7] A graduate in Sustainable Food Systems embodies the ability to promote positive change in the world in ways that are both transformational and practical. Graduates understand how to employ a values-rich worldview to work toward community, equality, integrity, simplicity, and stewardship, learning to identify and support positive change. And, as practical skills are critical components of our program, graduates will reflect the belief that their work should promote "civil and useful" skills needed for realizing the changes needed. The Sustainable Food Systems program at Guilford seeks to stand apart from these early generations of traditional agricultural programs and provide a values-rich educational and practical learning environment that

---

6 "Bonner Center for Community Service and Learning," Guilford College, accessed January 2019, http://guilford.edu/academics/departments/bonner-center.

7 "Guilford College Catalog (2018-19)," 7.

challenges students to see a larger, systems view of food, society and nature.[8] In this way, the essential core of the new program embodies Guilford's mission, values and Quaker heritage while also embracing emerging understandings of food systems as an academic discipline.

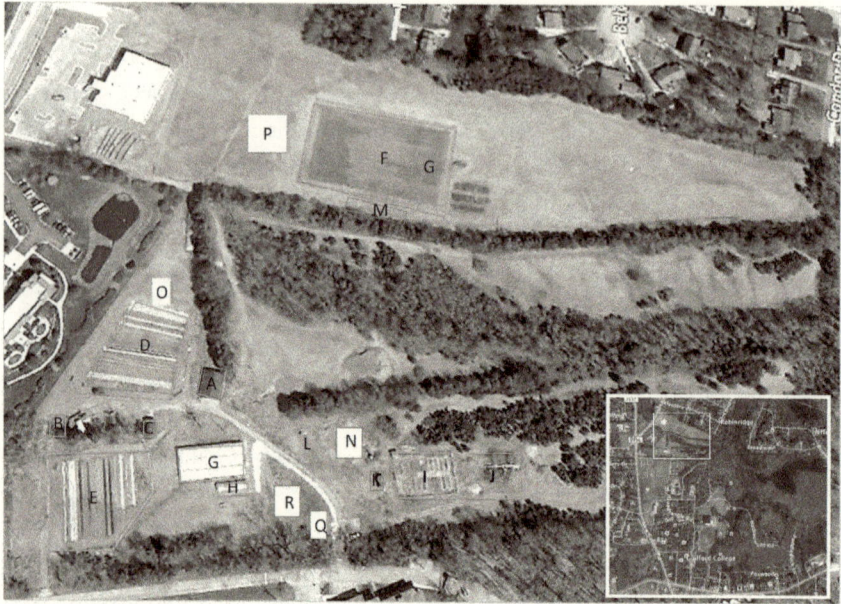

Image 1. The Guilford College Farm. Modified from Google Earth.

Current Structures A: Barn, B: Farmhouse, C: Wash shed, D-F: Fields, G: High tunnels, H: Greenhouse, I: Community garden, J: Compost curing, K: Gazebo, L: Permaculture beds, M: Beehives.

Proposed Structures N: Student co-op housing, O: Mobile chicken coop, P: Classroom, commercial kitchen and office space, Q: Farm stand, R: Outdoor classroom/event space.

---

[8] Molly Anderson, "Higher education revisited: Sustainability science and teaching for sustainable food systems," in *Future of Food,* ed. Stephan Allbrecht (Munich: Green Books, 2016).

The footprint of the farm on campus embodies these values and reflects a different approach to education with regard to food systems. As the figure above demonstrates, you'll find no hundred-acre fields or contained animal feed operations. Instead, you'll find beehives, oak logs with hand-inoculated mushrooms, permaculture beds, and solar-panel powered equipment.

During the development of the program in summer 2015, the farm served as an inspiration for the Summer Research Scholars team of faculty, staff and students working on the project. The team made an intentional choice to spend one day per week working on the farm together. This had a number of positive effects and reflected our commitments related to mission in a number of ways.

First, when working on the farm, it is difficult, even unconsciously, to revert to an artificial hierarchy related to faculty, staff and students. Doctoral degrees matter very little when weeding a new field, harvesting produce, or putting together CSA bags.

Second, as we worked on the farm together, the unstructured time exhibited a less pressured tone, leaving open the chance to talk and listen more deeply and in ways that would not be available in a seminar room, office, or across a conference table with laptops open. Finally, as a matter of integrity, our team wanted to practice what we were preparing to preach: if it was important for our future students to get their hands dirty in required practicum experiences, would not such experiences be equally, if not more important, when creating the foundation for the program? In fact, they were. Working on the farm each week together allowed our team to establish a common rhythm around a practical goal that had, at times, unforgiving needs and demands apart from ourselves. Nevertheless, farm days were the favorite days of the week for our team and all of us agreed our experience together would not have been anywhere near the same without this important time in community.

Image 2. The team that created the proposal for the Guilford College Sustainable Food System program at the Guilford College farm on a workday in summer 2015. Members of the team (from left to right): Hannah Brewer-Jensen, '17; Kyle Dell, political science professor and Environmental & Sustainability Studies chair; Moira O'Neill, '17; Bronwyn Tucker, Environmental & Sustainability Studies visiting lecturer; Marlene McCauley, geology professor; Seren Homer, '17; and Gail Webster, chemistry professor. Photo by Dan Nonte.

2. Student Demand for the New Major and Minor

The project of creating the new program emerged rather organically by student demand, which manifested itself in a number of ways. First, we experienced increasing requests on our cafeteria for local, organic, and sustainably raised food that was nutritious, tasty, and fresh. These appeals increased over time and reflect larger trends on campus toward sustainably grown and harvested food, concern for environmental impacts of food choices, and culturally appropriate meal selections. Second, experimental courses across campus that centered food as an interdisciplinary platform for learning (e.g., history of food, geology of wine, chemistry of food and cooking, food and justice, eating disorders and education, etc.) experienced record enrollments and promoted additional faculty interest in expanding offerings with food as a common theme. Finally, as mentioned earlier, a number of co-curricular programs on campus including those related to food hardship and our Bonner Center, the college farm, and other local opportunities reinforced the professional and social justice work available to students interested in engaging with values-driven education beyond the classroom. Taken together, these multiple streams of student interest resulted in the initial faculty and staff conversations concerning a new program.

One additional note is worth mentioning here. As a key principle of sustainable development, economic sustainability, and the triple bottom line—people, planet, profit[9]—suggests that graduates intent on representing change and doing so in a professional and rewarding environment should be able to secure gainful employment in the fields most relevant to sustainable development. Sustainable food systems is a rapidly growing field, so some of the jobs that our graduates will fill have not been created yet. The following list gives some examples of possible careers for SFS graduates:

1. **Farm, or work on someone else's farm.**
2. **Start or run a program directly serving farmers or communities**, such as by working with beginning farmers, managing urban gardens, starting a Farm-to-School program, or addressing community needs for healthy food. The program might be through a governmental agency (such as Cooperative Extension or the Natural Resources Conservation Service) or a non-governmental organization.
3. **Teach children (or adults)** about gardening, nutrition, where food comes from, and making better food choices.
4. **Start or run a food- or farm-related business**. Such a business might add value to farm products (such as by processing) or fill another niche in the food system, such as distributing or marketing food. Many graduates in this field become entrepreneurs.
5. **Work with an NGO that advocates for food or agricultural policy** in the US or abroad.
6. **Work with or start an NGO that addresses issues of food insecurity** in the US or abroad.
7. **Conduct research on improving practices in farming or the food system.** (This will require a master of science degree and perhaps a PhD to get funding to design and conduct research.)
8. **Report on food systems in traditional, online or social media.**

---

[9] Freer Spreckley, *Social Audit: A Management Tool for Co-operative Working* (Leeds: Beechwood College, 1987).

3. Benchmarking and Research of Curriculum from Other Colleges and Universities

During the 2015 Summer Research Scholars Program (SRSP), one of the chief goals of our team of four faculty and three students was to research existing academic programs related to sustainable food systems.

Our team quickly became aware of the wide variety of different approaches to the academic study of food at colleges and universities across the US. Programs ranged from large land-grant universities focused on existing industrial agricultural practices, to programs designed to train a new generation of sustainable farmers, to small colleges with specialized and narrow food programs that ranged from animal husbandry to culinary arts.

Given Guilford's unique mission and Quaker heritage, as well as the history of agriculture and food production on the New Garden campus, we wanted to design an academic program that would reflect our mission, our legacy, and our core values of community, equality, integrity, justice, and stewardship. The program we proposed is distinctive compared to sustainable food programs at other small colleges. This program promotes an understanding of food systems that emphasizes sustainability, food justice, and food advocacy, guided by our core values, and reflecting the heritage of our college.

We looked at dozens of programs across the country. Eventually we narrowed them down to colleges and universities that (a) have a similar degree program, (b) have a college farm, and (c) are relevant as peer and aspirant institutions for Guilford.

A common theme of programs we studied is a requirement for high-impact experiential learning courses, such as internships, student research, service-learning, and skills courses. We included such requirements in our curriculum as well. This brings the total number of credits to 45, which is in line with similar programs. Of the 45 credits in our program, 13 credits are earned in experiential courses, leaving 32 credits in traditional academic classroom settings.

4. SFS Program Purpose, Learning Outcomes, and Curriculum

In addition to benchmarking and research by the Summer Research Scholars Program team of students and faculty, the program and its curriculum was informed by the work of Dr. Molly Anderson, William R. Kenan, Jr. Professor of Food Studies at Middlebury College in Middlebury, Vermont. Dr. Anderson is a globally-recognized leader among academics and researchers associated with food studies. Prior to her appointment at Middlebury, she served as the inaugural holder of the Partridge Chair in Food and Sustainable Agriculture Systems at College of the Atlantic. As a consultant for our work, she provided our team with valuable research data and resources, and shepherded a contingent of Guilford faculty to an academic conference on food studies at Chatham University in Pittsburgh in June 2105. Dr. Anderson also visited Guilford, spending time working with our team and touring our campus facilities. As a Friend who is familiar with Guilford College, Dr. Anderson was well-placed to provide thoughtful, reflective, and informed guidance for creating the program. This curriculum also reflects valuable feedback and input from Guilford College alumni working in fields related to sustainable food systems. Sarah Campbell (2010), a farmer in Maryland and the education director of the National Farmers Union in Washington, DC; Joel Slezak (2007), a farmer in Charlottesville, Virginia; and Rania Campbell-Bussiere (2008), director of the rooftop farming organization Cloud 9 Rooftop Farms in Philadelphia, Pennsylvania all provided valuable input and feedback on our curricular and experiential goals.

Sarah Campbell, in particular, suggested that we pay close attention to building a curriculum that recognizes and problematizes the historical and social roots of inequality related to gender and farming. Sarah's work on this issue with the National Farmers Union provided her the perspective to correct oversights our team had made, in spite of the fact that our team was highly interdisciplinary and with strong representation by female faculty, staff and students. We continue to utilize our alumni friends of the program to assist us in regularly reviewing the program and for networking opportunities for students majoring in SFS. Following this research and in light of the information we gleaned from consultants, we defined and structured our program in the following ways.

The SFS program statement of purpose. The sustainable food systems program will develop graduates that demonstrate a range of knowledge, skills and values essential to effective professional and social engagement that advances and improves the sustainability of food systems within diverse cultural communities.

The SFS Program Student Learning Outcomes.

1. Define sustainable food practices and principles particular to historical and cultural settings.
2. Demonstrate specific skills associated with professional development related to sustainable food production, advocacy, or research.

3. Articulate a personal philosophy and engage in practice reflective of the needs and best practices related to the advocacy for social change and improvement on issues related to food, equality, justice, and diversity.
4. Develop a comprehensive professional plan that reflects interdisciplinary coursework, skills development, practical engagement with different cultural contexts, and the core values of Guilford College.

The SFS Curriculum. The curricula for the SFS major and minor consist of three levels of courses: required core courses, required liberal artisan courses, and elective courses. The structure, breadth, distribution and length of the curriculum reflects the best practices discovered through our benchmarking research as well as the college's mission, core values and Quaker heritage. We also sought ways to leverage the current and future facilities and learning opportunities provided both by the Guilford College Farm as well as existing service-learning opportunities with the Bonner Center.

(a) Required core courses: The required core courses include core academic courses and hands-on work.

- *SFS 120, Introduction to Food Systems:* an interdisciplinary overview of food systems along with the challenges facing them, and an introduction to food insecurity issues facing the region.
- *SFS 220, Sustainable Regional Food:* a place-based, interdisciplinary look at solutions to the challenges facing food systems and regional innovations.
- *SFS 110, Practicum in Sustainable Agriculture:* hands-on experience working on the College Farm.
- *SFS 310, Advanced Practicum in Sustainable Food Systems:* a student's signature work, including research and project development.

(b) Liberal artisan and experiential courses: This group of courses was designed to incorporate many best practices in higher education and give students a solid grounding in the hands on work of sustainable food.

SFS 210, Liberal Artisan Skills Courses: typically 1- to 2-credit courses that require students to master a specific skill. To date, we have offered topics such as permaculture design certification, food preservation, forest management and trail building, beer brewing, cooking from the local foodshed, basic farm construction techniques, farmers market management, and beekeeping. Many other topics will be developed in the future, perhaps including urban farming, season extension, composting, cheese making, grant writing, and more.

We also require either an off campus internship or study abroad at an approved program which focuses on food systems and sustainability. This allows students to grapple with sustainable food systems beyond the Guilford College Farm.

One of our major study abroad partners is the award-winning Guilford College Brunnenburg Program in the Italian Alps.[10] SFS faculty worked with our Brunnenburg partners to sharpen the focus on sustainability and sustainable food. The program features a weekly work day on the castle's farm and vineyards, which is now given academic focus as a Practicum In Sustainable Agriculture. Dr. Siegfried De Rachewiltz, director of the program, is an expert in the history of agriculture in the region, and teaches a course on Agro-archeology in the Sudtirol. Other courses include Environmental Ethics and regional courses taught by Guilford College faculty-in-residence, such as Sculpture and the Environment, Medicinal Plants, Chemistry of Food and Cooking, Just Food, and more.

(c) Elective courses: SFS students work with their academic advisor to determine a focus area, such as food production, food enterprises and entrepreneurship, food justice, food advocacy, food policy, food economics, food education, and food and health. Someone who aspires to become a farmer or entrepreneur needs a different skill set than someone who intends to work for a non-profit organization focused on food justice or policy. Based on the student's intended path, they choose a coherent group of five academic (4-credit) courses to help them achieve their goals.

For example, a potential farmer might select courses in accounting, marketing, soils, animal husbandry, and agroecology, while someone interested in food justice might select courses in community problem solving, food justice, food policy, non-profit management, and grant writing.[11]

Our students are also encouraged to take courses at North Carolina Agricultural and Technical University (NC A&T) under a consortium agreement. We work closely with colleagues at NC A&T to ensure that our curricula have little overlap; rather, they are complementary, and focus on the different strengths of each institution. For instance, NC A&T already offers topics suited

10 "The 25 Best Study Abroad Programs," College Rank, 2016, accessed January 2019, http://collegerank.net/best-places-to-study-abroad/.

11 A list of currently-approved courses can be found on the SFS web page: "Sustainable Food Systems," Guilford College, http://guilford.edu/sfs.

to a land grant institution, such as soil science and animal husbandry. We will not reproduce their courses, instead focusing on new topics.

IV. Results to Date

The results to date for the SFS program at Guilford have been impressive. With the launch of the program in the fall of 2016, students could begin declaring SFS as their major in January 2017. Although the college only began marketing the program to prospective students starting in the fall of 2017, we recorded over 30 students as majors in the first three semesters. We anticipate such recruiting to pick up as marketing of the new major is integrated into a full two-year cycle of admissions and recruiting efforts. Our current number of students majoring in SFS puts our program "mid-pack" among all majors on campus, and we expect to be among the largest interdisciplinary programs on campus in the next two to three years.

Additional measures of success are also important to share. First, the SFS program has been important in recruiting a number of new, young faculty to Guilford, teaching such diverse topics as food policy, gender and food, and food with an international perspective. In addition to recruiting faculty that have traditional academic backgrounds, Guilford has also been able to partner with local practitioners in beekeeping, farmers cooperatives and advocacy groups, and local farmers to provide much needed on-the-ground, practical engagement in issues contextual and local to Guilford College's place in the Piedmont of North Carolina. Recruiting and retaining these new faculty to the program will be important measures of success for SFS in the years ahead.

Second, Guilford's SFS program has been able to secure, in a short amount of time, funding sources in local foundation grants important to the start-up costs for a new major. For example, generous funding from the Hillsdale Family Foundation provided critical support in the early days of the program, allowing us to make improvements and additions to farm infrastructure, and to purchase equipment needed for new course development. This funding let us add another high tunnel to the farm for season extension, add a larger wash shed and cold storage to the barn to process and preserve produce, and heat the barn for winter classes. These improvements were critical, as larger numbers of SFS students working on the farm needed to be wisely and usefully accomodated. For new course development, the Hillsdale funding allowed us to outfit a food lab to teach courses related to food preservation, cooking, and fermentation. Alumni and community partners continue to provide funding from small to large donations. A recent donation allowed us to hire an assistant farm manager to help manage the larger number of student workers, and act as liaison between the farm and the SFS major.

A partnership between Guilford County and the college's Bonner Center has provided US Department of Agriculture (USDA) funding for the Guilford College to run the Mobile Oasis Farmers Market, which brings fresh produce to urban food deserts and poorly-served areas in the county. SFS students are active in this initiative, and SFS skills courses have provided a way for students to link academics with this co-curricular work.

Third, the practicum courses that are key pieces of the curriculum in supporting engaged "dirty hands" experiences for students have also provided important results for the SFS program. Over 96% of practicum students report in course evaluations that the practicum experience was of high quality, and 100% of practicum students (introductory and advanced) have achieved all learning outcomes associated with the courses. Most interestingly, reinforcing the positive and successful experience that students have working on the farm as part of the practicum courses, is that over 80% of practicum students voluntarily spent more than twice as many hours working on the farm than required for the course. This level of student-driven engagement in the practicum experience on the farm reflects not only the level of preparation for the practicum course and the oversight provided by our faculty and staff, but also the immediate feedback and visible results available to students working on projects as part of these "dirty hands" courses.[12]

Finally, by partnering with other offices on campus, the SFS program has been able to support activities that were critical in bringing additional visibility to our efforts. In partnering with our award-winning Bryan Series of speakers to campus, we were able to bring Michael Pollan to campus to launch our new program.

A similar partnership on campus with the faculty development program supports emerging scholarship in the field of sustainable food systems. This partnership resulted in an award-winning presentation at the Small Business Institute in 2017, given by program faculty in partnership with faculty in food programs at another local university.[13]

---

[12] In addition to the farm supporting SFS practicums and the student learning associated with these courses, the farm also produced impressive levels of produce. Between 2014 and 2017, the farm produced nearly 30,000 pounds of produce for commercial accounts, over 2,000 pounds were donated to various programs designed to address local food hardship, and nearly 20,000 pounds were shared through members of the college farm's CSA program.

[13] Chyi Lyi (Kathleen) Liang, Marlene McCauley, and Kyle Dell, "Building a Collaborative Effort of Training and Education in Sustainable Food System for the 22nd Century

V. Conclusions: Keys to Successful Development of a Food Systems Program

The Sustainable Food Systems Program at Guilford College is unique in many ways. It went from a vague idea in the minds of a few faculty, to a full major, in less than two years. This success would not have been possible without a perfect storm of assistance: a working college farm, the strong support of President Jane Fernandes, the support of the Summer Research Scholars program, and more. Even so, several aspects of our experience are useful and instructive to other schools interested in developing similar programs.

1. A Clear Connection to the College's Mission, Core Values, and Distinctiveness

The rapid development and approval of the SFS program was rooted in its deep connection to the college's mission and core values. The program embodies "living our values" of stewardship, equality, justice, community, and integrity. By making a clear connection to the values of the institution, the SFS program demonstrated to faculty and administrators, some of whom were unfamiliar with the details of the program, how such an academic major would represent important conceptual elements of the college in very real, tangible ways for students and friends of the college.

2. Establish Student Interest Early in Process

Without student demand, the SFS program would not exist. As the campus climate trended toward an increase in concern for environmental impacts on food choice, and culturally appropriate and diverse meal selections, student interest and involvement in the College Farm and sustainability followed suit. Existing courses across campus that focused on food as an interdisciplinary platform for learning had strong enrollments and led to increasing numbers of courses offered with food as a common theme. Finally, co-curricular programs on campus, particularly the Bonner Center, had large numbers of students interested in and actively working on local issues of food hardship and food justice. The academic program in SFS allows students to link curricular and co-

---

through Urban Agriculture Programs, 2017," Small Business Institute Conference Proceedings 41, no. 1 (2017): 139–142, http://smallbusinessinstitute.biz/resources/Pictures/SBI%202017%20Conference%20Proceedings.pdf.

curricular opportunities and interests in food justice, allowing them to engage in values-driven experiential education.

3. Effective Partnerships with Guilford College Faculty, Staff, and Community Groups and Individuals

Team members spent considerable time meeting with and learning from Guilford faculty and staff already involved in some way with the food system, ranging from academic departments that offered courses which could become a part of the new interdisciplinary major, to offices such as the Bonner Center, which were already deeply engaged in issues of food hardship. We also worked with potential community partners and faculty and staff from other local colleges and universities. Successful program development means mapping the local terrain first, and honoring existing programs and expertise. Our goal was to not reproduce what was already being done, but to use our resources to add to existing efforts.

4. Support and Sufficient Time for a Focused Team to Design the Program

Our team spent the summer of 2015 completely focused on this project. Additionally, one team member had a sabbatical leave the following fall to focus on seeing the SFS proposal through the approval process. This would not have been possible without support from President Jane Fernandes, Faculty Development, and the Summer Research Scholars Program. Considerable, focused research time is imperative, as is a diverse team of faculty, staff, and students from different backgrounds.

Part III: Quaker Approaches to the Environment in the Academy – Discussion Questions

1. **Chapter 11. A Quaker Educator in Dialogue with Teilhard on the Universe Story, by Stephen Potthoff**

   1. Drawing on some of the mystical experiences with nature described by Teilhard, George Fox, and Potthoff, what responsibility do educators have in shaping a sustainable future in light of both natural history and religion?

   2. How might Quaker educators go about bridging the gap that exists in the minds of many students between the natural sciences and religion in the classroom?

   3. Why might it be important to appreciate and be familiar with the findings of the scientific community as well as the findings of mystical, spiritual, or religious figures and experiences when discussing the environment?

2. **Chapter 12. Reclaiming Natural History: Quakers, Nature, and Education, by James W. Hood**

   1. In what ways are natural history and literature connected, in relation to the environment? Why might it be important to cross disciplines and include both the humanities and sciences when discussing environmental concerns in an educational setting?

   2. What are some of the benefits of learning to tell anecdotal stories such as the "animal stories" mentioned by Hood? How do these stories help address environmental issues?

   3. What did you learn about historical Friends through Hood's inclusion of a section on eighteenth and nineteenth century Quaker naturalists? In what ways does this impact your understanding of the Society of Friends?

3. **Chapter 13. Ecotone: Quakerism, Sustainability, Art, and the Boundaries Between, by Craig Goodworth with Cherice Bock**

    1. What role can artwork and artists such as Goodworth play in the engagement of Quaker communities with the environmental crisis?
    2. Does the metaphor of an ecotone help you imagine the human-earth relationship in any new ways? What ecotones do you live in or near, either in the physical landscape, your interior landscape, or your academic or occupational work?
    3. What might emerge if Friends collectively consider the ecotone between beauty and utility when addressing the environment?
    4. If Friends have not traditionally incorporated art in their worship, meetinghouses, and other aspects of their corporate life due to an emphasis on simplicity and knowing God inwardly, do you think this should change? Why or why not? What are some ways you can imagine Friends incorporating more art into their common life, and what does this have to do with environmental concerns?

4. **Chapter 14. How are We to Live? A Quaker Approach to Environmental Ethics and Economics, by Robert Howell**

    1. Howell suggests that a difficult future is inevitable due to the trajectory of climate change brought on by outdated societal and economic systems. What does this future look like and how do Quakers fit into it?
    2. How should Friends balance the task of preventing further environmental damage, and the task of managing the dystopian human condition that may occur due to the climate crisis?
    3. In what ways have Friends lived in line with neoclassical economics and human-centered ethical frameworks? Are there ways in which Friends have resisted these ideologies and/or offered different worldviews?
    4. How might Friends and others go about shifting ethical and economic practices toward systems that take the human-Earth relationship into account?

5. **Chapter 15. Seeking Truth in History and Pedagogy: ReMembering and Decolonizing are Crucial for Sustainability, by Sara Jolena Wolcott**

   1. Do you think it is possible to live in a world free of the attitudes of unsustainable expansion that were constructed out of colonialism? Why or why not? What were some of the ingredients for colonialism's rise in the first place?

   2. Educators like Wolcott seek to correct inaccurate and misleading notions about historical colonialism in order to interrupt the unsustainable systems it generated. Do you think learning more accurate histories can affect our actions moving forward? In what ways?

   3. Is it possible to explore the natural world sustainably in the future? In what ways might colonial ideals have played a role in more recent discoveries on our own planet (e.g., discovery of new species, or subterranean and oceanic exploration), or even extraterrestrial bodies like Mars or the Moon? What are the implications of what we are learning about the last several centuries of colonization as we imagine colonizing other planets?

   4. With Wolcott's focus on historical colonialism, what steps in the process of "ReMembering" do we as individuals, meetings, schools, or other organizations need to take in order to develop an equitable Quaker ecotheology?

6. **Chapter 16. Nuclear Power from a Quaker Physicist's Perspective, by Donald A. Smith**

   1. Did Smith convince you nuclear energy could be a necessary stepping stone from the use of fossil fuels to the use of solar and other renewables? What was most convincing? What questions do you still have?

   2. When reading this essay in combination with Appendix E, Quaker Earthcare Witness's "Minute on Nuclear Power," do you feel Smith addresses the concerns raised by QEW members? What might QEW members continue to be concerned about? Do you agree? Why or why not?

   3. What values do you consider most important as Friends and others weigh the costs and benefits relating to various forms of energy generation?

7. **Chapter 17. The Sustainable Food Systems Major at Guilford College: Food, Environment, and Community, by Kyle Dell, Marlene McCauley, and Gail Webster**

    1. What can other institutions learn from the success of Guilford College's Sustainable Food Systems (SFS) major? How could this change the way existing programs operate at your school, or the way your meeting or organization approaches food or sustainability ministries?
    2. Guilford's SFS major focuses on campus assets, student interest, and community need. When you think about your own community, what assets, interests, and needs might you focus on to create a program particular to your context?

8. **Part III General Questions**

    1. When thinking about environmental concerns from the angle of your own academic discipline or occupational focus, what do you need from other fields in order to develop a more holistic approach to environmental solutions?
    2. What do you notice about the ways these educators use the Friends values to inform their approaches to teaching and other work?
    3. What themes do you see in these Quaker approaches to various academic disciplines, and what differences are in evidence?

PART IV
Stories of Sustainability:
Individuals and Organizations Living Quaker Ecotheology in Action

18 | Earthcare as a Quaker Value: The Formation and Continued Work of Quaker Earthcare Witness

By Shelley Tanenbaum

Abstract: *Growing awareness of environmental concerns led to the formation of Quaker institutions to address the environmental crisis and inspired many Friends to change the way they were living. These institutions include Quaker Earthcare Witness (QEW), formed in 1987 to inspire and empower Friends on their own and in their meetings/churches. However, the rising existential crises of our times have outpaced Friends' witness in the world. Traditional Quaker values such as peace and equality are impacted by ecological stress and environmental justice. Earthcare is both a problem (the crises we are facing) and a solution (growing our connections with spirit). Technology, along with an insistence on a just transition, may be able to meet the environmental challenges we are facing, but needs to be combined with a growing sense of eco-spirituality to avoid continually facing one crisis after another. Embracing earthcare is a pathway to removing the occasion for war and creating a thriving world.*

In the mid-1980s, many Friends felt a strong leading to live their lives in harmony with nature and to support policies and programs that supported these lifestyles. In addition to Friends' personal lifestyle changes—thousands of light bulbs switched to compact fluorescents and now light-emitting diodes (LEDs), and generating tons of recycling and homegrown veggies—we also created Quaker institutions that pushed for broader societal change. Quaker Earthcare Witness (QEW), then called "Friends Committee on Unity with Nature," formed in 1987 as a North American organization to connect Friends with an Earthcare leading and to advocate for a sustainable world. Many Friends General Conference yearly meetings and some monthly meetings formed Unity with Nature committees. QEW's programs and publications stem from a conviction and consciousness that the global crisis of ecological sustainability is at root a spiritual crisis.

I. Quaker Earthcare Witness

Quaker Earthcare Witness (QEW) is a network of the Religious Society of Friends (Quakers) in North America and other like-minded people who are taking action to address ecological and social crises from a spiritual perspective, emphasizing Quaker process and testimonies, including continuing revelation. Connecting with others who share our leadings and concerns can make all the difference between feeling overwhelmed by today's environmental challenges and being a part of a growing community working for positive change. For over thirty years, QEW has been bringing together Friends and caring souls from all over North America who are seeking to live in right relationship with all of creation and aspiring for the peace and justice that can result when the earth's ecological integrity is restored.

Friends and like-minded individuals participate in QEW activities in numerous ways. As a network, we showcase what Friends are doing to support earthcare, ranging from frontline actions of resistance, to development of projects and programs that build resilient and sustainable communities, to reflections on eco-spirituality. We share these stories in our quarterly publications, on our website, and in social media. Friends are welcome to send us articles and let us know what is going on in their community, and we share the news with our network.

In addition to our quarterly newsletter, we produce background material and curricula on current topics such as climate change, environmental justice, and population. We offer material in downloadable format from our website and, on request, in print. We support a lively online discussion group, with Friends from all over North America sharing resources. These discussions are inspiring and provocative, often leading to creative solutions to thorny problems. All Friends are welcome to join.[1]

We also serve as a Quaker voice on earthcare. We offer workshops and presentations at Quaker events and interfaith gatherings, and support and lift up earthcare-related causes by publicizing these causes and collaborating as allies. As an accredited NGO with the United Nations, we participate in events sponsored by their Economic and Social Council (ECOSOC) and the United Nations

---

[1] Resources and information for joining the listserv can be found at QEW's website: http://quakerearthcare.org.

Framework Convention on Climate Change (UNFCCC). Most recently, connected with the UN, we have sent observers to the annual climate conferences and sponsored side events on water and food sovereignty in the African Diaspora. Even as individuals in our network and on our steering committee support political and social action in numerous areas, such as mitigating climate change, slowing population growth, and enhancing biodiversity, each of us tries to bring awareness to the essential spiritual dimension present in any given ecological issue. This is integral to the belief we are "one in the Spirit," which has formed the foundation for Quakers' powerful peace and social justice work in the past.

The conviction we are one in Spirit is closely tied to the Quaker principle that our actions necessarily reflect our true core beliefs. Many Friends also share the concern of mainstream environmental groups that significant changes are needed in legislation, technology, education, and social structures. But without a profound transformation in heart and consciousness, in our fundamental relationship with the rest of creation, there is little chance, given the destructive powers currently wielded by the human race, of averting a major collapse of the systems that support all life on earth.

II. Existential Threat

However, despite the establishment of QEW over 30 years ago, Quakers did not become leaders in the environmental movement; there was no sea change within the Society of Friends. Since then, the number of Quaker organizations working on environmental issues has increased, but our efforts have shifted our Society's collective environmental impact only slightly.[2] These institutions serve Friends as well as they can, and earthcare has started to register as a Quaker value. However, our response has not kept pace with accelerating environmental threats.

We find ourselves in 2019 facing an existential crisis: Will our civilizations survive climate change and resource depletion? How many people will be at enhanced risk from climate change, either directly from extreme weather or indirectly through long-term drought, or due to conflict and displacement over natural resources? How many generations will suffer due to our lack of awareness and action today? How many species will not be here in 100 years? Those of us

---

[2] Read the stories and descriptions of the earthcare work of many of these Friends organizations in other chapters in this section, including Quaker Institute for the Future (ch. 20), Friends Committee on National Legislation (ch. 24), Earth Quaker Action Team (ch. 19), and Friends World Committee for Consultation (FWCC, ch. 22). Also notable is the work of the Quaker United Nations Organization (QUNO) in Geneva, which has been engaging in "quiet diplomacy" around climate change issues, and in 2015 partnered with QEW and FWCC to release a "Quaker Statement on Climate Change." See Appendix H for full text.

doing this work are struggling to pedal faster, up steeper and steeper hills. How can the Religious Society of Friends shift into a higher gear to meet this existential challenge?

Friends pride ourselves on being at the forefront of social change. We are rightly pleased to have supported abolition of slavery, as well as women's rights and civil rights, long before these views were socially acceptable. When we support something, we do more than mouth the words. We act, whether that is promoting government policies, spreading information, or agitating in the streets. With earthcare, we are woefully behind. In my view, earthcare is a Quaker value that connects with our testimonies as Friends, and there is much we can do as individuals and the Society of Friends to more directly face into this crisis with our denomination's historic combination of courage and spirit.

III. Earthcare as an Expression of the Peace Testimony

We can all agree that the testimonies on peace and equality, along with respecting all people, are values that Friends embrace. But these same values call on us to fully embrace earthcare if we are to make significant progress in creating a peaceful, fair, and just world.[3] Most Quaker activists I know throughout North America share my concern for the environment and find ways in their personal lives to reduce their carbon footprint, yet many do not make the connection to earthcare as part of their peace and justice witness in the world.

We sum up our peace testimony with the words, "Take away the occasion for all war."[4] Yet ignoring the consequences of resource depletion and climate change seriously limits how much we actually can take away the occasion for war. The civil war in Syria is a prime example of how climate change triggers violence. Syria was hit with an especially long drought. With failing crops several years running, farmers and their families fled to the cities. Increasing numbers of internal refugees led to crowded cities with limited resources to absorb the newcomers. The already-existing authoritarian regime imposed rules that the people resisted; political unrest increased and people were jailed. Ultimately, civil war

---

[3] Keith Helmuth, "Ecological Integrity and Religious Faith," *Friends Journal* (August 2001), http://friendsjournal.org/2001065/.

[4] A phrase from the letter Friends delivered to King Charles II in 1660, "A Declaration from the Harmless and Innocent People of God Called Quakers, against all plotters and fighters in the world." George Fox also uses the phrase in his journal. George Fox, *The Journal of George Fox*, ed. John L. Nickalls, revised edition (Cambridge: Cambridge University Press, 1952), 379.

broke out, causing the loss of more than 400,000 lives and 5 million people becoming refugees to date.[5] Climate change is not the only cause of this war, but it served as a trigger in a resource-poor and authoritarian political system. This is one of several current examples of climate disruption sparking violence. More will surely follow as climate impacts become more severe.

IV. Earthcare as an Expression of the Testimony of Equality

In our Quaker community, we value equality; even more, we value equity for individuals and social groups. We strive to ensure that each person's voice is heard and valued. We search for better ways to fully welcome Friends of color into the Society of Friends, even though we often fall short. We are examining the role white privilege has played in all of society, including our faith. We support policies and programs that will create a more equitable world. There is much we can do better, but we recognize equality and equity as a value.

Yet, how many of us fully understand environmental justice? Friends were outraged to learn about the water crisis in Flint, but do we understand that many American communities, mostly communities of color, have similar problems with dirty water, polluted air, and limited food resources?[6] Do we notice that poorer people are most often located next to major sources of pollution, such as the fence-line communities adjacent to petrochemical industries in Louisiana, just to name one example?[7] Do we know that climate-induced sea level rise is already changing the lives of Floridians and other coastal dwellers?[8]

One way we express respect for the equality of all individuals is to worship together in a way that allows any person in attendance to minister during a Meeting for Worship. Another way we express this is to listen deeply and re-

---

[5] "Syria: Events of 2017," Human Rights Watch, accessed January 2019, http://hrw.org/world-report/2018/country-chapters/syria/. Peter Gleick, "Water, Drought, Climate Change and Conflict in Syria," *American Meteorological Society* 6 (July 2014): 331–340, doi/10.1175/WCAS-D-13-00059.1.

[6] "Learn About Environmental Justice," United States Environmental Protection Agency, accessed January 2019, http://epa.gov/environmentaljustice/learn-about-environmental-justice.

[7] "Life at the Fenceline: Understanding Cumulative Health Hazards in Environmental Justice Communities," Environmental Justice for All, accessed January 2019, http://ej4all.org/life-at-the-fenceline.

[8] *Patterns and Projections of High Tide Flooding Along the US Coastline Using a Common Impact Threshold*, NOS CO-OPS 086, Silver Spring, MD: National Oceanic and Atmospheric Administration, February 2018, accessed January 2019, http://tidesandcurrents.noaa.gov/publications/techrpt86_PaP_of_HTFlooding.pdf.

spectfully during discernment and decision-making, often holding listening meetings or worship-sharing before making any important decisions. Could we imagine respectfully listening to nature?

Earthcare requires a spiritual transformation within the Society of Friends. Quakers acknowledge that we see that of God in everyone. Earthcare calls us to extend that value to see that of God in everything—in the community of all life. This is not nature worship; it is more like worship in kinship with nature, living our lives in recognition that we are all connected through the soil, air, and water, through our common journey around the Sun. Unfortunately, it is all too easy to continue the practice of our culture, seeing nature as something to be exploited and used up before moving on to the next opportunity. We find ourselves now in a time in which there are no more opportunities, no other places on the planet to exploit, and no other planets to colonize. The time is long overdue to embrace our spiritual connection to all things, ask for guidance, and live as if we are part of the universe, not its dominators.

V. How Do We Live If We Value Earthcare?

I have felt called to work on environmental concerns all my life. Early on, I felt a tremendous affinity with the natural world, reveling in spending time at the ocean near where I grew up, and later finding beauty and solace in redwood forests close to where I settled as an adult. My first inkling of a sense of spirit came to me in nature.

I became an environmental scientist because I felt a spiritual and physical connection to the land and water around me. Intellectually, I wanted to learn everything I could about the places where I felt most alive and most in tune with the world.

When I found Friends and Quaker worship in my thirties, I immediately recognized that the mystical sense of connection that was palpable in a gathered meeting was something that I had felt all along in nature. Many of us drawn to QEW find our deepest connection with spirit when we are in nature.

I believe that the Society of Friends is on the brink of a transition in our relationship with Earth. What are our assumptions about environmental concerns? Why isn't this prioritized in our lives as much as our traditional peace and justice work? We understand that climate change poses a mortal threat, but when do we start taking action? Why haven't we? What needs to change in our assumptions, lifestyle, worship, and in our meetinghouses/church buildings to embrace earthcare as a core part of our faith and practice as Friends? How do I, and we, address the question of how to live as if we value Earthcare? We are facing an existential crisis; we need to embrace as much spiritual guidance as we can get. I would start with the overwhelming joy that exists when we embrace our oneness with the universe. We are made of stardust and the stars are us—how beautiful is that!

Readers might feel like you are the only one who cares about the environment in your meeting or church. You are not alone. I have found joy and strength in the network of Friends that is Quaker Earthcare Witness. Alone and reading the news, I can easily feel distraught and frozen. When I connect with QEW Friends either at our biannual meetings or on calls, reading our newsletter, *BeFriending Creation*, or sharing stories over our listserv, I am uplifted and empowered. Our organization connects a steadfast group of Friends who have faithfully reoriented their lives and positively impacted their local communities and national politics. I look to them for wisdom, insight, and inspiration as the host of environmental crises worsens. I also look toward many younger Friends who are more often taking the lead.

As a Quaker and a scientist, I am also heartened by recent advances in technology that will help us live more sustainably. These advances address one of our greatest environmental crises, climate change. Human influence on climate is predominantly due to acquisition and use of fossil fuels. We now know that it is possible for renewable energy to fill most of our energy needs.[9] The development of those technologies is advancing at a rapid pace. The times we live in have been compared to major technology shifts in the past. For example, in the early decades of the twentieth century, transportation in the United States shifted from horses to motor vehicles. In the first 15 years of the twenty-first century, cell phone usage rose from around 700 million to 7 billion. Many visionaries and scientists see us on the brink of such a change when it comes to energy use.

Rapidly changing energy technology along with a just transition for people working in the energy sector will allow us to move from fossil fuels to renewable energy sources, but technology alone will not solve our problems. We will continue to face one environmental crisis after another unless we confront our missing spiritual connection with the natural world. These dire environmental times should serve as a Quaker wake-up call for all the environmental threats we are facing. In addition to climate change, our world is experiencing depleted fisheries, decreasing biodiversity, soil erosion, declining water resources and growing human population. Technology will not solve all these problems.

---

[9] Robert Bruninga with Judy Lumb, Frank Granshaw, and Charles Blanchard, *Energy Choices: Opportunities to Make Wise Decisions for a Sustainable Future* (Belize: Quaker Institute for the Future, 2018).

Let us build on our tremendous history of faithful action and amplify our faith to include all that surrounds us. Embracing earthcare will help us find a way to live in harmony with nature. This is how we remove the occasion for war and inequity, and create a thriving world.

19 | Earth Quaker Action Team: Reclaiming the Lamb's War for Justice and Sustainability in the Twenty-first Century

By Walter Hjelt Sullivan

Abstract: *This essay argues that the nonviolent direct action practiced today by the Earth Quaker Action Team (EQAT) finds its philosophical roots in the cultural revolution that many seventeenth century Quakers called "The Lambs War." Starting with a brief overview and historical context for the Lamb's War, Sullivan then uses "remix theory," as developed by C. Wess Daniels, to help show how both difference and continuity link EQAT with early Friends. The second half of the article describes EQAT's history, theoretical framework, and activist praxis and outlines a challenge that the organization invites all Friends to consider today.*

On March 9, 2010, a small group of Quakers gathered outside of the Philadelphia Flower Show, one of the city's largest and most popular cultural attractions. They sang songs about the threat of climate disruption, mourned the destruction of mountains in Appalachia, and called out the Flower Show's chief sponsor, PNC Bank. The Earth Quaker Action Team (EQAT), made up at that time of a few dozen people, mostly members of the Religious Society of Friends, had the gall to confront the sixth largest bank in the United States.[1] They demanded that PNC cease all financing of companies that practiced a particularly horrific form of coal extraction called mountaintop removal coal mining. Senior management of the institution, which reported $3,397,000,000 in net income that year, scoffed at the group and totally discounted the threat. Five years and about 125 EQAT actions later, PNC Bank did change their policy. Standing on the legacy of 350

---

[1] Learn more about the Earth Quaker Action Team by visiting: http://eqat.org.

years of Quaker nonviolent action for social change, EQAT (pronounced equate) declared victory and threw a party.

Image 1: Early EQAT carolers outside PNC Bank Regional Headquarters, Philadelphia, PA, December 17, 2010. Photograph used by permission from Earth Quaker Action Team.

I. The Lamb's War: Historical Context

One hundred years after the first printed English translation of the full Bible, seventeenth century Quakers lived in a world where it was not uncommon to be well on Monday, fall ill on Tuesday, and be buried by week's end. Friends also lived in a Christian culture, controlled by the state church, focused heavily on salvation and everlasting life for the chosen. It was an era of both spiritual and political searching, radical experimentation, and civil war.

To proto-Friends, part of a larger community of progressive religious seekers of the day, the apocalyptic spirit of the times posed questions of ultimate concern. Aligning one's soul with falsehood instead of truth could be the difference between eternal redemption and condemnation. At any moment, the day of reckoning could be just around the corner.

For some, like early Quaker leader and organizer George Fox (1624–1691), there was an urgent spiritual motivation to see the Truth and to get right with God. His early years of searching, questioning, and eventual rejection of the Church of England is famously described in Chapter 1 of his *Journal*. So, too, is the moment of revelation where he uncovered the key to a new life guided by the inward Christ: "And when all my hopes in them and in all [people] were gone, so that I had nothing outwardly to help me, nor could tell what to do; then, Oh! then I heard a voice which said, 'There is one, even Christ Jesus, that can speak to thy condition.' And when I heard it, my heart did leap for joy."[2]

Having discovered the liberation experienced in true relationship with the Inner Light, Fox, and other Friends who joined the movement, could also see more clearly the oppressive political structures and cultural practices that separated people from their true spiritual inheritance. As Howard Brinton notes in *Friends for 300 Years*, early Friends understood that the powers and principalities of the day were no benign force: "As [Isaac] Penington points out, "the shadow is a real shadow" and not illusion of the mind. Throughout Fox's writings there appears a constant reference to that which is contrary to the Light, a real opposing power which [one] is free to choose instead of choosing the Power which comes from God."[3]

Friends came to understand the ways that the structures of church and society oppressed the minds and bodies of the common people and kept them in a state of unknowing, spiritual death, and political oppression. They saw how hierarchical structures that kept the poor and working people in their place were reinforced by the practice of hat honor, the celebration of religious feasts, the use of honorific pronouns, and the imposition of mandatory tithes. Early Quakers uncovered a profound conspiracy of social practices, economic structures, and religious conventions that they believed threatened their eternal souls.

Friends could also see how pride, position, and finery separated the rich and powerful from that true grace which was given freely and directly by God to all. One hundred years later and an ocean away, American Quaker tailor and abolitionist John Woolman (1720–1772) explained this effect most directly:

Where that spirit which loves riches works, and in its working gathers wealth and cleaves to customs which have their root in self-pleasing, this spirit, thus separating from universal love, seeks help from that

---

[2] George Fox, *The Journal of George Fox*, ed. Rufus M. Jones (Richmond, IN: Friends United Press, 1976), 72.

[3] Howard H. Brinton, *Friends for 300 Years* (Wallingford, PA: Pendle Hill Quaker-back, 1964), 24.

power which stands in the separation; and whatever it hath, it still desires to defend the treasures thus gotten. This is like a chain where the end of one link encloses the end of another. The rising up of a desire to attain wealth is the beginning. This desire being cherished moves to action, and riches thus gotten please self, and while self hath a life in them it desires to have them defended.... Thus cometh the harvest spoken by the prophet, which is "a heap in the day of grief, and of desperate sorrow." (Is 17:11)[4]

Isaac Penington (1616–1679) and his wife Mary (1623–1682) were among the affluent of England who gave up their position and wealth—and at times went to jail—upon the conviction of Friends in order to take up life faithful to the Light:

Then, one day, when they were out walking in the grounds of a friend's house Mary and Isaac were accosted by a passer-by, who turned out to be a rather newly convinced Quaker.... [T]he next day two well-known Quakers came to call.... Mary...wrote "Their solid and weighty carriage struck a dread over me. I now knew that they came in the power and authority of the Lord."[5]

After this encounter, Isaac Penington became one of the most affluent and politically connected converts to Quakerism, spent many extended periods in prison for his strict faithfulness to Quaker ways, lost most of the family property for refusing to swear an oath during court proceedings, and yet became one of the most prolific and poetic advocates for the transformational experience of giving oneself over to the inner life of the true guide.

II. Waging the Lamb's War

Friends felt urgently that profound social transformation was necessary. Part of the needed change was structural, and many Friends hoped that the military rebellion led by Oliver Cromwell in the late 1640s and 1650s would sweep in an era of political and social righteousness. The execution of King Charles I in 1649

---

[4] John Woolman, *The Journal and Major Essays of John Woolman*, ed. Phillips P. Moulton (New York: Oxford University Press, 1971), 255.
[5] Mary Penington in R. Melvin Keiser and Rosemary Moore, *Knowing the Mystery of Life Within: Selected Writings of Isaac Penington in their Historical and Theological Context* (London, UK: Quaker Books, 2005), 15.

and the establishment of a government theoretically more accountable to the people fostered hope for a new day. But corruption, the imposition by force of a new Cromwellian government, its fall, and finally the re-establishment of the monarchy in 1660, led Friends to see that violent, political revolution could not transform society in the ways spiritual necessity required.

Friends championed a new path, a Spirit-led revolution that some called the Lamb's War, in reference to the Book of Revelations. As historian Doug Gwyn argues:

> The Lamb's War might best be described as a *cultural revolution*: a wide ranging attack on the many norms and institutions that sustained the existing order, and the modeling of a different social order. ...
>
> [The] movement remaining subject to the existing state sought to transform social consciousness, codes, and institutions from below, from the base of society. Such activity can be destabilizing to the political regime, and may even topple it. But such political outcomes are not actual goals, since the appropriation of political power only creates new forms of domination and deforms the revolutionary process, which must unfold from the grassroots, where the Lamb moves freely.[6]

As a result, the Lamb's War was necessarily nonviolent, using spiritual rather than outward weapons, literally "the whole armor of God" (Eph 6:10–20). Friends took on practices that directly challenged the corrupt social contract. They refused to perform hat honor or to distinguish social status. They met illegally in the open and spoke out in the village square. Some went naked in public, a deeply embarrassing and shame-filled act, as a sign of how seriously they felt about the movement. Some Friends refused the payment of tithes. When brought to court, many refused to swear oaths on the Bible. They disrupted worship services, called common folk to step into the freedom that was their birthright, and confronted the rich and powerful. For all these acts of defiance—carefully planned and freely taken—Friends risked arrest, conviction, and imprisonment.

Historical estimates differ, but in 1660, at the height of the Quaker disruptions, somewhere between 3,400 and 4,000 Friends were tried and sentenced

---

[6] Douglas Gwyn, *The Covenant Crucified: Quakers and the Rise of Capitalism* (Wallingford, PA: Pendle Hill Publications, 1995), 106.

for their provocative behavior.[7] Some willingly remained and ultimately died in jail for the right to worship God as inwardly led rather than repent and be released. Gwyn goes on to describe the significant social impact the Quaker movement achieved:

> Perhaps many common people were not affected by the [first political] Civil War, and remained unmoved by the advanced political ideas of the Levellers and other radical Puritans. But nearly everyone was effected and moved (towards convincement or reaction) by the Lamb's War. There was probably no parish in England left untouched by the mercurial Quaker preachers and agitators of the 1650s.[8]

Among those affected and moved by the Quakers' spiritual campaign was Margaret Fell (1614–1702). The often-referenced story of her convincement, as laid out in her biography, provides particular insight into the powerful impact that the Lamb's War had upon many seekers of the day. Fell's story starts, as others' often did, with a personal encounter with a Quaker. In her case it was with George Fox, one Sunday in 1652 when he brought the revolutionary message to those gathered for worship in the Ulverston steeplehouse:

> [Fox] came in; and when they had done singing, he stood up upon his seat or form and desired that he might have liberty to speak. And he that was in the pulpit said he might. And the first words that he spoke were as followeth: 'He is not a Jew that is one outward, neither is that circumcision which is outward, but he is a Jew that is one inward, and that is circumcision which is of the heart'. And so he went on and said, How that Christ was the Light of the world and lighteth every man that cometh into the world; and that by this Light they might be gathered to God, etc. And I stood up in my pew, and I wondered at his doctrine, for I had never heard such before.[9]

Fox challenged those gathered to lay down the normative, passive understanding of God's Word and to experience the direct power of God within:

---

[7] William Wayne Spurrier, "The Persecution of the Quakers in England: 1650–1714," (PhD diss., University of North Carolina at Chapel Hill, 1976), 112.

[8] Gwyn, *The Covenant Crucified*, 107.

[9] Margaret Fell Fox, *The Life of Margaret Fox, Wife of George Fox* (Ann Arbor, MI: University of Michigan Library, 2005), 7.

[T]hen he…opened the Scriptures, and said, 'The Scriptures were the prophets' words and Christ's and the apostles' words, and what as they spoke they enjoyed and possessed and had it from the Lord'. And said, 'Then what had any to do with the Scriptures, but as they came to the Spirit that gave them forth. You will say, Christ saith this, and the apostles say this; but what canst thou say? Art thou a child of Light and hast walked in the Light, and what thou speakest is it inwardly from God?'[10]

As Margaret tells the story, she was convicted then and there into a new understanding:

This opened me so that it cut me to the heart; and then I saw clearly we were all wrong. So I sat me down in my pew again, and cried bitterly. And I cried in my spirit to the Lord, 'We are all thieves, we are all thieves, we have taken the Scriptures in words and know nothing of them in ourselves'…. I saw it was the truth, and I could not deny it; and I did as the apostle saith, I 'received the truth in the love of it'. And it was opened to me so clear that I had never a tittle in my heart against it; but I desired the Lord that I might be kept in it, and then I desired no greater portion.[11]

This new understanding led to new commitments and new behavior. She went on to take George Fox as her second husband. They established her home, Swarthmoor Hall, as a central hub of the Quaker movement where Margaret played a key role as correspondent and organizer.

Friends challenged the social codes and the institutions that held the common folk in a state of subservient acceptance. One particular victory of note was the outcome of the trial of William Penn (1634–1718), named by the *New York Times* as one of the most consequential trials in western history.[12] Arrested for speaking to a group in public, Penn and his collaborator William Mead (1628–1713) were put on trial in 1670 for convening an illegal religious assembly. When the judge insisted that the two Quakers be found guilty, the members of the jury, impressed by Penn's sincerity, refused. In spite of being jailed to force their compliance with the magistrate's demands, the jury stood firm in an act of defiance "establishing the unquestioned sovereignty of a jury to acquit without fear of

---

[10] M. Fell Fox, *The Life of Margaret Fox*.

[11] M. Fell Fox, *The Life of Margaret Fox*.

[12] Scott Turow, "Best Trial; Order in the Court," *New York Times*, April 18, 1999, http://nytimes.com/1999/04/18/magazine/best-trial-order-in-the-court.html.

Government reprisal."[13] The trial also became an important step in establishing the modern right of religious freedom for all people, brought on, not by violent revolution, not granted by the State voluntarily, but claimed by the people themselves.

III. EQAT: Carrying on the Lamb's War

The Earth Quaker Action Team, founded in late 2009 by Quakers from Philadelphia Yearly Meeting, is dedicated to building a just and sustainable economy through nonviolent direct action. EQAT stands quite consciously in the historic legacy of the Lamb's War and the continued Quaker history of direct action for change as exemplified by George Fox, Mary Dyer, Benjamin Lay, Lucretia Mott, Alice Paul, Bayard Rustin, and others.

The United States in the twenty-first century, though, is not the same as seventeenth century England. The world today does face its own existential crisis in the form of climate change, whose long-term effects pose ultimate threats to human and biological life as we know them. Climate disruption is already causing extreme harm, particularly to the poor and people of color in marginalized communities. "A 2010 report from the World Meteorological Organization predicted a laundry list of biblical-scale catastrophes for Africa if greenhouse gases continue to rise: drought, flood, famine, increasing number of pests, shrinking lakes, deforestation, and temperature increases."[14] Researchers are also documenting the role of human impact on climate in the causes of wars leading to the death and displacement of hundreds of thousands of people, a major driver of the current global refugee crisis.[15]

Yet the scientific and secular culture of the twenty-first century generally does not understand these as issues of ultimate personal spiritual concern. While many feel an urgent need to get public policy and social practice right in order to alleviate the worst long-term effects of climate change—and we individually and collectively may feel a moral and spiritual responsibility to act quickly—the imminent impacts are most frequently framed in concrete physical terms like public health, climate disruption, impacts on food production, or species extinction. The fear is more for the threat of physical extinction than that of personal, eternal, moral condemnation. As a result, this historical moment is not as ripe for an

---

[13] Turow, "Best Trial."

[14] Eileen Flanagan, "Temperature rising: Climate crises in Africa," *The Christian Century*, August 12, 2013, http://christiancentury.org/article/2013-08/temperature-rising.

[15] Craig Welch, "Climate Change Helped Spark Syrian War, Study Says," *The National Geographic*, March 2, 2015, http://news.nationalgeographic.com/news/2015/03/150302-syria-war-climate-change-drought/.

appeal for foundational cultural transformation built primarily upon the promise of eternal salvation or the threat of spiritual condemnation as it was in previous centuries of Friends history.

In his 2015 book, *A Convergent Model of Renewal*, Quaker educator C. Wess Daniels offers "remix theory" within what he calls "participatory culture" as a metaphor for understanding the relationship between a powerful, but in some ways outdated, spiritual tradition, and a dynamic and vibrant present.

> Remix reveals the interplay between the old and the new, between tradition [Read Only culture] and innovation [Read/Write culture]. Both need to co-exist…. Thus, even within participatory culture there is the tension between what we might call an "antiquarianism of tradition" and the impulse to innovate at the expense of R/O culture. Instead, remix shows tradition and innovation working together to create something new; it shows how apprentices can pay homage to their tradition while also creating something original.[16]

Therefore, Daniels' remix culture sees "tradition as grounds for innovation and imagination."[17] His concept of remix can be a helpful frame for understanding how the roots of EQAT's culture, grounded in Spirit-led nonviolent direct action, can be tied to the Lamb's War of seventeenth century England.

From its founding, EQAT has worked intentionally at the intersections of the movements for environmental, economic, and racial justice. The organization is deeply concerned about climate change and the future viability of the planet's ecosystems but also understands these issues to be inextricably yoked with concerns for economic and racial justice. Racism and the dehumanization of entire communities of color and the poor are crucial pieces of the logic that justifies the destruction of whole ecosystems, flushing poison into our drinking water, and pumping toxins into our air. Many of the most immediate impacts of our domination culture are borne by marginalized populations.[18] Those of us with social privilege are significantly less inconvenienced and reap most of the economic and political benefits. As a result, the dominant culture powerfully "desires to defend the treasures thus gotten," as Woolman reminds us.[19]

---

[16] C. Wess Daniels, *A Convergent Model of Renewal: Remixing the Quaker Tradition in a Participatory Culture* (Eugene, OR: Pickwick Publications, 2015), 83.

[17] Daniels, *A Convergent Model of Renewal*, 83.

[18] Dorceta E. Taylor, *Introduction: The Evolution of Environmental Justice Activism, Research, and Scholarship*, January 3, 2017, doi.org/10.1017/S1466046611000329.

[19] Woolman, *Journal*, 255.

EQAT understands that this desire to justify and defend the accumulation of treasure is a real power in direct opposition to the sustainable and beloved community that God desires. Like early forebears, the group also believes that violent political revolution cannot usher in the just or peaceful society envisioned by many modern progressive and radical people. As a result, EQAT's core technology for creating social change is the use of Spirit-led nonviolent direct action.

While standing in the tradition of the Lamb's War, EQAT also weaves in the principles of twentieth century Gandhian nonviolence as understood and practiced in the US civil rights movement, insights from the peace movement during the American/Vietnam War era, and teachings from the leading contemporary advocates for social justice work, like the Philadelphia area organization Training for Change.[20] One of EQAT's favorite frames for understanding their work is that of "the four roles of social change," developed by Quaker sociologist and writer Bill Moyer.[21]

EQAT acknowledges the important role of (i) advocates who work for social change within the political arena, of (ii) organizers who work to create mass movements for environmental and racial justice, and of (iii) helpers who work to alleviate the impact of racism and environmental destruction on individuals and communities, but EQAT clearly understands itself as a (iv) rebel organization within Moyer's framework.[22] The group sees its role as getting into the public square to challenge power through creative and strategic action. EQAT is committed to putting direct pressure on decision makers who have sided with the dirty fossil fuel past, failed to embrace a renewable energy future, and are willing to overlook the immense life-threatening impacts disproportionately laid upon poor and marginalized communities.

This does not mean that everyone who is a member of EQAT is by nature a rebel or that EQAT does not employ some of the wisdom and tactics of the organizer, the helper, or the advocate. But EQAT's strategic plans and campaign arc are guided by the spirit of the rebel. As Lakey says: "Bill Moyer's Four Roles is about effectiveness. Instead of one organization trying to do many things and risking scatter, his vision was that of a proliferation of groups, each

---

[20] Learn more about Training for Change by visiting: http://trainingforchange.org/.

[21] George Lakey, "What role were you born to play in social change?," Waging Nonviolence, February 3, 2016, http://wagingnonviolence.org/feature/bill-moyer-four-roles-of-social-change/.

[22] Bill Moyer, JoAnn McAllister, Mary Lou Finley and Steve Soifer, *Doing Democracy: The MAP Model for Organizing Social Movements* (Gabriola Island, BC: New Society Publishers, 2001).

maximizing strength through focus while networking and supporting a broader sense of unity. That's what a powerful movement looks like."[23]

Unlike some other activist groups, EQAT makes a long-term commitment to a particular campaign against a specific target, and with a set of specific demands for change. Occasionally collaborations with allies on other issues or with sympathetic campaigns are considered when those activities make strategic sense, could raise EQAT's profile, or strengthen important organizational relationships. Politicians, because they are so heavily influenced by financial contributions from the carbon energy industry, are not generally seen as likely targets for an EQAT campaign. Instead, EQAT finds the CEOs and boards of directors of corporations and industries more susceptible to public pressure. As policy deciders and implementers, they can choose directly between the destructive policies of the carbon energy past and the sustainable policies of the renewable future. While unlikely to do so without organized external pressure, they have the capacity to become the lever for progressive social transformation. In fact, with their legitimacy withdrawn, corporations could lose the power to implement their destructive policies.[24]

IV. EQAT and PNC Bank: Lamb's War in the Twenty-First Century

EQAT's first campaign against PNC Bank, BLAM! (Bank Like Appalachia Matters!) brought the small group of Friends to stand outside the 2010 Flower Show. EQAT chose PNC because it was a historically Quaker financial institution that branded itself as the greenest bank in the industry but was one of the largest US investors in mountaintop removal.

The narrative arc of the campaign was not a straight line, but the result of an iterative dance between EQAT and PNC management. Nimbleness, regular strategic planning retreats, on-going training, and new skill development were hallmarks of the campaign.

EQAT organized a two-hundred mile walk from Philadelphia to Pittsburgh, worshiped in numerous bank branches, challenged corporate leadership in public spaces, and increasingly disrupted annual shareholder meetings. In March 2015, PNC Bank announced a new corporate policy, essentially agreeing

---

[23] Lakey, "What role were you born to play in social change?"

[24] "Upside-Down Triangle: Understanding the Consent Theory of Power," Training for Change, accessed September 2, 2018, http://trainingforchange.org/training_tools/upside-down-triangle-understanding-the-consent-theory-of-power/.

to end all financing of companies engaged in mountaintop removal.[25] While all such statements from PNC on this issue had to be read with a healthy dose of skepticism, EQAT was adequately convinced of PNC's core intention to fundamentally change its relationship with the extreme practice and declared victory in its campaign.

EQAT's success sent ripples throughout the banking industry. *The American Banker* responded, "The recent decision by PNC Financial Services Group to scale back lending to companies that conduct mountaintop-removal coal mining may have other banks mulling whether they should follow suit."[26] In fact, several other banks did.

Image 2: Author arrested at PowerShift Action, part of the BLAM! campaign against PNC Bank, Pittsburgh, PA, October 23, 2013. Photograph used by permission from Earth Quaker Action Team.

---

[25] Timothy Cama, "PNC Bank restricts mountaintop removal financing," *The Hill*, March, 4, 2015, http://thehill.com/policy/energy-environment/234550-pnc-bank-restricts-mountaintop-removal-financing.

[26] Andy Peters, "Activists Target More Banks After PNC Curtails Loans to Coal Miners," *The American Banker*, March 26, 2015, http://americanbanker.com/news/activists-target-more-banks-after-pnc-curtails-loans-to-coal-miners.

Image 3: Author leads the Band-Aid Action at PECO Headquarters, Philadelphia, PA, December 8, 2015. Photo credit: Rachael Warriner, www.rachaelwarriner.com.

Image 4: "Worship Under the Weight of Justice," PECO Headquarters, Philadelphia, PA, January 30, 2018. Photo credit: Kaytee Ray-Riek, www.kayteerayriek.com.

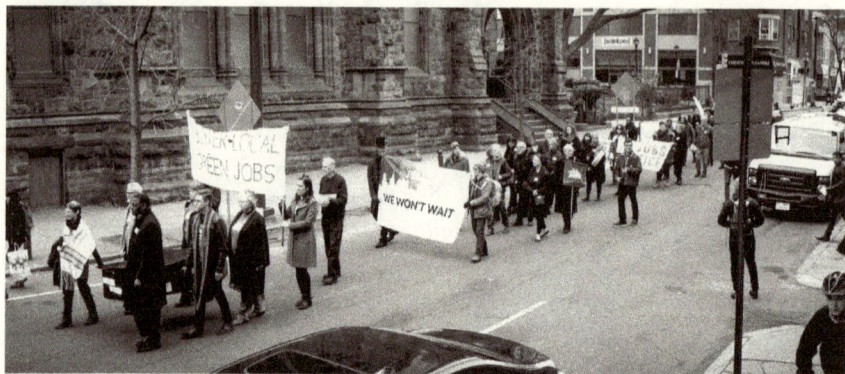

Image 5: EQAT Day of Mourning Action, Philadelphia, PA, March 27, 2018. Photo credit: Rachael Warriner, www.rachaelwarriner.com.

Image 6: EQAT Day of Mourning Action, PECO Headquarters, Philadelphia, PA, March 27, 2018. Photo credit: Kaytee Ray-Riek, www.kayteerayriek.com.

Image 7: Worship in PECO pay center, Day of Mourning Action, Philadelphia, PA, March 27, 2018. Photo credit: Rachael Warriner, www.rachaelwarriner.com.

Image 8: "Die-in for Justice," Day of Reckoning Action, Philadelphia, PA, March 29, 2018. Photo credit: Rachael Warriner, www.rachaelwarriner.com.

Image 9: EQAT members arrested outside PECO Headquarters, Day of Reckoning Action, Philadelphia, PA, March 29, 2018. Photo credit: Rachael Warriner, www.rachaelwarriner.com.

V. EQAT Today

EQAT began a new campaign, PLGJ: Power Local Green Jobs, in 2015. PLGJ targets the Philadelphia area electric utility, PECO (formerly the Philadelphia Electric Company), and demands that they:

- dramatically increase the purchase of local rooftop solar power so that 20% of PECO's electricity comes from roofs in its service area by 2025,
- spur solar installation on suitable roofs in high unemployment areas, starting in North Philadelphia, to economically benefit those communities, and
- prioritize installation by local workers, especially from high unemployment areas.[27]

The challenges of this ongoing campaign, initiated in the fall of 2015, are somewhat different than BLAM! Rather than calling on a private corporation to stop

---

[27] "Campaign," Earth Quaker Action Team, accessed September 1, 2018, http://eqat.org/campaign.

doing something harmful that contradicts their public brand, PLGJ focuses on a privately held, but publicly-regulated, utility. The demands challenge PECO to do something new and ethical that could require significant change to their core business model. The current campaign also challenges EQAT to work more intentionally on issues of race and institutional racism both within the organization itself and in the larger society. EQAT remains a small social justice organization with a primarily middle class culture and mostly white membership. The campaign goals seek to effect positive change for communities of color in Philadelphia with a long history of struggling with racism, disinvestment, false promises, and neglect. To take on this work with integrity, EQAT must develop new skills, explore new power relationships, and live into new strategic arcs. The organization, like the campaign, remains a work in progress.

Another difference between BLAM! and PLGJ is that EQAT has been joined in this campaign by POWER, a broad multi-faith network of 60 congregations,[28] well known for its successful campaign to significantly increase wages for Philadelphia airport workers.[29] Former clerk of the EQAT board, Eileen Flanagan, summarized the campaign's progress:

> [T]hree years ago PECO was not putting any resources into solar. Three years ago they didn't even have a form on their website for solar applications, let alone be talking about solar publicly. Since our campaign started, they have:
>
> - set up an internal committee of high ranked folks to work on solar issues, including for low-income people.
> - hosted two "Solar Stakeholder Collaborative" meetings, which advocates thought were a huge deal for PECO.
> - taken several small steps to make installing solar easier.
> - met with solar contractors several times about this.
> - hired people to coordinate these solar efforts.
> - consulted with their "sister" utilities in the Exelon "family" who are doing more solar to learn from them.
> - put out...surveys to test language around solar.

---

[28] Learn more about POWER by visiting: http://powerinterfaith.org/.

[29] Juliana Feliciano Reyes, "It took 6 years for PHL airport workers to double their pay to $12 an hour. Here's how they did it," *Philadelphia Inquirer*, June 11, 2018, http://www2.philly.com/philly/news/philadelphia-airport-workers-union-contract-20180611.html.2018.

- worked with PEA (Philadelphia Energy Authority) around solar initiatives, including job training.
- gave $100,000 to a North Philly based training group....
- encouraged a state representative to sponsor solar legislation....
- seriously pursued some pilot projects (which they cancelled when Trump's election eliminated the government money they were hoping would subsidize them).[30]

EQAT has not yet achieved its goals and the campaign is not yet won, but the organization has engaged important issues, and the target is paying attention.

In both campaigns, EQAT's tactics have been intentionally nonviolent, using the same spiritual weapons as those early Friends employed in the Lamb's War. EQATers have directly challenged the targets' unsustainable practices and the ideologies that justify them. They have challenged the environmentally friendly branding and community-partnered narratives propagated by PNC Bank and PECO. They have disrupted business as usual by worshipping in bank branches and corporate lobbies. At carefully selected times, Friends refused to disband when asked, risking citation and arrest. They called on the public to join the campaign of resistance and publicly confronted senior management as decision makers personally responsible for the impacts of their corporate practices.

From its founding, EQAT has also carried a challenge to the Religious Society of Friends in the twenty-first century. EQAT's campaign invites Friends to reconsider some current understandings and practices. When a Meeting writes and sends a minute to legislators on the issue of the week, one might ask: Has anything significant been done, and does the work stop there? Protest in this day of dissent is important. Yet, if one marches for one cause on Monday, another on Tuesday, and yet a third on Wednesday, only to feel exhausted and confused by week's end, have one's energies been well spent? EQAT urges members of the Religious Society of Friends to reclaim their birthright—almost four centuries of Spirit-led nonviolent direct action for justice and transformation.

EQAT believes these times require Friends to stand up out of the pews and move into the town square, leaving no parish in the land untouched. If we are faithful in this work, might we usher into being something new, just, and sustainable? Might it not only prove good for the planet, but also be liberating for the poor and the marginalized, including our own impoverished spirits?

Just perhaps, our eternal souls might depend on it.

---

[30] Eileen Flanagan, EQAT Discussion Group, personal post to EQAT listserv, August 31, 2018, used by permission.

20 | Collective Discernment at Quaker Institute for the Future

By Judy Lumb

Abstract: The Quaker Institute for the Future (QIF) is a Quaker think-tank established in 2003. Since then, QIF has used Quaker worship-sharing for collaborative research applied to the serious problems of the human-Earth relationship. From climate change to genetic engineering, from the economic growth dilemma to right relationship to finance, Quaker collaborative research has led to eleven QIF Focus Books. This paper summarizes the process of collaborative research and the QIF Focus Books.

I. Origins of Quaker Institute for the Future and Circles of Discernment

The Quaker Institute for the Future is the product of a 2003 gathering at Pendle Hill of Quaker environmentalists, economists, and public policy analysts to explore the connections between the current economic system and ecological crises. Those present at the gathering recognized the need for much more research in order to address issues of destruction of ecological integrity, climate change, biological extinctions, and the role of our economic structure as causation of these crises. A proposal for a Quaker think tank circulated at that meeting and a working group convened afterward to establish the Quaker Institute for the Future (QIF). Since 2003 QIF has conducted collaborative research as applied to the development of knowledge within the context of Friends' "experiments with truth," Quaker testimonies, and discernment.

For the past fifteen years, QIF engaged in the following three activities to address issues of importance to our future:

1.   The first major project was the Moral Economy Project (MEP), which resulted in the book, *Right Relationship: Building a Whole Earth Economy*.
2.   QIF holds Summer Research Seminars in which researchers of topics important to our future present their work in an atmosphere of Quaker worship, a Quaker Meeting for Worship for the Conduct of Research.
3.   QIF sponsors Circles of Discernment (CoD), a form of collaborative research by groups of Friends using the Quaker process of worship-sharing to advance the work.

Except for the work of the Moral Economy Project that resulted in the book *Right Relationship: Building a Whole Earth Economy,* which was funded by a grant, the rest of the work of QIF is done by volunteers, with the sales of previous books covering the expenses involved in the publication of new volumes.

Some CoDs have resulted in the preparation of a book in the series *QIF Focus Books*. Initially these were called "Quaker Institute for the Future Pamphlets" because we envisioned the products of this research being something like a Pendle Hill Pamphlet: 10,000 words that can be read in one sitting. But from the first QIF "pamphlet" they have grown to small books, so the series name was eventually changed to *QIF Focus Books*. In the current internet era, communication often comes either as a sound-byte or a massive research tome. The intention of *QIF Focus Books* is to take a topic of concern, research it, and boil it down to an accessible book—around 100 pages—somewhere between a sound-byte and a massive tome. As of 2018, 42 Friends have participated in CoDs, and the *QIF Focus Book* series now includes 11 books.[1]

This paper will focus on the CoDs and the resulting *QIF Focus Books* in hopes that Friends become aware (if they are not already) of the books that are presently available. We invite Friends to learn about the process we have developed for Quakers and others to use collective discernment to develop knowledge that can move us toward ethical and sustainable solutions to environmental concerns.

II. Quaker Process as Applied to Research

In two of the *QIF Focus Books*, our process was the subject of research. The fourth book, *How Does Societal Transformation Happen? Values Development, Collective*

---

[1] A bibliography of all 11 books can be found at the end of this chapter. See the Quaker Institute for the Future website, http://www.quakerinstitute.org/, to learn more about QIF and to read the full text of the *QIF Focus Books* online. Books can be ordered from Keith Helmuth, keithhelmuth@gmail.com.

Wisdom, and Decision Making for the Common Good by Leonard Joy (with a Foreword by QIF board members Phil Emmi and Keith Helmuth) studies how transformation happens. The analysis of the development of values was grounded in the work of Brian Hall.[2] Stages of personal development are described in the context of shifting values. Our values and priorities are manifested in our behavioral choices. Shifts in values are a consequence of changes in the ways we see the world and our emotional attachments to these perceptions. For example, a key stage in development is reached when self-reflective awareness emerges with a concern for integrity and personal identity formation. Personal transformation is the essential first step in societal transformation. Based on current literature in developmental psychology, we need to move from a "me-focus" to a "we-focus." Leonard Joy ends *How Does Societal Transformation Happen?* with a description of Quaker process as a way of arriving at collective wisdom. Using a process similar to a Quaker meeting for clearness, a meeting can be convened for discerning the common good. The practice holds up well in secular contexts. The essentials of specific Quaker practices translated into secular terms include the grounding of all participants, ensuring that all voices are heard, respect for all persons, equality for all voices, commitment to air dissent, maintaining community by a loving relationship, speaking out of the silence, essential role of the clerk, addressing the clerk not one another, speaking simply, being authentic with the expression of feeling, and all decisions made by unity.

Gray Cox was interested in the epistemology of QIF work and wrote a philosophical analysis of the first ten years of QIF work. A CoD was then formed with six Friends who expanded on his work. This is an example of a CoD with a primary author and group discernment on that work. *A Quaker Approach to Research: Collaborative Practice and Communal Discernment* grew out of a decade of experiments by QIF employing Quaker processes of communal discernment in research in the context of public policy, academic study, and community-based research. This *QIF Focus Book* is itself the product of a collaborative process, which began in 2003 with discussions of practicing "Meeting for Worship for the Conduct of Research" to use a collaborative, communal approach instead of the current competitive, argumentative approach to research.

During the last decade, people associated with QIF seminars and projects have engaged in reflective discussions, worshipful meditations, and practical experiments exploring this question. In considering how to do research that may offer us the understanding we need to respond to urgent calls to better our world, we have much to learn about how to practice humility, enter silence, and use

---

[2] Brian Hall, *Values Shift* (Eugene, OR: Resource Publications, 2006).

collective discernment. Quaker and other traditions offer resources for our continued experiments with communal discernment and collaborative research, and assurance that in the silence we can have openings, not only of seeking, but of finding as well. *A Quaker Approach to Research* may be our most important book. In each *QIF Focus Book* interest group, while the various topics have been of interest, most participants have expressed deep interest in our process, and this book offers an excellent exploration of QIF process, an analysis of our first ten years. The books explained in what follows focus on the results of this process as applied to environmental and economic concerns.

III. QIF Discernment and Research Process Applied to Energy Solutions

The first and the most recent *QIF Focus Books* address the topic of energy. *Fueling our Future (QIF Focus Book #1)* was published in 2009, coordinated by Ed Dreby and Keith Helmuth, and edited by Judy Lumb. In 2007 QIF and the Earthcare Working Group of Philadelphia Yearly Meeting held two symposia on the ethical implications of various energy technologies in the context of climate change. Friends who were professionally involved in the energy industries were invited to give presentations. At that time some environmentalists were making the argument that because renewable energy technologies were not developed enough to provide all the energy needed and the uses of fossil fuels were endangering human life on Earth through climate change, a period of time where we depend on nuclear energy would be required. The issue was what would fuel our future: coal, nuclear, or biofuels? A CoD of five persons met at Pendle Hill over a long weekend in August of 2008. We had the transcripts of the two symposia as a starting point. We sat in worship-sharing for three days in discernment over these issues.

Fueling Our Future is about advancing dialogue, not closing the argument. As will be clear in what follows, participants in the process were not neutral. We were in close agreement on some aspects of our discernment and divided on others—most notably nuclear power. We agreed on a set of framing principles that we advanced as a context for further dialogue:

1) For a sustainable future, carbon emissions must be in equilibrium with the capacity of the earth to absorb carbon.
2) Carbon emissions should be decreased as soon as possible to prevent catastrophic effects of climate change.
3) Full cost accounting must include net energy benefit and life cycle cost of each option considered.

4) Decisions made today must not put burdens on future generations who have no part in making these decisions.

5) Decisions that we make must not transfer the burdens onto the poor and disadvantaged or onto other areas of the world.

6) Decision making on energy options must be inclusive, fair, equitable, grassroots driven, and consensus based.

7) We must seek solutions that scale to the needs of all people on earth.

8) We must seek solutions that preserve the rest of the biosphere beyond human needs.

Areas of controversy and disunity centered around the question of whether a resurgence of nuclear energy is necessary as an interim measure before we can get to the point where all energy for human activities is generated by sustainable methods from renewable sources with carbon emissions in equilibrium with carbon absorption.

In 2018 QIF returned to the subject of energy with the most recent *QIF Focus Book # 11, Energy Choices: Opportunities to Make Wise Decisions for a Sustainable Future.* Three of us joined author Bob Bruninga in group discernment by conference call for about a year. Ten years after the first *QIF Focus Book* the energy situation has radically changed. Nuclear disasters and unfavorable economics have led to closures of some nuclear energy plants and less interest in new nuclear operations. Concern for climate change is now more acute. Renewable options have developed rapidly—so rapidly, in fact, that public awareness of the opportunities has not yet caught up.

Energy Choices focuses on steps that we can take as individuals to reduce fossil fuel emissions in our daily lives. Opportunities to make the switch to renewable energy arise regularly:

- when we buy a car or a lawnmower,
- when the roof needs replacing,
- when the water heater stops heating water,
- when the furnace breaks down,
- when we move,
- when we pay our utility bill, we might be able to buy energy generated by wind or solar.

In this practical guide, *Energy Choices* shows that renewable options are not only feasible but are cheapest in the long run. Practical information is provided for making these decisions: selecting your next electric vehicle, installing solar panels on your roof or signing up for community solar, replacing your water heater with a heat pump, replacing your furnace with a heat pump, planning your new house. Whether you live in an apartment in an urban area, on a farm, or in a single-family house, *Energy Choices* will lead you through making the changes needed for a sustainable future.

While this book is intensely practical and packed with important information for understanding and making clean energy choices, it is also a guide that addresses an overriding spiritual and ethical issue of our time: the human-Earth relationship. Reconfiguring energy use away from fossil fuels to clean, renewable electricity is a big step toward creating a mutually enhancing human-Earth relationship. *Energy Choices* shows how we can individually move in that direction, and how our cumulative individual choices have a huge effect on society.

IV. QIF Discernment and Research Process Applied to Economics

The vision of the Moral Economy Project was "that the global political-economic order shifts from one of unrestrained economic growth, ecological degradation, and social inequity to one that preserves and enhances social and ecological well-being." After considerable research by a dedicated group of Friends supported by a major grant, the flagship book *Right Relationship: Building a Whole Earth Economy* was published and launched with a number of symposia. Its distribution has reached beyond North America to Europe and Africa, it has now been translated into several languages, and is used in college and university courses throughout the academic world where considerations of changing economic systems to make them sustainable and supportive of all communities of life on Earth are taking place.

Right Relationship concludes that the predominant economic system used throughout the planet:

- is incapable of providing an adequate answer to the question, "What is the economy for?"
- fails to understand how the economy works,
- is unable to put any boundaries on consumption and waste,
- has no means to even attempt fair distribution of both benefits and burdens to present and future generations of people and other species, and
- lacks a system of governance that protects life's commonwealth.

Right Relationship issues this call to action: Economic and governance changes are necessary for building a whole earth economy, but a more profound new direction is also required. More fundamental is a required change in values. Instead of the pursuit of more money and possessions, people need to think about pursuing joyful, grateful, and fulfilling lives in right relationship with life's commonwealth. Values progression of this kind is needed not only at a personal level, but also in institutions and enterprises at the community, national, and international levels. Many indigenous peoples already have cultural values and belief systems that support right relationships, which rest primarily on respect and gratitude for all that is. Following this call to action, several of the CoDs and *QIF Focus Books* have dealt directly with economic issues.

How on Earth Do We Live Now? came out of the editorial team of *Quaker Eco-Bulletin (QEB)* published under Quaker Earthcare Witness. In 2007 we edited a paper by David Ciscel, "It's the Economy, Friend," which proposed consideration of the services provided by ecosystems as "natural capital" so that ecology can be included in economic calculations. Ciscel suggested that bringing natural capital under the management of the mainstream economic system will result in full-cost accounting of the human impact on the environment and is essential to reversing our current destructive trends.

Prompted by Ciscel's article, the QEB editorial team felt it was important to explore the larger question emerging from the field of ecological economics: Is Earth a subset of the human economy or is the human economy a subset of the biosphere? The predominant, technological, human-centered approach assumes that Earth is a subset of the global economy that functions primarily to benefit humanity. Drawing on both science and ancient indigenous wisdom, the approach of deep ecology assumes that human beings are one species among many in the larger community of life on Earth, and we cannot thrive economically, or otherwise, unless the whole web of life thrives.

For two years we worked in Canada, the USA, and Belize. We met in worship sharing by conference call, paying for Quaker silence at international phone rates. Each of these bimonthly calls led to new and surprising realizations that could not have been reached by discussion and debate of a conventional sort.

We lifted up the natural capital approach on the one hand, and the deep ecology approach on the other. We hoped that by working out their similarities, contrasts, and conflicts, we might arrive at their mutually beneficial contributions to an emerging worldview. While our work was in process, Elinor Ostrom was awarded the 2009 Nobel Prize in Economics, drawing our attention to the nature of commons and common-pool resources. We deemed the commons to be the middle ground between deep ecology and natural capital. We explored the history and development of current public policies in regard to two essential parts of Earth's commons: property and water. We studied systems of governance from private property to self-governing, community-based, trust organizations and the nature of human behavior from individualistic to cooperative. We asked what unique contributions Friends bring to the table as we all face the realization of the enormity of the change that is needed for a sustainable and just human-Earth relationship.

Between calls we wrote pieces of the story, some of which became new QEBs. We wrote chapters on natural capital, deep ecology, the commons, property, water, governing the commons, and human development. As the pieces fell together, the title came to us, "how on Earth do we live now?" When Sandra Lewis brought work on human development, we knew that was the last piece and we were ready to finish *How on Earth Do We Live Now*, the second *QIF Focus Book*. We understood how the natural capital approach and the deep ecology approaches to the human-Earth relationship are integrated into the reality of the commons. Engagement with the commons must be based on the best scientific and indigenous knowledge and guided by the precautionary principle.[3] Systems of governance of the commons must involve decision-making processes that are inclusive, fair, equitable, grassroots driven, and consensus based. Economic activity must include full-cost accounting in monetary value and ecological integrity for all operations. In that way the commons can support the flourishing of all human and other communities of life on Earth.

It's the Economy, Friends and *Beyond the Growth Dilemma, QIF Focus Books #5 and #6,* were published at the same time with chapters written by members of the Growth Dilemma Project of Philadelphia Yearly Meeting (PYM). The Growth Dilemma Project website states: "Humanity faces a profound dilemma. The economies of virtually all nations require growth to function. Yet more growth makes the wealthiest even wealthier, while unemployment, hunger, and violence are widespread, and human economies are already larger than Earth's ecosystems can continue to support."[4] Philadelphia Yearly Meeting approved a set of core principles that reflect this truth and are rooted in values we share with many of our sisters and brothers from other faith traditions. PYM charged the

---

[3] The precautionary principle suggests that new technology or innovations are not introduced on a large scale prior to thorough testing. See section V for further discussion of the precautionary principle.

[4] Beyond the Growth Dilemma Project, Philadelphia Yearly Meeting, Philadelphia, PA, n.d., http://pym.org/eco-justice-collaborative/wp-content/uploads/sites/58/2016/05/GDP-Brochure.pdf.

Growth Dilemma Project to promote a Quaker witness on ecology and the economy. While Friends may be in broad agreement about the values we should promote and the problems that must be addressed, we do not agree on what causes these problems, or what should be done about them.

Some Friends think that with sufficient political will and wisdom, and with a strategic adjustment of incentives, the existing economic model can enable society to shift from its environmentally destructive trajectory to an ecologically sound mode of adaptation. They are convinced that "good" economic growth is essential to meet humanity's needs, and to build an ecologically sustainable economy.

Other Friends are convinced that the current system makes economic growth inseparable from increased material and energy consumption. They think an alternative system must be devised so a society can prosper as its economy's demand for physical resources is brought within Earth's bio-productive capacity. This will require overdeveloped regions to use substantially fewer resources so poorer regions can develop and use the resources they need for a decent and dignified way of life.

As the two titles suggest, *It's the Economy, Friends* explains the growth dilemma, and *Beyond the Growth Dilemma* shows how we can get beyond that economic quandary. While they were written for the general education of Friends, these two *QIF Focus Books* were launched at the 2012 Annual Meeting of Friends Committee on National Legislation (FCNL) with the hope that these economic ideas can be incorporated into the FCNL lobbying efforts in the US Congress. Both *QIF Focus Books* #5 and #6 comprise a series of essays by different authors, representing the work of the members of the Growth Dilemma Project. While these books did not result from a CoD, they are both products of group discernment.

It's the Economy, Friends ends with a "Call to Action" with some policy changes that will move us toward a better future:

- Forgive sovereign debt.
- Educate women.
- Encourage a shorter workweek and job sharing.
- Question the fractional reserve banking system.
- Work on monetary system reform.

In chapter three of *Beyond the Growth Dilemma*, J. Tucker Taylor argues that the economic system can be clean and green if the inequality in the current economic system that began in the 1970s is reversed by raising the minimum wage, making the tax system more progressive, instituting a massive public works program, and generally restoring the safety net. In chapter four, Keith Helmuth makes the argument that prosperity does not require economic growth. In chapter five Steve Loughlin suggests improvements in our work systems, such as shortening the workweek, job sharing, and establishing a guaranteed income. In chapter six Pamela Haines describes essential earth-friendly changes in our production systems, such as worker-owned corporations, cooperatives, and circular production. David Watkins describes governance of the commons and new technologies such as open source that lend themselves to earth-friendly operations. *Beyond the Growth Dilemma* ends with Ed Dreby's description of an ecologically integrated economy, how we can get there, and some specific things to do for the way forward.

Toward a Right Relationship with Finance was initiated after a financial report at Philadelphia Yearly Meeting (PYM) in 2014. PYM had been through financial difficulties associated with the 2008 Great Recession. Finally, at the annual business sessions in the summer of 2014, the financial difficulties came to an end. Spending was stable, resources were up, and income was showing a tendency to rise. If the stock market would just continue to grow, PYM could anticipate more reassuring financial statements for years to come. "If the stock market would just continue to grow...." Members of PYM who had written *It's the Economy, Friends* and *Beyond the Growth Dilemma* were shocked to learn that PYM finances were so completely dependent on the stock market. Individuals realized their own retirement funds were also dependent on the stock market. They requested a CoD under the auspices of QIF on the issue of a right relationship with finance, their own and that of Quaker institutions like PYM.

By conference call, the authors worked for two years studying various options for managing personal and organizational finances. *Toward a Right Relationship with Finance* offers background on our current economic system, its basis on unearned income and debt with built-in momentum toward economic inequality and ecological overshoot. Consideration of their deepest values and beliefs framed the conversation, which led the authors to find alternative investments to finance individual retirement and organizations. The book ends with an invitation to imagine new forms of durable economic and social security, and ideas for how to create the relationships and institutions that would make them a reality.

V. QIF Discernment and Research Process Applied to Technology

Canadian Friend Anne Mitchell brought to QIF the topic of *Genetically Modified Crops*. She has devoted much of her life to a concern for genetic modification of life forms, first raising a concern about the patenting of the "oncomouse" with the Religious Society of Friends and then with the Canadian Council of Churches (CCC). The CCC agreed to intervene before the Supreme Court of Canada, arguing that the patenting of the oncomouse was a commodification of life. The Supreme Court overturned the decision of a lower court to legally permit patenting the oncomouse. Canada is now the only G8 country that does not allow the patenting of higher life forms.

She then turned to issues of agricultural biotechnology and invited three colleagues to write chapters for the third *QIF Focus Book* (*Genetically Modified Crops*): Pinayur Rajagopal, ("Why is Public Policy so Private?"), Keith Helmuth ("Genetic Engineering: Challenging the Worldview of Right Relationship"), and Susan Holtz ("A Framework for Discernment and Action on Biotechnology Policy").

The agricultural application of biotechnology evolved rapidly and brought GM seeds for such crops as soybeans, maize (corn), canola, and cotton to the market beginning in 1996. This technology is being pushed into use before farmers, consumers, and local policy makers can assess its potential negative consequences. However, an abundance of published information can be found in refereed journals that contradicts the claims of GM industries. The first chapter reviews this information and makes the following conclusions:

- Farmers are the principal generators and stewards of crop genetic resources.
- The social and economic impacts of GM crops benefit large-scale producers, but there is less evidence of positive impact for small producers in developing countries.
- The safety of GM foods and feed is controversial due to limited available data, particularly for long-term nutritional consumption and chronic exposure.
- Implications of GM crops for biodiversity are unknown.
- The number of properly designed and independently peer-reviewed studies on human health remains limited due to industry pressure.

The precautionary principle obliges governments to assess environmental risks, warn potential victims of such risks, and behave in ways that prevent such risks.

It puts the onus on the developer to show that an action is environmentally benign. A major limitation in the present regulatory framework is the lack of any clear sense of what constitutes environmental harm. Despite considerable debate, there are no guidelines that establish the magnitude of change that should trigger concern over ecosystem impacts. There are practical questions of how to assess long-term risks, and how much risk citizens are willing to accept. This ambiguity makes it even more difficult to develop an appropriate environmental risk assessment framework for agriculture.

Quakers, and all others who share these concerns about biotechnology, could take action in various ways on all of the areas for institutional change—and a number of people are indeed doing just that. But to pick only a couple of priorities, the strategic actions would be to concentrate on:

1) public awareness;
2) energizing NGOs, including Quaker and other church organizations; and
3) organizing a major consumer boycott coupled with organized, collective, well-publicized commitments to buying organic products.

VI. QIF Discernment and Research Process Applied to Climate Change

A CoD of six participants meeting by conference call every two months over two years wrote *Climate, Food, and Violence*. The subject of this CoD resulted from a conversation with FCNL staff. The topic was so broad we struggled to find a coherent approach as we were pulled in different directions. Early in our work we developed a set of guiding principles. Any action proposed should be in alignment with these principles:

- Earth is best understood as a living entity whose various interacting systems support the health of the planet as a whole.
- All species in the commonwealth of life on Earth have a right to equitable access to the resources of the ecosystems in which they exist.
- The human species is but one form of life among many with no special right to Earth's natural resources.
- All people have the right of access to sufficient clean water, clean air, and nutritious food that meets their caloric and dietary needs for a healthy and active life.
- No human community, government, or corporate entity has the right to degrade Earth's natural resources and fragile ecosystems in a way that

reduces the overall resilience and flourishing of present and future generations of human and other life.

- Carbon emissions and other wastes from human activity must be in equilibrium with the absorptive capacity of Earth.
- Indigenous peoples have gained wisdom and experience living sustainably on Earth for millennia, so their interests and perspective must be considered in any decision-making, planning, and subsequent actions.
- A community has the right to give or withhold its consent to proposed projects that may affect the lands they customarily own, occupy, or otherwise use (free prior and informed consent).
- Decision-making on matters of community interest is best handled by the smallest community-based, or least centralized, authority capable of addressing them effectively (subsidiarity).

We made several outlines, finally settled on one, and divided up the sections. The rest of the team reviewed all sections. In the midst of the work of this CoD, we attended the 2013 QIF Summer Research Seminar, presenting our work to the assembled Friends, after which we went into worship-sharing. Very important questions emerged, and in the silence, we were all led to new insights.

Rising to the Challenge: The Transition Movement and People of Faith is by Ruah Swennerfeldt, with a Foreword by Rob Hopkins, one of the founders of the Transition Town Movement. Because of Ruah Swennerfelt's extensive study of the very positive, hopeful Transition Town Movement, QIF asked her to write a QIF Focus Book.

Rising to the Challenge describes the emergence of the Transition Town Movement, inspired by the sustainable agriculture principles of Permaculture and adding a community component. Transition Towns aim to be fully sustainable systems, including food and energy production not requiring fossil fuels, and with a focus on collaborative and innovative approaches to developing resilient communities. The Transition Town Movement then spread rapidly around the world because of its uniquely positive approach toward the transition to a fossil fuel-free future by implementing local initiatives. The author focused on the role of faith communities in what started as a secular movement but is spreading among people of faith. Interviews from participants in the Transition Town Movement around the world provide a model of how we can approach the future with hope, joy, and confidence.

VII. The Future Work of the Quaker Institute for the Future

To determine future QIF work, the QIF Research Committee has conducted discussions in board meetings and at a board retreat, grounding this discernment in the process we developed for collective discernment combined with strong research. Given the current condition of the world, we approach solutions to climate change and ecological destruction with goals focused on Truth. We hope this spurs Quakers and others to know and live our collective Truth, and to contribute an explicitly Quaker perspective of what it will take to move from the current dystopian path to a symbiotically healthy human-Earth relationship.

BIBLIOGRAPHY OF *QIF FOCUS BOOKS*

Learn more and read the full text of these books online at http://quakerinstitute.org

1. *Fueling our Future: A Dialogue about Technology, Ethics, Public Policy and Remedial Action,* coordinated by Ed Dreby and Keith Helmuth, edited by Judy Lumb, 2008.

2. *How on Earth Do We Live Now? Natural Capital, Deep Ecology, and the Commons,* by David Ciscel, Barbara Day, Keith Helmuth, Sandra Lewis, and Judy Lumb, 2011.

3. *Genetically Modified Crops: Promises, Perils, and the Need for Public Policy,* by Anne Mitchell with Pinayur Rajagopal, Keith Helmuth, and Susan Holtz, 2011.

4. *How Does Societal Transformation Happen? Values Development, Collective Wisdom, and Decision Making for the Common Good,* by Leonard Joy, 2011.

5. *It's the Economy, Friends: Understanding the Growth Dilemma,* edited by Ed Dreby, Keith Helmuth, and Margaret Mansfield, 2012.

6. *Beyond the Growth Dilemma: Toward an Ecologically Integrated Economy,* edited by Ed Dreby and Judy Lumb, 2012.

7. *Quaker Approach to Research: Collaborative Practice and Communal Discernment,* by Gray Cox with Charles Blanchard, Geoff Garver, Keith Helmuth, Leonard Joy, Judy Lumb, and Sara Wolcott, 2014.

8. *Climate, Food and Violence: Understanding the Connections, Exploring Responses,* by Judy Lumb, Phil Emmi, Mary Gilbert, Leonard Joy, Laura Holliday, and Shelley Tanenbaum, 2014.

9. *Toward a Right Relationship to Finance: Debt, Interest, Growth, and Security,* by Pamela Haines, Ed Dreby, David Kane, and Charles Blanchard, 2016.

10. *Rising to the Challenge: The Transition Movement and People of Faith,* by Ruah Swennerfelt with a Foreword by Rob Hopkins, 2016.

11. *Energy Choices: Opportunities to Make Wise Decisions for a Sustainable Future,* by Robert Bruninga with Judy Lumb, Frank Granshaw, and Charles Blanchard, 2018.

21 | How Aotearoa New Zealand Quakers Care for the Planet

By Robert Howell

Abstract: What do members of the Religious Society of Friends in Aotearoa New Zealand believe and do about living in the planet Earth? What is the spiritual basis of their human-Earth relationship? What are their attitudes to the use of the Earth's resources, and current economic models that determine that use? How do they care for the planet? This paper briefly explains the history and culture of Friends in Aotearoa New Zealand, and then describes steps toward earthcare Aotearoa New Zealand Friends have made and the work still to do.

I. Quakers in Aotearoa New Zealand[1]

A little over a century after the Religious Society of Friends started in England, a Quaker named Sydney Parkinson arrived in Aotearoa New Zealand. He was a graphic artist on Captain Cook's first voyage in 1776. The links between Aotearoa New Zealand and Britain have remained strong since then. Thomas and Jane Mason were among the first settlers in Wellington, and several Quakers worked in Nelson for the New Zealand Land Company when the town was being established. Regular Meetings for Worship began in Nelson in 1842 (but discontinued after twenty years) and in Auckland in 1885 (and have continued since).

One name that stands out in the history of early Quakers in New Zealand is that of Ann Fletcher Jackson. She came to New Zealand with her husband Thomas in 1879, and they settled on bush-covered land north of Whangarei. She was instrumental in the establishment of a nationwide network

---

[1] Aotearoa is the Māori word for the islands that make up the area we refer to in English as New Zealand. "Aotearoa" means "land of the long white cloud," which is how one of the early Māori explorers first saw the islands. People who want to acknowledge the significance of Māori history and heritage use "Aotearoa New Zealand."

of Friends, and in encouraging the establishment of regular Meetings for Worship in a number of places. Today there are about 1,400 adults and children associated with Quakers in Aotearoa New Zealand with meetings in all the main centres.[2]

Aotearoa New Zealand Friends try to live according to three sources of inspiration: the Bible, the historical examples of Friends, and their own conscience, or Inner Light. Worldwide amongst Quakers there is and has been wide variation in the balance of these three sources. While some Aotearoa New Zealand Friends use the term "God," others do not. In the late 1980s, the Māori Commissioner of Names gave the Aotearoa New Zealand Religious Society of Friends a Māori name: *Te Haahi Tuuhauwiri*. A rough translation is: "the people / group / tribe that stand swinging / buffeted / shoved around by and in the wind of the Spirit." Most Quakers recognize that people can be Spirit-led within other religious and non-religious traditions.

There is also variation in worship practices internationally among Quakers, including programmed and unprogrammed meetings. In New Zealand, there are only unprogrammed meetings and it is most common to give qualified priority to internal leadings. There is no creedal affirmation required, but the testimonies of peace, integrity, simplicity, and equality are usually recognized. In recent years, a testimony of earthcare has been added.[3]

Anne Adams, in introducing a modern anthology of Friends' writing on earthcare, stated: "there is a huge gap in Quaker writing about the earth between the seventeenth and late twentieth centuries (apart from the remarkable John Woolman in the eighteenth)."[4] The primary emphasis within the Quaker historical record is of human-human concern. This has led to many admirable initiatives by Quakers over the years in peacemaking initiatives to resolve conflict, heal hurts resulting from conflict, and build ways of preventing violence. Quakers are one of the three historic peace churches, and were awarded the Nobel Peace prize in 1947.[5] More recently the importance of an earth testimony has emerged, moving us to consider concerns beyond the human-human

---

[2] "History of Quakerism in New Zealand," Quakers in Aotearoa, accessed January 2019, http://quaker.org.nz/history-of-quakerism-in-new-zealand. The total population of Aotearoa New Zealand is just under 5 million.

[3] "Statement on Environmental Sustainability," Aotearoa New Zealand Yearly Meeting, 2000, retrieved from http://quaker.org.nz/ym-statement-on-environmental-sustainability.

[4] Anne Adams, compiler, *The Creation Was Open To Me: An anthology of Friends' Writings on That of God in all Creation* (Suffolk: Lavenham Press, Quaker Green Concern, 1996).

[5] Gunnar Jahn, "Award Ceremony Speech," The Nobel Peace Prize 1947, The Nobel Prize website, accessed January 2019, http://nobelprize.org/nobel_prizes/peace/laureates/1947/press.html.

relationship. This essay shares some of the ways Friends in Aotearoa New Zealand are thinking about and responding to earthcare concerns.

II. The Inward and Outward Spiritual Experience

In Quaker worship, silent meetings tend to promote the inner search (the God within), rather than an experience of the divine outside of oneself. Rudolph Otto, in his book *The Idea of the Holy*, talks about an awe that he calls the *mysterium tremendum* that has a transcendent or numinous quality.[6] Otto sees mystical experiences as part of the *mysterium tremendum*. I understand mysticism as consisting of an interior quest, to be distinguished from the experience of mystery and awe of the exterior world. For Ursula Goodenough, a scientist (but not a Quaker), it is the mystery of why there is anything at all, the mystery of where the laws of physics came from, the mystery of why the universe is so strange: these generate wonder, and wonder generates awe.[7]

Although for many Quakers today the starting point may be the inner search, it is not the end point. Quakers use many images to talk about their spiritual life and journey. A number are committed gardeners, and the garden is a common metaphor. My wife, Gael, saw it that way. She was a gardener, and she saw the world as a garden. She did not treat the garden or the world like a coal mine—to be exploited for economic growth to benefit the rich. To grow a garden, it is necessary to harvest the water, nourish the soil, plan and plant within the seasons and Earth's capacity to support life, and then share the surplus. She told me off one year for putting too much netting under the feijoa tree—"You need to leave some feijoas on the ground for the birds." She did not believe in a Great Gardener in the Sky. She saw God as a spirit, an internal experience where you go when looking for guidance. For her as for many of us as New Zealand Friends, there is a spiritual element to sustainability, intertwined with the natural and non-natural world. There is no *why* to Creation. It just happened. Just marvel at its intricacy, feel connected, and revere it.

The Australian Quaker Jenny Spinks states that we need to embrace a way of thinking about ourselves that sees us as we truly are: completely integrated into a whole.[8] The Spirit flows through all things. It flows through trees, flowers,

---

[6] Rudolph Otto, *The Idea of the Holy*, paperback edition (London: Oxford University Press, 1958).

[7] Ursula Goodenough, *The Sacred Depths of Nature* (New York: Oxford University Press, 1998).

[8] Jenny Spinks, "Support for our true selves—Nurturing the space where leadings flow," James Backhouse Lecture, 2007, Australia Yearly Meeting of the Religious Society of Friends.

QUAKERS AND THE DISCIPLINES

birds, fish, animals, the stars, the moon, the sun, mountains, rivers, rocks, plastic ducks, nuclear weapons, and railway lines. It flows through earthquakes, hurricanes, tidal waves, and traffic jams.[9]

Living holistically in the planet Earth involves living in the spirit of a place that is local, vulnerable, and fragile. The Spirit is shaped by the mysteries and contrasts of the landscape, the climate, our rivers, and oceans. The Spirit is not an unchanging universal influence. Place and connection to that place are important for developing a spiritual respect for the earth. This lesson can also be learned from the spiritual insights of many indigenous peoples.

One of the most famous sayings of the founder of Quakerism, George Fox, is "to walk cheerfully over the world, answering that of God in every one."[10] But if we are to live in awe, we need to live in awe of where we are in this time and this place, and stop walking over the world. Thomas Berry, a Catholic, wrote that we must be true to the earth in the place or community where we live. If we are in the desert, we live in a desert community. If we are in a valley, we live in a valley community. We make our home in these communities, with all the other modes of being, and if these communities do not survive, we do not survive. We do not get a second chance. If we kill the earth, it is all over for our species.[11] When this awe and respect is grounded in place, and when our ethics and economics are based on this human-Earth principle, then human society has a chance of promoting a flourishing life.

III. Ecological Integrity and Aotearoa New Zealand Friends

A number of Quakers recognize the limits of the earth to support current human civilization and that this is in significant part due to the kind of model that dominates international economic behavior. That model is based on outdated science and an unacceptable utilitarian ethic focused solely on human utility, and is linked to an incoherent money supply theory based on preference for market allocation of demand and supply.[12] It ignores the global issues such as population, climate warming, price increases for hydrocarbons, water, food, and

---

[9] This does not commit one to an ethical position that everything has intrinsic value. See Robert Howell, "An Environmental Ethic," a-resilient-world blog, August 28, 2018, accessed January 2019, http://a resilient-world.blogspot.com/.

[10] Yearly Meeting of the Religious Society of Friends (Quakers) in Britain, *Quaker Faith and Practice* (London: Britain Yearly Meeting, 1994), 19.32.

[11] Thomas Berry with Thomas Clarke, *Befriending the Earth* (New London, CT: Twenty-Third Publications, 1991).

[12] See my other essay in this volume, chapter 14, Robert Howell, "How Are We to Live? An Overview of Ethics, Economics and Science."

toxins. Each of these factors contains significant threats to continued human life on Earth.[13] The prophetic Quaker economist Kenneth Boulding, in his famous 1966 essay, talked about the need for a spaceship economy, rather than the cowboy economy that sees the earth as a source to exploit for human utility.[14] Boulding states that rather than continue down the road of unlimited economic expansion and increasing energy use until a convergence of ecological breakdowns stops our cultural momentum, we should instead place ecologically sustainable adaptation at the leading edge of human settlement and economic behavior.[15]

Many aspects of these concerns have been shared by Aotearoa New Zealand Friends. They have adopted declarations such as the "Kabarak Call for Peace and Ecojustice," and "Facing the Challenge of Climate Change: A shared statement by Quaker groups."[16] A Futures Committee of the Yearly Meeting was established in 2005 to grapple with many of these issues. Aotearoa New Zealand Friends have been concerned about ethical investments (particularly assisting the Council for Socially Responsible Investment), and in 2014 supported the call to divest Yearly Meeting investments from the fossil fuel industry. They have been slow, however, to follow North American and British Friends in engaging with companies such as banks who provide finance for the fossil fuel industry.

Another example of the recognition that the current dominant economic model is unacceptable to a number of Aotearoa New Zealand Friends is the warm reception given to *Right Relationship: Building a Whole Earth Economy* produced for the Quaker Institute for the Future, and this was warmly received by a number of Friends.[17] We argue that without a rapid change to an economy premised on the need for human beings to live within the capacity of the earth to support human life, industrial civilization is heading toward widespread disaster. A post-industrial civilization is unlikely to replace our existing civilization in time to avoid major catastrophe and significant loss of human life.

It is hard to say how many Aotearoa New Zealand Friends agree with all this analysis. A number would, but it would not be universally accepted. There

---

[13] "Strong Sustainability for New Zealand," Sustainable Aotearoa New Zealand, 2009, accessed January 2019, http://earthslimits.org/.

[14] Kenneth Boulding, "The Economics of the Coming Spaceship Earth," in *Environmental Quality Issues in a Growing Economy*, ed. Henry Jarrett (Baltimore, MD: Resources for the Future/Johns Hopkins University Press, 1966). Now available at http://dieoff.org/page160.htm.

[15] Keith Helmuth, "Ecological Integrity and Religious Faith," *Friends Journal* 47, no. 8 (August 2001): 6–9.

[16] See Appendices F and H for the full text of these statements.

[17] Peter G. Brown et al., *Right Relationship: Building a Whole Earth Economy* (San Francisco: Berrett-Koehler Publishers, 2009).

is still discussion how best to respond to putting our leadings fully into effect. Practically, many Quakers are working in response to earthcare sentiments: interest groups at Quaker Summer Gathering involve discussions of water tanks, solar electricity, composting toilets, electric cars, permaculture, and sustainable houses. However, many Quakers are not opposed to air travel.

The average ecological footprint of Aotearoa New Zealand Quakers is likely to be below that of the average New Zealander, but not below the level needed for the planet's capacity to support the ecological systems necessary for flourishing human life. We are all dependent on the existing social and economic systems: housing, energy, transport, food, and water systems in New Zealand are not sustainable, yet we use them in order to live within existing cities and towns. We are caught in the dilemma of caring for ourselves and the vulnerable in our community (the old, disabled and ill, people in insecure work, and the young) that requires using existing infrastructures and organizations that are unsustainable, but convenient.

Many of us are impatient for the necessary changes. We yearn for a spiritual community based on awe, reverence, and respect, critical for living in the planet Earth in this space and time. We feel very apprehensive about the future for our children. The following is an opportunity for reflection on our individual and collective impact on the earth and our calling as Friends:

> *Try to live simply. A simple lifestyle freely chosen is a source of strength. Do not be persuaded into buying what you do not need or cannot afford. Do you keep yourself informed about the effects your style of living is having on the global economy and environment?*

> *We do not own the world, and its riches are not ours to dispose of at will. Show a loving consideration for all creatures, and seek to maintain the beauty and variety of the world. Work to ensure that our increasing power over nature is used responsibly, with reverence for life. Rejoice in the splendour of God's continuing creation. How aware are you of the threats to our planet by our current economic system, and the organisations that we are dependent on for our goods and services? Are you working to change the values of human dominance, greed and arrogance that drive our exploitation and destruction of the Earth? Do you search out whatever in your use of money, investments and resources contain the seeds for destroying the planet?[18]*

---

[18] Robert Howell, "Do Your Investments Destroy or Care for the Planet?" *Friends Quarterly*, May 2011. See also Aotearoa New Zealand Yearly Meeting Advices and Queries E7 and E14 at http://quaker.org.nz/advices-and-queries.

22 | The Building of a Collective Conviction Among Quakers Around Sustainability: Friends World Committee for Consultation

By Susanna Mattingly

Abstract: The Quaker community circles the globe, spanning a rich diversity of regional cultures, beliefs, and styles of worship. The underlying spiritual imperative to take action on climate change to protect life on earth unites many within the Quaker community—ultimately, it is a spiritual issue for Friends, and not just a material one.

Friends World Committee for Consultation (FWCC) encourages fellowship among all the branches of the Religious Society of Friends and acts in a consultative capacity to promote better understanding among Friends the world over. Following recent significant global Quaker commitments such as the Kabarak Call for Peace and Ecojustice (2012) and the Pisac Sustainability Minute (2016), FWCC has continued its work internationally to build Friends' collaborative efforts around the concern of sustaining life on Earth. Part of this work involves supporting yearly meetings around the world to take further action.

In 2017, FWCC launched a dedicated program to promote sustainability action in the global Quaker community, designed to generate interest and engage a greater number of Friends more deeply on the issue of sustainability and to articulate the spiritual imperative to sustain life on Earth.

This essay tells the story of FWCC's recent work relating to environmental concerns, and also shares stories of Friends' experiences of climate change across the globe. The examples contained in this chapter show the understanding of environmental challenges developing in the Quaker world, and represent a few of the many inspiring ways in which Friends are responding to this concern.*

I. Sustainability in Line with Global Quaker Witness

Quakers have historically played an important role at the forefront of social change movements with the goal of working toward a better world, compelled by their faith to alleviate suffering and destructive tendencies. This is the Quaker way; working with collective conviction and never giving up.

Equally, the concern for sustainability is not new. Quakers have been proponents of earthcare for centuries. The eighteenth century Quaker John Woolman wrote: "The produce of the earth is a gift from our gracious creator to the inhabitants, and to impoverish the earth now to support outward greatness appears to be an injury to the succeeding age."[1]

Today, in the twenty-first century, this Quaker commitment still holds strong as more and more Friends are recognizing and experiencing the threat of climate change. Joining other Quaker organizations that are embodying the Quaker testimonies through climate advocacy, lobbying, and spirit-led action, Friends World Committee for Consultation (FWCC) launched a dedicated program to promote sustainability action in the global Quaker community in 2017.[2] This program is designed to generate interest and engage a greater number of Friends more deeply on the issue of sustainability and to articulate the spiritual imperative to sustain life on Earth. This work of nurturing a global Quaker sustainability movement is now developing a strong, faith-driven, collective conviction to act. This chapter will explain the history of FWCC's sustainability focus, describe the connection between climate change and social justice as well as the spiritual aspects of sustainable living, and highlight the stories of global Friends as they strive to put their Quaker faith in action through earthcare.

II. Building a Sustainability Movement

Friends World Committee for Consultation (FWCC) is the global body representing Friends worldwide. It encourages fellowship among all the branches of

---

[1] John Woolman, *A Journal of the Life, Gospel Labours, and Christian Experiences, of that Faithful Minister of Jesus Christ, John Woolman, Late of Mount Holly, in the Province of New Jersey* (Philadelphia, PA: T. E. Chapman, 1837), 364.

[2] In addition to the Quaker organizations contributing chapters to this section in the present volume, there are other Quaker groups focused on environmental concerns including: Britain Yearly Meeting's Quaker Peace & Social Witness, and the Quaker United Nations Office (QUNO), which continues to work as accredited observers (through FWCC) of the UNFCCC negotiations, highlighting the human impacts of climate change, offering quiet diplomacy, and supporting climate negotiators' work with effective arguments for urgent climate action.

the Religious Society of Friends and acts in a consultative capacity to promote better understanding among Friends the world over.

The Quaker community of around 400,000 Friends circles the globe, spanning a rich diversity of regional cultures, beliefs, and styles of worship. Across this diversity, the underlying spiritual imperative to take action on climate change to protect life on Earth unites many within the Quaker community. It is a spiritual issue for Friends, not just a material one.

In 2007 at the FWCC Triennial in Dublin, Friends approved that FWCC would pursue consultations on Global Change, in response to an ever-growing concern from Friends in many different countries. The FWCC Central Executive Committee took it forward and in 2010 convened a series of worldwide consultations on Global Change specifically to address the question of the broken covenant between humanity and God that causes changes in the environment, climate, economy, and society. This consultation gathered the voices of Friends impacted by global change and convened several gatherings to discern what Friends could offer this global movement.

A few years later the Sixth World Conference of Friends was held in 2012 on the campus of Kabarak University, in Kenya. The theme of the conference was "Being Salt and Light: Friends Living the Kingdom of God in a Broken World." This was the largest worldwide Conference of Friends since 1967 with over 850 Friends gathered from 51 counties, from parts of Asia, Australia, New Zealand, Africa, the Middle East, Europe, Latin America, and North America.

The Kabarak Call for Peace and Ecojustice, approved at the World Conference of Friends in 2012, was the culmination of FWCC's three-year Global Change Consultation with Quakers on every inhabited continent. It recognized the dangers of climate change and its effect on famine, migrations, and war. The powerful and moving statement calls for Friends to "work for the peaceable Kingdom of God on the whole earth, in right sharing with all peoples. However few our numbers, we are called to be the salt that flavours and preserves, to be a light in the darkness of greed and destruction."[3]

The call recounts the impact of melting mountain glaciers, deforestation, changing seasons, and natural disasters including disease, drought, floods, fires, and famines, and directly attributes these to human greed and the prevailing economic systems, which in turn lead to war, inequality, violence, and desperate migrations. It questions, "Is this how Jesus showed us to live?" and asks Friends to consider what love can do and how to teach right relationship. It calls on

---

[3] "Kabarak Call for Peace and Ecojustice," World Conference of Friends, Kenya, 2012. See Appendix F for full text. It can also be found online at http://fwcc.world/call.pdf.

Friends to do justice and walk humbly and be patterns and examples in a twenty-first century campaign for peace and ecojustice.

While the Kabarak Call was moving and inspirational, Friends desired something that would call Quakers to action, and it needed to come from a group of Friends that included voices from both the Global South and North. Friends approved the Pisac Sustainability Minute nearly four years later at the World Plenary Meeting in Peru in 2016, answering this need. It provided something that was more action-oriented, and resulted from the joining of voices across the world. The Minute on Living Sustainably and Sustaining Life on Earth asks Friends and Yearly Meetings to take action to promote sustainability at all levels and to initiate two concrete actions on sustainability, involving young Friends in key roles.[4]

Building on these two significant global Quaker commitments, FWCC has continued to work internationally to build Friends' collaborative efforts around the concern of sustaining life on Earth. Part of this work is supporting yearly meetings around the world to take further action. The global Quaker sustainability movement is shaped by stories of Friends' concerns and actions on sustainability and how they are driven by the spiritual imperative to make the world a better place.

III. Climate Change as a Peace and Justice Concern

Friends worldwide increasingly understand climate change as a peace and justice issue and as an issue of faith. While the principal cause of climate change is high consumption, those who are most responsible rarely feel the worst impacts of climate change. The communities who bear the brunt are those most reliant upon the land for their livelihoods, those who are already vulnerable to extreme weather events, natural disasters and rising sea levels—often those who are socially marginalized due to their economic status, race, and gender. Climate change is creating greater inequality and as a result, leading to conflict and violence. It is a testament to this understanding that the Quaker United Nations Office has named its stream of work in this area the Human Impacts of Climate Change.

Given that climate change is a global problem, almost all of us will be required to make changes to our lives in order to be part of the solution, but lifestyle change is a sensitive subject. In developed countries, these conversations can make Friends feel anxious about loss of comfort or convenience, and guilty

---

[4] Pisac Minute: Living Sustainably and Sustaining Life on Earth, World Plenary Meeting, Peru 2016. See Appendix I for full text of the Pisac Minute. It can be viewed online at http://fwcc.world/wp-content/uploads/2019/01/Pisac-Sustainability-Minute-2016.pdf.

for their contribution to the problem. In developing countries, where increased consumption might alleviate poverty, where Global North lifestyles often hold great appeal, and where having such choice is often a luxury, promoting reduced consumption can be insensitive and inappropriate.

Different parts of the world exhibit different needs; therefore, the challenges needing to be overcome vary depending on the context. Whereas some parts of the world need to address overconsumption, other parts of the world are grappling with the unsustainable exploitation of their natural resources by outside interests for short-term gain. The story of overconsumption that occupies the Global North simply isn't exhibited in a large part of the world.

The actions that are appropriate for different Quaker communities around the world will vary, too, as there is not a "one size fits all" approach. But it is important for Friends, meetings, and churches to reflect and ask of themselves, without judgement or guilt, what could we do to make a difference? Then Friends must have the courage to be faithful and listen to the answer.

How do we keep trying to find solutions to inequality? It's true that there are inequalities between the Global North and South but Friends are also addressing the many local inequalities experienced in our own communities. Wherever Friends are in the world, we problem solve and help empower one another, what Isaac Penington in 1667 described as "helping one another up with a tender hand."[5]

IV. The Spiritual Journey to Sustainability

There are some troubling questions Friends are grappling with today. Looking back through Quaker history, our rightly celebrated past raises some challenging questions about the present. When will the Quaker commitment to sustainability become as embedded in Quaker faith and practice as the peace and equality testimonies are? That sustainability and stewardship have become testimonies in some parts of the world speaks of our desire for it to become more integral to our faith and practice. In reflecting on this question, it is helpful to consider how Friends around the world are already experiencing climate disruption and how Friends from different theological traditions are called to be faithful in responding to the challenges within our own Quaker family. Simply put, telling stories about the people we love and care about helps bring urgency to the situation and

---

[5] Isaac Penington, *The Works of Isaac Penington*, WWW edition (Farmington, ME: Quaker Heritage Press, 1995), accessed January 2019, http://qhpress.org/texts/penington/index.html.

helps us focus on the need to achieve a shift in our practices and attitudes as a global community.

It is hoped that sharing testimonies of the human impacts of climate change and stories of Friends' responses will inspire Quakers around the world to take action and join together to celebrate positive Quaker contributions. What follows are several examples of sustainability in action within yearly meetings from each of the four FWCC Sections.

V. Quaker Sustainability Concerns and Actions around the Globe

1. Africa Section[6]

Friends in Rwanda are working with church communities, particularly in rural areas, to help make Rwanda more resilient to the impacts of climate change through the "Forever Green Rwanda Friends" initiative. This includes promoting sustainable farming practices, water preservation, soil management, tree planting on church land and at home, anti-erosion measures for those living in mountainous areas, the use of solar energy to reduce the amount of firewood consumed, and a shift from electricity to biofuels. This work is inspired by the recommendations of the Pisac Sustainability Minute but it also ties in with the many opportunities provided by government initiatives in the country.

2. Europe and Middle East Section

Ireland Yearly Meeting's EcoQuakers Ireland committee has supported meetings in their efforts to live sustainably and peacefully since 2009. Following the call to action on sustainability from FWCC World Plenary in Peru, Ireland Yearly Meeting has been particularly focused on supporting Quaker Meetings in divesting from destructive industries including fossil fuels and reinvesting funds in sustainable, ethical companies. In 2018 Ireland Yearly Meeting produced a short film exploring the spiritual journey to earthcare, introducing the idea that Friends should be living with action, not just words.[7]

---

[6] FWCC is organized in "sections," each one representing all the Friends in that geographical area of the world.

[7] Brían Ó. Suílleabháin, "Quakers: The Spiritual Journey of Earthcare," Eco-Quakers Ireland, Ireland Yearly Meeting, 2018, video, 6:47, http://youtu.be/g1ZcfbpYgbE.

3. Section of the Americas

The Bolivian city of La Paz has experienced severe drought in recent years, a situation which has been exacerbated by climate change as the Andes Mountains receive less snowfall and the rapidly retreating glaciers fail to provide enough running water to the cities and towns below, removing an important source of fresh water for many communities. The Friends International Bilingual Center, set up by Quaker volunteers in Bolivia, offers educational programs to children, young people, and adults focused on social concerns and stewardship of creation. Following a prolonged drought in 2016, the Center ran a program for its students on the challenges posed by climate change and explored practical ways to help others who are affected.

The Baltimore Yearly Meeting Unity with Nature Committee originated in 1988 with the simple leading of a Friend to visit monthly meetings to speak of the urgency around environmental issues. The mission of the committee is "to work into the beliefs and practices of the Yearly Meeting the twin principles that God's creation is to be respected, protected and held in reverence, and that human aspirations for peace and justice depend upon restoring the Earth's ecological integrity."[8] This mission has led the committee to prepare a set of queries to help Friends navigate the subject called "Are Quakers called to Live Sustainably?" In addition, on a practical level the committee encourages monthly meetings and individual Friends to calculate their carbon footprint, and has called on Friends to disavow the use of single-use plastic bags in all stores.

4. Asia West-Pacific Section

Friends in Aotearoa New Zealand have responded in a variety of ways across the country.[9] Many meetings are introducing video conferencing in place of in-person meetings, installing electric car charging points at meeting houses, and supporting campaigns and lobbying groups promoting sustainability. Friends have established a series of online seminars featuring international speakers involving several sites across the country including the Wanganui Settlement. This simple solution allows Friends to meet to consider concerns such as earthcare, removing the need to travel long distances.

---

[8] *2015 Annual Report: Unity with Nature Committee*, Baltimore Yearly Meeting, Sandy Spring, MD, accessed January 2019, http://bym-rsf.org/what_we_do/committees/nature/unityrpts.html.

[9] See chapter 21, Robert Howell, "How Aotearoa New Zealand Quakers Care for the Planet."

In India, many people drink polluted water from rivers and wells, making waterborne diseases prevalent. In some villages, the water in the wells has never been tested so it's not known if it is clean and safe to drink. Quakers are working in rural areas to connect with people in the villages and help provide clean water and improve health. The Friends Rural Center, Rasulia in Hoshangabad, India runs a BioSand Water Filter project, with support from Friendly Water for the World. They make BioSand Water Filters and provide training for others on how to make them. The filters are easy to make, the raw materials such as sand, gravel, and cement are readily available, and they are low-cost (equivalent to around $45–50 USD each). The center provides both local and national-level training and equips participants with the skills and knowledge to go back to their villages and provide safe water for their community. Friends United Meeting (FUM) has also supported the installation of many BioSand Water Filters in East Africa, working with communities who have difficulty accessing clean water.

VI. Young Adult Friends' Stories

In addition to these examples of sustainability work at the local and yearly meeting level, there are individual Friends working diligently in their communities to advance the sustainability agenda and encourage collective progress. Many of these individuals regard their service in this field as Quaker ministry. Two such examples come from young adult Friends who have shared their stories with the wider Quaker world.

1. The Impact of Changing Weather Patterns in Western Kenya

Geylord Asimba from Nairobi Yearly Meeting comes from a small village in Western Kenya called Mukuyu where most people are farmers, reliant on agriculture. He has three siblings, his mother is a nurse, his father a farmer. He recognizes the impact climate change is having on their daily lives as a result of the changing weather patterns. There used to be set seasons; you knew that if you planted in April, the rains would follow and the plants would be able to germinate. But today, weather patterns have become unpredictable and there is no guarantee it will rain when the plants need it. Growing up, his parents largely relied on farm produce to support the family; this income could feed the family and help pay the children's school fees. While Geylord was still studying, the farm produced enough to pay his school fees and those of his siblings. But now, as a result of the changing weather patterns, produce has significantly dropped and it is very hard to earn enough from the farm to cover the school fees of his youngest sister, who is still in school.

When asked how this concern speaks to him as a Quaker, Geylord replied, "While my siblings and I are now old enough to help pay school fees for our last born, the fate of other families in my village, which still heavily rely on agriculture, is something that keeps me awake at night. How will they survive? This is an issue that affects us personally, and as Christians."

2. A Quaker Ministry Against Plastic Pollution

Another story of environmental degradation comes from Ludwig Bon Quirog from the Bohol Worship Group in the Philippines, which has over 7,000 islands and very poor solid waste management—the consequences of which are very real and immediate.

Ludwig volunteers with a local environmental group formed in November 2015 when they walked 100 km in solidarity with the March for Climate Justice in Paris, France. Their aim was to protest against the prospect of a coal power plant being built on their island, but since then their focus has expanded to include other environmental concerns. They collect non-biodegradable rubbish from different coastal areas around the islands and afterwards give brief educational talks on plastic pollution and introduce sustainable alternatives. Some of the group also lobby for legislation banning single-use disposable plastics, while others run campaigns with business owners.

The group is made up of people from different faith backgrounds, but Ludwig considers his participation as Quaker ministry. He sees it an expression of basic testimonies. As he explains, "In striving to live an ecologically sound Earthly existence, one learns to live with simplicity; one is compelled to always express one's truth so that others may follow suit; one empathizes with other creatures and recognizes the inherent equality between all beings; and one also endeavors to make peace with the Earth."

VII. Building a Quaker Approach

While the scale of the challenge remains so vast, it is worth touching on the reasons people may hesitate to get involved in a global Quaker sustainability movement. Friends may resist being told how to live by another, or may resist making changes to their habits and lifestyles. Or, Friends might not be aware of the impact of their behavior and choices. They may not be cognizant of the spiritual call to protect creation.

The hope is that sharing stories will offer fresh ideas, tools, and inspiration to help each of us find our own way to contribute to the global Quaker sustainability movement while also serving as a reminder of the spiritual call to take action that grows out of hope, optimism, and love for one another and our world, not out of fear and guilt. Quakers have the opportunity to develop a community of shared values and mutual support, and extend a loving hand to invite others to join.

It is clear that we all have a role to play. Each and every one of us belonging to the Quaker community is part of this movement. We need to have the courage to be faithful and listen to the Spirit. We do not need to have all the answers. We do not need to attempt to single-handedly solve all the problems we face. But we must not turn our backs and give up because the scale of the challenge is too daunting.

The solution may lie in the Quaker witness of putting faith into practice. Sustainability ultimately underlies all the other Quaker testimonies: peace, truth, simplicity, equality and community. **Peace** is threatened as climate change contributes to increased conflict and leads to violence and war. Friends are called to speak truth to power and live with **integrity**, attempting to challenge a wider crisis in our political and economic systems and stand up for those without a voice. As humanity consumes more resources than nature can support, embracing **simplicity** is essential to living in a sustainable way on earth, in right sharing with all people. Climate change undermines development gains and leads to shortages in basic necessities, creating greater in**equality**. As the common home we all share is misused, our health and wellbeing suffers, and global and local **community** is weakened. These testimonies, each intertwined with sustainability, are integral to Quaker faith and practice all over the world. Let us embrace this position freely and joyfully as a global community of Friends, and join with others and act now, so that life on earth will continue.

It is what God asks of us: to love and care for each other and the whole of creation.

23 | Practicing Quaker Stewardship: One Student's Experience Implementing Recycling and Food Waste Reduction Programs at Wilmington College

By April Mays

Abstract: Learning sustainability through both tradition and necessity, I grew up with a high-level view of stewardship. When I arrived on campus at Wilmington College, a Quaker school in Ohio, I noticed ways to enhance sustainability on campus, and I met faculty and staff who were supportive, encouraging students to push for these changes.

My understanding of sustainability was immediately put into a larger scale practice. Building off an existing (but low-functioning) recycling program, with the guidance of Tony Staubach and support of Tara Lydy, I was able to help develop a functioning recycling program. This opened the door to an internship position with Sodexo dining on campus to make the cafeteria more sustainable. Later, we proposed and implemented trayless dining, reducing water and food waste, and an experimental composting project, paired temporarily with the Ameri-Corps program Good Food, Grow Hope. Some of these efforts became part of the culture, others dwindled away, but the lasting lessons of stewardship and service still live on at Wilmington College and in my own personal practices. This chapter tells my experience, one student coming to a Quaker college, learning about Quakerism, and getting involved in caring for the planet.*

I. Sustainability as a Family Value

My love for the environment began very early in life. As a child, my mother taught me that when an animal was killed for food, the Great Spirit and the spirit of the animal were to be thanked for their sacrifice; it was considered an insult not to use every imaginable part, wasting as little as possible. I only ever heard stories of my mom's hunting experiences, never witnessed them, but I knew that when she did kill an animal, she prayed a prayer of gratitude. She exhibited the same gratitude and desire not to waste in the kitchen through daily prayers of thanksgiving over our meals before we ate and saving leftovers for another meal. My mom would also explain that our ancestors would never have sent their trash away, making it someone else's problem; rather, they would have kept it close as a reminder not to abuse the earth by creating more waste than necessary. She always found ways to reduce consumption, from mending worn clothing to making her own cleaning products using general household sundries.

My father shared these values, having been reared on a farm as a member of a large family. His interpretation was different, perhaps, but his actions echoed the same sentiments. He would repair old cars, patch tires, reuse nails, and find new purposes for used shingles. As a family, we practiced reusing by using handkerchiefs, cloth hand towels, passing clothes from child to child, and sharing and taking care of our toys. When every ounce of value and usefulness had been stripped from each product and it finally came time to discard, it was with a lengthy lecture and reminder that this is not what our ancestors would have done. We did not live in an area where recycling was feasible but we were all well aware of it. In this small slice of the world I felt the Earth was largely protected and I was doing my part; however, as I grew older, I realized many people did not practice sustainable living. It became grossly clear that our economy was organized around consuming more and more, with little commitment to reuse and recycling. I felt something needed to be done, and during my years as a student at Wilmington College I got a chance to do so.

II. Getting Involved in Sustainability at Wilmington College

I initially applied to Wilmington College (WC), a Quaker college in Wilmington, OH, because of my mother; she thought it had a great reputation and admired its beautiful campus. Neither of us knew much about Quaker values and practices. In fact, I knew more about recycling than I did about the Religious Society of Friends. I would soon come to learn that some of the core values of the faith, such as stewardship of the planet and service to others, matched those I held most dear. At the time, I was yet unaware that I would spend the next four years discovering far more about those two concepts than I had ever expected.

Right at the beginning of my college career, I met Tony Staubach and Tara Lydy. Tony was working as an AmeriCorps VISTA member, serving as Campus Sustainability Coordinator, and Tara was the Director for the Center for Service and Civic Engagement. Both were very excited to meet a self-proclaimed environmentalist who was ready to roll up her sleeves and get her hands dirty. They were not Quakers but, like me, they strived to embody the testimonies of stewardship and service, and so they recruited me to join a student organization called the Service Leader Executive Board (SLEB) as the Recycling Coordinator. It was not long before I was involved in recycling, sustainability, and community outreach.

III. Building a Thriving Recycling Program

Tony had discovered that a recycling program was started in the 1990s at WC and he had been working to revive and improve it ever since his time as a student. Unhappy with the lack of availability of recycling facilities, Tony began educating others about the necessity of recycling. He obtained some fifty-five gallon drums, placed them strategically around campus and, with the help of a few volunteers, started collecting the recycling himself. After graduation and during his service years with AmeriCorps VISTA, he continued to fuel the programs in which he had already invested so much. This is where I came into the picture.

I became one of Tony's volunteers within my first month on campus as a freshman. As the newly-installed student recycling chairperson of SLEB, it was my duty to both collect recycling and recruit others to do the same. A few times a week I went from office to office, apartment to apartment, collecting the recyclables and hauling them to the local recycling center, just as Tony had done. Things that could be recycled for money, such as aluminum cans, were taken to Wilmington Iron & Metal Company where a nominal payment would be exchanged for the materials collected. The funds received were used to buy more liners for the recycling bins to continue the collection effort. Over time, as interest and awareness increased, Tony was able to secure grant funding for nicer communal bins, as the fifty-five gallon drums looked well loved after years of service. At first we received a few new bins for events only; however, we were eventually able to get enough bins to leave at permanent locations around campus. Over time, every communal area and office (that wanted one) got a bin.

The next step was to place recycling bins in the student residence halls. Tony knew that doing so would mean we would also need to have recycling dumpsters along side the trash dumpsters on campus. Students would not be likely to recycle if they had to personally drive their recycling to the local recycling collection center. Many students did not have cars and those who did most likely did not have pick-up trucks suitable for hauling recyclables. The bins at offices and common areas were being utilized more and more, which presented a great problem as well. It was wonderful to see the campus recycling, but this success brought with it a real challenge: finding ways to properly dispose of materials, even with the help of the volunteers.

Tony set to work obtaining funding for individual bins for each student in the residence halls while simultaneously working on approval for recycling receptacles to be placed around campus. He proved successful and the college ended up with recycling collection spots at each dumpster site. Students were responsible for their personal bins, but the need grew for more volunteers to empty the ever-larger number of bins in common areas. I found a handful of reliable individuals to help me with recycling but I soon recognized the undeniable need for collecting as a team, due to the weight and volume. I began soliciting help from student organizations such as Greek Life and Athletics. Depositing the recyclables on campus at the recycling receptacles made volunteering more feasible for everyone and more appealing to those seeking community service hours. It was no longer as critical for volunteers to have a truck to move the collected materials. Groups volunteered to empty select bins on certain days, which made managing the process easier. If a bin was at capacity, I had someone to call for a helping hand.

After the first year of residents having their own individual bins, many of these same volunteers offered to hand wash them to prepare for use the following year. This proved a daunting task that we all—staff and volunteers alike—decided would not be repeated. Going forward, it became part of the checkout process to check the recycling bins for cleanliness. If they were dirty upon inspection, the resident was charged a cleaning fee: one more step toward a sustainable program.

Outside of having a paid service, the recycling program arrived at a fairly self-sustaining level. I continued to volunteer with the program and manage it until I graduated in 2011, adjusting here or there when improvements were necessary. According to recent conversations with Michael Allbright, assistant vice president for student affairs, and Chip Murdock, director of multicultural affairs, the recycling program is still alive and well today. The student recycling chairperson of SLEB continues to bring awareness to the campus population as both Tony and I did when we served in that role. Some of the communal bins have since been replaced after years of use. Student organizations and other volunteers continue to collect recyclables from those bins and there are still recycling receptacles on site near residence halls, classrooms, and offices.

IV. Tackling Food Waste

Recycling was not the only area of stewardship I participated in during my tenure at WC. While working in the recycling program, an opportunity for sustainability within our cafeteria opened up my senior year. I was aware of food waste, mostly due to my upbringing, and I witnessed it in excess in the cafeteria. The movement toward less food waste had already started, and I was not the only one who took notice. With the campus being such a small place, everyone knew I would be interested in a newly created sustainability internship position, including Janet Renshaw, the General Manager of Sodexo, our food service vendor. She invited me to apply, and I felt excited to be able to fill this role and help the campus reduce our food waste.

The first step toward improvement is always education. Many people do not realize how much food and water are wasted in the food service industry. Fuel waste can also be a factor when food is purchased outside of local areas. Our campus food service provider, Sodexo, had recently launched a sustainability initiative, and employees were being trained in many aspects of waste reduction. One example was proper thawing techniques in an effort to reduce water consumption. This meant that frozen food was defrosted according to a proper schedule to make sure it was ready to cook on time. This avoided the need for thawing food in running warm water. Educational signs were also displayed throughout the dining area regarding the source of the food we were eating and about food waste (both from customer's plates and that which was prepared but not served).

With education must also come action. Company-wide, Sodexo took on the project of sourcing local food and then showcasing the changes to increase student awareness. I worked to cut down on food waste by implementing a new composting project. The project germinated simultaneously with a new garden initiative called Grow Food, Grow Hope. I also tackled food waste by eliminating the use of trays in the dining room—a movement that came to be known as "trayless dining" which reduced the use of water, since there were no trays to wash. Trayless dining also encouraged people to only take what they would eat instead of taking food that would be wasted. Students were notorious for loading up their trays with multiple entrees and desserts only to barely nibble at a few. Trayless dining meant being intentional about what was gathered for dinner so students threw less food away. Initially, these projects were met with a great deal of resistance; however, I am pleased to say that trayless dining stuck. It took some adjustment and there was a lot of complaining, but it was eventually accepted. Trays are now available by request only and are not a large part of the eating culture.

Change is hard. When a concept is new, it often does not take root immediately. Composting was a good way to repurpose the food that would have been wasted, but it came with a few concerns: Sodexo rules regarding what could be taken off-site, exposure to rodents, and the even greater need for volunteers to commit to a smelly and dirty act of service. Composting did not stand the test of time, but the seed was planted. Much like the recycling program that began in the 1990s and got its wings in the 2000s, it is my hope that WC and all campuses alike will, in time, embrace composting as a normal part of the food system.

Grow Food, Grow Hope (GFGH) was a natural next step for me after I graduated from college. Tara Lydy presented me with an opportunity to work for AmeriCorps VISTA for six weeks as a summer intern for the gardening initiative. The program was intended to fill several needs: education, awareness, and impact. Many people are not aware that hunger is a serious issue in the United States, nor do they know about the concept of food deserts.[1] With so much food being wasted, it can be difficult to see hunger in one's own area. One of the impacts of the program was to bridge the food gap, helping low-income families who are struggling with hunger. When I was involved in the program, people were taught how to plant gardens on their own land (if they had land) or on campus grounds designated for community gardens, learning to grow food locally, a sustainable option for those living in the Midwest. Afterward, training was provided to demonstrate how to cook and prepare the homegrown food in healthy ways. Another component of the program was to provide advocacy to make EBT (commonly known as food stamps) available for use at local farmers markets.

The program evolved as needs changed. Some functions became their own non-profits and others were absorbed by different entities. The Clinton County Chamber of Commerce absorbed the "buy local" campaign. The school-based agriculture program became a joint effort between the Wilmington Agriculture department, Ohio State University Extension (where Tony Staubach went on to work), and the local grade schools. The community gardens that are located on Wilmington College property still serve the community today. Half of the produce grown on campus is donated to local food pantries and the other half benefits those who tend the gardens: students, faculty, staff, and community

---

[1] Food deserts are urban areas where healthy, fresh food is either not available at all or not affordable to the residents in the area. In these areas it is common to see convenience stores with processed salty and sweet snacks, but not food of healthy substance.

members. The project is still supported by the community. Most recently, funds that were donated by various community members were used to purchase seeds from Seed Savers Exchange, heirloom seeds used for planting and education. The materials needed to maintain the raised garden beds are donated by campus and community members, as well as the local Lowe's Home Improvement store. More resources to repair the garden beds will be donated by Timbertech in the future.

Learning is a lifelong endeavor and I am thankful that the Quaker values of stewardship of the planet and service to others were such a major part of my experience at WC. Even though my exposure began when I was a child, my higher education at WC was critical in refining my view of the world and my responsibility in it. Quakers take a global perspective, which pushed my efforts beyond the walls of my childhood kitchen and yard. I learned firsthand that recycling has many challenges on the ground level for diverse groups of people in one space, which I continue to see on a daily basis in my subsequent work-places. I am aware that sustainability is a lifestyle, sometimes requiring a commit-ment to what is right and not necessarily what is easy. Finally, I have accepted that communities working together make the largest impact.

24 | Lobbying for an Earth Restored: Friends Committee on National Legislation

By Emily Wirzba and Emmett Witkovsky-Eldred

Abstract: The Friends Committee on National Legislation's (FCNL) concerns for earthcare and the environment became a formal legislative priority in 2003, after decades of advocating for the United States government to address sustainability considerations in international development and agricultural systems since FCNL's founding in 1943. Friends recognize that "all on this earth are interdependent," which draws our attention to how environmental issues intersect with other important problems facing our world. Through grassroots and Washington, DC-based advocacy efforts, FCNL takes strategic steps to bridge the policy gaps to achieve its prophetic vision of "an earth restored."

In recent years, FCNL recognized that lasting and meaningful progress on climate change could only come through moral, bipartisan action in Congress. FCNL worked to introduce the Republican Climate Resolution in 2015, which acknowledged climate change as real and requiring congressional action. FCNL also worked closely with the House Climate Solutions Caucus, which followed a "Noah's Ark" rule of members joining "two-by-two" across political lines, to build relationships and cultivate a space for bipartisan dialogue and action on climate change in Congress. These actions helped pave the way for two Republican-supported bills placing a price on carbon to be ultimately introduced in the 2018. FCNL's prophetic and persistent work is made possible because of engaged constituents across the country, who build respectful relationships with their members of Congress and echo the moral call to action, regardless of political party or position.

In 2014, when a group of middle school students from Yardley (PA) Friends Meeting walked into a lobby meeting with Rep. Mike Fitzpatrick (R-PA-8) to talk about climate change, they were nervous but excited. There was some reason for optimism—Rep. Fitzpatrick would later be rated the tenth most bipartisan member of the 114th Congress.[1] But Rep. Fitzpatrick hadn't taken a strong position on climate change since 2006, at least not publicly.[2] As a Republican, he was toeing his party's line.

The students were there with the Friends Committee on National Legislation (FCNL), a nonpartisan Quaker lobby. They weren't there to get sweeping climate change legislation passed the next day. They were there to tell their stories, to build a relationship with their representative, and to ask a simple question: "Will you publicly state that Congress must act on climate change, out of concern for your own six children and all future children?"[3]

I. Environmental Concerns Emerge as Legislative Priorities at FCNL, 1990–2014

"An Earth restored" is one of the four pillars that describes FCNL's current mission statement, "The World We Seek."[4] Since FCNL's founding in 1943, care for our planet and agricultural systems have been central values, but not always a top legislative priority. In FCNL's first five decades, our work for a sustainable planet included advocating for sustainability considerations in international development in the 1970s and 1980s. In 1992, FCNL consulted with administration officials, congressional offices, and NGOs ahead of the Rio Earth Summit, which led to UN Conventions on Biological Diversity and Climate Change, but it wasn't until 2003 that we adopted climate change as a formal legislative priority with the introduction of our legislative program on energy and the environment.[5] FCNL added environmental issues as a legislative priority thanks to persistent and faithful encouragement from Friends across the country. In the late 1990s, Friends who were active in environmental stewardship and advocacy noticed that FCNL didn't have a specific program on environmental issues. They started urging FCNL to take action. Groups like Philadelphia Yearly Meeting's Environmental Working Group and the Friends Committee on Unity with Nature (later renamed Quaker Earthcare Witness) were already working among Friends and

---

[1] "The Lugar Center — McCourt School Bipartisan Index: 114th Congress," The Lugar Center, accessed August 12, 2018, http://thelugarcenter.org/ourwork-53.html.

[2] Jose Aguto and Emily Wirzba, "Affirming the Heart of Climate Advocacy," *Friends Journal*, last modified December 31, 2014, http://friendsjournal.org/affirming-the-heart-of-climate-advocacy.

[3] Jose Aguto and Emily Wirzba, "Affirming the Heart of Climate Advocacy."

[4] "The World We Seek: Statement of Legislative Policy" (Washington, DC: Friends Committee on National Legislation, 2014), 31.

[5] "Working for an Earth Restored," Friends Committee on National Legislation, accessed August 15, 2018, http://fcnl.org/timelines/page/working-for-an-earth-restored-3.

in ecumenical circles for climate and environmental action. Some of these Friends identified a need for leadership on environmental policies and saw FCNL as a natural fit. They even offered to raise money for an intern to start working on the issue.[6]

At the same time, Friends in meetings around the US were urging FCNL to begin advocating on climate change through the "priorities process," the process of discernment that FCNL's general committee undergoes every two years to set the organization's legislative agenda for each new Congress with input from Friends meetings, organizations, and individuals.[7]

Development of an FCNL policy priority around environmental concerns began in earnest in 2002, when war with Iraq seemed imminent. FCNL's policy committee suspended the normal priorities process to prepare for the rapidly developing issues that FCNL would have to address in the post 9/11 United States. One proposal that FCNL's policy committee brought forward was a program on energy and the environment, partly because of the relationship between oil and the Iraq war.[8] They said, "achieving lasting peace involves not just a cessation of war, but addressing the injustices and disparities that give rise to violent conflict among people."[9] FCNL's general committee followed by calling on the staff to work to "remove dependence on oil as a source of violent conflict, injustice, and environmental degradation by reducing United States' energy consumption and encouraging the development of renewable sources of energy and alternative modes of transportation."[10] FCNL's sustainable energy and environment program formally began in 2003, at the start of the 108th Congress.

What started as a concern relating to the long-standing Quaker testimony against war developed into a twin concern regarding the impact of climate change and environmental degradation on human conflict, and the recognition that caring for our planet is also a matter of calling for people of faith. Quakers receive from scripture and the stirring of the Spirit a moral calling to cherish and steward creation for future generations, as well as vulnerable populations living

---

[6] Ed Dreby, email to author, October 3, 2017. Used by permission.

[7] "Friends Committee on National Legislation: Policy Committee Meetings July 12–14, 2002 Minutes," in 2002 Newsletters, Minutes, Publications, Friends Committee on National Legislation Archives, 3.

[8] Dreby, email.

[9] "FCNL's Legislative Priorities for the 108th Congress," *Washington Newsletter*, January 2003, n.p.

[10] "FCNL's Legislative Priorities for the 108th Congress," *Washington Newsletter*, January 2003, n.p.

today.[11] Friends recognize that "all on this earth are interdependent," which draws our attention to how environmental issues intersect with other important problems facing our world.[12] In our policy statement, FCNL recognizes how "environmental degradation and the scarcity and inequitable distribution of resources are underlying causes of large-scale migration, violence, and war."[13] Climate disruption, pollution, and the strain on natural resources contribute to poverty, displacement, poor public health, war, and other pressing concerns. We cannot have a world free of war, equitable communities, or a just society without a planet whose climate sustains human and other life. Friends around the world have affirmed this, saying: "We see this Earth as a stunning gift that supports life. It is our only home. Let us care for it together."[14]

II. FCNL's Leadership in Encouraging Bipartisan Environmental Policy

From the beginning of our work on climate change, FCNL recognized lasting and meaningful progress could only come through moral, bipartisan action in Congress. FCNL has prophetic and visionary goals, so we strive to identify concrete and strategic steps that can be taken in DC and with our grassroots network across the country to bridge the policy gaps. We believe that US action on climate change at the federal level is essential to seeing the necessary international cooperation and action to keep global temperatures from rising more than 1.5 degrees Celsius. As a nonpartisan, Quaker organization, FCNL frequently seeks to bring about change by building bipartisan consensus. This has been particularly essential to our change strategy for energy and environment issues.

In a polarized political environment, meaningful legislative action is more achievable and more durable if it has a bipartisan majority behind it. Control of Congress can change hands every two years, and control of the White House every four. In that tumult, defined by a frequently divided government with shifting and conflicting policy agendas, getting Congress to act means getting Congress to first agree that a problem exists. Getting laws to last means passing laws that members of both parties have an interest in standing behind and that the White House is committed to upholding through regulation and enforcement.

---

[11] "A Shared Quaker Statement: Facing the Challenge of Climate Change," Quaker Earthcare Witness, last modified June, 2017, http://quakerearthcare.org/article/shared-quaker-statement-facing-challenge-climate-change. See Appendix H for the full text.

[12] *The World We Seek*, 31.

[13] *The World We Seek*, 31.

[14] "A Shared Quaker Statement."

While President Barack Obama had several major accomplishments on climate policy, many of them have since been endangered or eliminated by President Donald Trump. This is because they were largely wrought by executive action rather than through legislation. The Clean Power Plan, the Paris Climate Agreement, and increases in fuel-efficiency standards for vehicles are all landmark climate policies under the Obama Administration that President Trump has threatened or eroded during his tenure.[15]

This is not to argue that President Obama should not have used his authority to do something about climate change. However, it exemplifies how partisan division creates instability on the issue of climate change that impedes meaningful and lasting action without bipartisan Congressional consensus. Outside of electing an overwhelming majority in Congress of a single party with pro-environmental policy priorities, building bipartisan consensus on climate change is the only way to get Congress to act.

Pursuing a bipartisan legislative strategy is also a way that FCNL stewards its Quaker values. Friends receive a calling to care for the Earth and its creatures for its own sake. Our values also compel us to see that of God in each person, including members of Congress who haven't yet embraced climate science.[16] We choose to believe that any member of Congress, regardless of political party or preconceptions, is willing and able to see truth. This is especially important when that truth is founded upon overwhelming scientific consensus, represents a serious threat to people around the world and future generations, and implicates urgent moral action.

While seeking to build an appetite for bipartisan action on climate change might be the most promising strategy, that doesn't make it easy. According to long-time FCNL supporter Ed Dreby, "The program on energy and environment got off to a slow start."[17] FCNL began working on environmental issues in 2003, when serious pro-environmental policies seemed unlikely as the country geared up for war in Iraq, and the administration proposed the Clear Skies Act, largely seen as a weakening of air pollution regulations.[18] The issue of climate change, in particular, was becoming more polarized.[19] Though both the major

---

[15] Sarah Wheaton, "Obama's Fragile Climate Legacy," Politico, last modified December 13, 2015, http://politico.com/story/2015/12/climate-change-obama-paris-216716.

[16] Margery Post Abbott, *A Theological Perspective on Quaker Lobbying* (Washington, DC: FCNL Education Fund, 2014), 25.

[17] Dreby, email.

[18] "Clear Skies: RIP," *The New York Times*, March 7, 2005, A00016, http://nytimes.com/2005/03/07/opinion/clear-skies-rip.html.

[19] Riley E. Dunlap and Aaron M. McCright, "A Widening Gap: Republican and Democratic Views on Climate Change," *Environment Magazine*, September/October 2008,

party 2008 presidential candidates, John McCain and Barack Obama, campaigned on the need for comprehensive climate action, the issue took a sharp partisan turn after the election. Among the public and especially within Congress, there was virtually no bipartisan acknowledgement that climate change is real and human-caused, let alone that it requires an urgent response. While most Americans agreed on the importance of environmental protection, support splintered along partisan lines when voters faced concrete climate agreements like the Kyoto Protocol.[20]

III. Environmental Legislation Introduced as a Result of FCNL's Bipartisan Lobbying, 2015–2018

One important breakthrough in FCNL's work was the introduction of HR 424, the Republican Climate Resolution, in 2015. The resolution was the result of several years of organizing by FCNL and other interfaith partners around a "Call to Conscience on Climate Disruption."[21] For over two years, more than 50 interfaith delegations, with the help of the Citizens' Climate Lobby, Interfaith Power and Light, and others, visited members of Congress to deliver a faith-centered appeal to moral action on climate change. One such delegation visited Rep. Chris Gibson (R-NY-19), who agreed to draft a resolution that would acknowledge climate change as real and requiring congressional action. Rep. Gibson and ten other House Republicans introduced the Republican Climate Resolution on September 17, 2015, one week before Pope Francis was scheduled to address Congress. Pope Francis called for action on climate change, drawing from his encyclical, "Laudato Si': On Care for our Common Home."[22]

When Rep. Gibson retired before the 2016 elections, we needed a new lead sponsor of the Republican Climate Resolution in the 115th Congress. Fortunately, there were three House Republicans clamoring for the right to introduce the resolution. Ultimately, Elise Stefanik (R-NY-21) introduced the resolution with Representatives Carlos Curbelo (R-FL-26) and Ryan Costello (R-PA-

---

http://environmentmagazine.org/Archives/Back%20Issues/September-October%202008/dunlap-full.html.

[20] Dunlap and McCright, "A Widening Gap."

[21] "Call to Conscience on Climate Disruption," Friends Committee on National Legislation, accessed August 12, 2018, http://fcnl.org/updates/call-to-conscience-on-climate-disruption-370.

[22] Pope Francis, "Laudato Si': On Care for Our Common Home [Encyclical]," Catholic Church, 2015, http://laudatosi.com/.

6) and 14 other House Republicans who were original cosponsors.[23] At the end of 2018, the resolution had garnered 23 cosponsors.[24]

The fact that several Republicans vied for the honor of taking the lead on climate change legislation shows the growing political salience of bipartisan climate action as Republicans in Congress strive to be known as climate leaders. Increasingly, Congressional Republicans are identifying the moral and economic consequences of climate change, especially as they seek to differentiate themselves from the current administration's stance on climate policy.

FCNL seeks to tap into this growing appetite for climate action among congressional Republicans. One important approach has been convincing Republicans who accept climate science and agree that Congress should act to publicly identify themselves as climate leaders who are willing to work across the aisle to advance solutions. Congressional Republicans can do this by joining the House Climate Solutions Caucus (CSC). Founded in February of 2016 by Rep. Carlos Curbelo (R-FL-26) and Rep. Ted Deutch (D-FL-22), the CSC has been nicknamed the "Noah's Ark Caucus" because new members can only join "two-by-two," one Republican and one Democrat.

When they join the CSC, members of the House publicly affirm that climate change is real and that Congress has a role to play in solving the problem. The bipartisan nature of the caucus means that members can discuss and negotiate possible solutions to climate change that satisfy both Democrats and Republicans. The CSC is fostering bipartisan relationships and building up political trust. Moreover, it helps caucus members build political power by forming a voting block that can shift the balance of power in the House towards climate solutions, regardless of which party has the majority.[25]

FCNL played an important role in growing the membership and supporting the legislative work of the CSC by promoting sign-on letters, amendment vote recommendations, member-level briefings, and legislation supported by the caucus. In just two years, the CSC grew from 20 members at the beginning of the 115th Congress to 90 members by the end of 2018, which means that 45

---

[23] "Republican Climate Change Resolution Introduce in the House," office of Representative Elise Stefanik, last modified March 15, 2017, http://stefanik.house.gov/media-center/press-releases/republican-climate-change-resolution-introduced-house.

[24] "HR 195 – Expressing the Commitment of the House of Representatives to Conservative Environmental Stewardship," United States Congress, accessed August 12, 2018, http://congress.gov/bill/115th-congress/house-resolution/195/cosponsors.

[25] Emily Wirzba, "A Noah's Ark for Congress," Friends Committee on National Legislation, last modified July 24, 2018, http://fcnl.org/updates/a-noah-s-ark-for-congress-1564.

House Republicans have put themselves on the record affirming that climate change is real and requires congressional action.

A House caucus alone won't stop climate change, especially because the CSC doesn't require its members to support any particular legislation or policy solution. But it's undeniable that as more Republicans have taken a public stand on climate change, more of them have taken tough votes against their party on climate, signed onto climate legislation, and some have even introduced ambitious bills of their own. The following stories offer a few examples.

In May 2017, 11 CSC members voted to protect the Bureau of Land Management's natural gas waste rule, which limits the venting and flaring of methane on public lands. This was enough to provide political cover to three Senate Republicans, who voted with Senate Democrats to uphold the rule.[26] In July of 2017, CSC members played a pivotal role in protecting language in the National Defense Authorization Act for FY 2018 (HR 2810) that recognizes climate change as a direct threat to our national security and allows the Department of Defense to report on its vulnerabilities to climate impacts.[27] CSC members played a key behind-the-scenes role in ensuring that smaller renewable energy tax credits—like combined heat and power, microturbine, and small wind—were included in the budget deal that was signed into law earlier in 2018.[28]

CSC members are also introducing their own legislative solutions. Rep. John Faso (R-NY-19) and Rep. Dan Lipinski (D-IL-03) introduced H.R. 5031, the Challenges & Prizes for Climate Act, which establishes a Department of Energy "Climate Solutions Challenges" program to fund clean energy prize competitions with direct benefits to the climate.[29]

Also notable is the introduction of the MARKET CHOICE Act in July 2018. Introduced by Rep. Curbelo and Rep. Brian Fitzpatrick (R-PA-08), the MARKET CHOICE Act is the first major Republican-led climate bill in almost a decade. It would establish a carbon tax to incentivize clean energy consumption, fund our nation's infrastructure, and reduce greenhouse gas emissions. The bill isn't perfect, and important questions remain unanswered. But there is no

---

[26] "Natural Gas Waste Rule Upheld," Friends Committee on National Legislation, last modified May 10, 2017, http://fcnl.org/updates/natural-gas-waste-rule-upheld-814.

[27] Emily Wirzba, "Climate Win in the NDAA," Friends Committee on National Legislation, last modified July 14, 2017, http://fcnl.org/updates/climate-win-in-the-ndaa-937.

[28] David Burton, "Bipartisan Budget Act Partially Reinstates Orphaned Energy Tax Credits," Tax Equity Times, last modified February 15, 2018, http://taxequitytimes.com/2018/02/bipartisan-budget-act-partially-reinstates-orphaned-energy-tax-credits/.

[29] Emily Wirzba, "FCNL Applauds Challenges and Prizes for Climate Act," Friends Committee on National Legislation, last modified February 15, 2018, http://fcnl.org/updates/fcnl-applauds-challenges-and-prizes-for-climate-act-1262.

doubt this ambitious bill would do a great deal to address climate change.[30] An analysis by Columbia University determined that the bill would reduce greenhouse gas emissions by 30-40% from 2005 levels.[31] This exceeds the goals set by the Paris Climate Agreement.

Several months later, in November 2018, the Energy Innovation and Carbon Dividends Act of 2018 was introduced, the first-ever bipartisan carbon tax. Led by Rep. Deutch, Rep. Fitzpatrick, Rep. Francis Rooney (R-FL-19), Rep. John Delaney (D-MD-06), and Rep. Charlie Crist (D-FL-13), this ambitious bill establishes a carbon tax with 100% of the net revenue returned to households in the form of a dividend. According to FCNL's analysis, the bill would reduce greenhouse gas emissions by 90% by 2050, and marks a serious contribution to the climate policy arena.[32]

The MARKET CHOICE Act and the Energy Innovation and Carbon Dividends Act of 2018 come just two years after every Republican in Congress voted for a resolution saying that a carbon tax would hurt the economy, including Rep. Curbelo. A similar resolution against a carbon tax passed again in 2018, but this time garnered six Republican defections.[33] While we have a long way to go, the cracks in the partisan bulwark are growing. Increasingly, Republicans in Congress want to work with Democrats to devise bipartisan solutions to climate change. While over half the Republican members of the CSC will not be returning to Congress in 2019, due to retirements and lost elections, including co-founder Rep. Carlos Curbelo (R-FL-26), there is still a robust group of bipartisan legislators committed to the work of the CSC in the 116th Congress.

IV. The Important Role of Constituents

FCNL has been working persistently and prophetically for bipartisan climate action for more than a decade, but none of this progress would be possible without engaged constituents who have refused to let their members of Congress toe the party line on climate. Just about every House Republican who has joined the

---

[30] Emily Wirzba, "The MARKET CHOICE Act," Friends Committee on National Legislation, last modified July 23, 2018, http://fcnl.org/updates/the-market-choice-act-1558.

[31] Noah Kaufman et al., "Emissions, Energy, and Economic Implications of the Curbelo Carbon Tax Proposal," Columbia University Center of Global Energy Policy, last modified July 19, 2018, http://energypolicy.columbia.edu/research/report/emissions-energy-and-economic-implications-curbelo-carbon-tax-proposal.

[32] Bill Analysis: The Energy Innovation and Carbon Dividend Act of 2018 (HR 7173) (Washington, DC: Friends Committee on National Legislation), November 27, 2018, http://fcnl.org/documents/783

[33] Nick Sobczyk, "House Kicks off Partisan Fight on Carbon Tax," E&E News, last modified July 18, 2018, http://eenews.net/stories/1060089427.

Climate Solutions Caucus has said that they did so at the urging of constituents who built relationships with them and their staff. Those constituents could have easily looked at their representative's political party and given up. Instead, they chose to believe that their representatives could see reason, would yield to evidence, and could be moved by moral calls to action. They spoke with a vocabulary their representatives could understand: words of faith and examples of why climate action matters for the economy.

Regardless of where your members of Congress stand on climate change, you can always convince them to do just a little bit more. If your representative has refused to acknowledge that climate change is happening and human-caused, you can continue to bear witness to the facts and evidence and share your personal stories of how climate change is already impacting your community. If your member of Congress is already a climate champion, you can implore them to use their relationships with their colleagues across the aisle to foster bipartisan action. Either way, you have the power to form a relationship with them and be a presence that reminds Congress to whom they are accountable.

During his meeting with middle school students from Newtown Friends Meeting, Rep. Fitzpatrick did something surprising: he listened intently. For 40 minutes, he listened as the students shared stories about why climate change mattered to them. One boy said that he was worried that climate disruption would keep him from playing soccer by intensifying his asthma. One girl thanked Rep. Fitzpatrick for supporting efforts to clean up a park where she and her friends liked to play.[34]

After listening, he did something even more surprising. He acted. During the meeting, Rep. Fitzpatrick agreed to cosponsor HR 5314, the Preparedness and Risk Management for Extreme Weather Patterns Assuring Resilience Act of 2014 (the PREPARE Act), a bipartisan bill that seeks to strategically address the many environmental and economic risks from extreme weather events.[35] It wasn't just one successful meeting, it was the beginning of a powerful relationship. The following year, Rep. Fitzpatrick met with the students two more times, and ultimately became one of the original cosponsors of the Republican Climate Resolution and an early member of the Climate Solutions Caucus. Can one delegation of middle school students take all the credit? Probably not.

---

[34] Aguto and Wirzba, "Affirming."

[35] Emily Wirzba, "FCNL Welcomes the Bipartisan PREPARE Act," Friends Committee on National Legislation, last modified November 2, 2017, http://fcnl.org/updates/fcnl-welcomes-the-bipartisan-prepare-act-1119.

But if it weren't for constituents from congressional districts around the US urging their members of Congress to act on climate, Rep. Fitzpatrick would never have had the chance.

FCNL relies on constituents like these students to speak up for climate action. All are welcome to get involved! Individuals and groups can participate in FCNL's work for an Earth restored by coming to lobby with us in DC, lobbying your local congressional offices in your hometowns, or sharing stories of work you're already doing to address climate change.[36]

---

[36] Get involved at http://fcnl.org/energy.

Part IV: Stories of Sustainability: Individuals and Organizations Living Quaker Ecotheology in Action – Discussion Questions

1. **Chapter 18. Earthcare as a Quaker Value: The Formation and Continued Work of Quaker Earthcare Witness, by Shelley Tanenbaum**

    1. Tanenbaum suggests earthcare is an expression of Quaker testimonies such as peace and equality. How might earthcare be an expression of some of the other Quaker testimonies such as simplicity, integrity, and community? Do you agree with the inclusion of another testimony to the "SPICE" acronym, that of stewardship? Why or why not?

    2. What is most interesting or inspiring to you regarding the work of Quaker Earthcare Witness?

2. **Chapter 19. Earth Quaker Action Team: Reclaiming the Lamb's War for Justice and Sustainability in the Twenty-First Century, by Walter Hjelt Sullivan**

    1. Does EQAT's success with instigating change in PNC Bank's policy impact how you think activist groups should go about achieving their goals? If so, how?

    2. Do you think it would be beneficial for other grassroots campaigns to target private corporations instead of politicians? Why or why not? What other targets can you imagine being effective for groups interested in encouraging environmental justice?

    3. What are some of the ways that BLAM! and other EQAT campaigns embody the ideals of the Lamb's War?

    4. What might be some of the reasons nonviolent direct action tactics are often successful?

3. **Chapter 20. Collective Discernment at Quaker Institute for the Future, by Judy Lumb**

    1. What do you think would be the benefits of writing a book about sustainability and environmental justice using Circles of Discernment, conference calls, worship-sharing, and Meetings for Worship for the Conduct of Research, compared to an individual writing such a text on their own?

    2. What are some relevant topics surrounding the environmental crisis that could be addressed at a QIF Circle of Discernment that haven't been addressed yet?

    3. How can you imagine research functioning differently when the researcher is involved in a Circle of Discernment? How might this practice change the way you approach research?

4. **Chapter 21. How Aotearoa New Zealand Quakers Care for the Planet, by Robert Howell**

    1. In what ways are New Zealand Friends striving toward Boulding's "spaceship economy"?

    2. How does this compare to Friends and other groups from the rest of the world, and in your own context?

5. **Chapter 22. The Building of a Collective Conviction Among Quakers Around Sustainability: Friends World Committee for Consultation, by Susanna Mattingly**

    1. In what way(s) does the FWCC sustainability movement reflect social movements led by Quakers in the past?

    2. What are some of the reasons that lifestyle differences between the Global North and Global South make it difficult to address climate change on a worldwide level?

    3. In what ways (if any) might the increasing globalization of societies worldwide affect FWCC's climate change prevention efforts?

6. **Chapter 23. Practicing Quaker Stewardship: One Student's Experience Implementing Recycling and Food Waste Reduction Programs at Wilmington College, by April Mays**

    1. Using April Mays's student-driven sustainability initiatives as examples, how might other environmental issues be addressed through grassroots approaches, or how might similar issues regarding recycling and food waste reduction be addressed on your own campus, meetinghouse property, or other area under your care?

    2. Why are stories like April Mays's so important when talking about solving the numerous issues that pertain to sustainability and the environment?

    3. What challenges emerge when attempting to implement sustainability programs in communities largely composed of those who were not raised with ecocentric worldviews? What are some ways to address these challenges?

7. **Chapter 24. Lobbying for an Earth Restored: Friends Committee on National Legislation, by Emily Wirzba and Emmett Witkovsky-Eldred**

    1. Do you agree with FCNL's bipartisan approach to environmental legislation? What are the positives and negatives of this approach?

    2. In keeping with the Friends traditions of speaking truth to power and also of listening together until there is unity, what is the place of compromise or incremental progress, particularly in relation to climate change legislation?

8. **Part IV General Questions**

1. Describe the similarities and differences between the approaches to Quaker-informed sustainability and environmental justice projects represented in these six stories.

2. Which organization or approach are you most drawn to? Why?

3. Having read these stories of individuals and organizations expressing their understanding of Quaker values in action, what themes do you notice?

4. In what ways do you feel called to new action to care for the earth, or in what ways do you feel inspired by these stories to continue the actions you are already doing?

APPENDICES

Appendix A: "Toward a Testimony on Conscious Stewardship," Palo Alto (California) Friends Meeting, 1984: first known statement from Friends relating to environmental concerns[1]

Palo Alto (California) Friends Meeting
Toward a Testimony on Conscious Stewardship
(approved June 1984)

Pacific Yearly Meeting is urged by Palo Alto Monthly Meeting to study the landmark series of articles by Marshall Massey (*Friends Bulletin*, Vol. 52, Nos. 6-9, March–June, 1984) and then to set about the task of implementing Friend Massey's recommendations, on which the very survival of life on this earth may depend. Three environmental crises loom before us:

- Limits to the carrying capacity of the land.
- Increasing rates of species becoming extinct and marked decrease in the diversity of life forms.
- Disruption of the carbon dioxide-oxygen balance, caused by our burning of fossil fuels.

Palo Alto Meeting suggests an umbrella organization that might be called "Trustees for Planet Earth" to carry this concern to the Religious Society of Friends and to other socially conscious groups, who can well unite to carry the message to people everywhere—that we can reverse our present downward spiral if we enlist the positive forces already at work; that we can re-educate ourselves to greater awareness of the consequences of our use of Earth's resources; that we can put all this forward as a new and vital Testimony, proposing a conscious stewardship of the riches entrusted to us.

---

[1] Although this is the first minute related to the environment and sustainability of which we are aware, earlier statements may exist. A number of other meetings and yearly meetings approved minutes relating to environmental concerns and sustainability in the 1990s and 2000s. A collection of these statements can be found on the Friends World Committee for Consultation website. See Appendix G.

Appendix B: "Environment and Sustainability Minute," Friends World Committee for Consultation (FWCC), 22nd FWCC Triennial in Dublin, Ireland, 2007

22/31 Working Group on Environment and Sustainability — Report The Working Group met to respond to concerns submitted by Australia, Chavakali, Central and Southern Africa, East Africa, Netherlands, New England and Ohio Valley Yearly Meetings and Hong Kong Monthly Meeting. It has brought us two minutes to be submitted to the CEC [Central Executive Committee], commending to the Sections the model of Trees for Africa adopted by Netherlands Friends as a way of compensating for air travel to FWCC meetings, and suggesting to QUNO [Quaker United Nations Office] to increase attention to the environment by possibly appointing a staff person to work on environmental issues. The statement included in a third minute was welcomed and the group was asked to do further work and return it to a later session.

22/39 Working Group on Environment and Sustainability — Report (continued)
Further to minute 22/31, we have received a revised statement. We adopt it with amendments as follows:

Environment and Sustainability

We believe it is vital to address the threat to life on Earth posed by environmental destruction.

We believe that we have a duty of responsible stewardship to all of God's creation, although we recognize we do not always achieve it fully. When we damage the natural world and its creatures, we damage God's creation. Reverence for human life cannot be separated from maintaining the integrity and health of the ecology of our planet.

Competition for land, water and other precious resources is leading to wars and ecological disasters. Overuse and misuse of resources is not sustainable.

We call upon all the peoples and governments of the world to recognise the equal worth of all people, the integral worth of the natural world and to work together for the common good of all the earth community.

Appendix C: The Purpose of Quaker Earthcare Witness

The Purpose of Quaker Earthcare Witness

To search and to help others to search
for that life which affirms
the unity of all creation.

To apply and to help others to apply
Friends' practice to live in
deep communion with all life spirit.

To be guided by and to help others to be guided by
the Light within us
to participate in the healing of the earth.

To provide resources, networking, and support
to yearly and monthly meetings of the Religious Society of Friends,
and to others of whatever persuasion; to help them in their search
for effective ways to achieve the above objectives.

To provide a reflective and energetic forum
that will strengthen and deepen that spiritual unity with nature
which values the integrity, diversity, and continuity of life on earth.

Appendix D: Quaker Earthcare Vision and Witness

WE ARE CALLED to live in right relationship with all Creation, recognizing that the entire world is interconnected and is a manifestation of God

WE WORK to integrate into the beliefs and practices of the Religious Society of Friends the Truth that God's Creation is to be respected, protected, and held in reverence in its own right, and the Truth that human aspirations for peace and justice depend upon restoring the earth's ecological integrity.

WE PROMOTE these Truths by being patterns and examples, by communicating our message, and by providing spiritual and material support to those engaged in the compelling task of transforming our relationship to the earth.

Appendix E: "Minute on Nuclear Power," Quaker Earthcare Witness, Burlington, Vermont, USA, 2007

Quaker Earthcare Witness cannot support nuclear power as part of the solution to harmful climate change.

As Friends, our peace testimony has long led us to witness against nuclear power because of its connection to nuclear war. Our deep caring for all creation leads us to affirm that witness, even in the face of growing calls for an expansion of nuclear power.

Based on everything we know about the current state of nuclear technology and our understanding of its impact and risks for people and the earth, we are strongly opposed—for moral, spiritual, and practical reasons—to current efforts to increase nuclear power. Additionally, we are strongly opposed to subsidies for funding new nuclear power plants, including proposed loan guarantees such as those in energy bills currently being considered by the U.S. Congress.

While nuclear power produces no greenhouse gases during electricity generation, in fact significant amounts of greenhouse gases are emitted when the complete cycle of nuclear power—from mining, milling, enrichment of uranium, transportation of nuclear fuel, and removal and guarding of nuclear wastes, as well as construction of nuclear power plants—is considered.

Nuclear power is extremely expensive when all costs, including subsidies, are included. We believe that funds proposed for more nuclear power plants would be far more effective in reducing greenhouse gas emissions if used for energy efficiency, conservation, and renewable power.

Nuclear power is closely linked to the war machine in many countries. The cumulative effects of radioactive waste from nuclear power will be lethal, carcinogenic, and mutagenic to humans and all species for hundreds of thousands of years. Finally, given nuclear power's unique destructiveness, the risk of just one catastrophic accident anywhere in the world renders nuclear power unacceptable.

QEW also affirms that providing more energy to support unconstrained economic growth is neither inevitable nor desirable.

We accept the responsibility of working for all socially responsible and environmentally sound solutions to global climate change, including phasing-out the use of oil, coal, and gas; and increasing energy efficiency, energy conservation; and renewable sources of energy. We accept the responsibility for using less energy in all that we do and for working to make reduction of energy use a goal for society at large.

Approved by the Steering Committee of Quaker Earthcare Witness in session, October 14, 2007, Burlington, Vermont.

(Jack Bradin, SEYM, wishes to be recorded as standing aside.)

Appendix F: "The Kabarak Call for Peace and Ecojustice," Friends World Committee for Consultation, Sixth World Conference of Friends at Kabarak University near Nakuru, Kenya, 2012

The Kabarak Call for Peace and Ecojustice

The Kabarak Call for Peace and Ecojustice was approved on 24 April 2012 at the Sixth World Conference Friends, held at Kabarak University near Nakuru, Kenya. It is the culmination of the FWCC World Consultation on Global Change which was held in 2010 and 2011.

In past times God's Creation restored itself. Now humanity dominates, our growing population consuming more resources than nature can replace. We must change, we must become careful stewards of all life. Earthcare unites traditional Quaker testimonies: peace, equality, simplicity, love, integrity, and justice. Jesus said, "As you have done unto the least... you have done unto me". We are called to work for the peaceable Kingdom of God on the whole earth, in right sharing with all peoples. However few our numbers, we are called to be the salt that flavours and preserves, to be a light in the darkness of greed and destruction.

We have heard of the disappearing snows of Kilimanjaro and glaciers of Bolivia, from which come life-giving waters. We have heard appeals from peoples of the Arctic, Asia and Pacific. We have heard of forests cut down, seasons disrupted, wildlife dying, of land hunger in Africa, of new diseases, droughts, floods, fires, famine and desperate migrations – this climatic chaos is now worsening. There are wars and rumors of war, job loss, inequality and violence. We fear our neighbors. We waste our children's heritage.

All of these are driven by our dominant economic systems – by greed not need, by worship of the market, by Mammon and Caesar.

Is this how Jesus showed us to live?

- ❖ We are called to see what love can do: to love our neighbor as ourselves, to aid the widow and orphan, to comfort the afflicted and afflict the comfortable, to appeal to consciences and bind the wounds.
- ❖ We are called to teach our children right relationship, to live in harmony with each other and all living beings in the earth, waters and sky of our Creator, who asks, "Where were you when I laid the foundations of the world?" (Job 38:4)
- ❖ We are called to do justice to all and walk humbly with our God, to cooperate lovingly with all who share our hopes for the future of the earth.
- ❖ We are called to be patterns and examples in a 21st century campaign for peace and ecojustice, as difficult and decisive as the 18th and 19th century drive to abolish slavery.

We dedicate ourselves to let the living waters flow through us – where we live, regionally, and in wider world fellowship. We dedicate ourselves to building the peace that passeth all understanding, to the repair of the world, opening our lives to the Light to guide us in each small step.

Bwana asifiwe. A pu Dios Awqui. Gracias Jesús. Jubilé. Salaam aleikum. Migwetch. Tikkun olam. Alleluia!

Appendix G: "Statement on the Doctrine of Discovery," Quaker Earthcare Witness, 2012

In the days of European exploration and colonization, governments relied on what we now call the Doctrine of Discovery to extinguish all rights of indigenous peoples. The doctrine has not disappeared or been revoked. Instead it has evolved into common property law, providing the underpinning of US and Canadian chains of title.

In 2012 the UN Permanent Forum on Indigenous Issues (UNPFII) will focus on encouraging global repudiation of the Doctrine of Discovery.

The Indigenous Peoples are our allies in protecting the Earth, and we need to be theirs. There is much to be learned from indigenous earth-connected wisdom and spirituality. We renounce what amounts to a policy of domination and instead join with indigenous people to protect and restore the health of our planet.

Quaker Earthcare Witness (QEW) joins other Friends, and Unitarian and Episcopal churches in repudiating the Doctrine of Discovery. We encourage Friends' Monthly Meetings and Churches, and Yearly Meetings, to renounce the Doctrine of Discovery.

Approved by the Quaker Earthcare Witness Steering Committee, January 9, 2012.

Appendix H: "Facing the Challenge of Climate Change: A shared statement by Quaker groups," Quaker United Nations Office, Quaker Earthcare Witness, and Friends Committee on National Legislation, 2015

Dear Friends worldwide,

The Statement below was developed by Quaker Earthcare Witness, the Quaker United Nations Office, and Friends Committee on National Legislation for their joint presence at events during the UN Climate Summit in September 2014.

A number of fellow Quaker organizations wished to add their name, including FWCC, which sent the Statement out to Quaker communities worldwide. As a result, we continue to receive signatures which we add to the Statement, uploading the most recent versions onto the QEW, FCNL and QUNO websites.

The Statement was originally written as a 'witness' of our role in anthropogenic climate change. Its aim was to inspire personal and community action; it was not meant to define a universal action, since the situation of Quakers worldwide is not universal. However, QUNO has produced a booklet describing individual Quaker actions, *A Call to Conscience*, which is available on its website, and we encourage you to write if your Meeting commits to community-wide action. We are also helping develop a resource for Quaker action on climate change.

The attached Statement was revised in January 2015 to reflect the following concerns: that it have longer life by being non-date specific to continue its relevance, and that the language be less anthropocentric and more strongly acknowledge the grave dangers we face from climate change. It was revised in August 2015, to add the word 'anthropogenic' in clarifying the statement relating greenhouse gas emissions to the combustion of fossil fuels on the second page.

We have attempted to do this, while holding to the core message that Quaker organizations and Meetings have already upheld and signed.

If you wish to add your Meeting to this Statement, please contact Lindsey Cook as suggested at the end of the Statement.

If you do not wish to sign, but wish to use this material as a base for a Meeting-specific Statement, you are most welcome, but please take off the signatures.

In peace and with gratitude,

QEW, QUNO and FCNL
August 2015

Facing the Challenge of Climate Change
A shared statement by Quaker groups
January 2015

"It would go a long way to caution and direct people in their use of the world, that they were better studied and knowing in the Creation of it. For how could [they] find the confidence to abuse it, while they should see the great Creator stare them in the face, in all and every part of it?"

William Penn, 1693

As Quakers, we are called to work for the peaceable Kingdom of God on the whole Earth, in right sharing with all peoples.[2] We recognize a moral duty to cherish Creation for future generations.

We call on our leaders to make the radical decisions needed to create a fair, sufficient and effective international climate change agreement.

As Quakers, we understand anthropogenic climate change (climate change due to human activities) to be a symptom of a greater challenge: how to live sustainably and justly on this Earth.

We recognize that the current rise of greenhouse gas emissions is leading to an unprecedented rate of increase in global average surface temperature of extreme detriment to the Earth's ecosystems and species, including human beings.

---

[2] Kabarak Call to Peace and Ecojustice, 2012, Appendix C in the current volume.

We recognize that catastrophic global climate change is not inevitable if we choose to act urgently.

We recognize a personal and collective responsibility to ensure that the poorest and most vulnerable peoples now, and all our future generations, do not suffer as a consequence of our actions. We see this as a call to conscience.

We recognize the connections between climate change and global economic injustice as well as unprecedented levels of consumption, and question assumptions of unlimited material growth on a planet with limited natural resources.

We recognize that most anthropogenic greenhouse gas emissions are created by fossil fuel combustion. We recognize that our increasing population continues to pursue fossil fuel-dependent economic growth. We recognize that the Earth holds more fossil fuel reserves than are safe to burn, and that the vast majority of fossil fuel reserves must remain in the ground if we are to prevent the catastrophic consequences of climate change. We therefore question profoundly the continued investment in, and subsidizing of, fossil fuel extraction.

We seek to nurture a global human society that prioritizes the well-being of people over profit, and lives in right relationship with our Earth; a peaceful world with fulfilling employment, clean air and water, renewable energy, and healthy thriving communities and ecosystems.

As members of this beautiful human family, we seek meaningful commitments from our leaders and ourselves, to address climate change for our shared future, the Earth and all species, and the generations to come. We see this Earth as a stunning gift that supports life. It is our only home. Let us care for it together.

Quakers in Ghana
Quakers in Britain
Living Witness, UK
EcoQuakers Ireland
Quakers in Australia
Quakers in Denmark
Ireland Yearly Meeting
Norway Yearly Meeting
Quaker Service Australia

Canadian Yearly Meeting
Netherlands Yearly Meeting
Pacific Yearly Meeting, USA
Miami Friends Meeting, USA
Quaker Institute for the Future
Northern Yearly Meeting, USA
Lake Erie Yearly Meeting, USA
York Friends Meeting, PA, USA
Memphis Friends Meeting, USA
New York Yearly Meeting, USA
Storrs Friends Meeting, CT, USA
Quaker Concern for Animals, UK
Davis Friends Meeting, CA, USA
Quaker Earthcare Witness (QEW)
Newtown Monthly Meeting, USA
Croton Valley Meeting, NY, USA
Valley Friends Meeting, VA, USA
Quakers in Aotearoa New Zealand
FWCC- Asia West Pacific Section
Cookeville Monthly Meeting, USA
Eugene Friends Meeting, OR, USA
Oak Park Friends Meeting, IL, USA
New England Yearly Meeting, USA
Winnipeg Monthly Meeting, Canada
Northside Friends Meeting, IL, USA
Duneland Friends Meeting, IN, USA
Lafayette Friends Meeting, IN, USA
Herndon Friends Meeting, VA, USA
Berkeley Friends Meeting, CA, USA
Princeton Friends Meeting, NJ, USA
Patuxent Friends Meeting, MD, USA
Nashville Friends Meeting, TN, USA
Trenton Meeting of Friends, NJ, USA
Bethesda Friends Meeting, MD, USA
Honolulu Monthly Meeting, HI, USA
Palo Alto Friends Meeting, CA, USA
Abingdon Friends Meeting, VA, USA
Baltimore Yearly Meeting, MD, USA
Frederick Friends Meeting, MD, USA

Humboldt Friends Meeting, CA, USA
Eau Claire Friends Meeting, WI, USA
Annapolis Friends Meeting, MD, USA
Mattaponi Friends Meeting, VA, USA
Santa Fe Monthly Meeting, NM, USA
Rochester Friends Meeting, MN, USA
Gettysburg Friends Meeting, PA, USA
Richmond Friends Meeting, VA, USA
Anchorage Friends Meeting, AK, USA
Geneva Monthly Meeting, Switzerland
Westtown Monthly Meeting, PN, USA
Joseph Rowntree Charitable Trust, UK
University Friends Meeting, WA, USA
Woodbrooke Quaker Study Centre, UK
Blacksburg Friends Meeting, VA, USA
Liskeard Local Meeting, Cornwall, UK
Quaker United Nations Office (QUNO)
Midlothian Friends Meeting, VA, USA
Jacksonville Friends Meeting, FL, USA
Ohio Valley Yearly Meeting, OH, USA
Sacramento Friends Meeting, CA, USA
Twin Cities Friends Meeting, MN, USA
Gunpowder Friends Meeting, MD, USA
Homewood Friends Meeting, MD, USA
Haddonfield Monthly Meeting, NJ, USA
Langley Hill Friends Meeting, VA, USA
Chena Ridge Friends Meeting, AK, USA
Maury River Friends Meeting, VA, USA
Salmon Bay Friends Meeting, WA, USA
Belgium & Luxembourg Yearly Meeting
FWCC - Europe and Middle East Section
Northampton Friends Meeting, MA, USA
Prospect Hill Friends Meeting, MN, USA
Little Falls Meeting of Friends, MD, USA
Minneapolis Monthly Meeting, MN, USA
Chesapeake Quarterly Meeting, MD, USA
Monongalia Friends Meeting, WVA, USA
Santa Monica Monthly Meeting, CA, USA
Charlottesville Friends Meeting, VA, USA

Sandy Spring Monthly Meeting, MD, USA
Yellow Springs Friends Meeting, OH, USA
Dunnings Creek Friends Meeting, PA, USA
Whidbey Island Friends Meeting, WA, USA
Yonge Street Monthly Meeting, Ontario, CA
Delta Monthly Meeting, Stockton, CA, USA
Canadian Friends Service Committee (CFSC)
Edinburgh Universities' Quaker Society, SCT
Quaker Council for European Affairs (QCEA)
American Friends Service Committee (AFSC)
Quaker City Unity Friends Meeting, NH, USA
Strawberry Creek Monthly Meeting, CA, USA
Société Religieuse des Amis (Quakers), France
Eggemoggin Reach Monthly Meeting, ME, USA
Mid-Ohio Valley Friends Meeting, OH/WV, USA
Baltimore Monthly Meeting, Stony Run, MD, USA
Friends Committee on National Legislation (FCNL)
Friends World Committee for Consultation (FWCC)
Goose Creek Monthly Meeting of Friends, VA, USA
South Central Yearly Meeting (TX, OK, AR, LA), USA

Please contact Lindsey Cook at lfcook@quno.ch if you need more information, or wish to add your Quaker group.

Latest signature updated: September 2017

Appendix I: "Living Sustainably and Sustaining Life on Earth — The Minute from the Plenary," Friends World Committee for Consultation, World Plenary Meeting of Friends, Pisac, Perú, 2016

IRM 16-20. Sustainability. The Consultation on Sustainability, facilitated by Jonathan Woolley (Mexico City MM/Pacific YM; Staff, QUNO-Geneva), Rachel Madenyika (Staff, QUNO-NY), and Charlotte Gordon (Aotearoa/New Zealand YM) have presented a minute for our consideration:

Living Sustainably and Sustaining Life on Earth

The Light of Christ has inspired Quakers throughout the generations. As we gather together in Pisac, Peru in 2016, we feel this light stronger than ever in our calling to care for the Earth on which we live. It is calling us from all traditions: programmed, unprogrammed, liberal, and evangelical. It calls us to preserve this Earth for our children, our grandchildren and all future generations to come, working as though life were to continue for 10,000 years to come. *Be ready for action with your robes hitched up and your lamps alight. (Luke 12:35, Revised English Bible)*

Our faith as Quakers is inseparable from our care for the health of our planet Earth. We see that our misuse of the Earth's resources creates inequality, destroys community, affects health and well-being, leads to war and erodes our integrity. We are all responsible for stewardship of our natural world. We love this world as God's gift to us all. Our hearts are crying for our beloved mother Earth, who is sick and in need of our care.

We are at a historical turning point. Internationally, the Paris Agreement and the Sustainable Development Goals oblige governments to take action. Faith groups and other civil society are playing a major role. As Quakers, we are part of this movement. The FWCC World Conference approved the Kabarak Call for Peace and Ecojustice in April 2012, while the FWCC World Office was a signatory to the Quaker statement on climate change in 2014 and divested from fossil fuels in June 2015.

We recognise that the environmental crisis is a symptom of a wider crisis in our political and economic systems. Our loving and well informed environmental actions as Friends, consistent with our spiritual values, must therefore work to transform these systems.

Many of us all over the Quaker world are taking practical actions as individuals and communities. At this Plenary, a consultation of more than sixty Friends from all over the world worked to build on these leadings with further practical action. The Annex attached to these minutes shows examples of what Friends are doing already or propose to do.

We must redouble our efforts right now. We must move beyond our individual and collective comfort zones and involve the worldwide Quaker community and others of like mind. Just as Jesus showed us, real change requires us to challenge ourselves to be effective instruments of change. We can do more.

On recommendation of this Consultation, and after some discussion, we adopt the following minute:

In this effort for sustainability, and mindful of the urgency of this work, this Plenary asks the FWCC World Office and Central Executive Committee to:

1. **Invest FWCC World funds ethically.**
2. **Share Quaker experiences with other faith groups** to inspire them to action, especially through the World Council of Churches.
3. **Seek ways of connecting Friends worldwide that are sustainable.**
4. **Facilitate dissemination of training materials on sustainability issues** for Quaker leaders, pastors and teachers.

This FWCC Plenary Meeting also asks all Yearly Meetings to:

1. **Initiate at least two concrete actions** on sustainability within the next 12 months. These may build on existing projects of individuals or monthly meetings or they may be new initiatives. We ask that they encourage Young Friends to play key roles. We ask that meetings minute the progress and results, so as to share them with FWCC and Quaker meetings.

2. **Support individuals and groups in their meetings** who feel called to take action on sustainability.

3. **Support the work done by Quaker organisations** such as the Quaker United Nations Office and the Quaker Council for European Affairs to ensure that international agreements and their implementation support sustainability.

This FWCC Plenary Meeting asks individual Friends and groups (such as Monthly Meetings, Worship Groups and ad hoc groups within Meetings) to **share inspiring experiences of living sustainably** [by emailing the FWCC World Office, sustainability@fwcc.world.] This [FWCC sustainability] webpage can be used as a source of ideas, inspiration and action [http://fwcc.world/sustainability-resources].

Annex to the Minute: Possibilities for practical sustainability action from the Pisac consultation

Individuals can:

1. Dedicate personal time to nature.
2. Reduce consumption and use your consumer buying power to create change.
3. Cut down on meat consumption, be aware of energy costs in production and transport of all foods and methane from ruminant animals, support sustainable agriculture.
4. Travel — cycle, walk, use public transport or alternatives to private cars, keep air travel to a minimum.
5. Grow your own food and plant trees.
6. Be politically active in promoting sustainability concerns.
7. Share environmental concerns through books, publications, conversations, electronic media
8. Reduce energy use.

9. Use less water and harvest water.
10. Make time for spiritual connection with God.

Monthly Meetings, Worship Groups and small groups within Meetings can:
1. Live in a community, share housing, participate in a transition town movement.
2. Educate yourself and others.
3. Share transport and equipment.
4. Develop urban agriculture, community gardens, community supported agriculture, tree planting.
5. Love nature and encourage others to do so: we protect the things we love; get children out in nature; take care of nature around your meeting house (e.g., picking up trash/litter).
6. Invest ethically and divest from fossil fuels.
7. Ensure meeting houses are carbon neutral.
8. Build alliances, seek visibility, approach legislators.
9. Share sustainability skills.

Yearly Meetings can:
1. Support the sustainability actions of Monthly Meetings.
2. Build solidarity with local people.
3. Support Quakers in politics and international work.
4. Form support networks and alliances to make more impact — we can only do so much on our own.
5. Invest ethically, including on sustainability issues.
6. Practice what we preach.
7. Discern and move concerns to action.
8. Set targets for increased sustainability.
9. Connect and share with other YMs, direct or via FWCC Sections and World Office.

We recognise that different actions are relevant to different Quaker meetings in different parts of the world.

Appendix J: Resources Relating to Friends and Environmental Concerns on the Web

Earth Quaker Action Team (EQAT): http://eqat.org/

Friends Committee on National Legislation (FCNL)

- Environment and Energy, A Faithful and Moral Call to Conscience: http://fcnl.org/about/policy/issues/environment-energy
- "The World We Seek: FCNL's Statement of Legislative Policy," including Part 4: We Seek an Earth Restored: http://fcnl.org/updates/the-world-we-seek-25

Friends World Committee for Consultation (FWCC)

- Minutes and Statements from Friends Meetings and Organizations: http://fwcc.world/gcpastminutes
- Quaker case studies, sustainability in action: http://fwcc.world/sustainability-resources

Living Witness: Quakers for Sustainability: http://livingwitness.org.uk/

Quaker Earthcare Witness (QEW): http://quakerearthcare.org/

Quaker Institute for the Future (QIF): http://quakerinstitute.org/

Quaker United Nations Office (QUNO)

- Human Impacts of Climate Change: http://quno.org/areas-of-work/human-impacts-climate-change

Collated Bibliography

"1992 World Scientists' Warning to Humanity." Union of Concerned Scientists. Accessed January 2019. http://ucsusa.org/about/1992-world-scientists.html#.VHuZd6SUc5k.

2015 Annual Report: Unity with Nature Committee. Sandy Spring, MD: Baltimore Yearly Meeting. http://bym-rsf.org/what_we_do/committees/nature/unityrpts.html.

Abbott, Margery Post. *To Be Broken and Tender.* N.p.: Western Friend, Friends Bulletin Corporation, 2010.

Adams, Anne, compiler. *The Creation Was Open To Me: An Anthology of Friends' Writings on That of God in All Creation.* Suffolk: Lavenham Press, Quaker Green Concern, 1996.

Afrasiabi, Kaveh L. *Mahdism, Shiism, and Communicative Eco-Theology: Selected Articles in Comparative Theology.* Scotts Valley, CA: CreateSpace Independent Publishing Platform, 2015.

Allen, Beth. *Ground and Spring: Foundations of Quaker Discipleship.* London: Quaker Books, 2007.

American Friends Service Committee. "Bulletin No. 58. Sixth Annual Report, June lst, 1922–May 31st, 1923." *American Friends Service Committee Bulletin,* Issues 51–100. Google Books.

American Friends Service Committee. "Bulletin No. 59. Seventh Annual Report, June lst, 1923–May 31st, 1924." *American Friends Service Committee Bulletin,* Issues 51–100. Google Books.

American Friends Service Committee. "Bulletin No. 62. Eighth Annual Report, June lst, 1924–May 31st, 1925." *American Friends Service Committee Bulletin,* Issues 51–100. Google Books.

Anderson, Molly. "Higher education revisited: Sustainability science and teaching for sustainable food systems." In *Future of Food,* ed. Stephan Allbrecht. Munich: Green Books, 2016.

Angell, Stephen W., and Pink Dandelion, eds. *The Oxford Handbook of Quaker Studies.* Oxford: Oxford University Press, 2013.

Angell, Stephen W. "Quaker Women in Kenya and Human Rights Issues." In *Freedom's Distant Shores: American Protestants and Post-Colonial Alliances with Africa*, ed. R. Drew Smith, 111–130. Waco, TX: Baylor University Press, 2006.

Arendt, Hannah. *The Human Condition*. Chicago, IL: The University of Chicago Press, 1958, 1998.

Aristotle. *Ethics*, transl. J. A. K. Thomson. London: Penguin, 1948.

Augustine. *Sermons III (51-94)*, ed. John E. Rotelle, transl. Edmund Hill. Brooklyn, NY: New City, 1991.

Augustine. "The Writings Against the Manichaeans and Against the Donatists." In *Nicene and Post-Nicene Fathers*, ed. Philip Schaff, Vol. 4. Hendrickson Publishers, Inc., 1995.

Baltzell, E. Digby. *Puritan Boston and Quaker Philadelphia: Two Protestant Ethics and the Spirit of Class Authority and Leadership*. New York: Free Press, 1979.

Bamberger-Scott, Barbara. (2018). "Ruth Stout: The No-Dig Duchess." Homestead.org. Accessed February 2019. http://homestead.org/gardening/ruth-stout/.

Bamford, Christopher. *The Voice of the Eagle: The Heart of Celtic Christianity*. New edition. Great Barrington, MA: Lindisfarne Books, 2000.

Bane, Peter. *The Permaculture Handbook: Garden Farming for Town and Country*. Gabriola Island, BC: New Society Publishers, 2012.

Barbour, Hugh. *The Quakers in Puritan England*. New Haven and London: Yale University Press, 1964.

Barclay, Robert. *An Apology for the True Christian Divinity: Being an Explanation and Vindication of the Principles and Doctrines of the People Called Quakers*, ed. Edward Marsh. Eleventh edition. Google Books. London: Arthur Wallis, Printer and Bookseller, 1849.

Barclay, William. *The Revelation of John, Vol. 2*. Philadelphia, PA: Westminster Press, 1976.

Barnes, Kenneth. *The Creative Imagination*. London: George Allen and Unwin, Ltd., 1960.

Bartram, John, and Francis Harper. "Diary of a Journey through the Carolinas, Georgia, and Florida from July 1, 1765, to April 10, 1766." *Transactions of the American Philosophical Society* 33, no. 1 (1942). doi.org10.2307/1005551.

Bartram, William. *Travels Through North & South Carolina, Georgia, East & West Florida, The Cherokee Country, The Extensive Territories of the Muscogulges, or Creek Confederacy, and the Country of the Chactaws: Containing an Account of the Soil and Natural Productions of Those Regions, Together With Observations on the Manners of the Indians. Embellished with Copper-Plates.* Philadelphia: James & Johnson, 1791.

Bauman, Whitney. *Theology, Creation, and Environmental Ethics: From Creatio Ex Nihilo to Terra Nullius.* New York & London: Routledge, 2014.

Becker, Ernest. *The Denial of Death.* New York, NY: Free Press Paperbacks, 1973, 1997.

Beinhocker, Eric. *The Origin of Wealth.* Cambridge, MA: Harvard Business School Press, 2006.

Bell, Jr., Whitfield J. "John Bartram: A Biographical Sketch." In *America's Curious Botanist: A Tercentennial Reappraisal of John Bartram, 1699–1777*, eds. Nancy E. Hoffmann and John C. Van Horne, 3–20. Philadelphia: American Philosophical Society, 2004.

Benezet, Anthony. *The Pennsylvania Spelling-Book.* Third edition. Providence, RI: 1782.

Benjamin, Alison. "Stern: Climate change a market failure." *The Guardian*, November 29, 2007. Accessed January 2019. http://theguardian.com/environment/2007/nov/29/climatechange.carbonemissions.

Benson, Lewis. "'That of God in Every Man'—What Did George Fox Mean by it?" *Quaker Religious Thought* 24 (1970): 2–25. http://digitalcommons.georgefox.edu/qrt/vol24/iss1/2.

Bentham, Jeremy. *Introduction to the Principles of Morals and Legislation.* Oxford: Basil Blackwell, 1948.

Bercovitch, Sacvan. *The American Jeremiad.* University of Wisconsin Press, 1978.

Bergant, Dianne. "The Bible's Wisdom Tradition and Creation Theology." In *God, Creation, and Climate Change: A Catholic Response to the Environmental Crisis*, ed. Richard W. Miller, 35–48. Maryknoll: Orbis Books, 2010.

Berry, Thomas, with Thomas Clarke. *Befriending the Earth*. New London, CT: Twenty-Third Publications, 1991.

Berry, Thomas. *The Great Work: Our Way into the Future*. New York: Random House, 1999.

———. *The Sacred Universe: Earth, Spirituality, and Religion in the Twenty-first Century*. New York: Columbia University Press, 2009.

———. "The Universe Story: Its Religious Significance." In *The Greening of Faith: God, Environment and the Good Life*, eds. John E. Carroll, Paul Brockelman, and Mary Westfall, 208–218. Twentieth anniversary edition. Durham, NH: University of New Hampshire Press, 2016.

Birkel, Michael L. *A Near Sympathy: The Timeless Quaker Wisdom of John Woolman*. Friends United Press, 2003.

Blake, William. *The Complete Poetry and Prose of William Blake*, ed. David V. Erdman. Revised edition. Berkeley, CA: University of California Press, 1982.

———. *The Marriage of Heaven and Hell*. Boston: John W. Luce & Co., 1906.

Bock, Cherice. "Quaker Pneumatology." In *T & T Companion to Pneumatology*, eds. Daniel M. Castelo and Kenneth M. Loyer. London: Bloomsbury T & T Clark, forthcoming.

———. "Scarcity vs. Abundance: Moving Beyond Dualism to 'Enough.'" *Christian Feminism Today* (June 2015), http://eewc.com/scarcity-vs-abundance-moving-beyond-dualism-enough/.

Boehme, Jacob. *The Signature of All Things*, transl. John Sparrow. London: James Clarke, 1969.

Boulding, Kenneth. "The Economics of the Coming Spaceship Earth." In *Environmental Quality Issues in a Growing Economy*, ed. Henry Jarrett Baltimore, MD: Resources for the Future / Johns Hopkins University Press, 1966.

Bouma-Prediger, Stephen. *For the Beauty of the Earth: A Christian Vision for Creation Care*. Second edition. Grand Rapids: Baker Academic, 2010.

Braithwaite, William C. *Spiritual Guidance in the Experience of the Society of Friends*. London: Headley Brothers, 1909.

Brayshaw, Shipley N. *Unemployment and Plenty*. London: George Allen and Unwin, Ltd., 1933.

Breen, T. H. *The Marketplace of Revolution: How Consumer Politics Shaped American Independence*. New York: Oxford University Press, 2004.

Berners-Lee, Mike. *There Is No Planet B: A Handbook for the Make or Break Years*. Cambridge, UK: Cambridge University Press, 2019.

Brink, David O. "Mill's Moral and Political Philosophy." In *Stanford Encyclopedia of Philosophy*. Redwood City, CA: Metaphysics Research Lab, Stanford University, 2007. Accessed January 2019. http://plato.stanford.edu/ entries/mill-moral-political.

Brinton, Howard. H. *Ethical Mysticism in The Society of Friends*. Pendle Hill Pamphlet 156. Wallingford, PA: Pendle Hill Publications, 1967.

Brinton, Howard and Margaret Hope Bacon. *Friends for 350 Years: The History and Beliefs of the Society of Friends Since George Fox Started the Quaker Movement*. Wallingford, PA: Pendle Hill Publications, 2002.

Brooke, John and Geoffrey Cantor. *Reconstructing Nature: The Engagement of Science and Religion*. Edinburgh: T & T Clark, 1998.

Brookes, George S. *Friend Anthony Benezet*. Philadelphia: University of Pennsylvania Press, 1937.

Brown, Ellen. *Web of Debt: The Shocking Truth about Our Money System and How We Can Break Free*. Baton Rouge: Third Millennium Press, 2007.

———. *Public Bank Solution*. Baton Rouge: Third Millennium Press, 2013.

Brown, Peter G., et al. *Right Relationship: Building a Whole Earth Economy*. San Francisco: Berrett-Koehler Publishers, 2009.

Bruninga, Robert, with Judy Lumb, Frank Granshaw, and Charles Blanchard. *Energy Choices: Opportunities to Make Wise Decisions for a Sustainable Future*. Belize: Quaker Institute for the Future, 2018.

Brunner, Daniel L., Jennifer L. Butler, and A. J. Swoboda. *Introducing Evangelical Ecotheology: Foundations in Scripture, Theology, History, and Praxis*. Grand Rapids: Baker Academic, 2014.

Buber, Martin. *Tales of the Hasidim*. New York, NY: Schocken Books, 1947, 1991.

Cadbury, Deborah. *Chocolate Wars: The 150-Year Rivalry Between the World's Greatest Chocolate Makers*. New York: PublicAffairs, 2010.

Caganoff, Gary, dir. *Garden at the End of the World: Permaculture and the Forgotten, Teaching Permaculture in Places that Absolutely Need It, a Message of Hope with Rosemary Morrow*. Sydney, Australia: Lysis Films, 2009. Last updated 2019. http://thegardenattheendoftheworld.info/.

Callicott, J. Baird. *In Defense of the Land Ethic: Essays in Environmental Philosophy*. Albany: State University of New York, 1989.

Cama, Timothy. "PNC Bank restricts mountaintop removal financing." *The Hill*, March, 4, 2015, http://thehill.com/policy/energy-environment/234 550-pnc-bank-restricts-mountaintop-removal-financing.

Cantelon, P. L. and R. C. Williams. *Crisis Contained, The Department of Energy at Three Mile Island*. Carbondale, IL: Southern Illinois University Press, 1982.

Carabine, Deirdre. *John Scottus Eriugena*. New York: Oxford University Press, 2000.

Carnot, Sadi. *Reflections on the Motive Power of Heat*, ed. and transl. Robert Henry Thurston. New York: J. Wiley & Sons, 1890.

Carson, Rachel. *Silent Spring*. London: Hamish Hamilton, 1963.

Cartwright, Wayne, ed. *Strong Sustainability for New Zealand: Principles and Scenarios*. New Zealand: New Zealand National Commission for UNESCO, Sustainable Aotearoa New Zealand, Inc., Nakedize Ltd., 2009.

Cassebaum, Anne. *Down Along the Haw*. North Carolina: McFarland and Company, 2011.

Castle, E. B. *The Undivided Mind*. London: George Allen & Unwin, Ltd., 1941.

Churchman, John. *An Account of the Gospel Labours, and Christian Experiences of a Faithful Minister of Christ, John Churchman: To Which Is Added a Short Memorial of the Life and Death of a Fellow Labourer in The Church...* Philadelphia: Joseph Crukshank, 1779.

Clarke, Larry R. "Quaker Background of William Bartram's View of Nature," *Journal of the History of Ideas* 46, no. 3 (1985): 435–448.

Clausius, Rudolf. *The Mechanical Theory of Heat – With Its Application to the Steam Engine and to Physical Properties of Bodies*. London: John van Voorst, 1867.

Clayton, Philip. "Panentheisms East and West." *Sophia* 49, no. 2 (2010): 183–191.

———. "The New Story and Quaker Belief & Practice." In *Quakers and the New Story: Essays on Science and Spirituality*, eds. Philip Clayton and Mary Coelho, 6–7. Burlington: Quaker Earthcare Witness, 2007. http://newuniversestory.com/images/QuakersNewStory.pdf.

Coase, Ronald H. "Ronald H. Coase – Biographical." In *Les Prix Nobel*, Nobel Lectures Series, The Nobel Prize website. Accessed January 2019. http://nobelprize.org/prizes/economic-sciences/1991/coase/biographical/.

Colley, Brent M. "Redding Ridge, Connecticut (CT) History, Past and Present." History of Redding. Last modified June 4, 2007, accessed February 2019. http://historyofredding.net/HRreddingridge.htm.

Conradie, Ernst M., Sigurd Bergmann, Celia Deane-Drummond, and Denis Edwards, eds. *Christian Faith and the Earth: Current Paths and Emerging Horizons in Ecotheology*. London: Bloomsbury T&T Clark, 2015.

"Continued Extracts from *Rural Hours*." *Friends' Intelligencer* 10, no. 46 (February 1854): 726–727.

Cooper, Wilmer. *A Living Faith: An Historical and Comparative Study of Quaker Beliefs*. Second Edition. Richmond, IN: Friends United Press, 1990.

Costanza, Robert, et al. "The Value of the World's Ecosystem Services and Natural Capital," *Nature* 387 (1997): 253–260.

Cowan, Eliot. *Plant Spirit Medicine*. Newberg, OR: Swan•Raven & Co., 1995.

Cresson, Os. "QEW: A Nature Walk for All Friends." Quaker Earthcare Witness. http://quakerearthcare.org/article/qew-nature-walk-all-friends.

Culp, John. "Panentheism." *Stanford Encyclopedia of Philosophy*, ed. Edward N. Zalta. Summer 2017 edition. December 4, 2008. Last updated June 3, 2017. http://plato.stanford.edu/archives/sum2017/entries/panentheism/.

Curle, Adam. *True Justice: Quaker Peace Makers and Peace Making*. London: Quaker Home Service, 1981.

Daly, Herman. *Beyond Growth*. Boston MA: Beacon Press, 1996.

———. *Ecological Economics and Sustainable Development*. Cheltenham, UK: Edward Elgar, 2007.

———. *Steady-State Economics*. Second edition. Washington, DC: Island Press, 1991.

Damrosch, Barbara. "More Vegetables, Less Work: Lessons from the Mother of Mulch." *Washington Post*, March 9, 2017.

Dandelion, Pink. *A Sociological Analysis of the Theology of the Quakers: The Silent Revolution*. Lewiston, NY: The Edwin Mellen Press, Ltd., 1996.

———. *The Quakers: A Very Short Introduction*. Oxford and New York: Oxford University Press, 2008.

Daniels, C. Wess. *A Convergent Model of Renewal: Remixing the Quaker Tradition in a Participatory Culture*. Eugene, OR: Pickwick Publications, 2015.

Davis, Christine A. M. *Minding the Future*. London: Quaker Books, 2008.

Davis, Ellen. *Scripture, Culture, and Agriculture: An Agrarian Reading of the Bible*. New York: Cambridge University Press, 2008.

Deane-Drummond, Celia. *A Handbook in Theology and Ecology*. London: SCM Press, 1996.

———. "Creation." In *The Cambridge Companion to Feminist Theology*, ed. Susan Frank Parsons, 190–205. Cambridge: Cambridge University Press, 2002.

———. *Eco-Theology*. London: Darton, Longman and Todd, 2008.

———. *Wonder and Wisdom: Conversations in Science, Spirituality and Theology*. London: Darton, Longman & Todd, 2006.

Diamond, Louise. *The Courage for Peace: Daring to Create Harmony in Ourselves and the World*. Berkeley: Conari Press, 2002.

Dietz, Rob, and Dan O'Neill. *Enough is Enough*. Oakland, CA: Berrett-Koehler, 2013.

Dillard, Annie. *Pilgrim at Tinker Creek*. New York: Harper Perennial Press, 2007.

Dockrill, Peter. "Transparent Solar Cells Like This Could Deliver 40% of America's Power." *Science Alert*, October 24, 2017. http://sciencealert.com/transparent-solar-cells-satisfy-40-of-american-power-needs-see-through-light.

Douglas, Steve. "Religious Environmentalism in the West. I: A Focus on Christianity." *Religion Compass* 3, no. 4 (2009): 717–737. doi-org/10.1111/j.1749-8171.2009.00161.x.

Duffy, Kathleen, SSJ. *Teilhard's Mysticism: Seeing the Inner Face of Evolution.* Maryknoll: Orbis Books, 2014.

Dunstan, Edgar G. *Quakers and the Religious Quest.* London: Allen & Unwin, 1956.

Eaton, Heather, and Lois Ann Lorentzen, eds. *Ecofeminism and Globalization: Exploring Culture, Context, and Religion.* Lanham, MD: Rowman & Littlefield Publishers, Inc., 2003.

Emerson, Ralph Waldo. "Nature." In *Emerson: Essays and Lectures*, 5–49. New York: Library of America, 1983.

Feser, Edward. "Robert Nozick." In *Internet Encyclopedia of Philosophy.* Accessed January 2019. http://.iep.utm.edu/nozick/.

Feynman, Richard. *The Feynman Lectures on Physics, Vol. 1.* Reading, MA: Addison-Wesley, 1963.

Fideler, David. *Restoring the Soul of the World: Our Living Bond with Nature's Intelligence.* Rochester: Inner Traditions, 2014.

Flanagan, Eileen. "Temperature rising: Climate crises in Africa." *The Christian Century,* August 12, 2013. http://christiancentury.org/article/2013-08/temperature-rising.

Fleischner, Thomas Lowe. "The Mindfulness of Natural History." In *The Way of Natural History*, ed. Thomas Lowe Fleischner, 3–15. San Antonio, TX: Trinity University Press, 2011.

Fletcher, Stevenson Whitcomb. *Pennsylvania Agriculture and Country Life: 1640–1840.* Harrisburg, PA: Pennsylvania Historical and Museum Commission, 1950.

"Forecast suggests Earth's warmest period on record." Met Office, February 6, 2019. Accessed February 2019. http://metoffice.gov.uk/news/releases/2019/forecast-suggests-earths-warmest-period.

Fothergill, Samuel. "Memoirs of the Life and Gospel Labours of Samuel Fothergill, with Selections from His Correspondence. Also an Account of the Life and Travels of His Father, John Fothergill; and Notices of Some of His Descendants." In *The Friends' Library; Comprising Journals, Doctrinal Treatises, and Other Writings of Members of the Religious Society of Friends*, eds. William Evans and Thomas Evans, vol. 9, 83–289. Philadelphia, PA: Joseph Rakestraw, 1845.

Fox, George. *The Journal of George Fox*, ed. John L. Nickalls. Revised edition. Philadelphia: Religious Society of Friends, 1997.

———. *The Works of George Fox*. Philadelphia: Marcus T. C. Gould, 1831. Digital Quaker Collection: http://esr.earlham.edu/dqc/

———. *To the Parliament and Protector of England*. In the Digital Quaker Collection: http://esr.earlham.edu/dqc/

Fox, Margaret Fell. *The Life of Margaret Fox, Wife of George Fox*. Ann Arbor, MI: University of Michigan Library, 2005.

Francis, Pope. "'Laudato Si': On Care for Our Common Home." Washington, DC: United States Conference of Catholic Bishops, 2015.

Fry, Elizabeth Gurney. *Memoir of the Life of Elizabeth Fry: With Extracts from Her Letters and Journal*, eds. Katharine Fry and Rachel Elizabeth Cresswell. Philadelphia: H. Longstreth, 1847.

Francis of Assisi. *Francis of Assisi in His Own Words: The Essential Writings*, ed. Jon M. Sweeney. Brewster, MA: Paraclete Press, 2013.

Frankena, William K. "Utilitarianism." In *Dictionary of Philosophy*, ed. Dagobert D. Runes (Whitefish, MT: Kessinger Publishing, 1942). Accessed January 2019. http://ditext.com/runes/u.html.

Frankl, Viktor E. *Man's Search for Meaning*. Boston, MA: Beacon Press, 1959, 2006.

"Further Extracts from *Rural Hours*." *Friends' Intelligencer* 10, no. 34 (November 1853): 534–536.

Gardner, Gary. "Invoking the Spirit: Religion and Spirituality in the Quest for a Sustainable World." *Worldwatch Paper* 164, Worldwatch Institute (2002).

Gauthier-Lafaye, F., et al. "The last natural nuclear fission reactor." *Nature* 387, no. 337 (1997): 337.

George Fisher, Sydney. *The Quaker Colonies, a chronicle of the proprietors of the Delaware*. Kindle edition. New Haven, CT: Yale University Press, 1919.

Gerard, Philip. *Down the Wild Cape Fear*. North Carolina: University of North Carolina Press, 2013.

Gerona, Carla. *Night Journeys: The Power of Dreams in Transatlantic Quaker Culture*. Charlottesville, VA: University of Virginia Press, 2004.

Gleick, Peter. "Water, Drought, Climate Change and Conflict in Syria." *American Meteorological Society* 6 (July 2014): 331–340. doi/10.1175/WCAS-D-13-00059.1.

Glen, Charlotte. "What is Organic Gardening?" North Carolina Cooperative Extension, March 22, 2012. Accessed February 2019. http://pender.ces.ncsu.edu/2012/03/what-is-organic-gardening/.

Glover, T. R. *The Nature and Purpose of a Christian Society.* London: Headley Brothers Publishers Ltd., 1912.

Goodenough, Ursula. *The Sacred Depths of Nature.* New York: Oxford University Press, 1998.

Gorman, George H. *The Amazing Fact of Quaker Worship.* London: Friends Home Service Committee, 1973.

Gowan, Donald E. "'Ecotheology': a review article." *Perspective (Pittsburgh)* 14, no. 2 (1973): 107–113.

Grande, John K. *Art Nature Dialogues: Interviews with Environmental Artists.* Albany: State University of New York Press, 2004.

Grayson, Russ. "A Short and Incomplete History of Permaculture." Pacific Edge. Last updated July 2007. http://pacific-edge.info/2007/07/a-short-and-incomplete-history-of-permaculture/.

Greco, Jr., Thomas H. *The End of Money and the Future of Civilization.* White River Junction, VT: Chelsea Green Publishing, 2006.

Green Bible, The. Reprint edition. New York: HarperOne, 2010.

Greider, Kathleen. *Reckoning with Aggression: Theology, Violence, and Vitality.* Louisville, KY: Westminster John Knox Press, 1997.

Grim, John and Mary Evelyn Tucker. *Ecology and Religion.* Washington, DC: Island Press, 2014.

Grove, Richard H. *Green Imperialism: Colonial Expansion, Tropical Island Edens, and the Origins of Environmentalism, 1600–1860.* Cambridge, UK: Cambridge University Press, 1995.

Grubb, Michael. "Seeking Fair Weather: Ethics and the International Debate on Climate Change." *International Affairs* 71, no. 3 (1995): 463–496.

———. "The economics of climate damages and stabilization after the Stern Review." *Climate Policy* 6 (2006): 505–508.

Guenther, Karen. *"Rememb'ring Our Time and Work Is the Lords"*: *The Experience of Quakers on the Eighteenth-Century Pennsylvania Frontier.* The Pennsylvania History and Culture Series. Selinsgrove, PA: Susquehanna University Press, 2005.

Guha, Ramachandra. *Environmentalism: A Global History.* New York: Longman, 2000.

Gwyn, Douglas. *A Sustainable Life: Quaker Faith and Practice in the Renewal of Creation.* Philadelphia: QuakerPress of Friends General Conference, 2014.

————. *The Covenant Crucified: Quakers and the Rise of Capitalism.* Wallingford, PA: Pendle Hill Publications, 1995.

Hall, Shannon. "Exxon Knew about Climate Change almost 40 years ago." *Scientific American*, October 26, 2015.

Hamilton, James. "Is a Sustainability Career on your Horizon?" 2012. Bureau of Labor Statistics.

Hansen, Jolene. "An American Timeline: Home Gardening in the US." Garden Tech. Last updated 2018. http://gardentech.com/blog/gardening-and-healthy-living/an-american-timeline-home-gardening-in-the-us.

Harley, Ruth. "Pest-Proofing Your Garden." *Storey's Country Wisdom Bulletin*, A–15, January 11, 1997, 18.

Hawley, Benjamin. *Diary of Benjamin Hawley of East Bradford Township.* Pennsylvania: Chester County Historical Society, 1775.

Heales, Brenda Clifft and Chris Cook. *Images and Silence: The Future of Quaker Ministry.* London: Quaker Home Service, 1992.

Helmuth, Keith. *If John Woolman were Among Us: Reflections on the Ecology of Flush Toilets and Motor Vehicles.* Canadian Quaker Pamphlet no. 32. Argenta, BC: Argenta Friends Press, 1987.

————. "Ecological Integrity and Religious Faith." *Friends Journal*, 47, no. 8 (August 2001): 6–9.

Helmuth, Keith, Judy Lumb, Sandra Lewis, and Barbara Day. "Changing World View and Friends Testimonies." *Quaker Eco-Bulletin* 6, no. 4 (July-August 2006). http://quakerearthcare.org/node/133.

Henkel, Marion. *21st Century Homestead: Sustainable Agriculture I.* Morrisville, NC: Lulu.com, 2015.

Herbert, George. *The Poems of George Herbert*, ed. Helen Gardner. London: Oxford University Press, 1961.

Hibbert, G. K. *The Inner Light and Modern Thought*. London: George Allen and Unwin, Ltd., 1924.

Hinds, Hilary. "Unity and Universality in the Theology of George Fox." In *Early Quakers and Their Theological Thought, 1647–1723*, eds. Stephen Angell and Pink Dandelion, 48–63. New York: Cambridge University Press, 2015.

Hodgkin, Henry T. *The Missionary Spirit and the Present Opportunity*. London: The Swarthmore Press, Ltd., 1916.

Hoffman, Ace. "Another View on Nuclear Power." *Friends Journal* (January 2009).

Hoffmann, Nancy E. and John C Van Horne, eds. *America's Curious Botanist: A Tercentennial Reappraisal of John Bartram, 1699–1777*. Philadelphia: American Philosophical Society, 2004.

Holt, Shan. "Open Space Adventures in William Penn's 'Greene Countrie Town.'" Supplement to the 120th Annual Meeting (American Historical Association, 2005). http://historians.org/annual-meeting/past-meetings/supplement-to-the-120th-annual-meeting/open-space-adventures-in-william-penns-greene-countrie-town.

Hopkins, Gerard Manley. *The Major Works, including all the poems and selected prose*, ed. Catherine Phillips. Oxford World's Classics series. Oxford: Oxford University Press, 2002.

Howard, Mary Matilda. *Ocean Flowers and their Teachings*. Bath: Binns & Goodwin, 1846.

Howell, Robert. "Do Your Investments Destroy or Care for the Planet?" *Friends Quarterly* (May 2011).

———. "Talking Past Each Other: Economics, Ethics, the IPCC and the UNFCCC." *International Journal of Transdisciplinary Research* 4, no. 1 (2009): 1–15.

Howenstein, Bill. "Loving the Universe," 1992 Jonathan Plummer Lecture. McNab, IL: Illinois Yearly Meeting of the Religious Society of Friends, July 26, 1992. http://quaker.org/legacy/iym/plummer/1992.html.

Hursthouse, Rosalind. "Environmental Virtue Ethics." In *Working Virtue*, eds. Rebecca L. Walker and Philip J. Ivanhoe, 155–172. Oxford: Oxford University Press, 2007.

Hvistendahl, Mara. "Coal Ash Is More Radioactive Than Nuclear Waste." *Scientific American* (December 13, 2007).

"Importance of the Study of Natural History as a Branch of Elementary Education." *Friends' Intelligencer* 19, nos. 16 (June 1862): 249–251; 17 (July 1862): 264–267; 18 (July 1862): 282–285; 20 (July 1862): 314–317.

Ingham, Geoffrey. *The Nature of Money*. Malden, MA: Polity Press, 2004.

Jackson, Tim. *Prosperity Without Growth? The Transition to a Sustainable Economy*. London: Earthscan, 2009.

James, Edwin, ed. *Account of an Expedition from Pittsburgh to the Rocky Mountains, performed in the years 1819, 1820, by order of the Hon. J.C. Calhoun, Secretary of War, under the command of Maj. S.H. Long, of the U.S. Top. Engineers. Compiled from the notes of Major Long, Mr. T. Say, and Other Gentlemen of the Party*. 3 volumes. London: Longman, Hurst, Rees, Orme, and Brown, Paternoster-Row, 1823.

Janney, Werner and Asay Moore Janney. *Ye Meetg Hous Smal: A Short Account of Friends in Loudoun County, Virginia, 1732–1980*. Elkton, VA: X-high Graphic Arts, 1980.

Jenkins, Willis. "After Lynn White: Religious Ethics and Environmental Problems." *Journal of Religious Ethics* 37, no. 2 (2009): 283–309.

Jensen, Joan M. *Loosening the Bonds: Mid-Atlantic Farm Women 1750-1850*. New Haven, CT: Yale University Press, 1986.

Jevons, William Stanley. "The Mathematical Theory of Political Economy." *Journal of the Statistical Society of London* 37, no. 4 (December 1874): 478–488. doi: 10.2307/2338697.

Johnson, Robert. "Kant's Moral Philosophy." In *The Stanford Encyclopedia of Philosophy*, 2008. Accessed January 2019. http://plato.stanford.edu/archives/sum2014/entries/kant-moral/.

Jolliff, William. "The Economy of the Inward Life: John Woolman and Henry Thoreau." *The Concord Saunterer*, New Series, 15 (2007): 91–111.

Jones, Rufus M. *New Studies in Mystical Religion*. New York: The Macmillan Company, 1927.

————. *Social Law in the Spiritual World: Studies in Human and Divine Inter-Relationship*. Philadelphia: The John C. Winston Co., 1904.

————. *The New Quest*. New York: The Macmillan Company, 1928.

————. "The Quaker Conception of God." In *Beyond Dilemmas: Quakers Look at Life*, ed. S. B. Laughlin. Philadelphia: J. B. Lippincott Co., 1937.

————. *The Testimony of the Soul*. New York: The Macmillan Company, 1936.

————. *The World Within*. New York: The Macmillan Company, 1918.

Jones, Rufus M., Isaac Sharpless, and Amelia M. Gummere. *The Quakers in the American Colonies*. Kindle edition. London: Macmillan and Co., Ltd., 1911, 1923; Charleston, SC: BiblioBazaar, 2010.

Judd, Richard W. "A 'Wonderfull Order and Ballance': Natural History and the Beginnings of Forest Conservation in America, 1730–1830." *Environmental History* 11, no. 1 (2006): 8–36.

Kearns, Laurel. "Con-spiring Together: Breathing for Justice." In *The Bloomsbury Handbook on Religion and Nature: The Elements*, eds. Laura Hobgood and Whitney Bauman, Bloomsbury Handbooks in Religion series, 117–132. New York: Bloomsbury Academic, 2018.

————. "Cooking The Truth: Faith, The Market, And The Science of Global Warming." In *Eco-Spirit: Religion, Philosophy and the Earth*, eds. Laurel Kearns and Catherine Keller, 97–124. New York: Fordham University Press, 2007.

————. "Quakerism and the Journey of the Universe." In *Living Cosmology: Christian Responses to Journey of the Universe*, eds. Mary Evelyn Tucker and John Grim, 300–310. Maryknoll, NY: Orbis, 2016.

Keier, R. Melvin and Rosemary Moore. *Knowing the Mystery of Life Within: Selected Writings of Isaac Penington in their Historical and Theological Context*. London, UK: Quaker Books, 2005.

Keiser, R. Melvin. *Inward Light and the New Creation*. Pendle Hill Pamphlet 295. Wallingford: Pendle Hill Publications, 1991.

Kelley, Donald Brooks. "'A Tender Regard to the Whole Creation': Anthony Benezet and the Emergence of an Eighteenth-Century Quaker Ecology." *The Pennsylvania Magazine of History and Biography* 106, no. 1 (1982): 69–88.

———. "Friends and Nature in America: Toward an Eighteenth-Century Quaker Ecology," *Pennsylvania History: A Journal of Mid-Atlantic Studies* 53, no. 4 (October 1986): 257–272.

———. "The Evolution of Quaker Theology and the Unfolding of a Distinctive Quaker Ecological Perspective in Eighteenth-Century America." *Pennsylvania History: A Journal of Mid-Atlantic Studies* 52, no. 4 (1985): 242–253.

Kemeny, John. "The President's Commission on the Accident at Three Mile Island, the Need for Change: The Legacy of TMI." US Government Printing Office (October 1979): 157–163.

Kenny, Kevin. *Peaceable Kingdom Lost: The Paxton Boys and the Destruction of William Penn's Holy Experiment.* New York: Oxford University Press, 2009.

Kent, Deirdre. *Healthy Money, Healthy Planet: Developing Sustainability Through New Money Systems.* Nelson, NZ: Craig Potton, 2005.

Kershner, Jon R. *John Woolman and the Government of Christ: A Colonial Quaker's Vision for the British Atlantic World.* New York: Oxford University Press, 2018.

———. *"To Renew the Covenant": Religious Themes in Eighteenth-Century Quaker Abolitionism.* Leiden: Brill, 2018.

———. "'A More Lively Feeling': The Correspondence and Integration of Mystical and Spatial Dynamics in John Woolman's Travels." *Quaker Studies* 20, no. 1 (December 1, 2015): 103–116. doi.org/10.3828/quaker.20.1.103.

———. "'Diminish Not a Word': The Prophetic Voice of John Woolman." In *Quakers and Literature*, ed. James W. Hood, 11–26. Quakers and the Disciplines, vol. 3. Philadelphia: Friends Association for Higher Education, 2016.

Keynes, John M. *The General Theory of Employment, Interest and Money.* Eugene, OR: Harvest / San Diego, CA: Harcourt, 1936, 1964.

King, Rachel Hadley. *George Fox and the Light Within, 1650–1660.* Philadelphia: Friends Book Store, 1940.

Kirchner, Robert. "On Quakers and Permaculture: Making a Living, Not a Killing." Neighbour Grow: An Edmonton Quaker Transitions to a Livelihood in Urban Permaculture. April 9, 2014. http://neighbourgrow.wordpress.com/2014/04/09/on-quakers-and-permaculture-making-a-living-not-a-killing/.

Kliever, Lonnie D. "Experience-Religious." In *New & Enlarged Handbook of Christian Theology*, eds. Donald W. Musser and Joseph L. Price. Nashville, TN: Abingdon Press, 2003.

Knauf, Sandra. "The Whole Ruth." *Greenwoman*, vol. 5. Colorado Springs, CO: Greenwoman Magazine, 2013, 32–45.

Korten, David. *The Great Turning: From Empire to Earth Community*. Second edition. Oakland, CA: Berrett-Koehler, 1997, 2007.

Krasner, Lee. "Oral history interview with Lee Krasner." Interviewed by Dorothy Seckler, December 14, 1964. In the Lee Krasny Papers, Archives of American Art, Smithsonian Institution, Washington, DC.

Kraushaar, Otto. "America: Symbol of a Fresh Start." In *Utopias: The American Experience*, eds. Otto Kraushaar and Gairdner Moment, 11–29. Metuchen, NJ: Scarecrow Press, 1980.

Kuh, George D. "High-Impact Educational Practices: What They Are, Who Has Access to Them and Why They Matter." Association of American Colleges and Universities. 2008.

Lakey, George. "What role were you born to play in social change?" Waging Nonviolence. February 3, 2016. http://wagingnonviolence.org/feature/bill-moyer-four-roles-of-social-change/.

Lane, Belden C. "Giving Voice to Place: Three Models for Understanding American Sacred Space." *Religion and American Culture: A Journal of Interpretation* 11, no. 1 (2001): 53–81.

———. *The Solace of Fierce Landscapes: Exploring Desert and Mountain Spirituality*. New York: Oxford University Press, 1998.

Lanza, Patricia. "Lasagna Gardening." *Mother Earth News*, April/May 1999. http://motherearthnews.com/organic-gardening/lasagna-gardening-zmaz99amztak.

Lawrence Livermore National Laboratory Visualization. LLNL-MI-410527. US Energy Information Agency, April 2018. http://flowcharts.llnl.gov/content/assets/docs/2017_United-States_Energy.pdf.

Leiserowitz, A., Maibach, E., Rosenthal, S., Kotcher, J., Ballew, M., Goldberg, M., & Gustafson, A. *Climate Change in the American Mind: December 2018.* Yale University and George Mason University. New Haven, CT: Yale Program on Climate Change Communication, 2018. http://climate communication.yale.edu/publications/climate-change-in-the-american-mind-december-2018/.

"Letter to Address the Urgent Threat of Climate Change." Center for Biological Diversity. January 10, 2019. Accessed January 26, 2019. http://biologicaldiversity.org/news/press_releases/2019/climate-legislation-01-10-2019.php.

Leopold, Aldo. *A Sand County Almanac.* Oxford: Oxford University Press, 1949.

———. "The Land Ethic." In *Environmental Ethics: An Anthology*, eds. Andrew Light and Holmes Rolston, III, 38–46. Oxford: Blackwell Publishing, 2003.

Levy, Barry. *Quakers and the American Family: British Settlement in the Delaware Valley.* Kindle edition. New York: Oxford University Press, 1988.

Liang, Chyi Lyi (Kathleen), McCauley, Marlene, and Dell, Kyle. "Building a Collaborative Effort of Training and Education in Sustainable Food System for the 22nd Century through Urban Agriculture Programs." 2017 Small Business Institute Conference Proceedings 41, no. 1 (2017): 139–142.

Lietaer, Bernard, et al. *Money and Sustainability: The Missing Link.* Devon, UK: Triarchy Press, 2012.

"Life at the Fenceline: Understanding Cumulative Health Hazards in Environmental Justice Communities." Environmental Justice for All. Accessed January 2019. http://ej4all.org/life-at-the-fenceline.

Loewenstein, David. "The War of the Lamb: George Fox and the Apocalyptic Discourse of Revolutionary Quakerism." In *The Emergence of Quaker Writing: Dissenting Literature in Seventeenth-Century England*, ed. Thomas M. Corns, 25–41. N.p.: Frank Cass and Company, Limited, 1995.

Logsdon, Gene. "Ruth Stout: Mulch Can Cover a Multitude of Sins as Well as Weeds." The Contrary Farmer Memorial Blogsite. Last updated December 16, 2008. http://thecontraryfarmer.wordpress.com/2008/12/16/mulch-can-cover-a-multitude-of-sins-as-well-as-weeds/.

Luther, Martin. "The Sacrament of the Body and Blood of Christ—Against the Fanatics." In *Martin Luther's Basic Theological Writings*, ed. Timothy F. Lull, 224–239. Minneapolis, MN: Fortress Press, 1989.

MacDonald, George. *Unspoken Sermons: Series I, II, and III, Complete and Unabridged.* Classics Reprint Series. Scotts Valley, CA: CreateSpace Independent Publishing Platform, 2016.

Macy, Joanna, and Chris Johnstone. *Active Hope: How to face the mess we're in without going crazy.* Novato, CA: New World Library, 2012.

Magie, W. F., ed. and transl. *The Second Law of Thermodynamics: Memoirs by Carnot, Clausius and Thomson.* New York: Harper, 1899.

Malthus, Thomas R. *An Essay on the Principle of Population.* London: J. Johnson, 1798.

Masson-Delmotte, V., and P. Zhai, H.-O. Pörtner, D. Roberts, J. Skea, P.R. Shukla, A. Pirani, Moufouma-Okia, C. Péan, R. Pidcock, S. Connors, J.B.R. Matthews, Y. Chen, X. Zhou, M.I. Gomis, E. Lonnoy, Maycock, M. Tignor, and T. Waterfield, eds. *Global Warming of 1.5°C. An IPCC Special Report on the impacts of global warming of 1.5°C above pre-industrial levels and related global greenhouse gas emission pathways, in the context of strengthening the global response to the threat of climate change, sustainable development, and efforts to eradicate poverty.* Intergovernmental Panel on Climate Change, 2018. World Meteorological Organization, Geneva, Switzerland. Accessed January 2019. http://ipcc.ch/sr15/.

McAleer, John. *Rex Stout: A Biography.* Boston: Little, Brown, 1977.

McBride, J. and R. Moore, J. Witherspoon, and R. Blanco. "Radiological impact of airborne effluents of coal and nuclear plants." *Science* 202, no. 4372 (December 1978): 1045–1050.

McFadden, David W., Clare Gorfinkel, and Sergei Nikitin. *Constructive Spirit: Quakers in Revolutionary Russia.* Altadena, CA: Intentional Productions, 2004.

McFague, Sallie. *A New Climate for Theology: God, the World, and Global Warming.* Minneapolis, MN: Augsburg Fortress Press, 2008.

————. *Super, Natural Christians: How We Should Love Nature*. Minneapolis, MN: Fortress Press, 2000.

McKenna, Phil. "Fossil Fuels are Far Deadlier than Nuclear Power." *New Scientist,* March 23, 2011. http://newscientist.com/article/mg20928 053.600-fossil-fuels-are-far-deadlier-than-nuclear-power/.

McKibben, Bill. "Global Warming's Terrifying New Math." *Rolling Stone,* July 19, 2012. http://rollingstone.com/politics/news/global-warmings-terrifying-new-math-20120719.

McLuhan, Marshall. *Understanding Media: The Extensions of Man*. Cambridge, MA: MIT Press, 1994.

Meadows, Donella, et al. *The Limits to Growth: a Report for the Club of Rome's Project on the predicament of Mankind*. New York: Universe Books, 1972.

Menger, Carl. *Principles of Economics*. Auburn, AL: Ludwig von Mises Institute, 1871, 2007.

Meshik, A. "The Workings of an Ancient Nuclear Reactor." *Scientific American* 293, no. 5 (2005): 82–91.

Metzger, Bruce M. *Breaking the Code: Understanding the Book of Revelation*. Nashville: Abingdon Press, 1993.

Mill, John Stuart. *Utilitarianism*. Oxford: Oxford University Press, 1998.

Mintz, Steven and Susan Kellogg. *Domestic Revolutions: A Social History of American Family Life*. New York: The Free Press, 1988.

Mokin, Arthur, dir. *Ruth Stout's Garden*. Documentary, filmed in 1976. Audio in English, 23:00. http://youtube.com/watch?v=GNU8IJzRHZk.

Moore, Rosemary. *The Light in their Consciences: Early Quakers in Britain, 1646–1666*. University Park, PA: The Pennsylvania University Press, 2000.

Morgan, Brandon Lee. "Reimaging Aesthetics: Sergius Bulgakov on Seeing the Wisdom of Creation." *Irish Theological Quarterly* 83, no. 2 (2018): 149–163.

Morrow, Rosemary Howe. *A Demanding and Uncertain Adventure*. Religious Society of Friends (Quakers) in Australia, Interactive Publications ebook, 2011.

Mossman, David J., et al. "Carbonaceous substances in Oklo reactors—Analogue for permanent deep geologic disposal of anthropogenic nuclear waste." *Reviews in Engineering Geology* 19 (2008): 1–13. doi.org/10.1130/2008.4119(01).

Moulton, Mary. "In Honor of Phillips P. Moulton." In *The Tendering Presence: Essays on John Woolman*, ed. Mike Heller, 311–313. Wallingford, PA: Pendle Hill Publications, 2003.

Moulton, Phillips P. "John Woolman: Exemplar of Ethics." *Quaker History* 54 (1965): 81–93.

———. "The Influence of the Writings of John Woolman." *Quaker History* 60, no. 1 (1971): 3–13.

Moyer, Bill, JoAnn McAllister, Mary Lou Finley, and Steve Soifer. *Doing Democracy: The MAP Model for Organizing Social Movements*. Gabriola Island, BC: New Society Publishers, 2001.

Muers, Rachel. *Testimony: Quakerism and Theological Ethics*. London: SCM Press, 2015.

Muller, Richard. *Energy for Future Presidents*. New York: Norton Publishing, 2012.

———. "The Dirty Bomb Distraction." *MIT Technology Review* (June 2004).

Musil, Caryn McTighe. "Department Designs for Civic Impact." *Peer Review* (Association of American Colleges & Universities) 19, no. 4 (2017).

Myers, Ched, ed. *Watershed Discipleship: Reinhabiting Bioregional Faith and Practice*. Eugene, OR: Cascade Books, 2016.

Naess, Arne. "The Deep Ecological Movement: Some Philosophical Aspects." In *Environmental Ethics: An Anthology*, eds. Andrew Light and Holmes Rolston, III, 10–31. Oxford: Blackwell Publishing, 2003.

Nash, Roderick Frazier. *Wilderness and the American Mind*. Fourth edition. New Haven, CT: Yale University Press, 2001.

Natural History Museum. "Conrad, Solomon White." Global Plants. Accessed June 1, 2018. http://plants.jstor.org/stable/10.5555/al.ap.person.bm000375110.

Nayler, James. *The Works of James Nayler*. Farmington, ME: Quaker Heritage Press, 1657. Accessed January 2019, www.qhpress.org/texts/nayler.

Nearing, Helen and Scott Nearing. *Living the Good Life*. New York: Schocken Books, 1954.

Neihardt, John, ed. *Black Elk Speaks: The Complete Edition*. Lincoln: University of Nebraska Press, 2014.

Newell, J. Philip. *Listening for the Heartbeat of God: A Celtic Spirituality*. New York: Paulist, 1997.

Newman, Andrew. *On Records: Delaware Indians, Colonists, and the Media of History and Memory*. Lincoln, NE: University of Nebraska Press, 2012.

New York Passenger Lists, 1820–1957 (database). Ancestry.com.

Norris, Kathleen. *The Cloister Walk*. New York, NY: Riverhead Books, 1997.

Nozick, Robert. *Anarchy, State, and Utopia*. New Jersey: Blackwell, 1974.

Nussbaum, Martha. "The Enduring Significance of John Rawls." *The Chronicle of Higher Education*. Accessed January 2019. http://evatt.org.au/papers/enduring-significance-john-rawls.html.

Oats, William N. *Backhouse and Walker: A Quaker View of the Australian Colonies, 1832–1838*. Sandy Bay, Tasmania: Blubber Head Press in association with the Australian Yearly Meeting Religious Society of Friends, 1981.

O'Brien, Kevin J. *The Violence of Climate Change: Lessons of Resistance from Nonviolent Activists*. Washington, DC: Georgetown University Press, 2017.

Olmsted, Sterling, and Mike Heller. *John Woolman: A Nonviolence and Social Change Source Book*. Second edition. Wilmington, OH, and Richmond, IN: Wilmington College Peace Resource Center and Friends United Press, 2013.

"On the Study of Natural History." *The Friend: A Religious & Literary Journal* 26 (April 1828): 203.

Otto, Rudolph. *The Idea of the Holy*. London: Oxford University Press, 1958.

Ouis, Soumaya Pernilla. "Islamic Ecotheology Based on the Qur'ān." *Islamic Studies* 37, no. 2 (1998): 151–181.

Pachauri, R. K., and L. A. Meyer, eds. Intergovernmental Panel on Climate Change, *Climate Change 2014: Synthesis Report. Contribution of Working Groups I, II and III to the Fifth Assessment Report of the Intergovernmental Panel on Climate Change*. Geneva, Switzerland, 2014.

Palmer, G. E. H., Philip Sherrard and Kallistos Ware, eds. and transls. *The Philokalia: The Complete Text,* compiled by St. Nikodimos of the Holy Mountain and St. Makarios of Corinth. London: Faber and Faber, 1995.

Patterns and Projections of High Tide Flooding Along the US Coastline Using a Common Impact Threshold. NOS CO-OPS 086. Silver Spring, MD: National Oceanic and Atmospheric Administration. February 2018. Accessed January 2019. http://tidesandcurrents.noaa.gov/publications/techrpt 86_PaP_of_HTFlooding.pdf.

Peirce, Walter. "A Farmer of the Early Republic." *Bulletin of Friends' Historical Association* 19, no. 1 (1930): 7–15, Project MUSE.

Penington, Isaac. *The Works of Isaac Penington.* WWW edition. Farmington, ME: Quaker Heritage Press, 1995. http://qhpress.org/texts/penington/index.html.

Penn, William. "Some Fruits of Solitude, in Reflections and Maxims, Relating to the Conduct of Humane Life." In *Collection of the works of William Penn,* vol. 1. London: J. Sowle, 1726. In the Digital Quaker Collection. http://esr.earlham.edu/dqc/.

———. "Excerpts from *Frame of Government of Pennsylvania.*" Constitution Society, 1682, accessed July 2018, http://constitution.org/bcp/frampenn.htm.

Peters, Andy. "Activists Target More Banks After PNC Curtails Loans to Coal Miners." *The American Banker,* March 26, 2015. http://americanbanker.com/news/activists-target-more-banks-after-pnc-curtails-loans-to-coal-miners.

Pinkney Pleasant Bell, James. *Our Quaker Friends of ye olden time; being in part a transcript of the minute books of Cedar Creek meeting, Hanover County, and the South River meeting, Campbell County, VA.* Google Books. Lynchburg, VA: J. P. Bell Company, 1905.

Plank, Geoffrey. "John Woolman and Land." In *Quakers, Politics, and Economics,* eds. David R. Ross and Michael T. Snarr, 304–321. Quakers and the Disciplines, vol. 5. Philadelphia: Friends Association for Higher Education, 2018.

———. *John Woolman's Path to the Peaceable Kingdom: A Quaker in the British Empire.* Philadelphia: University of Pennsylvania Press, 2012.

———. "The Flame of Life Was Kindled in All Animal and Sensitive Creatures": One Quaker Colonist's View of Animal Life." *Church History* 76, no. 3 (2007): 569–590.

Power, Rosemary. *The Celtic Quest: A Contemporary Spirituality.* Blackrock, Ireland: The Columba Press, 2010.

Priestland, Gerald. *Reasonable Uncertainty.* London, Quaker Books, 2007.

Proud, James. "A Note on John Woolman's Paternal Ancestors: The Gloucestershire Roots; The West New Jersey Plantation." *Quaker History* 96, no. 2 (2007): 28–53.

Prowell, George R. *History of York County Pennsylvania, Volume I.* Chicago: J. H. Beers and Co., 1907.

Quaker Faith and Practice. Yearly Meeting of the Religious Society of Friends (Quakers) in Britain. London: Britain Yearly Meeting, 1994.

"Quaker Research in Virginia — Hopewell Meeting." Hay Genealogy. Accessed July 2018, http://haygenealogy.com/hay/quaker/quaker-VA.html.

Radice, Betty, transl. *The Letters of Abelard and Heloise.* New York: Viking Penguin, 1974.

Rawls, John. *A Theory of Justice.* Cambridge, MA: Harvard University Press, 1971.

Raworth, Kate. *Doughnut Economics: Seven Ways to Think Like a 21st-Century Economist.* White River Junction, VT: Chelsea Green Publishing, 2017.

Rees, William E. "Ecological Footprints and Appropriated Carrying Capacity: What Urban Economics Leaves Out." *Environment and Urbanization* 4, no. 2 (1992): 120–130.

Regan, Tom. *The Case for Animal Rights.* Berkeley, CA: University of California Press, 1983.

"Review of *Letters to a Young Naturalist*, part 1." *The Friend: A Religious & Literary Journal* 5, no. 11 (December 1831): 81–83.

"Review of *Letters to a Young Naturalist*, part 2." *The Friend: A Religious & Literary Journal* 5, no. 12 (December 1831): 89–91.

"Review of *Rural Hours*." *Friends' Intelligencer* 10, no. 31 (October 1853): 489–491.

"Review of *Rural Hours*." *The Friend: A Religious & Literary Journal* 24, no. 25 (March 1851): 194–196.

Reyes, Juliana Feliciano. "It took 6 years for PHL airport workers to double their pay to $12 an hour. Here's how they did it." *Philadelphia Inquirer*, June 11, 2018. http://www2.philly.com/philly/news/philadelphia-airport-workers-union-contract-20180611.html.2018.

Reynolds, Reginald. *The Wisdom of John Woolman*. London: Friends Home Service Committee, 1948.

Rhodes, Richard. *Energy: A Human History*. New York: Simon & Schuster, 2018.

———. *The Making of the Atomic Bomb*. New York: Simon & Schuster, 1986.

Ricardo, David. *On the Principles of Political Economy and Taxation*. First edition. London: John Murray, 1817.

Ridner, Judith. *A Town In-Between: Carlisle, Pennsylvania, and the Early Mid-Atlantic Interior*. Philadelphia: University of Pennsylvania Press, 2010.

Ripple, William J., and Christopher Wolf, Thomas M. Newsome, Mauro Galetti, Mohammed Alamgir, Eileen Crist, Mahmoud I. Mahmoud, William F. Laurance, and 15,364 scientist signatories from 184 countries. "World Scientists' Warning to Humanity: A Second Notice." *BioScience* 67, no. 12 (December 2017): 1026–1028. doi.org/10.1093/biosci/bix125.

Robertson, James. *Future Money: Breakdown or Breakthrough?* Devon, UK: Green Books, 2012.

Robinson, Andrea L. "The Ecosapiential Theology of Psalms." *Evangelical Review of Theology* 42, no. 1 (2018): 21–34.

Robishaw, Sue. "A Few Good Gardening Books." Many Tracks Organic Gardening. Last updated 2018. http://manytracks.com/Garden/Books.htm.

Rolston, III, Holmes. *Environmental Ethics: Duties to and Values in the Natural World*. Philadelphia: Temple University Press, 1988.

Ross, Ellen M. "The Solace of History: Reflections on Quakers and the Environment." *Friends Journal*, February 17, 2012. http://friends journal.org/the-solace-of-history-reflections-on-quakers-and-the-environment/.

Rosso, Randy. "How Hungry is America? Food Hardship in America: A Look at National, Regional, State, and Metropolitan Statistical Area Data on Household Struggles With Hunger." Washington, DC: Food Research Action Center. August 2018.

"Ruth Stout, September 8, 1923." US Passport Applications, 1795–1925 (database). Ancestry.com.

"Ruth Stout System of Permanent Hay Mulching." Veganic Agricultural Network. Last updated June 18, 2013. http://goveganic.net/article 182.html.

"Ruth Stout's System for Gardening." *Mother Earth News*, February/March 2004. http://motherearthnews.com/organic-gardening/ruth-stouts-system-zmaz04fmzsel.

Sayre, Robert. "William Bartram and Environmentalism." *American Studies* 54, no. 1 (March 2015): 67–87.

Schaefer, Jame. *Theological Foundations for Environmental Ethics: Reconstructing Patristic and Medieval Concepts.* Washington, DC: Georgetown University, 2009.

Schumacher, Eric. *Small is Beautiful: A Study of Economics As If People Mattered.* Vancouver, BC: Hartley and Marks Publishers, 1973.

Schurman, Virginia. "A Quaker Theology of the Stewardship of Creation." *Quaker Religious Thought* 24, no. 4 (1990): 27–41.

Schweitzer, Albert. *Out of My Life and Thought.* New York: Henry Holt and Company, Inc., 1949.

Scott, Richenda C. *Tradition and Experience.* Swarthmore Lecture. London: Allen and Unwin, 1964.

Scott, Robert. "A Critical Review of Permaculture in the United States." PhD diss., University of Illinois at Urbana/Champaign, 2010.

Seeger, Daniel A. "Why Do the Unbelievers Rage? The New Atheists and the Universality of the Light." *Friends Journal* (January 2011): 6–11.

Shapiro, Ian, ed. *Two Treatises of Government and A Letter Concerning Toleration: John Locke.* New Haven, CT: Yale University Press, 2003.

Shue, Henry. "Ethics, the Environment and the Changing International Order," *International Affairs* 71, no. 3 (1995): 453–461.

———. "Global Environment and International Inequity," *International Affairs* 75, no. 3 (1999): 531–545.

———. "Human rights, climate change, and the trillionth ton." In *The Ethics of Climate Change*, ed. Denis G. Arnold, 292–314. Cambridge, UK: Cambridge University Press, 2011.

Silver, Bruce. "Clarke on the Quaker Background of William Bartram's Approach to Nature." *Journal of the History of Ideas* 47, no. 3 (1986): 507–510.

Singer, Peter. *Animal Liberation: A New Ethics for Our Treatment of Animals*. New York: HarperCollins, 1975.

———. *Practical Ethics*. Cambridge, UK: Cambridge University Press, 2011.

Slaughter, Thomas P. *The Natures of John and William Bartram*. Philadelphia: University of Pennsylvania Press, 1996.

Smith, Robert V. "Soil Survey of Adams County, Pennsylvania." US Department of Agriculture, 2005. Accessed January 2019. http://nrcs.usda.gov/Internet/FSE_MANUSCRIPTS/pennsylvania/PA001/0/PA_Adams.pdf.

Sobrino, Jon. *Christology at the Crossroads: A Latin American Approach*. Maryknoll, NY: Orbis Books, 1976.

Somé, Malidoma P. *Of Water and the Spirit: Ritual, Magic, and Initiation in the Life of an African Shaman*. New York: Tarcher/Putnam, 1994.

Spencer, Carole Dale. "Quakers in Theological Context." In *The Oxford Handbook of Quaker Studies*, eds. Stephen W. Angell and Pink Dandelion. New York: Oxford University Press, 2013.

Spent Nuclear Fuel: Legislative, Technical, and Societal Challenges to Its Transportation. GAO-16-121T. Government Accountability Office, Oct 1, 2015.

Spinks, Jenny. "Support for our true selves—Nurturing the space where leadings flow," James Backhouse Lecture, 2007, Australia Yearly Meeting of the Religious Society of Friends.

Spreckley, Freer. 1987. *Social Audit: A Management Tool for Co-operative Working*. Beechwood College.

Spurrier, William Wayne. "The Persecution of the Quakers in England: 1650–1714." PhD diss., University of North Carolina at Chapel Hill, 1976.

Stashower, Gloria. "Poverty Hollow." *The New York Times,* May 29, 1977, 377. http://nytimes.com/1977/05/29/archives/long-island-opinion-poverty-hollow-priestess.html

Stiglitz, Joseph. "Macroeconomics, Monetary Policy and the Crisis." In *In the Wake of the Crisis*, eds. Olivier Blanchard, et al., 31–44. Cambridge, MA: MIT Press, 2012.

Stob, William S. *The Life and Times of William Pettit Raley and His Family in America: A Glimpse at Life in the 18th and 19th Centuries.* Kindle edition. N.p.: Trustees of the Stob Living Trust, 1993, 2017.

Stocker, Brad. "Earth Literacy?" *Befriending Creation* 27, no. 3 (2014): 4–5. http://quakerearthcare.org/bfc/volume-27-number-3.

Stout, Ruth. *As We Remember Mother: A Lifetime of Love and Laughter With a Mother Light Years Ahead of Her Nineteenth Century Peers.* New York: Exposition Press, 1975.

———. *Company Coming: Six Decades of Hospitality, Do-It-Yourself and Otherwise.* New York: Exposition Press, 1958. Reprinted by Norton Creek Press, 2016.

———. *Gardening Without Work: For the Aging, the Busy & the Indolent.* New York: Devin-Adair, 1963. Reprinted by Norton Creek Press, 2011.

———. *How to Have a Green Thumb Without an Aching Back: A New Method of Mulch Gardening.* New York: Exposition Press, 1955.

———. "Verdict: Iris Are Wonderful, Interview with Rex Stout." *Popular Gardening,* June, 1956, 48–52.

Stout, Ruth and Richard Clemence. *The Ruth Stout No-Work Garden Book: Secrets of the Year-round Mulch Method.* Emmaus, PA: Rodale Press, 1973.

Street, Karen. "A Friend's Path to Nuclear Power." *Friends Journal* (October 2008).

———. "The Nuclear Energy Debate among Friends: Another Round." *Friends Journal* (July 2009).

Stroud, Patricia Tyson. "'At What Do You Think the Ladies Will Stop?' Women at the Academy." *Proceedings of the Academy of Natural Sciences of Philadelphia* 162 (2013): 195–205.

———. "Forerunner of American Conservation: Naturalist Thomas Say." *Forest & Conservation History* 39, no. 4 (1995): 184–190.

Suílleabháin, Brían Ó. "Quakers: The Spiritual Journey of Earthcare." Eco-Quakers Ireland. Ireland Yearly Meeting, 2018, video, 6:47. http://youtu.be/g1ZcfbpYgbE.

Suzuki, David. *The Sacred Balance: Rediscovering Our Place in Nature.* Toronto: Greystone, 2007.

Swimme, Brian and Mary Evelyn Tucker. *Journey of the Universe*. New Haven, CT: Yale University Press, 2014.

Swimme, Brian and Thomas Berry. *The Universe Story*. San Francisco: HarperOne, 1994.

Sylvan, Richard. *Transcendental Metaphysics*. Cambridgeshire, UK: White Horse Press, 1997.

Taylor, Dorceta E. "Introduction: The Evolution of Environmental Justice Activism, Research, and Scholarship." *Journal of Environmental Practice* 13, no. 4 (2011): 280–301. doi.org/10.1017/S1466046611000329.

Taylor, Paul W. *Respect for Nature: A Theory of Environmental Ethics*. New Jersey: Princeton University Press, 1986.

Teilhard de Chardin, Pierre. *Divine Milieu*. Paris: Editions du Seuil, 1957.

———. *Human Phenomenon*. Portland: Sussex Academy Press, 1999.

———. *Journal*. Paris: Fayard, 1975.

———. *The Phenomenon of Man*, transl. Bernard Wall. New York: Harper & Row, 1959.

Temple, James. "Let's keep the Green New Deal grounded in science." *MIT Technology Review*. January 18, 2019. Accessed January 26, 2019. http://technologyreview.com/s/612780/lets-keep-the-green-new-deal-grounded-in-science/.

Terres, John. *From Laurel Hill to Siler's Bog: The Walking Adventures of a Naturalist*. New York: Alfred K. Knopf, 1969.

["The study of Natural History."] *The Friend: A Religious & Literary Journal* 29, no. 28 (March 1856): 231.

The Theology of Creation: A Position Paper for the Church's Investment Policy Relating to environmental ethics. London: Central Finance Board of the Methodist Church, 2009. Accessed January 2019. http://cfbmethodist church.org.uk/downloads/position_papers/cfb_climate_change_posit ion_paper.pdf.

Thompson, Silvanus P. *Calculus Made Easy*. Second edition. London: Macmillan and Co., Ltd., 1910, 1914.

———. *The Quest for Truth*. London: Headley Brothers, 1915.

Thoreau, Henry David. *Walden; or, Life in the Woods*. New York: Avanel Books, 1845, 1985, 321–587.

Thorpe, William H. *Quakers and Humanists*. London: Friends Home Service Committee, 1968.

Today in Energy. US Energy Information Agency, December 28, 2018. http://eia.gov/todayinenergy/detail.php?id=37817.

Tony Reichhardt, "The Deadliest Air Raid In History," *Smithsonian Air and Space Magazine* (March 9, 2015).

Troster, Lawrence. "Tikkun Olam and Environmental Restoration: A Jewish Eco-Theology of Redemption." *Jewish Education News* (Fall 2008): 1–6.

Trueblood, Elton. *The People Called Quakers*. Richmond, IN: Friends United Press, 1989.

Tuckness, Alex. "John Locke." In *Stanford Encyclopedia of Philosophy*, 2005. Accessed January 2019. http://plato.stanford.edu/entries/locke/.

Turner, Graham M. "On the Cusp of Global Collapse? Updated Comparison of the Limits to Growth with Historical Data," *GAIA — Ecological Perspectives for Science and Society* 21, no. 2 (2012): 116–124.

Turow, Scott. "Best Trial; Order in the Court." *New York Times*, April 18, 1999. http://nytimes.com/1999/04/18/magazine/best-trial-order-in-the-court.html.

United States Department of Agriculture. "Employment Opportunities for College Graduates in Food, Agriculture, Renewable Natural Resources, and the Environment, United States, 2015–2020." 2015. http://purdue.edu/usda/employment/.

"Universal Declaration of Human Rights, The." United Nations. Accessed January 2019. http://un.org/en/universal-declaration-human-rights/.

"Upside-Down Triangle: Understanding the Consent Theory of Power." Training for Change. Accessed September 2, 2018. http://trainingfor change.org/training_tools/upside-down-triangle-understanding-the-consent-theory-of-power/.

Vanderjagt, Arjo and Klaus van Berkel, eds. *The Book of Nature in Early Modern and Modern History*. Leuven, Belgium: Peeters Publishers, 2006.

Vaux, Robert. *Memoirs of the life of Anthony Benezet*. Kindle edition. Philadelphia: J.P. Parke, 1817.

Victor, Peter. *Managing Without Growth.* Cheltenham, UK: Edward Elgar, 2008.

Vitousek, Peter M., et al. "Human appropriation of the products of photosynthesis." *Bioscience* 36, no. 6 (1986): 368–373.

Von Shulze-Gaevernitz, Gerhart. *Democracy and Religion: A Study in Quakerism.* London: George Allen and Unwin, Ltd., 1930.

Walras, Léon. *Elements of Pure Economics.* Reprint edition. London: American Economic Association and the Royal Economic Society, Allen and Unwin, 1874, 1954.

Walters, Kerry S. "The 'Peaceable Disposition' of Animals: William Bartram on the Moral Sensibility of Brute Creation." *Pennsylvania History: A Journal of Mid-Atlantic Studies* 56 (1989): 157–176.

Weekley, Carolyn J. *The Kingdoms of Edward Hicks.* New York, NY: The Colonial Williamsburg Foundation, 1999.

Welch, Craig. "Climate Change Helped Spark Syrian War, Study Says." *The National Geographic*, March 2, 2015. http://news.nationalgeo graphic.com/news/2015/03/150302-syria-war-climate-change-drought/.

Wesley, John. Sermon 23, "Upon Our Lord's Sermon on the Mount, Discourse III," I.11. http://ccel.org/ccel/wesley/sermons.v.xxiii.html#v.xxiii-p0.3.

Westra, Laura. *Living in Integrity: Toward a Global Ethic to Restore a Fragmented Earth.* Lanham, MD: Rowman Littlefield, 1998.

White, Gilbert. *The Natural History and Antiquities of Selborne.* 1789. London: Methuen & Co., 1901.

White, Jr., Lynn. "The Historical Roots of Our Ecologic Crisis." *Science* 155, no. 3767 (March 1967): 1203–1207.

Whitehead, Alfred North. *Dialogues of Alfred North Whitehead: As Recorded By Lucien Price.* New York: New American Library, 1954.

———. *Modes of Thought.* New York: Macmillan Co., 1938.

———. *Process and Reality: An Essay in Cosmology*, eds. David Ray Griffin and Donald W. Sherburne. Corrected edition. New York: The Free Press, 1978.

———. *Religion in the Making.* New York: Macmillan Co., 1926.

VOLUME 6: QUAKERS, CREATION CARE, AND SUSTAINABILITY

————. *Science and the Modern World*. New York: The Free Press, 1925.

————. *The Function of Reason*. Boston: Beacon Press, 1929.

Wildwood, Alex. *A Faith to Call Our Own: Quaker Tradition in the Light of Contemporary Movements of the Spirit*. London: Quaker Home Service, 1999.

Willcuts, Jack L. *Why Friends are Friends*. Newberg, OR: Barclay Press, 1984.

Wolf, Martin. *The Shifts and Shocks — What We Have Learned and Have Still to Learn from the Financial Crisis*. London: Penguin, 2014.

Wolff, Jonathan. *Robert Nozick*. Cambridge, UK: Polity Press, 1991.

Wood, Herbert G. *Quakerism and The Future of the Church*. London: The Swarthmore Press, Ltd., 1920.

Woodley, Randy S. *Shalom and the Community of Creation: An Indigenous Vision*. Prophetic Christianity series. Grand Rapids, MI: Eerdmans Publishing Co., 2012.

Woody, Thomas. *Early Quaker Education in Pennsylvania*. Kindle edition. New York: Teachers College, Columbia University, 1920.

————. *The Journal and Major Essays of John Woolman*, ed. Phillips P. Moulton. 1971. Richmond, IN: Friends United Press, 1989.

"World Charter for Nature." United Nations, 1982. Accessed January 2019. http://un.org/documents/ga/res/37/a37r007.htm.

Wray, Randall. *Modern Money Theory*. New York: Palgrave Macmillan, 2012.

Wynward, Todd. *Rewilding the Way: Break Free to Follow an Untamed God*. Harrisonburg, VA: Herald Press, 2015.

Zencey, Eric. "Mr. Soddy's Ecological Economy." *The New York Times*, April 11, 2009.

www.ingramcontent.com/pod-product-compliance
Lightning Source LLC
Chambersburg PA
CBHW031228090426
42742CB00007B/118